GABRIELLE LANGHOLTZ

AMERICA

THE COOKBOOK

GUEST CONTRIBUTIONS: ESSAYS & RECIPES BY STATE

50 STATES BY REGION

NORTHEAST

CONNECTICUT - CT
MAINE - ME
MASSACHUSETTS - MA
NEW HAMPSHIRE - NH
NEW YORK - NY
RHODE ISLAND - RI
VERMONT - VT

MID-ATLANTIC

DELAWARE - DE
MARYLAND - MD
NEW JERSEY - NJ
PENNSYLVANIA - PA

SOUTH

ALABAMA - AL
ARKANSAS - AR
FLORIDA - FL
GEORGIA - GA
KENTUCKY - KY
LOUISIANA - LA
MISSISSIPPI - MS
NORTH CAROLINA - NC
SOUTH CAROLINA - SC
TENNESSEE - TN
VIRGINIA - VA
WEST VIRGINIA - WV

SOUTHWEST

ARIZONA - AZ
NEW MEXICO - NM
OKLAHOMA - OK
TEXAS - TX
UTAH - UT

WEST

ALASKA - AK
CALIFORNIA - CA
COLORADO - CO
HAWAII - HI
IDAHO - ID
MONTANA - MT
NEVADA - NV
OREGON - OR
WASHINGTON - WA
WYOMING - WY

MIDWEST

ILLINOIS - IL
INDIANA - IN
IOWA - IA
KANSAS - KS
MICHIGAN - MI
MINNESOTA - MN
MISSOURI - MO
NEBRASKA - NE
NORTH DAKOTA - ND
OHIO - OH
SOUTH DAKOTA - SD
WISCONSIN - WI

LEGEND

REGIONS

NORTHEAST	NE	MID-ATLANTIC	MA
SOUTH	S	SOUTHWEST	SW
WEST	W	MIDWEST	MW

STATES

NY

DAIRY-FREE

DF

GLUTEN-FREE

GF

ONE-POT

1

VEGAN

V

VEGETARIAN

VEG

LESS THAN 30 MINUTES

30

LESS THAN 5 INGREDIENTS

5

INTRODUCTION

"We need a burger."

The four-word email from my editor, Emily, came months after I had turned in the massive manuscript. Hundreds of recipes were tested and typed, when she noticed I had omitted the iconic food for which my country is best known.

How did something called *America: The Cookbook* make it this far without a burger? I can explain.

In 1492, Columbus discovered America—or so I learned in grade school. Nevermind the people who already called it home. Despite having been here all along, the so-called New World was a revelation—to the people who had never noticed it.

Five hundred years later, something similar happened to American food. You could say it has been discovered. A continent of crab cakes and cracklins, fiddleheads and fatback, huckleberries and huevos, corn and conch, peanuts and peaches had been hidden in plain sight, missed by the modern mapmakers of taste. These longstanding foodways were the daily bread for millions of Americans, but to the culinary Columbuses, the world was flat and French. American food was not on the map—or the menus that "mattered."

People who hadn't discovered American food included, foremost, Americans. European techniques and imported ingredients were hailed as superior. Like couture and concertos, fine cuisine came from another continent. None foresaw the day when chefs would boast of California wine, New Jersey asparagus, Colorado lamb, or American cheese.

I didn't foresee it either. But I was fortunate to have eaten my way from sea to shining sea, thanks to two people who knew the world was round: my parents. They grew up in New York suburbs, but in pursuit of their Manifest Destiny, headed west to Kentucky, Indiana, California and Alaska. With PhDs in psychology and anthropology, they sought to experience it all. We sucked the marrow out of America.

They were not foodies. Dinner was homemade meatballs atop spaghetti with sauce from a jar, and parmesan cheese from a Kraft canister. But we paddled past icebergs and feasted on salmon, king crab, halibut bigger than I was, and mussels pulled from the frigid Pacific shore. Wearing bells to scare off bears, we picked wild blueberries and fiddlehead ferns. Dad took us ice fishing and when the snow melted we planted peas. We vacationed in Hawaii, where I ate my weight in pineapple and papaya.

One summer we packed the Jeep and moved to Oklahoma, land of chicken-fried steak with sweet tea. Our snowless backyard was home to apple, cherry, and pecan trees. My brother's hunting landed squirrel and venison. Mom's research meant pow wows and fry bread. We drove to Texas for chili and steak. To New Mexico for chiles and sopapillas. To graduate students' backyards for tastes of their native India, Vietnam, and the Phillipines.

And occasionally, to McDonald's for chicken nuggets and a cup of Coke.

Over the years I lived in Virginia, Colorado, New York, and Pennsylvania. Eventually I had been to all fifty states, eating pit barbecue, jambalaya, nopalitas, potato donuts, fried alligator, guava pastries, and prairie oysters. I visited dozens of farms, left my corporate job for food writing, and explored place-based taste. I married a farmer and learned about raising pigs, keeping bees, milking sheep, tapping maple trees, as well as foraging milkweed, pokeweed, and chickweed. I visited Argentina, Italy, Brazil, and Spain, but was glad to eat my way through Charleston, Portland, Oakland, Boulder, and Nashville, or a signless shack where locals line up for lunch.

A decade into editing food magazines, Emily, a friend-of-a-friend, asked if I was interested in a major book project called *America: The Cookbook*. Yes, I was.

To those who have not discovered America, the phrase "American cuisine" is an oxymoron. True, the Standard American Diet is devoid of both meaning and fiber. But I wrote this book to refute this misconception that American food means homogenized processed blandness. I come to bury the burger, not to praise it.

While researching this book, I hopped trains and planes. I re-read James Beard, Karen Hess, Betty Fussell, Clementine Paddleford, and Harvey Levenstein. I pored over *Mama Dip's Kitchen*, *Oregon's Cuisine of the Rain*, *Walnut Pickles and Watermelon Cake*, *Texas on the Half Shell*, *Cooking From Quilt Country*, and mountains more. I interviewed chefs and academics, historians and home cooks, farmers and foragers, butchers and fishers. I visited seashores and mountains, downtowns and backwoods. I ate off both fine china and paper plates. I studied regional, demographic, and immigration data. With my Oxford-trained research assistant, Annie, I sorted elaborate spreadsheets parsing everything from pies, preserves, and potato donuts to chefs and refugee resettlements. I cooked and tasted a lot during my research. And with my editor's thoughtful guidance, I curated contributions by leading chefs and writers across the country who celebrate American food's past and are forging its future. The responses poured forth from culinary luminaries who were so proud to be asked to represent their home state.

While many contributors wrote love letters to the foods of their roots, I was struck by how many included a variation of the sentence: "When I left Alabama, I was never coming back." Many of our country's greatest cooks once dismissed American food. They watched Julia Child and read *Gourmet*, perfected French pastries and Italian pasta, bought tickets to Europe or Asia. Only later did many realize, like Dorothy, that they had gone over the rainbow, but longed for what they'd left in their Kansas backyard.

Today, Americans are discovering American food—and as a result, American food is getting even better. We have followed our noses to farmers' markets. We prize local beer, bread, cheese, and charcuterie. We buy books on the foods of the Midwest and Appalachia. We envy the bankers-turned-distillers, wait hours for a taste of Texas barbecue, and vie for upscale riffs on pimento cheese and shrimp and grits.

These pages also proudly include national standards: Steak and meatloaf. Roast chicken and fried chicken. Hot dogs and pork chops. Creamed corn and mashed potatoes. Green bean gratin and cole slaw. French fries and onion rings. Peach pie and strawberry shortcake. But those dishes aren't America's full menu—not by a long shot.

So I also include recipes for antelope and rabbit. Beach plum jam and scallop stew. Fried smelt and soft-shelled crabs. Saltwater taffy and whoopee pies. Chitterlings and burgoo. Collard greens and crawfish. Benne wafers and frogmore stew. Pierogi and paczki. Persimmon pudding and pickled pike. Swedish limpa and nannyberry butter. Pawpaw ice cream and chokecherry wojapi. Bratwurst and booyah. Chiles rellenos and mutton stew. Panfried trout and huckleberry pie. Green chile cornbread and blackberry buckle. Chilaquiles and barbacoa. Injera and Horchata.

Our culinary canon is wild and wonderful. It is old and it is young. It is slippery and sticky, sour and sweet, and searingly spicy. It's black and white and brown. It's messy and it's meaningful.

And yes, I added a burger, because it belongs. Eat it in the backyard, barefoot. Depending on where you are, crown it with Monterey Jack or Vermont Cheddar. Top it with a Jersey tomato, wild watercress, a slice of pineapple, roasted poblanos, or Vidalia onion. Pour a cold glass of sweet tea, sumac punch, or mint julep. Raise it high.

Discover America.

Gabrielle Langholtz

RECIPES FROM 50 STATES

STARTERS

JAMAICAN PLANTAIN CHIPS

PREPARATION TIME: 15 MINUTES
(5 MINUTES INACTIVE)
COOKING TIME: 10 MINUTES
MAKES: AS MUCH AS YOU'D LIKE

- Green plantains
- Vegetable oil, for frying
- Salt

[Use green plantains in order to make crisp chips. Ripe plantains will yield soft chips. Serve plain or with Ackee Dip (recipe below).]

Slice the ends off of the plantains. Cut a lengthwise slit in the thick skin of each plantain from end to end along one side. Place plantains in a bowl and cover with very hot water. Set aside for 5 minutes. Remove the skin completely. Slice the plantains very thinly crosswise and set aside.

In a heavy pot, heat oil to a depth of 2 inches (5 cm) until very hot. Working in batches, fry the plantain slices until golden brown and crisp, 1–2 minutes depending on thickness. Drain on paper towels. Sprinkle with salt.

ACKEE DIP

PREPARATION TIME: 10 MINUTES
SERVES: 6–8

- 1 can (19 oz/540 g) ackee, drained
- 1 small onion, diced
- 2 cloves garlic, peeled but whole
- ½ habanero pepper, seeded
- ½ teaspoon salt
- 2 tablespoons olive oil
- Plantain Chips (recipe above), for serving

In a blender, combine all of the ingredients and purée until smooth. Pour into a serving bowl and serve with plantain chips.

ROASTED PUMPKIN SEEDS

PREPARATION TIME: 15 MINUTES
COOKING TIME: 40 MINUTES
MAKES: ABOUT 2 CUPS

- Seeds from 1 medium pumpkin (about 2 cups/130 g), well rinsed
- 2 tablespoons plus ¼ teaspoon salt
- 2 tablespoons (30 g) butter, melted
- ¼ teaspoon freshly ground black pepper

[These seeds are easy to make, delicious, and high in protein.]

Preheat the oven to 275°F (140°C/Gas Mark 1).

In a medium pot, combine 4 cups (950 ml) water and 2 tablespoons salt and bring to a boil. Reduce the heat to medium, add the pumpkin seeds, and simmer for 10 minutes. Drain and dry on paper towels.

Transfer the seeds to a baking sheet. Toss with the melted butter, black pepper, and ¼ teaspoon salt. Distribute in a single layer and roast, stirring every 10 minutes, until crispy and lightly browned, about 30 minutes. Let sit to crisp up before serving.

BOILED PEANUTS

PREPARATION TIME: 5 MINUTES, PLUS
  9 HOURS SOAKING AND STANDING TIME
COOKING TIME: 6 HOURS 30 MINUTES
SERVES: 10–12

- 2 lb (910 g) raw shell-on peanuts
- ⅔ cup (195 g) salt

[Warm, salty, chewy boiled peanuts are so beloved in South Carolina that they were declared the state snack in 2006. Freshly harvested green peanuts are best for boiling, and the in-the-shell treats can be found at roadside stands, farmers' markets, fairs, and events throughout the South (see essay on boiled peanuts on page 666).]

Place the peanuts in a large pot. Cover with water, press plastic wrap (clingfilm) onto the surface of the water, then top with a plate to weigh the peanuts down and keep them submerged. Soak for 8 hours or overnight. Drain and rinse the peanuts.

In a large pot, combine the peanuts, salt, and 5 quarts (4.7 liters) water. Bring to a boil over high heat. Cover, reduce the heat to medium-low, and cook at a low simmer until the shells are leathery and the peanuts inside are tender, about 6 hours. (Add hot water as needed to keep the peanuts covered.)

Remove from the heat and let stand for 1 hour. Serve the peanuts in liquid or pull out of liquid in small batches to serve (keeping the remaining peanuts warm and moist).

Peanuts will keep for up to 10 days in the refrigerator. Reheat the peanuts until warm before serving.

GUACAMOLE

PREPARATION TIME: 15 MINUTES
SERVES: 4

- 3 tablespoons fresh lime juice
- 1 clove garlic, minced
- 4 tablespoons finely chopped red onion
- 1 small jalapeño pepper, seeded and finely chopped
- 3 avocados, diced
- 4 tablespoons chopped fresh cilantro (coriander)
- Salt

In a medium bowl, combine the lime juice, garlic, and red onion. Let rest for at least 5 minutes and up to 10 minutes while you prepare the other ingredients. Add the jalapeño and avocado and mash with a fork to combine. Fold in the cilantro (coriander) and salt to taste. Serve immediately, or press plastic wrap (cling-film) onto the surface of the guacamole and refrigerate for up to 24 hours.

TORTILLA CHIPS

PREPARATION TIME: 10 MINUTES
COOKING TIME: 15 MINUTES
MAKES: 180 CHIPS (10–12 SERVINGS)

- 30 corn tortillas, cut into 6 wedges each
- Peanut (groundnut) oil, for deep-frying
- Salt

Preheat the oven to 200°F (95°C).

Spread the tortillas in a single layer on a rimmed baking sheet and bake until the tortillas begin to harden and dry out, 20–25 minutes. Remove from the oven.

Meanwhile, pour 2–3 inches (5–7.5 cm) oil into a large heavy pot or deep-fryer and heat to 350°F (180°C). Set a wire rack over a rimmed baking sheet.

Working in batches of 12–15 chips, fry until golden brown, 45–60 seconds. Using a spider/skimmer or slotted spoon, transfer to the wire rack. Blot with paper towels to remove any excess oil. Season to taste with salt.

Serve or store in an airtight container for up to 3 days.

GUACAMOLE

POPCORN BALLS

PREPARATION TIME: 15 MINUTES
COOKING TIME: 5 MINUTES
MAKES: TWELVE 3-INCH (7.5 CM) BALLS

- 4 tablespoons (60 g) butter, softened, plus more for greasing the pan and forming the balls
- 12 cups (130 g) popped corn
- ½ cup (120 ml) corn syrup (dark or light)
- 1 cup (200 g) sugar
- ½ teaspoon salt
- 1 teaspoon any type of vinegar
- 1 teaspoon pure vanilla extract

[Native Americans taught settlers how to grow and pop corn. The oldest ears of corn were found in New Mexico; Nebraska and Indiana now produce the most corn. According to a Nebraska legend, popcorn balls were created in the "year of the striped weather," when extreme heat made the corn in the valley pop, and heavy rain caused the sorghum on the hilltop to drain downwards, thus forming huge popcorn balls. Some people still flavor the balls with molasses, but much more popular is corn syrup, sugar, and flavorings of choice.]

Preheat the oven to 250°F (120°C/Gas Mark ½).

Butter a large roasting pan and add the popped corn. Place in the oven to keep warm while preparing the syrup.

In a heavy-bottomed saucepan, combine the corn syrup, 4 tablespoons (60 g) butter, and sugar and bring to a boil, stirring constantly. Continue to boil the syrup for 2 more minutes, stirring. Remove from the heat and stir in the salt, vinegar, and vanilla.

Pour the syrup over the warm popped corn, mixing well with a wooden spoon. When the mixture is cool enough to handle, butter your hands and form into 3-inch (7.5 cm) balls. Place them on a wire rack to cool completely before eating.

CHEESE BALL

PREPARATION TIME: 20 MINUTES, PLUS 2 HOURS CHILLING TIME
COOKING TIME: 5 MINUTES
SERVES: MANY

- 1 lb (455 g) cream cheese, at room temperature
- 4 tablespoons minced onion
- 1 cup (115 g) grated cheddar cheese
- ¾ cup (85 g) crumbled blue cheese
- 1 tablespoon Worcestershire sauce, or more to taste
- ½ teaspoon cayenne pepper
- 1 cup (100 g) pecans, toasted and finely chopped
- Crackers or bread, for serving

In a stand mixer fitted with the paddle attachment, beat together the cream cheese and onion. Beat in the cheddar, blue cheese, Worcestershire sauce, and cayenne until well combined. Cover the bowl and refrigerate until somewhat firm, about 2 hours.

Form the mixture into a ball, roll in the chopped nuts, and serve with crackers or bread.

CHILE CON QUESO

PREPARATION TIME: 5 MINUTES
COOKING TIME: 15 MINUTES
SERVES: 4

- 1 tablespoon vegetable oil
- 1 small yellow onion, chopped
- 2 cloves garlic, finely grated
- ½ teaspoon ground cumin
- 1 tablespoon cornstarch (cornflour)
- 1 cup (240 ml) chicken stock
- 1 can (4.5 oz/130 g) chopped green chilies
- ½ lb (225 g) block Velveeta or American cheese, cut into small cubes
- Kosher (coarse) salt and freshly ground black pepper
- 1 cup (150 g) store-bought refrigerated salsa
- Tortilla chips, for serving

[This ubiquitous appetizer is little more than melted queso (cheese) spiked with chicken broth and chilies, eaten with salty tortilla chips.]

In a medium saucepan, heat the oil over medium heat. Add the onion and cook until it is golden brown and tender, 5–7 minutes. Stir in the garlic, cumin, and cornstarch (cornflour) and stir in a few tablespoons of the stock. Stir in the remaining stock until well incorporated, then stir in the chilies and cheese. Cook, stirring, until the cheese melts and the sauce thickens, about 2 minutes. Season to taste with salt and pepper. Transfer to a warm dish, top with the salsa, and serve with tortilla chips.

PIMIENTO CHEESE

PREPARATION TIME: 15 MINUTES,
    PLUS CHILLING TIME
SERVES: 8–10

- 4 oz (115 g) cream cheese, at room temperature
- ½ cup (105 g) mayonnaise
- 1 teaspoon Dijon mustard
- ½ teaspoon Worcestershire sauce
- 4 tablespoons grated white onion
- ½ teaspoon Tabasco-style hot sauce
- ½ teaspoon kosher (coarse) salt
- ¼ teaspoon sugar
- ⅛ teaspoon cayenne pepper
- 1 lb (455 g) sharp cheddar cheese, grated on the large holes of a box grater
- 1 jar (8 oz/225 g) diced pimientos, drained
- Toast or crudités, for serving

[Southerners, particularly Georgians, are serious about this appetizer. Some make it with mayonnaise, some with butter, and some even use both. Serve with raw vegetables for dipping or slather on toast.]

In a medium bowl, beat the cream cheese with a wooden spoon until softened. Blend in the mayonnaise, mustard, Worcestershire sauce, onion, hot sauce, salt, sugar, and cayenne. Add the cheddar and stir again. Gently fold in the diced pimientos.

Cover and refrigerate for at least 1 hour for the flavors to permeate. Tightly covered, the pimiento cheese will keep for up to 3 days in the refrigerator.

CHEESE STRAWS

PREPARATION TIME: 25 MINUTES
COOKING TIME: 1 HOUR
MAKES: 8–10 DOZEN

- 3 sticks (340 g) unsalted butter, softened
- 1 lb (455 g) sharp cheddar cheese, shredded
- 1½ teaspoons salt
- 1½ teaspoons cayenne pepper
- ½ teaspoon paprika
- 4 cups (520 g) all-purpose (plain) flour

[Popular in Virginia, and overall a staple of Southern cocktail parties, open houses, and holiday gatherings, cheese straws are a savory shortbread made of flour, butter, and cheese — usually cheddar, but sometimes with cheddar and Parmesan. "Straws" refers to the shape when made with a cookie press, though cheese straws can also be round like biscuits.]

Position a rack in the middle of the oven and preheat to 350°F (180°C/Gas Mark 4). Line a baking sheet with parchment paper.

In a stand mixer fitted with a paddle attachment, combine the butter, cheddar, salt, cayenne, and paprika. Beat at medium speed until well blended, about 1 minute. On low speed, beat in the flour, ½ cup (65 g) at a time, and continue to mix until blended completely. Place the dough in a piping bag or a 1-gallon (3.8-liter) resealable plastic food bag with a ½-inch (1.25 cm) long opening cut from one corner. Pipe 2-inch (5 cm) long strips ½ inch (1.25 cm) apart onto the parchment paper.

Bake until lightly browned, about 12 minutes. Transfer to wire racks to cool.

DEEP-FRIED CHEESE CURDS

PREPARATION TIME: 10 MINUTES
COOKING TIME: 5 MINUTES
SERVES: 6–10

- Vegetable oil, for deep-frying
- 1 egg, beaten
- 1 cup (240 ml) beer
- 1 cup (130 g) all-purpose (plain) flour
- ½ teaspoon salt
- 1 lb (455 g) fresh cheese curds, at room temperature

[Cheese curds were made famous at the Wisconsin State Fair, where they are served deep-fried.]

In a large heavy-bottomed pot, heat the oil to 375°F (190°C).

Meanwhile, in a bowl, whisk together the egg, beer, flour, and salt until smooth.

When ready to fry, dip the cheese curds, a handful at a time, into the batter, coating them well. Working in batches, lower the battered curds into the hot oil and fry, turning occasionally, until they turn golden brown, 1–2 minutes. Remove the curds with a slotted spoon or mesh sieve and drain on paper towels. Serve hot.

CHEESE STRAWS

BAKED GOAT CHEESE

PREPARATION TIME: 10 MINUTES
COOKING TIME: 10 MINUTES
SERVES: 4–6

- 2 logs (4 oz/115 g each) goat cheese, cut into 5 slices each
- ⅓ cup (80 ml) extra-virgin olive oil
- ½ teaspoon salt
- ¼ teaspoon freshly ground black pepper
- 4 tablespoons chopped fresh mixed herbs such as dill, chives, parsley, and tarragon
- ⅔ cup (75 g) panko breadcrumbs

[Goat cheese was not commonly found in America until the 1970s, when it gained a foothold in Northern California. Now it is a supermarket and farmers market staple across the country.]

Preheat the oven to 350°F (180°C/Gas Mark 4).

Place the cheese slices on a small rimmed baking sheet. Drizzle with the olive oil, then sprinkle with the salt and pepper. Top with the mixed herbs, then the panko. Bake until the panko starts to brown and the cheese is warm and soft, about 10 minutes. Let rest for 1 minute on the baking sheet. Serve warm.

TUPELO HONEY AND GOAT CHEESE-STUFFED FIGS

PREPARATION TIME: 15 MINUTES
COOKING TIME: 5 MINUTES
SERVES: 6–8

- 8 oz (225 g) goat cheese, at room temperature
- 24 fresh figs, stems removed
- ¼ cup (60 ml) olive oil
- 1 teaspoon fine sea salt
- ½ teaspoon freshly ground black pepper
- ½ cup (170 g) tupelo honey

Preheat the broiler (grill) to high.

Fill a piping bag with goat cheese (or fill a plastic food storage bag and cut a small hole in the corner of the bag). Cut an "x" ½ inch (1.25 cm) deep in the top of each fig, to reveal a small opening. Pipe goat cheese into the figs, to rise above the opening by about ¼ inch (6 mm). Drizzle the prepared figs with olive oil and sprinkle with the salt and pepper.

Arrange the figs on a rimmed baking sheet and broil until the figs are lightly golden and the goat cheese is beginning to melt, about 2 minutes. Let cool for 5 minutes. Transfer to a serving platter and drizzle with the honey.

TUPELO HONEY AND GOAT CHEESE-STUFFED FIGS

QUESADILLAS

PREPARATION TIME: 15 MINUTES
COOKING TIME: 25 MINUTES
SERVES: 4

- 2 tablespoons vegetable oil
- 3 poblano peppers, seeded and diced
- ½ red onion, diced
- ¼ teaspoon salt
- 2 cloves garlic, minced
- 8 flour tortillas (8-inch/20 cm)
- 1 cup (115 g) grated asadero or Monterey Jack cheese
- 4 tablespoons chopped fresh cilantro (coriander) leaves
- Salsa, guacamole, or sour cream (optional), for serving

Place 1 tablespoon of oil in a 10-inch (25 cm) nonstick frying pan over medium heat. Add the poblanos, onion, and salt and cook until the onions have slightly softened, 4-5 minutes. Add the garlic and cook for 2 more minutes. Transfer mixture to a bowl and set aside. Wipe the pan clean with a paper towel.

Place 4 flour tortillas on a work surface. Top each with 2 tablespoons cheese, one-fourth of the poblano mixture, and 1 tablespoon cilantro (coriander). Top with another 2 tablespoons cheese and cover each with another flour tortilla.

Reheat the frying pan over medium heat. Add 1 teaspoon oil to the pan and swirl to thinly coat the bottom of the pan. Place a quesadilla in the pan and cook, flipping halfway, until golden brown and the cheese is melted, 3–4 minutes per side. Let rest 1 minute before cutting. Repeat with the remaining oil and quesadillas.

Cut each quesadilla into wedges and serve with salsa, guacamole, or sour cream, if desired.

KOREAN PANCAKES

PREPARATION TIME: 10 MINUTES
COOKING TIME: 40 MINUTES
SERVES: 8

- 1 cup (230 g) kimchi, finely chopped
- 2 eggs
- 3 tablespoons vegetable oil
- 1 cup (130 g) all-purpose (plain) flour
- 1 cup (160 g) rice flour
- ½ teaspoon salt
- 6 scallions (spring onions), thinly sliced
- 4 tablespoons chopped fresh chives
- 4 tablespoons chopped fresh cilantro (coriander)
- Soy sauce, for dipping

[Los Angeles is home to the largest Korean-American community in the country. Serve these pancakes with a soy dipping sauce, if desired.]

Place the kimchi in a sieve and press to remove as much liquid as possible.

In a medium bowl, whisk together the eggs and 1 tablespoon of the oil until lightly beaten. Add both flours, the salt, and 1½ cups (355 ml) water and whisk to combine into a smooth batter. Stir in the kimchi, scallions (spring onions), chives, and cilantro (coriander).

Heat an 8-inch (20 cm) nonstick frying pan over medium-high heat. Add 1 tablespoon of the oil and swirl to coat the bottom of the pan. Add one-fourth of the batter and spread to cover the entire bottom of the pan. Cook until the bottom is browned, about 5 minutes. Flip in one piece and cook an additional 5 minutes. Repeat with the remaining batter, using the remaining 1 tablespoon oil to grease the pan, as needed, between batches.

Cut the pancakes into wedges and serve.

KOREAN PANCAKES

TEXAS CAVIAR

PREPARATION TIME: 10 MINUTES,
  PLUS CHILLING TIME
SERVES: 6–8

- 2 cans (15 oz/425 g each) black-eyed peas (beans), rinsed and drained, or 3 cups (900 g) fresh black-eyed peas
- 1 jalapeño pepper, seeded and finely chopped
- ¾ cup (110 g) finely chopped red bell pepper
- ½ cup (60 g) thinly sliced red onion
- ¼ cup (60 ml) extra-virgin olive oil
- ¼ cup (60 ml) red wine vinegar
- 1 teaspoon salt
- ½ teaspoon freshly ground black pepper
- ½ cup roughly chopped fresh cilantro (coriander)

[Serve on top of lettuce leaves or with tortilla chips.]

In a large bowl, mix together the black-eyed peas (beans), jalapeño, bell pepper, onion, oil, vinegar, salt, and black pepper. Stir to combine. Refrigerate for 4 hours or overnight. Stir in the cilantro (coriander) just before serving.

CHANTERELLE RISOTTO

PREPARATION TIME: 15 MINUTES
COOKING TIME: 30 MINUTES
SERVES: 4

- 4–5 cups (1–1.2 liters) mushroom broth
- 3 tablespoons (45 g) butter
- 2 shallots, finely chopped
- 4 cups (300 g) fresh chanterelles, sliced
- 1½ cups (295 g) Arborio rice
- ½ cup (120 ml) dry white wine
- Pinch of saffron
- ⅓ cup (80 ml) heavy (whipping) cream
- 2 oz (55 g) Parmesan cheese, grated
- Salt

[Chanterelles thrive in Oregon, Washington, and Georgia and are Oregon's official state mushroom. They typically appear from late spring in the South through late summer and early fall in the North, preferring moisture, shade, and plenty of woodland matter.]

In a saucepan, bring the mushroom broth to a simmer; keep hot.

In a heavy-bottomed pan, melt the butter over medium heat. Add the shallot and cook until translucent, about 4 minutes. Add the chanterelles and cook for 5 minutes, stirring. Add the rice, stirring and toasting it until the grains are glistening. Increase the heat to high and add the wine, allowing it to come to a brief boil. Stir well. Reduce the heat to medium-high.

Add the saffron and the warm broth, ½ cup (120 ml) at a time, stirring constantly and cooking until it is absorbed before adding the next ½ cup (120 ml). This will take about 20 minutes. Taste the rice grains to see if they are still chalky in the middle. If they are, add more broth.

Just before serving, stir in the cream and Parmesan. Taste and season with salt.

FRIED PICKLES

PREPARATION TIME: 10 MINUTES,
    PLUS CHILLING TIME
COOKING TIME: 15 MINUTES
SERVES: 6

- 2½ cups (325 g) cornmeal
- 1½ cups (195 g) all-purpose (plain) flour
- 2 teaspoons dried dill weed
- 4 teaspoons paprika
- ¼ teaspoon cayenne pepper
- 3 teaspoons garlic salt
- 3 teaspoons freshly ground black pepper
- 1¾ cups (415 ml) milk
- ¼ cup (60 ml) dill pickle juice
- 2 eggs
- 24 dill pickle spears, chilled
- Canola (rapeseed) oil, for deep-frying
- Ranch Dressing, for serving
  (see page 480)

[An Arkansas drive-in lays claim to the first sale of the fried dill pickle in 1963. The snack has become a favorite at sports bars and state fairs across the South.]

Set up a dredging station: In a wide shallow bowl, whisk together the cornmeal, flour, dill weed, paprika, cayenne, and 2½ teaspoons each of garlic salt and black pepper. In a second shallow bowl, whisk together the milk, pickle juice, eggs, and remaining ½ teaspoon each garlic salt and black pepper.

Working with one at a time, dip a pickle spear into the egg mixture, then into the cornmeal mixture. Chill the pickles for 30 minutes.

Pour 3 inches (7.5 cm) oil into a large heavy pot or deep-fryer and heat to 375°F (190°C).

Working in batches, carefully add the chilled pickle spears to the hot oil and cook until golden, 2–3 minutes. Drain on paper towels. Serve hot, with ranch dressing on the side.

ELDERFLOWER FRITTERS

PREPARATION TIME: 10 MINUTES
COOKING TIME: 25 MINUTES
MAKES: 18 FRITTERS

- 1⅓ cups (170 g) all-purpose (plain) flour
- 1 teaspoon baking powder
- Pinch of salt
- ⅔ cup (160 ml) sparkling water
- 1 egg white, beaten to soft peaks
- Vegetable oil, for shallow-frying
- 18 elderflower umbels, with stems
  attached (for handles)
- Powdered (icing) sugar, for dusting

[Elderberry, also known as blue elderberry, grows wild across the country. Elderflower cordial and elderflower fritters are two wild delights of early summer, using just the white flower umbels. In late summer, ripe elderberry fruit is good for juices, wine, syrups, jams, and sauces, once the seeds have been removed (a food mill works best).]

In a bowl, whisk together the flour, baking powder, and salt. Stir in the sparkling water until smooth. Fold in the egg white.

Pour 1 inch (2.5 cm) oil into a frying pan and heat over medium-high heat until hot but not smoking.

Working in batches, dip an umbel into the batter and place gently in the hot oil. As soon as the fritters are golden, about 1 minute per side, remove and drain on paper towels. Dust at once with powdered (icing) sugar. Eat immediately while crisp (do not eat the green stems).

COLD SESAME NOODLES

PREPARATION TIME: 30 MINUTES,
  PLUS NOODLE CHILLING TIME
COOKING TIME: 10 MINUTES
SERVES: 4–6

- 1 lb (455 g) cucumbers, halved lengthwise, seeded, and thinly sliced crosswise
- ½ teaspoon salt
- ½ cup (120 ml) tahini
- 3 tablespoons soy sauce
- 2 tablespoons sesame oil
- 1 tablespoon fresh lime juice
- 2 teaspoons Sriracha sauce
- 1 teaspoon minced fresh ginger
- 1 tablespoon sugar
- ½ teaspoon freshly ground black pepper
- 12 oz (340 g) fresh Chinese egg noodles, cooked and chilled
- ½ cup (50 g) chopped scallions (spring onions)
- 2 tablespoons toasted sesame seeds

In a large colander, toss the cucumbers and salt to combine. Let stand for 15 minutes. Press well to drain and squeeze dry with paper towels.

In a large bowl, whisk together the tahini, soy sauce, sesame oil, lime juice, Sriracha, ginger, sugar, and pepper. Thin the sauce with hot water, 1 tablespoon at a time, until it is easy to whisk and similar in consistency to crêpe batter. Gently stir in the noodles, then the cucumbers until well combined. Serve garnished with scallions (spring onions) and sesame seeds.

BUFFALO WINGS

PREPARATION TIME: 15 MINUTES
COOKING TIME: 50 MINUTES
SERVES: 6

- 3 lb (1.4 kg) chicken wings, tips removed, remaining wing separated at the joint
- Salt and freshly ground black pepper
- 3 tablespoons (45 g) butter
- 1 clove garlic, minced
- ½ cup (120 ml) Tabasco-style hot sauce
- 1 tablespoon cider vinegar
- Vegetable oil, for deep-frying
- Blue cheese dressing and celery sticks, for serving

[In 1964, a bar in Buffalo, New York, created this preparation of chicken wings, fried and bathed in a spicy sauce and accompanied by blue cheese dressing and celery.]

Preheat the oven to 250°F (120°C/Gas Mark ½). Season the chicken wings with salt and pepper. Set aside.

In a small saucepan, melt the butter over medium heat. Add the garlic, hot sauce, and vinegar and bring to a simmer. Remove from the heat and set aside.

Pour 3 inches (7.5 cm) oil into a large heavy pot or deep-fryer and heat to 375°F (190°C).

Working in batches, fry the wings, turning occasionally, until deep brown and crisp, 10–12 minutes. Transfer to an ovenproof dish and keep warm in the oven while you fry the rest of the wings.

After all of chicken wings have been fried, rewarm the sauce. Pour over the wings and stir to coat. Serve with blue cheese dressing and celery sticks on the side.

COLD SESAME NOODLES

RAW OYSTERS

PREPARATION TIME: 1 MINUTE PER
OYSTER
SERVES: AS MANY AS YOU'D LIKE

- Local oysters
- Lemon wedges, for serving
- Horseradish, for serving
- Hot sauce, such as Tabasco, for serving

[Cold and just-shucked, you can eat them with lemon, horseradish, or hot sauce.]

To shuck an oyster, hold it with a towel or thick glove in one hand (your weak hand). Using your dominant hand, slip an oyster knife, held horizontally, into the hinge of the oyster. Don't force—if it's not going in, wiggle it. Once it's in, twist gently and listen for a pop. After the pop, slide the knife around edge of shell, under and over the oyster to release the muscle. In the absence of an oyster knife, try a flathead screwdriver or even a sturdy butter knife.

Serve the oysters on the half shell with lemon wedges for squeezing, freshly grated horseradish, and hot sauce. Let guests dress their oysters to taste.

OYSTERS ROCKEFELLER

PREPARATION TIME: 10 MINUTES
COOKING TIME: 25 MINUTES
SERVES: 4–6

- 1½ sticks (170 g) plus 3 tablespoons (45 g) unsalted butter, softened
- ½ cup (30 g) chopped fresh parsley
- ¼ cup (25 g) chopped scallions (spring onions)
- ¼ cup (25 g) chopped fennel
- 1 teaspoon chopped fresh tarragon
- 2 cups (70 g) roughly chopped watercress
- ⅓ cup (35 g) fine dried breadcrumbs
- 2 tablespoons Pernod
- ½ teaspoon salt
- ¼ teaspoon freshly ground black pepper
- ¼ teaspoon Tabasco-style hot sauce
- 2 lb (910 g) edible rock salt
- 2 dozen shucked oysters, with half shells
- 2 lemons, cut into 6 wedges each (optional)

[These oysters are as rich as John D. Rockefeller, for whom the dish was named. The recipe, which calls for baking the oysters with aromatic greens, and plenty of butter, was born at Antoine's restaurant in New Orleans in 1899.]

Preheat the oven to 450°F (230°C/Gas Mark 8).

In a medium frying pan, melt 3 tablespoons (45 g) of the butter over medium-high heat. Add the parsley, scallions (spring onions), fennel, and tarragon and cook for 2–3 minutes. Add the watercress and cook until wilted, 2–3 minutes. Let cool, then transfer to a food processor.

Add the remaining 1½ sticks (170 g) butter to the food processor along with the breadcrumbs, Pernod, salt, pepper, and hot sauce. Pulse until smooth.

Fill a large rimmed baking sheet with the rock salt. Dampen the salt slightly and arrange the oysters in their half shells on the bed of salt so that they sit straight. Top each oyster with a spoonful of the parsley mixture. Bake until lightly browned and bubbling, 12–15 minutes. Transfer the bed of rock salt to a serving platter. Arrange the oysters on top and garnish with lemon wedges, if desired.

GRILLED OYSTERS

PREPARATION TIME: THE TIME NEEDED
TO HEAT THE GRILL OR BUILD A FIRE
COOKING TIME: 5 MINUTES
SERVES: AS MANY AS YOU'D LIKE

6–12 OYSTERS PER PERSON

Preheat a gas or charcoal grill (barbecue) to high heat. (Or start a wood fire.) Grill the oysters in their shells, with the rounded side facing down until they begin to open (time varies, but usually is less than 5 minutes). Transfer them to a dish, being careful not to spill their liquor. At this point the oyster can be shucked and eaten, or carefully returned on its half shell to the grill, where it can be grilled "well-done."

FRIED OYSTERS

PREPARATION TIME: 10 MINUTES
COOKING TIME: 20 MINUTES
SERVES: 4

- Vegetable oil, for deep-frying
- 4 eggs
- ½ cup (120 ml) milk
- 3 cups (340 g) fine dried breadcrumbs or finely crushed saltine crackers
- 1½ cups (196 g) all-purpose (plain) flour
- ½ teaspoon freshly ground black pepper
- Generous pinch of cayenne pepper
- 1 teaspoon salt (optional)
- 48 shucked oysters
- Optional accompaniments: lemon wedges, tartar sauce, hot sauce, Worcestershire sauce

Pour 6 inches (15 cm) oil into a large heavy pot or deep-fryer and heat to 375°F (190°C).

Meanwhile, set up a dredging station: In a wide shallow bowl, beat the eggs with the milk. In a second bowl, spread out the breadcrumbs or saltine crumbs. In a third bowl, whisk the flour, black pepper, and cayenne. If using breadcrumbs, whisk in the salt; if using saltines, omit the salt.

Drain and thoroughly dry the oysters. When the oil is ready, dredge the oysters one at a time, first in the flour, then the egg, then the breadcrumbs or cracker crumbs. Working in batches of a few at a time, add the oysters to the hot oil and fry for about 2 minutes (or less if they are very small).

Drain on paper towels. Serve hot with lemon wedges, tartar sauce, hot sauce, or Worcestershire sauce, if desired.

STUFFIES

PREPARATION TIME: 25 MINUTES
COOKING TIME: 40 MINUTES
MAKES: ABOUT 2 DOZEN STUFFED
    CLAMS

- 10 lb (4.5 kg) quahogs (large hardshell clams), scrubbed
- ¼ cup (60 ml) dry white wine
- 1 stick (115 g) butter
- 1 large onion, minced
- 1 tablespoon minced garlic
- ½ teaspoon salt
- ¼ teaspoon freshly ground black pepper
- 1½ cups (75 g) fresh breadcrumbs
- 2 tablespoons minced fresh parsley
- Paprika
- Lemon wedges and hot sauce, for serving

Place the quahogs in a large pot with 1 inch (2.5 cm) of water and the wine. Cover and cook over high heat until the clams have opened, 6 minutes or more. Remove them from the pot and set aside to cool. Strain the cooking liquid through a fine-mesh sieve lined with several layers of cheesecloth and reserve. Remove the clams from their shells. Clean the shells and set them aside. Mince the clam meats and set aside.

Preheat the oven to 350°F (180°C/Gas Mark 4).

In a large frying pan, melt the butter over medium heat. Add the onion and garlic and cook until softened, about 5 minutes. Remove from the heat. Stir in the salt, pepper, breadcrumbs, and parsley. Stir in the clams and enough of the reserved cooking liquid to moisten the mixture so that it can be formed but is not wet.

Using a large soup spoon, fill the reserved shells with the stuffing. The filling should be slightly mounded in the shell. Sprinkle the stuffed shells with paprika. Place them on a rimmed baking sheet and bake until they are golden brown, about 20 minutes. Serve with lemon wedges and hot sauce.

PERUVIAN CEVICHE

PREPARATION TIME: 20 MINUTES,
    PLUS CHILLING AND MARINATING TIME
SERVES: 2–4

- 1½ lb (680 g) very fresh white fish fillets (such as halibut, escolar, or fluke)
- Salt
- ¾ cup (180 ml) fresh lime juice (preferably from key limes)
- 1 medium red onion, halved lengthwise and very thinly sliced crosswise
- ¼ cup (15 g) fresh cilantro (coriander), finely chopped
- 1 habanero pepper, seeded, deribbed, and minced
- 1–2 cloves garlic, minced
- Freshly ground black pepper

[More Peruvians live in New Jersey than in any other state. Ceviche is a major part of Peru's culinary heritage. The fresh seafood is "cooked" not with heat but in a cold bath of citrus juice. Peruvian limes (*limón sutil*) have a flavor similar to key limes and a high acid content, so use key limes if possible. Serve this refreshing dish on a hot day with grilled corn and sweet potato slices on the side.]

Cut the fish into small cubes. Place in a bowl and cover with cold water and 1 tablespoon salt. Refrigerate for at least 15 minutes.

Meanwhile, in a bowl, combine the lime juice, onion, cilantro (coriander), habanero, and garlic.

Remove the fish from the salted water, rinse with cold water, and add to the lime juice mixture, tossing everything together. Season to taste with salt and pepper. Cover and refrigerate for 15 minutes before serving.

WALLEYE FINGERS

PREPARATION TIME: 10 MINUTES
COOKING TIME: 10 MINUTES
SERVES: 4

- 2 cups (260 g) all-purpose (plain) flour
- ½ teaspoon salt
- 1 teaspoon baking powder
- ¾ cup (180 ml) dry white wine
- Vegetable oil, for deep-frying
- 1½ lb (680 g) skinless walleye pike fillets, cut into 1-inch (2.5 cm) wide strips
- Tartar sauce and lemon wedges, for serving

[Walleye fingers are served in bars throughout Minnesota and are especially common near Lake Superior.]

Place 1 cup (130 g) flour in a large bowl. Whisk in the salt and baking powder. Stir in the wine and ¾ cup (180 ml) cold water and set aside.

Pour 2 inches (5 cm) oil into a deep, heavy-bottomed frying pan and heat to 375°F (190°C).

Spread the remaining 1 cup (130 g) flour on a plate. Dredge the fish pieces first in the flour, then dip in the batter. Working in batches, fry a few at a time in the hot oil, turning as necessary, until golden brown and crispy, 1–2 minutes. Drain on paper towels. Serve with tartar sauce and lemon wedges on the side.

SPAM MUSUBI

PREPARATION TIME: 15 MINUTES, PLUS COOLING TIME
COOKING TIME: 25 MINUTES
MAKES: 10

- 2 cups (400 g) short-grain sushi rice
- 6 tablespoons unseasoned rice vinegar
- ¼ cup (60 ml) soy sauce
- ½ cup (100 g) sugar
- 1 can (12 oz/340 g) Spam, cut horizontally into 10 slices
- 2 tablespoons vegetable oil
- 5 sheets nori, halved

[Hawaiians lead the country in Spam consumption. In their state the canned "spiced ham" is affectionately known as Hawaiian steak. Here it's marinated and rolled into sushi. It can be served warm or cool. You can use the Spam can as a mold for the rice that sits under the meat.]

Cook the rice according to the package directions. While still hot, stir in the vinegar and set aside to cool.

Meanwhile, in a large bowl, mix together the soy sauce and sugar until dissolved. Add the Spam slices and toss them gently to coat. Set aside to marinate for 10 minutes.

In a large frying pan, heat the oil over medium-high heat. Add the Spam and cook until crispy on the edges, about 2 minutes per side.

Use the Spam can or a musubi maker to mold the cooked rice: cut the outer side off of the Spam can. Place the rice on the counter and press to a depth of ½ inch (1.25 cm). Set a rice block in the middle of a strip of nori. Press a piece of Spam on top, then use the can as a cutter to shape into a rectangle. Roll the musubi up in the nori, dampening it to seal.

CRISPY SNOOTS

PREPARATION TIME: 10 MINUTES
COOKING TIME: 3 HOURS
SERVES: AS MANY AS YOU'D LIKE

Per person:
- 1 pig snout
- Salt and freshly ground black pepper
- Barbecue sauce or hot sauce, for serving

[Grilled pig snouts are a favorite in St. Louis, Missouri barbecue joints. Like pork cracklin' (pig skin), snoots can be eaten alone or added to barbecue sandwiches, chili, soups, and stews. Raw snouts (and ears and tails) can often be found at international food markets or farmers' markets.]

Clean the snout under cold water. Using a sharp knife, slice lengthwise. Discard the hard cartilage and slice off the nostrils. Place the meat in a large pot of salted water, bring to a boil, and simmer, uncovered, for 1 hour. Drain and rinse under cold water. Preheat a gas or charcoal grill (barbecue) to 275°F (135°C).

Salt the snout, place on the grill rack, and cook, turning often with tongs, until very crispy, 1½–2 hours. Watch closely as dripping fat can cause flare-ups.

Transfer the snout to a serving plate. Season with salt and pepper and drizzle with barbecue sauce or hot sauce.

FRITO PIE

PREPARATION TIME: 10 MINUTES
COOKING TIME: 1 HOUR 15 MINUTES
SERVES: 10–12

- 1 tablespoon vegetable oil
- 1 medium onion, chopped
- 2 cloves garlic, chopped
- 1 tablespoon chili powder
- 1 teaspoon ground cumin
- 1 teaspoon dried oregano
- 1 lb (455 g) ground (minced) beef chuck
- 1 can (14.5 oz/410 g) diced (chopped) tomatoes
- Kosher (coarse) salt and hot sauce
- 1 large bag (19 oz/540 g) Fritos corn chips
- Optional toppings: shredded cheddar cheese, sliced jalapeños, sour cream, and diced onion

[Dallas, home to the Texas State Fair and Frito-Lay headquarters, is said to be the birthplace of this recipe known throughout Texas, as well as across the American South and the Midwest. Sometimes presented in a Fritos Original Corn Chips bag (and if split open then referred to as a "Frito Boat"), the dish consists of chips topped with chili, onions, jalapeño, cheese, and/or sour cream. While the Chili Con Carne (page 214) could work, this is a recipe for more traditional ground beef chili.]

In a large Dutch oven (casserole), heat the oil over medium heat. Add the onion and garlic and cook until softened, 5–7 minutes. Stir in the chili powder, cumin, and oregano and cook until fragrant, about 1 minute. Add the beef, tomatoes, and 2 cups (475 ml) water. Bring to a boil, then reduce to a simmer and cook until the broth is dark red, about 1 hour. (Skim off the fat that rises to the surface, if desired.) Season to taste with salt and hot sauce.

To assemble, place the corn chips in the bottom of a large serving dish. Spoon the chili over top and scatter with desired toppings.

CHISLIC

PREPARATION TIME: 10 MINUTES,
   PLUS MARINATING TIME
COOKING TIME: 5 MINUTES
SERVES: 6

- 1 lb (455 g) steak (or mutton, lamb, or venison), cut into 1-inch (2.5 cm) cubes
- 1 teaspoon garlic powder
- 1 teaspoon salt
- ½ teaspoon freshly ground black pepper
- 2 teaspoons Worcestershire sauce
- Vegetable oil, for deep-frying
- Hot sauce and saltine crackers, for serving

[Chislic is cubed red meat that is skewered, then deep-fried rare or medium-rare, and seasoned with salt.]

In a bowl, toss the meat with the garlic powder, salt, pepper, and Worcestershire sauce. Cover and refrigerate for at least 2 hours to marinate.

Pour 2 inches (5 cm) oil into a large heavy pot or deep-fryer and heat to 375°F (190°C).

Working in batches (do not crowd the pan), fry the meat until rare or medium-rare, 1–2 minutes. Remove and drain on paper towels. Skewer the cooked meat with cocktail picks and serve with hot sauce and saltine crackers on the side.

FRIED ALLIGATOR BITES

PREPARATION TIME: 10 MINUTES,
PLUS OVERNIGHT MARINATING TIME
COOKING TIME: 10 MINUTES
SERVES: 4–6

- 1 lb (455 g) alligator meat, cut into 1-inch (2.5 cm) chunks
- 2 cups (475 ml) buttermilk
- 2 tablespoons Cajun seasoning
- 1 teaspoon salt
- ½ teaspoon freshly ground black pepper
- 1½ cups (195 g) all-purpose (plain) flour
- ½ cup (65 g) cornmeal
- 2 tablespoons Tabasco-style hot sauce
- Peanut (groundnut) or vegetable oil, for deep-frying

[The well-known Florida alligators live in the wild, but they're also farmed for food: Alligator butchers in Florida, Alabama, Mississippi, and Louisiana do a thriving business, including mail order. The taste and texture of the tail meat are akin to veal, and it can be grilled, fried, or slow-simmered in stews like gumbo and étouffée.]

Place the alligator meat, 1 cup (240 ml) of the buttermilk, and the Cajun seasoning in a 1-gallon (3.8-liter) resealable plastic food bag. Seal and massage to combine. Marinate in the refrigerator for 8 hours or overnight.

Remove the alligator from the marinade (discard the marinade). Season the meat with the salt and pepper.

Set up a dredging station: In a wide shallow bowl, combine the flour and cornmeal. In a second shallow bowl, whisk together the remaining 1 cup (240 ml) buttermilk with the hot sauce. Place a wire rack over a rimmed baking sheet. Working with a few pieces at a time, dredge the gator pieces in the flour mixture, then in the buttermilk mixture, then back into the flour mixture. Transfer to the wire rack.

Pour 3 inches (7.5 cm) oil into a large heavy pot or deep-fryer and heat to 375°F (190°C).

Working in batches, fry the gator pieces until golden brown, about 3 minutes. Drain on paper towels. Serve hot.

ROCKY MOUNTAIN OYSTERS

PREPARATION TIME: 20 MINUTES,
  PLUS FREEZING AND SOAKING TIME
COOKING TIME: 10 MINUTES
SERVES: 4–6

- 2 lb (910 g) calf testicles (see Note)
- 2 cups (475 ml) buttermilk
- Canola (rapeseed) oil, for deep-frying
- 1 cup (115 g) panko breadcrumbs
- Salt and freshly ground black pepper
- 2 eggs
- Lemon wedges and hot sauce,
  for serving

Note:
  To remove the tough skin surrounding the
  testicles, place the testicles in the freezer
  for about 30 minutes (the skin comes off
  more easily if the testicles are slightly
  frozen). Use a sharp paring knife to first
  make a slice through the skin, then peel
  it off.

[When calves were branded at roundups in the Old West, their testicles were cut off and thrown in a bucket of cold water. They were then peeled, washed, rolled in flour and pepper, and pan-fried. Also known as prairie oysters, Montana tendergroins, cowboy caviar, swinging beef, and calf fries, deep-fried testicles remain a Rocky Mountain delicacy. They are the size of a walnut and much more tender than the larger bull testicles.]

Place the peeled testicles in a bowl, cover with buttermilk, and let sit at least 2 hours and up to 6 hours. Drain the testicles and pat dry.

Pour 5 inches (13 cm) oil into a large heavy pot or deep-fryer and heat to 375°F (190°C).

Set up a dredging station: In a wide shallow bowl, season the panko with salt and pepper. In a second shallow bowl, beat the eggs. Dip each testicle first in the egg, then roll in the seasoned panko. Working in batches, fry until golden brown, turning them as they cook. They will rise to the top when they are done, about 3 minutes. Drain on paper towels. Serve hot, with lemon wedges and hot sauce on the side.

MINER'S LETTUCE SALAD

PREPARATION TIME: 20 MINUTES
SERVES: 2

- 1 teaspoon white wine vinegar
- ½ teaspoon smooth Dijon mustard
- Pinch of salt
- Pinch of sugar
- Freshly ground black pepper
- 1 tablespoon grapeseed oil
- 1 orange, peeled and segmented
- 2 handfuls miner's lettuce, washed
  and dried

[Miner's lettuce appears at the end of mild West Coast winters, growing prolifically in moist and shaded habitats. This salad green is mild in flavor, succulent in texture, and best used raw.]

In a bowl, whisk together the vinegar, mustard, salt, sugar, and pepper. Whisk in the oil to emulsify. Add the orange segments and toss. Scoop out the orange and arrange the segments on a plate. Toss the miner's lettuce in the vinaigrette and lay on top of the orange segments. Serve at once.

SHAVED ARTICHOKE SALAD

PREPARATION TIME: 20 MINUTES
SERVES: 4

- Juice of 2 lemons
- 10 baby artichokes
- ¼ cup (60 ml) extra-virgin olive oil
- Salt and freshly ground black pepper
- 4 tablespoons shaved Parmesan cheese
- 8–10 basil leaves, torn

Set up a bowl of cold water and stir in half of the lemon juice. Clean the artichokes by removing the first 3 or 4 outer layers of fibrous leaves. Cut 1–2 inches (2.5–5 cm) off the tip of the artichoke to expose the furry center. Use a spoon with a pointy tip to dig into the center of the artichoke and remove all the fur. Use a paring knife to peel the fibrous outer layer of the stem. Add trimmed artichokes to the bowl of lemon water as you work (the artichokes can be kept in the lemon water until you're ready to continue, for up to 1 hour).

Shave the artichokes lengthwise using a mandoline, returning the slices to the lemon water as you work. Drain the artichoke slices, transfer to a bowl, and toss immediately with the olive oil, remaining lemon juice, ½ teaspoon salt, and ¼ teaspoon pepper.

Spread on a platter and top with the Parmesan shavings and basil. Season to taste with salt and pepper. Serve immediately.

VIDALIA ONION AND CUCUMBER SALAD

PREPARATION TIME: 10 MINUTES,
   PLUS CHILLING TIME
COOKING TIME: 5 MINUTES
SERVES: 6–8

- 4 cucumbers, peeled and cut into ½-inch (1.25 cm) thick slices
- 1 large Vidalia onion, cut into ⅛-inch (3 mm) wide slices
- ½ cup (120 ml) distilled white vinegar
- 1 tablespoon sugar
- 1 teaspoon salt
- 2 cloves garlic, minced
- 1 teaspoon freshly ground black pepper

[Georgia's famously mild and sweet Vidalia onions have been a favorite of Southerners since the Great Depression in the 1930s. The fat, white onions are harvested in May and June, and are available for much of the year.]

Place the cucumber and onion slices in a large heatproof bowl.

In a small saucepan, combine the vinegar, sugar, salt, garlic, and ½ cup (120 ml) water. Heat over medium heat, stirring frequently, just to dissolve the sugar and salt. Pour over the cucumbers and onions, add the pepper, and mix gently to coat. Cover tightly and refrigerate to chill completely, about 6 hours. Serve in the pickling liquid with a slotted spoon.

CAESAR SALAD

PREPARATION TIME: 15 MINUTES
SERVES: 4

- 1 clove garlic, peeled
- 3 or 4 oil-packed anchovy fillets, to taste
- 2 tablespoons fresh lemon juice
- 1 teaspoon Dijon mustard
- 1 egg yolk
- 6 tablespoons extra-virgin olive oil
- Worcestershire sauce (optional)
- 1 large head romaine lettuce, torn into pieces (about 8 cups)
- ½ cup (50 g) freshly shredded Parmesan cheese
- 1 cup (30 g) croutons
- Salt and freshly ground black pepper

[Created a century ago by an Italian immigrant working in Tijuana, Mexico this salad became hugely popular in neighboring Southern California and remains a favorite on menus nationwide.]

Mince the garlic and anchovy fillets together. Using the side of the knife, mash them into a fine paste. Place the garlic-anchovy paste in a large bowl. Whisk in the lemon juice and mustard, then the egg yolk. Whisk in the oil, 1 tablespoon at a time. Add the Worcestershire sauce (if using). Add the lettuce and toss well. Sprinkle the Parmesan and croutons over the top. Mix well and season to taste with salt and pepper. Serve immediately.

CAESAR SALAD

ICEBERG WEDGE SALAD
WITH BLUE CHEESE DRESSING

PREPARATION TIME: 10 MINUTES
COOKING TIME: 10 MINUTES
SERVES: 4

- ½ lb (225 g) thick-cut bacon (streaky),
  cut into 1-inch (2.5 cm) pieces
- 1 cup (240 ml) buttermilk
- ½ cup (120 ml) sour cream
- 2 tablespoons cider vinegar
- 1 tablespoon finely chopped fresh chives
- ½ lb (225 g) crumbled blue cheese
- Salt and freshly ground black pepper
- 1 head iceberg lettuce
- 1 small red onion, sliced thinly

Heat a medium frying pan over high heat. Add the bacon and cook, stirring frequently, until the bacon is crispy and browned, 6–8 minutes. Drain on paper towels.

In a small bowl, mix together the buttermilk, sour cream, vinegar, and chives. Fold in the blue cheese. Season to taste with salt and pepper.

Cut the iceberg lettuce into 4 wedges, removing the core but keeping the wedges intact. Place each wedge on a plate. Spoon the dressing over each wedge and top with slices of red onion and the reserved bacon. Serve at once.

SEVEN-LAYER SALAD

PREPARATION TIME: 20 MINUTES,
  PLUS CHILLING TIME
COOKING TIME: 20 MINUTES
SERVES: 12

- 2 heads iceberg lettuce, chopped
- 6 hard-boiled eggs, chopped
- 1 lb (455 g) bacon (streaky), cooked
  and finely chopped
- 1 small white onion, finely diced
- 8 oz (225 g) cheddar cheese, grated
- 10 oz (285 g) frozen green peas, thawed
- ½ cup (105 g) mayonnaise
- ½ cup (120 ml) sour cream
- 1 tablespoon sugar

[This Utah standby appears at many potlucks. Variations are endless, but here's the classic combination.]

In a large clear glass bowl or a 9 x 13-inch (23 x 33 cm) glass baking dish, place the chopped lettuce in an even layer. Sprinkle the chopped eggs over the lettuce, followed by the bacon, then the onion, cheese, and peas.

In a small bowl, whisk together the mayonnaise, sour cream, and sugar. Using a rubber spatula, spread the dressing evenly over the green pea layer. Cover the entire salad with plastic wrap (clingfilm), being careful not to let the wrap touch the dressing. Refrigerate for at least 1 hour and up to 8 hours.

To serve, either toss the salad in the bowl or serve the salad straight from the glass bowl, cutting the salad into 12 servings and using a metal spatula (fish slice) to lift it out of the pan.

ICEBERG WEDGE SALAD WITH BLUE CHEESE DRESSING

WALDORF SALAD

PREPARATION TIME: 15 MINUTES
COOKING TIME: 5 MINUTES
SERVES: 4

- 4 large Granny Smith apples, diced
- 4 stalks celery, halved lengthwise and chopped
- 1 carrot, grated
- ½ cup (105 g) mayonnaise
- 2 tablespoons fresh lemon juice
- Salt and freshly ground black pepper
- ½ cup (50 g) walnuts, toasted and chopped
- 4 tablespoons raisins (optional)

[This salad was invented in the late 1800s at The Waldorf Astoria Hotel in New York City.]

In a bowl, combine the apples, celery, carrot, mayonnaise, and lemon juice and stir well to combine. Season to taste with salt and pepper. Fold in the walnuts and raisins (if using).

WALDORF SALAD

COBB SALAD

PREPARATION TIME: 15 MINUTES
COOKING TIME: 40 MINUTES
SERVES: 6

- 1 large head romaine lettuce, finely chopped
- 6 slices bacon (streaky), cooked and finely chopped
- 2 chicken breasts, cooked and sliced
- 1 large tomato, diced
- 2 hard-boiled eggs, quartered
- 2 avocados, diced
- ½ cup (55 g) finely crumbled blue cheese
- ¼ cup (60 ml) red wine vinegar
- ½ cup (120 ml) extra-virgin olive oil
- 1 tablespoon Dijon mustard
- Salt and freshly ground black pepper

Spread the lettuce on a large serving platter. Arrange the bacon, chicken, tomato, eggs, avocado and blue cheese in neat strips on top of the lettuce. In a small bowl, whisk together the vinegar, oil, mustard, and salt and pepper to taste. Drizzle over the salad and serve at once.

MEMPHIS-STYLE COLESLAW

PREPARATION TIME: 15 MINUTES,
    PLUS 1 HOUR REFRIGERATION TIME
SERVES: 4

- ¾ cup (155 g) mayonnaise
- 1½ tablespoons Dijon mustard
- 1½ tablespoons cider vinegar
- 2 teaspoons sugar
- ¾ teaspoon salt
- ½ teaspoon freshly ground black pepper
- 2 tablespoons grated onion
- 1½ teaspoons celery seeds
- 4 cups (300 g) thinly sliced cabbage
- ½ cup (75 g) minced green bell pepper
- 1 carrot, grated

In a small bowl, whisk together the mayonnaise, mustard, vinegar, sugar, salt, black pepper, onion, and celery seeds. In a large bowl, combine the cabbage, bell pepper, and carrot. Add the dressing to the vegetable mixture and toss well to combine. Cover and refrigerate for at least 1 hour and up to 2 days before serving.

COBB SALAD

MEXICAN SLAW

PREPARATION TIME: 20 MINUTES,
PLUS 1 HOUR CHILLING TIME
SERVES: 8–10

- ¼ cup (60 ml) fresh lime juice
- 2 tablespoons distilled white vinegar
- 1 small clove garlic, minced
- 2 tablespoons minced jalapeño
- ⅓ cup (80 ml) olive oil
- 8 cups (560 g) thinly sliced cabbage
- 3 medium carrots, grated
- 1 green bell pepper, diced
- ½ cup (50 g) thinly sliced scallions (spring onions)
- 1 teaspoon salt
- ½ teaspoon freshly ground black pepper
- 4 tablespoons chopped fresh cilantro (coriander)

In a large bowl, whisk together the lime juice, vinegar, garlic, and jalapeño. While whisking constantly, slowly add the olive oil in a steady stream. Add the cabbage, carrots, bell pepper, scallions (spring onions), salt, and black pepper and toss well to combine. Cover and refrigerate for 1 hour. Toss with cilantro (coriander) and serve.

LEXINGTON BARBECUE SLAW

PREPARATION TIME: 20 MINUTES
SERVES: 10–12

- 1 large head cabbage (about 3½ lb/ 1.6 kg), finely shredded
- 1 large carrot, grated
- ⅔ cup (130 g) sugar
- ⅓ cup (45 g) kosher (coarse) salt
- 1½ cups (355 ml) Lexington Barbecue Sauce (page 468)
- Freshly ground black pepper

[Lexington, North Carolina, lays claim to the first barbecue joint, circa 1919, when one local set up a tent in the center of town each Saturday to sell his pit-cooked pork. Red slaw is another of the town's claims to fame. Lexington's coleslaw skips the mayonnaise and instead calls for saucing the chopped cabbage salad with a spicy ketchup and vinegar mixture.]

In a large bowl, combine the cabbage and carrot. Sprinkle with the sugar and salt and toss to combine. Let stand for 5 minutes, then transfer to a large colander and rinse thoroughly under cold running water. Squeeze well to dry and blot with paper towels. (It's very important to remove as much liquid as possible!) Transfer to a large dry bowl.

Pour the barbecue sauce over vegetables and toss to coat. Adjust the seasoning to taste with salt, pepper, and/or sugar.

MEXICAN SLAW

CUCUMBER SALAD WITH SOY AND GINGER

PREPARATION TIME: 15 MINUTES
SERVES: 4

- 1½ lb (680 g) seedless (English) cucumbers (about 2)
- 3 tablespoons unseasoned rice vinegar
- 3 tablespoons grated fresh ginger (from 1½ inches/4 cm fresh ginger)
- 1½ teaspoons light brown sugar
- 3 tablespoons soy sauce
- 2 tablespoons chopped fresh cilantro (coriander)
- Salt and freshly ground black pepper

Slice the cucumbers into ¼-inch (6 mm) thick rounds. In a large bowl, whisk to combine the vinegar, ginger, brown sugar, and soy sauce. Add the cucumbers and toss to coat. Let rest for 5 minutes, then toss again with the cilantro (coriander). Season to taste with salt and pepper.

CUCUMBERS IN SOUR CREAM

PREPARATION TIME: 10 MINUTES, PLUS 4 HOURS CHILLING TIME
SERVES: 6

- 4 medium cucumbers
- ¾ cup (180 ml) sour cream
- 2 tablespoons white wine vinegar
- 1 tablespoon sugar
- ½ teaspoon salt
- ¼ teaspoon freshly ground black pepper
- 2 tablespoons chopped fresh dill (optional)

Peel the cucumbers, or don't, or peel long strips off, leaving thin stripes of skin. Very thinly slice the cucumbers and place in a bowl. Add the sour cream, vinegar, sugar, salt, pepper, and dill (if using). Cover and refrigerate for at least 4 hours.

REDBUD COUSCOUS SALAD

PREPARATION TIME: 10 MINUTES
COOKING TIME: 10 MINUTES
SERVES: 4

- ⅔ cup (125 g) couscous, cooked and cooled
- 2 tablespoons extra-virgin olive oil or walnut oil
- ¼ teaspoon sugar
- Pinch of salt
- 1 tablespoon fresh lemon juice
- 1 cup (25 g) fresh redbud buds
- ¼ cup (32 g) dried apricots, finely sliced
- 8 fresh mint leaves, torn up

[The eastern redbud is a small tree, a popular ornamental, and the state tree of Oklahoma. Unopened clusters of spring buds, as well as their very fresh flowers, have a sweet shell-pea flavor. You can also sprinkle them over green salads, yogurt, or even ice cream. This salad could be made with grain, such as bulgur or quinoa, instead of couscous.]

In a large bowl, toss the couscous with the oil. In a small bowl, whisk together the sugar, salt, and lemon juice. Pour over the couscous. Add the redbud buds, apricots, and mint and toss well. Serve at once.

MAC SALAD

PREPARATION TIME: 10 MINUTES,
  PLUS COOLING AND CHILLING TIME
COOKING TIME: 15 MINUTES
SERVES: 8–10

- 1 lb (455 g) elbow macaroni
- ¼ onion, grated
- 2 carrots, grated
- 2 stalks celery, finely chopped
- 2 tablespoons apple cider vinegar
- 2 cups (420 g) mayonnaise
- ¼ cup (60 ml) milk
- 1½ teaspoons sugar
- ½ teaspoon salt
- ½ teaspoon freshly ground black pepper

[This simple island standard is tangy, sweet, and popular for lunch. Don't drain the pasta al dente — Hawaiians cook it until it's completely soft, which allows it to soak up more dressing.]

In a pot of boiling salted water, cook the macaroni until very tender, almost mushy. Drain and transfer to a large bowl. Stir in the onion, carrots, celery, and vinegar and let cool to room temperature.

In a small bowl, whisk together the mayonnaise, milk, and sugar. Stir into the macaroni mixture. Season with the salt and pepper. Refrigerate for at least 4 hours and up to 24 hours.

BEET, AVOCADO, AND CITRUS SALAD

PREPARATION TIME: 15 MINUTES
COOKING TIME: 50 MINUTES
SERVES: 4

- 1¼ lb (565 g) medium beets (beetroots)
- Salt
- 3 tablespoons fresh lemon juice
- ½ teaspoon Dijon mustard
- ¼ teaspoon freshly ground black pepper
- ⅓ cup (80 ml) extra-virgin olive oil
- 1 tablespoon chopped fresh tarragon
- 2 avocados, cut into ½-inch (1.25 cm) thick slices
- 2 blood oranges, peeled and segmented
- ½ cup (50 g) thinly sliced red onion

Bring a medium pot of water to a boil and salt generously. Add the beets (beetroots), reduce to a simmer, cover, and cook until the beets can be pierced easily with a knife, 30–45 minutes. Meanwhile, set up a bowl of ice and water. When the beets are done, drain and shock in the ice water until cool enough to handle. Drain and peel. Slice each beet into 8 wedges.

In a medium bowl, whisk together the lemon juice, mustard, ½ teaspoon salt, and the pepper. Whisking constantly, add the olive oil in a stream until creamy and emulsified. Whisk in the tarragon.

On a small platter, arrange the beets, avocados, blood oranges, and onions. Drizzle with the vinaigrette and season to taste with salt. Serve immediately.

TABBOULEH

PREPARATION TIME: 35 MINUTES
SERVES: 4–6

- 1½ cups (300 g) finely diced tomatoes (about 2 medium)
- ¼ cup (55 g) bulgur wheat
- 4 bunches fresh parsley
- 1 bunch fresh mint
- 4 scallions (spring onions), finely chopped
- 1 teaspoon kosher (coarse) salt
- ¼ teaspoon freshly ground black pepper
- ⅓ cup (80 ml) extra-virgin olive oil
- ¼ cup (60 ml) fresh lemon juice
- Romaine lettuce or green cabbage leaves (optional), for serving

[Descended from Lebanese and Syrian recipes, this parsley-studded Middle Eastern salad or side dish is common across the country.]

In a large bowl, stir together the tomatoes (and all of their juices) and the bulgur wheat. Let rest for 20 minutes.

Meanwhile, remove the large stems from the parsley and mint (small/medium stems are okay). Thinly slice the parsley and place in a medium bowl. Finely chop the mint and add to the parsley along with the scallions (spring onions).

Just before serving, combine the herb/scallion mixture with the tomato/bulgur mixture. Season with the salt and pepper and stir in the olive oil and lemon juice. If desired, serve alongside lettuce or cabbage leaves.

BEET, AVOCADO, AND CITRUS SALAD

PALISADE PEACH AND BASIL SALAD

PREPARATION TIME: 10 MINUTES
SERVES: 4

- 6 peaches
- 1 cup (150 g) cherry tomatoes, halved
- 1 tablespoon fresh lemon juice
- 1 tablespoon honey
- ¼ cup (30 g) very thinly sliced red onion
- ¼ teaspoon salt
- 8 large basil leaves
- ¾ cup (85 g) crumbled sheep's milk feta
  or goat cheese

[The hot days and cool nights in the Palisade area of Colorado yield spectacular stone fruit. Palisade peaches are known for being sweet, juicy, and big.]

Slice the peaches and toss with the tomatoes, lemon juice, honey, red onion, and salt. Tear the basil into small pieces and add to the salad. Serve topped with crumbled cheese.

THREE-BEAN SALAD

PREPARATION TIME: 25 MINUTES,
   PLUS MARINATING TIME
COOKING TIME: 15 MINUTES
SERVES: 6-8

- 1 lb (455 g) green beans, trimmed and cut
  into 1-inch (2.5 cm) pieces
- 1 lb (455 g) yellow wax beans, trimmed
  and cut into 1-inch (2.5 cm) pieces
- ⅓ cup (65 g) sugar
- ⅔ cup (160 ml) cider vinegar
- ⅓ cup (80 ml) vegetable oil
- 1 teaspoon celery seeds
- 1 medium onion, thinly sliced
- 2 cans (15 oz/425 g each) kidney beans,
  rinsed and drained
- 2 tablespoons minced fresh parsley
- Salt and freshly ground black pepper

Set up a large bowl of ice and water. Bring a large pot of water to a boil. Blanch the green and yellow wax beans in the boiling water until just tender, about 5 minutes. Drain and plunge them into the ice bath. Drain well.

In a large bowl, whisk together the sugar, vinegar, oil, and celery seeds. Stir in the onion and let stand for 5 minutes. Add the kidney beans, the blanched beans, and the parsley. Season to taste with salt and pepper. Let salad marinate at room temperature for about 1 hour before serving.

PALISADE PEACH AND BASIL SALAD

WILD RICE SALAD

PREPARATION TIME: 5 MINUTES,
   PLUS COOLING AND STANDING TIME
COOKING TIME: 1 HOUR 10 MINUTES
SERVES: 8

- 2 cups (360 g) wild rice
- 1 medium red onion, thinly sliced
- 1 cup (160 g) dried cranberries
- 1 cup (140 g) slivered (chopped) almonds
- 4 tablespoons chopped fresh parsley
- ½ cup (120 ml) extra-virgin olive oil
- ¼ cup (60 ml) red wine vinegar
- Salt and freshly ground black pepper

[Wild rice, Minnesota's state grain, is actually the seed of an aquatic grass. Naturally abundant in Minnesota's rivers and lakes, wild rice was a staple in the diet of the native Chippewa and Sioux people. Today some still harvest it by canoe.]

In a medium saucepan, bring 6 cups (1.4 liters) water to a boil. Stir in the wild rice and return to a boil. Reduce the heat, cover, and simmer until the rice begins to pop open, 50–60 minutes. Uncover, stir, and cook 5 minutes longer. Drain any remaining liquid and pour the rice into a large bowl. Let cool to room temperature.

Add the onion, cranberries, almonds, parsley, oil, and vinegar and season to taste with salt and pepper. Let the salad stand at room temperature for 1 hour. (The salad may be made ahead and refrigerated, but tastes best when served at room temperature.)

CORN SALAD

PREPARATION TIME: 20 MINUTES
SERVES: 4

- 4 ears of corn, kernels cut from cob
- 1 avocado, diced
- 1 cup cherry tomatoes, halved
- 4 tablespoons thinly sliced scallions
  (spring onions)
- 2 tablespoons olive oil
- 1 tablespoon white balsamic vinegar
- 1 tablespoon fresh lime juice
- Kosher (coarse) salt and black pepper

In a large bowl, combine the corn, avocado, tomatoes, scallions (spring onions), oil, vinegar, lime juice, ½ teaspoon salt, and ¼ teaspoon black pepper (or more to taste). Toss well to combine.

Let rest for 10 minutes before serving to let the flavors come together.

WILD RICE SALAD

POTATO SALAD

PREPARATION TIME: 15 MINUTES,
   PLUS CHILLING TIME
COOKING TIME: 40 MINUTES
SERVES: 4–6

- 1½ lb (680 g) waxy potatoes (such as red or Yukon Gold)
- ½ cup (105 g) mayonnaise, or more to taste
- 1 tablespoon Dijon mustard
- 2 stalks celery, diced
- 3 tablespoons finely diced red onion
- 2 tablespoons finely chopped fresh chives
- Salt and freshly ground black pepper

Scrub the potatoes. Put in a pot and cover with cold water by 2 inches (5 cm). Bring to a boil over high heat, then reduce the heat to medium and boil until tender, 20–30 minutes depending on the size of the potatoes. A knife will easily pierce the potatoes when they are done. Drain in a colander. Refrigerate the potatoes in a single layer until they are quite cold. This could take several hours. (You may boil the potatoes the day before you plan to make the salad and chill them overnight.)

Cut the potatoes in 1-inch (2.5 cm) chunks and place in a bowl. Stir in the mayonnaise and mustard, then stir in the celery, onion, and chives. Season to taste with salt and pepper. Chill for 1 hour or so before serving.

HOT GERMAN POTATO SALAD

PREPARATION TIME: 15 MINUTES
COOKING TIME: 35 MINUTES
SERVES: 8

- 3 lb (1.4 kg) small red or other waxy potatoes, scrubbed
- ½ lb (225 g) bacon (streaky)
- 1 large red onion, diced
- ½ cup (120 ml) cider vinegar
- ¼ cup (50 g) sugar
- 1 tablespoon Dijon mustard
- 1½ teaspoons salt
- 2 tablespoons minced fresh chives
- 1 tablespoon minced fresh parsley

[Despite its name, this dish is best served warm.]

Place the potatoes in a medium saucepan and add cold water to cover by 2 inches (5 cm). Bring to a boil and cook until tender, about 20 minutes.

Meanwhile, in a frying pan, cook the bacon over medium-high heat until crisp, about 5 minutes. Reserving the fat in the pan, drain the bacon on paper towels. Add the onion to the frying pan and cook, stirring, until just tender, about 5 minutes. Whisk in the vinegar, sugar, mustard, and salt.

Drain the potatoes and slice into ¼-inch (6 mm) thick rounds. Place the potato slices in a large bowl and toss with the onion mixture. Crumble the bacon over the top and mix in along with the chives and parsley. Serve warm.

HOT GERMAN POTATO SALAD

GREEN JELL-O SALAD

PREPARATION TIME: 10 MINUTES,
 PLUS CHILLING AND SETTING TIME
COOKING TIME: 5 MINUTES
SERVES: 12

- 1 box (3 oz/85 g) lime Jell-O
- 1 box (3 oz/85 g) lemon Jell-O
- 1 can (8 oz/225 g) juice-packed crushed
  pineapple
- 1 cup (225 g) full-fat cottage cheese
- ½ cup (105 g) mayonnaise

[Utah eats far more Jell-O, especially in "green," than any other state. This is mostly attributed to the large Mormon population, which typically has big families, eschews alcohol, and enjoys sweets. The Jell-O though is not always served for dessert. Carrots, peas, and cubed ham are often suspended in jiggling "salads." Utah Jell-O may also be studded with pistachios and mandarin orange segments or, in this classic version, crushed pineapple.]

Empty the boxes of Jell-O into a large heatproof bowl. Drain the pineapple liquid into a 2-cup measuring cup (500 ml measuring jug) and set the fruit aside. To the juice, add enough water to equal 2 cups (475 ml), pour into a saucepan, and bring to a boil. Pour over the Jell-O powders and mix to dissolve. Transfer to the refrigerator to chill until the Jell-O has thickened to the consistency of thick syrup, about 30 minutes. Stir in the pineapple, cottage cheese, and mayonnaise until smooth. Pour the Jell-mixture into a mold or bowl. Cover and refrigerate until set, 2–3 hours.

AHI POKE

PREPARATION TIME: 10 MINUTES,
 PLUS CHILLING TIME
SERVES: 2–4

- 1 lb (455 g) sashimi-grade ahi tuna
- 4 tablespoons very thinly diagonally
  sliced scallions (spring onions)
- 1 clove garlic, very thinly sliced
- ¼ cup (60 ml) soy sauce
- 2 tablespoons sesame oil
- 1 tablespoon toasted sesame seeds
- 2 teaspoons very finely chopped roasted
  macadamia nuts
- 1 teaspoon crushed chili flakes

[This simple seafood staple, named for the Hawaiian word for "slice" or "cut" and pronounced poke-eh, is chunks of tuna (or other spectacularly fresh Pacific catch) marinated in sesame oil and soy sauce. It's classically served atop a bowl of white rice.]

Using a very sharp knife, cut the tuna into 1-inch (2.5 cm) cubes. Place the tuna in a glass or ceramic bowl and toss with the remaining ingredients. Cover and refrigerate for at least 2 hours to chill. Best eaten the day it is prepared.

POKE WITH WILD KUKUI

PREPARATION TIME: 15 MINUTES,
   PLUS CHILLING TIME
SERVES: 6

- 2 lb (910 g) sushi-grade ahi tuna, cubed
- ½ cup finely sliced scallions (spring onions) tops
- ½ cup (80 g) finely diced sweet onion, such as Maui or Vidalia
- Scant ⅓ cup (25 g) chopped limu kohu or soaked hijiki seaweed
- ¼ cup (60 ml) soy sauce
- 2 teaspoons sesame oil
- 2 tablespoons 'Inamona (page 457)

[Here poke, the traditional raw fish salad, is finished with ground roasted nuts of the kukui tree, a condiment known as 'inamona. Kukui, the fruit of Hawaii's state tree, also known as candlenut, kemiri (*Aleurites moluccanus*), was considered to be brought to Hawaii from the South Pacific. Kukui trees have a long history of traditional uses, including wood for canoes, nut shells for leis, and nut oil as a moisturizer and lamp oil.]

In a bowl, combine all ingredients except the 'inamona, and chill for 1 hour. Just before serving, stir in the 'inamona and plate.

LOMI-LOMI SALMON

PREPARATION TIME: 15 MINUTES,
   PLUS 1 DAY CURING TIME
SERVES: 4

For the salmon cure:
- ½ cup (100 g) sugar
- 1 cup (135 g) kosher (coarse) salt
- 1 lb (455 g) very fresh wild salmon fillet, skinless

For the salad:
- 3 tomatoes, seeded and diced
- 1 medium white onion, diced
- 3 scallions (spring onions), very thinly sliced on the diagonal
- 1 tablespoon sesame oil
- Juice of 1 lime

For the salmon cure: In a bowl, mix together the sugar and salt. Cover a baking sheet or long platter with plastic wrap (clingfilm), letting some hang over the edges. Scatter half of the sugar/salt combo over the plastic and place the fish fillet on top. Scatter the remaining sugar/salt over the fish and pat all around to distribute it evenly. Wrap the fish well and refrigerate for 24 hours.

Remove the salmon from the refrigerator. Rinse it well under cold running water. Drain the fish and pat dry with paper towels. Using a very sharp knife, cut the salmon into roughly ½-inch (1.25 cm) cubes.

For the salad: Place the salmon in a large bowl. Add the tomatoes, onion, scallions, sesame oil, and lime juice and massage them all together. Serve immediately.

CRAB SALAD

PREPARATION TIME: 10 MINUTES
SERVES: 4

- 2 cups (330 g) chilled crabmeat, picked over for shells and cartilage
- 1 cup (100 g) diced celery
- 1 tablespoon fresh lemon juice
- 4 tablespoons mayonnaise
- Bibb (round) lettuce leaves and avocado slices, for serving

In a bowl, stir together the crabmeat, celery, lemon juice, and mayonnaise. Serve the crab salad on lettuce leaves and garnish with avocado slices.

PICKLED SHRIMP

PREPARATION TIME: 35 MINUTES,
   PLUS OVERNIGHT CHILLING TIME
COOKING TIME: 10 MINUTES
SERVES: 4–6

- 3 tablespoons Old Bay seasoning
- 1 lb (455 g) medium shrimp (prawns), peeled and deveined
- 1 teaspoon celery seeds
- ½ teaspoon mustard seeds
- 1 cup (240 ml) extra-virgin olive oil
- ½ cup (120 ml) unseasoned rice vinegar
- ¼ cup (14 g) packed fresh parsley, finely chopped
- 1 tablespoon kosher (coarse) salt
- ½ teaspoon crushed chili flakes
- 2 cloves garlic, finely chopped
- 6 bay leaves, halved
- 1 cup (115 g) thinly sliced yellow onion
- 2 lemons, thinly sliced

[Seafood spices and bay leaves are the dominant flavors in these Lowcountry cocktail party favorites. Bay laurel trees are grown as evergreen plants in many gardens in and around the Charleston area.]

Set up a bowl of ice and water. Fill a medium saucepan halfway with water. Add the Old Bay and bring to a low boil. Add the shrimp (prawns), reduce the heat to low, and cook until they turn pink, about 2 minutes. Drain and transfer to the ice bath to chill. Drain and place on a plate lined with paper towels.

In a large bowl, whisk together the celery seeds, mustard seeds, oil, vinegar, parsley, salt, chili flakes, garlic, bay leaves, and ¼ cup (60 ml) water. In a 1-quart (950 ml) glass jar, layer the shrimp, onion, and lemons. Pour the olive oil mixture over the shrimp to let it sink in between the layers. Ensure that the shrimp are completely submerged by pressing gently with your hands to cover them with liquid. Close the lid and refrigerate overnight to chill before serving. The pickled shrimp will keep for up to 48 hours.

PICKLED NORTHERN PIKE

PREPARATION TIME: 10 MINUTES,
  PLUS COOLING TIME AND 2 DAYS
  BRINING AND PICKLING TIME
COOKING TIME: 30 MINUTES
MAKES: ABOUT 1 QUART (950 ML)

- 1 cup (290 g) salt
- 1 lb (455 g) northern pike (or other white firm-fleshed fish) fillets, skin-on, cut into 1-inch (2.5 cm) pieces, frozen first
- 2 cups (475 ml) cider vinegar
- ½ cup (100 g) sugar
- 2 teaspoons black peppercorns
- 2 teaspoons allspice berries
- 2 teaspoons mustard seeds
- 2 teaspoons coriander seeds
- 2 bay leaves
- 1 large red onion, thinly sliced

In a saucepan, combine 4 cups (1 liter) water and the salt and bring to a boil. Remove from the heat and let cool to room temperature.

Place the fish in a large nonreactive container (glass or ceramic) and pour the cooled brine over it. Make sure the fish is submerged. Cover and refrigerate for 24 hours.

In a medium saucepan, combine 1 cup (240 ml) water, the vinegar, sugar, spices, and bay leaves and bring to a boil. Reduce to a simmer and cook for 15 minutes. Remove from the heat and let cool. (The pickling liquid can be made in advance and refrigerated.)

Drain the fish. In a large jar (or other deep nonreactive container), layer the fish with the sliced onion and pour the pickling liquid over. Cover and refrigerate for 24 hours before eating.

PUERTO RICAN SALT COD SALAD (ENSALADA DE BACALAO)

PREPARATION TIME: 35 MINUTES,
  PLUS 8 HOURS SOAKING TIME
COOKING TIME: 20 MINUTES
SERVES 4

- 1 lb (455 g) bacalao (salt cod)
- 3 medium potatoes, peeled and cubed
- 2 chayotes, cubed
- 1 large red onion, diced
- 2 medium tomatoes, diced
- ½ cup (120 ml) olive oil
- 3 tablespoons vinegar
- 1 teaspoon dried Mexican oregano
- Salt and freshly ground black pepper
- Cooked white rice, for serving
- 2 avocados, sliced
- 4 hard-boiled eggs, sliced

Rinse the salt cod, place in a large bowl, cover with cold water, and soak for 8 hours. Rinse the cod well under cold running water for several minutes, then transfer to a large pot. Cover with water, bring to a boil, and drain. Repeat this process two more times.

In the same pot, place the drained cod and plenty of water to cover. Bring to a boil, then add the potatoes and chayotes. Return to a boil and cook until the vegetables are tender, about 10 minutes. Drain everything in a colander.

Separate the cod from the vegetables. Transfer the vegetables to a large bowl and add the onion, tomatoes, oil, vinegar, and oregano. Flake the fish, removing any bones, and add to the bowl. Mix well and season to taste with salt and pepper.

Arrange the salad on top of cooked rice and garnish with slices of avocado and hard-boiled eggs.

WARM SALMON SALAD

PREPARATION TIME: 15 MINUTES,
   PLUS 4 ½ TO 8 HOURS MARINATING TIME
COOKING TIME: 20 MINUTES
SERVES: 4

For the salmon:
- ½ cup (120 ml) extra-virgin olive oil
- 2 tablespoons cider vinegar
- 1 tablespoon fresh lemon juice
- 2 cloves garlic, minced
- 2 teaspoons minced fresh thyme
- ½ teaspoon salt
- ½ teaspoon freshly ground black pepper
- 4 salmon fillets or steaks (about
  8 oz/225 g each)

For the salad:
- 12 cups (510 g) torn greens (lettuces,
  frisée, baby kale, mustard greens,
  or a mixture)
- 4 tablespoons extra-virgin olive oil
- 1 medium red onion, thinly sliced
- 1 clove garlic, thinly sliced
- 1 tablespoon fresh lemon juice
- 1½ cups (50 g) fresh sourdough
  bread cubes
- Salt and freshly ground black pepper
- 2 large tomatoes, cut into wedges

For the salmon: In a container big enough to hold the salmon, combine the oil, vinegar, lemon juice, garlic, thyme, salt, and pepper. Add the salmon and turn to coat. Cover and refrigerate for at least 4½ hours and up to 8 hours.

Preheat the broiler (grill) with the rack about 6 inches (15 cm) from the heat source.

Cook the salmon until medium-rare, about 3–4 minutes per side (depending on the thickness of the salmon). Set aside to keep warm.

For the salad: Place the greens in a large bowl and have the bowl near the stove. In a large frying pan, heat the olive oil over medium heat. Add the onion and cook, stirring often, for 6 minutes, to soften. Stir in the garlic and cook for another few minutes. Stir in the lemon juice. Add the bread cubes and cook, stirring, until the cubes are beginning to toast. Pour the hot bread mixture onto the greens and toss well. Season to taste with salt and pepper.

Divide the greens among 4 plates. Place the salmon on top and garnish with tomato wedges.

HAM SALAD

PREPARATION TIME: 10 MINUTES
COOKING TIME: 10 MINUTES
MAKES: ABOUT 4 CUPS

- 3 cups (455 g) finely diced or ground
  cooked ham
- 2 hard-boiled eggs, finely diced
- 1 cup (100 g) finely diced celery
- 1 small onion, finely diced
- ⅔ cup (150 g) mayonnaise
- ½ cup (120 g) sweet relish
- 1 tablespoon Dijon mustard

[This recipe is a good use for leftover ham. The salad makes enough for a lot of crackers or about 8 sandwiches.]

Mix all of the ingredients together and serve.

WARM SALMON SALAD

WEST INDIES SALAD

PREPARATION TIME: 15 MINUTES
SERVES: 4

- ¾ cup (100 g) sliced white onion
- 2 tablespoons cider vinegar
- 2 tablespoons fresh lemon juice
- 2 tablespoons vegetable oil
- ¾ teaspoon salt
- ¼ teaspoon freshly ground black pepper
- 1 lb (455 g) lump crabmeat, picked over for shells and cartilage
- 8 butter lettuce leaves
- Saltine crackers, for serving (optional)

[Despite the name, this simple dish was born in Alabama, the 1947 creation of a Mobile restaurateur named Bill Bayley. While doing a heavy business in fried blue crab claws, he needed a way to move the lump crabmeat he was quickly accumulating. Spurning the ubiquitous mayonnaise-bound crab salad, he created a ceviche-inspired version, as delicious as it is simple, that has since become a regional staple, still available at most Lowlands crab shacks.]

In a medium bowl, combine the onion, vinegar, lemon juice, oil, salt, and pepper. Let rest for 10 minutes. Add the crabmeat and toss very gently to combine. Serve the salad on a bed of lettuce leaves. Serve with saltine crackers, if desired.

EGG SALAD

PREPARATION TIME: 25 MINUTES
COOKING TIME: 10 MINUTES
SERVES: 4

- 6 eggs
- ¼ cup (50 g) mayonnaise
- 1 tablespoon Dijon or yellow mustard
- 2 scallions (spring onions), thinly sliced
- Salt and freshly ground black pepper

Set up a bowl of ice and water. Place the eggs in a pot and cover with cold water. Bring to a boil over medium-high heat. Remove from the heat, cover, and let sit for 8 minutes. Using a slotted spoon, transfer the cooked eggs to the ice bath and let sit for a few minutes. Peel the eggs and refrigerate them for 15 minutes to chill.

Chop the eggs and place them in a bowl. Stir in the mayonnaise, mustard, and scallions (spring onions). Season to taste with salt and pepper.

WEST INDIES SALAD

CHICKEN SALAD

PREPARATION TIME: 10 MINUTES
SERVES: 4

- 2 cups (280 g) diced cooked chicken
- 2 stalks celery, diced
- 1 small onion, diced
- ½ cup (105 g) mayonnaise
- 1 tablespoon finely chopped fresh parsley
- Salt and freshly ground black pepper

[This is a lunch classic, served on lettuce leaves or tucked into a sandwich.]

Mix everything together in a bowl. Season to taste with salt and pepper.

BUTTERNUT SQUASH–APPLE SOUP

PREPARATION TIME: 30 MINUTES
COOKING TIME: 1 HOUR
SERVES: 6

- 2 tablespoons olive oil
- 1 large onion, chopped
- 3 cloves garlic, chopped
- 1 large butternut squash, peeled
  and cut into 2-inch (5 cm) chunks
- 4 cups (950 ml) apple cider
- ¼ teaspoon freshly grated nutmeg
- Salt and freshly ground black pepper

In a large soup pot, heat the oil over medium heat. Add the onion and cook, stirring frequently, until the onion has softened, about 7 minutes. Add the garlic and cook for a few more minutes. Add the squash, cider, and 3 cups (710 ml) water. Cover and bring to a boil. Reduce the heat and simmer until the squash is tender, about 40 minutes. Remove from the heat and, working in batches, purée the soup in a blender or food processor until smooth. As each batch is puréed, pour into another large pot.

Place the puréed soup over medium heat and return to a simmer. Stir in the nutmeg and season to taste with salt and pepper. Serve hot.

CHICKEN SALAD

ROASTED BEET BORSCHT

PREPARATION TIME: 10 MINUTES
COOKING TIME: 1 HOUR 30 MINUTES
SERVES: 4

- 2 lb (910 g) beets (beetroots)
- Salt and freshly ground black pepper
- 6 sprigs fresh thyme
- 6 tablespoons extra-virgin olive oil
- 1 medium onion, chopped
- 2 carrots, chopped
- 2 cloves garlic, chopped
- 6 cups (1.4 liters) chicken stock, heated
- 2 tablespoons red wine vinegar
- 1 tablespoon honey
- 4 tablespoons sour cream
- 2 tablespoons chopped fresh dill

Preheat the oven to 400°F (200°C/Gas Mark 6).

Scrub the beets, put them in a baking pan, and season with 1 teaspoon salt and ½ teaspoon pepper. Add 3 thyme sprigs and drizzle with 3 tablespoons of the olive oil. Cover with foil and bake until tender, about 1 hour. Once the beets are cool enough to handle but still warm, slip off their skins and chop the beets into large chunks.

Heat a large soup pot over medium heat. Add the remaining 3 tablespoons olive oil. Add the onion, carrots, and garlic and cook until softened and just starting to color, about 10 minutes. Add the chicken stock and remaining 3 thyme sprigs and simmer until the vegetables are tender, about 20 minutes. Discard the thyme stems.

Transfer the mixture to a blender and blend on high until smooth. Add the vinegar, honey, and salt and pepper to taste and purée. Serve warm or refrigerate to serve chilled. Garnish each bowl with a dollop of sour cream and a sprinkle of fresh dill.

CHIPOTLE PUMPKIN SOUP

PREPARATION TIME: 15 MINUTES
COOKING TIME: 30 MINUTES
SERVES: 6–8

- 3 tablespoons olive oil
- 1 large onion, diced
- 1 teaspoon kosher (coarse) salt
- 2 cloves garlic, chopped
- 1 tablespoon ground cumin
- 1 sugar pumpkin (2 lb/910 g), peeled, seeded, and diced
- 6–6½ cups (1.4–1.5 liters) chicken stock
- 1 canned chipotle pepper in adobo sauce plus 1 tablespoon sauce

In a large Dutch oven (casserole) or soup pot, heat the oil over medium heat. Add the onion and salt and cook until translucent, 5–7 minutes. Stir in the garlic and cumin and cook for 2 minutes. Add the pumpkin, chicken stock, chipotle pepper, and adobo sauce. Increase the heat to medium-high and simmer, stirring occasionally, until the pumpkin is tender, 18–20 minutes.

Working in batches, transfer the soup to a blender and purée until very smooth. If needed, add up to ½ cup (120 ml) stock or water, 2 tablespoons at a time, to reach desired consistency. Serve warm.

ROASTED BEET BORSCHT

CARROT–GINGER SOUP

PREPARATION TIME: 20 MINUTES
COOKING TIME: 40 MINUTES
SERVES: 4–6

- 1½ lb (680 g) carrots, cut into ½-inch (1.25 cm) thick rounds
- 3 tablespoons (45 g) butter
- 1½ tablespoons grated fresh ginger
- ½ teaspoon grated orange zest
- ¼ cup (60 ml) fresh orange juice
- 1 teaspoon sugar
- Salt and freshly ground black pepper
- 6 cups (1.4 liters) vegetable stock
- Parsley leaves, for garnish

In a large soup pot or saucepan, combine the carrots, ½ cup (120 ml) water, the butter, ginger, orange zest, orange juice, sugar, ½ teaspoon salt, and ¼ teaspoon pepper. Cover and cook over medium-low heat until the liquid is almost all absorbed and the carrots are tender, about 20 minutes.

Add the vegetable stock and bring to a simmer over medium-high heat. Stir well to incorporate the syrup at the bottom of the pan. Cook until the carrots are very tender, about 15 minutes.

Working in batches, purée the soup in a blender until very smooth, 1–2 minutes. Add the soup back to the saucepan and season to taste with salt and pepper.

VICHYSSOISE

PREPARATION TIME: 25 MINUTES, PLUS CHILLING TIME
COOKING TIME: 35 MINUTES
SERVES: 4–6

- ¾ lb (340 g) leeks (about 3 large)
- 4 tablespoons (60 g) butter
- Salt
- 1½ lb (680 g) russet (baking) potatoes (about 3 large), peeled and diced
- Freshly ground black pepper
- 1 quart (1 liter) chicken stock
- 4 sprigs fresh thyme
- ½ cup (115 g) crème fraîche, plus more for serving
- 2 tablespoons chopped fresh chives

[This cold, creamy potato-leek soup was conceived at The Ritz-Carlton in New York City. Legend has it that the day it debuted, steel magnate Charles Schwab ate it and promptly ordered more.]

Halve the leeks lengthwise, then thinly slice crosswise. Place in a large bowl and fill with water. Break the leek slices up with your hands and let rest 10 minutes (the grit and sand should fall to the bottom). Lift the leeks from the water and drain in a colander. Repeat if the leeks are very sandy.

In a large pot, melt the butter over medium heat. Add the leeks and 1 teaspoon salt and cook until softened and translucent, about 5 minutes. Add the potatoes, ½ teaspoon pepper, the chicken stock, thyme and 1 cup (240 ml) water. Increase the heat to medium-high and bring to a simmer. Reduce the heat to medium-low and simmer until the potatoes are tender, 20–25 minutes. Remove from the heat and discard the thyme stems.

Working in batches, purée the soup in a blender until very smooth. Return to the pot. Stir in the crème fraîche and water, if needed, to reach the desired consistency (it should have a thinner texture, as it will thicken as it cools.) Cover and refrigerate until well chilled. Keep refrigerated until ready to serve.

Whisk well before serving. Garnish each bowl with chives and an additional spoonful of crème fraîche, if desired.

CARROT-GINGER SOUP

GREEN BEAN AND DUMPLING SOUP

PREPARATION TIME: 30 MINUTES
COOKING TIME: 25 MINUTES
SERVES: 4

For the soup:
- 2 medium potatoes, peeled and diced
- 1 teaspoon salt
- 2 cups (200 g) cut green beans (1-inch/ 2.5 cm lengths)
- 2 tablespoons all-purpose (plain) flour
- 2 tablespoons (30 g) butter or bacon fat
- 1 cup (240 ml) heavy (whipping) cream

For the dumplings:
- 1 cup (130 g) all-purpose (plain) flour
- ½ teaspoon salt
- 1 egg yolk

For the soup: In a heavy-bottomed pot, combine 4 cups (950 ml) water, the potatoes, and salt and bring to a boil over high heat. Add the green beans. Reduce the heat and keep at a low simmer while you prepare the rest of the ingredients.

In a small saucepan, melt the butter or bacon fat over medium heat. Stir in the flour and cook for 2–3 minutes, stirring constantly. Pour in the cream and stir well. Reduce the heat to low and cook, stirring constantly, until thickened, about 6 minutes.

For the dumplings: In a bowl, whisk together the flour and salt. Add the egg yolk and stir in with a fork. Turn the dough out onto a lightly floured surface and knead for 1 or 2 minutes, until the dumpling dough is smooth. Pinch off a small bit at a time and roll into balls, dusting your hands with flour as necessary.

To cook the dumplings, bring the soup to a vigorous simmer. Add the dumplings, stir gently, and let them cook until they rise to the top.

Stir the reserved cream sauce into the soup. Serve hot.

AMISH BEAN SOUP

PREPARATION TIME: 10 MINUTES,
    PLUS SOAKING TIME
COOKING TIME: 1½–2 HOURS
SERVES: 6–8

- 1 lb (455 g) dried navy beans, rinsed and picked over
- 1 ham hock
- 1 large onion, chopped
- 2 stalks celery, chopped
- 3 carrots, chopped
- 1 teaspoon dried oregano
- ½ teaspoon celery seeds
- Salt and freshly ground black pepper

In a large soup pot, bring the beans and 8 cups (2 liters) water to a rolling boil. Remove from the heat, cover, and let sit for 1 hour. Return the beans to a boil and add the ham hock, onion, celery, carrots, oregano, and celery seeds. Reduce the heat and simmer until the beans are tender, 1½–2 hours.

Remove the ham hock; then remove the meat from the bone and add it back to the pot. Season to taste with salt and pepper.

BEER CHEESE SOUP

PREPARATION TIME: 10 MINUTES
COOKING TIME: 25 MINUTES
SERVES: 4

- 4 tablespoons (60 g) butter
- 1 medium onion, diced
- 1 medium carrot, diced
- 4 tablespoons all-purpose (plain) flour
- 1½ cups (355 ml) beer
- 1 cup (240 ml) chicken stock or water
- 1 cup (240 ml) milk
- 1 cup (240 ml) heavy (whipping) cream
- 2 teaspoons Dijon mustard
- Dash of Worcestershire sauce
- 10 oz (285 g) sharp cheddar cheese, grated
- Salt and freshly ground black pepper

[Wisconsin is best known for producing cheese and beer. This soup stars both. It's rich, orange, and delicious.]

In a soup pot, melt the butter over medium-low heat. Add the onion and carrot and cook, stirring, until the onion has softened, about 5 minutes. Add the flour and cook, stirring constantly, for 3 minutes. Whisk in the beer, chicken stock, milk, and cream. Simmer on low, stirring occasionally, for 15 minutes. Whisk in the mustard and Worcestershire sauce. Whisk in the cheese a handful at a time until melted. Season to taste with salt and pepper.

CREAM OF MUSHROOM SOUP

PREPARATION TIME: 10 MINUTES
COOKING TIME: 30 MINUTES
SERVES: 4

- 4 tablespoons (60 g) butter
- 1 lb (455 g) mushrooms, sliced
- 1 large onion, finely diced
- 3 cloves garlic, minced
- 1 teaspoon salt
- ½ teaspoon freshly ground black pepper
- 2 tablespoons all-purpose (plain) flour
- 1 quart (1 liter) chicken stock, vegetable stock, or water
- 1 cup (240 ml) heavy (whipping) cream

[This soup is also used as an ingredient in many Midwestern casseroles, particularly in Minnesota. While tradition often calls for the popular canned soup, here is a homemade version.]

In a heavy-bottomed pot, melt the butter over medium-high heat. Add the mushrooms and onion and cook, stirring frequently, until the onion has softened and the mushrooms have released their juices, about 5 minutes. Stir in the garlic and sprinkle with the salt and pepper. Stir in the flour, coating the vegetables. Cook for 1 to 2 minutes, stirring constantly.

Stir in the stock and bring almost to a boil, then reduce to a simmer and cook over low heat, stirring occasionally, for 15 minutes to blend the flavors. Add the cream and heat through. Do not allow the soup to boil.

SUNCHOKE SOUP

PREPARATION TIME: 10 MINUTES
COOKING TIME: 40 MINUTES
SERVES: 4

- 1 lb (455 g) sunchokes (Jerusalem artichokes), well scrubbed
- 2 tablespoons (30 g) butter
- 1 large onion, sliced
- 2 cloves garlic, chopped
- Salt and freshly ground black pepper
- 2 tablespoons sherry
- 4 cups (1 liter) vegetable stock
- 1 Yukon Gold potato (about 6 oz/170 g), peeled and diced
- 4 sprigs fresh thyme
- ½ cup (120 ml) heavy (whipping) cream

You can peel the sunchokes if you'd like, but it is not necessary. Cut into 1-inch (2.5 cm) pieces.

Heat a large pot over medium heat. Add the butter to melt, then the onion, sunchokes, garlic, ½ teaspoon salt, and ¼ teaspoon pepper. Cook until the onion is translucent, 8–10 minutes. Increase the heat to medium-high, add the sherry, and cook 1 minute to dissipate the alcohol. Add the vegetable stock, potato, and thyme sprigs. Simmer until the sunchokes and potatoes are tender, 15–20 minutes. Remove from the heat.

Discard the thyme stems. Purée the soup with an immersion blender or in a stand blender until very smooth, 1–2 minutes. Return the soup to the pot and add the cream. Warm over low heat, but do not let boil. Season to taste with salt and pepper.

KNOEPHLA SOUP

PREPARATION TIME: 20 MINUTES
COOKING TIME: 40 MINUTES
SERVES: 8

For the soup:
- 1 stick (115 g) butter
- 3 medium potatoes, peeled and diced
- 1 medium onion, finely diced
- 3 cups (720 ml) milk

For the knoephla:
- 1½ cups (187 g) all-purpose (plain) flour
- ½ teaspoon salt
- 1 egg, beaten
- 5 tablespoons milk
- 6 cups (1.4 liters) chicken stock
- Salt and freshly ground black pepper
- 3 tablespoons finely chopped fresh parsley

For the soup: In a 2-quart (2-liter) saucepan, melt the butter over medium-high heat. Add the potatoes and onion and stir to coat. Add enough water to just barely cover the vegetables. Bring to a boil over medium-high heat. Reduce the heat to a simmer, stirring occasionally, until the vegetables are cooked through, about 10 minutes. Add the milk and cook just until the milk is hot. Do not let the milk boil. Remove from the heat.

Meanwhile, for the knoephla: In a bowl, whisk together the flour and salt. Stir in the egg and milk. Turn the dough out onto a lightly floured surface and knead to form a stiff dough. Knead the dough just until it comes together. Divide the dough into 4 pieces. Roll each piece into a rope ½ inch (1.25 cm) thick. Cut crosswise into ¼-inch (6 mm) pieces and set aside.

In a large soup pot, bring the chicken stock to a boil. Drop in the knoephla, stir them gently, reduce the heat to a simmer, cover, and cook for 10 minutes. Add the potato/milk mixture and cook to heat through. Season to taste with salt and pepper. Garnish with the parsley.

KNOEPHLA SOUP

SPLIT PEA SOUP

PREPARATION TIME: 10 MINUTES
COOKING TIME: 1 HOUR 10 MINUTES
SERVES: 6–8

- 2 tablespoons (30 g) butter
- 1 medium onion, diced
- 2 medium carrots, peeled and diced
- 2 stalks celery, diced
- 2 cups (370 g) green split peas, rinsed and picked over
- 8 cups (2 liters) vegetable stock
- ½ lb (225 g) ham hock (optional)
- 1 bay leaf
- Salt and freshly ground black pepper
- Sliced scallions (spring onions), for garnish

In a large pot, melt the butter over medium-high heat. Add the onion, carrots, and celery and cook until the vegetables are softened and the onion is translucent, about 7 minutes. Add the split peas, stock, ham hock (if using), bay leaf, 1½ teaspoons salt, and ¾ teaspoon pepper. Increase the heat to medium-high to bring to a high simmer, then reduce to a low simmer and cook until the split peas are very soft, 50–55 minutes.

Remove the ham hock and bay leaf. Use an immersion blender to pulse the soup to a consistency somewhere between slightly chunky and smooth. Season to taste with salt and pepper. Thin with water to reach desired consistency. Serve garnished with sliced scallions.

WILD BUTTERNUT SOUP

PREPARATION TIME: 10 MINUTES,
   PLUS COOLING TIME
COOKING TIME: 1 HOUR 10 MINUTES
SERVES: 4

- 2 cups (250 g) whole shelled butternuts
- 3 tablespoons (45 g) butter
- 1 cup (160 g) finely chopped onion
- 1 stalk celery, thinly sliced
- 2 cups (475 ml) chicken stock
- 1 cup (240 ml) milk
- ½ cup (120 ml) half-and-half (single cream)
- ¼ teaspoon salt
- Freshly ground black pepper
- ½ lime

[Butternut, a tree nut also known as white walnut, grows wild throughout the country. Like fresh walnuts, the hulling of the green rind or outer covering will stain, so use gloves. Once the outer hull is removed there is still a shell – and cracking the shell is easier if you let the nuts dry first in single layer in the sun, or an oven set to its lowest temperature. Crack with a hammer and extract the nutmeats with a nut pick or skewer. The rich flavor of butternuts works well in soup; otherwise, roast the nuts and use in any way that you would walnuts or pecans.]

Preheat the oven to 300°F/150°C. Place the butternuts on a rimmed baking sheet and roast until cooked through, about 45 minutes. Shake the pan frequently to prevent sticking and scorching. Let nuts cool, then grind in a spice grinder into a fine meal.

In a medium saucepan, melt the butter over medium heat. Add the onion and celery and cook until translucent, 5–8 minutes. Add the ground butternuts and toast for 1 minute. Pour in the stock, milk, and half-and-half (cream). Increase the heat and cook at a simmer for 10 minutes. Season with the salt and pepper to taste. Finish with a squeeze of lime. Serve hot.

SPLIT PEA SOUP

TORTILLA SOUP

PREPARATION TIME: 15 MINUTES
COOKING TIME: 45 MINUTES
SERVES: 6

- 2 large dried New Mexico chilies
- 1 can (14.5 oz/410 g) diced (chopped) tomatoes, undrained
- Vegetable oil
- 1 medium yellow onion, diced
- 3 cloves garlic, minced
- 12 corn tortillas
- 6 cups (1.4 liters) chicken stock
- Salt
- 2 cups (340 g) shredded cooked chicken
- 2 tablespoons fresh lime juice
- ½ teaspoon salt
- 1 large avocado, diced
- ½ cup (55 g) crumbled queso fresco
- ⅓ cup (15 g) loosely packed fresh cilantro (coriander) leaves

Heat a large soup pot over medium heat. Gently press the dried chilies into the bottom of the pot to toast, until slightly darkened in color and fragrant, about 2 minutes per side. Remove from the pan. When cool enough to handle, discard the stem and seeds and tear or chop chilies into pieces. Place in a blender with the tomatoes and their juices. Purée on high for about 1 minute.

Return the pot to medium-high heat. Add 3 tablespoons vegetable oil, then the onion and cook until translucent, 5–7 minutes. Add the garlic and cook for 2 minutes. Add the tomato-chili mixture and cook until slightly reduced, stirring occasionally, 10–12 minutes.

Meanwhile, cut 6 tortillas into strips 2 inches (5 cm) long by ½ inch (1.25 cm) wide.

Add the chicken stock and tortilla strips to the soup and simmer until the tortilla strips begin to break down and thicken the soup, 15–20 minutes.

While the soup is simmering, pour ½ inch (1.25 cm) oil into a medium frying pan and heat to 350°F (180°C). Cut the remaining 6 tortillas into 2 x ½ inch (5 x 1.25 cm) strips. Fry the strips until lightly golden and crispy, 1–2 minutes. Drain on paper towels and season to taste with salt.

Just before serving, stir the chicken, lime juice, and ½ teaspoon salt (or more to taste) into the soup and cook for 5 minutes to heat the chicken through.

Serve topped with fried tortilla strips, sliced avocado, queso fresco, and cilantro (coriander).

PEANUT SOUP

PREPARATION TIME: 10 MINUTES
COOKING TIME: 35 MINUTES
SERVES: 6–8

- 4 tablespoons (60 g) unsalted butter
- 1 medium onion, finely chopped
- 2 stalks celery, finely chopped
- 3 tablespoons all-purpose (plain) flour
- 6 cups (1.4 liters) chicken stock
- 2 cups (510 g) smooth peanut butter
- 1½ cups (355 ml) heavy (whipping) cream
- 4 tablespoons chopped salted roasted peanuts

[A descendant of the African goober stew, this recipe appeared in George Washington Carver's 1925 collection of ways to cook peanuts. It became a staple in countless church and Junior League cookbooks throughout the South.]

In a large saucepan, melt the butter over medium heat. Add the onion and celery and cook, stirring often, until softened, 3–5 minutes. Stir in the flour and cook until lightly golden, about 3 minutes. Pour in the chicken stock, increase the heat to high, and bring to a boil, stirring well to combine. Reduce the heat to medium and cook, stirring frequently, until slightly reduced and thickened, about 15 minutes. Pour into a sieve set over a large bowl and strain out the solids. Return the liquid to the saucepan. Whisk the peanut butter and the cream into the liquid. Warm over low heat, whisking frequently, for about 5 minutes. Do not boil. Serve warm, garnished with the chopped peanuts.

TORTILLA SOUP

HMONG RED CURRY NOODLE SOUP (KHAUB POOB)

PREPARATION TIME: 40 MINUTES
COOKING TIME: 1 HOUR
SERVES: 6

- 1 whole chicken (3½ lb/1.6 kg), cut into 8 pieces
- 2 red bell peppers, roasted and peeled (see Corn and green Chili Chowder, page 86)
- 2 cups (260 g) canned thinly sliced bamboo shoots
- ¼ cup (60 ml) vegetable oil
- 2 whole heads garlic, peeled and minced
- 1 heaping teaspoon Thai red curry paste, or more to taste
- 1 heaping teaspoon Thai namya curry paste, or more to taste
- 2 cans (13.5 oz/400 ml each) coconut milk
- Salt
- 1 package (14 oz/398 g) rice noodles
- ½ large head cabbage, finely shredded
- 1 bunch scallions (spring onions), thinly sliced
- 1½ cups (60 g) fresh cilantro (coriander) leaves
- ½ cup (45 g) fresh mint leaves
- Fish sauce, for serving

[Large populations of Hmong people, from Southeast Asia, have immigrated to the Midwest, specifically Minnesota and Wisconsin. Red namya curry pastes can be found in Asian food markets.]

For the soup: Place the chicken in a large pot, cover with 12 cups (3 liters) cold water, and bring to a boil over high heat, skimming any foam that rises to the top. Reduce the heat to medium-high and continue to boil the chicken until tender and cooked through, about 20 minutes.

Meanwhile, roast and peel the peppers as directed. Purée the roasted peppers in a blender until smooth. Set aside.

Reserving the cooking broth, drain the chicken in a colander set over another large pot. When the chicken is cool enough to be handled, remove the meat from the bones. Set the meat aside and discard the skin and bones.

Heat the pot of chicken broth and the bamboo shoots over medium heat.

In a separate saucepan, heat the oil over high heat. Add the garlic and cook, stirring, until golden, about 3 minutes. Add both curry pastes and cook for 1 minute. Stir in the red pepper purée and cook, stirring, for a few minutes. Add the coconut milk and bring to a simmer. Add this mixture to the chicken broth along with the chicken meat. Season to taste with salt. Reduce to a simmer while you cook the noodles.

Prepare the noodles according to the package directions. Divide the noodles among 6 large bowls. Ladle the hot soup over the top. Garnish each bowl with cabbage, scallions (spring onions), cilantro (coriander), and mint. Pass the fish sauce for diners to season the soup to taste.

VIETNAMESE PHO

PREPARATION TIME: 50 MINUTES,
   INCLUDING FREEZING TIME
COOKING TIME: 4 HOURS
SERVES: 6

- 5 lb (2.3 kg) beef bones
- 2 medium onions, quartered
- 4-inch (10 cm) piece fresh ginger,
  thinly sliced
- 1 large or 2 small cinnamon sticks
- 1 tablespoon coriander seeds
- 2 teaspoons fennel seeds
- 1 star anise
- 1 black cardamom pod or 3 green
  cardamom pods
- 6 whole cloves
- 2 tablespoons sugar
- 1 tablespoon salt
- 1 lb (455 g) banh pho noodles
  (thin rice noodles)
- ½ lb (225 g) beef sirloin, very thinly sliced
- ½ cup (50 g) thinly sliced scallions
  (spring onions)
- ½ cup (20 g) fresh cilantro (coriander)
  leaves
- Leaves of fresh Thai basil or mint
- Bean sprouts
- Thai red chilies, thinly sliced
- Lime wedges
- Fish sauce
- Hoisin sauce
- Sriracha sauce

[Vibrant Vietnamese-American communities can be found in California, as well as Arizona, Louisiana, and Mississippi. This signature soup is now popular across the country.]

For the broth: Place the beef bones in a large pot. Cover with cold water, bring to a boil, and boil for 5 minutes. Drain and rinse the bones. Rinse the pot and place the bones back in the pot. Cover with 6 quarts (5.7 liters) cold water and bring to a boil.

Meanwhile, preheat the broiler (grill) to high. Arrange the onions and ginger on a rimmed baking sheet and broil until they are charred, about 15 minutes.

Add the onions and ginger to the broth. Place the spices in a mortar and crush them lightly with a pestle. Add to the broth. When the broth comes to a boil, skim the foam from the surface. Reduce the heat to a simmer and cook for 3 hours. Strain the broth (discard the bones and spices) and return the broth to the pot. Bring back to a simmer and season with the sugar and salt.

Meanwhile, for the soup bowls: Prepare the noodles according to the package directions. Also, place the beef in the freezer for 30 minutes to make it easier to slice.

Divide the noodles, thinly sliced beef, scallions (spring onions), and cilantro (coriander) leaves among the bowls. Ladle in the hot broth and serve with garnishes on the side.

CALDO VERDE

PREPARATION TIME: 15 MINUTES
COOKING TIME: 1 HOUR
SERVES: 6

- 1 tablespoon olive oil
- 1 large onion, diced
- 3 cloves garlic, minced
- 6 medium potatoes, peeled and diced
- 1 lb (455 g) kale, cleaned and thinly sliced
- 6 oz (170 g) chouriço or Spanish-style chorizo sausage, cut into ¼-inch (6 mm) thick coins
- Salt and freshly ground black pepper

[This kale-*chouriço* soup is beloved by Rhode Island's Portuguese communities. *Chouriço* is a cousin of chorizo.]

In a large pot, heat the oil over low heat. Add the onion and cook, stirring occasionally, until soft and translucent, about 8 minutes. Add the garlic and cook for 2–3 more minutes, until the garlic is softened. Add 2 quarts (2 liters) water and the potatoes, cover, increase the heat, and bring to a boil. Reduce the heat and simmer until the potatoes just begin to soften, about 15 minutes. Add the kale and simmer 10 minutes. Add the chouriço and season to taste with salt and pepper. Cook for 10 more minutes to blend the flavors.

CORN AND GREEN CHILI CHOWDER

PREPARATION TIME: 25 MINUTES
COOKING TIME: 1 HOUR 15 MINUTES
SERVES: 6–8

- 12 Hatch green chilies
- 6 ears of corn, kernels cut from cobs, cobs reserved
- 4 tablespoons (60 g) butter
- ½ cup (50 g) chopped white onion
- 4 tablespoons all-purpose (plain) flour
- 4 cups (950 ml) milk
- 1 cup (240 ml) heavy (whipping) cream
- 1 russet (baking) potato, peeled and cut into ½-inch (1.25 cm) dice
- 2 tablespoons fresh lime juice
- 2 tablespoons chopped fresh cilantro (coriander)

To roast and peel the chilies, preheat the broiler (grill) to high with the rack about 6 inches (15 cm) from the heat source. Place the chilies on a rimmed baking sheet and broil (grill), turning the chilies frequently, until very charred on all sides, about 15 minutes. Transfer the chilies to a bowl, cover with plastic wrap (clingfilm), and let steam for 15 minutes. Peel the charred skin from the chilies (rinse under cold water, if necessary). Discard the stems and seeds.Finely chop the chilies and set aside.

In a large soup pot, place 4 corncobs in a single layer, discarding the remaining 2. Add 2 cups (475 ml) water and bring to a simmer over medium-high heat. Reduce the heat to low, cover, and cook for 30 minutes. Discard the cobs and transfer the broth to another container until ready to make the soup.

In the same soup pot, melt the butter over medium-high heat. Add the onion and cook, stirring occasionally, until translucent and softened, 5–7 minutes. Reduce the heat to medium-low, stir in the flour, and cook until the flour is lightly golden, about 2 minutes. Add the reserved corn broth, milk, cream, potato, corn kernels, and chopped green chilies. Increase the heat to medium-high and stir or whisk frequently until the flour is blended into the liquid. Reduce the heat to medium-low and simmer until the potato is tender and the soup is thickened, about 15 minutes. Stir in the lime juice and cilantro (coriander) and serve.

CALDO VERDE

SHE-CRAB SOUP

PREPARATION TIME: 20 MINUTES
COOKING TIME: 1 HOUR 10 MINUTES
SERVES: 4

- Kosher (coarse) salt
- 6 live female crabs (with roe intact)
- ¾ lb (340 g) lump crabmeat, picked over for shells and cartilage
- 1½ tablespoons all-purpose (plain) flour
- 3 tablespoons (45 g) unsalted butter
- ¾ cup (120 g) finely minced yellow onion
- Freshly ground black pepper
- 2 cups (475 ml) milk
- 2 cups (475 ml) heavy (whipping) cream
- 2 tablespoons dry sherry
- 1 tablespoon chopped fresh chives

[A few areas vie to call she-crab soup their own: Tidewater (southeastern Virginia and northeastern North Carolina), Coastal Georgia, and the South Carolina Lowcountry. What sets the soup apart from a crab bisque or chowder is the addition of crab roe, hence the reference to "she" in the soup base.]

Set up a large bowl of ice and water. Fill a large pot two-thirds full of water and bring to a boil over high heat. Season generously with salt. Working in two batches, place the crabs in the boiling water and cook until their shells turn bright orange, about 3 minutes. Immediately plunge the crabs in the ice bath and let rest 1 minute, or until cool enough to handle. Remove and place on a tray and refrigerate until ready to use. Repeat with remaining crabs until all are cooked and cooling. Measure out 4 cups (1 liter) of the crab cooking liquid, transfer to a saucepan, and set aside.

Remove the soft outer shell and the gills from the belly side of each crab. With a small coffee spoon, scoop any orange roe from the crab into a bowl. (Use a wooden pick to scrape the roe from the deep parts.) Cover and refrigerate the roe. Split the crab bodies and legs in half and pick out the meat. Reserve the bodies and combine the meat with the lump crabmeat.

Add the crab bodies to the crab cooking liquid in the saucepan. Bring to a boil over high heat, then reduce to a simmer and cook for 12–15 minutes to reduce to about 3 cups (710 ml) of cooking liquid (once the crab bodies are removed). Discard the crab bodies.

Return the broth to a boil over high heat. Reduce the heat to medium and keep at a simmer. Measure out ½ cup (120 ml) of the broth and place in a small bowl. Add the flour and whisk to create a smooth paste. Whisk the flour mixture back into the pot of broth, along with the crab roe. Simmer until slightly thickened, 5–7 minutes. Cover and hold over a burner on low heat.

In a medium pot, melt the butter over medium heat until bubbling. Add the onion, ½ teaspoon salt, and ¼ teaspoon pepper. Cook, stirring occasionally, until the onion is softened and translucent, 5–7 minutes. Add the milk, cream, reserved broth mixture, and sherry. Bring to a simmer and cook until slightly reduced and thickened, 12–15 minutes. Add the crabmeat and cook for 2 more minutes, just to warm through. Season the soup to taste with salt and pepper. Serve garnished with chives.

HALIBUT BISQUE

PREPARATION TIME: 15 MINUTES
COOKING TIME: 1 HOUR 5 MINUTES
SERVES: 4

For the stock and fish:
- ½ cup (120 ml) dry white wine
- 1 small onion, quartered
- 1 stalk celery, cut into large pieces
- 1 carrot, cut into 1-inch (2.5 cm) pieces
- ½ lemon
- ½ teaspoon black peppercorns
- 1 small bundle fresh thyme
- 2 lb (910 g) skinless halibut fillets

For the bisque:
- 4 tablespoons (60 g) butter
- 1 large onion, diced
- 2 stalks celery, diced
- 2 cloves garlic, minced
- 4 tablespoons all-purpose (plain) flour
- 2 cups (475 ml) heavy (whipping) cream
- 2 tablespoons tomato paste (purée)
- ⅓ cup (80 ml) dry sherry
- ½ teaspoon paprika
- Pinch of cayenne pepper
- Salt and freshly ground black pepper
- Worcestershire sauce
- Crusty bread, for serving

For the stock and fish: In a medium pot or fish poacher, combine 3 cups (710 ml) water, the wine, onion, celery, carrot, lemon, peppercorns, and thyme and bring to a boil. Reduce to a simmer and cook, uncovered, for 15 minutes. Add the halibut and gently poach just until the fish barely flakes and is opaque throughout, 5–10 minutes depending on the thickness of the fillets. Remove the fish with a slotted spoon and set aside. Strain the cooking liquid through a fine-mesh sieve into a bowl. Measure 2½ cups (590 ml) of this liquid and set aside.

For the bisque: In a soup pot, melt the butter over medium heat. Add the onion, celery, and garlic and cook until the onion is translucent, about 8 minutes. Stir in the flour and cook, stirring constantly, about 3 minutes. Whisk in the reserved fish stock. Whisk in the cream. Bring just to a boil, then reduce to a simmer and whisk in the tomato paste (purée), sherry, paprika, and cayenne. Simmer for 15 minutes.

Add the halibut to the soup and simmer for another 5 minutes to heat the fish through. Season to taste with salt, pepper, and Worcestershire sauce. Serve hot, with nice crusty bread.

LOBSTER BISQUE

PREPARATION TIME: 25 MINUTES
COOKING TIME: 1 HOUR 40 MINUTES
SERVES: 4

- 2 live lobsters (1 lb/455 g each), boiled (see page 104)
- 2 tablespoons (30 g) butter
- 1 medium onion, chopped
- 1 stalk celery, chopped
- 1 carrot, chopped
- 1 head garlic, halved at the equator
- 2 bay leaves
- A small bunch fresh thyme
- 2 tablespoons chopped fresh tarragon
- 2 teaspoons black peppercorns
- ½ cup (120 ml) dry sherry
- 5 cups (1.2 liters) fish or chicken stock
- 2 tablespoons tomato paste (purée)
- 1 cup (240 ml) heavy (whipping) cream
- Salt and freshly ground black pepper

Working over a bowl to save the juices, remove the meat from the lobsters, chop roughly, and set aside. Cut the shells into pieces.

In a large pot, melt the butter over medium-high heat. Add the shells and cook, stirring, until they begin to brown, 8–10 minutes. Stir in the onion, celery, carrot, garlic, bay leaves, thyme, tarragon, peppercorns, and sherry. Bring to a boil, add the stock, and return to a boil. Reduce to a simmer and cook, uncovered, for 1 hour.

Strain the stock through a sturdy sieve into a clean saucepan, pressing on the solids to release all of the juices (discard the solids). Set the pan over low heat and whisk in the tomato paste (purée) and cream. Bring just to a simmer, add the reserved lobster meat, and simmer for 2 minutes to heat the lobster meat through. Season to taste with salt and pepper.

SMOKED FISH CHOWDER

PREPARATION TIME: 15 MINUTES
COOKING TIME: 45 MINUTES
SERVES: 4–6

- 6 tablespoons (85 g) butter
- 2 medium onions, diced
- 2 cloves garlic, minced
- 2 medium carrots, diced
- 2 stalks celery, diced
- 4 small potatoes, peeled and diced
- 6 cups (1.4 liters) fish stock
- 1 teaspoon minced fresh thyme
- 2 bay leaves
- 2 cups (475 ml) heavy (whipping) cream
- Freshly grated nutmeg
- 1½ lb (680 g) flaked smoked fish (salmon or halibut, skinless)
- Salt and freshly ground black pepper

In a soup pot, melt the butter over medium heat. Add the onions and cook, stirring frequently, for 3 minutes. Add the garlic and cook for 1 minute. Stir in the carrots, celery, potatoes, fish stock, thyme, and bay leaves and bring just to a boil. Reduce to a simmer and cook until the potatoes and carrots are almost tender, about 10 minutes. Stir in the cream and nutmeg. Return to a simmer, add the fish, and cook for 10–15 minutes to develop the flavors. Season to taste with salt and pepper.

RHODE ISLAND RED CLAM CHOWDER

PREPARATION TIME: 15 MINUTES
COOKING TIME: 50 MINUTES
SERVES: 6–8

- 2 dozen quahogs (large hardshell clams), scrubbed
- ¼ lb (115 g) salt pork, diced
- 1 large onion, diced
- 3 large potatoes, peeled and diced
- ⅓ cup (80 ml) tomato purée (passata)
- 2 teaspoons paprika
- 1 teaspoon salt
- ½ teaspoon freshly ground black pepper

Place the clams in a large heavy-bottomed pot with 4 cups water. Cover and bring to a boil over high heat. Cook until the clams have opened, about 10 minutes. Remove the clams, strain the cooking liquid through a fine-mesh sieve lined with cheesecloth and reserve. Remove the clam meat from the shells and set aside. Rinse the pot and place over medium-high heat. Add the salt pork and cook, stirring, until it has browned, about 5 minutes. Remove the pork with a slotted spoon and set aside. Add the onion to the pork fat, reduce the heat to medium, and cook, stirring, until the onion is softened, 6–8 minutes. Add the reserved clam broth, 1 cup (240 ml) water, the potatoes, tomato purée (passata), and paprika. Bring to a boil, then reduce to a simmer and cook until the potatoes are tender, about 15 minutes. Chop the clams and add them to the pot along with the salt and pepper. Simmer for another 5 minutes to heat the clams through. Serve hot.

RAZOR CLAM CHOWDER

PREPARATION TIME: 15 MINUTES
COOKING TIME: 45 MINUTES
SERVES: 4

- ½ lb (225 g) bacon (streaky), cut into ½-inch (1.25 cm) pieces
- 1 medium onion, chopped
- 2 cloves garlic, minced
- 2 stalks celery, chopped
- 1 tablespoon fresh thyme leaves
- 4 Yukon Gold potatoes, cut into 1-inch (2.5 cm) chunks
- 1 lb (455 g) clam meat (ideally razor clams), chopped, with their juices
- 2 tablespoons (30 g) butter
- 2 tablespoons all-purpose (plain) flour
- 1 cup (240 ml) milk
- 1 cup (240 ml) heavy (whipping) cream

[Named for its resemblance to a straight razor, this succulent shellfish can be found along the Pacific coast from California to Alaska. The clams may grow up to six inches long and their meat is a favorite food of Dungeness crabs — and of local people.]

In a large pot, cook the bacon over medium-high heat until crisp, about 6 minutes. Remove the bacon with a slotted spoon and set aside. Add the onion, garlic, celery, and thyme to the bacon fat and cook, stirring, until soft and tender, about 8 minutes. Add the potatoes and the clam juice. Add enough water to just cover the potatoes; bring to a boil, then reduce to a simmer and cook until the potatoes are soft, about 15 minutes.

Meanwhile, in a small saucepan, melt the butter over medium heat. Whisk in the flour, then whisk in the milk and cream. Cook, whisking, until the mixture is bubbling and has thickened, about 10 minutes.

Pour the cream sauce into the simmering vegetables and stir well to combine. Add the clams and reserved bacon and simmer for 5 more minutes.

NEW ENGLAND CLAM CHOWDER

PREPARATION TIME: 10 MINUTES
COOKING TIME: 30 MINUTES
SERVES: 4

- 4 slices thick-cut smoked bacon (streaky), cut into 1-inch (2.5 cm) pieces
- 1 large onion, diced
- 2 tablespoons all-purpose (plain) flour
- 4 medium waxy potatoes (such as red or Yukon Gold), diced
- 3 cups (720 ml) fish stock or chicken stock
- 1½ cups (355 ml) heavy (whipping) cream
- 2 dozen any type clams, shucked, with their liquor, cut in pieces if large
- Salt and freshly ground black pepper
- 1 tablespoon minced fresh parsley or chives

In a heavy-bottomed pot, cook the bacon over medium high heat, stirring frequently, until browned and crisp, about 5 minutes. Drain the bacon on paper towels.

Add the onion to the bacon drippings and cook, stirring, until the onion has softened, about 5 minutes. Stir in the flour. Add the potatoes and stock. Cook, stirring occasionally, until the potatoes are tender, about 15 minutes.

Add the cream and bring to a simmer. Add the clams and reserved bacon and simmer for another few minutes. Season to taste with salt and pepper. Serve garnished with parsley or chives.

CORN CHOWDER

PREPARATION TIME: 25 MINUTES
COOKING TIME: 1 HOUR
SERVES: 6–8

- 6 large ears of corn, kernels cut from cobs, cobs reserved
- 4 tablespoons (60 g) butter
- ½ cup (80 g) chopped white onion
- 4 tablespoons all-purpose (plain) flour
- 3½ cups (830 ml) milk
- 1 cup (240 ml) heavy (whipping) cream
- 1 russet (baking) potato, peeled and cut into ½-inch (1.25 cm) pieces
- Salt and freshly ground black pepper
- 2 tablespoons chopped fresh chives

In a large soup pot, combine the corncobs and 4 cups (1 liter) water and bring to a simmer over medium-high heat. Reduce the heat to low, cover, and simmer for 30 minutes. Pour the corn broth into a bowl and discard the cobs.

In the same pot, melt the butter over medium-high heat. Add the onion and cook, stirring occasionally, until translucent and softened, 5–7 minutes. Reduce the heat to medium-low, add the flour, and stir to combine. Cook until the flour is lightly golden, about 2 minutes. Add 2 cups (475 ml) reserved corn broth, the milk, cream, potato, and corn kernels. Increase the heat to medium-high and stir or whisk frequently until the flour is blended in. Reduce the heat to medium-low and simmer until the potato is tender and the soup is thickened, about 15 minutes. Adjust the consistency with any remaining corn broth. Season with salt and pepper to taste and serve topped with chives.

NEW ENGLAND CLAM CHOWDER

CONCH CHOWDER

PREPARATION TIME: 15 MINUTES
COOKING TIME: 2 HOURS 20 MINUTES
SERVES: 6–8

- 4 tablespoons (60 g) salted butter
- 2 medium onions, chopped
- 1 red bell pepper, chopped
- 3 cloves garlic, finely chopped
- 2 lb (910 g) cleaned conch meat, finely chopped or ground
- 1 can (28 oz/795 g) chopped tomatoes, drained
- 2 bottles (8 oz/240 ml each) clam juice
- 1 quart (1 liter) fish stock or water
- 1 bay leaf
- 1 teaspoon thyme leaves
- ⅛ teaspoon ground allspice (optional)
- Pinch of cayenne pepper, or more to taste (optional)
- 1 large russet (baking) potato, peeled and diced
- 2 tablespoons fresh lime juice

[The cuisine of the Florida Keys is influenced by The Bahamas, and conch is a staple of the native Floridian and Bahamian diet. The conch itself has become a symbol of Key West and the Bahamian people who live there. Conch meat is quite tough and benefits from being ground in a meat grinder or very finely chopped in a food processor, rather than chopped by hand.]

In a Dutch oven (casserole) or other large pot, melt the butter over medium heat until foamy. Add the onions, bell pepper, and garlic and cook, stirring, until onions and peppers are tender, 10–12 minutes. Add the conch, canned tomatoes, clam juice, fish stock, bay leaf, thyme, allspice (if using), and cayenne (if using). Bring the chowder to a boil over medium-high heat, then reduce to a simmer and cook for 1 hour to blend the flavors. Add the potato and simmer until tender, 30–45 minutes. Discard the bay leaf and stir in the lime juice before serving.

PHILLY CHEESESTEAK

PREPARATION TIME: 15 MINUTES,
  PLUS FREEZING TIME
COOKING TIME: 10 MINUTES
SERVES: 2

- ¾ lb (340 g) beef sirloin, ribeye, or eye of round
- 2 tablespoons olive oil
- 1 large onion, sliced into very thin rings
- ½ cup (40 g) sliced mushrooms (optional)
- Salt and freshly ground black pepper
- 4 slices provolone cheese, or more to taste
- 2 hoagie, sub, or hero rolls, split lengthwise
- Dill pickles, for serving

[The Philly Cheesesteak is such a quintessential Philadelphia, Pennsylvania food that residents have even developed a gesture known as the "Philly lean," a way of bending forward to the cheesesteak, rather than bringing it to the mouth.]

Place the beef in the freezer for 1 hour. Slice the beef paper thin, then into 1-inch (2.5 cm) pieces.

In a large frying pan, heat the oil over high heat until almost at the smoking point. Reduce the heat to medium, add the onion and mushrooms (if using), and cook, stirring occasionally, until the onion is wilted and the mushrooms have browned, about 5 minutes. Add the "chipped" steak and cook for 3 minutes, stirring. Season to taste with salt and pepper.

Still in the pan, divide the meat mixture into 2 mounds. Top each mound with the provolone and melt the cheese, then transfer to the rolls. Serve with a dill pickle.

CLASSIC BURGER

PREPARATION TIME: 10 MINUTES
COOKING TIME: 7 MINUTES OR MORE
SERVES: 4

- 1½ lb (680 g) ground (minced) beef
- Salt and freshly ground black pepper
- 4 hamburger rolls
- 4 slices cheese, such as cheddar or American (optional)

For the toppings (optional):
- 1 large tomato, sliced
- 1 medium red onion, thinly sliced
- 4 lettuce leaves
- Ketchup and mustard

[The classic burger is cooked over coals in parks and backyards, afternoon into evening, all summer long.]

Preheat a gas or charcoal grill (barbecue) to high heat.

Divide the beef into 4 equal portions. Shape into patties roughly 1 inch (2.5 cm) thick. Using your thumb, make a depression in the center of each patty. This will keep the burger flat as it cooks and the center swells. Season the patties on both sides with salt and pepper.

Place the patties on the hot grill and cook, without moving them, until slightly charred, grill marks form, and the meat no longer sticks to the grill, about 3 minutes. Flip and cook until slightly charred and deep brown all over, another 4 minutes for medium-rare, 5 or more for medium, 7–8 for well-done. If making a cheeseburger, place the cheese on the burger during the last minute of cooking time.

Place the burgers on the rolls and garnish with toppings, if desired.

GYRO

PREPARATION TIME: 30 MINUTES,
   PLUS REFRIGERATION TIME
COOKING TIME: 40 MINUTES
SERVES: 4

For the tzatziki sauce:
- 1 cup (240 ml) whole-milk yogurt
- 1 small cucumber, peeled, seeded, and finely diced
- 2 cloves garlic, minced
- 2 teaspoons minced fresh mint or ½–1 teaspoon dried mint, crumbled
- 1 teaspoon fresh lemon juice
- Salt and freshly ground black pepper

For the meat:
- 1 pound (455 g) ground (minced) beef, lamb, or pork
- 4 cloves garlic, minced
- 1 teaspoon sea salt
- ½ teaspoon freshly ground black pepper
- 1 teaspoon dried oregano
- ½ teaspoon dried thyme
- 1 teaspoon ground cumin
- ¼ teaspoon ground cinnamon
- ¼ teaspoon freshly grated nutmeg
- 1 small onion, chopped

For the gyros:
- 4 pita breads, halved
- 2 medium tomatoes, sliced
- 1 medium white onion, thinly sliced
- 4 large leaves romaine lettuce, thinly shredded

[This Greek sandwich of spiced meat, served in a pita with a cooling cucumber-yogurt sauce, is popular across the country. Traditionally the meat is roasted on a spit; this version allows home cooks to easily roast it in the oven.]

For the tzatziki sauce: In a bowl, whisk together the yogurt, cucumber, garlic, mint, and lemon juice. Season to taste with salt and pepper. Cover and refrigerate for at least 2 hours and up to 24 hours.

For the meat: In a stand electric mixer fitted with the paddle attachment, combine the ground meat, garlic, salt, pepper, oregano, thyme, cumin, cinnamon, and nutmeg. Mix on low speed for about 4 minutes, until the spices are evenly distributed with the meat. Remove the meat and place in a bowl, cover, and refrigerate for at least 4 hours (and up to overnight) to allow the flavors to develop.

Preheat the oven to 325°F (160°C/Gas Mark 3).

In a food processor, pulse the onion to grind. Remove the meat from the refrigerator and add a small handful of the cold meat to the onion and pulse to blend. Continue to add a handful of meat at a time and pulse to blend until the meat and onion are completely combined and have the consistency of a thick paste.

Line a rimmed baking sheet with parchment paper or foil. Place the meat in the center of the sheet and form into a short square loaf, about 1 inch (2.5 cm) thick.

Bake until browned and no longer pink in the center, about 30 minutes. Remove from the oven and transfer to a carving board. Leaving the oven on but increase the temperature to 400°F (200°C/Gas Mark 6).

Let the meat cool slightly, then cut into slices ¼ inch (6 mm) thick, placing them back on the baking sheet. Bake until the meat is deep brown and crispy on the edges, about 6 minutes.

To make the gyros: Stuff each pita half with meat, tomato, onion, and lettuce. Garnish with spoonfuls of tzatziki. Serve immediately.

ITALIAN BEEF SANDWICH

PREPARATION TIME: 20 MINUTES
COOKING TIME: 2 HOURS 50 MINUTES
SERVES: 8

- 3 lb (1.4 kg) boneless beef top round (topside)
- Salt and freshly ground black pepper
- 2 tablespoons olive oil
- 3 cups (710 ml) beef stock
- 4 cloves garlic, smashed
- 1 teaspoon dried basil
- 1 teaspoon dried oregano
- 1 teaspoon crushed chili flakes
- 1 large onion, thinly sliced
- 3 green bell peppers, cut into ¼-inch (6 mm) wide strips
- 8 hoagie rolls (sub rolls), split lengthwise
- 1 cup (320 g) spicy giardiniera (Italian pickled vegetables)

[Created on the South Side of Chicago, Illinois, around former stockyards, this juicy beef sandwich holds a place of honor and can be found throughout the city. Some versions are made with thinly sliced roast beef and jus; this recipe uses a more economical cut, cooked slowly until tender.]

Preheat the oven to 325°F (160°C/Gas Mark 3).

Season the beef liberally with salt and pepper. In a large Dutch oven (casserole), heat 1 tablespoon of the oil over high heat. Add the beef and sear on all sides until deeply browned, about 8 minutes. Add the beef stock, garlic, basil, oregano, chili flakes, and onion. Bring to a boil, then cover and transfer to the oven. Roast until the beef is tender, about 2½ hours.

Remove the beef from the cooking liquid and set aside. Strain the liquid, then return it to the pot. Shred the beef and add it to the liquid. Keep warm over low heat.

In a large frying pan, heat the remaining 1 tablespoon oil over medium heat. Add the bell peppers and cook until softened and just beginning to brown, about 7 minutes.

To assemble the sandwiches, place a heaping portion of shredded beef along with plenty of liquid onto each roll. Top with bell peppers and giardiniera.

LOOSEMEAT SANDWICH

PREPARATION TIME: 5 MINUTES
COOKING TIME: 1 HOUR
SERVES: 6

- 2 tablespoons vegetable oil
- 2 lb (910 g) ground (minced) beef
- 1 large onion, diced
- 1 teaspoon garlic powder
- 2 tablespoons Worcestershire sauce
- 1 tablespoon white or apple cider vinegar
- 2 cups (475 ml) beef stock
- Salt and freshly ground black pepper
- 6 burger buns
- Ketchup and mustard, for serving

[This is the signature Ohio sandwich that's also immensely popular in Iowa. It's as messy as a Sloppy Joe, but with a flavor all its own.]

In a heavy-bottomed pot, heat the oil over high heat. Add the beef and cook, breaking it up with a wooden spoon, until browned, about 15 minutes. Stir in half the onion, the garlic powder, Worcestershire sauce, vinegar, and beef stock. Cook until the stock has almost completely reduced, about 40 minutes. Season to taste with salt and pepper. Serve on burger buns with the remaining diced onions and ketchup and mustard on the side.

SLOPPY JOE

PREPARATION TIME: 10 MINUTES
COOKING TIME: 30 MINUTES
SERVES: 4

- 2 tablespoons (30 g) butter or olive oil
- 1 lb (455 g) ground (minced) beef
- 4 tablespoons diced onion
- 4 tablespoons diced green bell pepper
- 4 tablespoons diced celery
- 2 cloves garlic, minced
- 1 cup (240 ml) tomato sauce
- 4 tablespoons ketchup
- 2 tablespoons light brown sugar
- 1 teaspoon yellow mustard
- Salt and freshly ground black pepper
- Worcestershire sauce (optional)
- 4 burger buns

In a heavy-bottomed pot, melt the butter over medium heat. Add the beef and cook, breaking it up with a wooden spoon, until the meat begins to brown, about 10 minutes. Add the onion, bell pepper, celery, and garlic and cook, stirring frequently, for 5 minutes, until the onion has softened. Add the tomato sauce, ketchup, sugar, and mustard. Season to taste with salt, pepper, and Worcestershire sauce (if using). Simmer for 15 minutes to develop the flavors. Serve on buns, open-faced.

CREAMED CHIPPED BEEF

COOKING TIME: 15 MINUTES
SERVES: 4

- 2 tablespoons (30 g) butter
- ¼ lb (115 g) dried shredded beef
- 3 tablespoons all-purpose (plain) flour
- 2 cups (475 ml) milk
- Freshly ground black pepper
- Toast or biscuits, for serving

[During World War II American soldiers were often served this dish of quick-cooking thinly sliced beef. Today it endures on diner menus throughout the Mid-Atlantic.]

In a small saucepan, melt the butter over medium heat. Add the beef and fry until the meat begins to brown and get barely crispy on the edges, about 3 minutes. Sprinkle the beef with the flour, stir to coat, and cook, stirring, for 2 minutes. Add the milk and cook, stirring constantly, until the mixture thickens and bubbles, about 10 minutes. Season to taste with pepper. Serve with toast or biscuits.

CHICAGO-STYLE HOT DOG

PREPARATION TIME: 5 MINUTES
COOKING TIME: 10 MINUTES
SERVES: 6

- 6 all-beef hot dogs
- 6 split hot dog rolls, preferably seeded
- 6 dill pickle (pickled cucumber) spears
- 12 thin slices tomato
- Yellow mustard
- Sweet relish
- 1 small white onion, finely chopped
- 6 sport peppers or pepperoncini
- Celery salt (optional)

[The Chicago Dog or Chicago Red Hot is a perennial favorite among Chicagoans. It is covered in toppings, without ketchup.]

Cook the hot dogs in a medium saucepan of boiling water to warm through. Transfer the hot dogs to the rolls and place a pickle spear on one side of each hot dog and 2 tomato slices on the other. Cover with yellow mustard and relish. Sprinkle with chopped onion and top with a sport pepper. Sprinkle with celery salt, if desired.

REUBEN SANDWICH

PREPARATION TIME: 5 MINUTES
COOKING TIME: 10 MINUTES
SERVES: 2

- ½ cup (120 g) Thousand Island dressing
- 1 cup (110 g) sauerkraut, drained
- 2 tablespoons (30 g) butter, softened
- 4 slices dark rye bread
- 4 slices Swiss cheese
- 1 lb (455 g) sliced corned beef

[According to legend, this sandwich is named for its creator, an Omaha, Nebraska grocer named Reuben Kulakofsky.]

In a small bowl, mix the Thousand Island dressing with the sauerkraut. Butter one side of each piece of bread. Place a slice of Swiss cheese on the unbuttered sides. Place the corned beef over the cheese on one side and the sauerkraut mixture on top of the corned beef. Place both sides together and cook in a frying pan over medium heat until both slices of bread are crispy and browned and the cheese is melted, about 4 minutes per side.

COUNTRY HAM BISCUITS

PREPARATION TIME: 15 MINUTES,
PLUS CHILLING TIME
COOKING TIME: 30 MINUTES
MAKES: ABOUT 12 BISCUITS

- 2½ cups (325 g) all-purpose (plain) flour
- 1 tablespoon baking powder
- 1 teaspoon baking soda (bicarbonate of soda)
- ½ teaspoon salt
- 1 stick (115 g) cold unsalted butter, cut into ½-inch (1.25 cm) dice, plus 2 tablespoons (30 g) butter, melted
- 1 cup (240 ml) cold buttermilk
- ½ lb (225 g) thinly sliced country ham

Position a rack in the middle of the oven and preheat to 450°F (230°C/Gas Mark 8).

In a medium bowl, combine the flour, baking powder, baking soda (bicarbonate of soda), and salt. Cut in the cold butter (using a pastry/dough blender or your fingertips) until small clumps form. Place the bowl in the freezer (or refrigerator) for 10 minutes to chill.

Gently stir the cold buttermilk into the flour/butter mixture until the dough just comes together. Turn dough onto a lightly floured surface and knead 5–6 times, until just combined. Lightly flour your hands and press the dough into a rectangle, about ¾-inch (2 cm) thick. Cut into 2-inch (5 cm) rounds with a biscuit cutter or glass and arrange on an ungreased baking sheet. Gently reshape the remaining dough and cut out more biscuits.

Bake until golden brown, 16–18 minutes. Brush the tops of the biscuits with the 2 tablespoons melted butter. Let sit for 10 minutes.

Meanwhile, heat a large frying pan over medium-high heat. Place the ham slices in a single layer, with 2 tablespoons water. Cook on each side, until warmed through, about 5 minutes total.

Split the biscuits in half, divide the ham among the biscuit bottoms, and close with the biscuit top.

PORK TENDERLOIN SANDWICH

PREPARATION TIME: 15 MINUTES
COOKING TIME: 30 MINUTES
SERVES: 4

- 1 lb (455 g) pork tenderloin (fillet)
- 1 egg
- 3 tablespoons buttermilk
- 1 teaspoon salt
- ½ teaspoon freshly ground black pepper
- ½ teaspoon paprika
- ½ teaspoon dried oregano
- 1 cup (115 g) fine dried breadcrumbs
- Vegetable oil, for frying
- 4 burger buns
- Shredded iceberg lettuce, sliced tomato, mayonnaise, ketchup, and mustard, for serving

[This sandwich features a thin, crisp fried pork cutlet served on a bun with traditional hamburger condiments.]

Cut the tenderloin into 4 equal pieces. Cut each piece about halfway through horizontally and open it up like a book. Flip the cutlets over and place on a sheet of plastic wrap (clingfilm). Cover with a second sheet of plastic wrap and pound with a meat mallet or heavy pan until they are about ¼-inch (6 mm) thick. Set aside.

In a bowl, whisk together the egg, buttermilk, salt, pepper, paprika, and oregano. Place the breadcrumbs on a plate. Dip each cutlet first in the egg mixture, then dredge in the breadcrumbs.

In a large skillet, pour in oil to a depth of 1 inch (2.5 cm) and heat over high heat until it shimmers. Fry 1 or 2 cutlets at a time until golden brown, about 4 minutes per side. Drain on paper towels.

Place each cutlet on a burger bun. Serve with lettuce, tomato, mayonnaise, ketchup, and mustard.

SAUSAGE AND PEPPER SUB

PREPARATION TIME: 10 MINUTES
COOKING TIME: 40 MINUTES
SERVES: 6

- 1½ lb (680 g) Italian pork sausage
  with fennel
- 2 tablespoons olive oil
- 2 medium red onions, cut into ¼-inch
  (6 mm) thick rings
- 4 cloves garlic, thinly sliced
- 2 large red bell peppers, cut into ½-inch
  (1.25 cm) wide strips
- 2 large green bell peppers, cut into
  ½-inch (1.25 cm) wide strips
- 1 teaspoon dried basil
- 1 teaspoon dried oregano
- 1 teaspoon crushed chili flakes (optional)
- ½ cup (120 ml) dry white wine
- Salt and freshly ground black pepper
- 6 crusty French rolls, split horizontally

In a large frying pan, cook the sausages over medium-high heat until browned on all sides, about 10 minutes (they will cook further in the next step). Transfer to a plate and when cool enough to handle, slice on the diagonal into 1-inch (2.5 cm) thick pieces.

Add the olive oil and onions to the pan and cook, stirring, over medium heat until the onions wilt, about 5 minutes. Stir in the garlic, bell peppers, basil, oregano, chili flakes, and wine and cook for 10 minutes, stirring occasionally. Stir the sausage into the pan, cover, reduce the heat to low, and cook for 15 minutes. Season to taste with salt and pepper.

Divide the sausage and peppers equally among the rolls.

CUBAN SANDWICH

PREPARATION TIME: 10 MINUTES
COOKING TIME: 15 MINUTES
SERVES: 2

- 2 loaves Cuban bread, or 6-inch
  (15.25 cm) long soft sandwich rolls
- 4 tablespoons yellow mustard
- 3 tablespoons (45 g) salted butter,
  softened
- 4 oz (110 g) boiled ham or thinly sliced
  Virginia ham
- 4 oz (110 g) roast pork
- 4 slices Swiss cheese
- Dill pickle slices, to taste

[This iconic sandwich, beloved far beyond the Little Havana community in Miami, Florida, is an ideal way to use meat left over from a traditional backyard whole hog roast. The type of bread is very important – it will be flattened and griddled, so a crusty loaf or hard hoagie roll will not work and slices are not traditional. Look for Hawaiian bread as a substitute, or a particularly pillowy Italian loaf.]

Split the bread in half lengthwise. Spread the mustard on one of the cut sides and about 2 tablespoons (30 g) butter on the other. Assemble the sandwich with ham, roast pork, cheese, and pickle slices. Spread the remaining 1 tablespoon (15 g) butter on the outside of the bread.

Heat a large cast-iron skillet over medium heat. Add the sandwich and place a second, smaller frying pan on top to press as it cooks. Cook the sandwich, turning halfway through, until it is browned on both sides and the cheese is melted, 10 to 12 minutes total. Slice in half and serve warm.

MUFFULETTA SANDWICH

PREPARATION TIME: 30 MINUTES,
    PLUS 24 HOURS MARINATING TIME
    AND SANDWICH CHILLING TIME
COOKING TIME: 15 MINUTES
SERVES: 4–6

For the olive salad:
- 2 cups (215 g) coarsely chopped cauliflower florets
- 1 cup (240 ml) extra-virgin olive oil
- 1 teaspoon chopped fresh oregano
- 1 teaspoon chopped fresh thyme
- 1 large carrot, halved lengthwise, thinly sliced crosswise
- 2 stalks celery, halved lengthwise, thinly sliced crosswise
- 1½ cups (215 g) pimiento-stuffed green olives, chopped
- ½ cup (85 g) Kalamata olives, pitted and chopped
- 3 tablespoons capers, drained
- 2 tablespoons white wine vinegar
- Salt and freshly ground black pepper

For the sandwiches:
- 2 round seeded Italian loaves (8–10-inch/20–25 cm diameter)
- ¾ lb (340 g) thinly sliced mortadella
- 6 oz (170 g) thinly sliced provolone
- 6 oz (170 g) thinly sliced salami
- 6 oz (170 g) fresh mozzarella cheese, thinly sliced
- 6 oz (170 g) thinly sliced capicola
- 2 tablespoons chopped fresh parsley

[This Italian-style sandwich is one of the pillars of French Quarter cuisine. Sicilian immigrant Salvatore Lupo created the round sandwich filled with cold cuts and "olive salad" (seasoned, chopped olives) at the Central Grocery on Decatur Street in New Orleans.]

For the olive salad: In a small pot, combine the cauliflower, oil, oregano, thyme, carrot, celery, and ⅓ cup (80 ml) water. Bring to a simmer over medium-high heat, then reduce the heat to medium-low. Cook, covered, until the vegetables just become tender, 10–12 minutes. Transfer contents of the pot to a quart-sized glass jar. Stir in both olives, the capers, vinegar, and salt and pepper to taste. Cover and refrigerate for 24 hours.

For the sandwiches: Halve the Italian loaves horizontally. Using your hands, hollow out and discard the soft inside portion of the bread. Layer ½ inch (1.25 cm) of the olive salad inside the bottom half of the loaves. Layer the mortadella, provolone, salami, fresh mozzarella, and capicola on the sandwiches. Layer with another ½ inch (1.25 cm) of olive salad on top. Sprinkle evenly with chopped parsley and cover with the top half of bread. Wrap very tightly in plastic wrap (clingfilm) and refrigerate for at least 4 hours or overnight.

Unwrap, slice each into 6 wedges and serve.

KENTUCKY HOT BROWN SANDWICH

PREPARATION TIME: 10 MINUTES
COOKING TIME: 30 MINUTES
MAKES: 8 OPEN-FACED SANDWICHES

- 6 tablespoons (85 g) unsalted butter
- 6 tablespoons (50 g) all-purpose (plain) flour
- 3½ cups (830 ml) milk, warmed
- 6 tablespoons grated Parmesan cheese, plus more for topping
- 1 egg yolk
- Salt and freshly ground black pepper
- 8 thick slices (½ inch/1.25 cm) white bread (such as Texas toast), toasted
- 1½ lb (680 g) cooked sliced turkey breast
- 16 slices bacon (streaky), fried until crisp
- 4 Roma (plum) tomatoes, sliced

[After dancing the night away at The Brown Hotel in Louisville, Kentucky, hungry 1920s revelers would head to the hotel restaurant for a Hot Brown, an open-faced turkey, bacon, and tomato sandwich doused in Mornay (cream) sauce and browned under the grill.]

In a medium saucepan, melt the butter over medium heat. Add the flour while whisking, until all the butter is absorbed and the mixture creates a thick roux. Whisking constantly, slowly add the warm milk, whisking until smooth. Reduce the heat to medium-low and cook, continuing to whisk frequently, until thickened, 4–5 minutes (do not let the sauce boil). Whisk in the Parmesan. Remove from the heat and whisk in the egg yolk until completely incorporated. Season the sauce to taste with salt and pepper.

Preheat the broiler (grill) to high.

Place the toast on a rimmed baking sheet. Top each piece of toast with 3 ounces (85 g) turkey and smother generously with the cream sauce. Sprinkle with additional Parmesan and broil until golden and bubbling, 2–3 minutes.

Top each open-faced sandwich with 2 slices bacon and sliced tomatoes. Serve immediately.

CRAB ROLL

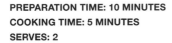

PREPARATION TIME: 10 MINUTES
COOKING TIME: 5 MINUTES
SERVES: 2

- ½ lb (225 g) lump crabmeat, picked over for shells and cartilage
- 4 tablespoons mayonnaise
- Salt and freshly ground black pepper
- Cayenne pepper (optional)
- 3 tablespoons (45 g) butter, softened
- 4 hot dog rolls, split lengthwise
- Bibb (round) lettuce, washed and dried

In a medium bowl, mix the crabmeat with the mayonnaise. Season to taste with salt, pepper, and cayenne (if using). Set aside. Butter the inside of the hot dog rolls. In a frying pan, toast the rolls over medium heat until golden. Fill the rolls with the crab salad and several leaves of lettuce. Serve immediately.

FALAFEL

PREPARATION TIME: 20 MINUTES,
   PLUS CHILLING AND OVERNIGHT
   SOAKING TIME
COOKING TIME: 20 MINUTES
MAKES: 32 PIECES

- 2 cups (1 lb/455 g) dried chickpeas
- 1 bunch fresh parsley, roughly chopped
- 3 cloves garlic, peeled but whole
- 2 teaspoons ground cumin
- 1 teaspoon ground coriander
- 1½ teaspoons kosher (coarse) salt
- ½ teaspoon freshly ground black pepper
- 1 teaspoon baking soda (bicarbonate of soda)
- Vegetable oil, for deep-frying

[These Middle Eastern fried nuggets of spiced chickpeas, often tucked into pita bread sandwiches with tahini, cucumber slices, and lemon juice, are popular across America. Detroit, Michigan, is home to one of the country's largest Middle Eastern communities.]

In a large bowl, combine the chickpeas with water to cover by 4 inches (10 cm) and soak overnight.

Drain the chickpeas and place a food processor with the parsley, garlic, cumin, coriander, salt, and pepper. Pulse to process the mixture into small pieces, like the texture of couscous. Sprinkle the baking soda (bicarbonate of soda) evenly over the surface of the mixture and continue to pulse until it sticks together when pinched. Transfer to a bowl. Cover and refrigerate for 1 hour.

Preheat the oven to 200°F (95°C). Line a baking sheet with parchment paper.

Pour 2 inches (5 cm) oil into a large heavy pot or deep-fryer and heat to 360°F (180°C). Using wet hands, scoop the falafel mixture and form into 1-inch (2.5 cm) balls. Working with batches of 8 falafel balls, gently transfer to the hot oil. Cook, turning frequently, until golden brown, about 5 minutes. Transfer to the baking sheet and keep warm in the oven while you fry the remaining batches. Serve warm.

MAINE LOBSTER ROLL

PREPARATION TIME: 20 MINUTES,
   PLUS COOLING AND CHILLING TIME
COOKING TIME: 30 MINUTES
SERVES: 4

Per person:
- 2 live lobsters (1½ lb/680 g each)
- 4 tablespoons mayonnaise
- 2 small stalks celery, minced (optional)
- 4 tablespoons (60 g) butter, softened
- 4 top-loader (split-top) hot dog rolls
- Lemon wedges

[Maine lobster meat, chilled and mixed with mayonnaise and celery, is spooned into a buttered, toasted bun. Choose an active lobster; it should flip its tail back and move its claws when handled. Live lobsters should ideally be cooked the same day they are purchased but they may be kept in the refrigerator, in a pan covered with a cold damp towel, for up to 24 hours.]

In a large stockpot fitted with a steamer rack, bring 4 inches (10 cm) water to a boil. Lower the lobsters into the pot, cover, and steam until deep red, about 14 minutes. Remove each lobster from the pot one at a time. Slice a crack in the shell. If the meat is white, then the lobster is cooked. If it is still translucent, then it needs more time to cook. Let the fully cooked lobsters cool until they can comfortably be handled. Remove the meat from the tails, knuckles, and claws. (Save the shells for stock.)

Cut the lobster meat into large chunks and mix with the mayonnaise and celery (if using). Chill for 1 hour.

Spread each bun with 1 tablespoon (15 g) butter on the inside. Heat a frying pan over medium heat, add the buttered rolls, and toast open side down. Fill the buns with the chilled lobster mixture and serve with lemon wedges.

MAINE LOBSTER ROLL

OYSTER PO' BOYS

PREPARATION TIME: 10 MINUTES,
   PLUS RESTING TIME
COOKING TIME: 10 MINUTES
SERVES: 4

For the rémoulade:
- 1 cup (210 g) mayonnaise
- ½ cup (120 ml) sour cream
- 4 tablespoons roughly chopped cornichons
- 1 tablespoon Creole mustard
- 1 tablespoon Louisiana-style hot sauce, such as Crystal
- 1 tablespoon chopped fresh parsley
- 2 tablespoons fresh lemon juice
- Salt and freshly ground black pepper

For the oysters:
- 36 shucked large oysters
- 2 cups (475 ml) buttermilk
- 2 tablespoons Louisiana-style hot sauce, such as Crystal
- Peanut (groundnut) or vegetable oil, for deep-frying
- 2 cups (260 g) cornmeal
- ½ cup (65 g) all-purpose (plain) flour
- 1½ tablespoons onion powder
- 1½ tablespoons garlic powder
- 1½ teaspoons smoked paprika
- Pinch of cayenne pepper
- Salt

For the sandwiches:
- 2 large hoagie/sub/po' boy rolls (each about 12 inches/30 cm long)
- 2 cups (150 g) finely shredded iceberg lettuce
- 2 tomatoes, sliced
- Louisiana-style hot sauce, for serving (optional)

[This New Orleans–style sandwich owes its name to streetcar union members—the "poor boys" striking in 1929 to whom the Martin Brothers Coffee Stand and Restaurant provided large sandwiches for free. Fried oyster po' boys remain the best known of the sandwiches, though at the annual Oak Street Po-Boy Festival in New Orleans, visitors can try shrimp, crawfish, catfish, soft-shell crab, and even schnitzel po' boys.]

For the rémoulade: In a medium bowl, combine the mayonnaise, sour cream, cornichons, mustard, hot sauce, parsley, and lemon juice. Season to taste with salt and pepper.

For the oysters: In a large bowl, soak the oysters in buttermilk and hot sauce for at least 20 minutes and up to 30 minutes.

Pour 3–4 inches (7.5–10 cm) oil into a large heavy pot or deep-fryer and heat to 375°F (190°C).

In a shallow dish, whisk together the cornmeal, flour, onion powder, garlic powder, smoked paprika, and cayenne. Drain the oysters and toss them in the seasoned cornmeal. Working in batches, fry the oysters until golden and crispy, about 3 minutes. Remove with a slotted spoon and drain on paper towels. Season to taste with salt.

For the sandwiches: Split the rolls and spread each with ⅓ cup (120ml) rémoulade. Line with shredded lettuce and tomato slices. Top with fried oysters. Close the rolls and cut each sandwich into 2 pieces. Serve immediately, with the remaining rémoulade and hot sauce alongside, if desired.

OYSTER PO' BOYS

CALZONE

PREPARATION TIME: 35 MINUTES,
   PLUS DRAINING TIME
COOKING TIME: 35 MINUTES
SERVES: 2–4

- 2 cups (310 g) ricotta cheese
- 2 tablespoons semolina flour or fine cornmeal
- 1 lb (455 g) pizza dough
- Flour, for the work surface
- 1½ cups (170 g) shredded mozzarella cheese
- 4 tablespoons freshly grated Parmesan cheese
- 4 tablespoons loosely torn basil leaves
- 1 egg white
- ¼ teaspoon fine sea salt
- 1 cup (240 ml) marinara sauce, warmed

Line a fine-mesh sieve with two layers of cheesecloth. Add the ricotta and spread to an even layer. Let drain for 30 minutes.

Position a rack in the middle of the oven and preheat to 425°F (220°C/Gas Mark 7). Dust a baking sheet with the semolina.

Divide the dough into 2 pieces and form into balls. On a lightly floured surface, stretch and lightly press each ball into a 10-inch (25 cm) round, adding a small amount of flour as needed to prevent sticking. Cover both rounds with plastic wrap (clingfilm) and let rest for 15 minutes.

In a large bowl, mix together the drained ricotta, mozzarella, Parmesan, and basil. Dividing evenly, dollop or spread over one-half of each dough round, leaving a ½-inch (1.25 cm) border at the edge. Whisk the egg white with 1 tablespoon water. Brush the bare edge with the egg wash. Bring the other side of the dough up and over the ricotta mixture and press to seal.

Using two large spatulas (fish slices), place both calzones onto the baking sheet. Brush the tops with the egg wash and sprinkle with the sea salt.

Bake until golden brown, 20–25 minutes. Let rest for 5 minutes before serving with warmed marinara sauce alongside.

AREPAS

PREPARATION TIME: 15 MINUTES
COOKING TIME: 20 MINUTES
SERVES: 4

- 1 teaspoon salt
- ¼ cup (50 g) lard, melted
- 2 cups (395 g) precooked white or yellow cornmeal, such as masarepa or harina precocida
- 2 tablespoons vegetable oil
- 2 cups preferred filling, such as shredded cooked meat, queso fresco, sautéed vegetables

In a medium bowl, whisk together 2½ cups (590 ml) very warm water and the salt, until dissolved. Whisk in the melted lard, then gradually stir in the cornmeal, eventually mixing with your hands to form a soft, moist, malleable dough. Divide the dough into 8 balls the size of golf balls and press each one into a patty about ½ inch (1.25 cm) thick.

In a large frying pan, heat the oil over medium heat. Working in batches, cook the corn patties in until golden brown, 4–5 minutes per side. Drain on paper towels until cool enough to handle.

Slice halfway through each cake horizontally with a thin serrated knife to form a pita-like pocket. Serve stuffed with shredded meat, cheese, or sautéed vegetables, as desired.

CALZONE

CLAM PIZZA

PREPARATION TIME: 30 MINUTES,
   PLUS DOUGH RISING TIME
COOKING TIME: 10 MINUTES
SERVES: 4

- 3½ cups (455 g) all-purpose (plain) flour
- 1½ teaspoons active dry yeast
- 2 teaspoons salt
- 2 teaspoons sugar
- 6 tablespoons olive oil
- 2 dozen littleneck (hardshell) clams, scrubbed and shucked, cut into pieces if large
- 2 cloves garlic, thinly sliced
- Coarse salt and freshly ground black pepper or crushed chili flakes
- 2 tablespoons chopped fresh parsley

[The coastal city of New Haven, Connecticut, lays claim to the original clam pizza, which is notable for the toppings it has (littleneck clams) and those it doesn't (tomato sauce and mozzarella cheese). Toppings aside, pizzas vary regionally based mostly on the thickness and texture of their crust. The crust on a classic clam pizza is Neapolitan style: thin.]

In a large bowl, whisk together the flour, yeast, salt, and sugar. Make a well in the center and add 3 tablespoons of the olive oil and 1 cup (240 ml) lukewarm water. Stir well. If necessary, add more water to make a workable but sticky dough. Turn out onto a floured surface and knead for a few minutes. Place 1 tablespoon of the oil in a clean bowl. Add the dough and turn to coat it with oil. Cover with a damp tea towel and let rise for 1 hour, until doubled in bulk. (The dough can be made ahead of time, before rising, and kept in the refrigerator for up to 24 hours. When ready to use, remove the dough from the refrigerator, punch down, and bring back up to room temperature before rolling and baking.)

Preheat the oven to 500°F (260°C/Gas Mark 10). If you have a pizza stone, preheat it in the oven.

On a pizza peel, roll the dough to ¼-inch (6 mm) thick. (If you don't have a pizza stone, roll the dough on a floured surface and slide the dough onto a baking sheet, reshaping it if necessary.) Allow the dough to rest for 10 minutes. Punch it down and stretch it slightly. Brush the remaining 2 tablespoons olive oil over the top of the pizza. Sprinkle the clams and garlic over the top and season to taste with coarse salt and black pepper or chili flakes.

Slide the pizza onto the hot stone with the pizza peel (or put the baking sheet in the oven). Bake until golden brown, about 10 minutes (a few minutes longer if using a baking sheet). Sprinkle with parsley and serve.

CLAM PIZZA

CHICAGO-STYLE DEEP-DISH PIZZA

PREPARATION TIME: 2 HOURS 15
    MINUTES
COOKING TIME: 1 HOUR 10 MINUTES
MAKES: 2 PIZZAS

For the dough:
- 3¼ cups (425 g) all-purpose (plain) flour, plus more for kneading
- ½ cup (65 g) cornmeal
- 1 tablespoon sugar
- 1½ teaspoons salt
- 1 packet (2 ¼ teaspoons/7 g) active dry yeast
- 1¼ cups (295 ml) warm water (110°F/43°C)
- 4 tablespoons (60 g) unsalted butter, melted and cooled to room temperature
- 4 tablespoons (60 g) unsalted butter, softened

For the sauce:
- 2 tablespoons olive oil
- 1 medium onion, minced
- 2 tablespoons olive oil
- 4 cloves garlic, minced
- 1 can (28 oz/795 g) crushed (finely chopped) tomatoes
- 1 teaspoon dried oregano
- ½ teaspoon crushed chili flakes
- 1 bay leaf
- 1 teaspoon salt
- ¼ teaspoon freshly ground black pepper
- Large pinch of sugar

For the pizzas:
- Olive oil, for the pans and brushing
- 4 cups (450 g) shredded mozzarella cheese
- Toppings (optional): pepperoni, thinly sliced onion, mushrooms, peppers, olives
- ½ cup (45 g) freshly grated Parmesan cheese

[In Chicago, Illinois, pizza has a thick, buttery crust, with the sauce baked *on top* of the cheese and other toppings.]

For the dough: In a large bowl, whisk together the flour, cornmeal, sugar, salt, and yeast. Stir in the water and melted butter. Turn the dough out onto a lightly floured surface and knead until the dough comes together and is smooth and elastic, about 5 minutes. Place the dough in a clean oiled bowl, turn it to coat, cover with a damp tea towel, and place in a warm, draft-free place. Let rise until doubled in volume, about 1 hour.

Meanwhile, for the sauce: In a medium saucepan, heat the oil over medium heat. Add the onion and cook, stirring frequently, until soft and translucent, about 5 minutes. Add the garlic and cook for another minute. Add the tomatoes, oregano, chili flakes, bay leaf, salt, black pepper, and sugar. Cook, stirring occasionally, for 30 minutes. Set aside.

Turn the risen dough out onto a clean work surface. Punch it down and form it into a large rectangle roughly 12 x 15 inches (30 x 40 cm). Spread the softened butter over the top and roll the dough into a log. Cut the log in half and form each half into a ball. Return the dough to the oiled bowl, cover, and let rise for 30 minutes.

Position a rack in the middle of the oven and preheat to 425°F (220°F/Gas Mark 7). Grease two 9-inch (23 cm) springform pans or deep cake pans.

For the pizzas: Press a ball of dough into the corners and 1½ inches (38 mm) up the sides of each pan. Brush the dough with olive oil. Divide the mozzarella between the pizzas. Follow with toppings, if desired. Smother with all of the sauce and finally top with the Parmesan. Bake until golden brown, 20–30 minutes. Allow to cool in the pan for 10 minutes before serving.

CHICAGO-STYLE DEEP-DISH PIZZA

BIEROCKS OR RUNZAS

PREPARATION TIME: 45 MINUTES,
   PLUS RISING AND COOLING TIME
COOKING TIME: 30 MINUTES
MAKES: 12 LARGE BIEROCKS OR RUNZAS

For the dough:
- 2 cups (475 ml) milk
- 2 tablespoons sugar
- 2 teaspoons salt
- 1 stick (115 g) unsalted butter
- 1 tablespoon active dry yeast
- 2 eggs
- 6 cups (780 g) all-purpose (plain) flour, plus more as needed

For the filling:
- 4 tablespoons (60 g) butter, or more as needed
- 1½ lb (680 g) ground (minced) beef
- 1 large onion, finely diced
- 1 head cabbage, shredded
- Salt and freshly ground black pepper

[Although slightly different shapes, bierocks and runzas are both yeast dough filled with a savory ground (minced) beef and cabbage filling. Bierocks, found throughout the Midwest, are a round bun shape, while runzas, in Nebraska, are oblong. Bierocks were made popular by Volga German immigrants.]

For the dough: In a small heavy-bottomed saucepan, bring the milk, sugar, and salt to a simmer. Remove from the heat and stir in the butter. Pour the milk mixture into a large bowl and let cool to lukewarm. Stir in the yeast and let sit for 5 minutes. Add the eggs, one at a time, and mix well. Add 5 cups (650 g) flour and stir well. Spread the remaining 1 cup (130 g) flour on a clean work surface, turn the dough out onto it, and knead the flour into the dough. Knead for 7–10 minutes, dusting the surface with additional flour as necessary, until the dough is smooth and elastic. Transfer the dough to a large buttered bowl and turn to coat. Cover with a clean tea towel and let the dough rise in a warm draft-free area until doubled in volume, about 1 hour.

Meanwhile, for the filling: In a large pot, melt the butter over medium-high heat. Add the beef and onion and cook, stirring frequently, until the beef and onions are cooked through and beginning to brown, about 10 minutes. Remove the beef and onion with a slotted spoon. If there isn't plenty of fat left in the pan, add more butter. Add the cabbage and cook over medium heat, stirring and scraping the bottom of the pan, until wilted and beginning to brown, about 15 minutes. Remove from the heat, return the beef/onion mixture to the pan, and season to taste with salt and pepper. Let cool.

Punch down the dough. On a floured work surface, divide the dough into 12 equal pieces.

For bierocks: Roll each dough piece into a ball shape, then flatten into a 6-inch (15 cm) round.

For runzas: Roll each dough piece into a log 6 inches (15 cm) long and flatten them into rectangles.

Spoon 4 tablespoons filling onto each dough piece. Pull the sides together, pinching them tightly. Place the bierocks or runzas on 2 parchment-lined baking sheets and cover them with a clean tea towel. Let them rest for 15 minutes.

Meanwhile, position a rack in the middle of the oven and preheat to 350°F (180°C/Gas Mark 4).

Bake until the pastries are golden brown, about 30 minutes. Serve hot or at room temperature.

PASTIES

PREPARATION TIME: 30 MINUTES,
    PLUS CHILLING TIME
COOKING TIME: 1 HOUR
MAKES: 12 PASTIES

For the dough:
- 5 cups (650 g) all-purpose (plain) flour
- 1 teaspoon salt
- 1 cup (225 g) cold lard, solid vegetable shortening, or unsalted butter, cut into small pieces
- Ice water, as needed

For the filling:
- 1½ lb (680 g) ground (minced) beef
- 4 medium potatoes, peeled and diced
- 2 medium carrots, peeled and diced
- 2 medium turnips, peeled and diced
- 1 medium onion, diced
- 1½ teaspoons salt
- ½ teaspoon freshly ground black pepper
- 1 egg or ⅓ cup (80 ml) heavy (whipping) cream (optional, for brushing)

For the dough: In a bowl, whisk together the flour and salt. Cut in the fat using a pastry (dough) blender or your fingers until the fat is evenly distributed and there are no pieces larger than a pea. Add 4 tablespoons ice water and mix, adding more as needed, 1 tablespoon at a time, until the dough forms a ball. Form the dough into a disk, wrap with plastic wrap (clingfilm), and refrigerate for at least 30 minutes or up to 24 hours.

For the filling: In a large bowl, combine the beef, potatoes, carrots, turnips, onion, salt, and pepper and use your hands to mix thoroughly.

Position racks in the upper and lower thirds of the oven and preheat to 350°F (180°C/Gas Mark 4). Grease 2 baking sheets or line with parchment paper.

Divide the dough into 12 pieces and form each into a ball. Flatten the balls and roll them into 8-inch (20 cm) rounds. Place about ¼ cup (4 tablespoons) filling on each round. Fold the dough over and crimp, using a fork or your fingers, to seal them shut.

Place the pasties on the baking sheets. Brush the pasties with egg or cream if desired. Cut three slits in the top of each pasty (this will allow steam to escape and keep the pasties from bursting). Bake until golden brown and steaming, about 1 hour, switching racks halfway through. Serve hot or at room temperature.

Baked pasties freeze well. To reheat from frozen, place the pasties in a 325°F (160°C/Gas Mark 3) oven or toaster (mini) oven and bake until heated through, 15–20 minutes.

PIEROGI

PREPARATION TIME: 1 HOUR 35 MINUTES
COOKING TIME: 50 MINUTES
SERVES: 4–6

For the dough:
- 3 cups (390 g) all-purpose (plain) flour
- 1 teaspoon salt
- 1 egg
- 2 teaspoons vegetable oil

For the filling:
- 1½ lb (680 g) russet (baking) potatoes, peeled and cut into 1-inch (2.5 cm) pieces
- Salt and freshly ground black pepper
- Freshly grated nutmeg
- 2 cups (225 g) grated mild white farmer cheese or mild white cheddar
- 4 tablespoons (60 g) butter
- 1 large onion, diced
- 4 tablespoons melted butter
- Sour cream and sauerkraut, for serving

[Pierogi are filled Polish dumplings that are fried or boiled. The dough can be as simple as flour and water, and some recipes also call for eggs and/or sour cream. Common fillings include potato, onion, cheese, ground meat, or fruit; this classic version contains potato and onion. Serve with sour cream and sauerkraut.]

For the dough: In a large bowl, whisk together the flour and salt. Make a well in the center, pour in 1 cup (235 ml) water, the egg, and oil. Whisk the water and egg together, then gradually bring the flour into the center, mixing it in. Use a wooden spoon to mix it as thoroughly as possible, then turn the dough out onto a lightly floured surface and knead until the dough is pliable and very soft, about 5 minutes. Place in a greased bowl, cover with a damp kitchen towel, and let rest for 1 hour.

Meanwhile, for the filling: Place the potatoes in a saucepan and add cold water to cover. Bring to a boil and cook until tender, about 8 minutes. Drain, return the potatoes to the pan, and cook over medium heat, stirring, until any remaining liquid has evaporated and the potatoes are quite dry, about 5 minutes. Remove from the heat, mash well, and season to taste with salt, pepper, and nutmeg. Stir in the cheese. Set aside.

In a large frying pan, melt the butter over medium heat. Add the onions and cook, stirring frequently, until golden brown, about 15 minutes. Remove from the heat, stir half of the onions into the potato mixture, and reserve the other half for garnish.

To assemble the pierogi, on a floured surface, roll the dough to a thickness of about ¼ inch (6 mm). Using a glass or biscuit cutter, cut the dough into 3-inch (7.5 cm) rounds, re-rolling scraps as necessary. Place a small spoonful of filling on one half of a round. Brush the edge of the dough with water, fold over, and crimp to seal. As you work, arrange the pierogi in a single layer on a baking sheet.

Bring a large pot of water to a boil. Add the pierogi and as soon as they float to the surface, boil them for about 2 minutes more, until cooked through. Remove with a slotted spoon to a bowl. Toss with melted butter. Garnish with the reserved browned onions. Serve with sour cream and sauerkraut.

PIEROGI

NATCHITOCHES MEAT PIES

PREPARATION TIME: 25 MINUTES,
  PLUS CHILLING AND COOLING TIME
COOKING TIME: 45 MINUTES
MAKES: 16–18 PIES

For the dough:
- 2½ cups (325 g) all-purpose (plain) flour
- 2 teaspoons salt
- ½ cup (120 ml) vegetable oil
- ½ cup (120 ml) ice water

For the filling:
- 3 tablespoons (45 g) unsalted butter
- ½ lb (225 g) ground (minced) beef chuck
- ¼ lb (115 g) ground (minced) pork
- 3 cloves garlic, minced
- ⅔ cup (110 g) chopped white onion
- ⅓ cup (50 g) chopped green bell pepper
- 1 bay leaf
- 4 teaspoons tomato paste (purée)
- ½ teaspoon cayenne pepper
- ½ teaspoon chopped fresh thyme
- Salt
- Louisiana hot sauce, such as Crystal
- Peanut (groundnut) oil, for deep-frying

[This Louisiana specialty is from the center of the state, where meat pies have been a favorite since the 18th century. What sets these hand pies apart is their crust, which is made from a type of biscuit dough.]

For the dough: In a food processor, combine the flour and salt. With the machine on, add the oil and process until the flour is moistened. Sprinkle on the ice water and pulse 5 or 6 times, just until the dough is moistened. Transfer the dough to a work surface and knead just until smooth. Form the dough into 2 disks, wrap in plastic wrap (clingfilm), and refrigerate for 30 minutes.

For the filling: In a large frying pan, melt the butter over medium-high heat. Add the ground (minced) beef and pork and cook, breaking it up with a wooden spoon, until browned, about 5 minutes. Reduce the heat to medium and add the garlic, onion, bell pepper, and bay leaf and cook, stirring occasionally, until the onion is translucent, 7–8 minutes. Stir in the tomato paste (purée), cayenne, and thyme and cook over medium-low heat for 3 minutes. Season to taste with salt and hot sauce and let cool. Discard the bay leaf.

Pour 3 inches (7.5 cm) oil into a large heavy pot or deep-fryer and heat to 375°F (190°C).

On a floured work surface, roll each disk of dough into a rectangle ⅛ inch (3 mm) thick. Using a 4-inch (10 cm) biscuit cutter, cut rounds from each piece of dough. Re-roll the scraps one time and cut out more rounds. Brush the edges of the rounds with water and place 2 tablespoons of filling to one side of each round. Fold the other half of the dough over the filling and press with a fork to seal.

Working in batches of 3 or 4, fry the pies until golden brown, turning once, about 5 minutes total. Drain on paper towels. Serve warm.

SHREDDED BEEF CHIMICHANGAS

PREPARATION TIME: 40 MINUTES
COOKING TIME: 6 HOURS
SERVES: 12

For the beef:
- 2½ lb (1.1 kg) beef chuck roast
- Salt
- 2 tablespoons vegetable oil
- 6 cloves garlic, peeled but whole
- 1 large onion, chopped
- 2 bay leaves
- 2 teaspoons dried oregano
- Freshly ground black pepper
- 2 cups (475 ml) dark Mexican beer, such as Negra Modelo
- About 3 cups (710 ml) beef stock

For the chimichangas:
- 2 tablespoons canola (rapeseed) oil
- 2 large onions, finely chopped
- 4 bell peppers, diced
- 4–5 cloves garlic, minced
- 1 can (4.5 oz/127 g) chopped green chilies
- 1 teaspoon dried oregano
- 2 teaspoons ground cumin
- 2 teaspoons chili powder
- 12 (10-inch/25.5 cm) flour tortillas
- 1 lb (455 g) Monterey Jack or mild cheddar cheese, shredded
- 6-inch (15 cm) skewers
- Vegetable oil, for frying
- Shredded lettuce, for serving
- Garnishes: sour cream, mild salsa, avocado chunks, chopped tomatoes, and cilantro (coriander)

[The "chimi," as it is known in Arizona, is a large, meat-stuffed, deep-fried burrito, served atop lettuce and smothered with cheese and sour cream. Tucson, Arizona's second-largest city, claims it as its own.]

Preheat the oven to 350°F (180°C/Gas Mark 4).

For the beef: Season the roast with salt. Heat 2 tablespoons oil in a Dutch oven (casserole) over medium heat, add the roast, and sear on all sides, about 10 minutes. Add the garlic, onion, bay leaves, oregano, black pepper to taste, the beer, and enough stock to cover the meat halfway. Bring to a boil, cover, transfer to the oven, and cook until meat can be shredded with a fork, 5–6 hours.

Remove the pot from the oven and transfer the beef to a carving board. Reserve 1 cup (240 ml) of the cooking liquid, discarding the rest. When cool enough to handle, shred the meat and mash in the softened garlic and onions with the reserved cooking liquid. Transfer the meat mixture to a large bowl to cool.

For the chimichangas: Heat 2 tablespoons canola (rapeseed) oil in a large skillet over medium heat, add the onions, bell peppers, and garlic, and cook until soft, about 5 minutes. Reduce the heat and stir in the chopped chilies, oregano, cumin, and chili powder. Add the vegetable mixture to the shredded beef and mix well.

Preheat the oven to 250°F (120°C/Gas Mark ½).

Lay out a flour tortilla and fill with ½ cup (120 ml) beef mixture and 2 tablespoons cheese. Roll the tortilla tightly and secure with a skewer. Repeat with the remaining tortillas.

Pour vegetable oil to a depth of 1 inch (2.5 cm) into a large deep frying pan and heat over medium heat until the oil shimmers (about 350°F/180°C). Carefully transfer the chimichangas to the hot oil and cook, turning once, until golden brown on each side, about 4 minutes. Drain on paper towels and hold in a warm oven.

Serve the chimichangas over lettuce and topped with sour cream, salsa, tomatoes, avocado, and cilantro (coriander).

PORK AND RED CHILI TAMALES

PREPARATION TIME: 2 HOURS
 15 MINUTES
COOKING TIME: 4 HOURS 45 MINUTES
MAKES: 7–8 DOZEN TAMALES

- 6–8 lb (2.7–3.6 kg) boneless pork shoulder, cut into 3-inch (7.5 cm) chunks
- 8 cloves garlic, smashed and peeled
- 6 cups (1.4 liters) New Mexico red chili sauce, plus more for serving (optional)
- 8 dozen dried corn husks
- 8 cups masa harina, such as Maseca
- 4 teaspoons baking powder
- 2 teaspoons salt
- 1⅔ cups (340 g) lard, melted

Place the meat in a large pot and add cold water to cover and the garlic. Bring to a boil over high heat, skimming off any foam that rises to the surface. Cover, reduce the heat to medium-low, and simmer until the meat is very tender, 2–2½ hours. Reserving the broth, remove the meat to a cutting board. When cool enough to handle, shred into 1-inch (2.5 cm) pieces. Discard all the fat and tendons. Place the meat in a large bowl and toss to combine with the red chile sauce until well coated.

While the meat is cooking, separate the corn husks into single leaves and rinse them individually under warm water. Place the husks in a bowl and cover with warm water. Let soak for 1 hour or until soft.

In a large bowl, combine the masa mix, baking powder, salt, and lard until well blended. Gradually stir in enough warm pork broth to make a soft dough. Knead well with your hands until you have a moist, but not sticky dough. Cover the bowl with a damp kitchen towel and set aside.

Working with one softened corn husk at a time, hold a husk in one hand with the pointy end facing you. With the back of a spoon, spread 2–3 tablespoons dough in an even layer across the wide end to within 1 inch (2.5 cm) of the top edge, 2 inches (5 cm) from the bottom point, and 3 inches (7.5 cm) from the right side. Spoon 1 tablespoon of the meat mixture into the center of the dough. Roll the husk toward the empty right side, so that the dough surrounds the filling and forms a tight roll. Fold the bottom under to close the tamale (the top should remain open). Set aside. Repeat with the remaining corn husks, dough, and filling.

In a large pot, pack the tamales upright (folded end down, open end up) and tightly together so that they stand up on their own. (You may need to use two pots, or else cook them in two batches.) Add water to the pot to come within ½ inch (1.25 cm) of the top of the tamales. Bring the water to a boil over high heat. Cover the pot, reduce the heat to medium-low, and simmer until the dough is firm yet still creamy, 1½–2 hours.

Serve the tamales warm. Unwrap the husks to eat, and serve with additional red chile sauce, if desired.

PUPUSAS WITH CURTIDO

PREPARATION TIME: 45 MINUTES, PLUS
AT LEAST 3 DAYS MARINATING AND
FERMENTING TIME FOR THE CABBAGE
COOKING TIME: 15 MINUTES
MAKES: 8 PUPUSAS

For the curtido:
- 1 medium head cabbage, shredded
- 1 large carrot, grated
- 1 medium onion, thinly sliced
- 2 jalapeño peppers, seeded and diced
- 1 teaspoon dried Mexican oregano
- 1 teaspoon crushed chili flakes
- 1 heaping tablespoon sea salt, or to taste

For the pupusas:
- 2 cups (240 g) masa harina
- Pinch of salt
- 1½ cups (355 ml) warm water
- 1 cup (115 g) grated queso fresco
- Vegetable oil
- Curtido, for serving
- Thinly sliced jalapeños, for serving
- Hot sauce, for serving

[Two million Americans claim Salvadoran roots and have brought this traditional dish to America, especially around Los Angeles, California, and Washington, D.C. Pupusas are similar to corn tortillas, only thicker and stuffed with cheese, beans, or meat. They're traditionally topped with curtido (fermented cabbage), jalapeños, and hot sauce.]

For the curtido: In a large bowl, combine the cabbage, carrot, onion, jalapeños, oregano, and chili flakes. Add enough salt so the cabbage tastes salty. Cover and marinate overnight. The next day, knead and pound the vegetables with your hands until the cabbage has softened and liquid is released. Pack the vegetables into a large jar, cover, and let sit out at room temperature until the mixture has fermented and soured to taste, 2–5 days. Use immediately or store in the refrigerator for up to 1 month.

For the pupusas: Place the masa in a large bowl. Add the salt and warm water and knead to form a moist, smooth dough. If the dough is too stiff or dry, add a little bit more water. If the dough is sticky, add a bit more masa. Cover the bowl with a clean tea towel and let rest for at least 10 and up to 15 minutes.

Using oiled hands, divide the dough into 8 pieces and form into balls. Make each ball into a bowl shape and fill with 1 tablespoon cheese. Seal the dough over the cheese and re-form into a ball. Form a disk by patting the dough back and forth between your hands. The disk should be about ½–¾ inch (1.25–2 cm) thick. Repeat with the remaining balls.

Pour enough oil to coat the bottom of a large frying pan and heat over medium-high heat. Working in batches, cook the pupusas until golden brown, 2–3 minutes per side.

Serve warm with the remaining cheese and the curtido on top, and jalapeños and hot sauce on the side.

MAIN

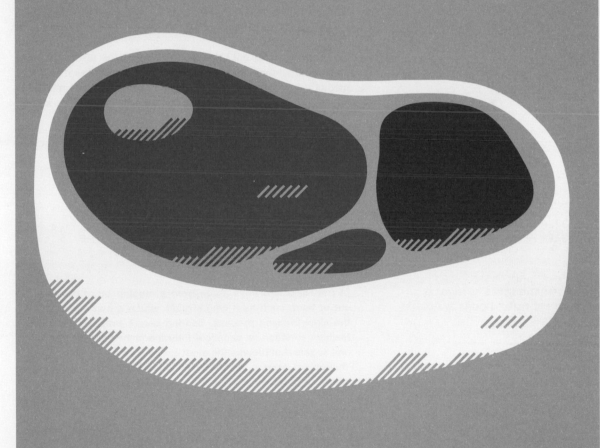

COURSES

PRIME RIB ROAST BEEF

PREPARATION TIME: 10 MINUTES,
   PLUS STANDING TIME
COOKING TIME: 1 HOUR 20 MINUTES
SERVES: ½–1 LB (227–455 G) PER PERSON

- 3 lb (1.4 kg) boneless prime rib roast (forerib), trimmed of excess fat and silverskin and tied
- Salt and freshly ground black pepper
- Whole cloves garlic (optional)

[Bone-in has more flavor, but many people prefer a boneless roast, trimmed and tied. The roasting time will vary greatly depending on the size and shape of the roast, as well as the animal itself. Searing the roast beforehand is an option, but not essential. A good piece of meat marbled with fat will form a beautiful brown crust and the flavor will benefit from a longer roasting time. The pan juices may be saved and served along with the roast.]

Let the beef stand at room temperature for at least 1 hour. Preheat the oven to 325°F (160°C/Gas Mark 3).

Wipe the roast with a damp cloth. Season liberally with salt and pepper. If using garlic, halve the cloves lengthwise. Pierce the roast all over with a sharp paring knife and insert a piece of garlic about ½ inch (1.25 cm) deep in each slit. Place the roast in a large roasting pan.

Roast, uncovered, until the beef is about 10°F (6°C) shy of its final cooked temperature (it will continue cooking as it sits): For medium-rare, remove the roast when its internal temperature reads 135°F (57°C). Timing will be roughly 20–30 minutes per pound (455 g).

Tent the roast with foil and let sit for 10–15 minutes. Slice the beef and serve with pan juices.

YANKEE POT ROAST

PREPARATION TIME: 10 MINUTES
COOKING TIME: 3 HOURS 20 MINUTES
SERVES: 6

- 4 lb (1.8 kg) boneless beef rump or chuck roast
- Salt and freshly ground black pepper
- 2 tablespoons olive oil
- 1 large onion, chopped
- 3 cloves garlic, sliced
- 1 cup (240 ml) red wine
- 3 cups (710 ml) beef stock
- 6 carrots, peeled and halved lengthwise
- 6 medium potatoes, peeled and halved lengthwise

[A pot roast is always made from a tougher but more flavorful cut of beef, such as a chuck roast, which grows tender during the slow braising process. Searing before braising produces a Maillard reaction, a chemical interaction between amino acids and sugars that browns the meat and gives it a rich flavor. Classic Yankee pot roast — which can include carrots, parsnips, turnips, celery, or potatoes — is rooted in New England.]

Preheat the oven to 325°F (160°C/Gas Mark 3).

Season the beef all over with salt and pepper. In a large Dutch oven (casserole), heat the oil over medium-high heat. Sear the beef on all sides, until it is well browned, about 12 minutes. Transfer the beef to a plate and set aside. Add the onion and garlic to the pan and cook, stirring, for a few minutes. Add the red wine and beef stock. Return the beef to the pan, cover, and bring to a boil.

Transfer to the oven and roast for 1 hour. Turn the beef over and roast for 1 hour. Check to make sure the roast is almost submerged in broth, adding some water if it isn't. Roast for 30 minutes. Add the carrots and potatoes to the pot, placing them in the liquid surrounding the beef. Roast until the vegetables and the meat are tender, 45 minutes to 1 hour.

BARBACOA

PREPARATION TIME: PIT-DIGGING
  AND FIRE-BUILDING TIME
COOKING TIME: 10 HOURS
MAKES: ABOUT 7 LB (3 KG) MEAT

   5

- 1 beef head (see headnote), about 20 lb (9 kg)
- Mesquite or preferred wood for fire-roasting, such as pecan, hickory, or oak

[Succulent Barbacoa meat — from a cow's head cooked in burlap in an in-ground fire pit — is a staple in border towns like El Paso, Texas, where it is shredded and served in a flour tortilla with onion, salsa, and cilantro. Buying a beef head can be illegal in various markets across the country, so finding one may require befriending a farmer or substituting lamb for beef. Note that in Mexican meat markets, beef head is called *cabeza*. Some place a pot of water among the coals for more moisture. This recipe is inspired by one from Vera's Backyard Bar-B-Que, which opened in 1955 in Brownsville, Texas.]

Dig a large round pit in the ground about 3 feet (1 m) in diameter and 2 feet (0.5 m) deep. Fill with firewood and light the fire, letting it burn for several hours or until the pit is full of glowing embers.

Soak two large burlap sacks in water (or use foil). Rinse the beef head and use a torch to burn off any hair. Trim any hide that remains. Wrap the head in one of the soaked burlap sacks (or foil).

Place the head in the center of the pit and cover with the remaining water-soaked burlap sack (or, traditionally, maguey leaves). Cook until the meat shreds from the bone, 7–10 hours, adding more wood to keep embers glowing steadily.

Peel the skin from the head and separate the cooked meat into *ojos* (eyes), *lengua* (tongue), and *mollejas* (sweetbreads), from the face meat.

TRI-TIP, SANTA MARIA STYLE

 CA

PREPARATION TIME: 5 MINUTES,
  PLUS RESTING TIME
COOKING TIME: 20 MINUTES
SERVES: 4

- 1 tablespoon garlic powder
- 1 tablespoon salt
- 2 teaspoons freshly ground black pepper
- 1 teaspoon cayenne pepper
- 1 teaspoon minced fresh rosemary
- 2½ lb (1 kg) beef tri-tip roast

[This recipe calls for simply seasoned beef to be grilled directly over red oak chips. Californians favor an unusual cut for this technique, the tri-tip, which comes from the bottom of the sirloin, and the dish is named after the town that popularized it.]

In a small bowl, mix together the garlic powder, salt, black pepper, cayenne, and rosemary. Rub all over the beef and let the meat rest at room temperature for 1 hour.

Preheat a gas or charcoal grill (barbecue) to medium-high heat.

Place the roast on the grill rack over direct heat and sear on both sides. Move to a cooler part of the grill and continue to cook until the internal temperature reads 120°F (49°C), about 20 minutes.

Transfer to a carving board and let rest for 5–10 minutes before slicing across the grain.

PREPARATION TIME: 15 MINUTES
COOKING TIME: 9 HOURS OR MORE
SERVES: 8–10

For the marinade:
- 2 cups (475 ml) beer
- ½ cup (120 ml) cider vinegar
- ⅓ cup (80 ml) Worcestershire sauce
- 4 cloves garlic, minced
- 4 tablespoons grated onion
- 1 bay leaf
- 1 teaspoon kosher (coarse) salt
- 1 teaspoon freshly ground black pepper
- 1 teaspoon Tabasco-style hot sauce
- Food-safe spray bottle or a grilling mop

For the rub:
- 3 tablespoons yellow mustard
- 2 tablespoons cider vinegar
- 2 tablespoons light brown sugar
- 1 tablespoon molasses (treacle)
- 2 tablespoons smoked sweet paprika
- 2 teaspoons chili powder
- 2 teaspoons garlic powder
- 2 teaspoons onion powder
- 2 teaspoons salt
- 1 teaspoon ground celery seeds
- 1 teaspoon ground cumin
- 1 teaspoon freshly ground black pepper

For the brisket:
- 7–10 lb (3–4.5 kg) beef brisket
- Hardwood chips or chunks, for smoking
- Kansas City–Style Barbecue Sauce (page 463)

[This double recipe yields a whole barbequed brisket—and the burnt ends beloved in Kansas City, Missouri.]

For the marinade: In a small saucepan, combine the beer, vinegar, Worcestershire, garlic, onion, bay leaf, salt, black pepper, and hot sauce and bring to a boil. Simmer over low heat for 10 minutes. Let cool, then transfer to a blender and purée. Strain through a fine-mesh sieve and transfer to a spray bottle or a bowl (if you're using a grilling mop). Set aside.

For the rub: In a bowl, combine the mustard, vinegar, brown sugar, molasses (treacle), and spices.

For the brisket: Score the brisket all over by making small slits about 1 inch (2.5 cm) apart with a sharp paring knife. Coat the brisket all over with the rub.

Set up a gas or charcoal grill (barbecue) for indirect cooking with a drip pan and preheat to medium-low. Toss 1 handful of the wood chips or chunks on the coals. If using a gas grill, place presoaked wood chips or chunks in a smoker box or in a smoker pouch and run the grill on high until you see smoke, then reduce the heat to medium. The temperature of the grill should be 250°–275°F (120°–135°C).

Place the brisket, fat side up, in the center of the grill rack, over the drip pan and away from the heat, and close the lid. Smoke the brisket for 1 hour 15 minutes per pound (455 g) of meat: A 7-lb (3 kg) brisket will take about 8 hours 45 minutes. If using a charcoal grill, every hour, add fresh charcoal and a handful of wood chips. As the brisket cooks, every hour, spray or mop with the marinade. When the brisket is thoroughly cooked (the internal temperature should read 185°F/85°C), transfer to a carving board and tent with foil. Let the meat rest for 30 minutes.

If making burnt ends, see below. Otherwise, thinly slice the brisket across the grain and serve with the barbecue sauce on the side.

For the burnt ends: Remove the point from the flat of the cooked brisket by separating it along the fat line. This can be done by simply pulling the meat apart, or use a knife to cut through the entire brisket. Cut the point into ½-inch (1.25 cm) cubes. Place the cubed meat in a metal pan and toss with barbecue sauce. Place the pan back on the grill, close the lid, and smoke for another hour or so, until the meat is beginning to burn a bit. Serve as is, or save for making Burnt Ends Chili (page 213).

SAUERBRATEN

PREPARATION TIME: 20 MINUTES,
PLUS COOLING TIME AND AT LEAST
2 DAYS MARINATING TIME
COOKING TIME: 3 HOURS 25 MINUTES
SERVES: 6

For the marinade and beef:
- 1 cup (240 ml) dry red wine
- 1 cup (240 ml) vinegar (wine or cider)
- 1 medium onion, thinly sliced
- 1 tablespoon black peppercorns, lightly crushed
- 1 tablespoon juniper berries, lightly crushed
- 1 tablespoon coriander seeds, lightly crushed
- 2 bay leaves
- 3 tablespoons sugar
- 1 teaspoon salt
- 4 lb (1.8 kg) boneless bottom or top round (topside) beef roast

For the sauerbraten:
- 3 tablespoons fat, lard, or oil
- 2 large onions, diced
- 4 carrots, diced
- 2 stalks celery, diced
- 1 cup (240 ml) sour cream
- 1 cup (100 g) crushed gingersnaps (ginger nuts)

For the marinade and beef: In a medium saucepan, combine 2 cups (475 ml) water, the wine, vinegar, onion, spices, bay leaves, sugar, and salt and bring to a boil. Let cool.

Pour the marinade into a glass or ceramic dish big enough to hold the roast. Add the beef and cover it with the marinade. Cover and refrigerate for at least 2 days and up to 3 days, turning the meat several times each day.

Preheat the oven to 325°F (160°C/Gas Mark 3).

For the sauerbraten: Remove the beef from the marinade. Strain the marinade into a bowl (discard the solids) and set aside.

In a large Dutch oven (casserole), heat the fat over high heat. Sear the meat on all sides until it is deep brown, 3–4 minutes per side. Add the onions, carrots, celery, 1 cup (240 ml) water, and the reserved marinade. Bring to a boil, cover, and transfer to the oven. Roast until the meat is tender and falling apart, about 3 hours.

Transfer the meat to a platter. Place the Dutch oven over medium heat, stir in the sour cream and gingersnaps, and cook to heat through. Pour over the meat and serve hot with a spoon.

CORNED BEEF AND CABBAGE

PREPARATION TIME: 10 MINUTES
COOKING TIME: 4 HOURS
SERVES: 6

- 4–5 lb (1.8–2.3 kg) corned beef
- 1 clove garlic, sliced
- ½ teaspoon lightly crushed peppercorns
- 3 medium onions, quartered
- 3 carrots, peeled and halved crosswise
- 1 medium head cabbage, cored and cut into wedges

Place the corned beef in a large pot and add cold water to cover by 3 inches (7.5 cm). Add the garlic and peppercorns and bring to boil, skimming off any scum that rises to the top. Reduce the heat, cover, and simmer until the beef is just tender, about 3 hours. Add the onions and carrots, simmer for 30 minutes. Add the cabbage and cook for another 15 minutes. Transfer the beef to a cutting board, slice, and serve on a platter with the vegetables.

PREPARATION TIME: 20 MINUTES
COOKING TIME: 6 HOURS 40 MINUTES
SERVES: 6–8

- 3 lb (1.4 kg) brisket, with a fatty layer on one side
- Kosher (coarse) salt and freshly ground black pepper
- 1 sweet onion, halved, with root end intact
- 2 tablespoons vegetable oil
- 1 head garlic (about 10 cloves), cloves smashed and peeled
- 1 teaspoon ground cumin
- Pinch of ground coriander (optional)
- ¼ cup (60 ml) cider vinegar
- 2 cups (475 ml) beef stock
- 1 jalapeño pepper, halved (seeded for less heat)
- 1 bay leaf
- 1 poblano or green bell pepper, thinly sliced
- 12 corn or flour tortillas (6 inch/15 cm), warmed according to package directions
- Shredded Monterey Jack or mild cheddar cheese, for serving (optional)

[Brisket and tacos are two pillars of Texas cuisine. This Dallas-born dish combines them in a Tex-Mex answer to the roast beef sandwich. The meat is tender and juicy, simply paired with a few strips of peppers and onions. It can be served with a small bowl of the brisket's pan juices, or a thickened gravy made from them. For a variation, use beer instead of cider vinegar.]

Position a rack in the lowest position and preheat the oven to 300°F (150°C/Gas Mark 2).

Season the brisket generously with salt and pepper. Cut one half of the onion into thin slices and set aside for serving. Cut the other half into 1-inch (2.5 cm) wedges through the intact root end (this holds the wedges together).

In a Dutch oven (casserole), heat 1 tablespoon of the oil over medium-high heat. Add the brisket and cook until browned on both sides, about 15 minutes total. Transfer the brisket to a plate. Add the onion wedges, garlic, cumin, and coriander (if using) and cook, stirring often, until the spices are toasted and the onion begins to release some liquid (stir in a tablespoon of the vinegar if the spices begin to burn), about 6 minutes. Add the vinegar, stirring to scrape up the browned bits from the bottom of the pan.

Return the brisket to the pan and add the stock, jalapeño, and bay leaf. Increase the heat to bring to a boil, then reduce to a simmer. Transfer to the oven and cook until the brisket shreds easily with a fork, about 6 hours. Transfer the brisket to a bowl and shred with two forks. Strain the juices through a sieve into a bowl (discard the solids). Return the strained broth to the pan, bring to a boil, and cook until thickened and reduced by half, about 10 minutes.

Meanwhile, preheat the broiler (grill) with the rack in the position closest to the heat source. In a sheet pan, toss the reserved sliced onion and the poblano with the remaining 1 tablespoon oil and season with salt and pepper. Broil the vegetables, tossing occasionally, until charred in spots and softened, about 5 minutes.

To serve, divide the brisket and vegetables among warmed tortillas. Serve with cheese.

BRISKET TACOS

NEW YORK STRIP STEAKS

PREPARATION TIME: 5 MINUTES
COOKING TIME: 10 MINUTES
SERVES: 2

- 2 boneless New York strip steaks, 1½–2 inches (4–5 cm) thick
- Salt
- 2 tablespoons olive oil
- Freshly ground black pepper

[Also called a Strip, Kansas City Strip, or Shell Steak, this cut is a steakhouse favorite. Marinate with olive oil, garlic, and rosemary if you like, but for prime meat, that's optional. Outside the United States, this cut is sometimes labeled sirloin steak or club steak.]

Remove the steaks from the refrigerator 15–20 minutes before cooking. Preheat the oven to 450°F (230°C/Gas Mark 8).

Season the steaks generously with salt. In a large cast-iron skillet, heat the oil over high heat until hot but not smoking. Sear the steaks until nicely browned on both sides, 1–2 minutes per side. Transfer the pan to the oven and roast until the internal temperature reads 130°F (54°C) for rare (the internal temperature will rise as the steaks rest), about 6 minutes.

Transfer the steaks to a carving board and let rest for 5 minutes. Season with salt and pepper, slice, and serve.

CHICAGO-STYLE STEAK

PREPARATION TIME: 5 MINUTES
COOKING TIME: 15 MINUTES
SERVES: 4

- 2 aged bone-in ribeye steaks (prime if possible), 1½–2 inches (4–5 cm) thick
- Salt
- Canola (rapeseed) oil or other high-heat oil, for the grill (barbecue)
- Freshly ground black pepper

[Chicagoans in Illinois take their steaks seriously. A rib eye Chicago-style is simply a great aged piece of beef charred on the outside, rare on the inside, seasoned with salt and pepper. In some parts of the country this is known as a "black and blue" steak.]

Leave the steaks in the refrigerator until ready to cook. Preheat a gas or charcoal grill (barbecue) to high heat. (Make sure the grill rack is clean.)

Salt both sides of the steaks. Oil the grill rack and place the steaks on the hottest part, close the lid, and cook for 3–4 minutes. Open, flip the steaks, and cook for 3–4 minutes. Repeat the process one more time or until the internal temperature reads 110°–115°F (43°–46°C). Transfer the steaks to a carving board and let rest for 3–5 minutes. The temperature of the steaks will continue to rise another 5°–10°F (3°–5°C).

Cut the meat from the bone, slice (the meat closest to the bone will be the most rare), and sprinkle with salt and pepper.

COWBOY STEAKS
WITH WHISKEY BUTTER

PREPARATION TIME: 25 MINUTES,
   PLUS 2 HOURS CHILLING TIME
COOKING TIME: 20 MINUTES
SERVES: 4

- 2 shallots, minced
- 9 teaspoons whiskey
- 1 stick (115 g) butter, softened
- 1 teaspoon minced fresh rosemary
- 1 tablespoon plus ½ teaspoon
  smoked paprika
- 1 tablespoon plus ½ teaspoon salt
- 2 tablespoons chili powder
- 1 tablespoon light brown sugar
- 1 teaspoon freshly ground black pepper
- 4 (1–1½-inch/2.5–4 cm) thick bone-in beef
  steaks, 12 oz (340 g) each

In a food processor, combine the shallots, whiskey, butter, rosemary, ½ teaspoon smoked paprika, and ½ teaspoon salt and process to blend. Transfer the butter to a piece of parchment paper or plastic wrap (clingfilm) and shape into a log. Wrap well and refrigerate until firm. The whiskey butter will keep for 2 weeks in the refrigerator or up to 6 months in the freezer.

In a small bowl, combine the chili powder, brown sugar, the remaining smoked paprika and salt, and the pepper and mix well.

Preheat a gas or charcoal grill (barbecue) to high heat. Crust the steaks with the rub and let rest for 5–10 minutes.

Place the steaks on the grill rack and sear each side until nicely browned, 2–3 minutes per side. Move the steaks to a cooler part of the grill and continue cooking until the internal temperature reads 110°F (43°C), 6–8 minutes. Transfer the steaks to a carving board and let rest for 5–10 minutes.

To serve, cut the steak from the bone, slice, and top each portion with 2 slices whiskey butter.

HANGER STEAK
WITH CHERRY SAUCE

PREPARATION TIME: 10 MINUTES
COOKING TIME: 25 MINUTES
SERVES: 4

For the steak:
- 3 lb (1.4 kg) hanger steak (beef skirt)
- Olive oil
- Salt and freshly ground black pepper

For the sauce:
- 2 teaspoons olive oil
- 2 large shallots, minced
- ¼ cup (60 ml) balsamic vinegar
- 1½ cups (225 g) whole fresh sweet
  cherries, pitted, or frozen, thawed,
  roughly chopped
- Salt and freshly ground black pepper
- 2 tablespoons (30 g) butter

[Michigan grows 70 percent of America's cherries. Here they are simmered into a sauce that is both sweet and tart, very nice with the robust flavor of hanger steak.]

Preheat the broiler (grill) with the rack about 6 inches (15 cm) from the heat source. Have the sauce ingredients ready.

For the steak: Rub the steak with olive oil and season all over with salt and pepper. Broil the steak for about 4 minutes per side, until the internal temperature reads 120°F (49°C). Transfer the steak to a carving board and let rest, uncovered, for 10 minutes.

Meanwhile, for the sauce: In a skillet, heat the oil over medium heat. Add the shallots and cook, stirring, until softened, about 3 minutes. Add the vinegar and cherries and season with salt and pepper. Bring to a boil, then stir in the butter. Remove from the heat.

Slice the beef and serve with the cherry sauce poured over.

GRILLED FLAT IRON STEAK WITH COWBOY COFFEE RUB

PREPARATION TIME: 5 MINUTES,
  PLUS SEASONING TIME
COOKING TIME: 10 MINUTES
SERVES: 2

- 2 teaspoons ground espresso
- 1 teaspoon chili powder
- 1 teaspoon garlic powder
- 1 teaspoon smoked paprika
- ½ teaspoon salt
- ¼ teaspoon ground black pepper
- Pinch of dark brown sugar
- 1 (12–16 oz/340–455 g) flat iron steak

[Coffee was a vital staple for pioneers, cowboys, and ranchers in the Old West. "Cowboy coffee," cooked over an open fire, is still appreciated in the Rockies and this recipe is reminiscent of those flavors — earthy and smoky. The flat iron steak, a flavorful and relatively tender cut from the shoulder, named for its resemblance to an old-fashioned metal flat iron, has flavor similar to a hanger or skirt steak; either can be substituted in this recipe. This is often served with rice and beans.]

In a bowl, mix together the coffee, spices, salt, pepper, and brown sugar. Season the steak with the coffee rub and let rest while the grill preheats.

Preheat a gas or charcoal grill (barbecue) to medium-high heat. Grill the steak for about 3 minutes per side, until the internal temperature reaches 130°F (54°C). Transfer the steak to a cutting board and let rest for 5 minutes. Slice across the grain and serve.

SWISS STEAK

PREPARATION TIME: 20 MINUTES
COOKING TIME: 2 HOURS 25 MINUTES
SERVES: 8

- 2 lb (910 g) beef top round (topside)
- ¾ cup (100 g) all-purpose (plain) flour
- 1 teaspoon salt
- 1 teaspoon freshly ground black pepper
- Vegetable oil, for frying
- 1 large onion, thinly sliced
- 2 cloves garlic, minced
- 1 can (4 oz/115 g) tomato paste (purée)
- 1 teaspoon paprika
- 1 tablespoon Worcestershire sauce
- 2 cups (475 ml) beef stock

[This dish is not named for Switzerland. Rather, it involves a processing method that takes its name from a manufacturing technique called "swissing," which softens fabric by running it back and forth through rollers. Swiss steaks (or cube steaks) are inexpensive, tougher cuts, like top round, that have been "swissed" to tenderness. Serve over buttered egg noodles.]

Preheat the oven to 325°F (160°C/Gas Mark 3).

Cut the beef into eight ½-inch (2.5 cm) thick slices. In a shallow dish, mix the flour, salt, and pepper and dredge the steaks in the seasoned flour. Place the steaks between sheets of plastic wrap (clingfilm) and pound with a meat mallet or heavy pan to flatten to ¼ inch (6 mm) thick.

In a large frying pan, heat 1 tablespoon oil over medium-high heat. Working in batches and adding oil as needed, brown the steaks on both sides, 1–2 minutes per side. Transfer to a Dutch oven (casserole).

Wipe the frying pan clean, add 1 tablespoon oil, and cook the onion over medium-high heat until it has softened, 2–3 minutes. Stir in the garlic, tomato paste (purée), paprika, and Worcestershire. Add the beef stock, bring to a boil, and pour over the steaks.

Cover the Dutch oven, transfer to the oven, and roast until the meat is fork-tender, 1½–2 hours.

CHICKEN-FRIED STEAK

OK

PREPARATION TIME: 15 MINUTES
COOKING TIME: 20 MINUTES
SERVES: 4

- 1 cup (130 g) plus 4 tablespoons all-purpose (plain) flour
- Kosher (coarse) salt and freshly ground black pepper
- 2 eggs, lightly beaten
- 1 lb (455 g) beef top round (topside), cut crosswise into 4 slices
- 4 tablespoons (60 g) lard
- Vegetable oil, for frying
- 1½ cups (355 ml) milk, plus more if needed

[In this ubiquitous family dinner, a thin steak — purists favor a humble cut like top round (topside) — is tenderized with a meat mallet, coated in flour, and shallow-fried like chicken, or "chicken-fried." Hot from the frying pan, the battered steak is served with a creamy white gravy, seasoned well with black pepper. Regional riffs may include dipping in buttermilk or egg between rounds of dredging in seasoned flour.]

Preheat the oven to 250°F (120°C/Gas Mark ½). Place a wire rack on a large rimmed baking sheet and place near the oven.

Set up a dredging station: In a wide shallow bowl, season 1 cup (130 g) of the flour generously with salt and pepper. Place the beaten eggs in a second shallow bowl. Line a baking sheet with wax (greaseproof) paper.

Place the beef between sheets of plastic wrap (clingfilm) on a sturdy surface. Use a meat mallet or large heavy frying pan to pound the meat into steaks ¼ inch (6 mm) thick. Dredge the steaks in the seasoned flour, then in the egg, and then back in the flour. Set aside on the lined baking sheet until ready to fry. Reserve the bowl of seasoned flour (the steaks will be dredged again).

Add the lard and 1 inch (2.5 cm) oil to a large (12-inch/30 cm) cast-iron skillet (or other large heavy high-sided frying pan) and heat to 350°F (180°C).

Dredge one steak at a time in the seasoned flour. Working in batches of two, fry the steaks until the coating is crisp and golden brown, about 3 minutes per side. Transfer the cooked steaks to the wire rack and place the baking sheet in the oven while you prepare the gravy.

Pour all but 4 tablespoons fat (a very thin layer) from the skillet. Add the remaining 4 tablespoons flour and 1 teaspoon pepper to the fat in the pan and cook, whisking constantly, until the flour paste darkens to a golden brown, about 3 minutes. Gradually whisk in the milk and bring to a boil. If you'd prefer a thinner gravy, whisk in more milk.

Serve the steaks with gravy spooned on top.

KOREAN BARBECUED BEEF SHORT RIBS

PREPARATION TIME: 5 MINUTES,
   PLUS OVERNIGHT MARINATING TIME
COOKING TIME: 15 MINUTES
SERVES: 8

- ½ cup (95 g) packed light brown sugar
- 1 cup (240 ml) soy sauce
- ½ cup (120 ml) mirin (Japanese sweetened rice wine)
- ¼ cup (60 ml) unseasoned rice vinegar
- 4 tablespoons minced garlic
- 2 tablespoons Sriracha sauce
- 1 tablespoon sesame oil
- 1 teaspoon ground white pepper
- 5 lb (2.3 kg) Korean-style beef short ribs

[Bergen County, in northern New Jersey, is home to the highest per capita Korean American population in the country. Unlike typical short ribs, Korean-style short ribs (also called *kalbi* or *galbi*) are cut lengthwise across the rib bones. The resulting thin "strips" of ribs make a great grilling cut — flavorful, juicy, and fun to gnaw on. Serve with steamed white rice and kimchi.]

In a bowl, whisk together the brown sugar, soy sauce, mirin, vinegar, garlic, Sriracha, sesame oil, and white pepper. Place the ribs in a large container and cover with the marinade. Cover and refrigerate overnight.

Preheat a gas or charcoal grill (barbecue) to medium heat.

Remove the ribs from the marinade and place over direct heat. Grill, turning once and basting with the marinade, about 4 minutes per side. Transfer the ribs to a carving board and let rest for 5 minutes. Cut the ribs into 1–2-inch (2.5–5 cm) chunks with a sharp knife or kitchen shears.

COWBOY SHORT RIBS

PREPARATION TIME: 20 MINUTES
COOKING TIME: 3 HOURS 15 MINUTES
SERVES: 6–8

- 4 lb (1.8 kg) beef short ribs
- ¾ cup (100 g) all-purpose (plain) flour
- 4 tablespoons (60 g) lard or butter
- 1 large onion, halved and sliced
- 3 cloves garlic, minced
- 1 can (15 oz/455 g) chopped tomatoes
- 1½ cups (355 ml) dark beer
- 1½ cups (355 ml) beef stock
- 2 canned chipotle peppers in adobo sauce, coarsely chopped
- 2 tablespoons soy sauce
- 2 tablespoons light brown sugar
- 2 teaspoons smoked paprika
- 1 teaspoon salt
- 1 teaspoon freshly ground black pepper

[The delicious smoky flavor of these ribs recalls the wood fires cowboys would cook over.]

Preheat the oven to 350°F (180°C/Gas Mark 4).

Cut the short ribs into pieces by slicing them between the bones. Dredge the ribs in the flour, shake off the excess, and set aside.

In a Dutch oven (casserole), melt 2 tablespoons of the lard over medium-high heat. Add half the short ribs and sear on all sides, about 8 minutes. Remove and set aside. Repeat with the remaining 2 tablespoons lard and short ribs, removing the ribs when seared. Add the remaining ingredients to the pot and bring to a boil. Return the ribs to the pot, cover, transfer to the oven, and bake for 3 hours. Uncover, skim the fat off the top, and bake, uncovered, until the beef is tender and falling off the bone, about 1 hour.

LOCO MOCO

PREPARATION TIME: 10 MINUTES
COOKING TIME: 40 MINUTES
SERVES: 4

For the hamburgers:
- 1 lb (455 g) ground (minced) beef
- ½ cup (80 g) minced sweet onion
- 1 egg
- Several dashes of Worcestershire sauce
- ½ cup (55 g) dried breadcrumbs
- 1 teaspoon salt
- ½ teaspoon freshly ground black pepper
- 1 tablespoon vegetable oil

For the gravy:
- 3 tablespoons (45 g) butter
- 3 tablespoons all-purpose (plain) flour
- 1¾ cups (415 ml) beef stock
- Salt and freshly ground black pepper
- Worcestershire sauce

For serving:
- At least 2 cups (320 g) freshly cooked sticky rice
- 4 eggs, cooked sunny-side up

[Loco moco is sticky rice topped with a hamburger patty, drizzled with gravy, and crowned with a runny, sunny-side egg. First created in the 1940s, it is now very popular in Hawaii and at Hawaiian restaurants across the country.]

For the hamburgers: In a bowl, combine the beef, onion, egg, Worcestershire sauce, breadcrumbs, salt, and pepper. Shape into 4 patties.

In a large frying pan, heat the oil over medium-high heat. Add the patties and cook to preferred doneness. Set aside and keep warm.

For the gravy: In the same frying pan, melt the butter over medium heat, scraping up the pan drippings as it melts. Whisk in the flour. Whisk in the beef stock and cook, whisking constantly, until the gravy has thickened, about 5 minutes. Season to taste with salt, pepper, and Worcestershire sauce. Keep warm.

For serving: Scoop some rice onto each plate and top with a hamburger, gravy, and then an egg.

MEAT LOAF

PREPARATION TIME: 15 MINUTES
COOKING TIME: 1 HOUR
SERVES: 4–6

- 1 lb (455 g) ground (minced) beef
- 3 tablespoons minced white onion
- 2 tablespoons chopped fresh parsley
- 1 egg yolk
- 1 tablespoon (15 g) butter, softened
- 1 teaspoon salt
- ½ teaspoon freshly ground black pepper

Preheat the oven to 350°F (180°C/Gas Mark 4). Butter a 9 x 5-inch (23 x 13 cm) loaf pan or use a nonstick pan.

In a large bowl, mix together the beef, onion, parsley, egg yolk, butter, salt, and pepper. Use your hands to mix thoroughly. Place the mixture into the loaf pan and bake for 1 hour, until the internal temperature reaches 160°F (70°C). Let the loaf rest for a few minutes before slicing.

CORN AND BEEF CASSEROLE

PREPARATION TIME: 15 MINUTES
COOKING TIME: 1 HOUR 10 MINUTES
SERVES: 4

- 2 tablespoons butter
- 1 lb (455 g) ground (minced) beef
- 1 medium onion, minced
- 1 red bell pepper, diced
- 1 green bell pepper, diced
- 8 ears of corn, kernels cut from the cob
- 1 cup (240 ml) heavy (whipping) cream
- Salt and freshly ground black pepper

Preheat the oven to 350°F (180°C/Gas Mark 4). Butter a 9 x 13-inch (23 x 33 cm) baking dish.

In a heavy-bottomed pot, melt the butter over medium-high heat. Add the beef and cook, breaking it up with a wooden spoon, until beginning to brown, about 10 minutes. Add the onion and cook, stirring, for about 8 minutes, until the onion has softened. Remove from the heat, stir in the bell peppers, corn, and cream, and season to taste with salt and pepper.

Pour the mixture into the baking dish. Bake until bubbling and golden brown, about 45 minutes.

NORWEGIAN MEATBALLS

PREPARATION TIME: 15 MINUTES
COOKING TIME: 35 MINUTES
SERVES: 4–6

- 2 lb (910 g) ground (minced) beef
- 2 eggs
- ¾ cup (30 g) fresh breadcrumbs
- ¾ cup (180 ml) milk
- 2 tablespoons minced onion
- 1 teaspoon freshly ground black pepper
- 1 teaspoon salt
- ½ teaspoon ground ginger
- ¼ teaspoon freshly grated nutmeg
- 4 tablespoons (60 g) butter
- 2 tablespoons all-purpose (plain) flour
- 2 cups (475 ml) beef stock

[Serve with mashed potatoes, or a combination of mashed rutabaga (swede) and potato.]

In a large bowl, mix the beef, eggs, breadcrumbs, milk, onion, pepper, salt, ginger, and nutmeg. Blend thoroughly, using your hands at first, then a spoon for several minutes. (You can also use an electric mixer for this: It makes a lighter meatball.) Using your hands, form the meat mixture into 12 balls the size of golf balls.

In a large frying pan, melt 2 tablespoons (30 g) of the butter over medium-high heat. Add 6 of the meatballs, turning so they brown evenly. They should still be pink inside, because they will cook further in the next step. Transfer to a plate. Repeat with the remaining 2 tablespoons (30 g) butter and meatballs. Transfer the second batch of browned meatballs to the plate. (You can also finish cooking the meatballs in a 350°F (180°C/Gas Mark 4) oven for 20 minutes. Just be sure you start off with an ovenproof frying pan.)

Reduce the heat to medium and stir the flour into the pan. Add the beef stock, whisking until smooth. Add the meatballs to the sauce, reduce the heat to medium-low, cover, and simmer until cooked through (160°F/70°C), about 25 minutes.

CHILES RELLENOS

PREPARATION TIME: 20 MINUTES
COOKING TIME: 30 MINUTES
SERVES: 6–8

- 6–8 large Anaheim, poblano, or Hatch chilies
- 1 tablespoon vegetable oil, plus more for shallow-frying
- ½ small onion, finely chopped
- ½ lb (225 g) ground (minced) beef
- 2 cloves garlic, finely chopped
- ½ teaspoon ground cumin
- ½ cup (80 g) cooked white rice
- ½ lb (225 g) Monterey Jack cheese, grated
- 4 eggs, separated
- Salt
- ½ cup (65 g) all-purpose (plain) flour
- Store-bought salsa, for serving

[Chiles Rellenos can be stuffed with many of the same items as enchiladas, from rice and cheese to picadillo. The battered-and-fried peppers also vary, as does the style of batters, whether eggy or crisp. Here is a recipe of classic chile relleno expectations: stuffed with a mixture of beef, cheese, and rice. Serve the peppers on their own or drenched in salsa.]

Char the peppers directly over a gas flame on the stove top, turning often, until they are blackened and the skin bubbles up, about 15 minutes. (Alternatively, place the peppers on a rack in the oven and broil for 15 minutes, turning peppers often.) Transfer the charred peppers to a bowl, cover with plastic wrap (clingfilm), and set aside to steam for 10 minutes.

Meanwhile, in a large nonstick frying pan, heat 1 tablespoon oil over medium heat. Add the onion and cook, stirring, until softened and golden brown, 5–7 minutes. Add the beef, garlic, and cumin and cook, breaking up the beef with a spoon, until browned and cooked through, about 5 minutes. Stir in the rice and Monterey Jack.

Peel the charred skin from the peppers (rinse under cold water if necessary). Cut a slit in the side of each pepper and remove the seeds and ribs, but leave the stem intact. Divide the filling evenly among the peppers, carefully placing it inside each pepper through the slit, then pressing the slit together to close.

Pour 1 inch (2.5 cm) oil into a Dutch oven (casserole) or other heavy pot and heat to 375°F (190°C).

Meanwhile, in a bowl, with an electric mixer, beat the egg whites until stiff peaks form. In a separate bowl, beat the egg yolks with a pinch of salt until foamy and pale. Fold the egg yolks into the egg whites.

Spread the flour in a shallow bowl. Working with 1 pepper at a time, dredge them in the flour, then dip into the egg mixture and transfer to the hot oil. Cook until golden brown, 3–5 minutes. Use a slotted spoon or spatula (fish slice) to gently lift the fried peppers from the pot as they're done. Serve hot, with salsa.

SMOTHERED LIVER AND ONIONS

PREPARATION TIME: 10 MINUTES,
  PLUS SOAKING TIME
COOKING TIME: 25 MINUTES
SERVES: 4

- 1½ lb (680 g) beef (calves') liver
- 1 cup (240 ml) milk
- 3 tablespoons (45 g) butter
- 1 large sweet onion, thinly sliced
- 1 cup (130 g) all-purpose (plain) flour
- Salt and freshly ground black pepper

[Inexpensive organ meats, especially liver, have long been a main-stay on tables across Appalachia, an inland mountain region that runs from southern New York into the South. Today this remains is a classic Southern dish. Soaking the liver in milk before cooking helps soften bitter flavors.]

Rinse the liver under cold running water and slice into ½-inch (1.25 cm) thick steaks. Place the liver in a bowl, cover with the milk, and refrigerate for 1 hour.

In a large skillet, melt 2 tablespoons (30 g) of the butter over medium heat. Add the onion and cook, stirring frequently, until the onion is golden brown and soft, about 15 minutes.

Meanwhile, remove the liver from the milk and drain in a colander. In a shallow bowl, season the flour with salt and pepper. Dredge the liver in the seasoned flour and set aside.

Remove the onions from the skillet and set aside. Melt the remaining 1 tablespoon (15 g) butter. Add the liver and cook until browned on both sides, about 3 minutes per side. Add the onions to the pan and pour ¾ cup (180 ml) water over the top. Bring to a simmer, then transfer the liver to plates and top with the onions.

PRAIRIE BUTTER (ROASTED BEEF MARROW)

PREPARATION TIME: 10 MINUTES
COOKING TIME: 25 MINUTES
SERVES: 6

- 12 beef marrow bones, about 2 inches (5 cm) long
- Salt and freshly ground black pepper

[Prairie butter, also known as roasted beef marrow, is nutrient-rich and delicious. The marrow can be eaten plain, or spread on toast or steaks. A butcher can cut marrow bones to any length: Shorter is better, to easily remove the marrow. The bones should smell fresh and the marrow itself should be whitish-pink in color — blood spots on the surface are normal.]

Preheat the oven to 425°F (220°C/Gas Mark 7). Line a rimmed baking sheet with parchment paper.

Place the bones upright (cut ends up and down) on the lined baking sheet. Sprinkle with salt and pepper. Roast until the marrow is bubbling and separating from the bone, 20–25 minutes. Do not over-roast (or you may lose some of the marrow). Remove from the oven, let stand for a few minutes, and serve with small knives to remove the marrow.

BRAISED OXTAILS

PREPARATION TIME: 10 MINUTES
COOKING TIME: 3 HOURS 25 MINUTES
SERVES: 6–8

- 4 lb (1.8 kg) oxtails
- 1 teaspoon salt
- ½ teaspoon freshly ground black pepper
- 1 tablespoon olive oil
- 2 medium yellow onions, thinly sliced
- 4 cloves garlic, thinly sliced
- 1 cup (240 ml) red wine
- 4 cups (1 liter) beef stock, or more
  as needed
- 2 bay leaves

[Many cultures cook a version of oxtails; in the South, these are a soul food classic. The flavor is even better on the second day. Serve with rice or mashed potatoes.]

Season the oxtails with the salt and pepper. In a large Dutch oven (casserole), heat the oil over medium-high heat until very hot. Working in batches (do not crowd the pot), brown the oxtails, about 5 minutes. Transfer the oxtails to a plate and set aside.

Add the onions to the pot and cook, stirring frequently, until softened, about 4 minutes. Add the garlic and cook for 1 minute. Add the red wine and bring to a boil, stirring and scraping the browned bits on the bottom of the pot. Return the oxtails to the pot and pour in enough beef stock to cover the oxtails by at least 1 inch (2.5 cm), adding more stock or water if necessary. Add the bay leaves. Bring to a boil, cover, reduce the heat, and simmer for 1½ hours.

Turn the oxtails, cover, and simmer until tender, another 1½ hours.

GRILLED BASQUE-SPICED LEG OF LAMB

PREPARATION TIME: 15 MINUTES,
   PLUS OVERNIGHT MARINATING TIME
COOKING TIME: 40 MINUTES
SERVES: 6

- 1 boneless leg of lamb (about 3 lb/1.4 kg)
- ¼ cup (60 ml) olive oil
- ½ cup (120 ml) dry white wine
- 1 tablespoon Dijon mustard
- 5 cloves garlic, minced
- 2 teaspoons fresh rosemary, chopped
- 1 teaspoon smoked sweet paprika
- Salt and freshly ground black pepper

[During the Gold Rush of the mid-1800s, Basque immigrants headed west in search of their fortunes; many became ranchers and shepherds settling in the western states, such as Nevada. Their culinary traditions still star in dishes like this one.]

Butterfly the lamb by opening it up and cutting through the thinnest part of the leg, at the natural seam. Score the thickest parts of the leg by slicing partially through the muscle. The leg will now lie flat and will grill more evenly.

In a large bowl (big enough to hold the lamb), combine the oil, wine, mustard, garlic, rosemary, and smoked paprika. Add the lamb to the bowl and massage it with the marinade. Cover and marinate in the refrigerator overnight or up to 24 hours.

Preheat a gas or charcoal grill (barbecue) to medium-high heat.

Season the lamb with salt and pepper. Grill the lamb until the internal temperature reaches 115°F (46°C), about 12 minutes per side. Transfer to a carving board, tent with foil, and let rest for 10–15 minutes (the lamb should reach an internal temperature of 125°–130°F/52°–54°C). Slice and serve.

LAMB TENDERLOINS WRAPPED IN SALTBUSH

PREPARATION TIME: 10 MINUTES
COOKING TIME: 30 MINUTES
SERVES: 4

- 2 tablespoons vegetable oil
- 4 lamb tenderloins (loin fillets)
- 2 cups (60 g) fresh saltbush leaves, well washed
- Boiling water
- 2 tablespoons olive oil
- Freshly ground black pepper
- 1 large lemon, halved

[Native Americans used saltbush extensively, burning dry twigs as fuel and eating the cooked leaves and parched seeds. As the name suggests, saltbush is indeed salty and thus very useful as a native seasoning, whether fresh or dried.]

Preheat the oven to 450°F (230°C/Gas Mark 8). Heat a cast-iron skillet over high heat until smoking hot. Add the vegetable oil and the lamb and sear until lightly browned, about 1 minute per side. Remove and set aside.

Place the saltbush leaves in a bowl and cover with just-boiled water. Let sit for 2 minutes. Remove the leaves, refresh under cold water, and squeeze dry. Separate the leaves somewhat.

Lay each tenderloin on a piece of foil large enough to enclose it completely. Lightly oil the lamb with the olive oil. Season with pepper. Pack a thin layer of blanched saltbush leaves around the lamb. Squeeze a little lemon juice over the length of the tenderloins and close the foil package. Repeat with the other packages and place in the hot oven for 8 minutes. Remove and let rest unwrapped for 10 minutes. Unwrap and thinly slice each tenderloin to serve.

CHOP SUEY

PREPARATION TIME: 15 MINUTES, PLUS MARINATING TIME
COOKING TIME: 15 MINUTES
SERVES: 2

- ½ lb (225 g) pork tenderloin, sliced into ¼-inch (6 mm) thick strips
- 1 tablespoon sherry
- 1 tablespoon oyster sauce
- ¼ teaspoon ground white pepper
- 1 cup (240 ml) chicken stock
- 2 teaspoons cornstarch (cornflour)
- 2 tablespoons sesame oil
- 2 cloves garlic, minced
- ¾ cup (70 g) chopped cabbage
- 4 mushrooms, sliced
- 1 stalk celery, diced
- 1 small onion, diced
- 1 carrot, thinly sliced on the bias
- Cooked white rice or Chinese noodles, for serving
- Soy sauce, for serving

[This is an American Chinese dish, made popular during the building of the Central Pacific railroad. The dish was adapted to ingredients that were available at the time, such as mushrooms, cabbage, and carrots. Additions that came later include bok choy, water chestnuts, and straw mushrooms. Different combinations of vegetables and meat can be used.]

In a bowl, combine the pork, sherry, oyster sauce, and white pepper and marinate for at least 1 hour, covered and refrigerated.

In a small bowl, stir the chicken stock into the cornstarch (cornflour) and set aside.

Heat a wok or large frying pan over high heat. Add 1 tablespoon of the sesame oil and the garlic and stir to cook for a few seconds. Add the pork and cook, stirring, until the meat is cooked through and no longer pink, about 5 minutes. Transfer the pork to a bowl and set aside.

Add the remaining 1 tablespoon sesame oil to the pan and add all the vegetables, stir-frying until they are just cooked through, 5–6 minutes. Return the cooked pork to the pan. Restir the stock mixture and add to the pan. Cook, stirring, until the sauce has thickened, about 6 minutes. Serve hot over rice or noodles, with soy sauce on the side.

MAPLE AND RUM-GLAZED PORK ROAST

PREPARATION TIME: 10 MINUTES
COOKING TIME: 1 HOUR
SERVES: 4–6

- 3 lb (1.4 kg) boneless pork loin roast, tied with kitchen twine
- 2 teaspoons salt
- 1 cup (240 ml) pure maple syrup
- 3 tablespoons (45 g) butter, melted
- 3 tablespoons cider vinegar
- 6 tablespoons dark rum
- 1 teaspoon ground cinnamon
- 1 teaspoon freshly grated nutmeg
- ½ teaspoon freshly ground black pepper

[Every year, as winter fades, people across the Northeast venture into the snowy woods to "tap" sugar maples, collect the sweet sap, and simmer it down into maple syrup. Vermont prides itself as the top producer in the country.]

Preheat the oven to 375°F (190°C/Gas Mark 5).

Rub the roast with salt and place in a roasting pan. In a small bowl, whisk together the maple syrup, melted butter, vinegar, 3 tablespoons of the rum, the cinnamon, nutmeg, and pepper.

Pour the glaze over the roast and transfer to the oven. Roast, basting every 15 minutes. Flip the roast over after 45 minutes and continue cooking, about 10 minutes more, until the internal temperature reads 155°F (68°C). Remove the roast from the oven, transfer to a carving board, and let rest for 10–15 minutes.

Place the roasting pan over medium heat. Add the remaining 3 tablespoons rum to deglaze the pan, scraping up the browned bits on the bottom of the pan. Slice the pork and serve with the sauce on the side.

SMOKED PORK SHOULDER

PREPARATION TIME: 30 MINUTES
COOKING TIME: 5-6 HOURS
SERVES: 10–12

- 5–6 lb (2.3–2.7 kg) boneless pork shoulder
- 1 tablespoon plus 1 teaspoon salt
- 1½ teaspoons freshly ground black pepper
- 10 lb (4.5 kg) hardwood charcoal
- Oil, for the grill rack
- 4 large handfuls hickory wood chips, soaked in cold water for 1 hour
- Your favorite barbecue sauce, for serving

[In some parts of the South, the pork shoulder is rubbed with spices or basted. Some pull (shred) the meat; others slice or dice it. The saucing varies widely by region.]

Trim all but ¼ inch (6 mm) fat from the pork roast. Pat very dry and season evenly with the salt and pepper, pressing gently.

Prepare a charcoal grill (barbecue) with one quarter of the charcoal. Move the hot coals to one side of the grill. Place a foil pan on the opposite side (without coals) and add 3 cups (710 ml) water. Lightly brush the grill rack with oil. Drain one quarter of the hickory wood chips and scatter them on the hot coals. Heat the chips until smoking.

Place the pork shoulder on the rack, skin side up, over the drip pan. Close the lid and smoke the pork until the skin is deeply browned, the meat easily pulls apart, and the internal temperature reads 190°F (88°C), 5–6 hours. Every hour, add more charcoal to maintain a grill temperature of 250°–275°F (120°–135°C) and add more hickory chips to keep the smoke going.

Transfer the cooked pork to a carving board, tent with foil, and let rest for 15 minutes. Pull off and discard any skin. Pull the pork into pieces and finely chop. Toss with the barbecue sauce to taste to season and keep moist until serving.

BARBECUE PORK SHOULDER

PREPARATION TIME: 15 MINUTES,
   PLUS WOOD CHIP SOAKING TIME
COOKING TIME: 6 HOURS
SERVES: 12–14

- 5–6 lb (2.3–2.7 kg) skin-on boneless pork shoulder roast
- 2½ tablespoons Alabama Dry Rub (page 456)
- 4 large handfuls pecan or hickory wood chips
- 10 lb (4.5 kg) hardwood charcoal
- Oil, for the grill rack
- Memphis-Style Barbecue Sauce (page 464), for serving

Trim the fat from the pork roast, leaving ¼ inch (6 mm). Pat very dry and evenly coat with the dry rub, pressing gently to adhere.

Soak the pecan wood chips in cold water for 1 hour.

Prepare a charcoal grill (barbecue) for indirect cooking, using one quarter of the charcoal. Place a drip pan on the side without coals and add 3 cups (710 ml) water to it. Lightly brush the grill rack with oil. Drain one quarter of the pecan wood chips and scatter them on the hot coals. Let the chips heat until smoking.

Place the pork shoulder on the rack, skin side up, over the drip pan. Close the lid and smoke the pork until the skin is deeply browned, the meat easily pulls apart, and the internal temperature reads 190°F (88°C), 5–6 hours. Every hour, add even amounts of charcoal and pecan chips to the grill to maintain the smoke and a grill temperature of 250°–275°F (120°–135°C).

Transfer the cooked pork roast to a carving board, tent with foil, and let rest for 15 minutes. Pull off and discard the skin. Pull the pork into pieces and finely chop, if desired. Serve with the barbecue sauce in the side.

KALUA PORK

PREPARATION TIME: 15 MINUTES
COOKING TIME: 6 HOURS
SERVES: 6–8

- 5 lb (2.3 kg) boneless pork shoulder
- 2 tablespoons smoked Hawaiian red salt
- 3–4 banana leaves, fresh or thawed if frozen

[A classic Polynesian pork preparation, often served with poi and sweet potatoes, and usually prepared by smoking salted pork, wrapped in banana leaves, in a pit for hours. The recipe calls for baking in an oven, but a slow cooker could also be used. Some people add liquid smoke, to mimic the traditional flavor of the outdoor smoking process. This recipe instead calls for smoked Hawaiian salt.]

Preheat the oven to 350°F (180°C/Gas Mark 4).

Using a sharp paring knife, cut ¼-inch (6 mm) deep slits roughly 1 inch (2.5 cm) apart, all over the pork roast. Rub with the salt, wrap in banana leaves, and tie with kitchen twine to secure. Place in a large roasting pan, pour 6 cups (1.4 liters) water into the pan, and wrap tightly with foil. Bake until very tender, 4–6 hours. Remove the pork from the roasting pan, reserving the cooking liquid. Skim some of the fat if desired. Unwrap the pork, shred it, and add back to the liquid in the roasting pan. Stir to distribute the pork and liquid evenly.

PREPARATION TIME: 15 MINUTES,
  PLUS MARINATING TIME
COOKING TIME: 5 HOURS 20 MINUTES
SERVES: 12–14

- 7 lb (3.2 kg) bone-in pork shoulder, with skin
- 8–9 cloves garlic, peeled but whole
- 1 teaspoon freshly ground black pepper
- 1 tablespoon dried Mexican oregano
- 1 tablespoon salt
- 2 tablespoons olive oil

[This Puerto Rican slow-roasted pork shoulder is served on nearly every block in northern Manhattan's Washington Heights neighborhood.]

Rinse the pork shoulder and pat dry. Using a very sharp knife, score the shoulder in a crosshatch pattern, cutting through the skin and fat layer almost to the muscle. Place the shoulder in a large deep roasting pan (make sure the pan is deep, as the pork will render quite a bit of fat during roasting).

Using a mortar and pestle, smash the garlic, pepper, oregano, salt, and olive oil into a paste. Rub the paste all over the pork. Let the pork sit at room temperature for 30 minutes.

Preheat the oven to 400°F (200°C/Gas Mark 6).

Place 2 cups (475 ml) water in the bottom of the roasting pan. Roast for 1 hour, reduce the heat to 300°F (150°C/Gas Mark 2), and roast, basting the roast every hour or so with the fat that is rendered, until the pork has crispy skin and is very tender, about 4 hours. If the skin is not crispy enough, increase the oven temperature to 400°F (200°C/Gas Mark 6) and cook until crisp (be careful — at this point, it will cook very quickly). Let the shoulder rest for 20 minutes before serving. Serve a chunk of the skin and fat with each portion of meat.

CARNE ADOVADA

PREPARATION TIME: 20 MINUTES,
  PLUS 24 HOURS MARINATING TIME
COOKING TIME: 3 HOURS
SERVES: 8

- 3–4 lb (1.4–1.8 kg) boneless pork shoulder, cut into 1-inch (2.5 cm) chunks
- ¾ cup (70 g) New Mexico chili powder (hot or mild)
- 2 teaspoons ground cumin
- 2 teaspoons ground coriander
- 2 teaspoons dried Mexican oregano
- 2 tablespoons distilled white vinegar
- 1 cup (120 g) toasted pumpkin seeds, ground
- 2 large onions, diced
- 6 cloves garlic, minced
- 4 cups (950 ml) chicken stock
- 2 teaspoons salt

[Pork in red chili sauce, this dish is also known as *adobada*: Spanish for "marinated." Traditionally the pork was fermented, which gave it a sour flavor. That flavor is now often achieved with vinegar. Serve with corn tortillas.]

Place the pork in a large bowl. Add the chili powder, cumin, coriander, oregano, and vinegar. Stir well to combine. Cover and refrigerate for 24 hours.

Preheat the oven to 350°F (180°C/Gas Mark 4).

Put the marinated pork into a large Dutch oven (casserole). Add the ground pumpkin seeds, onions, garlic, stock, and salt and bring to a boil over high heat. Cover, transfer to the oven, and roast until the pork is very tender and falling apart, 2½–3 hours.

PORK ADOBO (ADOBONG BABOY)

PREPARATION TIME: 10 MINUTES,
  PLUS MARINATING TIME
COOKING TIME: 1 HOUR
SERVES: 4

- 4 tablespoons soy sauce
- 4 tablespoons any vinegar
- 7–8 cloves garlic, smashed and peeled
- 4 bay leaves
- 1 tablespoon black peppercorns
- 1 tablespoon sugar
- 2 lb (910 g) pork belly, cut into chunks
- Cooked rice, for serving

[This dish is a staple in the Philippines, where it is served for breakfast, lunch, and dinner. It remains popular in the states with the largest Filipino populations, which are in Hawaii, California, Nevada, and Arizona.]

In a ceramic or glass bowl, stir together 1 cup (240 ml) water, the soy sauce, vinegar, garlic, bay leaves, peppercorns, and sugar. Add the pork, stirring to coat. Cover and refrigerate for at least 1 and up to 24 hours.

Transfer the pork and marinade to a heavy pot and bring to a boil. Reduce the heat to medium and cook, stirring occasionally, until most of the liquid has been absorbed, about 40 minutes. Reduce to a simmer and cook until only the oily sauce is left in the pan, about 20 minutes. Serve with rice.

FRIED PORK CHOPS

PREPARATION TIME: 10 MINUTES
COOKING TIME: 15 MINUTES
SERVES: 4–6

- 1 cup (130 g) all-purpose (plain) flour
- 2 teaspoons salt
- 1 teaspoon freshly ground black pepper
- 1 teaspoon onion powder
- 6 boneless pork loin chops, ½ inch
  (1.25 cm) thick (about 4 oz/115g each)
- ½ cup (120 ml) canola (rapeseed) oil

In a shallow dish, whisk together the flour, salt, pepper, and onion powder.

Place the pork chops on a cutting board. Using a meat mallet, pound each out to a cutlet about ⅛ inch (3 mm) thick. Dredge both sides of the cutlets in the flour mixture.

Set a wire rack in a rimmed baking sheet. In a large cast-iron skillet or heavy-bottomed frying pan, heat ¼ cup (60 ml) of the oil over medium-high heat until very hot. Working in batches, add the pork chops (do not crowd the pan) and fry until golden brown on both sides, about 6 minutes total. Transfer to the wire rack. Add the remaining ¼ cup (60 ml) oil for the second batch. Serve hot.

SAUSAGE AND APPLE STUFFED PORK CHOPS

PREPARATION TIME: 20 MINUTES
COOKING TIME: 1 HOUR 10 MINUTES
SERVES: 4

- 4 bone-in pork chops (12–16 oz/340–450 g each), about 1½ inches (4 cm) thick
- Salt and freshly ground black pepper
- 2 tablespoons olive oil
- 1 cup (160 g) diced onion
- ½ lb (225 g) sausage (sausagemeat), loose or removed from casings
- 1 cup (120 g) peeled and diced apples
- ½ cup (120 ml) apple cider
- 1 cup (35 g) bread cubes
- 2 teaspoons minced fresh thyme
- 2 teaspoons minced fresh sage

Season the pork with salt and pepper. In a large ovenproof frying pan, heat the oil over high heat. Add the chops and brown them, about 3 minutes per side. Transfer to a plate and set aside.

Reduce the heat to medium-high, add the onions, and cook for a few minutes to soften them. Add the sausage and cook, breaking it up with a wooden spoon as it browns, about 10 minutes. Add the apples and apple cider and bring to a boil. Remove from the heat and stir in the bread cubes, thyme, sage, and ¼ teaspoon black pepper. Set aside to cool.

Preheat the oven to 375°F (190°C/Gas Mark 5). Grease a 9 x 13-inch (23 x 33 cm) baking dish.

Cut a pocket in the side of each pork chop by making a horizontal cut on the meaty side through the chop, almost to the bone. Stuff each chop with ½ cup (100 g) stuffing. Place the chops in the baking dish and cook until the juices run clear, about 45 minutes.

SMOTHERED PORK CHOPS

PREPARATION TIME: 10 MINUTES
COOKING TIME: 30 MINUTES
SERVES: 6

- 1½ cups (195 g) all-purpose (plain) flour
- 3 tablespoons onion powder
- 1½ teaspoons cayenne pepper
- Salt and freshly ground black pepper
- 6 bone-in pork chops, ¾ inch (2 cm) thick (about 2 lb/900 g)
- ⅓ cup (80 ml) peanut (groundnut) oil
- 1½ cups (355 ml) chicken stock
- ¾ cup (180 ml) heavy (whipping) cream
- 1 tablespoon fresh lemon juice
- 2 tablespoons chopped fresh parsley (optional)

In a shallow dish, whisk together the flour, onion powder, cayenne, 1½ teaspoons salt, and 1 teaspoon black pepper. Pat the pork chops dry with paper towels, then dredge them in the seasoned flour, tapping to remove the excess. Measure out 3 tablespoons of the seasoned flour and set aside (discard the remainder).

Heat a large cast-iron skillet over medium-heat and add the oil, swirling to coat. Working in batches, cook the pork chops until golden brown on both sides, 3–4 minutes per side. Drain on paper towels, then transfer to a platter and keep warm.

Add the 3 tablespoons reserved seasoned flour to the pan drippings, stirring until incorporated, then cook until lightly golden, about 3 minutes. Slowly whisk in the chicken stock. Cook until the liquid is slightly reduced and thickened, 5–6 minutes. Reduce the heat to low and whisk in the cream and lemon juice. Remove from the heat. Season to taste with salt and pepper.

Pour the sauce over the pork chops on the platter. Garnish with the parsley, if desired.

MEMPHIS-STYLE BARBECUED PORK RIBS

PREPARATION TIME: 15 MINUTES,
PLUS 8 HOURS CHILLING TIME
COOKING TIME: 6 HOURS
SERVES: 6–8

- 2 racks spare ribs (about 6 lb/2.7 kg)
- ¼ cup (25 g) paprika
- 1½ tablespoons freshly ground black pepper
- 1½ tablespoons dark brown sugar
- 1 tablespoon salt
- 1½ teaspoons celery salt
- 1½ teaspoons cayenne pepper
- 1½ teaspoons ground cumin
- 1½ teaspoons onion powder
- 2 cups (475 ml) cider vinegar
- ¼ cup (60 g) brown mustard
- ¼ cup (60 g) yellow mustard
- 10 lb (4.5 kg) charcoal
- 3–5 large handfuls wood chips, soaked in water for 30 minutes
- Memphis-Style Barbecue Sauce (page 464) (optional)

Rinse the ribs in water, then pat dry. Remove the membrane from the underside of each rack.

In a small bowl, stir together the paprika, black pepper, brown sugar, salt, celery salt, cayenne, cumin, and onion powder. Measure out 2 tablespoons of the rub and set aside. Rub the remainder evenly over the ribs. Cover and refrigerate for 8 hours or overnight. Remove from the refrigerator 30 minutes before grilling.

In a small bowl, whisk to combine the vinegar and both mustards. Set the sauce aside.

Start a charcoal fire in a grill (barbecue) with half the charcoal. Distribute the coals in a ring around the whole outside edge of the grill, leaving an opening in the center. Evenly distribute the soaked wood chips over the hot charcoal and wait until they start to smoke. Place the ribs on the grill rack, close the lid, and smoke the ribs until the meat is tender and easily pulls away from the bone, 4–5 hours. Every hour, "mop" the sauce on the ribs. If the temperature starts to dip below 225°–250°F (110°–120°C), heat more charcoal and add it to the outer ring. If the smoke begins to dissipate, add more soaked wood chips, a handful at a time. When the ribs are tender, scatter the reserved 2 tablespoons dry rub over the ribs and smoke an additional 30 minutes.

Let the ribs rest for 30 minutes, then slice and serve with Memphis-Style Barbecue Sauce, if desired.

MEMPHIS-STYLE BARBECUED PORK RIBS

BARBECUED PORK RIBS

PREPARATION TIME: 15 MINUTES,
  PLUS WOOD CHIP SOAKING TIME
COOKING TIME: 5 HOURS, PLUS MEAT
  RESTING TIME
SERVES: 6

- 2 racks baby back ribs (about 2½ lb/
  1.1 kg)
- Alabama Dry Rub (page 458)
- 10 lb (4.5 kg) charcoal
- 4 handfuls wood chips, soaked in cold
  water for 30 minutes
- Your favorite barbecue sauce (optional)

Rinse the ribs and pat dry. Remove the membrane from the underside of each rack. Evenly coat the ribs with the dry rub. Set aside at room temperature while you prepare the grill.

Prepare a charcoal grill (barbecue) using half the charcoal. Distribute the coals in a ring around the whole outside edge of the grill, leaving an open circle inside. Evenly distribute half the wood chips over the coals. Place the ribs in the center of the grill rack, close the lid, and smoke the ribs until the meat is tender and easily pulls away from the bone, 4–5 hours. If using a barbecue sauce, apply during the last 30 minutes of cooking. Maintain a grill temperature of 225°–250°F (107°–121°C), adding more charcoal as needed. As the smoke begins to decrease, add additional handfuls of wood chips.

Let the ribs rest for 30 minutes, then slice and serve alongside additional barbecue sauce, if desired.

SMOKED ST. LOUIS–STYLE RIBS

PREPARATION TIME: 15 MINUTES,
  PLUS RESTING TIME
COOKING TIME: 6 HOURS
SERVES: 4

For the rub:
- ½ cup (95 g) packed light brown sugar
- 2 tablespoons paprika
- 1 tablespoon chili powder
- 1 tablespoon garlic powder
- 1 tablespoon onion powder
- 1 tablespoon freshly ground black pepper
- 2 teaspoons ground cumin

For the ribs:
- 2 slabs pork ribs (2½–3 lb/1–1.4 kg
  per rack)
- Kosher (coarse) salt
- ½ lb (225 g) hardwood chips
- Your favorite barbecue sauce, or Kansas
  City Barbecue Sauce (see page 463), for
  basting and serving

For the rub: In a small bowl, combine the brown sugar, paprika, chili powder, garlic powder, onion powder, pepper, and cumin.

For the ribs: Peel the membrane off the bone side of the ribs. Sprinkle salt over both sides of the ribs and let sit at room temperature for at least 1 hour and up to 2 hours.

Coat each side of the ribs generously with the rub.

Preheat a gas or charcoal grill (barbecue) or smoker to 225°F (107°C). Add a small handful of wood chips to the coals or smoker box. Place the ribs on the grill rack, close the lid, and slowly smoke (adding more charcoal and wood chips as necessary) until tender, 5–6 hours. To test the ribs for doneness, lift them with tongs and give them a gentle bounce; if they crack they are done.

Increase the grill temperature to high. Baste the ribs with barbecue sauce and grill until the sauce is sizzling and starting to caramelize, about 5 minutes. Remove from the heat and let rest for 5–10 minutes before slicing. Serve with more sauce on the side.

FRIED COUNTRY HAM WITH RED-EYE GRAVY

**PREPARATION TIME: 5 MINUTES,
   PLUS SOAKING TIME**
COOKING TIME: 30 MINUTES
SERVES: 4

- 4 slices (¼ inch/6 mm thick) country ham, about 1½ lb (680 g)
- ⅓ cup (80 ml) brewed coffee

In a shallow baking dish, cover the ham with cold water and soak for 1 hour. Drain and thoroughly pat dry with paper towels.

Slice the ham in half crosswise. Working in batches, cook the ham in a single layer in a large cast-iron skillet or heavy frying pan over medium heat until lightly browned, turning occasionally, 10–12 minutes. Drain well on paper towels. Reserve the pan drippings in the skillet. Transfer the ham to a large serving platter and cover to keep warm.

Add 3 cups (710 ml) water and the coffee to the skillet and bring to a boil. Reduce to a simmer and cook for 5–7 minutes, stirring occasionally, until reduced by half. Remove from the heat — the gravy will be thin. Serve the gravy over the fried country ham.

HAM LOAF

PREPARATION TIME: 20 MINUTES
COOKING TIME: 55 MINUTES
SERVES: 6

For the ham loaf:
- 1½ lb (680 g) smoked ham (fully cooked)
- ½ lb (225 g) ground (minced) pork
- 2 eggs
- 1 cup (240 ml) milk
- 1 cup (50 g) fresh breadcrumbs
- 1 small onion, minced
- ¼ teaspoon mustard powder
- ¼ teaspoon ground allspice
- ¼ teaspoon freshly ground black pepper

For the glaze:
- ⅓ cup (65 g) packed light brown sugar
- ¼ cup (60 ml) cider vinegar
- 1 tablespoon Dijon mustard

Preheat the oven to 350°F (180°C/Gas Mark 4). Grease a 9 x 5 x 3-inch (23 x 13 x 7.5 cm) loaf pan.

For the ham loaf: Cut the ham into cubes. Place in the bowl of a food processor and pulse to grind. In a large bowl, combine the ham, pork, eggs, milk, breadcrumbs, onion, mustard powder, allspice, and pepper. Use your hands to mix thoroughly. Form the mixture into a loaf in the pan.

For the glaze: In a small bowl, mix the brown sugar, vinegar, and mustard, stirring until the sugar is dissolved.

Spoon half of the glaze over the loaf. Bake the ham loaf for 20 minutes. Spoon the remaining glaze on top. Continue baking until the loaf is deeply browned and crusty around the edges and the internal temperature reads 165°F (74°C), 30–35 minutes. Let the loaf sit for a few minutes before slicing.

COCA-COLA GLAZED HAM

PREPARATION TIME: 15 MINUTES
COOKING TIME: 4 HOURS
SERVES: 12–16

- 10–12 lb (4.5–5.4 kg) bone-in cured ham
- ½ cup (95 g) packed light brown sugar
- ⅓ cup (80 ml) Dijon mustard
- 1 large orange, washed and cut into 8 wedges (optional)
- 1½ cups (355 ml) Coca-Cola

[Coca-Cola, the major beverage brand born in Georgia, now serves almost 2 billion drinks worldwide daily. Its global headquarters are in downtown Atlanta, and some people cook with the soda.]

Position a rack in the bottom third of the oven and preheat to 325°F (160°C/Gas Mark 3).

Trim any excess skin and/or fat from the ham. Using a sharp knife, score the ham in a diamond pattern, making ¼-inch (6 mm) deep cuts spaced 1 inch (2.5 cm) apart. Place on the rack of a roasting pan.

In a small bowl, combine the brown sugar and mustard. Rub the mixture all over the ham. Place the orange wedges on the roasting rack, around the edges of the ham. Pour the Coca-Cola into the bottom of the roasting pan (not over the ham). Cover the pan tightly with foil, wrapping it around the edges of the pan to seal. Using a small, sharp knife, make three small slits in the top of the foil.

Roast until the internal temperature reads 165°F (74°C), 3–3½ hours; after the first hour, baste with the pan juices every 30 minutes.

Cover the ham with foil and let the ham rest in the pan for 30 minutes. Baste once more with the Coke mixture at the bottom of the roasting pan, then transfer to a carving board and slice.

BARBECUE SPAGHETTI

PREPARATION TIME: 10 MINUTES
COOKING TIME: 30 MINUTES
SERVES: 5–6

- Salt and freshly ground black pepper
- 3 tablespoons vegetable oil, such as peanut (groundnut)
- 1 cup (160 g) diced onions
- ½ cup (75 g) diced green bell pepper
- 2 cups (475 ml) barbecue sauce
- ¼ cup (50 g) sugar
- 2 teaspoons chili powder
- 1 teaspoon garlic powder
- 1 teaspoon onion powder
- 1 teaspoon paprika
- 1 teaspoon dried oregano
- ¾ lb (340 g) cooked pork shoulder (preferably smoked), pulled into 1-inch (2.5 cm) pieces
- 1 lb (455 g) spaghetti

[Italians add meat to tomato sauce for spaghetti Bolognese. Cooks in Memphis, Tennessee, add pulled pork and barbecue sauce for barbecue spaghetti. At James Neely's Interstate Barbecue, the pasta is cooked soft, not al dente, and cut into shorter lengths for easier eating as a side dish.]

Bring a large pot of water to a boil for the pasta. Season generously with salt.

Meanwhile, in a large frying pan, heat the oil over medium-high heat. Add the onion and bell pepper and cook until tender, 5–7 minutes. Add the barbecue sauce, sugar, chili powder, garlic powder, onion powder, paprika, and oregano. Reduce the heat to a simmer and cook for 10–12 minutes, stirring occasionally, to blend the flavors. Season to taste with salt and black pepper. Add the pork shoulder and keep warm while you cook the pasta.

Cook the spaghetti according to package directions. Drain the pasta and transfer to a large serving bowl. Pour the sauce over the pasta and toss gently. Serve hot.

COCA-COLA GLAZED HAM

SHEBOYGAN BRATS

PREPARATION TIME: 10 MINUTES
COOKING TIME: 35 MINUTES
SERVES: 4

- 8 uncooked bratwurst
- 1½ cups (355 ml) beer
- 1 stick (115 g) butter
- 1 large onion, thinly sliced
- 4 hard rolls
- Minced raw onions, for serving
- Pickles, for serving
- Whole-grain or grainy mustard, for serving

["Brats" are beloved in Wisconsin – especially when cooked in a brew from Milwaukee, once hailed as the beer capital of the world. For this recipe, grill the bratwurst, then simmer them in beer. Wash them down with some cold beers. Pabst Blue Ribbon is the traditional choice.]

Preheat a gas or charcoal grill (barbecue) to high heat.

Meanwhile, pierce the brats with a fork so that they don't split open during grilling.

When the grill is heated, place the brats on the grill rack, close the lid, and cook until deep golden brown with an internal temperature of 165°F (74°C), about 20 minutes, turning several times during cooking.

Meanwhile, in a saucepan big enough to hold the brats, combine the beer, 4 tablespoons (60 g) of the butter, and the onion slices and bring to a boil. Reduce to a simmer and cook for 10 minutes.

Add the cooked brats to the beer sauce and keep warm until ready to serve. At serving time, split each hard roll in half, slather with the remaining butter, place 2 brats in each roll, and, using a slotted spoon, smother them with the cooked onions. Serve with minced raw onions, pickles, and mustard on the side.

SAUERKRAUT AND KIELBASA

PREPARATION TIME: 15 MINUTES
COOKING TIME: 1 HOUR 30 MINUTES
SERVES: 6

- 2 lb (910 g) sauerkraut
- 1 tablespoon caraway seeds
- 4 tablespoons light brown sugar
- 3 apples, peeled and diced
- ½ lb (225 g) bacon (streaky), cut into 1-inch (2.5 cm) pieces
- 1 large onion, diced
- 1½ lb (680 g) kielbasa (Polish sausage), cut into 1-inch (2.5 cm) slices

[This dish is delicious served with good bread (rye especially) and butter, or with mashed potatoes.]

In a medium saucepan, combine the sauerkraut, caraway, brown sugar, and apples and simmer over very low heat for 1 hour. Stir occasionally and add a bit of water if necessary to prevent scorching.

Meanwhile, in a large heavy frying pan, cook the bacon (streaky) over medium-high heat until crisp. Remove with a slotted spoon and set aside.

Add the onion to the bacon fat in the pan and cook over medium-high heat, stirring often, until it is soft and translucent. With a slotted spoon, transfer the onion to the sauerkraut mixture, leaving the fat in the pan.

Add the kielbasa to the pan and brown over medium-high heat for 10 minutes. Add to the sauerkraut along with the reserved bacon. Simmer all together for another 10 minutes.

MILK CAN SUPPER

PREPARATION TIME: 20 MINUTES
COOKING TIME: 35 MINUTES
SERVES: 6–8

- 1–2 tablespoons vegetable oil
- 4 lb (1.8 kg) bratwurst
- 2 lb (910 g) red potatoes, scrubbed
- 1 head cabbage, cut into 8 wedges
- 3 ears of corn, husked and cut into
  3 pieces each
- 8 carrots, roughly chopped
- 2 medium onions, cut into 8 wedges each
- 4 cloves garlic, peeled
- 1 small bunch fresh thyme
- 2 bay leaves
- 2 teaspoons salt
- 1 teaspoon freshly ground black pepper
- 1½ cups (355 ml) light beer

[Milk can supper is the western version of New England boiled dinner. Traditionally, cowboys would layer meat and vegetables in a large milk can and cook it over an open fire. The modern version uses a large Dutch oven (casserole), or a sturdy covered pot on top of the stove.]

In a large Dutch oven (casserole) or heavy-bottomed pot, heat 1 tablespoon of the oil over medium-high heat. Working in batches, brown the bratwurst, adding more oil if necessary. Transfer the bratwurst to a plate and set aside to cool slightly. Halve the bratwurst lengthwise.

Place the potatoes in the bottom of the pot, then layer the bratwurst and vegetables over. Add the garlic, thyme, and bay leaves. Sprinkle with the salt and black pepper. Pour in the beer, cover, and bring to a boil. Reduce the heat to medium and cook, covered, for 30 minutes, until the vegetables are tender.

Discard the thyme stems and bay leaves. Transfer everything to a large bowl or platter. Serve hot.

CHITTERLINGS

PREPARATION TIME: 15 MINUTES,
  PLUS SOAKING TIME
COOKING TIME: 4 HOURS 30 MINUTES
SERVES: 12

- 10 lb (4.5 kg) chitterlings
- 2 medium yellow onions, diced
- ¼ cup (60 ml) cider vinegar
- 1 tablespoon minced garlic
- 2 teaspoons salt
- 1 teaspoon crushed chili flakes

["Chitlins" (how this food is pronounced) sounds so much nicer than pig intestines, which is what this Southern country-style dish really is. What was once a common dish created to use every bit of meat has become something of a rare delicacy today, when few farmers and cooks still butcher their own hogs. Chitterlings are often served fried, but can also be boiled and drizzled with vinegar.]

Set up a big bowl of cold water. Place the chitterlings in a large stockpot and add water to cover by 2 inches (5 cm). Bring to a boil over high heat, reduce to a simmer, and cook for 5 minutes. Drain in a colander, then transfer to the cold water. Let soak for 15 minutes to let any debris or dirt fall out. Change the water in the bowl 4 or 5 times, until clear. (Each chitterling can also be run individually under cold water, in order to remove all foreign matter.) Note that you want to remove all debris, but leave some fat on the chitterlings.

Place the chitterlings in a medium pot and fill with cold water to cover. Bring to a boil, then add the onions, vinegar, garlic, salt, and chili flakes. Continue to simmer until tender, 3–4 hours. Drain and serve warm.

ROAST CHICKEN

PREPARATION TIME: 10 MINUTES
COOKING TIME: 45 MINUTES TO 1 HOUR
SERVES: 4

- 1 whole chicken (3–4 lb/1.4–1.8 kg)
- 3 tablespoons (45 g) butter, softened
- Salt and freshly ground black pepper
- 1 small bunch fresh thyme, rosemary, or sage (optional)
- ½ lemon

Preheat the oven to 400°F (200°C/Gas Mark 6).

Rub the chicken all over with the softened butter and season with salt and pepper. If desired, stuff the thyme and lemon into the cavity of the chicken. Place the chicken in a roasting pan and roast until the juices run clear (pierce the thigh to the bone to test this) and the internal temperature is 160°F (71°C), 45 minutes to 1 hour, depending on the size of the chicken. Discard the herbs and lemon half.

Transfer the chicken to a serving platter. Pour the pan juices into a pitcher (jug) and skim off excess fat. Serve alongside the chicken.

CORN DOGS

PREPARATION TIME: 15 MINUTES
COOKING TIME: 50 MINUTES
SERVES: 8

- Vegetable oil, for deep-frying
- 8 hot dogs
- Eight 12-inch (30 cm) bamboo skewers
- ½ cup (65 g) all-purpose (plain) flour
- ⅔ cup (85 g) cornmeal
- 1 tablespoon sugar
- 1½ teaspoons baking powder
- ½ teaspoon baking soda (bicarbonate of soda)
- ½ teaspoon salt
- 2 tablespoons (30 g) salted butter, melted
- 1 egg, lightly beaten
- 1¼ cups (295 ml) buttermilk, plus more if needed
- Yellow mustard, for serving

[State fairs across the country are known as annual harvest-season meccas of prized pigs, pie competitions, and fried foods served on sticks. Corn dogs, popularized there, are frankfurters dipped in a cornbread batter and cooked in boiling oil. They are best enjoyed while riding a Ferris wheel.]

Preheat the oven to 250°F (120°C/Gas Mark ½).

Pour 3 inches (7.5 cm) oil into a large heavy pot or deep-fryer and heat to 375°F (190°C). Place a wire rack on a large rimmed baking sheet and place near the fryer.

Thread the hot dogs onto skewers, keeping the pointed end inside the hot dog and leaving enough of the room (about 3 inches/7.5 cm) at the other end so you can grasp it in your hand.

In a large bowl, combine the flour, cornmeal, sugar, baking powder, baking soda (bicarbonate of soda), and salt. Stir in the melted butter, egg, and buttermilk to create a thick batter.

Working with 1 hot dog at a time, dip a hot dog in the batter and fry in the hot oil to fry until the coating is crisp and a dark golden brown, 6–8 minutes. As the corn dogs are cooked, transfer to the wire rack and place in the oven while you fry the remaining corn dogs. Serve with yellow mustard.

ROAST CHICKEN

FRIED CHICKEN

PREPARATION TIME: 10 MINUTES
COOKING TIME: 40 MINUTES
SERVES: 8

- 4 cups (520 g) all-purpose (plain) flour
- Kosher (coarse) salt and freshly ground
  black pepper
- 2 eggs
- 2 cups (475 ml) milk
- Peanut (groundnut) oil, for deep-frying
- 2 whole chickens (3–4 lb/1.4–1.8 kg each),
  quartered

Set up a dredging station: In a wide shallow bowl, whisk the flour with 2 teaspoons kosher (coarse) salt and 1 teaspoon pepper. In a second shallow bowl, beat the eggs and milk.

Pour 3 inches (7.5 cm) oil into a large cast-iron Dutch oven (casserole) and heat to 325°F (160°C).

Season the chicken with 1 teaspoon each kosher (coarse) salt and pepper. Working in batches, dip the chicken quarters in the milk and egg mixture, then dredge in the flour, shaking off any excess. Carefully place in the oil and fry, turning occasionally, until the chicken is cooked through and well browned on all sides, 12–15 minutes for white meat, 16–18 minutes for dark meat. Season to taste with salt. Drain on paper towels and let cool for 5 minutes before serving.

NASHVILLE HOT CHICKEN

PREPARATION TIME: 30 MINUTES,
  PLUS CHILLING TIME
COOKING TIME: 1 HOUR
SERVES: 3–4

For the hot bird spice mixture:
- 4 tablespoons cayenne pepper
- 1 tablespoon plus 1 teaspoon
  light brown sugar
- 1 teaspoon chili powder
- 1 teaspoon salt
- ½ teaspoon garlic powder
- ½ teaspoon onion powder
- ½ teaspoon paprika
- ½ teaspoon freshly ground black pepper
- ½ teaspoon dried oregano

For the chicken:
- 1 whole chicken (about 4 lb/1.8 kg),
  cut into 10 pieces
- 1 teaspoon freshly ground black pepper
- 1 tablespoon plus 2 teaspoons kosher
  (coarse) salt
- 2 eggs
- 2 cups (475 ml) buttermilk
- 1 tablespoon Tabasco-style hot sauce
- 2 cups (260 g) all-purpose (plain) flour
- Peanut (groundnut) oil, for deep-frying
- White bread and sliced pickles,
  for serving

[This spicy chicken dish has become so popular that there's now a hot chicken festival held in Nashville, Tennessee each year.]

For the hot bird spice mixture: In a medium bowl, whisk together the cayenne, brown sugar, chili powder, salt, garlic powder, onion powder, paprika, black pepper, and oregano. Set aside.

For the chicken: Season the chicken pieces with the black pepper and 2 teaspoons of the kosher (coarse) salt. Cover and refrigerate for 2 hours.

Set up a dredging station: In a shallow dish, whisk together the eggs, buttermilk, and hot sauce. In a second shallow dish, whisk together the flour and remaining 1 tablespoon kosher salt.

Pour 3 inches (7.5 cm) oil into a large heavy pot or deep-fryer and heat over medium-high heat to 330°F (165°C).

With a paper towel, pat the chicken pieces very dry. Working in batches, dredge the chicken pieces in the flour mixture, then dip in buttermilk mixture. Dredge again in the flour mixture and set aside.

Working in batches of 2–3 pieces at a time, fry the chicken until the internal temperature of the thickest part of the chicken reads 160°F (71°C), 8–10 minutes. Drain on paper towels, then transfer to a serving platter. While there is still oil glistening on the chicken, season immediately with as much spice mixture as desired. Serve with white bread and pickles.

FRIED CHICKEN

BARBERTON CHICKEN AND HOT SAUCE

PREPARATION TIME: 20 MINUTES,
  PLUS BRINING TIME
COOKING TIME: 1 HOUR 30 MINUTES
SERVES: 4

For brining the chicken:
● ½ cup (145 g) salt
● 1 whole chicken (about 3 lb/1.4 kg)

For the hot sauce:
● 2 tablespoons (30 g) butter
● 1 large onion, chopped
● 1 hot pepper, such as jalapeño, sliced
● 2 cans (15 oz/425 g each) crushed (finely chopped) tomatoes
● 2 tablespoons sugar
● ½ teaspoon salt
● ½ cup (100 g) rice

For frying the chicken:
● 1 cup (130 g) all-purpose (plain) flour
● 1½ teaspoons salt
● 1 teaspoon freshly ground black pepper
● 3 eggs
● 3 cups (340 g) fine dried breadcrumbs
● Lard, for deep-frying (about 4 lb/1.8 kg)

[A local Ohio specialty based on a Serbian recipe, this chicken is dredged in flour, egg, and breadcrumbs. It's then fried in lard; and served with "hot sauce" (rice cooked with tomatoes and a hot pepper), sweet and sour coleslaw, and French fries. The chicken is cut into small pieces, leaving the bone in, and includes the back. Some locals specifically order "backs only."]

For brining the chicken: In a large pot, dissolve the salt in 2 quarts (2 liters) cold water. Cut the chicken into 11 pieces: back, wings, drumsticks, thighs, and breasts each breast cut halved across. Add the chicken pieces to the brine, cover, and refrigerate for 1 hour.

For the hot sauce: In a large pot, heat the butter over medium heat. Add the onion and pepper and cook, stirring, until golden brown, 12–15 minutes. Stir in the crushed tomatoes, sugar, salt, rice, and 1 cup (240 ml) water. Bring to a boil, reduce the heat, cover, and cook, stirring occasionally, for 40 minutes, until the rice is tender.

For frying the chicken: Set up a dredging station. In a wide shallow bowl, combine the flour with ½ teaspoon each of the salt and pepper. In a second shallow bowl, beat the eggs. In a third bowl, season the breadcrumbs with the remaining 1 teaspoon salt and ½ teaspoon pepper. Drain the chicken pieces and blot dry with paper towels.

In a large deep frying pan, heat the lard to a depth of 3 inches (7.5 cm) to 275°F (135°C).

Dredge the chicken pieces by first dipping them in the flour, then the beaten eggs, and finally the breadcrumbs, pressing the crumbs lightly to adhere. Fry the chicken, in batches if necessary, until golden brown and done all the way through. Smaller pieces will cook more quickly (about 10 minutes), the larger ones will take roughly 20 minutes. Serve immediately, with the hot sauce.

MARYLAND FRIED CHICKEN

PREPARATION TIME: 20 MINUTES
COOKING TIME: 40 MINUTES
SERVES: 4

- 1¼ cups (160 g) all-purpose (plain) flour
- 1 teaspoon salt
- ½ teaspoon freshly ground black pepper
- 1 whole chicken (3 lb/1.4 kg),
  cut into 8 pieces
- Vegetable oil or lard, for shallow-frying
- 2 tablespoons (30 g) butter
- 1½ cups (355 ml) milk

[This "chicken-fried chicken" is made in the style of chicken-fried steak, covered in gravy. Serve with mashed potatoes and corn on the cob.]

Season the flour with the salt and pepper. Dredge the chicken pieces in the seasoned flour. Reserve any remaining flour for the gravy.

In a large heavy frying pan, heat ¼ inch (6 mm) oil (or enough lard to come to the same depth) over high heat. When the oil is very hot, fry the chicken, skin side down, until golden brown, 5–6 minutes. Flip the chicken and fry until golden, another 5 minutes. Flip again, add ½ cup (120 ml) water, reduce the heat to medium, cover, and cook until the chicken is cooked through, 15–20 minutes. Transfer the chicken to a plate and cover to keep warm while you make the gravy.

In the same frying pan, melt the butter over medium heat. Stir in 2 tablespoons of the reserved seasoned flour. Add the milk and cook, stirring, until it bubbles and thickens, 6–7 minutes. To serve, top the chicken with the gravy.

CAROLINA RICE PILAU

PREPARATION TIME: 20 MINUTES
COOKING TIME: 1 HOUR 40 MINUTES
SERVES: 4–6

- 1 whole chicken (4 lb/1.8 kg)
- 2 stalks celery
- 1 onion, quartered
- 3 teaspoons salt
- 1 teaspoon freshly ground black pepper
- 1 teaspoon paprika
- ¼ teaspoon cayenne pepper
- 4 sprigs fresh thyme
- 2 cups (400 g) long-grained rice, such as Carolina Gold
- 1 lb (455 g) smoked sausage, cut into ¼-inch (6 mm) thick rounds

[New Orleans, Louisiana has its jambalayas, and South Carolina has pilau (pronounced pee-low, per-low, or per-loo). Pilau refers to pilaf-style rice dishes that have a little extra something like chicken, crab, shrimp, or tomatoes (also called red rice).]

Place the chicken in a large pot or Dutch oven (casserole). Add enough cold water to just cover the chicken, along with the celery, onion, 2 teaspoons of the salt, the black pepper, paprika, cayenne, and thyme sprigs. Bring to a simmer over medium heat. Cover, reduce the heat to low, and simmer until the chicken is tender and falling off the bone, about 1 hour 15 minutes.

Remove the chicken from the broth. Strain the broth (discard the solids) and measure out 4 cups (1 liter). Skim the fat and set the broth aside. When the chicken is cool enough to handle, pull the meat into 1-inch (2.5 cm) pieces (discard the skin and bones).

Return the reserved broth to the Dutch oven and add the chicken pieces, remaining 1 teaspoon salt, rice, and sausage. Bring to a boil over medium-high heat. Reduce the heat to medium-low, cover tightly, and cook until the rice is tender, 15–20 minutes. If liquid remains, uncover and cook another 5 minutes.

JAMBALAYA

PREPARATION TIME: 20 MINUTES
COOKING TIME: 55 MINUTES
SERVES: 8–10

- 3 tablespoons vegetable oil
- ¾ lb (340 g) skinless, boneless chicken thighs
- ½ teaspoon salt
- ¼ teaspoon freshly ground black pepper
- ¾ lb (340 g) smoked sausage, sliced
- 1 yellow onion, diced
- 3 stalks celery, thinly sliced
- 1 large red bell pepper, diced
- 4 cloves garlic, minced
- 1 bay leaf
- 1 tablespoon Creole seasoning
- 3 cups (540 g) chopped tomatoes
- 3 cups (710 ml) chicken stock
- 2 cups (400 g) rice
- 1 lb (455 g) peeled and deveined medium shrimp (prawns)
- 1 tablespoon fresh lemon juice
- 4 tablespoons chopped fresh parsley
- 4 tablespoons sliced scallions (spring onions)

[The name of this dish comes from the French *jambon* (ham) and *à la* (with or on top of), plus the African *ya* (rice). It is a Cajun-Creole rice dish, which is now topped with much more than ham, though some pork is usually involved.]

Place a large Dutch oven (casserole) over medium heat. Add the oil to the pan. Season the chicken with the salt and pepper, add to the hot oil, and cook on both sides until cooked through, about 10 minutes total. Remove the chicken and set aside. Once the chicken is cool enough to handle, shred into 1-inch pieces.

Return the pan to medium heat, add the sausage, and cook for 5 minutes, turning once. Transfer the sausage to a plate and leave the fat in the pan. Add the onion, celery, bell pepper, garlic, bay leaf, and Creole seasoning and cook until the vegetables are softened and the onion is translucent, 5–7 minutes. Stir in the tomatoes, stock, and rice and return the chicken and sausage to the pan. Bring to a boil over medium-high heat. Cover, reduce the heat to medium-low, and simmer, stirring occasionally, until the rice is tender, about 20 minutes.

Top with the shrimp (prawns), cover, and cook until the shrimp turn pink, about 5 minutes. Stir in the lemon juice, parsley, and scallions (spring onions). Serve immediately.

HULI-HULI CHICKEN

PREPARATION TIME: 5 MINUTES,
    PLUS MARINATING TIME
COOKING TIME: 45 MINUTES
SERVES: 4

- 1 cup (240 ml) unsweetened pineapple juice
- ⅓ cup (80 ml) soy sauce
- ½ cup (95 g) packed light brown sugar
- ⅓ cup (90 g) ketchup
- ¼ cup (60 ml) sherry or chicken stock
- 2-inch (5 cm) knob fresh ginger, smashed
- 5 cloves garlic, smashed and peeled
- 2 chickens (3 lb/1.4 kg each), split in half

In a container big enough to hold the 4 chicken halves, combine all the ingredients (except the chicken), stirring until the brown sugar has dissolved. Add the chicken and turn to coat well. Cover and refrigerate for at least 3 hours and up to overnight.

Preheat a gas or charcoal grill (barbecue) to medium-high heat. Reserving the marinade for basting, place the chicken on the grill rack, close the lid, and cook, occasionally turning and basting with marinade, until dark and crisp, about 45 minutes.

PREPARATION TIME: 30 MINUTES
COOKING TIME: 20 MINUTES
SERVES: 4

For the sauce:
- 3 tablespoons sugar
- 2 teaspoons cornstarch (cornflour)
- ½ cup (120 ml) chicken stock or water
- 3 tablespoons soy sauce
- 2 tablespoons rice wine
- 2 tablespoons unseasoned rice vinegar
- 1 tablespoon sesame oil

For the chicken:
- 2 egg whites
- 2 tablespoons rice wine
- 2 tablespoons soy sauce
- 2 lb (910 g) skinless boneless chicken thighs, cut into ½-inch (1.25 cm) pieces
- 3 cups (710 ml) peanut (groundnut) oil, for frying
- ¾ cup (95 g) cornstarch (cornflour)
- ¼ cup (30 g) all-purpose (plain) flour
- ¼ teaspoon salt

For the stir-fry:
- 1 tablespoon sesame oil
- 2 cloves garlic, minced
- 1 tablespoon minced fresh ginger
- 5 or 6 small fresh or dried red chilies, such as árbol, left whole but stems removed
- 4 scallions (spring onions), cut into 1-inch (2.5 cm) lengths
- 1 tablespoon sesame seeds
- Cooked white rice, for serving

[A favorite "Chinese" dish, it was born in New York and popularized nationwide in the 1970s. It is little-known in Asia.]

For the sauce: In a medium bowl, whisk together the sugar and cornstarch (cornflour). Whisk in the chicken stock, soy sauce, wine, vinegar, and sesame oil. Set aside.

For the chicken: In a bowl, whisk together the egg whites, wine, and soy sauce. Add the chicken, toss to coat, and let the chicken marinate for 15 minutes while the oil is heating.

Pour the oil into a wok and heat to 375°F (190°C).

In a medium bowl, whisk together the cornstarch, flour, and salt. Dredge the chicken pieces in the mixture. Working in batches, fry the chicken until golden brown and crispy, about 4 minutes. Drain on paper towels. When all of the chicken has been fried, carefully drain the oil from the wok. Wipe the wok clean with paper towels.

For the stir-fry: In the wok, heat the sesame oil over medium-high heat. Add the garlic, ginger, and chilies and cook until fragrant, about 30 seconds. Add the reserved sauce and cook, stirring, until the sauce is bubbling and thickened, about 4 minutes. Stir in the fried chicken and cook to heat through. Stir in the scallions (spring onions) and sesame seeds. Serve with rice.

CHICKEN POT PIE

PREPARATION TIME: 15 MINUTES
COOKING TIME: 1 HOUR
SERVES: 6–8

For the filling:
- ⅓ cup (75 g) butter
- 1 medium onion, diced
- 1 medium carrot, diced
- ⅓ cup (43 g) all-purpose (plain) flour
- 1½ cups (355 ml) chicken stock
- ½ cup (120 ml) milk
- 2 teaspoons finely chopped fresh thyme
- 3 cups (420 g) cooked chicken, diced
- 10 oz (285 g) frozen green peas
- Salt and freshly ground black pepper

For the dough:
- 2 cups (260 g) all-purpose (plain) flour
- 1 teaspoon salt
- 1½ sticks (170 g) cold butter or solid vegetable shortening
- 4–8 tablespoons ice water

For the filling: In a large heavy-bottomed pot, melt the butter over medium-high heat. Add the onion and carrot and cook, stirring, until the onion has softened, about 4 minutes. Add the flour and stir to coat the vegetables. Add the chicken stock and milk and bring to a simmer, stirring frequently. Stir in the thyme, chicken, peas, and salt and pepper to taste. Remove from the heat and set aside.

Position a rack in the middle of the oven and preheat to 375°F (190°C/Gas Mark 5).

For the dough: In a bowl, whisk together the flour and salt. Cut in the butter (using a pastry/dough blender or 2 knives) until the fat is well incorporated and small crumbs form. Add ice water 1 tablespoon at a time, stirring, just until the dough comes together. It is helpful to gather the dough up with your hands and knead it a few times to see if it needs more water. Turn the dough out onto a floured surface. Divide the dough in half. Roll each piece a few inches bigger than a 9-inch (23 cm) pie plate. Line the bottom of the pie plate with 1 crust.

Pour the filling into the pie shell (pastry case), then top with the second crust. Fold the edges of the dough together, or crimp it using a fork. Cut one or more vents in the top of the pie. Bake until the crust is golden brown and the filling is bubbling and steaming, 40–45 minutes.

CHICKEN POT PIE

PREPARATION TIME: 30 MINUTES
COOKING TIME: 2 HOURS
SERVES: 6

- 1 whole chicken (4 lb/1.8 kg), cut into 8 pieces
- 1 bay leaf
- 1 lb (455 g) thin spaghetti, broken into 2-inch (5 cm) pieces
- 2½ cups (280 g) shredded sharp cheddar cheese
- ½ cup (80 g) diced onion
- 4 tablespoons diced celery
- 4 tablespoons diced red bell pepper
- 1 teaspoon seasoned salt
- ⅛ teaspoon cayenne pepper
- 1 can (10.5 oz/295 g) cream of mushroom soup
- 1 can (14.5 oz/410 g) diced (chopped) tomatoes with juice

[From 1957 to 1986, Craig Claiborne was the food editor (and often the restaurant critic) of the *New York Times*, also becoming one of the most important culinary forces in America. A Mississippi native, he maintained that this dish, made by his mother, was the best thing he ever tasted.]

In a large pot, combine the chicken pieces, bay leaf, and 4 quarts (3.8 liters) water. Bring to a boil, then reduce to a simmer and cook over medium-low heat until the chicken is no longer pink, 40–45 minutes. Remove the chicken from the broth. When cool enough to handle, remove the meat from the bones (discard the skin and bones) and, using forks, shred the meat. Measure out 2 cups (475 ml) of the chicken broth and set aside. Return the pot with the remaining broth to the stove.

Preheat the oven to 350°F (180°C/Gas Mark 4).

Bring the pot of chicken broth to a boil over high heat. Add the spaghetti to the boiling broth and cook to 1 minute less than the cooking time in the package directions. Drain the spaghetti and place in a large bowl. Add the chicken, 1½ cups (170 g) of the cheddar, the onion, celery, bell pepper, seasoned salt, cayenne, soup, and tomatoes. Stir in 1 cup (240 ml) of the reserved chicken broth, adding the remaining 1 cup (240 ml) if needed to achieve a stew-like consistency.

Transfer the mixture to a 9 x 13-inch (23 x 33 cm) baking dish and top with the remaining 1 cup (110 g) cheddar. Cover with foil and bake for 25 minutes. Remove the foil and bake until bubbling, about 20 minutes.

DEEP-FRIED TURKEY

PREPARATION TIME: 20 MINUTES,
  PLUS RESTING TIME
COOKING TIME: 50 MINUTES,
  PLUS TIME TO BRING THE OIL TO
  FRYING TEMPERATURE
SERVES: 12

- 1 whole turkey (12–14 lb/5.4–6.4 kg), neck and giblets removed
- 4–5 gallons (15–19 liters) peanut (groundnut) or canola (rapeseed) oil
- 3 tablespoons Creole seasoning, such as Zatarain's
- 2 tablespoons fresh thyme leaves, finely chopped
- 2 tablespoons kosher (coarse) salt
- 1½ tablespoons freshly ground black pepper

[The turkey was almost chosen to be America's national bird. And deep-frying is a particularly American food preparation. This dish is often made outside, such as on a driveway, on Thanksgiving Day.]

Place the turkey in a 30-quart (28-liter) stockpot and add water to cover it by 2 inches (5 cm). Remove the turkey from the pot, dry it thoroughly with paper towels, and set aside at room temperature. Mark the water level on the inside or outside of the pot (to indicate how much oil to heat in the pot). Discard the water and wash and dry the pot thoroughly.

Place the pot over an outdoor propane burner. Fill the pot with oil, up to the water level that you marked earlier. Heat the oil over medium heat to 375°F (190°C).

In a small bowl, combine the Creole seasoning, thyme, salt, and pepper. Starting with the breasts, carefully slide your hand between the skin and the meat of the breast and thighs to separate the flesh from the skin. Massage the rub into the flesh. Spread any extra rub on the skin of the turkey and inside the cavity. Pull the neck cavity open and cut small slits in the skin between the bottom of the breast and the thigh meat.

Once the oil reaches 375°F (190°C), turn off the burner. Slowly lower the turkey into the oil, until it is fully submerged (do not lower too fast or the moisture from the turkey will cause grease to splatter out of the pot). Turn the burner back on and bring the oil to 350°F (180°C). Fry the turkey for 40 minutes (adjusting the burner as needed to maintain an oil temperature of 350°F/180°C). To test if the turkey is done, slowly remove the fried turkey from the oil and place it on a carving board or large rimmed baking sheet. Insert an instant-read thermometer into the thickest part of the breast, close to the bone; the thermometer should read 155°–160°F (68°-71°C). If it reads lower than 155°F (68°C), slowly lower the turkey back into the oil to finish frying.

Once the internal temperature reaches 155°F (68°C), transfer the turkey to a carving board, cover with foil, and let rest for 30 minutes before carving and serving.

WILD RICE HOTDISH

PREPARATION TIME: 10 MINUTES
COOKING TIME: 1 HOUR
SERVES: 4

- 1 package (6 oz/170 g) long-grain white and wild rice mix, unseasoned
- 2 tablespoons (30 g) butter
- ½ cup (80 g) diced onion
- ½ cup (50 g) diced celery
- 2 tablespoons all-purpose (plain) flour
- 2 cups (475 ml) chicken stock
- 1 teaspoon chopped fresh thyme or ½ teaspoon dried
- ½ cup (120 ml) white wine
- ½ cup (120 ml) sour cream
- 2 cups (280 g) diced cooked chicken or turkey
- Salt and freshly ground black pepper
- 4 tablespoons grated Parmesan cheese

["Hotdish" refers to a wide variety of casseroles popular in the upper Midwest, particularly in Minnesota. Served straight from the baking dish, they are frequently found at church suppers. This version includes the region's famous wild rice.]

Preheat the oven to 350°F (180°C/Gas Mark 4). Butter a 4-quart (3.8-liter) deep baking dish.

Rinse the rice in a fine-mesh sieve. Set aside.

In a large pot, melt the butter over medium heat. Add the onion and celery and cook, stirring, until the onions are just translucent, about 4 minutes. Stir in the flour. Add the chicken stock and bring to a simmer. Remove from the heat and stir in the rice, thyme, white wine, and sour cream. Add the chicken or turkey and season to taste with salt and pepper.

Pour the mixture into the buttered baking dish. Cover tightly and bake for 35 minutes. Uncover, sprinkle with the Parmesan, and bake, uncovered, until the top is golden brown, about 15 minutes.

LUTEFISK

PREPARATION TIME: 5 MINUTES,
   PLUS SOAKING TIME
COOKING TIME: 30 MINUTES
SERVES: AS MANY AS YOU'D LIKE

- ½ lb (225 g) lutefisk per person
- Softened butter, for the baking dish

[Traditionally served at Christmas or Thanksgiving in Scandinavian households, of which there are many in Minnesota, lutefisk is cod (or sometimes haddock) that has been soaked in a lye solution to soften it. At home, cooks boil or bake it and serve it with plenty of melted butter, riced potatoes, and green peas.]

Rinse the lutefisk with cold water. Place the fish in a bowl, cover with ice water, and refrigerate for 3 hours (or more if necessary, to soften), changing the water once or twice.

Preheat the oven to 350°F (180°C/Gas Mark 4).

Drain the lutefisk. Place it in a buttered glass or ceramic baking dish, cover with foil, and bake until the fish flakes easily with a fork, 25–30 minutes.

SALT COD CAKES

PREPARATION TIME: 5 MINUTES,
  PLUS SOAKING TIME
COOKING TIME: 30 MINUTES
SERVES: 4

- ½ lb (225 g) salt cod, cut into pieces
- 2 cups (420 g) plain mashed potatoes
  (see page 256)
- 3 scallions (spring onions), sliced
  very thin
- 1 clove garlic, minced
- Salt and freshly ground black pepper
- 2 egg yolks
- 2 cups (100 g) fresh breadcrumbs
- 1 stick (115 g) butter

[Cod was long essential to the Atlantic Ocean fishing economy, and heavy salting preserved the harvest. "Salt cod" became a major, shelf-stable export as well as a popular ingredient.]

Rinse the cod with cold water, place in a bowl, cover with fresh water, and refrigerate for at least 6 hours and up to 24 hours, changing the water several times.

Rinse the salt cod a final time, place in a small saucepan, cover with cold water, and bring to a boil. Reduce the heat to a simmer and cook until the fish can be flaked easily with a fork, about 15 minutes. Drain well. When cool enough to handle, flake the fish into a bowl.

Add the mashed potatoes, scallions (spring onions), and garlic. Season with salt and pepper. Stir in the egg yolks. Form the mixture into small 2-inch (5 cm) balls, flatten into cakes, and press them in the breadcrumbs.

In a large frying pan, melt the butter over medium heat. Add the cod cakes and cook until golden brown on the first side, about 3 minutes. Flip and brown the other side, about 3 minutes. Serve hot.

BOILED COD WITH MUSTARD SAUCE

PREPARATION TIME: 5 MINUTES
COOKING TIME: 35 MINUTES
SERVES: 4

- 1 teaspoon salt
- 4 (1½-inch/4 cm thick) cod fillets
- ½ cup (120 ml) white wine
- 3 tablespoons (45 g) butter
- 2 tablespoons all-purpose (plain) flour
- 1 tablespoon mustard powder
- 1 tablespoon Dijon mustard
- ½ cup (120 ml) heavy (whipping) cream
- Salt and freshly ground black pepper

[This Scandinavian-style preparation is usually served with boiled buttered potatoes.]

Preheat the oven to 200°F (93°C). In a large heavy saucepan, bring enough water to cover the fish to a boil. Add the salt, fish, and wine. Cook over medium heat until the fish is opaque throughout and flakes easily with a fork, 10–15 minutes, depending on the thickness of the fillets. Using a slotted spatula, carefully transfer the fish to a covered baking dish and place in the oven to keep warm. Measure out 1½ cups (355 ml) of the fish cooking liquid and set aside.

In a saucepan, melt the butter over medium heat. Stir in the flour and mustard powder and cook, stirring, until the mixture is bubbling, several minutes. Add the Dijon mustard and the reserved fish broth and bring to a simmer, stirring. Cook until the sauce has thickened, about 6 minutes. Stir in the cream and bring just to a simmer. Remove from the heat and season to taste with salt and pepper. Serve the fish with the sauce poured over it, or serve the sauce in a pitcher (jug) on the side.

COD ROASTED WITH POTATOES AND ONIONS

PREPARATION TIME: 20 MINUTES
COOKING TIME: 45 MINUTES
SERVES: 4

- ⅓ cup (80 ml) olive oil
- 3 lb (1.4 kg) small red potatoes, scrubbed and halved
- 1 large onion, thinly sliced
- Salt and freshly ground black pepper
- 2 lb (910 g) cod fillets

[Cod is a common name used for several fish in the genus *Gadus* that are known for their white, mild flesh. When Europeans settled New England, many communities were built around cod fishing grounds.]

Preheat the oven to 425°F (220°C/Gas Mark 7).

Put the olive oil in a 9 x 13-inch (23 x 33 cm) ovenproof dish. Add the potatoes and turn to coat them with the oil. Bake for 10 minutes. Stir and bake for another 10 minutes. Stir in the onion, season with salt and pepper, and bake for another 10 minutes.

Place the cod fillets on top of the vegetables. Season the fish with a little more salt and pepper. Bake until the cod is opaque throughout and flakes easily, 8–15 minutes, depending on the thickness of the fillets.

BOILED BURBOT

PREPARATION TIME: 5 MINUTES
COOKING TIME: 10 MINUTES
SERVES: 4

- ½ cup (60 ml) white wine
- 2 tablespoons fresh lemon juice
- 4 teaspoons salt
- 2 lb (910 g) burbot, cut into bite-size pieces
- Melted butter and lemon wedges, for serving

[From the Latin *burba* meaning "*beard*," this long-bodied, flat-headed, cod-like freshwater fish has a single chin whisker. It requires cold to reproduce and lives under ice part of the year. Known as "poor man's lobster" and "Minnesota lobster," the flesh is firm, white, sweet, and delicious prepared simply by boiling in water with wine, vinegar, or lemon and smothered with melted butter. Native to Alaska, the northern Great Lakes states, and as far east as New Brunswick, Canada, it is also known as freshwater ling, the lawyer, lingcod, lush, and eelpout.]

In a 4-quart (4-liter) saucepan, bring 2 quarts (2 liters) water, the wine, lemon juice, and salt to a boil. Add the burbot and cook until the fish is cooked through, about 2 minutes. Drain and toss with melted butter to taste. Serve with lemon wedges on the side.

COD ROASTED WITH POTATOES AND ONIONS

SMOKED MULLET

PREPARATION TIME: 15 MINUTES,
   PLUS COOLING AND BRINING TIME
COOKING TIME: 1–3 HOURS
SERVES: 10–12

For the brine:
- 1 cup (290 g) salt
- 1 cup (190 g) packed light brown sugar
- 2 teaspoons cayenne pepper
- ¼ cup (60 ml) fresh lemon juice or vinegar

For the smoked mullet:
- 5 lb (2.3 kg) mullets, gutted and butterflied for smoking (ask your fishmonger to do this)
- 1 lb (455 g) hickory wood chips
- Oil, for brushing the fish

For the brine: In a large pot, combine the salt, brown sugar, cayenne, lemon juice, and 1 gallon (3.8 liters) water. Bring just to a boil. Remove from the heat and let cool. (The brine can be made ahead to this point and refrigerated.)

For the mullet: place the mullet in a deep ceramic or glass bowl and cover with the brine. Place a plate or other weight on the fish to keep them submerged. Refrigerate for at least 4 hours and up to 24 hours. (The fish will get increasingly salty the longer it brines.)

Soak the wood chips in water to cover while the fish is brining.

Transfer the fish from the brine to wire racks. Let the fish air-dry while you prepare the fire.

Preheat a gas or charcoal grill (barbecue) to low heat. (For a charcoal fire, you need a fire hot enough to keep going, but low enough to smoke slowly.) Once the coals are hot, spread them out and cover them with one-third of the soaked wood chips, or use a smoker box as directed.

Brush both sides of the fish with oil and place them skin side down on the grill rack. Close the lid to the grill, open the vents a little, and keep the fire low. The temperature should be around 175°–200°F (80°–95°C). The fish will be done when they are golden brown and flake easily with a fork, about 1 hour if the fillets are thin, up to 3 hours if the fish is very thick. Add more soaked wood chips as necessary to keep the smoke going.

BAKED WALLEYE PIKE

PREPARATION TIME: 10 MINUTES
COOKING TIME: 10 MINUTES
SERVES: 4

- 6 tablespoons (90 g) butter, melted
- 4 large (½ lb/225 g each) walleye pike fillets, skin on
- Salt and freshly ground black pepper
- 4 cloves garlic, finely minced
- 4 teaspoons chopped fresh dill
- 4 tablespoons fresh lemon juice
- Paprika

Preheat the oven to 450°F (230°C/Gas Mark 8). Brush 2 tablespoons (30 g) of the melted butter in a 9 x 13-inch (23 x 33 cm) ovenproof dish.

Season the fish with salt and pepper. Place the fish in the dish, skin side down. In a small bowl, mix the garlic, dill, and lemon juice together and pour over the fish. Drizzle with the remaining 4 tablespoons (60 g) melted butter and sprinkle with the paprika. Bake the fish until it's opaque and flakes easily with a fork, about 10 minutes.

PAN-FRIED GREAT LAKES FISH WITH LEMON-PARSLEY BUTTER SAUCE

PREPARATION TIME: 5 MINUTES
COOKING TIME: 10 MINUTES
SERVES: 4

- ¾ cup (95 g) all-purpose (plain) flour
- 1 teaspoon salt
- ½ teaspoon freshly ground black pepper
- Pinch of sugar
- 2 tablespoons vegetable oil
- 4 (½ lb/225 g each) skinless fish fillets (walleye pike, northern pike, or lake trout)
- 2 tablespoons fresh lemon juice
- 3 tablespoons (45 g) butter
- 1 tablespoon chopped fresh parsley
- Lemon wedges, for serving

In a large bowl, whisk together the flour, salt, pepper, and sugar.

In a large frying pan, heat the vegetable oil over medium-high heat. Dip the fish fillets in the flour mixture, shaking any excess off into the bowl. Place the fish in the hot oil and cook for 3 minutes or so, then lip and cook until the fish is opaque and flakes easily with a fork, another 3–4 minutes, depending on the thickness of the fish. Transfer the fish to a plate.

Reduce the heat to low and add the lemon juice. Quickly whisk in the butter. Pour the sauce over the fish and sprinkle with the parsley. Serve with extra lemon wedges on the side, if you'd like.

BROILED FLOUNDER WITH HAZELNUT BUTTER SAUCE

PREPARATION TIME: 10 MINUTES
COOKING TIME: 20 MINUTES
SERVES: 4

- 1 cup (140 g) hazelnuts
- 2 lb (910 g) flounder or other flatfish fillets
- 8 tablespoons (115 g) butter, melted
- Salt and freshly ground black pepper
- 1 lemon

[Oregon produces 99 percent of the American hazelnut crop. Here they are paired with local flounder.]

Preheat the oven to 350°F (180°C/Gas Mark 4). Place the hazelnuts in a single layer on a rimmed baking sheet. Bake 10–12 minutes, until the nuts are lightly toasted and the skins begin to pop open. Remove from the oven and let cool slightly. Place the nuts in a tea towel and rub to remove the skins. Chop the nuts coarsely and set aside.

Preheat the broiler (grill) with the rack about 6 inches (15 cm) from the heat source.

Brush the fish with 4 tablespoons (60 g) of the melted butter and season to taste with salt and pepper. Broil until lightly browned, about 5 minutes.

In a small saucepan over medium heat, combine the remaining 2 tablespoons (30 g) butter and the hazelnuts. Cook until fragrant and the butter and nuts are browning, about 4 minutes. Add a squeeze of lemon.

Serve the fish hot with the hazelnut butter sauce spooned over.

SWEET AND SOUR FLATFISH

PREPARATION TIME: 15 MINUTES,
   PLUS OPTIONAL CHILLING TIME
COOKING TIME: 20 MINUTES
SERVES: 4

- 2 large onions, halved and thinly sliced
- ½ cup (120 ml) sherry
- ½ cup (120 ml) white wine
- 1 tablespoon any vinegar
- 2 bay leaves
- 1 teaspoon black peppercorns
- 1 teaspoon minced fresh thyme
  or ½ teaspoon dried
- 2 teaspoons sugar
- 2 lb (910 g) flounder or other flatfish fillets
- Salt and freshly ground black pepper
- 2 tablespoons olive oil

[This dish can be made with flounder, fluke, or any other flatfish, and eaten warm over hot buttered rice, or chilled and served on lettuce as a salad.]

In a saucepan, combine the onions, sherry, wine, ¼ cup (60 ml) water, the vinegar, bay leaves, peppercorns, thyme, and sugar. Bring to a boil, then reduce the heat and simmer just until the onions begin to soften, about 4 minutes. Remove from the heat and set aside.

Season the fillets with salt and pepper. In a large frying pan, heat the oil over medium-high heat. Add the fish and cook until the skin is beginning to brown, about 5 minutes. Flip the fish and cook the other side for about 4 minutes, until the fish is cooked through and turns opaque. Pour the onions and sauce over the fish. If serving hot, let sit about 10 minutes. If serving chilled, refrigerate it in the sauce for at least 1 hour and up to 24 hours.

HALIBUT CADDY GANTY

PREPARATION TIME: 10 MINUTES,
   PLUS MARINATING TIME
COOKING TIME: 20 MINUTES
SERVES: 6

- 2½ lb (1 kg) skinless Alaskan halibut
  fillets, cut 1 inch (2.5 cm) thick
- 2 cups (475 ml) dry white wine
- 3 tablespoons (45 g) butter, softened
- 2 cups (475 ml) sour cream
- 1 cup (210 g) mayonnaise
- 1 cup (160 g) minced onion
- 1 teaspoon paprika
- 2 teaspoons minced fresh dill or tarragon
- 2½ cups (280 g) dried sourdough
  breadcrumbs
- Salt and freshly ground black pepper

Place the halibut in a bowl and cover with the wine. Cover and refrigerate for at least 1 hour and up to 2 hours.

Preheat the oven to 375°F (190°C/Gas Mark 5). Generously butter a 9 x 13-inch (23 x 33 cm) glass baking dish.

Meanwhile, in a small bowl, combine the sour cream, mayonnaise, onion, paprika, and dill. Set aside. In a separate bowl, season the breadcrumbs with salt and pepper.

Drain the fish and pat dry. Roll each halibut fillet in the crumbs and place in the prepared baking dish. Spread the sour cream mixture evenly over the fish. Bake until the fish flakes easily and the top is golden brown and bubbling, 15–20 minutes. Serve hot.

HALIBUT WITH RHUBARB SAUCE

PREPARATION TIME: 10 MINUTES
COOKING TIME: 20 MINUTES
SERVES: 4

- 1 lb (455 g) rhubarb, as red as possible, diced
- 2 tablespoons sugar
- 4 (½ lb/225 g each) halibut steaks
- Salt and freshly ground black pepper

In a small saucepan, combine the rhubarb, sugar, and 1 tablespoon water. Cook over medium heat, stirring, until the rhubarb begins to break down, about 6 minutes. Remove from the heat.

Season the fish with salt and pepper. In a steamer basket set over a pot of boiling water, steam the fish just until opaque in the center, about 10 minutes per 1 inch (2.5 cm) of thickness. Do not oversteam.

Transfer the halibut to a serving dish and ladle the rhubarb compote on top.

BEER-BATTERED HALIBUT

PREPARATION TIME: 10 MINUTES
COOKING TIME: 10 MINUTES
SERVES: 4

- Vegetable oil, for deep-frying
- 1¼ cups (163 g) all-purpose (plain) flour
- 1 teaspoon baking powder
- 1½ teaspoons salt
- ½ teaspoon freshly ground black pepper
- 1½ cups (355 ml) beer
- 1 egg
- 1½ lb (680 g) boneless, skinless halibut, cut into 2-inch (5 cm) cubes

Pour 3 inches (7.5 cm) oil into a large heavy pot or deep-fryer and heat to 375°F (190°C).

While the oil is heating, in a large bowl, whisk together the flour, baking powder, salt, and pepper. Whisk in the beer and egg.

Dip the pieces of fish into the batter and lower into the oil. Cook, in batches if necessary, until the fish is golden brown and floats to the top, about 2 minutes. Drain on paper towels. Serve hot.

HALIBUT POACHED WITH POTATOES, LEEKS, AND CREAM

PREPARATION TIME: 10 MINUTES
COOKING TIME: 35 MINUTES
SERVES: 4

- 3 tablespoons (45 g) butter
- 1 medium onion, diced
- 1 large leek, well rinsed and cut into 1-inch (2.5 cm) pieces
- 2 cloves garlic, sliced
- 3 medium red potatoes, diced
- 1 teaspoon minced fresh thyme
- ¼ cup (60 ml) white wine
- 2 cups (475 ml) chicken stock
- 1 cup (240 ml) heavy (whipping) cream
- Salt and freshly ground black pepper
- 2 large halibut steaks (about 1 lb/455 g each), cut into 4 pieces

[These flat, mild-tasting fish lie on the ocean floor. Males can grow up to sixty pounds, while the females are enormous: up to 600 pounds (over 270 kg). Halibut can live up to thirty years and some grow to be over eight feet (about 2.5 m) long and five feet (about 1.5 m) wide.]

In a large saucepan, melt the butter over medium heat. Add the onion and cook, stirring, for a few minutes, until softened. Add the leek and garlic and stir for a few more minutes, until softened. Add the potatoes, thyme, and wine and bring to a boil. Add the chicken stock and cream, bring to a simmer, and cook until the potatoes are beginning to get tender, about 5 minutes. Season to taste with salt and pepper.

Bring back to a simmer. Season the fish with salt and pepper and place in the pot on top of the vegetables. Cover and simmer until the fish is opaque throughout, 12–15 minutes. Transfer the fish to serving bowls with a slotted spoon. Ladle the vegetables and creamy broth over the top. Serve at once.

SPICY FRIED CATFISH

PREPARATION TIME: 5 MINUTES,
   PLUS 30 MINUTES RESTING TIME
COOKING TIME: 15 MINUTES
SERVES: 2

- 1 lb (455 g) catfish fillets
- 1 cup (240 ml) milk
- 1 cup (130 g) cornmeal
- 4 tablespoons all-purpose (plain) flour
- 1 tablespoon freshly ground black pepper
- ½ teaspoon cayenne pepper
- 1 teaspoon salt
- Vegetable oil, for deep-frying
- Lemon wedges and tartar sauce, for serving

[Named for their "whiskers" and also called bullheads and channel cats, catfish used to weigh up to several hundred pounds in the wild. Now they're almost exclusively farmed and harvested small: between one and two pounds (455 g and 910 g).]

Cut the fillets into 3- or 4-inch (7.5 or 10 cm) pieces. Place in a bowl, add the milk, and soak in the refrigerator for 30 minutes. In a bowl, whisk together the cornmeal, flour, black pepper, cayenne, and salt.

Pour 4 inches (10 cm) oil into a large heavy pot or deep-fryer and heat to 375°F (190°C).

Working in batches, drain the fish and pat dry, dredge in the cornmeal mixture, shaking off any excess, and fry, turning, until golden, about 3 minutes per side. Drain on paper towels. Serve with lemon wedges and tartar sauce.

HALIBUT POACHED WITH POTATOES, LEEKS, AND CREAM

FRIED RIVER HERRING

PREPARATION TIME: 10 MINUTES
COOKING TIME: 30 MINUTES
SERVES: 4

- 8 river herring (¾–1 lb/340–455 g each), cleaned and gutted
- Peanut (groundnut) or vegetable oil, for deep-frying
- 3 cups (390 g) cornmeal
- 1 cup (130 g) all-purpose (plain) flour
- Salt and freshly ground black pepper

[Tiny river herring are a local delicacy in North Carolina, celebrated with an annual festival each spring. This herring dish is served alongside boiled potatoes, hush puppies, and coleslaw.]

With a sharp knife, score each side of the herring with 3–4 cuts ½ inch (1.25 cm) deep, placing them 1–1½ inches (2.5–4 cm) apart.

Pour 3 inches (7.5 cm) oil into a large heavy pot or deep-fryer and heat to 350°F (180°C).

In a 9 x 13-inch (23 x 33 cm) glass baking dish, combine the cornmeal, flour, and 1 tablespoon salt. Mix well. Working in batches of 3 or 4 herring at a time, dredge the fish in the cornmeal mixture. Fry until dark golden brown, 4–5 minutes per side. Remove from the oil and season to taste with salt and pepper.

BAJA FISH TACOS

PREPARATION TIME: 20 MINUTES
COOKING TIME: 25 MINUTES
SERVES: 4

For the sauce:
- ¾ cup (155 g) mayonnaise
- ¼ cup (60 ml) sour cream
- 1 tablespoon fresh lime juice
- 1 clove garlic, minced
- ½ teaspoon ancho chili powder
- ¼ teaspoon salt

For the cabbage:
- 2 cups (180 g) finely sliced red cabbage
- ½ cup (20 g) chopped fresh cilantro (coriander)
- 1 tablespoon fresh lime juice
- ½ teaspoon salt

For the fish:
- 1 cup (130 g) all-purpose (plain) flour
- 1 teaspoon salt
- ½ teaspoon freshly ground black pepper
- 1 cup (240 ml) beer
- Vegetable oil, for deep-frying
- 1¼ lb (565 g) firm white fish

For the tacos:
- 12 corn tortillas
- 1 avocado, sliced
- Fresh salsa and lime wedges, for serving

[Halibut or another firm white fish is a perfect choice for these tacos.]

For the sauce: In a medium bowl, combine all the sauce ingredients. Cover and chill until ready to use.

For the cabbage: In a medium bowl, toss the cabbage, cilantro (coriander), lime juice, and salt together and set aside.

For the fish: In a large bowl, whisk together the flour, salt, and pepper. Stir in the beer.

Pour 3 inches (7.5 cm) oil into a large heavy pot or deep-fryer and heat to 375°F (190°C).

Cut the fish into 2-inch (5 cm) pieces. Dip the fish pieces in the batter. Cooking in batches, cook the fish until golden brown on both sides, 2–3 minutes. Drain on paper towels.

For the tacos: Using tongs, heat the tortillas over the open flame of a burner (alternatively, heat them in a dry frying pan). Cover the tortillas with a towel to keep them warm as you work.

To assemble, top each tortilla with a spoonful of the cabbage, a few pieces of fried fish, a spoonful of sauce, and an avocado slice. Serve immediately, with fresh salsa and lime wedges.

DOOR COUNTY FISH BOIL

PREPARATION TIME: 15 MINUTES
COOKING TIME: 30 MINUTES
SERVES: 10–12

- 1 lb (455 g) salt
- 3 dozen small red potatoes
- 4 dozen small white onions (pearl onions), peeled but whole
- 7 lb (3.2 kg) white fish steaks, 2 inches (5 cm) thick
- 2 sticks (225 g) butter, melted

[Scandinavians brought the fish boil to Wisconsin. Originally, the outdoor event fed large groups of workers and it's still a tradition in Wisconsin (and northern Lake Michigan and Lake Superior). In Door County, Wisconsin, the fish boil typically consists of a pot of potatoes, onions, and whitefish cooked over an open fire. After the oils from the fish rise to the top, sometimes kerosene is added to the fire, causing it to swell and the pot to boil over, indicating that it's time to feast. The dish can also be made on top of the stove; just be careful not to let it boil over. The fish boil is traditionally followed by Sour Cherry Pie (page 290).]

Fill a 5-gallon (19-liter) stockpot (or a cast-iron pot if you're cooking over an outside fire) three-quarters with water. Add the salt and bring to a boil.

Add the potatoes to the boiling water and cook for 10 minutes. Add the onions and boil for 5 minutes. Add the fish and boil until the fish is opaque and flakes easily, 10–15 minutes. Remove the pot from the heat and use a wide mesh spider/skimmer or big slotted spoon to remove the contents from the pot. Serve drizzled with melted butter.

BLACKENED RED SNAPPER

PREPARATION TIME: 10 MINUTES
COOKING TIME: 20 MINUTES
SERVES: 6

- 2 teaspoons paprika
- 2 teaspoons onion powder
- 2 teaspoons salt
- 1 teaspoon dried thyme
- 1 teaspoon freshly ground black pepper
- ½ teaspoon dried oregano
- ½ teaspoon cayenne pepper
- 6 red snapper fillets (6–7 oz/ 170–200 g each)
- 4 tablespoons vegetable oil

[Firm, sweet, mild red snapper is native to the coastal South, from North Carolina to Texas.]

In a small bowl, mix together the paprika, onion powder, salt, thyme, black pepper, oregano, and cayenne. Coat the fillets generously with the seasoning mixture.

Heat a large cast-iron skillet over high heat until very hot. Add 2 tablespoons of the vegetable oil and swirl to coat the bottom of the pan. Working in batches, add the snapper fillets in a single layer, skin side down. Reduce the heat to medium and cook until well seared, about 4 minutes. Flip and cook until cooked through, 2–3 minutes, then transfer to a platter. Wipe the pan clean with a paper towel and repeat with the remaining 2 tablespoons oil and fish. Serve hot.

GRILLED MAHI-MAHI
WITH FRESH MANGO SALSA

PREPARATION TIME: 15 MINUTES,
  PLUS MARINATING TIME
COOKING TIME: 10 MINUTES
SERVES: 4

- 2 tablespoons olive oil
- 3 tablespoons fresh lime juice
- 1 teaspoon cayenne pepper
- 4 (1-inch/2.5 cm) thick mahi-mahi steaks, skinned
- Salt and freshly ground black pepper
- 2 mangoes, peeled and chopped
- 1 small red onion, diced
- 2 tablespoons chopped fresh cilantro (coriander)
- 1 jalapeño pepper, seeded and minced

In a small bowl, mix together the oil, 2 tablespoons of the lime juice, and the cayenne. Brush the fish with the oil mixture. Season with salt and pepper. Let marinate, turning now and then, for at least 20 minutes and up to 1 hour.

Meanwhile, in a bowl, combine the mangoes, onion, cilantro (coriander), jalapeño, and remaining 1 tablespoon lime juice. Season to taste with salt and pepper. Set the salsa aside.

Preheat a gas or charcoal grill (barbecue) to medium heat.

Grill the fish until opaque throughout, about 4 minutes per side. Serve with the salsa.

SLOW-ROASTED SALMON
WITH YOGURT SAUCE

PREPARATION TIME: 15 MINUTES,
  PLUS CHILLING TIME
COOKING TIME: 30 MINUTES
SERVES: 4

For the yogurt sauce:
- 2 cups (455 g) whole-milk yogurt
- ½ cup (120 ml) sour cream
- ¾ cup (100 g) peeled, seeded, and diced cucumber
- 4 tablespoons minced onion
- 1 clove garlic, minced
- 2 tablespoons fresh lemon juice
- 1 tablespoon minced fresh dill
- Salt and freshly ground black pepper, to taste

For the salmon:
- ¼ cup (60 ml) olive oil
- 1 side of wild salmon (about 1½ lb/680 g)
- Juice of 1 lemon
- 4 tablespoons chopped fresh parsley
- 4 tablespoons chopped fresh dill or fennel fronds
- ½ teaspoon salt
- ½ teaspoon freshly ground black pepper

[Wild salmon is the pride of the Pacific Northwestern states.]

For the yogurt sauce: In a small bowl, stir all the ingredients together. Cover and refrigerate for at least 1 hour to chill. Store in the refrigerator for up to 2 days.

For the salmon: Line a rimmed baking sheet with foil or parchment and brush with some of the olive oil. Place the salmon, skin side down, on the parchment.

In a small bowl, whisk together the remaining olive oil, the lemon juice, herbs, salt, and pepper. Rub the mixture over the top of the salmon. Let the salmon rest while you preheat the oven to 275°F (140°C/Gas Mark 1).

Bake until the fish is just opaque in the center, 25–30 minutes. Serve with the yogurt sauce.

SLOW-ROASTED SALMON WITH YOGURT SAUCE

WHOLE POACHED SALMON

PREPARATION TIME: 10 MINUTES,
   PLUS CHILLING TIME
COOKING TIME: 45 MINUTES
SERVES: 8–10

- 2 medium onions, chopped
- 3 stalks celery, chopped
- 2 lemons, halved
- 3 cups (710 ml) dry white wine
- 1 teaspoon freshly ground black
  peppercorns
- 3 bay leaves
- 1 small bunch fresh parsley
- 1 whole salmon (6–8 lb/2.7–3.6 kg),
  cleaned and gutted
- Yogurt Sauce (page 178)

In a fish poacher large enough to hold the fish, place the onions, celery, lemon halves (squeeze them slightly), wine, peppercorns, bay leaves, and parsley. Pour in enough water so that the fish will be submerged. Bring to a boil. Let simmer for about 15 minutes. Gently lower the fish into the simmering stock. Poach the fish for about 10 minutes per 1 inch (2.5 cm) of thickness. Transfer to a platter, cover, and refrigerate overnight.

Serve the salmon cold, with the yogurt sauce.

GRILLED MARINATED SALMON
WITH SESAME AND GINGER

PREPARATION TIME: 10 MINUTES,
   PLUS MARINATING TIME
COOKING TIME: 10 MINUTES
SERVES: 4

- ⅓ cup (80 ml) sesame oil
- ¼ cup (60 ml) dry white wine
- 1 tablespoon fresh lime juice
- 2 teaspoons soy sauce
- 1 tablespoon minced fresh ginger
- 2 cloves garlic, minced
- 1 teaspoon sugar
- ½ teaspoon salt
- ½ teaspoon freshly ground black pepper
- 4 salmon steaks (6–8 oz/170–225 g each)

In a deep bowl, combine the sesame oil, wine, lime juice, soy sauce, ginger, garlic, sugar, salt, and pepper. Add the salmon and turn to coat well on all sides. Cover and refrigerate for at least1 hour and up to 3 hours.

Preheat a gas or charcoal grill (barbecue) to high heat. Remove the salmon from the marinade and grill until the fish flakes easily but is still moist in the center, about 5 minutes per side (depending on the thickness of the steaks).

MASSACHUSETTS FRIED SMELT

PREPARATION TIME: 10 MINUTES
COOKING TIME: 10 MINUTES
SERVES: 2

- 1 cup (130 g) all-purpose (plain) flour
- 1 teaspoon salt
- ½ teaspoon freshly ground black pepper
- 1 lb (455 g) smelt, 2–5 inches
  (5–13 cm) long
- Vegetable or olive oil, for frying
- Tartar sauce and/or lemon wedges, for
  serving (optional)

[Smelt are traditionally caught in estuaries and river mouths. When extremely fresh, smelt can be eaten whole. Or they can be gutted, and their heads removed. Their bones are pliable and completely edible.]

In a shallow bowl, whisk together the flour, salt, and pepper. Dredge the fish in the seasoned flour.

Pour oil to a depth of 1 inch (2.5 cm) into a heavy frying pan. Heat the pan over medium-high heat until the oil just starts to smoke. Add the smelt and fry for 2–3 minutes, flip, and cook for another 2 minutes or so. Remove the smelt with a slotted spoon and drain on paper towels. Serve hot, with tartar sauce and/or lemon wedges, if desired.

CAMPFIRE TROUT

PREPARATION TIME: 10 MINUTES,
   PLUS THE TIME TO BUILD A CAMPFIRE
COOKING TIME: 15 MINUTES
SERVES: 2

- 2 trout, cleaned and gutted
- Salt and freshly ground black pepper
- 1 lemon, thinly sliced
- 1 small bunch fresh thyme
- 4 slices bacon (streaky) (optional)

[In Wyoming, freshly caught mountain trout is roasted over an open fire. A fish basket makes the process easier, but isn't essential.]

Build a nice fire. When the flames have gone down and the embers are red hot, place a grill rack over the top, about 6 inches (15 cm) from the fire. Open the trout and season with salt and pepper. Stuff the fish with lemon slices and thyme. Wrap each trout with 2 slices of bacon around the middle of the fish, if desired. Place the fish on the rack and cook until the fish flakes easily, 4 minutes per side, depending on the size of the fish.

MACKEREL ROASTED WITH POTATOES, BACON, AND ONIONS

PREPARATION TIME: 10 MINUTES
COOKING TIME: 30 MINUTES
SERVES: 2

- 2 medium potatoes, cut into ¼-inch (6 mm) thick slices
- 1 medium onion, cut into ¼-inch (6 mm) thick slices, separated into rings
- 3 tablespoons olive oil
- Salt and freshly ground black pepper
- 2 whole mackerel (about 1 lb/455 g each), gutted, heads on or off
- 4 slices thick-cut smoked bacon (streaky)

Preheat the oven to 425°F (220°C/Gas Mark 7).

In a 9 x 13-inch (23 x 33 cm) ovenproof dish, toss the potatoes and onion with the olive oil and season with salt and pepper. Spread the vegetables out in a single layer. Wrap 2 slices bacon around each mackerel. Place the fish on top of the potatoes and onions. Roast, uncovered, until the bacon is somewhat crisp and the fish is opaque throughout, about 30 minutes.

MACKEREL GRILLED WITH HERBS AND LEMON

PREPARATION TIME: 5 MINUTES
COOKING TIME: 20 MINUTES
SERVES: 2

- 2 whole mackerel (about 1 lb/455 g each), gutted
- 3 tablespoons olive oil
- Salt and freshly ground black pepper
- 2 lemons, thinly sliced
- 1 bunch herbs such as thyme, rosemary, or sage (or a mixture)

Preheat a gas or charcoal grill (barbecue) to medium-high heat.

Place the fish on a plate and coat with the olive oil. Season with salt and pepper. Line each fish cavity with the lemon slices and herbs. Place on the preheated rack and grill until the fish is opaque and flakes easily, 15–20 minutes, turning the fish as necessary to keep it from burning.

MACKEREL WITH GINGER AND SESAME

PREPARATION TIME: 5 MINUTES,
   PLUS MARINATING TIME
COOKING TIME: 15 MINUTES
SERVES: 2

- 2 large (½ lb/225 g each) or 4 small (¼ lb/115 g) mackerel fillets, skin on
- 2 tablespoons sesame oil
- 2 tablespoons soy sauce
- 1 tablespoon unseasoned rice vinegar
- 1 tablespoon minced fresh ginger
- 2 large cloves garlic, minced
- 1 teaspoon crushed chili flakes

Place the mackerel fillets in a long dish. In a small bowl, stir together 1 tablespoon of the sesame oil, the soy sauce, vinegar, ginger, garlic, and chili flakes. Pour the marinade over the fillets and turn to coat well on both sides. Let marinate at room temperature for at least 30 minutes and up to 1 hour.

In a large heavy frying pan, heat the remaining 1 tablespoon sesame oil over medium-high heat until very hot. Add the fillets, skin side down, and press them flat with a spatula (fish slice). Cook until the fish are deeply browned and the flesh flakes easily, 4–5 minutes per side.

BROILED POMPANO

PREPARATION TIME: 5 MINUTES
COOKING TIME: 10 MINUTES
SERVES: 4

- 4 pompano fillets (4 oz/115 g each)
- Olive oil, for brushing
- Blackened seasoning (optional)
- 4 tablespoons (60 g) butter, melted, for serving (optional)
- Lemon wedges, for serving

Preheat the broiler (grill) with the rack in the closest position to the heat source.

Arrange the fish on a broilerproof rimmed baking sheet. Brush with oil and rub with seasoning (if using). Broil the fish until just cooked through, 5–6 minutes, rotating the pan occasionally. Serve the fish brushed with melted butter, if desired, with lemon wedges for squeezing.

BLUEFISH WITH TOMATOES

PREPARATION TIME: 5 MINUTES
COOKING TIME: 20 MINUTES
SERVES: 2

- 2 tablespoons olive oil
- 2 bluefish fillets (about ½ lb/225 g each), skin-on
- 1 small onion, diced
- 2 cloves garlic, sliced
- 1 teaspoon minced fresh thyme or rosemary
- 2 cups cherry tomatoes, halved
- Salt and freshly ground black pepper
- ¼ cup (60 ml) white wine

[Due to its high oil content, bluefish must be served very fresh, before the flavor turns overly fishy. Its silver skin is edible and delicious when crisp. New Jersey has excellent tomatoes, which pair beautifully with this summer fish.]

In a large heavy frying pan or cast-iron skillet, bring the oil almost to the smoking point over medium-high heat. Add the bluefish fillets to the pan, skin side down. Press the fillets with a spatula (fish slice) to sear them evenly and flatten them. Cook the fish, pressing them often, for about 5 minutes.

Without moving the fish, add the onions. Cook them for a few minutes, then add the garlic. Continue cooking the fish with the onions for a few minutes, until the onion and garlic have softened and the skin of the fish is very browned and crispy. Flip the fish. Add the herbs and tomatoes and season to taste with salt and pepper. Cook for a few more minutes, again without moving the fish. When the tomatoes are hot and sizzling and the flesh of the fish is opaque and flakes easily, remove the fish from the pan. Add the wine to the pan and boil for a few minutes. Pour over the fish.

CORNMEAL FRIED FROG LEGS

PREPARATION TIME: 15 MINUTES
COOKING TIME: 25 MINUTES
SERVES: 4–6

- Vegetable oil, for deep-frying
- 1 cup (130 g) cornmeal
- Kosher (coarse) salt and freshly ground black pepper
- 2 eggs, lightly beaten
- ¼ cup (60 ml) milk
- 3 lb (1.4 kg) frog legs, rinsed and patted dry
- Ranch dressing (page 480), for serving

[The Florida town of Fellsmere, near Vero Beach in Indian River County, holds an annual festival that sells about 3,500 pounds (over 1,500 kg) of frog legs to visitors. Otherwise, frog legs can be readily sourced online. Any variety of dipping sauces is accepted with frog legs at the Fellsmere Frog Leg Festival; in many restaurants in Florida, ranch dressing is a common accompaniment.]

Pour 2 inches (5 cm) oil into a large deep cast-iron skillet or heavy frying pan and heat to 350°F (180°C).

Set up a dredging station: In a wide shallow bowl, combine the cornmeal and a generous amount of salt and pepper. In a second shallow bowl, beat the eggs and milk.

Dip the frog legs in the milk mixture, then in the cornmeal. Working in batches of 5 at a time, gently drop the frog legs into the hot oil and cook until golden brown, 3–5 minutes. Serve hot, with ranch dressing.

MAINE STEAMER CLAMS

PREPARATION TIME: 10 MINUTES,
    PLUS CLAM PURGING TIME
COOKING TIME: 15 MINUTES
SERVES: 4

- 4 lb (1.8 kg) steamer (soft-shell) clams
- Sea salt
- Chopped parsley (optional)
- Melted butter, for dipping the clams

[Use tightly closed, unbroken, fresh, soft-shell clams. For a sea-side version of this recipe, purge the clams in seawater for a few hours, before boiling them in fresh water on the beach.]

Clean and sort the clams. If the shells are very sandy, use a soft vegetable brush to clean them. Place the clams in a large bowl or pot and cover with cold water mixed with sea salt (about 2 tablespoons per gallon/3.8 liters of water). Keep the submerged clams in a dark cool place or the refrigerator. After a few hours they will have purged some sand. Rinse them and cover with fresh salty water. Repeat until all of the sand has been purged. The water will be clear. Rinse the clams a final time.

In a large pot, bring several inches (7–8 cm) water to a boil. Reduce to a simmer and add the clams to the pot. Cover and let steam until the clams have all opened and are just done, 6–8 minutes.

Reserving the broth in the bottom of the pot, fish out the clams. Add the parsley (if using) to the broth. Serve the clams, including broth, in a big bowl, with individual bowls of melted butter on the side for dunking.

FRIED CLAMS

PREPARATION TIME: 15 MINUTES,
    PLUS CLAM PURGING TIME
COOKING TIME: 10 MINUTES
SERVES: 4

- Fine sea salt
- 30–40 steamer (soft-shell) clams, scrubbed and rinsed
- Vegetable oil, for deep-frying
- 3 cups (390 g) all-purpose (plain) flour
- 1 teaspoon freshly ground black pepper
- ½ teaspoon cayenne pepper
- 1 teaspoon sugar

To purge the clams, fill a large pot with cold water, and add enough salt to make the water taste as salty as the sea. Soak the clams in the salt water. If they spit out a lot of sand, repeat the process, changing the salt water every once in a while if necessary. (This can be a quick process if the clams are very clean, or it may take up to 4 hours or more.) When the clams have stopped purging sand, remove them from the water and shuck them, being careful to keep them whole. Drop the clams into ice water as they are shucked. Rinse the clams and drain well in a sieve. Dry them very thoroughly by laying them on a clean lint-free tea towel.

Pour 3 inches (7.5 cm) oil into a deep-fryer or a large heavy pot with a deep-fry basket and heat to 375°F (190°C).

Meanwhile, in a shallow dish, whisk together the flour, 1½ tea-spoons sea salt, the black pepper, cayenne, and sugar.

Dredge the clams in the flour mixture and shake off any excess. Working in batches, place the clams in the fryer basket and cook until they are light golden brown, about 2 minutes. Drain on paper towels and serve immediately.

CLAM BAKE

NE

PREPARATION TIME: 20 MINUTES
COOKING TIME: 50 MINUTES
SERVES: 8

- 1 bottle (750 ml) dry white wine
- 16 small red or Yukon Gold potatoes, scrubbed
- 8 live lobsters, 1–1½ lb (455–680 g) each
- 8 eggs
- 8 ears of corn, husked and halved crosswise
- 1 lb (455 g) spicy chouriço, cut into 2-inch (5 cm) slices
- 8 cloves garlic, peeled but whole
- 1 large onion, cut into wedges
- 2 lemons, sliced
- 6 lb (2.7 kg) clams, any type, scrubbed
- Old Bay seasoning
- 2 sticks (225 g) butter, melted

[This recipe is for a traditional New England–style clam bake, best made on the beach over an open fire. It makes a large amount, so requires a large stockpot (at least 7½ gallons/28 liters), with a steamer basket to fit. Traditionally, this clam bake is served with Boston Brown Bread (page 421).]

In a very large (7½-gallon/28-liter) stockpot with a steamer basket, combine 1 gallon (4 liters) water and the wine and bring to a boil.

Place the potatoes in the bottom of the steamer basket, cover, and cook for 10 minutes. Add the lobsters and eggs, cover, and cook for another 10 minutes. Add the corn, chouriço, garlic, onion, and lemons. Cover and cook for 5 minutes. Add the clams, cover, and cook until the clams have opened, 6–10 minutes. Remove an egg from the basket. Cut it in half. If it is hard-boiled, the lobster is done.

Transfer the contents of the basket to a large platter or a table covered with newspaper. Sprinkle Old Bay over everything. Pour the cooking liquid into bowls, leaving any sediment behind. Use the liquid for dipping clams or as a broth. Serve everything with melted butter, for dipping.

PORTUGUESE CLAMS WITH LINGUIÇA AND KALE

RI

PREPARATION TIME: 10 MINUTES
COOKING TIME: 40 MINUTES
SERVES: 4

- 1 tablespoon olive oil
- ½ lb (225 g) linguiça, cut into ½-inch (1.25 cm) slices
- 1 medium onion, diced
- 1 lb (455 g) kale, cleaned and chopped
- 2 medium russet (baking) potatoes, peeled and cut into ¼-inch (6 mm) slices
- 4 cups (1 liter) chicken stock
- 1 dozen hardshell clams, scrubbed
- Salt and freshly ground black pepper

[With over 400 miles of coastline, Rhode Island is home to great seafood, and also to many seafaring people and their culinary traditions. Portuguese immigrants began settling in Rhode Island in the late 1600s, and the state now has the highest per capita population of people with Portuguese heritage. The introduction of linguiça, a smoke-cured pork sausage, is one of their many legacies.]

In a large pot, heat the oil over high heat. Add the linguiça and cook until beginning to brown. Add the onion and cook, stirring, for several minutes. Add the kale, potatoes, and stock. Cover and bring just to a boil. Reduce the heat and simmer until the greens and potatoes are just tender, about 15 minutes. Add the clams, stir gently, season with salt and pepper, cover, and simmer until the clams have opened, about 10 minutes.

PORTUGUESE CLAMS WITH LINGUIÇA AND KALE

CLAM CAKES

PREPARATION TIME: 10 MINUTES
COOKING TIME: 30 MINUTES
MAKES: ABOUT 30 CAKES

- 1 quart (1 liter) shucked clams
  in their liquid
- 2½ cups (325 g) all-purpose (plain) flour
- 2 teaspoons baking powder
- 1 teaspoon salt
- ½ teaspoon paprika
- ¼ teaspoon freshly ground black pepper
- ½ cup (120 ml) milk
- 1 egg
- 2 tablespoons (30 g) butter, melted
- Vegetable oil, for deep-frying
- Lemon wedges, tartar sauce, and hot
  sauce, for serving

Drain the clams, reserving ½ cup (120 ml) of the liquid. Check for shells and discard if any found. Chop the clams coarsely and set aside.

In a large bowl, whisk together the flour, baking powder, salt, paprika, and pepper. Stir in the clams, the reserved clam liquid, the milk, egg, and melted butter.

Pour 3 inches (7.5 cm) oil into a large heavy pot or deep-fryer and heat to 375°F (190°C). Using 2 spoons, scoop and scrape 1 tablespoon of batter into the hot oil. Fry a few at a time, turning halfway through cooking, until golden brown, 2–3 minutes. Drain on paper towels. Serve hot with lemon wedges, tartar sauce, and hot sauce.

NEW ENGLAND CLAM PIE

PREPARATION TIME: 30 MINUTES,
  PLUS DOUGH CHILLING TIME
COOKING TIME: 10 HOURS 40 MINUTES,
  INCLUDING RESTING TIME
SERVES: 6–8

- Basic Pie Dough (page 280) for a double-
  crust pie
- 1 quart (1 liter) shucked clams
  in their liquid
- 3 large potatoes, peeled and diced
- 2 cups (475 ml) bottled clam juice,
  or chicken stock
- 6 slices bacon (streaky), cut into ½-inch
  (1.25 cm) pieces
- 1 medium onion, diced
- 3 tablespoons all-purpose (plain) flour
- ¼ cup (60 ml) heavy (whipping) cream
- 1 tablespoon minced fresh thyme
- 3 tablespoons minced fresh parsley
- Salt and freshly ground black pepper
- 3 tablespoons (45 g) butter

Prepare the pie dough and chill as directed.

Drain the clams, reserving ½ cup (120 ml) liquid. Check for shells and discard if found. Chop the clams coarsely and set aside.

In a medium saucepan, combine the potatoes and clam juice or chicken stock and bring to a boil over medium-high heat. Cook until the potatoes are tender, about 10 minutes. Reserve the liquid, drain and set aside.

Position a rack in the middle of the oven and preheat to 350°F (180°C/Gas Mark 4).

In a large deep frying pan, cook the bacon over medium-high heat, stirring, until crisp, about 6 minutes. Remove with a slotted spoon and set aside. Reduce the heat to medium, add the onion, and cook until tender, about 5 minutes. Stir in the flour and cook, stirring constantly, for 2 minutes. Add the cream and reserved 1 cup (240 ml) clam liquid. Cook, stirring constantly, until the mix-ture is bubbling and thickened, several more minutes. Remove from the heat, stir in the reserved potatoes, bacon, clams, thyme, and parsley, and season to taste with salt and pepper.

Pour the clam mixture into the pie shell (pastry case). Dot with the butter and cover with the top crust. Crimp the edges together and cut vents in the top. Bake until the crust is deep golden brown and the filling is bubbling, about 1 hour. Let the pie rest for 10 minutes before serving.

PASTA WITH FRESH CLAMS

PREPARATION TIME: 10 MINUTES
COOKING TIME: 35 MINUTES
SERVES: 4

- Salt
- 1 lb (455 g) linguine
- ½ cup (120 ml) olive oil
- 4 large cloves garlic, sliced
- 1 teaspoon crushed chili flakes
- 1 cup (240 ml) dry white wine
- 2 dozen littleneck (hardshell) clams, scrubbed, rinsed, and dried
- 2 tablespoons chopped fresh parsley
- Freshly ground black pepper

Bring a large pot of salted water to a boil. Add the pasta and cook until al dente according to package directions.

Meanwhile, in a second large pot, heat the olive oil over medium heat. Add the garlic and cook until light golden brown, about 5 minutes. Add the chili flakes and wine and bring to a boil. Add the clams a small handful at a time, stirring gently. Cover and cook until most of the clams have opened, about 12 minutes. Check them while they're cooking, as once they start to open, they will cook fast. Stir in the parsley. Season with salt and pepper.

Drain the pasta and toss in a bowl with the cooked clams and sauce. Serve at once.

OYSTER PAN ROAST

PREPARATION TIME: 10 MINUTES
COOKING TIME: 15 MINUTES
SERVES: 4

- 4 tablespoons (60 g) butter
- 2 tablespoons minced shallot
- ½ cup (120 ml) white wine
- 2 cups (475 ml) heavy (whipping) cream
- 2 teaspoons Worcestershire sauce
- Dash of celery salt
- Hot sauce or cayenne pepper (optional)
- 4 dozen shucked oysters, with their liquor
- Buttered toast, for serving

In a saucepan, melt the butter over medium heat. Add the shallot and cook, stirring, for a few minutes. Add the wine and cook until the wine has reduced a bit. Add the cream, Worcestershire sauce, celery salt, and hot sauce (if using) and bring to a simmer. Add the oysters and their liquor and cook just until their edges begin to curl and they are heated through, about 5 minutes. Serve hot, with buttered toast.

PENN COVE MUSSELS IN WHITE WINE

PREPARATION TIME: 10 MINUTES
COOKING TIME: 15 MINUTES
SERVES: 4

- 2 tablespoons olive oil
- 4 cloves garlic, thinly sliced
- 2 large shallots, halved and thinly sliced
- 2 cup (475 ml) dry white wine
- 4 lb (1.8 kg) mussels, debearded and well scrubbed
- 4 teaspoons minced fresh tarragon
- 4 teaspoons minced fresh parsley
- 4 tablespoons (60 g) butter
- Crusty French bread, for serving

[Mussels from the clean, cold waters of Penn Cove, sixty miles northwest of Seattle, Washington, have won international taste tests.]

In a large heavy-bottomed pot, heat the olive oil over medium heat. Add the garlic and shallot and cook, stirring, until softened, about 2 minutes. Pour in the wine and 2 cups (475 ml) water and bring to a boil. Add the mussels, cover, and cook until all the mussels have opened, 6–8 minutes.

Add the herbs and butter to the mussels, stirring gently to distribute and melt the butter. Divide the mussels among 4 bowls, pour the cooking liquid over them, and serve with French bread.

FLORIDA STONE CRAB

COOKING TIME: 15 MINUTES
SERVES: AS MANY AS YOU'D LIKE

- Cooked stone crab claws
- Melted butter and lemon wedges, for serving

[The stone crab has a rock–hard shell (hence its name), and large powerful claws, which are usually the only part eaten. Unless you are harvesting your own claws, they are almost exclusively sold already cooked and frozen.]

Set up a bowl of ice and water. Bring a pot of water to a boil. Add the claws to the pot and return to a boil. Cook for 5 minutes for medium-large, a little longer if very large. Drain and plunge into the ice bath. Drain and serve. Diners can crack the hard shells using a nutcracker, hammer, or mallet. Serve with melted butter and lemon wedges.

PENN COVE MUSSELS IN WHITE WINE

BOILED DUNGENESS CRAB

PREPARATION TIME: 5 MINUTES
COOKING TIME: 20 MINUTES
SERVES: AS MANY AS YOU'D LIKE

Per person:
- 1 live Dungeness crab (1–1¼ lb /455–565 g)
- Salt
- Melted butter

[Named for a small Washington fishing village, the Pacific Ocean famous Dungeness crab has been commercially harvested since the 1880s. The delicacy is now so popular that annual, sustainable harvesting can top fifty million pounds (over 22 metric tons).]

Bring a pot of water to a boil. (The number of crabs you are cooking will determine the pot size; the crabs should not be crowded.) Salt the water generously.

Plunge the crabs into the boiling water and boil until the crab has turned red, 8–10 minutes. The flesh should be opaque throughout. Serve with melted butter.

GRILLED KING CRAB LEGS

PREPARATION TIME: 5 MINUTES
COOKING TIME: 8 MINUTES
SERVES: AS MANY AS YOU'D LIKE

Per person:
- 1–2 king crab legs
- Melted butter, for serving

Note:
If the crab legs are intact, they can be cooked over a hot fire, turning them and charring the shells. If they have been split open, grill the legs over medium heat on the unsplit side only, so the juices don't run out.

Preheat a gas or charcoal grill (barbecue) to hot heat (see Note).

Grill the legs just until they are hot, 6–8 minutes. Serve the legs with melted butter.

SNOW CRAB LEGS WITH HERBED BUTTER SAUCE

PREPARATION TIME: 10 MINUTES
COOKING TIME: 20 MINUTES
SERVES: 4

- 4 lb (1.8 kg) frozen snow crab legs
- 1 stick (115 g) butter
- 4 cloves garlic, minced
- 4 tablespoons minced fresh chives
- 2 tablespoons minced fresh tarragon
- 2 tablespoons minced fresh parsley
- Salt and freshly ground black pepper
- Lemon wedges, for serving

[*Chionoecetes*, which means "snow," is a genus of crabs living in the cold waters of northern oceans, and includes Queen Crab, Spider Crab, and Tanner Crab.]

Bring a pot of water to a boil. Boil the crab legs, about 5 minutes, or more if they are very big. Remove a leg and crack it open: If the meat is opaque throughout, the crab is done. Remove the crab legs from the pot. Let cool slightly and remove the meat from the shells. Set aside.

In a medium frying pan, melt the butter over medium heat. Add the garlic and cook just until it becomes fragrant, but before it has browned. Stir in the herbs. Remove from the heat, add the crab meat, and season to taste with salt and pepper. Toss to coat well with the butter sauce. Serve with lemon wedges.

SAUTÉED SOFT-SHELL CRABS

PREPARATION TIME: 15 MINUTES
COOKING TIME: 10 MINUTES
SERVES: 4

- 4 live soft-shell crabs
- ¾ cup (100 g) all-purpose (plain) flour
- ½ teaspoon salt
- Pinch of cayenne pepper
- 1 egg
- 4 tablespoons (60 g) butter

[Considered quintessential Maryland, this dish is also commonly found in Delaware and throughout the mid-Atlantic. Soft-shell crabs aren't a species but rather a stage: blue crabs just after molting. Caught in late spring at the precise moment before their new shells harden, they can be eaten whole, "soft shell" and all. Once a crab has molted, it must be kept out of the water to prevent its shell from hardening, so it should be eaten as soon as possible. Soft-shell crabs are often served in sandwiches and seasoned with Old Bay, a blend of herbs and spices made in the Chesapeake Bay and liberally applied to area seafood.]

Make sure the crabs are very fresh and alive. They should smell clean and be lively. Using sharp kitchen shears, cut the face off the crab by cutting just behind the eyes and the mouth, cutting off a strip about ¼ inch (6 mm). Remove the gills by lifting a corner of the top shell and ripping the gills out at the base. Turn the crab over and remove the apron by pulling it from the base.

In a shallow bowl, mix the flour, salt, and cayenne. Set up a dredging station: in a second bowl, beat the egg. Dip each crab first in the flour, then egg, then the flour again.

In a frying pan, melt the butter over medium-high heat. When the butter has melted and the pan is very hot, use long tongs to add the crabs. They will spatter as they cook. Cook until golden brown, about 4 minutes per side. Serve hot.

MARYLAND-STYLE CRAB CAKES

PREPARATION TIME: 10 MINUTES,
   PLUS CHILLING TIME
COOKING TIME: 15 MINUTES
SERVES: 4

- 1 lb (455 g) lump crabmeat, picked over for shells and cartilage
- 2 slices white bread, crusts removed
- 1 egg, beaten
- 2 tablespoons minced white onion
- 2 teaspoons Dijon mustard
- 1 teaspoon Worcestershire sauce
- 2 teaspoons Old Bay seasoning
- 4 tablespoons (60 grams) butter
- Lemon wedges, for serving
- Parsley, for serving

Break the crabmeat into smaller pieces and place in a large bowl. Tear the bread into small pieces and add to the crab. Stir in the beaten egg. Add the onion, mustard, Worcestershire sauce, and Old Bay. Cover and refrigerate for 1 hour to chill.

Form the mixture into 8 small patties. Preheat a large frying pan over medium-high heat. Add the butter and let melt, then add the crab cakes and cook until light golden brown on the bottom, about 5 minutes. Flip gently and cook until the other side is done, about 5 minutes. Serve with lemon wedges and parsley.

STUFFED DEVILED CRABS

PREPARATION TIME: 30 MINUTES
COOKING TIME: 25 MINUTES
SERVES: 3–4

- 1 lb (455 g) lump crabmeat, picked over for shells and cartilage
- 1 cup (115 g) panko breadcrumbs
- 1 tablespoon chopped fresh parsley
- 2 teaspoons smoked paprika
- 1 teaspoon mustard powder
- 1 teaspoon salt
- ¼ cup (40 g) finely chopped onion
- 2 tablespoons minced jalapeño pepper
- 1 teaspoon minced garlic
- 4 tablespoons (60 g) butter, melted
- ¼ cup (60 ml) milk
- 2 tablespoons dry sherry
- 6–8 cleaned crab shells, for serving (or ramekins)
- ⅓ cup (30 g) freshly grated Parmesan cheese

Preheat the oven to 375°F (190°C/Gas Mark 5).

In a large bowl, combine the crabmeat, panko, parsley, smoked paprika, mustard powder, salt, onion, jalapeño, garlic, melted butter, milk, and sherry. Gently toss to combine well. Let rest for 10 minutes.

Loosely fill the crab shells with the mixture and place on a rimmed baking sheet. Top evenly with the Parmesan. Bake until hot and golden, 20–25 minutes. Serve hot.

MARYLAND-STYLE CRAB CAKES

NORFOLK-STYLE CRABMEAT

PREPARATION TIME: 5 MINUTES
COOKING TIME: 5 MINUTES
SERVES: 4

- 4 tablespoons (60 g) butter
- 1 lb (455 g) lump crabmeat, picked over for shells and cartilage
- 1 tablespoon tarragon vinegar, lemon juice, or white wine vinegar
- ½ teaspoon sea salt
- ¼ teaspoon freshly ground black pepper
- Hot sauce
- Cooked white rice or buttered toast, for serving
- Paprika, for garnish
- Vinegar, for serving

In a frying pan, melt the butter over medium heat. Add the crabmeat, vinegar, salt, and pepper. Cook until the crab is hot. Season to taste with hot sauce.

To serve with rice: Plate the rice on a large platter and top with the crab. To serve with toast: Spoon a heaping spoonful of crab onto each slice. Sprinkle with paprika. Serve with more hot sauce or vinegar on the side.

CRAB IMPERIAL

PREPARATION TIME: 10 MINUTES
COOKING TIME: 45 MINUTES
SERVES: 4

- 5 tablespoons (75 g) butter
- 4 tablespoons all-purpose (plain) flour
- 2 cups (475 ml) half-and-half (single cream)
- 1 lb (455 g) jumbo lump crabmeat, picked over for shells and cartilage
- 1 cup (50 g) fresh breadcrumbs
- ½ cup (50 g) diced pimientos
- 3 tablespoons finely chopped shallot
- 2 tablespoons finely chopped fresh parsley, plus more for garnish
- 2 tablespoons fresh lemon juice
- 2 teaspoons Worcestershire sauce
- 1 teaspoon mustard powder
- ½ teaspoon crushed chili flakes
- ¾ teaspoon salt
- ½ teaspoon freshly ground black pepper
- 1 tablespoon olive oil

[This creamy casserole is made with meat from local blue crabs. The flavorings and fillings can vary, but the dish always has a crumb (cracker or bread) topping that gets browned in the oven. To elevate the dish, the filling can be baked inside cleaned blue crab shells.]

Preheat the oven to 375°F (190°C/Gas Mark 5). Grease an 8-inch (20 cm) square baking dish with 1 tablespoon (15 g) of the butter.

In a medium saucepan, melt the remaining 4 tablespoons (60 g) butter. Whisk in the flour and cook until golden, 2–3 minutes. Slowly whisk in the half-and-half (single cream), bring to a simmer, and cook until thickened, 8–10 minutes. Remove from the heat and gently stir in the crabmeat, half of the breadcrumbs, the pimientos, shallot, 2 tablespoons parsley, lemon juice, Worcestershire sauce, mustard powder, chili flakes, salt, and pepper.

Spoon the crab mixture into the baking dish. In a small bowl, mix together the remaining breadcrumbs and the olive oil. Distribute evenly over the crab mixture. Bake until lightly browned and bubbling in the center, 25–30 minutes. Garnish with parsley and serve.

CRAWFISH BOIL

PREPARATION TIME: 25 MINUTES
COOKING TIME: 1 HOUR 10 MINUTES
SERVES: 8–10

- 3 packets (4 oz/115 g each) seafood boil seasoning, such as Zatarain's Crawfish, Shrimp, and Crab Boil
- 3 cups (400 g) kosher (coarse) salt
- ½ cup (95 g) Creole seasoning, plus more to taste
- 8 bay leaves
- 8 lemons, halved
- 4 heads garlic, halved horizontally through the equator
- 8 small yellow onions, halved
- 4 lb (1.8 kg) small red potatoes, halved
- 20 lb (9 kg) crawfish, cleaned
- 8 ears of corn, husked and quartered crosswise
- Hot sauce and ice-cold beer, for serving (optional)

[New Englanders have their clam bakes and Louisianans have their crawfish boils. Both call for cooking the namesake seafood with potatoes and corn on the cob.]

In a 16-gallon (60-liter) stockpot over an outdoor gas burner, bring 9–10 gallons (34–38 liters) water to a rolling boil. (Start early! This could take 30–40 minutes.) Add the seafood boil seasoning, salt, Creole seasoning, bay leaves, lemons, garlic, and onions. Stir to dissolve the seasonings. Add the potatoes, return to a boil, and cook for 20 minutes. Add the crawfish and simmer for 5 minutes. Add the corn and simmer for 5 minutes. (If you lose your boil at any point, cover with a lid to return it to a simmer.)

Line 2 large baking sheets (or a long table) with newspaper or parchment paper. Drain the mixture in a large colander set in the sink, or use a large spider/skimmer or slotted spoon to the remove crawfish and vegetables from the water. Dump everything onto the newspaper or parchment. Season to taste with additional Creole seasoning. Serve with hot sauce and ice-cold beer, if desired.

BOILED LOBSTER

COOKING TIME: 30 MINUTES
SERVES: AS MANY AS YOU'D LIKE

Per person:
- Seawater or sea salt
- 1 live lobster (1½ lb/680 g)
- Melted butter and lemon wedges, for serving (optional)

[Most Mainers keep a tool kit for cracking lobster shells and digging out each morsel of succulent meat.]

If you can obtain fresh seawater, bring a large pot of it to a boil; otherwise use sea salt to make salty water. Plunge the live lobster into the boiling water, bring the water back to a boil, and cook for roughly 8 minutes per pound (455 g). An instant-read thermometer, inserted between the body and tail joint, should read 140°F (60°C).

Remove the lobster and let it sit for 5 minutes before serving. Serve with melted butter and lemon wedges, if desired.

CRAWFISH ÉTOUFFÉE

PREPARATION TIME: 15 MINUTES
COOKING TIME: 1 HOUR, INCLUDES
    COOKING RICE
SERVES: 6–8

- ½ cup (120 ml) vegetable oil
- 1 cup (130 g) all-purpose (plain) flour
- 3 stalks celery, chopped
- 1 green bell pepper, chopped
- 1 small yellow onion, chopped
- 3 cloves garlic, chopped
- 1 jalapeño pepper, chopped and seeded
- 1 tablespoon paprika
- 2 teaspoons kosher (coarse) salt
- 1 teaspoon freshly ground black pepper
- 1 teaspoon dried oregano
- ½ teaspoon cayenne pepper
- 2 cups (475 ml) chicken stock
- 2 lb (910 g) peeled crawfish tails or medium shrimp (prawns), peeled and deveined
- 4 tablespoons chopped fresh parsley
- 3 tablespoons fresh lemon juice
- 1 tablespoon Worcestershire sauce
- 1 tablespoon Tabasco-style hot sauce, plus more for serving
- 9 cups cooked white rice (from 3 cups/600 g uncooked)
- ½ cup (50 g) thinly sliced scallions (spring onions)

[This Cajun seafood dish gets its name from the French verb *étouffer*, which means "to smother". The crawfish are cooked, or "smothered," in a covered pot with the simmering sauce at the end of the cooking time. You can use shrimp instead, just cook until they turn pink and are opaque throughout, 3–5 minutes.]

In a large soup pot, heat the oil over medium-high heat. Add the flour and stir well to combine. Reduce the heat to medium-low and cook, stirring frequently, until the roux is medium brown, 15–20 minutes. Add the celery, bell pepper, and onion. Cook, stirring, until the vegetables are tender, about 10 minutes. Add the garlic, jalapeño, paprika, salt, black pepper, oregano, and cayenne. Cook for 2 minutes.

Meanwhile, in a saucepan, heat the stock to simmering.

Stirring constantly, slowly add the hot stock to the pot. Return to a simmer over medium-high heat. Stir in the crawfish, parsley, lemon juice, Worcestershire sauce, and hot sauce. Cook for 2–3 minutes to warm through. Serve on the hot rice, topped with the scallions (spring onions), with hot sauce on the side.

LOBSTER NEWBERG

PREPARATION TIME: 10 MINUTES
COOKING TIME: 15 MINUTES
SERVES: 2–4

- 4 tablespoons (60 g) butter
- 2 cups (300 g) cubed (½ inch/1.25 cm) cooked lobster
- ½ teaspoon salt
- ¼ teaspoon cayenne pepper
- 1 cup (240 ml) heavy (whipping) cream
- 3 egg yolks
- ¼ cup (60 ml) Cognac or sherry
- Toasted bread, for serving

In a large frying pan, melt the butter over medium-low heat. Add the lobster and cook, stirring, for 2 minutes. Add the salt, cayenne, and cream. Cook, stirring, until heated through. In a bowl, whisk the egg yolks. Whisk a large spoonful of the hot cream into the egg yolks, then whisk the warmed yolks back into the cream and lobster. Reduce the heat, add the Cognac or sherry, and cook, stirring constantly, until thickened, about 12 minutes. Do not let boil. Serve hot, with toast.

FRIED GULF SHRIMP

PREPARATION TIME: 30 MINUTES
COOKING TIME: 25 MINUTES
SERVES: 6

- 2 lb (910 g) large (16–20) shrimp (prawns), peeled and deveined
- 2 cups (475 ml) buttermilk
- 2 tablespoons Louisiana hot sauce, such as Crystal
- 1½ cups (195 g) finely ground cornmeal
- 1 cup (130 g) all-purpose (plain) flour
- 1½ tablespoons onion powder
- 1½ tablespoons garlic powder
- 1½ teaspoons smoked paprika
- ⅛ teaspoon cayenne pepper
- Salt
- Peanut (groundnut) or vegetable oil, for deep-frying

In a large bowl, combine the shrimp (prawns), buttermilk, and hot sauce. In a shallow dish, whisk together the cornmeal, flour, onion powder, garlic powder, smoked paprika, cayenne, and 1 teaspoon salt.

Pour 3–4 inches (7.5–10 cm) oil into a large heavy pot or deep-fryer and heat to 375°F (190°C).

Working in batches, remove a few shrimp (prawns) from the buttermilk, toss in the seasoned cornmeal, and fry until golden and crispy, about 4 minutes. Drain on paper towels. Repeat with remaining shrimp. Season to taste with salt.

SHRIMP AND GRITS

PREPARATION TIME: 40 MINUTES
COOKING TIME: 55 MINUTES
SERVES: 4–6

- 2 cups (475 ml) milk
- 1 cup (140 g) coarsely ground grits
- Salt and freshly ground black pepper
- 2 tablespoons all-purpose (plain) flour
- 1½ cups (355 ml) chicken stock
- 6 slices bacon (streaky)
- 2¼ cups (335 g) chopped red bell pepper
- 1¼ cups (200 g) chopped yellow onion
- 3 cloves garlic, minced
- 1½ lb (680 g) large (26–30) shrimp (prawns), peeled and deveined
- ¼ teaspoon cayenne pepper
- 1 tablespoon Worcestershire sauce
- 2 tablespoons fresh lemon juice
- 2 tablespoons (30 g) butter
- 1 cup (115 g) grated sharp cheddar cheese
- 4 tablespoons sliced scallions (spring onions)

In a medium saucepan, whisk well to combine 3 cups (710 ml) water, the milk, and grits. Bring to a boil over medium-high heat. Reduce the heat to low and simmer, stirring frequently, until the grits are thickened and tender, 25–30 minutes. Season to taste with salt and pepper. Remove from the heat and cover to keep warm.

In a separate medium bowl, whisk together the flour and chicken stock. Set aside.

In a large frying pan, cook the bacon over medium heat until browned, 7–8 minutes. Drain on paper towels. Crumble and set aside. Add the bell pepper, onion, and garlic to the bacon fat in the pan and cook until the onion is softened and translucent, 5–7 minutes. Add the shrimp (prawns) and season with ½ teaspoon salt and the cayenne. Cook until the shrimp turn pink, 2–3 minutes, turning once. Remove from the pan.

Whisk the flour-stock mixture into the pan, increase the heat to medium-high, and simmer until thickened slightly, 2–3 minutes. Return the bacon and shrimp to warm through. Reduce the heat to low and stir in the Worcestershire sauce, lemon juice, and butter. Remove from the heat and cover to keep warm.

Mix the cheddar into the grits until melted. Serve the grits topped with the shrimp mixture and garnished with scallions (spring onions).

PREPARATION TIME: 20 MINUTES,
  PLUS NOODLE SOAKING TIME
COOKING TIME: 15 MINUTES
SERVES: 4

- ½ lb (225 g) rice noodles
- 3 tablespoons fish sauce
- 3 tablespoons tamarind juice
- 2 tablespoons palm sugar
- 4 tablespoons peanut (groundnut) oil
- ½ lb (225 g) shrimp (prawns), peeled, deveined, and halved lengthwise
- ½ lb (225 g) extra-firm tofu, julienned
- 5 cloves garlic, minced
- 3 tablespoons dried shrimp
- 2 teaspoons crushed chili flakes, or more to taste
- 3 cups (300 g) fresh bean sprouts
- 3 eggs
- ½ cup (75 g) chopped unsalted roasted peanuts
- Cilantro (coriander) leaves, sliced scallions (spring onions), and lime wedges, for serving

[This noodle dish has become the most popular order at casual Thai restaurants across the country.]

Place the rice noodles in a large bowl and cover with lukewarm water. Soak until they have softened but are still firm, 40 minutes to 1 hour. Drain well.

In a small bowl, stir together the fish sauce, tamarind juice, and palm sugar. Set aside.

In a wok, heat 2 tablespoons of the peanut oil over high heat. Add the shrimp (prawns) and cook, stirring, until they are just cooked through and have turned pink, about 4 minutes. Remove and set aside.

Add 1 tablespoon of the oil to the wok. Stir in the tofu and fry, stirring, until golden, about 2 minutes. Add the garlic and cook, stirring, for 1 minute. Add the dried shrimp and cook for 30 seconds. Stir in the chili flakes. Add one-third of the bean sprouts and the drained noodles and return the shrimp to the pan. Cook, stirring, until the noodles have softened even more and everything is steaming hot.

Push everything to one side and add the remaining 1 tablespoon peanut oil, then the eggs, one at a time. Scramble the eggs, then chop them with a spoon and distribute evenly. Add the reserved sauce, stir well, and cook to heat through.

Divide among 4 plates and top with the remaining bean sprouts and the peanuts. Serve with cilantro (coriander) leaves, scallions (spring onions), and lime on the side .

ROAST QUAIL
WITH WILD JUNIPER RUB

PREPARATION TIME: 10 MINUTES,
   PLUS 24 HOURS MARINATING TIME
COOKING TIME: 25 MINUTES
SERVES: 4

- 4 tablespoons fresh ripe juniper berries
- ½ cup (15 g) loosely packed fresh oregano leaves (preferably Mexican)
- 3 tablespoons corn oil
- 2 tablespoons chili powder
- 2 teaspoons unsweetened cocoa powder
- 1 teaspoon salt
- 4 cloves garlic, peeled
- 8 quail

[Cedar berry, also known as one-seed juniper, grows wild in the Southwest, especially New Mexico. The berries are edible in the fall, when they become ripe and purple. Native Americans have used one-seed juniper as a food, an aromatic, and a medicine and it plays a part in some of their ceremonies. The tree gum is also chewed as a delicacy. It is typically paired with game, but is versatile and also works well in baked goods and sweet dishes.]

Grind the juniper berries in a blender. Add 3 tablespoons water, the oregano, oil, chili powder, cocoa powder, salt, and garlic and grind to a paste. Scrape the paste out of the blender and immediately wipe the blades of the blender with a warm, damp cloth to remove the juniper resin.

Rub the paste onto the skins of the quail and inside their cavities. Cover and refrigerate at least 1 hour and up to 24 hours.

Preheat the oven to 425°F (220°C/Gas Mark 7).

Place the quail in a roasting pan and roast until the skin is turning dark and the juice runs clear when the thigh meat is pierced with a skewer or sharp knife, 20–25 minutes.

FRIED RABBIT

PREPARATION TIME: 15 MINUTES,
  PLUS MARINATING TIME
COOKING TIME: 40 MINUTES
SERVES: 4

- 2 rabbits, cut into pieces
- 2 cups (475 ml) buttermilk
- 1 teaspoon dried thyme
- 1 teaspoon dried tarragon
- 1½ cups (195 g) all-purpose (plain) flour
- 2 teaspoons paprika
- 2 teaspoons salt
- ½ teaspoon freshly ground black pepper
- Vegetable oil, for deep-frying

[Wild rabbit has long been a staple on southern tables. If you don't want to hunt your own, you can buy the meat at many fine butcher shops.]

Place the rabbit pieces in a large bowl. Add the buttermilk, thyme, and tarragon and mix well to coat. Cover and refrigerate for at least 4 hours.

Drain the rabbit in a colander. In a large bowl, whisk together the flour, paprika, salt, and pepper. Dredge the rabbit in the flour mixture and set aside.

Pour 1–2 inches (2.5–5 cm) oil into a large heavy frying pan and heat to 325°F (160°C). Working in batches (do not crowd the pan), fry until the rabbit is golden brown and the internal temperature reads 160°F (71°C), 8–10 minutes per side. Drain on paper towels. Serve hot.

JALISCO-STYLE GOAT (BIRRIA)

PREPARATION TIME: 10 MINUTES
COOKING TIME: 5 HOURS IN THE SLOW
  COOKER
SERVES: 6

- 3 lb (1.4 kg) bone-in goat shoulder
- Salt and freshly ground black pepper
- 1 tablespoon vegetable oil
- 1 medium white onion, diced
- 7–8 cloves garlic, peeled but whole
- ¼ cup (25 g) ancho chili powder
- 2 teaspoons ground cumin
- 1 teaspoon ground cinnamon
- 2 teaspoons dried oregano
- ¼ cup (60 ml) cider vinegar
- 1 can (14.5 oz/410 g) diced (chopped) tomatoes
- Chopped white onion, cilantro (coriander) leaves, lime wedges, for serving
- Corn tortillas, for serving

[In Jalisco, Mexico, birria is often cooked in an open fire pit, in quantities great enough to feed large groups of people. Birria can be served soupy or dry with a bowl of broth on the side.]

Season the goat shoulder generously with salt and pepper. In a large cast-iron skillet, heat the vegetable oil over high heat to the smoking point. Add the goat shoulder and cook until deeply browned and getting a bit charred on the edges, about 5 minutes. Flip and brown the other side. Remove the shoulder to a plate. Add the onion and garlic and cook, stirring occasionally, to char, about 3 minutes. Remove from the heat, add ½ cup (120 ml) water, and scrape up all of the browned bits from the pan.

Place the meat, onion, and garlic in a slow cooker or a 3-quart (3 liter) Dutch oven (casserole). Add 1½ quarts (1.4 liters) water, or more (enough to cover the shoulder), the chili powder, cumin, cinnamon, oregano, vinegar, and tomatoes. Cover and slow-cook until the shoulder is extremely tender and falling off the bone, 5 hours in the slow cooker on high. Serve with chopped onion, cilantro (coriander) leaves, lime wedges, and corn tortillas.

JALISCO-STYLE GOAT (BIRRIA)

PAN-SEARED BISON FILLETS

PREPARATION TIME: 5 MINUTES
COOKING TIME: 25 MINUTES
SERVES: 4

- 4 bison fillets (also called filet mignon or tenderloin), 6 oz (170 g) each
- Salt and freshly ground black pepper
- Canola (rapeseed) oil
- 4 tablespoons (60 g) butter

[Bison are so important to North Dakota culture that they're featured on the state quarter. They're also delicious. Take care not to overcook, which can cause the lean meat to become tough — rare to medium-rare is the perfect way to serve these steaks.]

Preheat the oven to 400°F (200°C/Gas Mark 6).

Season the fillets with salt and pepper. In a cast-iron skillet, heat 2 tablespoons oil over high heat until shimmering. Add half of the filets to the pan and sear on all sides, about 5 minutes. Remove the pan from the heat and add half of the butter. Baste the fillets with the melted butter and transfer from the heat to an ovenproof dish. Repeat with the remaining steaks. Transfer the meat to the oven and roast until the internal temperature reads 115°F (46°C), 4–5 minutes. Let the steaks rest for at least 10 minutes before slicing.

SMOKY CHIPOTLE BISON POT ROAST

PREPARATION TIME: 25 MINUTES
COOKING TIME: 4 HOURS 30 MINUTES
SERVES: 6

- 3½–4 lb (1.6–1.8 kg) bison shoulder roast or boneless chuck roast
- Salt and freshly ground black pepper
- 3 tablespoons vegetable oil
- 1 large onion, finely diced
- 2 medium carrots, finely diced
- 2 stalks celery, finely diced
- 2 cloves garlic, minced
- 1 tablespoon tomato paste (purée)
- 2 canned chipotle peppers in adobo sauce, minced
- 1 cup (240 ml) red wine
- 3 cups (710 ml) beef stock

[Bison are essential to the West, in both fact and fable. Millions of the great beasts roamed North America into the early 19th century — until an estimated 50 million were used for their meat or hides. This dish is best made a day ahead: Refrigerate the roast in its sauce. Reheat for 1 hour and 15 minutes, covered, in a 300°F (150°C/Gas Mark 2) oven.]

Preheat the oven to 275°F (140°C/Gas Mark 1).

Season the roast with salt and pepper. In a Dutch oven (casserole), heat the oil over medium-high heat. Add the roast and brown on all sides, 8–10 minutes. Remove the roast and set aside.

Add the onion, carrots, and celery and cook, stirring, until the vegetables have softened, about 7 minutes. Stir in the garlic, tomato paste (purée), chipotle peppers, wine, and beef stock and bring to a boil. Return the roast to the pan, cover, transfer to the oven, and roast for about 4 hours, until tender.

Transfer the roast to a carving board and let rest for 10 minutes before slicing. Serve with the roasted vegetables.

ANTELOPE MEDALLIONS WITH WHITE WINE AND MUSTARD SAUCE

PREPARATION TIME: 10 MINUTES
COOKING TIME: 20 MINUTES
SERVES: 4

- 1½–2 lb (680–910 g) antelope loin
- Salt and freshly ground black pepper
- 1 tablespoon olive oil
- 4 tablespoons (60 g) butter
- 2 large shallots, minced
- 1 teaspoon minced fresh thyme
- ½ cup (120 ml) white wine
- ½ cup (120 ml) chicken stock
- 1 tablespoon Dijon (French) mustard
- 2 tablespoons finely chopped fresh parsley

[The American pronghorn antelope was an essential source of food when the West was wild. At the turn of the 20th century, their extinction loomed, but habitat preservation and hunting restrictions allowed the herds to recover, and until recently they outnumbered people in many western states. They are now legally hunted again.]

Remove the silverskin from the loin. Slice the loin across the grain into ¾-inch (2 cm) thick medallions. Season with salt and pepper and set aside.

In a large frying pan, heat the oil over medium-high heat. When the pan is very hot, add the medallions and cook until browned, about 3 minutes. Flip and cook until almost medium-rare, about 4 minutes (the internal temperature should read 125°F/52°C but will increase as the medallions rest). Transfer the medallions to a plate, very loosely tent with foil, and let rest while the sauce is cooking.

Add 1 tablespoon (15 g) of the butter to the pan and reduce the heat to medium. Add the shallots and cook, stirring constantly, until softened, about 3 minutes. Add the thyme and wine. Increase the heat to high and boil, scraping the browned bits on the bottom of the pan. Cook until the wine is syrupy, about 4 minutes. Add the stock and boil again until the sauce has reduced by one-third, about 3 minutes. Whisk in the mustard until combined; then whisk in the remaining 3 tablespoons (45 g) butter, 1 tablespoon at a time, and stir in parsley. Pour over the medallions and serve.

ELK BURGUNDY

PREPARATION TIME: 20 MINUTES
COOKING TIME: 3 HOURS 20 MINUTES
SERVES: 4–6

- ½ cup (65 g) all-purpose (plain) flour
- Salt and freshly ground black pepper
- 2 lb (910 g) elk stew meat, cut into cubes
- 6 slices thick-cut bacon (streaky), coarsely chopped
- 3 tablespoons (45 g) butter
- 3 cups (710 ml) red wine, preferably Burgundy
- 2 cups (475 ml) beef stock
- 1 can (6 oz/170 g) tomato paste (purée)
- 4 cloves garlic, minced
- 1 bouquet garni: 2–3 sprigs each parsley, thyme, and rosemary, tied together with kitchen twine
- 1 cup (180 g) pearl onions, peeled
- 1 lb (455 g) white mushrooms, halved or quartered

[Serve over mashed potatoes or polenta.]

Preheat the oven to 350°F (180°C/Gas Mark 4).

Season the flour with salt and pepper. Toss the stew meat with the seasoned flour and set aside.

In a Dutch oven (casserole), cook the bacon over medium-high heat until lightly browned, about 6 minutes. Remove with a slotted spoon and set aside. Melt the butter in the bacon fat. Add the elk meat and brown all over, about 8 minutes. Stir in the wine and beef stock. Bring to a boil, then stir in the tomato paste (purée) and garlic. Add the bouquet garni, cover, and transfer to the oven. Bake for 2 hours. Uncover, add the onions, bacon, and mushrooms, and cook uncovered until the sauce has reduced and the elk is very tender, about 1 hour.

VENISON STEW WITH WILD RICE

PREPARATION TIME: 15 MINUTES
COOKING TIME: 2 HOURS 30 MINUTES
SERVES: 4–6

- 2 lb (910 g) venison chuck roast, cut into 1-inch (2.5 cm) pieces
- Salt and freshly ground black pepper
- 2 tablespoons olive oil
- 1 cup (240 ml) port wine
- 6 cups (1.4 liters) beef stock
- 1 medium onion, chopped
- 2 carrots, peeled and chopped
- 3 stalks celery, chopped
- 1 teaspoon minced fresh thyme
- 2 bay leaves
- 1 cup (180 g) wild rice, rinsed

Preheat the oven to 300°F (150°C/Gas Mark 2).

Season the venison with salt and pepper. In a heavy pot, heat the oil over medium-high heat. Add the venison and brown, about 8 minutes. Add the port and bring to a boil. Add 2 cups (475 ml) of the beef stock and stir in the onion, carrots, celery, thyme, and bay leaves. Bring to a boil, then reduce the heat to a simmer and cook until the meat is tender, about 1½ hours.

Meanwhile, in a medium saucepan, combine the wild rice and remaining 4 cups (950 ml) beef stock. Bring to a boil over high heat, then reduce to a simmer, cover, and cook until tender, about 45 minutes.

When the stew meat is tender, stir the rice into the pot and season to taste with salt and pepper.

HUNGARIAN GOULASH

PREPARATION TIME: 15 MINUTES
COOKING TIME: 1 HOUR 45 MINUTES
SERVES: 6

- 2 tablespoons (30 g) butter
- 2 lb (910 g) beef chuck or round, cut into 1-inch (2.5 cm) cubes
- 1 large onion, chopped
- 2 cloves garlic, minced
- 1 teaspoon salt
- 1 tablespoon Hungarian sweet paprika
- 2 tablespoons tomato paste (purée)
- 2 cups (475 ml) beef stock
- ½ cup (120 ml) sour cream
- Freshly cooked egg noodles, for serving

In a heavy-bottomed pot, melt the butter over medium-high heat. Add the meat and brown to a deep caramel color, about 10 minutes. Using a slotted spoon, remove the meat and set aside.

Add the onion to the pot and cook, stirring, for 2–3 minutes. Stir in the garlic, salt, paprika, and tomato paste (purée). Return the meat to the pan, add the beef stock, and bring to a boil. Cover, reduce to a simmer, and cook until the meat is tender, about 1½ hours. Remove from the heat and stir in the sour cream. Serve over freshly cooked egg noodles.

AMERICAN-STYLE GOULASH

PREPARATION TIME: 10 MINUTES
COOKING TIME: 35 MINUTES
SERVES: 8

- 1 tablespoon (15 g) butter
- 1 lb (455 g) ground (minced) beef
- 1 large onion, chopped
- 1 green bell pepper, diced
- 2 cloves garlic, minced
- ½ tablespoon Hungarian sweet paprika
- 1 can (28 oz/795 g) diced (chopped) tomatoes
- 1 can (15 oz/425 g) tomato sauce or passata
- Salt and freshly ground black pepper
- 1 lb (455 g) elbow macaroni
- 1 cup (115 g) shredded cheddar or Colby cheese

[A descendant of the Hungarian dish first brought to America by immigrants in the mid-19th century, this more assimilated version of goulash retains the beef and paprika of its culinary ancestor, now rounded out with plenty of tomato sauce and elbow macaroni.]

In a medium pot, melt the butter over high heat. Add the ground (minced) beef and cook, breaking it up with a wooden spoon, until browned, about 8 minutes. Add the onion and cook for a few minutes. Stir in the bell pepper, garlic, and paprika. Cook for a few more minutes, until the vegetables are slightly softened. Stir in the tomatoes and tomato sauce. Bring to a simmer and season to taste with salt and pepper. Reduce the heat and simmer gently while you cook the pasta.

In a large pot of boiling water, cook the macaroni to al dente, according to package directions. Drain and stir into the meat sauce. Serve sprinkled with the cheese.

GREEN GUMBO
(GUMBO Z'HERBES)

PREPARATION TIME: 25 MINUTES
COOKING TIME: 1 HOUR 50 MINUTES
SERVES: 8–10

- 3 lb (1.4 kg) greens
- Kosher (coarse) salt
- ½ cup (120 ml) peanut (groundnut) oil
- ½ cup (65 g) plus 2 tablespoons all-purpose (plain) flour
- 1 medium yellow onion, diced
- 1 large poblano pepper, diced
- 4 stalks celery, thinly sliced
- 4 cloves garlic, finely chopped
- 3 cups (710 ml) vegetable stock
- 1 tablespoon paprika
- 1 teaspoon cayenne pepper
- 1 teaspoon dried oregano
- 2 bay leaves
- ½ cup (50 g) thinly sliced scallions (spring onions)
- Freshly cooked white rice, for serving

[What was once a meat-free dish served during Lent is now a flavorful year-round riff that can include pork, poultry, and seafood. The gumbo gets its name from seven different types of leafy greens—for good luck—that are slow-cooked to melting tenderness. You can take your pick among collards, turnip greens, mustard greens, spinach, watercress, carrot tops, beet (beetroot) greens, radish tops, flat-leaf parsley, arugula, chicory, sorrel, romaine lettuce, dandelion greens, or pepper grass (an indigenous Louisiana green, used in Creole cooking).]

Rinse and trim the greens, removing any tough stems or thick center ribs. Soak or rinse the greens well to clean. Tear the greens into 3-inch (7.5 cm) pieces and place in a large Dutch oven (casserole) or pot. Add 2 cups (475 ml) water and season with 2 tablespoons salt. Bring to a simmer over medium-high heat, then cover, reduce the heat to medium-low, and cook, stirring occasionally, until very tender, 25–30 minutes. Add water by the ¼ cup (60 ml), if needed, to keep the greens moist.

Reserving the cooking liquid, drain the greens. When they are cool enough to handle, roughly chop the greens. Measure out 1 cup (240 ml) of the greens and transfer to a blender with ¼ cup (60 ml) the reserved cooking liquid. Purée until smooth. Set the chopped greens, puréed greens, and cooking liquid aside.

Heat a large Dutch oven (casserole) or heavy-bottomed pot over medium-low heat. Add the oil, then whisk in the flour. Reduce the heat to low and cook, stirring slowly but constantly, until the roux is medium brown, 15–20 minutes. Add the onion, poblano, and celery. Increase the heat to medium and cook, stirring frequently, until the vegetables are tender, 8–10 minutes.

Whisk in 1 cup (240 ml) of the reserved cooking liquid and the vegetable stock. Increase the heat to medium-high and bring the mixture to a simmer. Stir in the paprika, cayenne, oregano, and bay leaves and simmer, stirring often, until slightly thickened, about 15 minutes.

Discard the bay leaves. Stir in the chopped and puréed greens and simmer for 10 minutes to meld the flavors. Season with additional salt as desired. Serve over cooked white rice and garnish with the scallions (spring onions).

GREEN GUMBO (GUMBO Z'HERBES)

PREPARATION TIME: 30 MINUTES
COOKING TIME: 1 HOUR
SERVES: 8

For the chicken:
- 1 whole chicken (4–5 lb/1.8–2.3 kg)
- Salt and freshly ground black pepper
- 1 tablespoon olive oil
- 2 medium onions, chopped
- 3 cloves garlic, minced
- 6 cups (1.4 liters) chicken stock
- 3 stalks celery, cut into 1-inch (2.5 cm) chunks
- 4 medium carrots, cut into 1-inch (2.5 cm) chunks
- 2 teaspoons minced fresh thyme

For the dumplings:
- 2 cups (260 g) all-purpose (plain) flour
- 2 teaspoons baking powder
- ½ teaspoon baking soda (bicarbonate of soda)
- Pinch of salt
- 1 egg
- 6 tablespoons (85 g) butter, melted and cooled
- ¾ cup (180 ml) buttermilk
- 3 tablespoons chopped fresh parsley, for garnish

For the chicken: Quarter the chicken, cutting it into 2 breasts (with wing attached) and 2 legs (thigh and drumstick attached). Season the chicken quarters with salt and pepper. In a large pot, heat the oil until very hot and almost smoking. Add the chicken pieces, in batches if necessary, and cook until golden all over, about 10 minutes. Remove the chicken and set aside.

Add the onions to the drippings and cook, stirring, over medium heat until the onions are beginning to wilt, about 5 minutes. Stir in the garlic and return the chicken to the pan. Add the stock, bring to a boil, then add the celery, carrots, and thyme. Cover, reduce to a medium simmer, and cook until the juices run clear when the chicken is pierced to the bone, 20–30 minutes. The thighs and legs may need more cooking time than the breast, so as each piece is done, remove from the pot and set aside to cool. Leave the pot on a low simmer as you make the dumplings.

For the dumplings: In a medium bowl, whisk together the flour, baking powder, baking soda (bicarbonate of soda), and salt. In a large bowl, whisk together the egg, melted butter, and buttermilk. Stir the flour mixture into the buttermilk mixture. Do not overmix.

Return the pot to a boil. Spoon 8 mounds of batter onto the boiling liquid. Bring the liquid back up to a boil, reduce the heat to low, cover, and gently simmer the dumplings for 10 minutes.

Meanwhile, remove the chicken meat from the bones. Keep the meat in large chunks.

Stir the chicken gently into the pot and cook just to heat through. Garnish with the chopped parsley.

CHICKEN AND DUMPLINGS

CARNE GUISADA

PREPARATION TIME: 20 MINUTES
COOKING TIME: 2 HOURS 15 MINUTES
SERVES: 4–6

- 3 tablespoons olive oil
- 1 large onion, diced
- 1 large red bell pepper, diced
- 4 cloves garlic, minced
- ½ teaspoon ground coriander
- 1 tablespoon paprika
- ½ teaspoon cayenne pepper
- ½ teaspoon ground turmeric
- 2 lb (910 g) beef stew meat, cut into 1½–2-inch (4–5 cm) pieces
- ½ lb (225 g) chouriço
- 1 cup (240 ml) red wine
- 1 can (14.5 oz/410 g) stewed tomatoes
- 1 can (6 oz/170 g) tomato paste (purée)
- 2 bay leaves
- 8 medium potatoes, peeled and cubed
- Salt and freshly ground black pepper

[This Portuguese beef stew is a taste of home for Rhode Island's vibrant Portuguese community. Serve with Portuguese rolls and a dash of *molho picante* or Portuguese hot sauce.]

In a Dutch oven (casserole), heat the oil over medium heat. Add the onion, bell pepper, garlic, coriander, paprika, cayenne, and turmeric and cook, stirring, for 5 minutes. Add the beef and stir well. Slice the chouriço into ½ inch (1.25 cm) rounds and add it, the wine, 2 cups (475 ml) water, stewed tomatoes, tomato paste (purée), and bay leaves. Cover and simmer over low heat until the meat is tender, 1–1½ hours.

Add the potatoes, season to taste with salt and pepper, and cook uncovered until the potatoes are tender, 20–30 minutes.

CHILI COLORADO

PREPARATION TIME: 15 MINUTES,
   PLUS SOAKING TIME
COOKING TIME: 2 HOURS 25 MINUTES
SERVES: 6

- 6 cups (1.4 liters) chicken stock
- 6 dried ancho chilies
- 4 dried pasilla chilies
- 2 lb (910 g) beef stew meat or pork shoulder
- 1 teaspoon salt
- ½ teaspoon freshly ground black pepper
- 2 tablespoons olive oil
- 1 large onion, chopped
- 6 cloves garlic, minced
- 1 tablespoon ground cumin
- 2 teaspoons dried oregano
- 2 bay leaves
- Corn tortillas, chopped cilantro (coriander), and lime wedges, for serving

[This traditional Mexican dish of beef or pork is made with red chilies. The word *colorado* means "colored red" in Spanish, a reference to the finished sauce's deep rich reddish-brown hue.]

In a medium pot, bring 3 cups (710 ml) of the chicken stock to a boil. Stem and seed the chilies and add them to the stock. Cover, and remove from the heat. Set aside to soak for 30 minutes.

Cut the meat into 1-inch (2.5 cm) cubes. Season the meat with the salt and pepper. In a heavy pot, heat the oil over medium-high heat. Add the meat and brown, about 8 minutes. Stir in the onion and cook until softened, about 5 minutes. Add the garlic, cumin, oregano, and bay leaves. Stir in the remaining 3 cups (710 ml) chicken stock and bring to a boil, then reduce to simmer. Simmer uncovered for 1 hour.

Meanwhile, in a blender, purée the reconstituted chilies with the 3 cups (710 ml) chicken stock used to soak the chilies until smooth.

Stir the pepper purée into the simmering stew and cook until the meat is tender and the sauce has reduced, about 1 hour. Serve with tortillas, cilantro (coriander), and lime wedges on the side.

BURNT ENDS CHILI

PREPARATION TIME: 15 MINUTES
COOKING TIME: 2 HOURS 50 MINUTES
SERVES: 8

- 2 tablespoons oil
- 2 medium onions, diced
- 1 lb (455 g) ground (minced) beef
- 1 can (15 oz/425 g) black beans, rinsed and drained
- 1 can (15 oz/425 g) dark red kidney beans, rinsed and drained
- 2 cans (14.5 oz/410 g each) crushed (finely chopped) tomatoes
- 1 cup (240 ml) beef stock
- 2 cloves garlic, minced
- 1 tablespoon minced canned chipotle pepper in adobo sauce
- 1 tablespoon chili powder
- 1 tablespoon ground cumin
- 1 teaspoon cayenne powder
- 2 lb (910 g) sliced Kansas City–Style Barbecued Brisket and Burnt Ends (page 126)
- 3 tablespoons Kansas City–Style Barbecue Sauce (optional; page 463)
- Corn chips, sour cream, grated cheddar cheese, diced onions, and diced jalapeño peppers, for serving

[This is a delicious way to use burnt ends after making brisket. See page 126 for more about burnt ends and brisket.]

In a large Dutch oven (casserole), heat the oil over medium-high heat. Add the onions and cook, stirring, until softened, about 8 minutes. Add the ground (minced) beef and cook, breaking it up with a wooden spoon, until the beef is browned, about 10 minutes. Stir in the beans, tomatoes, beef stock, garlic, chipotle pepper, and spices. Bring to a boil, reduce the heat to low, and simmer for about 2 hours, until the juices are reduced.

Preheat a gas or charcoal grill (barbecue) to medium heat.

Place the sliced brisket in a shallow roasting pan and brush with the barbecue sauce. Place the pan on the grill, close the lid, and cook until the sauce is glistening and the edges of the beef are burnt, 20–30 minutes.

Add the burnt ends to the chili. Serve in bowls, topped with any or all of the condiments.

CHILI CON CARNE

PREPARATION TIME: 30 MINUTES
COOKING TIME: 2 HOURS
SERVES: 8

- 6 dried ancho or pasilla chilies
- 4 dried hot chilies, such as guajillo, árbol, or chipotle
- ½ lb (225 g) bacon (streaky), thinly sliced
- 2 medium white onions, chopped
- 4 large cloves garlic, minced
- 3 bay leaves, finely crumbled
- 4 teaspoons dried oregano
- 1 tablespoon paprika
- 1 teaspoon ground cumin
- 1 teaspoon freshly ground black pepper
- ½ teaspoon dried thyme
- 1 teaspoon salt
- 3 lb (1.4 kg) boneless beef chuck, cut into ½-inch (1.25 cm) cubes
- 3 tablespoons cornmeal
- 1¾ cups (415 ml) beef stock
- 1 can (28 oz/795 g) tomato purée (passata)
- Corn tortillas, for serving
- Grated cheddar cheese (optional)

[Classic Texas chili contains no beans. A meat-loving state, Texas has more cattle than any other state. In true Texas spirit, this recipe calls for three pounds (1.4 kg) of boneless chuck, but you could also use buffalo or venison.]

In a bowl of hot water, soak the dried chilies to soften, about 20 minutes. Drain. Discard the stems and seeds and coarsely chop.

Heat a Dutch oven (casserole) over medium heat. Add the bacon and cook until golden brown, about 8 minutes. Drain the bacon on paper towels. Add the chopped chilies, onions, garlic, bay leaves, oregano, paprika, cumin, black pepper, thyme, and salt to the pan and cook until the onions soften, about 10 minutes. Add the meat and cook, stirring, until well browned on all sides, about 6 minutes. Stir in the cornmeal. Add the stock, tomato purée (passata), cooked bacon, and 1 cup (240 ml) water and bring to a boil. Reduce the heat to low, cover, and simmer until the meat is tender, about 2 hours.

With a slotted spoon, remove the meat and set aside. Let the sauce cool, then purée it in a blender or food processor. Return the sauce and beef to the pan and mix well. Simmer for a few minutes and serve with corn tortillas.

CHILI CON CARNE

CINCINNATI CHILI

PREPARATION TIME: 10 MINUTES,
PLUS OVERNIGHT CHILLING
COOKING TIME: 2 HOURS 15 MINUTES
SERVES: 6

- 1 lb (455 g) ground (minced) beef
- 4 cups (950 ml) beef stock or water
- 2 bay leaves
- 1 tablespoon chili powder
- 2 teaspoons Worcestershire sauce
- 1 teaspoon ground cinnamon
- ½ teaspoon cayenne pepper
- ¼ teaspoon ground allspice
- ¼ teaspoon ground cloves
- 1 teaspoon salt
- 1 can (15 oz/425 g) tomato purée (passata)
- Cooked spaghetti, for serving
- Crushed oyster crackers, for topping
- Optional garnishes: grated cheddar cheese, chopped white onions, cooked kidney beans

[Called a chili, this is more of a soupy ground (minced) beef sauce seasoned with sweet and savory spices. Now a regional standby, the Cincinnati, Ohio dish was created in 1922 by Macedonian immigrant brothers and showcases a blend of spices that may include cinnamon, allspice, Worcestershire sauce, and sometimes chocolate. Many crown it with chopped onions, shredded cheese, kidney beans, and crushed oyster crackers. Serve it over spaghetti.]

In a large pot, combine the ground (minced) beef and beef stock. Bring to a boil over medium-high heat while simultaneously breaking apart the beef with a wooden spoon. Reduce the heat and simmer, continuing to break up the beef so that it is very fine. Cook for 20 minutes. Add the bay leaves, chili powder, Worcestershire sauce, cinnamon, cayenne, allspice, cloves, salt, and tomato purée (passata) and simmer, stirring occasionally, for 1½ hours. Remove from the heat, cover, and refrigerate overnight or longer.

Before serving, skim the fat from the top and discard. Reheat the chili. Sprinkle with oyster crackers and garnishes of choice after the chili is put atop the spaghetti.

BEEF TIPS WITH RICE AND GRAVY

PREPARATION TIME: 5 MINUTES
COOKING TIME: 1 HOUR 30 MINUTES
SERVES: 6

- 2 tablespoons vegetable oil or butter
- 2 medium onions, thinly sliced
- 3 lb (1.4 kg) beef sirloin tips, cut into 1-inch (2.5 cm) chunks
- Salt and freshly ground pepper
- 5 cups (1.2 liters) beef stock
- 3 tablespoons cornstarch (cornflour)
- 5 cups cooked white rice (from 1⅔ cups/335 g raw), for serving

[Arkansas is a leading producer of rice in America. Here a simple beef stew is served over top — feel free to swap in other cuts, just adjust the cooking time accordingly.]

In a large Dutch oven (casserole), heat the oil over medium-high heat. Add the onions and beef and season with salt and pepper. Cook, stirring frequently, until the beef is slightly browned and the onions have softened, about 10 minutes. Add the beef stock and bring to a boil. Reduce the heat, cover, and simmer until the beef is tender, about 45 minutes.

Place the cornstarch (cornflour) in a small bowl and stir in 3 tablespoons cold water. Add to the stew and cook, stirring constantly, until the stew has thickened, about 5 minutes. Adjust the seasoning and serve over the rice.

CINCINNATI CHILI

PHILADELPHIA PEPPER POT

PREPARATION TIME: 20 MINUTES
COOKING TIME: 2 HOURS 40 MINUTES
SERVES: 6

- 1½ lb (680 g) cleaned, precooked honeycomb tripe
- 5 slices bacon (streaky), diced
- 2 cloves garlic, minced
- 2 onions, chopped
- ½ teaspoon dried marjoram
- ¼ teaspoon dried thyme
- 2 bay leaves
- 3 whole cloves
- 3 teaspoons black peppercorns, coarsely ground
- 6 cups (1.4 liters) beef stock
- 2 stalks celery, diced
- 2 carrots, diced
- 1 large potato, peeled and diced
- Crusty bread, for serving

[This hearty stew of beef tripe and abundant black pepper is steeped in patriotic legend: Many say this economical, warming dish sustained the Continental Army through the punishingly cold winter of 1777–1778, playing a key role in its winning of the Revolutionary War.]

Place the tripe in a Dutch oven (casserole), cover with cold water, and simmer for 20 minutes. Drain, let cool, and chop into small pieces. Set aside.

In the same Dutch oven (casserole), cook the bacon over medium-high heat until the fat is rendered, about 5 minutes. Add the garlic and onions and continue to cook until the onion is soft, about 10 minutes. Add the marjoram, thyme, bay leaves, whole cloves, and peppercorns. Return the tripe to the pan and add the stock. Bring to a simmer and skim off any scum. Simmer gently, covered, for about 1 hour.

Add the celery, carrots, and potatoes and continue to cook, uncovered, for 30 minutes, until the potatoes are tender. Discard the bay leaves and cloves. Serve the stew with crusty bread.

SON-OF-A-GUN STEW

PREPARATION TIME: 30 MINUTES
COOKING TIME: 8 HOURS
SERVES: 10

- 3 lb (1.4 kg) beef offal, including heart and tongue, cut into bite-size pieces
- 1 lb (455 g) beef neck, cut into 1-inch (2.5 cm) pieces
- 1 lb (455 g) marrow gut, cut into ½-inch (1.25 cm) pieces
- ¼ lb (115 g) calves' liver, chopped
- 4 cloves garlic, chopped (optional)
- 4 jalapeño peppers (optional), chopped (seeded for less heat)
- 1 can (14.5 oz/410 g) diced (chopped) tomatoes
- Kosher (coarse) salt and freshly ground black pepper
- Hot sauce, for serving

[This is a classic from chuck wagon days, when a spicy beef stew was thrown together on the trail after butchering an animal. Cooks would toss various less-loved cuts into a pot, simmer for hours, and serve the results with an abundance of hot sauce.]

In a Dutch oven (casserole) or other large pot, combine all the meat. Add the garlic, jalapeños (if using), tomatoes, salt, pepper, and enough water to cover the meat. Bring to a boil, then reduce to a simmer and cook, occasionally skimming off any scum, until the meat is cooked through and tender, 6–8 hours. Serve with hot sauce.

PREPARATION TIME: 35 MINUTES
COOKING TIME: 3 HOURS 15 MINUTES
SERVES: 10–12

- 3 lb (1.4 kg) bone-in beef short ribs
- 3 lb (1.4 kg) bone-in, skin-on chicken thighs
- Salt and freshly ground black pepper
- 1–2 tablespoons vegetable oil
- 2 large onions, chopped
- 6 cloves garlic, chopped
- 10 cups (2.4 liters) chicken stock
- 1 tablespoon cider vinegar
- 3 large carrots, chopped
- 2 stalks celery, chopped
- 1 large rutabaga (swede), peeled and diced
- 3 large russet (baking) potatoes, peeled and diced
- 1 medium head cabbage, shredded
- 1 tablespoon minced fresh thyme
- 1 can (28 oz/795 g) diced (chopped) tomatoes
- 1 cup (135 g) green peas
- 1 cup (150 g) corn kernels
- 3 tablespoons minced fresh parsley
- 2 teaspoons grated lemon zest
- 1 tablespoon fresh lemon juice
- Salt and freshly ground black pepper

[The name refers to both the dish and the event in which giant batches of this meat and vegetable stew are made in special iron booyah kettles (some can hold more than 50 gallons [190 liters]). "Booyah!" is yelled when the stew is ready. It is served at community events throughout Wisconsin, Minnesota, and Michigan. This is often prepared in stages, with the meats cooked the night before and the vegetables added the next day.]

Season the beef and chicken with salt and pepper. In a large heavy-bottomed pot, heat 1 tablespoon oil over medium-high heat. Add the beef and cook until browned all over, about 10 minutes. Transfer the beef to a plate and set aside.

Add the remaining 1 tablespoon of vegetable oil to the pot (if needed), then add the chicken and brown all over, turning as necessary, about 10 minutes. Transfer the chicken to a plate.

Add the onions to the pot and cook, stirring, for 3 minutes. Add the garlic and cook for another minute. Stir in the chicken stock and vinegar, then return the browned beef and chicken. Bring to a boil, reduce the heat, cover, and simmer until the chicken is done, about 30 minutes.

Remove the chicken from the pot. When cool enough to handle, remove the skin and pull the meat from the bones (discard the skin and bones or save for stock). Cover the chicken meat and refrigerate.

Continue simmering the beef until it is tender and falling off the bone, about 1½ hours.

Transfer the beef to a plate. When cool enough to handle, remove the meat from the bones (discard the bones or save for stock).

Return the cooked beef to the broth. Add the carrots, celery, rutabaga (swede), and potatoes and return to a boil. Cook until the vegetables are just tender, about 20 minutes. Add the cabbage, thyme, and tomatoes and simmer until the cabbage is tender, about 15 minutes.

Stir the reserved chicken meat into the pot along with the peas, corn, parsley, lemon zest, and lemon juice. Season to taste with salt and pepper. Simmer the stew for 10 minutes more before serving.

KENTUCKY BURGOO

PREPARATION TIME: 30 MINUTES
COOKING TIME: 2 HOURS 40 MINUTES
SERVES: 6–8

- 2 lb (910 g) beef flank steak, cut into 2-inch (5 cm) chunks
- 1 lb (455 g) lamb or pork shoulder, cut into 2-inch (5 cm) chunks
- Salt and freshly ground black pepper
- 1 tablespoon olive oil
- 2 cups (480 ml) white wine
- 1 whole chicken (about 4 lb/1.8 kg), quartered
- 4 large dried chilies (negro or ancho)
- ½ lb (225 g) dried small white beans or small lima beans (butter beans), rinsed and picked over
- 2 cups (255 g) diced carrots
- 2 cups (290 g) corn kernels
- 2 cups (200 g) chopped okra
- 2 cups (320 g) diced onions
- 2 cups (300 g) diced potatoes
- 1 can (28 oz/794 g) diced (chopped) tomatoes
- 2 tablespoons cider vinegar
- 2 teaspoons chili powder
- Bread and hot sauce, for serving

[The ingredients in this hunters' stew can vary wildly. Traditionally, they included a combination of different game meats, such as venison and squirrel, but these days, beef and pork are common.]

Season the steak and lamb with salt and pepper. In a large heavy frying pan, heat the oil over medium-high heat. Working in batches, cook the meat until browned, about 15 minutes. Using a slotted spoon, transfer the meat to a large soup pot.

Deglaze the frying pan with 1 cup (240 ml) of the wine, scraping up all the browned bits. Add that liquid to the soup pot, along with the chicken quarters, chilies, beans, 10 cups (2.4 liters) water, and remaining 1 cup (240 ml) wine. Bring to a boil, reduce to a simmer, and cook until the meat and beans are tender, 1½–2 hours.

Add the cut-up vegetables, canned tomatoes, vinegar, and chili powder and simmer for another 30 minutes, until the vegetables are cooked through. Adjust the seasoning. Serve in bowls, with bread and hot sauce on the side.

PREPARATION TIME: 20 MINUTES
COOKING TIME: 2 HOURS 40 MINUTES
SERVES: 6–8

- Flour, for dredging
- Salt and freshly ground black pepper
- 2 lb (910 g) boneless pork shoulder, cut into 1½-inch (4 cm) cubes
- 4 tablespoons olive oil
- 1 large onion, chopped
- 4 stalks celery, chopped
- 2 carrots, peeled and chopped
- 1½ cups (355 ml) apple cider
- 2 tablespoons cider vinegar
- 1 cup (240 ml) chicken stock
- Bouquet garni: thyme, sage, bay leaf, and parsley tied with kitchen twine
- 3 medium potatoes, peeled and cut into 2-inch (5 cm) chunks
- 2 large crisp, slightly tart apples, peeled and cut into 2-inch (5 cm) chunks

[New England boasts some of the best apple orchards in the world, complete with many heirloom varieties. This recipe calls for crisp, slightly tart apples like Macouns, Granny Smiths, or Honeycrisps.]

Preheat the oven to 325°F (160°C/Gas Mark 3).

Season the flour with salt and pepper. Dredge the pork in the seasoned flour and set aside.

In a large Dutch oven, heat 3 tablespoons of the oil over very high heat. Add the pork and sear on all sides, about 10 minutes. Remove the meat and set aside.

Reduce the heat to medium and add the remaining 1 tablespoon oil. Add the onions, celery, and carrots and cook, stirring frequently, until softened, about 6 minutes. Add the apple cider and cider vinegar, increase the heat, and bring to a boil.

Add the chicken stock and herbs and return the pork to the pan. Bring to a boil, cover, and transfer to the oven. Bake for 1½ hours. Add the potatoes, re-cover, and cook for 30 minutes. Add the apples, re-cover, and cook until the apples, potatoes, and meat are fork-tender, another 15–20 minutes.

PORK POSOLE

PREPARATION TIME: 20 MINUTES,
 PLUS OVERNIGHT SOAKING TIME
COOKING TIME: 3 HOURS 25 MINUTES
SERVES: 8

- 1½ lb (680 g) dried posole
- 3 lb (1.4 kg) bone-in pork shoulder
- Salt and freshly ground black pepper
- Vegetable oil (optional)
- 7 whole cloves garlic
- 2 large onions, chopped
- 1 tablespoon dried oregano
- 2 teaspoons ground cumin
- 1 teaspoon cayenne pepper
- 12 Hatch green chilies, roasted and
  peeled (see page 86)
- ½ cup (20 g) chopped fresh cilantro
  (coriander), plus more for serving
- 2 tablespoons fresh lime juice
- Lime wedges and warm tortillas,
  for serving

[This pork posole recipe is in the New Mexican style, using green chilies. The dish can also be made with red chilies. Posole, or hominy, is large-kernel white corn soaked in a lime solution (made from limestone), then dehydrated.]

Rinse the posole until the water runs clear. Cover with cold water and soak for 8 hours or overnight.

If the pork is very fatty, trim some of the fat off, but leave enough to add flavor and richness to the stew.

Cut the pork into 2-inch (5 cm) chunks, leaving some meat on the bone. Season with salt and pepper. Heat a large cast-iron skillet or frying pan over medium-high heat, with a small amount of oil if necessary (there may be enough fat on the pork that it can brown in its own fat). When the pan is very hot, add the pork and brown, in batches if necessary, not crowding the pan. Add the bone to the pan and brown it too. Transfer the pork and bone into a large soup pot or slow cooker. Deglaze the pan with ½ cup (120 ml) water and add the scrapings to the pot. Drain the posole and add it to the pot. Add the garlic and onions and cover with 10 cups (2.4 liters) water. Bring to a boil.

Reduce the heat to a simmer (or set the slow cooker on low). Add the oregano, cumin, and cayenne. Cook until the pork and posole are very tender (the meat will have fallen off the bone), about 2½ hours (3 or more in the slow cooker).

Finely chop the chilies and add to the stew. Simmer for another 30 minutes. Add the cilantro (coriander) and lime juice. Season to taste with salt and pepper.

Serve in bowls, with chopped cilantro, lime wedges, and warm tortillas on the side.

PORK POSOLE

SCHNITZ UN KNEPP

PREPARATION TIME: 10 MINUTES,
   PLUS SOAKING TIME
COOKING TIME: 3 HOURS 45 MINUTES
SERVES: 6–8

- 4 cups (470 g) dried apples
- 1 bone-in ham (about 3 lb/1.4 kg)
- 3 tablespoons dark brown sugar
- 1 large onion, chopped
- 2 cups (260 g) all-purpose (plain) flour
- 4 teaspoons baking powder
- 1 teaspoon salt
- ½ teaspoon freshly ground black pepper
- 1 egg
- 3 tablespoons (45 g) butter, melted
- ½ cup (120 ml) milk

[Pennsylvania Dutch refers to regional groups of Amish and Mennonites. This recipe's name comes from the German for "apples and buttons," otherwise known as dried apples and dumplings.]

Place the dried apples in a large bowl. Pour over enough hot water to just cover and let soak for at least 2 hours.

Meanwhile, place the ham in a large pot, and add cold water to cover by 3 inches (7.5 cm). Bring to a boil, reduce the heat, and simmer, covered, for 2 hours.

Add the apples and the soaking liquid, brown sugar, and onion. Cover and cook for 1½ hours.

In a bowl, whisk the flour with the baking powder, salt, and pepper. Stir in the egg, butter, and milk to make a stiff batter. Bring the ham and apples to a boil and drop the batter by the tablespoonful into the boiling liquid. Reduce the heat, cover, and simmer until the dumplings are fully cooked, 12–15 minutes. Transfer the ham to a deep serving dish. Pour the cooked apples, dumplings, and cooking liquid over and around the ham. Serve hot.

GREEN CHILI LAMB STEW

PREPARATION TIME: 30 MINUTES
COOKING TIME: 2 HOURS 30 MINUTES
SERVES: 4

- 12–15 Hatch green chilies
- 2 lb (910 g) lamb shoulder, well trimmed
- Salt
- 2 tablespoons vegetable oil
- 1 large onion, finely chopped
- 4 cloves garlic, minced
- 6 cups (1.4 liters) chicken stock
- ¾ cup (180 ml) beer (ale or lager)
- 3 bay leaves
- 1 teaspoon ground cumin
- ½ teaspoon dried Mexican oregano
- 1 teaspoon freshly ground black pepper
- 1 can (15 oz/425 g) diced (chopped) tomatoes
- 2 cans (15 oz/425 g each) hominy, drained
- 3 large potatoes, diced
- 2 carrots, diced
- Corn tortillas, warmed, for serving

[If Hatch chilies aren't available, you can substitute Anaheim peppers. Because Anaheims are milder, add one to two diced jalapeño peppers to bring up the heat.]

Roast and peel the chilies (see Note, page 86). Chop the chilies, including the seeds. Cut the lamb into 1-inch (2.5 cm) chunks

Season the lamb with salt and set aside.

In a large Dutch oven (casserole), heat the oil over medium-high heat. Add the lamb and onion and brown, stirring frequently, about 8 minutes. Add the garlic, chopped chilies, chicken stock, beer, bay leaves, cumin, oregano, pepper, and 1 teaspoon salt and bring to a boil. Reduce the heat and simmer, uncovered, for 1½ hours.

Add the tomatoes, hominy, potatoes, and carrots and continue to cook until the potatoes and carrots are tender, about 30 minutes.

Serve with warm corn tortillas.

NAVAJO MUTTON STEW (ATOO)

PREPARATION TIME: 35 MINUTES
COOKING TIME: 3 HOURS
SERVES: 4

- 3 Hatch green chiles, roasted and peeled (see Note, page 86)
- 2 tablespoons vegetable oil
- 1 lb (455 g) mutton or lamb stew meat, cut into 2-inch (5 cm) pieces
- 1 lb (455 g) winter squash, peeled and cut into 1-inch (2.5 cm) chunks
- 1 onion, diced
- 2 large potatoes, cut into 1-inch (2.5 cm) chunks
- 1 cup (150 g) corn kernels
- Pinch of salt
- Cornbread, for serving

[The Navajo tribe, native to the Four Corners region (Arizona, New Mexico, Utah, and Colorado), raise sheep for both meat and wool. This stew stars slow-simmered mutton (meat from an older sheep), showcasing its stronger, gamey flavor.]

Chop the peeled chilies and set aside.

In a Dutch oven (casserole), heat the oil over medium-high heat. Add the mutton in batches and brown on all sides, about 5 minutes per batch. Remove from the pan and set aside.

Add the onion and cook until soft, about 10 minutes. Return the mutton to the pan. Add the squash, potatoes, chilies, and 4 cups (1 liter) water. Simmer over low heat until the meat is just tender, about 2 hours. Add the corn and salt and continue to cook until the meat is fork-tender, 20–30 minutes. Serve with cornbread.

CIOPPINO

PREPARATION TIME: 40 MINUTES
COOKING TIME: 1 HOUR
SERVES: 6

- 1 (1 lb/455 g) live lobster
- ½ cup (120 ml) olive oil
- 1 large onion, chopped
- 2 cloves garlic, minced
- 1 green bell pepper, diced
- 4 large tomatoes, peeled and diced
- 1 cup (240 ml) tomato purée (passata)
- 2 cups (475 ml) dry red wine
- Salt and freshly ground black pepper
- 1½ lb (680 g) sea bass fillets, cut into 2-inch (5 cm) pieces
- 1 lb (455 g) shrimp (prawns), peeled and deveined
- 2 dozen clams or mussels, well scrubbed
- 3 tablespoons chopped fresh parsley
- Garlic bread, for serving

Kill the lobster by inserting a sharp knife through the spinal cord, directly behind the lobster's eyes. Cut the lobster into large pieces, leaving the shell on.

In a medium saucepan, heat the oil over medium heat. Add the onion, garlic, and bell pepper and cook for 5–6 minutes, until softened, stirring frequently. Add the tomatoes, tomato purée (passata), and wine. Reduce to a simmer and cook the sauce for 20 minutes. Season to taste with salt and black pepper.

In a large pot with a tight-fitting lid, layer the fish and lobster and pour the tomato sauce over. Cover, bring to a simmer, and cook for 20 minutes. Add the shrimp (prawns) and clams and cook just until the shells open or until the shrimp is pink, 6–7 minutes.

Transfer the stew to a serving bowl and garnish with the parsley. Serve with garlic bread on the side.

FROGMORE STEW

PREPARATION TIME: 20 MINUTES
COOKING TIME: 1 HOUR
SERVES: 8

- 3 tablespoons kosher (coarse) salt
- 2 bay leaves
- ½ cup (55 g) Old Bay seasoning
- 1 Vidalia onion, peeled and quartered, with root end intact
- 4 large stalks celery, halved crosswise
- 2 lemons, quartered
- 1 (12 oz/355 ml) bottle beer
- 2 lb (910 g) small red new potatoes
- 2 lb (910 g) smoked sausage, cut into 1½-inch (4 cm) thick pieces
- 3 mild green chili peppers (such as poblano, cubanelle, or Anaheim), quartered and seeded
- 8 ears of corn, husked and cut crosswise into 2-inch (5 cm) pieces
- 4 lb (1.8 kg) shell-on jumbo shrimp (prawns)
- Cocktail sauce and warm bread (optional), for serving

[The seasoning is the signature ingredient of this shrimp and sausage boil from South Carolina's Lowcountry, the tidewater region along the state's coast.]

In a large stockpot, combine 2 gallons (7.6 liters) water, the salt, bay leaves, Old Bay, onion, celery, lemons, beer, and potatoes. Bring to a boil over high heat, then reduce to a simmer. Cook until the potatoes are fork-tender, 15–20 minutes. Remove the celery and lemons with a slotted spoon and discard. Remove the onion and potatoes and set aside.

Add the sausage and peppers to the broth and return to a simmer over medium-high heat. Reduce the heat to medium-low and cook for 5 minutes. Add the corn and cook for 5 more minutes. Add the reserved potatoes and onion, then the shrimp (prawns), and cook until the shrimp turn pink and float to the top, 3–4 minutes.

Measure out 4 cups (950 ml) broth for dipping, then pour the remainder of the stew through a colander and drain well. Transfer to platters and serve on tables covered with newspaper, alongside bowls of broth, cocktail sauce, and warm bread, if desired.

FROGMORE STEW

SEAFOOD GUMBO

PREPARATION TIME: 35 MINUTES
COOKING TIME: 2 HOURS 15 MINUTES
SERVES: 6–8

- ¾ cup (180 ml) vegetable oil
- ¾ cup (100 g) all-purpose (plain) flour
- 1 cup (160 g) finely chopped onion
- ½ cup (150 g) finely chopped green bell pepper
- ½ cup (50 g) chopped celery
- 6 cups (1.4 liters) fish or shrimp stock
- 1 teaspoon salt
- ½ teaspoon freshly ground black pepper
- ½ teaspoon cayenne pepper
- ½ teaspoon dried thyme
- 1 bay leaf
- 1 lb (455 g) medium shrimp (prawns), peeled and deveined
- 18–24 shucked oysters and their liquor
- 1 lb (455 g) lump crabmeat, picked over for shells and cartilage
- 2 cups (227 g) cut okra, ½-inch (1.25 cm) rounds
- 2 scallions (spring onions), thinly sliced
- 1 tablespoon finely chopped fresh parsley
- Filé powder (optional garnish)
- 9 cups freshly cooked white rice (from 3 cups/600 g raw), for serving
- Louisiana hot sauce, such as Crystal (optional), for serving

[Gumbo is most often associated with Louisiana cuisine, but the Creole stew is prepared throughout the Gulf Coast region and lends itself to endless variations.]

Heat a large Dutch oven (casserole) or heavy-bottomed pot over medium-low heat. Add the oil, then whisk in the flour. Reduce the heat to low and cook, stirring slowly but constantly, until the roux is medium dark brown, 25–30 minutes. Add the onion, bell pepper, and celery. Increase the heat to medium and cook, stirring frequently, until the vegetables are tender, 8–10 minutes.

Meanwhile, in a large saucepan, heat the stock to simmering.

Whisking constantly, slowly add the hot stock to the pot. Add the salt, black pepper, cayenne, thyme, and bay leaf and bring to a simmer, stirring frequently. Reduce the heat to low and simmer uncovered for 1 hour, stirring occasionally.

Increase the heat to medium. Add the shrimp (prawns), oysters, crab meat, and okra and cook until the shrimp are opaque and the oysters have firmed up slightly, 3–5 minutes. Remove from the heat and stir in the scallions (spring onions) and parsley. Serve with white rice, hot sauce, and filé powder, if desired.

SCALLOP STEW

PREPARATION TIME: 10 MINUTES,
  PLUS MARINATING TIME
COOKING TIME: 1 HOUR
SERVES: 4

- 2 lb (910 g) sea scallops
- ½ cup (120 ml) dry vermouth
- 2 cloves garlic, minced
- ¼ cup (60 ml) olive oil
- 2 medium onions, thinly sliced
- 2 cups (360 g) peeled and chopped Roma (plum) tomatoes
- 3 tablespoons (45 g) butter
- 2 tablespoons chopped fresh parsley
- 1 teaspoon salt
- ½ teaspoon freshly ground black pepper
- Toasted French bread, for serving

In a large deep bowl, toss the scallops with the vermouth and garlic. Cover and refrigerate for at least 30 minutes and up to 1 hour.

In a large pot, heat the oil over medium-low heat. Add the onions and cook, stirring frequently, until tender, 12 minutes. Add the tomatoes and cook for 10 minutes. Add the scallop mixture and cook until they are opaque throughout, 8–10 minutes. Stir in the butter, parsley, salt, and pepper. Serve hot, with toasted French bread.

BLACKFISH STEW

PREPARATION TIME: 10 MINUTES
COOKING TIME: 30 MINUTES
SERVES: 4

- 4 tablespoons olive oil
- 1 large onion, thinly sliced
- 2 cloves garlic, thinly sliced
- 1 teaspoon minced fresh thyme
- 1 teaspoon crushed chili flakes
- ½ cup (120 ml) dry white wine
- 2 cups (475 ml) fish stock
- 1½ cups (355 ml) heavy (whipping) cream
- Salt and freshly ground black pepper
- 2 lb (910 g) blackfish fillets, cut into 4 pieces

[Also called chowderfish, tautog, black porgy, or oysterfish, blackfish live from Nova Scotia, Canada, to South Carolina. Their firm flesh and rich, mellow flavor hold up well to stewing and grilling.]

In a medium saucepan, heat 2 tablespoons of the oil over medium heat. Add the onion and cook, stirring frequently, until it begins to wilt. Stir in the garlic and cook until the onion and garlic are soft and beginning to turn golden, about 10 minutes. Add the thyme and chili flakes. Stir in the wine and bring to a boil. Add the stock and bring to a simmer. Add the cream and season to taste with salt and pepper. Return to a simmer, add the fish, and cook until the fish is opaque and tender, about 8 minutes.

SIDE

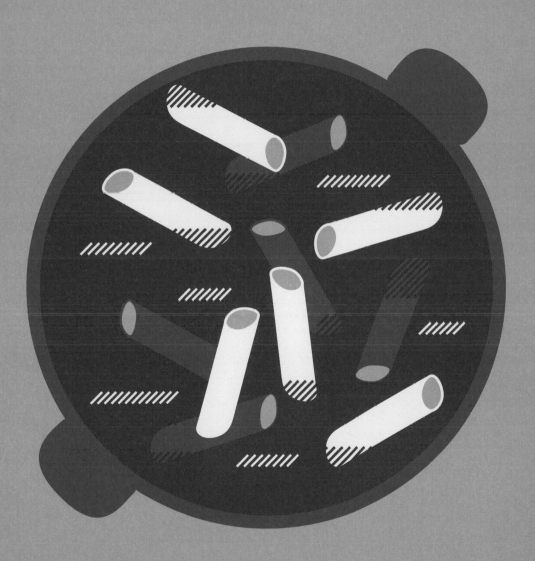

DISHES

STEAMED ARTICHOKES

PREPARATION TIME: 5 MINUTES
PER ARTICHOKE
COOKING TIME: 20–40 MINUTES
SERVES: AS MANY AS YOU'D LIKE

    5

- Fresh artichokes

Fit a large pot with a steamer basket and fill with water at least 3 inches (7.5 cm) deep. Bring to a boil.

Meanwhile, trim off the sharp points of the artichoke leaves with kitchen shears. Discard any tough, brown, or split leaves. Trim the stem slightly if it is brown on the end.

Place the artichokes in the steamer basket with the stems facing up and without crowding. Cover the pot and steam until a sharp knife can easily pierce the base. Keep a kettle of boiling water to replenish the water in the pot if it looks like it might boil off. Cooking times will vary, depending on the size of the artichokes: A small one could be fully cooked in 20 minutes, a large artichoke may take as long as 40 minutes. When the base is tender, transfer the artichoke to a plate and serve warm or at room temperature.

SAUTÉED JERUSALEM ARTICHOKES

PREPARATION TIME: 15 MINUTES
COOKING TIME: 35 MINUTES
SERVES: 4

- 1 lb (455 g) Jerusalem artichokes, very well scrubbed and sliced
- 4 tablespoons walnut oil
- 2 cloves garlic (or wild onion bulbs), finely chopped
- Salt
- 1 tablespoon cider vinegar
- ½ cup (25 g) finely chopped fresh chives (or wild onion greens)

[Jerusalem artichokes grow wild in the Plains and beyond (but not the Southwest). They grow especially well in North Dakota. The invasive tendencies of this native sunflower made it a useful food for Native Americans, who cultivated it in the Northern Great Plains before it spread. Raw, the tubers are crisp and taste very nutty and slightly sweet. Cooked, their texture is similar to a cross between potato and turnip. Wild onions in place of garlic are a great substitution.]

In a pot of boiling salted water, cook the Jerusalem artichokes until tender, 12–15 minutes. Drain well.

In a saucepan, heat the oil over medium heat. Add the drained Jerusalem artichokes. Add the garlic and cook gently for a couple of minutes. Stir well to coat the vegetables with oil. Cook for 10 minutes until lightly golden brown, turning once with a spatula (fish slice). Sprinkle in the vinegar, add the chives, stir well, and cook for another 2 minutes, until the flavors have melded. Serve hot.

BEETS WITH SOUR CREAM AND HORSERADISH

PREPARATION TIME: 20 MINUTES
COOKING TIME: 1 HOUR 10 MINUTES
SERVES: 4

- 6 medium beets (beetroots)
- 3 tablespoons (45 g) butter
- 1 medium onion, diced
- 2 tablespoons all-purpose (plain) flour
- 2 tablespoons cider vinegar
- ¾ cup (180 ml) sour cream
- 3 tablespoons prepared horseradish
- ½ teaspoon freshly ground black pepper
- Salt

Preheat the oven to 375°F (190°C/Gas Mark 5).

Scrub the beets (beetroots) and place them in a roasting pan with 1 inch (2.5 cm) of water. Cover the pan with foil. Roast the beets until they are fork-tender, about 1 hour. Let them cool enough to handle, then remove their skins. Dice the beets and set them aside.

In a large frying pan, melt the butter over medium heat. Add the onion, reduce the heat to low, and cook until soft and translucent, about 5 minutes. Add the flour, stirring and scraping the bottom of the pan. Add the vinegar and 1½ cups (355 ml) water and cook for 2–3 minutes, stirring as the mixture thickens. Add the beets and cook until they are heated through. Remove from the heat and stir in the sour cream, horseradish, pepper, and salt to taste. Serve warm.

HARVARD BEETS

PREPARATION TIME: 15 MINUTES
COOKING TIME: ABOUT 1 HOUR
SERVES: 4

- 3 lb (1.4 kg) medium beets (beetroots)
- ⅓ cup (65 g) sugar
- 1 tablespoon cornstarch (cornflour)
- ⅓ cup (80 ml) cider vinegar
- 3 tablespoons (45 g) butter
- Salt and freshly ground black pepper

In a large pot, cover the beets (beetroots) with cold water. Bring to a boil, then reduce to a simmer and cook until just tender, approximately 40 minutes (time will vary according to the freshness and size). Drain the beets, let them cool slightly, and slip off their skins. Cut into ¼-inch (6 mm) dice and place in a large frying pan.

In a small bowl, mix the sugar and cornstarch (cornflour). Stir into the beets, followed by the vinegar and ⅓ cup (80 ml) water. Bring to a boil over medium-high heat, stirring constantly. Reduce the heat and simmer, stirring frequently, until the sauce is thick and glossy, about 8 minutes. Stir in the butter and season to taste with salt and pepper.

CABBAGE COOKED IN MILK

PREPARATION TIME: 5 MINUTES
COOKING TIME: 15 MINUTES
SERVES: 4

- 1½ cups (355 ml) milk
- 4 cups (280 g) shredded green cabbage
- ½ teaspoon salt
- ¼ teaspoon freshly grated nutmeg
- 2 tablespoons (30 g) butter
- 2 tablespoons all-purpose (plain) flour

In a heavy-bottomed saucepan, bring the milk to a simmer. Add the cabbage and cook over medium heat for 5–6 minutes, until the cabbage is just tender. Stir in the salt and nutmeg.

Meanwhile, in a small saucepan, melt the butter, stir in the flour, and add some of the hot milk from the cabbage pot. Stir until smooth.

Add the milk sauce to the cabbage pot and cook, stirring frequently, over medium heat for another 4 minutes, until the sauce has thickened and the cabbage is very tender.

SWAMP CABBAGE WITH BACON

PREPARATION TIME: 10 MINUTES
COOKING TIME: 3 HOURS 15 MINUTES
SERVES: 4

- 6 slices smoked bacon (streaky), cut into small pieces
- Small head swamp cabbage, tender interior part only, chopped
- 1 tablespoon distilled white vinegar
- Salt and freshly ground black pepper

[Swamp cabbage, also called cabbage palm or palmetto (sabal palmetto), grows wild in southeastern Gulf states, especially Florida, South Carolina, and North Carolina. It grows in a wide variety of habitats including upland areas and wetlands, riverbanks and coastal plains. Sable palm fruits are edible and were used by Native Americans to make a flour, but heart of palm is the better known food part of the plant. The bud tastes somewhat like cabbage and can be eaten raw or cooked. This is often served with fried biscuits.]

In a pot with a lid, cook the bacon over medium-high heat until crisp, about 10 minutes. Reserving the bacon fat, remove the bacon with a slotted spoon and drain on paper towels.

Using the same pot, heat the bacon fat over medium-high heat. Add the swamp cabbage and stir for a few minutes. Add the vinegar, cook for another minute, and add 1 cup (240 ml) water and the pieces of bacon. Simmer, covered, until tender, about 3 hours. Add more water if the cabbage is drying out.

SPAETZLE

PREPARATION TIME: 15 MINUTES
COOKING TIME: 20 MINUTES
SERVES: 4

- 2 cups (260 g) all-purpose (plain) flour
- ½ teaspoon salt
- Freshly grated nutmeg
- 4 eggs
- ½ cup (120 ml) milk
- Butter or gravy, for serving

[Spaetzle is German for "little sparrow," which the tiny dumplings resemble. Best served tossed with butter or gravy.]

In a large bowl, whisk together the flour, salt, and nutmeg. In a separate bowl, whisk the eggs and milk. Add the egg mixture to the flour mixture and stir until all comes together. Cover and let rest for 10 minutes.

Meanwhile, bring a large pot of water to boil.

Set a colander over the boiling water and use a rubber spatula to press the dough into the boiling water through the holes. Cook until the spaetzle float to the surface, 3–4 minutes. Drain and toss with butter or gravy.

FRESH EGG NOODLES

PREPARATION TIME: 45 MINUTES
COOKING TIME: 10 MINUTES
SERVES: 6

- 2 cups (260 g) all-purpose (plain) flour
- 1 teaspoon salt
- 1 egg
- 3 egg yolks
- Butter, for serving
- Chopped fresh parsley, for garnish (optional)

In a medium bowl, whisk the flour and salt. Make a well in the center and add the whole egg, egg yolks, and enough water to make a pliable dough (about ¼ cup/60 ml). Mix thoroughly; if the dough feels dry, add more water.

Turn out the dough onto a floured surface. Knead until smooth and workable, adding flour as needed, about 2 minutes. Wrap with plastic (clingfilm) and let rest at room temperature for 30 minutes.

Roll the dough very thin, cut into ½-inch (1.25 cm) wide strips and again into 2-inch (5 cm) lengths. Toss the noodles with flour to keep them from sticking.

Bring a pot of water to a rapid boil. Stir in the noodles and boil until they rise to the top, about 3 minutes. Drain and transfer to a bowl. Toss with butter and chopped parsley (if using).

MACARONI AND CHEESE

PREPARATION TIME: 10 MINUTES
COOKING TIME: 1 HOUR 10 MINUTES
SERVES: 6–8

- Salt
- 1 lb (455 g) penne pasta
- 4 cups (1 liter) milk
- 1 bay leaf
- 6 tablespoons (85 g) butter
- 6 tablespoons all-purpose (plain) flour
- 2 cups (230 g) shredded extra-sharp cheddar cheese
- 2 cups (230 g) shredded mild cheddar cheese
- 1½ teaspoons Tabasco-style hot sauce
- ½ teaspoon freshly ground black pepper
- 1½ cups (75 g) fresh breadcrumbs
- 2 teaspoons olive oil

Preheat the oven to 375°F (190°C/Gas Mark 5). Butter a 9 x 13-inch (23 x 33 cm) baking dish.

Bring a large pot of water to a boil and season generously with salt. Add the pasta to the boiling water and cook for 8 minutes. Drain and set aside.

In a medium saucepan, heat the milk and the bay leaf over medium heat until very warm.

Heat a large cast-iron skillet over medium heat. Add the butter and let melt. Add the flour and cook, whisking constantly, until lightly golden, about 3 minutes. Discard the bay leaf and gradually whisk in the hot milk. Increase the heat to medium-high, bring to a low boil, and cook, whisking often, for about 6 minutes. Remove from the heat and whisk in the cheeses, hot sauce, 1 teaspoon salt, and the pepper. Add the pasta to the pan and fold together to combine. Transfer the macaroni and cheese to the prepared baking dish.

In a small bowl, stir together the breadcrumbs and olive oil. Distribute evenly over the top of the pasta. Bake until the breadcrumbs are golden brown, 25–30 minutes. Serve hot.

CRANBERRY SAUCE

PREPARATION TIME: 5 MINUTES, PLUS
    CHILLING TIME
COOKING TIME: 10 MINUTES
MAKES: ABOUT 2½ CUPS (590 ML)

- 1 cup (200 g) sugar
- 3 cups (300 g) fresh cranberries
- 1 teaspoon grated orange zest (optional)

In a medium saucepan, combine the sugar and 1 cup (240 ml) water and bring to a boil over medium-high heat. Add the cranberries and cook until the berries begin to pop open, about 10 minutes. Remove from the heat and stir in the orange zest (if using). Chill for at least 30 minutes before serving. Can be stored in the refrigerator for 1 month.

MACARONI AND CHEESE

MAPLE-GLAZED BRUSSELS SPROUTS WITH BACON

PREPARATION TIME: 15 MINUTES
COOKING TIME: 30 MINUTES
SERVES: 8

- 1 lb (455 g) bacon (streaky), cut into 1-inch (2.5 cm) pieces
- 2 lb (910 g) Brussels sprouts, trimmed and halved lengthwise
- ¼ cup (60 ml) pure maple syrup
- Salt and freshly ground black pepper

In a large frying pan, cook the bacon over medium-high heat until crisp, about 10 minutes. Remove the bacon with a slotted spoon, leaving the bacon fat in the pan. Add the Brussels sprouts and cook over medium heat, stirring, until the sprouts are golden brown and barely tender, about 15 minutes. Add the maple syrup and cook for another 5 minutes. Toss in the bacon and season to taste with salt and pepper. Serve immediately.

TOMATO ASPIC

PREPARATION TIME: 15 MINUTES,
   PLUS 8 HOURS CHILLING TIME
COOKING TIME: 5 MINUTES
SERVES: 8

- 4 cups (950 ml) tomato juice
- 6 tablespoons cider vinegar
- 1 tablespoon Worcestershire sauce
- 2¼ cups (335 g) diced green bell pepper
- 2¼ cups (225 g) diced celery
- ¾ cup (120 g) diced white onion
- 2 teaspoons salt
- 2 tablespoons plus 1 teaspoon unflavored gelatin powder

[Savory jellied salads were once a hallmark of sophistication at Southern lunches.]

In a large saucepan, combine the tomato juice, cider vinegar, Worcestershire sauce, bell pepper, celery, onion, and salt. Bring almost to a boil over medium-high heat. Remove from the heat.

Meanwhile, pour 2 cups (475 ml) cold water into a bowl. Sprinkle the gelatin over the water and set aside.

Add the gelatin mixture to the hot tomato mixture. Whisk well to evenly incorporate the gelatin.

Coat an 8-cup (1.9-liter) Bundt pan with cooking spray. Fill with the tomato mixture. Cover and refrigerate for 8 hours or overnight to set.

To unmold, fill a large bowl with warm water. Dip the Bundt pan into the water for 10 seconds. Cover with an inverted dinner plate and flip over. Shake the pan to release the aspic onto the plate. Serve immediately or refrigerate until serving time.

MAPLE-GLAZED BRUSSELS SPROUTS WITH BACON

CARROTS AND HONEY

UT

PREPARATION TIME: 5 MINUTES
COOKING TIME: 10 MINUTES
SERVES: 2–3

- Salt
- 3 medium carrots, thinly sliced on the diagonal
- 1 tablespoon (15 g) butter
- 1 tablespoon Utah honey

Bring a pot of salted water to a boil. Add the carrots and boil until just tender, about 5 minutes. Drain and toss with the butter and honey.

BUTTERED FIDDLEHEADS

AK

PREPARATION TIME: 5 MINUTES
COOKING TIME: 10 MINUTES
SERVES: 4

- 32 ostrich fern fiddleheads
- Salt
- 3 tablespoons (45 g) unsalted butter

["Fiddlehead" refers to the young, unfurled fronds (crosiers) of any fern. For eating, ostrich fern is the safe choice. Its fiddleheads are ready to collect in spring. While markets and restaurants usually sell only the tightly rolled coil, the straight shaft beneath the unfurled fiddlehead is also tender and delicious. Note: If preparing ahead of time, cook the fiddleheads as directed, then refresh in a bowl of ice water and pat dry. Just before serving, add them to a hot saucepan with the butter.]

Dunk the batch of fiddleheads in a bowl of water and wash carefully.

In a large saucepan of boiling salted water, cook the fiddleheads until just tender, about 5 minutes (see Note). Drain, return the fiddleheads to the empty saucepan, place over medium heat, and add the butter. Shake the saucepan to coat the fiddleheads, season to taste with salt, and serve at once.

CARROTS AND HONEY

SUCCOTASH

PREPARATION TIME: 10 MINUTES
COOKING TIME: 20 MINUTES
SERVES: 4–6

- 2 tablespoons olive oil
- 1 sweet onion, chopped
- 3 cups (440 g) corn kernels
- 1½ cups (225 g) cherry tomatoes, halved
- 2 cups (340 g) drained canned lima beans (butter beans)
- ¾ cup (180 ml) chicken stock
- 3 tablespoons (45 g) butter
- 1 tablespoon fresh lemon juice
- 1 tablespoon plus 1 teaspoon chopped fresh parsley
- ¾ teaspoon salt
- ½ teaspoon freshly ground black pepper

[The word *succotash* comes from a Native American word for boiled corn. This side dish can be gilded with red and green bell peppers, which are also plentiful in Southern gardens in the summer.]

In a cast-iron skillet, heat the oil over medium heat. Add the onion and cook until softened and translucent, about 5 minutes. Stir in the corn and cook, stirring frequently, until tender, about 6 minutes. Stir in the tomatoes, lima beans, and stock and simmer until the tomatoes start to break down, 3–5 minutes. Remove from the heat and stir in the butter, lemon juice, parsley, salt, and pepper. Serve.

SOUTHERN SKILLET CORN

PREPARATION TIME: 15 MINUTES
COOKING TIME: 40 MINUTES
SERVES: 6

- 6 ears of corn, husked
- 2 tablespoons all-purpose (plain) flour
- 2 teaspoons sugar
- 1 teaspoon salt
- ¼ teaspoon freshly ground black pepper
- ½ cup (120 ml) milk
- 6 tablespoons (85 g) butter

Slice the kernels off the cobs and into a large bowl. With the back of the knife, scrape up and down the cob to extract the milk.

In a medium bowl, whisk together the flour, sugar, salt, and pepper. Stir in the milk and ¾ cup (180 ml) water. Whisk until smooth.

In a large cast-iron skillet, melt the butter over medium heat. Add the corn and cook for 3 minutes. Add the flour mixture and cook, stirring occasionally, until the corn is tender and the mixture has thickened slightly, 30–35 minutes.

SUCCOTASH

CREAMED CORN

PREPARATION TIME: 10 MINUTES
COOKING TIME: 20 MINUTES
SERVES: 4

- 3 large ears of corn, husked
- 1 tablespoon sugar
- 1 tablespoon all-purpose (plain) flour
- 3 tablespoons (45 g) butter, melted
- 1 cup (240 ml) heavy (whipping) cream
- Salt and freshly ground black pepper

Cut the kernels off the cobs and into a large bowl. Using the back of the knife blade, scrape the cobs, exuding the milk and any remaining bits of corn. Toss the corn kernels with the sugar, flour, butter, and cream.

Transfer the corn mixture to a large frying pan and cook over medium heat, stirring constantly, for about 20 minutes, until very thick. Season to taste with salt and pepper. Serve hot.

CORN PUDDING

PREPARATION TIME: 15 MINUTES
COOKING TIME: 55 MINUTES
SERVES: 8–10

- ¼ cup (50 g) sugar
- 3 tablespoons all-purpose (plain) flour
- 2 teaspoons baking powder
- 2 teaspoons salt
- 6 eggs
- 2 cups (475 ml) heavy (whipping) cream
- 1 stick (115 g) butter, melted and cooled
- Kernels from 6 ears of husked corn

Preheat the oven to 350°F (180°C/Gas Mark 4). Generously butter an 8-inch (20 cm) square baking dish.

In a small bowl, whisk together the sugar, flour, baking powder, and salt. In a large bowl, whisk together the eggs, cream, and melted butter. Gradually whisk the sugar mixture into the egg mixture, whisking until smooth. Stir in the corn.

Pour the mixture into the baking dish. Bake until the top is deep golden and the custard is set, 40–45 minutes. Let stand for 5 minutes before serving.

EASTERN SHORE CORN FRITTERS

PREPARATION TIME: 10 MINUTES
COOKING TIME: 15 MINUTES
MAKES: ABOUT 1 DOZEN

- 1 cup (130 g) all-purpose (plain) flour
- 1 teaspoon baking powder
- 1 teaspoon salt
- 2 eggs
- ½ cup (120 ml) milk
- 1 tablespoon (15 g) butter, melted
- 1 cup (150 g) corn kernels
- 2 tablespoons minced onion (optional)
- Vegetable oil or lard, for shallow-frying
- Butter and maple syrup, for serving (optional)

In a large bowl, whisk the flour with the baking powder and salt. In a medium bowl, whisk the eggs with the milk. Stir the milk mixture into the dry ingredients. Stir in the melted butter, corn, and onions (if using) and mix well.

Pour about ½ inch (1.25 cm) oil (or enough lard to come up to the same depth) into a large frying pan over medium-high heat until very hot. When the oil is hot, drop the fritter batter by the tablespoonful into the pan. Fry until the fritters puff a little and are golden brown, about 4 minutes. Flip and cook on the second side. Drain on paper towels. If desired, serve with butter and maple syrup.

GREEN BEAN GRATIN

PREPARATION TIME: 10 MINUTES
COOKING TIME: 45 MINUTES
SERVES: 6–8

- Salt
- 2 lb (910 g) green beans or yellow wax beans, ends trimmed
- 2 cups (226 g) unsalted nuts, such as cashews
- 6 tablespoons (85 g) butter
- 2 cups (475 ml) heavy (whipping) cream
- Freshly ground black pepper
- 1½ cups (60 g) fresh coarse breadcrumbs

Preheat the oven to 375°F (190°C/Gas Mark 5).

Bring a large pot of water to a boil over high heat. Season the water generously with salt. Add the green beans and cook until crisp-tender, about 3 minutes. Drain into a colander and rinse well under cool water.

In a food processor, grind the nuts to the consistency of a coarse meal, about 2 minutes.

Heat a large frying pan over medium heat. Add the butter to melt, then add the ground nuts. Stir until the mixture is fragrant, about 1 minute. Reduce the heat to medium-low and continue to cook, stirring frequently, until the mixture darkens and forms a paste, about 8 minutes. Add the cream, season to taste with salt and pepper, and whisk well. Continue to cook over low heat, stirring frequently, until the sauce thickens, 6–8 minutes.

Mix together the sauce and the green beans and spread in an even layer in a 8-inch (20 cm) square baking dish. Top with the breadcrumbs and bake until warmed through and the breadcrumbs are toasty, 15–20 minutes.

LEATHER BRITCHES

 WV

PREPARATION TIME: DEPENDS ON
   HOW MUCH YOU MAKE
COOKING TIME: 1 HOUR
MAKES: AS MUCH AS YOU'D LIKE

- String beans
- Sturdy thread
- Darning needle
- Salt

[Long before mountain homes had a freezer, people across Appalachia dried string beans (green or wax beans) into "leather britches" by stringing them up or placing them on screens to dry. The drying process would vary according to climate and often takes several weeks. Once dried, the beans can be added to soups and stews.]

Clean the beans and drain well. Remove the stem ends. Using a needle and thread, pierce the beans through the center and pull the thread through. Tie off the end for the first bean (this will be the "anchor" for the whole string, making sure it is secure. You can make the string of beans any length, as long as it is manageable. Hang the beans to dry in a sheltered area that has good air circulation. Let them dry until they are brittle.

To reconstitute and cook, remove the thread, place the dried beans in a pot, and just barely cover them with cold water. Bring to a boil, reduce the heat, and simmer for about 1 hour, until the beans are tender. Remove the beans with a slotted spoon and set aside. Reduce the liquid in the pot by one half. Return the beans to the pot and season to taste with salt.

STEAMED GREENBRIAR SHOOTS

PREPARATION TIME: 5 MINUTES
COOKING TIME: 10 MINUTES
SERVES: 4

- 1 lb (455 g) greenbriar shoots, rinsed
- 4 tablespoons (60 g) butter
- Salt and freshly ground black pepper

[Greenbriar—also known as cat briar, carrion flower, or sarsaparilla (smilax species)–grows wild east of the Rocky Mountains and across the South. Smilax is generally seen as a tumbling vine in woodland areas. Tuberous smilax roots were traditionally used for flours and baking by Native Americans as well as in beverages. The ripe fruit is edible and varies considerably in flavor from species to species. The shoots can be eaten raw or cooked and are good in an omelet or with lightly scrambled eggs.]

In a steamer basket set over a pot of boiling water, steam the shoots until tender, about 6 minutes. Remove the shoots, empty the pot of water, and add the butter to the hot pot. When it has melted, return the shoots to the pot and stir until coated with butter. Season with salt and pepper and serve right away.

BABY BOK CHOY

PREPARATION TIME: 10 MINUTES
COOKING TIME: 10 MINUTES
SERVES: 4

- 1½ lb (680 g) baby bok choy
- 2 tablespoons peanut (groundnut) oil or vegetable oil
- 1 small clove garlic, finely chopped
- ½ cup (120 ml) chicken stock
- ½ teaspoon salt
- ¼ teaspoon freshly ground black pepper

Separate the leaves from the stems of the bok choy. Cut each part into 1-inch (2.5 cm) pieces.

In a large frying pan, heat the oil over medium-high heat until very hot. Add the stems and cook until slightly softened, but still somewhat firm, 3–5 minutes. Add the leaves, garlic, chicken stock, salt, and pepper and cook until the liquid is almost evaporated and the leaves are wilted, about 5 minutes.

BRAISED TURNIP GREENS WITH POTLIKKER

PREPARATION TIME: 15 MINUTES
COOKING TIME: 1 HOUR 45 MINUTES
SERVES: 8–12

- 8 slices thick-cut bacon (streaky), cut into ½-inch (1.25 cm) pieces
- 1 medium onion, diced
- ½ lb (225 g) country (salt cured) ham, diced
- 1 teaspoon crushed chili flakes
- ¼ cup (50 g) packed light brown sugar
- ⅔ cup (160 ml) cider vinegar
- 4 lb (1.8 kg) turnip greens, stems removed, leaves torn into 2-inch (5 cm) pieces
- Salt

[In the rural South, greens with potlikker — the flavorful broth that yields after cooking greens in water low and slow on the stove — has long been served with cornbread. It's now commonly served as a side dish and locals know to ask for "extra potlikker."]

In a large soup pot, cook the bacon over medium heat to render its fat, about 5 minutes. Add the onion and cook until translucent, 5–7 minutes. Add the ham, chili flakes, brown sugar, vinegar, and 6 cups (1.4 liters) water and bring to a boil. Working in batches, add the turnip greens to fill three-fourths of the pot. As the greens wilt, continue to add more. Once all the greens are wilted, reduce the heat to medium-low, cover, and simmer, stirring occasionally, until the greens are tender, 1–1½ hours. If the greens are sticking to the bottom of the pan, add ¼ cup (60 ml) water at a time as needed. Season to taste with additional salt.

COLLARD GREENS WITH HAM HOCKS

PREPARATION TIME: 10 MINUTES
COOKING TIME: 55 MINUTES
SERVES: 6–8

- 4 big bunches collard greens (about 2¼ lb/1 kg)
- ¾ lb (340 g) ham hocks (2–3 hocks)
- ½ teaspoon seasoned salt
- Salt and freshly ground black pepper
- 4 cloves garlic, sliced
- 1–2 tablespoons hot-pepper vinegar (optional)

[Bitter greens slow-cooked with smoked pork are found throughout the South.]

Wash the greens in cold water to remove any dirt. Cut out and discard the thick center ribs. Tear the leaves roughly into 2-inch (5 cm) pieces. Cut any pieces of meat off the hocks and chop into ½-inch (1.25 cm) pieces. Reserve both the meat and bones.

In a large Dutch oven (casserole) or heavy-bottomed pot, bring 4 cups (1 liter) water to a simmer over medium heat. Add the seasoned salt, ½ teaspoon each salt and pepper, the garlic, chopped ham, and ham bones. Increase the heat to high and bring the mixture to a full boil. Working in batches, add the greens to fill about three-fourths of the pot. As the first batch of greens boils down, stir in more handfuls, one at a time, until all the greens are added. Reduce the heat to medium-low, cover, and simmer, stirring occasionally, until the greens are uniformly soft, about 45 minutes, adding more liquid as necessary. Finish with hot-pepper vinegar (if desired). Season to taste with salt and pepper.

SUDANESE GREENS COOKED WITH PEANUT BUTTER

PREPARATION TIME: 15 MINUTES
COOKING TIME: 35 MINUTES
SERVES: 4–6

- 1 small onion, diced
- 2 large bunches Swiss chard, washed and chopped (including stems)
- 5 tablespoons no-sugar-added peanut butter
- 1 tomato, diced
- Salt and freshly ground black pepper
- Asida (page 277), for serving

[Nebraska is home to a refugee community from South Sudan that packed their cookbooks when they came. Southern Sudanese cooking, influenced by East African and Arabic cuisine, is now at home on the American prairie. This dish can be made with spinach, but chard is more traditional in the South. Peanuts are a common savory ingredient in sub-Saharan Africa, and peanut butter is often used to thicken sauces. Serve with Asida (page 277).]

In a large saucepan, bring 1 cup (240 ml) water to a boil over medium-high heat. Add the onion and chard, cover, reduce the heat, and simmer for 15 minutes, stirring occasionally. Add a bit of water if necessary to keep the greens from scorching. Stir in the peanut butter, cover, and simmer for 10 minutes. Add the tomato and season to taste with salt and pepper. Simmer, uncovered, for 5 minutes. Serve with asida.

SPICY WILD BUTTERED HOPNISS

PREPARATION TIME: 5 MINUTES
COOKING TIME: 25 MINUTES
SERVES: 4

- 2 cups (600 g) hopniss tubers, well washed
- 4 tablespoons (60 g) butter
- ½ lemon
- 2 large pinches of chili powder
- Salt

[Hopniss, also known as American groundnuts, grows wild east of the Rocky Mountains. The most nutritious part hides underground: Hopniss tubers are like miniature potatoes, but with a unique flavor. Hopniss should be eaten cooked.]

In a medium pot of boiling water, cook the hopniss tubers until tender then drain. With the tip of a sharp knife and your fingers, remove the skins. The time this takes is highly variable, as the pieces will be of different sizes.

In a saucepan, melt the butter over medium-high heat until foaming. Add the hopniss, turning to coat them with butter. Add 2 squeezes of lemon juice and toss the hopniss again, until they are beginning to brown. Add the chili powder and salt to taste. Serve hot.

ROASTED ASPARAGUS

PREPARATION TIME: 5 MINUTES
COOKING TIME: 15 MINUTES
SERVES: 4

- 1 lb (455 g) asparagus, woody ends trimmed
- 2 tablespoons olive oil
- ½ teaspoon salt
- ¼ teaspoon freshly ground black pepper
- Lemon wedges, for serving

[This is also delicious served with freshly grated Parmesan cheese.]

Preheat the oven to 450°F (230°C/Gas Mark 8). Line a rimmed baking sheet with foil.

Arrange the asparagus on the lined baking sheet. Drizzle with the olive oil and sprinkle with the salt and pepper. Toss to coat the asparagus in the oil, salt, and pepper and distribute in a single layer. Roast until tender and slightly charred, 10–12 minutes. Serve hot or at room temperature, with lemon wedges for squeezing.

SAUTÉED WILD MUSHROOMS

PREPARATION TIME: 5 MINUTES
COOKING TIME: 15 MINUTES
SERVES: 2–4

- 4 tablespoons (60 g) butter
- 1 teaspoon fresh rosemary, finely chopped
- 1 clove garlic, minced
- 1 lb (455 g) wild mushrooms (chanterelle, morel, hedgehog, or a mix), left whole if small, or sliced if large, trimmed and cleaned if necessary
- ½ teaspoon salt
- 2 tablespoons sherry

[Hikers in the Northwest know to watch for delicacies growing on the forest floor. Dozens of edible varieties, with names like hedgehog, apricot jelly, lion's mane, and lobster mushroom, grow wild across the region. This simple preparation works for any combination.]

In a large frying pan, melt the butter over medium heat. Add the rosemary and garlic and cook, stirring until slightly softened, about 2 minutes. Add the mushrooms, sprinkle with the salt, and cook, stirring often, until the liquid has evaporated, 10–12 minutes. Increase the heat to high and add the sherry, stirring to deglaze the pan. Remove from the heat and serve.

MAITAKE MUSHROOM "BACON"

PREPARATION TIME: 10 MINUTES
COOKING TIME: 40 MINUTES
SERVES: 2

- 2 lb (910 g) hen-of-the-woods (maitake) caps, washed and dried well (see note)
- 3 tablespoons soy sauce
- 2 teaspoons sugar
- 3 tablespoons grapeseed oil

[The hen-of-the-woods mushroom — also known as maitake, ram's head, and sheep's head – grows wild in the Northeast, and sometimes beyond. It is a large mushroom that resembles a fat gray-brown hen sitting on her nest, with feathers ruffled. It has a very strong and meaty flavor. When young and tender, it can be eaten in numerous ways, cooked, from soup to sautés to oven-dried chips. Older mushrooms (as well as the interior white core or stem) can be dried, powdered, and used for flavoring broths, soups, and sauces. Note: Caps are the smaller overlapping outer parts of wild maitake; they have large, tough interiors or cores. Caps are preferable.]

Preheat the oven to 350°F (180°C/Gas Mark 4).

Slice the hen-of-the-woods into pieces no thicker than ¼ inch (6 mm). They can be as long as you like.

In a medium bowl, whisk together the soy sauce and sugar to dissolve the sugar. Add the oil. Add the mushroom pieces and toss until they are thoroughly coated with the mixture.

Arrange the mushrooms pieces evenly in a single layer on 1 or 2 baking sheets. Bake until the mushrooms begin to brown, 15–20 minutes. Flip over every piece and bake until well cooked and almost crispy, 15–20 minutes longer, taking care that they do not burn.

PREPARATION TIME: 15 MINUTES
COOKING TIME: 1 HOUR 50 MINUTES
SERVES: 4

- 2 tablespoons olive oil
- 3 cloves garlic, minced
- 1 medium onion, finely chopped
- 1 carrot, finely chopped
- 2 stalks celery, finely sliced
- ⅓ cup (85 g) tomato paste (purée)
- 3 tomatoes, chopped
- 6 cups (325 g) chopped
  hen-of-the-woods mushrooms
- 1 cup (240 ml) red wine
- 2 cups (475 ml) mushroom broth or stock
- 2 bay leaves
- ½ cup (30 g) fresh parsley, chopped
- Salt and freshly ground black pepper

[The wild mushroom known as hen-of-the-woods grows widely throughout the United States and is found in the forests of Connecticut and other states east of the Rocky Mountains. Its flavor is very mild and takes well to seasoning. Use this ragu in lasagna or with noodles or polenta.]

In a large saucepan, heat the oil over medium heat. Add the garlic and onion and cook until translucent, about 3 minutes. Add the carrot and celery and cook until the vegetables take on a little color, another 8 minutes. Add the tomato paste (purée), stir well, and cook for 4 minutes to caramelize. Increase the heat to high and add the tomatoes and mushrooms, stirring well. Add the wine and bring it to a brief boil before adding the broth and bay leaves. Reduce the heat to medium-low and gently simmer for 30 minutes. Stir in the parsley. Cook for 1 hour, until the flavors come together. Season to taste with salt and pepper.

MOREL SAUCE

PREPARATION TIME: 10 MINUTES
COOKING TIME: 15 MINUTES
MAKES: ABOUT 2 CUPS (475 ML)

- 3 tablespoons (45 g) butter
- 8 oz (225 g) fresh morels, cleaned
  and halved lengthwise
- Salt and freshly ground black pepper
- 1 shallot, finely chopped
- ⅓ cup (80 ml) fruity white wine
- ½ cup (120 ml) heavy (whipping) cream
- 1 tablespoon snipped fresh chives
  (or ramp leaves)

[This sauce is served on toast or accompanies sautéed chicken or beef. Note that morel mushrooms must be cooked to be eaten.]

In a saucepan, heat the butter over medium-high heat. Add the morels and season with salt and pepper. Cook until just tender, 3–4 minutes. Reduce the heat to medium, stir in the shallot, and cook until soft, about 3 minutes. Add the wine and simmer for 1 minute. Add the cream and cook until the sauce thickens a little, about 5 minutes. Taste for seasoning and keep warm until needed. Add the chives or ramp leaves just before serving. Store in the refrigerator for up to 3 days.

HUSH PUPPIES

PREPARATION TIME: 5 MINUTES
COOKING TIME: 15 MINUTES
SERVES: 4

- ½ cup (65 g) all-purpose (plain) flour
- ½ cup (65 g) cornmeal
- ½ teaspoon salt
- ¼ teaspoon baking soda (bicarbonate of soda)
- ¼ teaspoon freshly ground black pepper
- 1 egg
- ½ cup (120 ml) buttermilk
- 4 tablespoons minced onion
- Peanut (groundnut) or vegetable oil, for deep-frying

[Popular in Mississippi and throughout the South overall, hush puppies are served as a side dish with seafood.]

In a large bowl, whisk together the flour, cornmeal, salt, baking soda (bicarbonate of soda), and pepper. In a medium bowl, whisk together the egg and buttermilk. Whisk the wet ingredients into the dry ingredients until just combined. Stir in the onion.

Pour 2 inches (5 cm) oil into a large heavy pot or deep-fryer and heat to 350°F (180°C).

Working in batches, carefully drop the batter by 1 tablespoon into the oil and fry, turning once, until golden and the center is cooked through, 5–6 minutes. Drain on paper towels. Serve hot.

WILD PUFFBALL PARMESAN

PREPARATION TIME: 15 MINUTES
COOKING TIME: 15 MINUTES
SERVES: 2

- 1 cup (130 g) all-purpose (plain) flour
- ½ teaspoon salt
- 2 eggs
- 1 cup (90 g) freshly grated Parmesan cheese
- 4 tablespoons (60 g) butter
- 2 tablespoons vegetable oil
- 1 lb (455 g) puffballs, cut into ½-inch (1.25 cm) thick slices
- Freshly cracked black pepper
- Lemon wedges, for serving

[Puffballs are mushrooms that appear like volleyballs on the grass in late summer. When cooked, tender puffball flesh is as soft as lightly melted cheese, tender tofu, or cooked bone marrow. Use it in any way that you would use those ingredients.]

Set up a dredging station: In a wide shallow bowl, mix the flour and salt. In a second bowl, beat the eggs with ¼ cup (60 ml) water. Place the Parmesan in a third bowl.

In large frying pan, heat the butter and oil over medium heat. Dip the mushroom slices in the flour, then the egg, and finally the Parmesan. Add the mushrooms to the pan and cook slowly over medium heat until golden brown, turning once, about 3 minutes per side. Drain briefly on paper towels. Season with cracked black pepper and serve hot, with lemon wedges for squeezing.

SPICY PIGWEED

PREPARATION TIME: 5 MINUTES
COOKING TIME: 10 MINUTES
SERVES: 4

- 1½ lb (680 g) pigweed leaves and tender stems (about 20 cups)
- Boiling water
- 1 tablespoon vegetable oil
- ½ juicy lime
- 1 teaspoon ancho chili powder
- Salt

[Palmer's pigweed, also known as careless weed, is native to the deserts of the Southwestern states. Native Americans cultivated this drought-tolerant species, using both seeds and leaves. It should always be blanched in boiling water before being squeezed and refreshed. A nice warm-weather leafy alternative to spinach and Swiss chard, it is delicious topped with warm eggs or folded into toasted tortillas.]

Place the clean pigweed in a large heatproof bowl and cover completely with boiling water. Let sit for 3 minutes.

Drain the pigweed in a colander and run under cold running water to refresh. When cool, squeeze dry.

In a cast-iron skillet or frying pan, heat the oil over medium heat. Pull the squeezed bundles of pigweed apart with your fingers and add to the pan. Cook for 1 minute before turning and stirring. Add a squeeze of lime juice, the ancho chili powder, and salt to taste. Serve hot.

FRIED WILD POKEWEED SHOOT TIPS

PREPARATION TIME: 10 MINUTES
COOKING TIME: 12 MINUTES
SERVES: 4

- 16 pokeweed shoot tips (up to 6 inches/15 cm long for ease of frying), with young leaves
- 2 cups (260 g) all-purpose (plain) flour
- 1¼ teaspoons salt
- 3 eggs
- 8 tablespoons bacon fat, oil, or butter

[Poke, polk, poke salad, and poke sallett are just a few of this American vegetable's many names, immortalized in the Elvis song "Poke Salad Annie." Pokeweed must be eaten young (while green, tender, and easily snapped) and cooked, not raw. Boil young stems until just tender, then prepare them any way you might eat asparagus, although the texture of pokeweed is much more succulent. While not traditional, lemon wedges are an excellent addition.]

Wash the pokeweed shoots and peel off any red membrane. Pat thoroughly dry or spread out in front of a fan until dry.

Preheat the oven to warm. Set up a dredging station: In a wide shallow bowl, combine the flour and 1 teaspoon of the salt. In a second shallow bowl, beat the eggs, ⅓ cup (80 ml) water, and the remaining ¼ teaspoon salt.

In a wide saucepan, heat 2 tablespoons of the fat over medium heat. Dip each pokeweed shoot in the egg mixture, shake off the excess, and dip into the flour mixture, coating each side. Dip into the egg a second time, and then again into the flour. Working in batches (do not crowd the pan), add the shoots to the hot fat and cook on each side until golden brown, about 4 minutes per side. Transfer the shoots to a platter lined with paper towels and keep warm in the oven. Fry more batches, adding fat to the pan as needed. Serve hot.

ONION RINGS

PREPARATION TIME: 10 MINUTES
COOKING TIME: 10 MINUTES
SERVES: 2

- peanut (groundnut) oil, for frying
- ¾ cup (98 g) all-purpose (plain) flour
- ¾ cup (115 g) cornmeal
- ½ teaspoon salt
- ½ teaspoon sugar
- Pinch of cayenne pepper
- 1 cup (240 ml) buttermilk
- 1 egg
- 1 large onion, sliced in ½-inch (1.25 cm) rings, separated

Pour oil to a depth of 2 inches (5 cm) into a large heavy pot or deep-fryer and heat to 375°F (190°C).

Meanwhile, set up a dredging station: In a wide shallow bowl, whisk together the flour, cornmeal, salt, sugar, and cayenne. In a separate bowl, whisk together the buttermilk and egg.

Dip the onion rings into the flour mixture first, then the egg mixture, then the flour mix again. Working in batches if necessary, add the onion rings to the hot oil and fry, turning occasionally, until golden brown, 3–4 minutes. Drain the rings on paper towels. Serve hot.

GRILLED WALLA WALLA ONIONS

PREPARATION TIME: 5 MINUTES
COOKING TIME: 10 MINUTES
SERVES: 4

- 4 medium Walla Walla onions
- 2 tablespoons olive oil
- ½ teaspoon salt
- ½ teaspoon freshly ground black pepper

[The pride of Washington State, Walla Walla County's eponymous onions are exceptionally mild and sweet. They are wonderful sliced raw on sandwiches, and their sweetness is played up on the grill.]

Preheat a gas or charcoal grill (barbecue) to high heat.

Peel the onions and either halve lengthwise or cut crosswise into 2-inch (5 cm) thick rings. Rub all over with the olive oil, then sprinkle with the salt and pepper. Grill until charred and soft, about 10 minutes.

ONION RINGS

TWICE-BAKED POTATOES

PREPARATION TIME: 20 MINUTES
COOKING TIME: 1 HOUR 15 MINUTES
SERVES: 8

- 4 large russet (baking) potatoes
  (about 2 lb/910 g)
- 1 tablespoon olive oil
- ½ teaspoon salt, plus more to taste
- 4 tablespoons (60 g) butter
- 4 tablespoons sour cream
- 1 tablespoon milk
- 1 cup (115 g) shredded cheddar cheese
- 2 tablespoons chopped fresh chives
- Freshly ground black pepper

Preheat the oven to 425°F (220°F/Gas Mark 7).

Scrub the potatoes well. Using a fork, prick each potato 3 or 4 times. Place on a baking sheet, brush with the olive oil, and sprinkle with ½ teaspoon salt. Bake until a paring knife can be easily inserted into and removed from the potato, 40–50 minutes. Take the potatoes out but leave the oven on.

When the potatoes are cool enough to handle, halve them lengthwise. Scrape the flesh of the potato into a bowl, leaving ⅛ inch (3 mm) of potato on the skin. Add the butter, sour cream, milk, half the cheddar, the chives, and salt and pepper to taste. With a potato masher or a fork, mash the mixture until smooth.

Divide the potato mixture evenly among the skins. Top with the remaining cheddar. Return to oven and bake until the potatoes are heated through and the cheddar is melted, 20–25 minutes.

MASHED POTATOES

PREPARATION TIME: 10 MINUTES
COOKING TIME: 35 MINUTES
SERVES: 4

- 2 lb (910 g) russet (baking) or
  Yukon Gold potatoes
- Salt
- 4 tablespoons (60 g) butter
- 1 cup (240 ml) milk
- Freshly ground black pepper

Scrub the potatoes. Place them in a large pot and add cold water to cover by about 3 inches (7.5 cm). Add ½ teaspoon salt, bring to a boil, and cook until they can easily be pierced with a knife, 15–30 minutes depending on the size.

Drain the potatoes. At this point, it is optional to peel the potatoes. Return the potatoes to the pot and set over low heat. Add the butter and milk. Heat until the butter has melted and the milk is hot. Remove from the heat and use a potato masher to mash the potatoes. Mash according to your preferred style: smooth or lumpy. Season to taste with salt and pepper.

SCALLOPED POTATOES

PREPARATION TIME: 15 MINUTES
COOKING TIME: 1 HOUR 20 MINUTES
SERVES: 8

- 6 large russet (baking) potatoes
- 4 tablespoons (60 g) butter
- 3 tablespoons all-purpose (plain) flour
- 1½ cups (355 ml) milk
- 1½ teaspoons salt
- ½ teaspoon freshly ground black pepper
- ¼ teaspoon cayenne pepper
- 1 cup (115 g) grated cheddar cheese

Preheat the oven to 350°F (180°C/Gas Mark 4). Butter a 9 x 13-inch (23 x 33 cm) baking dish.

Set up a bowl of cold water. Peel and thinly slice the potatoes, as thinly and evenly as possible, using a mandoline or a very sharp knife, adding the slices to the bowl of water as you slice them to keep them from browning.

In a small saucepan, melt the butter over medium heat. Stir in the flour. Add the milk and cook over medium heat, whisking, until the mixture begins to bubble and thicken, about 8 minutes. Remove from the heat and stir in the salt, black pepper, cayenne, and cheddar. Continue stirring until the cheese is melted.

Drain the potatoes. Layer them in the baking dish, ladling some cheese sauce over each layer. Cover with foil and bake for 1 hour. Remove the foil and bake until golden brown and crispy around the edges, another 15 minutes.

FUNERAL POTATOES

PREPARATION TIME: 10 MINUTES
COOKING TIME: 1 HOUR 10 MINUTES
SERVES: 12

- 6 tablespoons (90 g) butter
- 1 medium onion, diced
- 3 cloves garlic, minced
- 2 lb (910 g) grated frozen hash brown potatoes (thawed)
- 1 can (10.5 oz/295 g) cream of chicken soup
- 2 cups (475 ml) sour cream
- 1½ teaspoons salt
- ½ teaspoon freshly ground black pepper
- 2 cups (230 g) shredded sharp cheddar cheese
- 4 tablespoons freshly grated Parmesan cheese
- 1½ cups (45 g) corn flakes

[This dish is popular for large crowds, particularly among the Mormon community and not only at funerals. The traditional recipe calls for frozen hash brown potatoes, but freshly grated potatoes work fine, too.]

Preheat the oven to 350°F (180°C/Gas Mark 4). Generously grease a 9 x 13-inch (23 x 33 cm) baking dish.

In a small saucepan, melt 2 tablespoons (30 g) of the butter over medium heat. Add the onion and cook until softened, about 5 minutes. Stir in the garlic and cook for 30 seconds. Remove from the heat.

In a large bowl, mix together the potatoes, cooked onions and garlic, soup, sour cream, salt, and pepper. Stir in the cheddar and Parmesan. Pour the mixture into the buttered pan.

Melt the remaining 4 tablespoons (60 g) butter and toss with the corn flakes. Sprinkle the corn flakes over the top of the cheesy potatoes. Bake until golden brown and bubbling, about 1 hour.

POTATO LATKES

PREPARATION TIME: 25 MINUTES
COOKING TIME: 30 MINUTES
MAKES: 12

- 2 lb (910 g) russet (baking) potatoes, peeled and grated
- 1 small onion, grated
- ½ teaspoon salt
- 2 eggs
- 4 tablespoons matzo meal
- ¼ teaspoon freshly ground black pepper
- Vegetable oil, for cooking the latkes

Place the grated potatoes and onion in a colander. Toss with ½ teaspoon salt and let rest for 15 minutes. Press well, first squeezing with your hands, then place on a paper towel to drain as much liquid as possible.

In a medium bowl, whisk the eggs. Stir in the potato/onion mixture, matzo meal, and black pepper and mix gently to combine.

Heat a large frying pan over medium heat. Pour about ⅛ inch (3 mm) vegetable oil into the pan, enough to coat the bottom of the pan. Working in batches, place ¼-cup (60 ml) spoonfuls of batter into the pan and press lightly into a flat round. Cook until golden brown, about 5 minutes. Flip and cook until golden brown and crispy on the second side, another 5 minutes. Drain on paper towels and season to taste with salt and pepper.

FRENCH FRIES

PREPARATION TIME: 15 MINUTES,
   PLUS 1 HOUR RESTING TIME
COOKING TIME: 20 MINUTES
SERVES: 6–8

- Peanut (groundnut) or vegetable oil, for deep-frying
- 1½ lb (680 g) russet (baking) potatoes
- Salt and freshly ground black pepper

Pour 3 inches (7.5 cm) oil into a large heavy pot or deep-fryer and heat to 300°F (150°C). Set up a wire rack in a rimmed baking sheet.

Cut the potatoes ½-inch (1.25 cm) thick and 3–4 inches (7.5–10 cm) long. Pat dry with paper towels. Carefully add the potatoes by the handful to the hot oil and cook, adjusting the heat to keep the oil at 300°F (150°C), until the potatoes are very lightly golden and just tender, 5–10 minutes. Using a spider/skimmer or slotted spoon, transfer potatoes to the wire rack to drain. Let rest for 1 hour (or refrigerate for up to 8 hours, until ready to finish).

Bring the same oil up to 350°F (180°C). Add half the potatoes to the oil and cook, adjusting the heat to keep oil at 350°F (180°C), until the potatoes are golden and crispy, 3–4 minutes. (Remove those that turn golden first, allowing the others to continue to cook and crisp.) Remove with a spider/skimmer or slotted spoon and drain on paper towels or a paper bag. Season to taste with salt and pepper. Serve hot.

FRIED OKRA

PREPARATION TIME: 15 MINUTES
COOKING TIME: 15 MINUTES
SERVES: 4–6

- Peanut (groundnut) or vegetable oil,
  for deep-frying
- 1 cup (130 g) cornmeal
- 1 cup (130 g) all-purpose (plain) flour
- Salt
- ¼ teaspoon freshly ground black pepper
- ⅛ teaspoon cayenne pepper
- 2 cups (475 ml) buttermilk
- 1½ lb (680 g) okra, cut crosswise into
  ½-inch (1.25 cm) thick slices

Pour 3 inches (7.5 cm) oil into a large heavy pot or deep-fryer and heat to 350°F (180°C).

Set up a dredging station: In a wide shallow bowl, combine the cornmeal, flour, ½ teaspoon salt, the black pepper, and cayenne. Place the buttermilk in a second shallow bowl. Dip a few okra slices into the buttermilk. With a slotted spoon, move them to cornmeal mixture and toss well to coat.

Working in batches (do not crowd the pan), separate the pieces of okra, add to the oil, and cook until tender and golden, about 3 minutes. Drain on paper towels. Season with salt.

RUTABAGA PURÉE

PREPARATION TIME: 15 MINUTES
COOKING TIME: 30 MINUTES
SERVES: 4

- 1 lb (455 g) rutabagas (swedes),
  peeled and diced
- Salt
- 1 Yukon Gold potato (about 6 oz/170 g),
  peeled and diced
- 2 tablespoons (30 g) butter, melted
- 2 tablespoons heavy (whipping) cream
- 2 tablespoons crème fraîche
- Freshly ground black pepper

Place the rutabagas (swedes) and potato in a large soup pot. Add water to cover and season the water with salt. Bring to a boil over high heat, then reduce to a simmer and cook over medium-low heat until the vegetables are tender when pierced with a fork, 15–20 minutes.

Reserving ½ cup (120 ml) of the cooking liquid, drain the vegetables. Place the rutabagas and potato in a blender and add the butter, cream, and crème fraîche. Purée on high, until very smooth, adding some of the cooking liquid 1 tablespoon at a time in order help the blender to blend. Season to taste with salt and pepper.

CREAMED SPINACH

PREPARATION TIME: 10 MINUTES
COOKING TIME: 15 MINUTES
SERVES: 4

- 1 stick (115 g) butter
- 1 small onion, diced
- 3 cloves garlic, minced
- ½ cup (65 g) all-purpose (plain) flour
- 2 cups (475 ml) milk
- ½ teaspoon salt
- ¼ teaspoon freshly ground black pepper
- Freshly grated nutmeg
- 3 large bunches spinach, cleaned and roughly chopped (tender stems included)

In a large pot, melt the butter over medium heat. Add the onion and cook, stirring occasionally, until the onions begin to wilt, about 5 minutes. Add the garlic and cook for another minute.

Stir in the flour and cook, stirring constantly, for 2 minutes. Add the milk and cook, stirring constantly, until the mixture comes up to a brisk simmer. Reduce the heat to low, add the salt, pepper, and a grating of nutmeg, and cook, stirring, until the mixture thickens and no longer tastes of flour. Add the spinach by the handful to the pot, stirring to let it wilt after each addition. Increase the heat to medium and cook, stirring constantly, until the creamed spinach is bubbling and thoroughly cooked, about 5 minutes.

PALAK PANEER

PREPARATION TIME: 15 MINUTES
COOKING TIME: 40 MINUTES
SERVES: 4

- 2 large bunches spinach, washed and chopped (including tender stems)
- 2 small red onions, chopped
- ½-inch (1.25 cm) piece fresh ginger, chopped
- 1–2 small green chilies, halved and seeded
- 2 tablespoons olive oil
- 1 cinnamon stick
- 2 teaspoons ground cumin
- ½ teaspoon freshly grated nutmeg
- ½ teaspoon chaat masala (spice mix)
- 2 cups (496 g) unseasoned paneer, cut into ½-inch (1.25 cm) cubes
- ¼ cup (60 ml) heavy (whipping) cream
- Salt and freshly ground black pepper

[New Jersey is home to the largest population of Indian-Americans in the country. This dish has become popular takeout with Americans of many backgrounds. Serve with naan bread or rice.]

Bring a large pot of water to a boil. Add the spinach and blanch for 2 minutes. Reserving 1 cup of the blanching water, drain the spinach in a colander. Transfer the spinach to a blender and add the onions, ginger, chilies, and the reserved liquid. Blend until smooth.

In a deep large frying pan, heat the oil over medium-high heat. Add the cinnamon stick, cumin, and nutmeg and cook, stirring, until fragrant, about 2 minutes. Stir in the spinach purée and the chaat masala. Cook, stirring, until bubbling, about 5 minutes. Add the paneer, cover, and cook for 20 minutes, stirring occasionally. Stir in the cream and cook for 5 more minutes. Season to taste with salt and pepper. Serve.

SQUASH CASSEROLE

PREPARATION TIME: 15 MINUTES
COOKING TIME: 1 HOUR
SERVES: 10–12

- 4 tablespoons (60 g) butter, melted
- 4 cups (600 g) sliced yellow squash
- 1 medium onion, chopped
- 2 eggs
- 1¼ cups (295 ml) milk
- 1½ cups (170 g) grated cheddar cheese
- ¼ teaspoon cayenne pepper
- ½ teaspoon salt
- ½ teaspoon freshly ground black pepper
- 1 sleeve (35 crackers) Ritz crackers, crushed to crumbs

[A classic, creamy side on "meat-and-three" plates that are popular in the South.]

Preheat the oven to 350°F (180°C/Gas Mark 4). Grease a 9 x 13-inch (23 x 33 cm) baking dish.

In a large frying pan, melt 2 tablespoons of the butter over medium-low heat. Add the squash and onion and cook until tender, about 10 minutes.

In a large bowl, whisk together the eggs and milk. Stir in the cheddar. Fold in the cooked squash mixture, the remaining 2 tablespoons butter, the cayenne, salt, and black pepper. Pour the mixture into the baking dish. Top evenly with the cracker crumbs.

Bake until the top has lightly browned and the center is set, about 45 minutes. Let rest for 5 minutes before serving.

CALABACITAS (SQUASH AND GREEN CHILI CASSEROLE)

PREPARATION TIME: 30 MINUTES
COOKING TIME: 35 MINUTES
SERVES: 8–10

- 6 Hatch green chilies, roasted and peeled (see Note, page 86)
- 3 tablespoons (45 g) butter
- 1 cup (160 g) diced yellow onion
- 3 cloves garlic, minced
- 1¾ lb (795 g) yellow squash, sliced crosswise into ¼-inch (6 mm) thick rounds
- 1 teaspoon kosher (coarse) salt
- ½ teaspoon freshly ground black pepper
- 4 tablespoons chopped fresh cilantro (coriander)
- 4 cups (450 g) shredded Monterey Jack or mild cheddar cheese
- 4 eggs
- ½ cup (120 ml) milk
- 3 tablespoons all-purpose (plain) flour
- 2 teaspoons baking powder
- ½ cup (45 g) dried breadcrumbs

Preheat the oven to 350°F (180°C/Gas Mark 4).

Finely chop the chilies and set aside.

In a large heavy-bottomed ovenproof frying pan, melt the butter over medium heat. Add the onion and cook until softened and translucent, 5–7 minutes. Add the garlic and cook for 2 more minutes. Add the squash and cook until softened, 5–7 minutes. Stir in the salt, pepper, and cilantro (coriander). Remove from the heat and stir in the diced chilies and cheese.

In a bowl, whisk together the eggs, milk, flour, and baking powder. Pour over the squash mixture and stir very gently to combine and mix evenly with the squash.

Top the squash mixture with the breadcrumbs. Bake, uncovered, until the casserole filling is set and the breadcrumbs are lightly golden, 30–35 minutes. Serve warm.

BRAISED BUTTERNUT SQUASH

PREPARATION TIME: 10 MINUTES
COOKING TIME: 30 MINUTES
SERVES: 4

- 3 tablespoons extra-virgin olive oil
- 3 cloves garlic, finely chopped
- 2 lb (910 g) butternut squash, peeled, seeded, and cut into 1-inch (2.5 cm) cubes
- ½ cup (120 ml) vegetable stock
- Salt and freshly ground black pepper
- 2 tablespoons (30 g) butter, diced
- 1 tablespoon chopped fresh parsley

Heat a large Dutch oven (casserole) or heavy-bottomed pot over medium heat. Add the oil and garlic and cook just until the garlic turns light golden, 1–2 minutes. Add the squash and stock and season with salt and pepper. Bring to a boil, cover, reduce the heat to low, and cook until the squash is tender, about 15 minutes.

Uncover, stir, increase the heat to medium-high, and cook, stirring occasionally, until the liquid has evaporated and the squash is golden brown, 8–10 minutes. Remove from the heat and toss with the butter and parsley. Serve hot.

CANDIED SWEET POTATOES

PREPARATION TIME: 10 MINUTES,
    PLUS COOLING TIME
COOKING TIME: 1 HOUR 20 MINUTES
SERVES: 8–10

- 6 tablespoons (90 g) butter
- 4 lb (1.8 kg) sweet potatoes
- Salt
- 1 cup (190 g) packed light brown sugar
- ½ cup (120 ml) apple juice
- 1 teaspoon ground cinnamon
- ½ teaspoon freshly grated nutmeg
- ½ teaspoon ground ginger
- ¼ cup (60 ml) bourbon (optional)
- 2 cups (100 g) mini marshmallows

[*Sweet potato* and *yam* are terms often used interchangeably to refer to the same vegetable with dark skin and golden to deep-orange flesh. The sliced or cubed tubers are baked in a sweet, buttery syrup until tender and glistening, then served as a "vegetable" even when sweeter than many desserts and crowned with marshmallows.]

Preheat the oven to 350°F (180°C/Gas Mark 4). Butter a 9 x 13-inch (23 x 33 cm) baking dish with 1 tablespoon (15 g) of the butter.

Place the sweet potatoes in a large soup pot, add water to cover, and season generously with salt. Bring to a boil over high heat, reduce the heat to medium-low, and simmer until sweet potatoes are just tender, about 25 minutes. Drain. When cool enough to handle, peel the sweet potatoes and cut into ¼-inch (6 mm) thick rounds. Layer the sweet potato rounds in the baking dish, shingling them to cover the whole dish.

In small saucepan, combine the remaining 5 tablespoons (75 g) butter, the brown sugar, apple juice, cinnamon, nutmeg, ginger, ½ teaspoon salt, and bourbon (if using). Bring the mixture to a boil and cook for 2 minutes. Pour over the potatoes.

Bake uncovered until browned, about 40 minutes. Increase the oven temperature to 500°F (260°C/Gas Mark 10) and top sweet potatoes with the mini marshmallows. Bake until the marshmallows are lightly browned, about 5 minutes.

BRAISED BUTTERNUT SQUASH

RUM-GLAZED ACORN SQUASH

PREPARATION TIME: 10 MINUTES
COOKING TIME: 1 HOUR
SERVES: 4

- 2 medium acorn squash
- 4 tablespoons dark brown sugar
- 4 tablespoons (60 g) butter
- 4 tablespoons dark rum
- Salt and freshly ground black pepper

Preheat the oven to 350°F (180°C/Gas Mark 4).

Cut the stems off the squash and halve lengthwise. Scoop out the seeds and discard (or save for roasting). Place the squash halves cut side up in a baking pan. Fill each half with 1 tablespoon brown sugar, 1 tablespoon (15 g) butter, and 1 tablespoon rum. Sprinkle salt and pepper over each one. Bake, basting every 15–20 minutes, until tender, about 1 hour.

MAPLE-GLAZED PARSNIPS

PREPARATION TIME: 10 MINUTES
COOKING TIME: 20 MINUTES
SERVES: 4

- 8 medium parsnips, peeled and cut into 1-inch (2.5 cm) pieces
- 3 tablespoons (45 g) butter
- 3 tablespoons maple syrup
- 1 teaspoon salt
- ½ teaspoon freshly ground black pepper

Place the parsnips in a medium saucepan, cover with cold water, and bring to a boil. Cook until just tender, about 5 minutes. Drain well.

In a large frying pan, melt the butter over medium-high heat. Add the parsnips and cook, stirring, until beginning to brown, about 5 minutes. Add the maple syrup, salt, and pepper. Reduce the heat to medium and cook until the sauce thickens, another 3–5 minutes. Serve hot.

RUM-GLAZED ACORN SQUASH

POI

PREPARATION TIME: 10 MINUTES WITH
A FOOD PROCESSOR, OR 20 MINUTES
WITH MORTAR AND PESTLE
COOKING TIME: 15 MINUTES
SERVES: 4

- 2 taro roots, scrubbed

[This starchy root, cooked until smooth, is a traditional, native Hawaiian staple. It is made from the root of the taro plant and is commonly paired with lomi-lomi salmon or kalua pork, or eaten alone, seasoned with salt and pepper, soy sauce, or sugar. Poi can also be fermented for two or more days before eating.]

In a large pot, cover the taro roots with cold water and bring to a boil. Reduce the heat and simmer until tender, 12–15 minutes. Drain and rinse with cold water. When cool enough to handle, peel and cut into small cubes.

Using a food processor, or a bowl with a mallet, or a large mortar and pestle, pound or blend the taro with 1 tablespoon of water at a time, to make a smooth paste. Add water and blend or pound until thick and sticky, similar in consistency to bread dough.

BRAISED TURNIPS

PREPARATION TIME: 10 MINUTES
COOKING TIME: 25 MINUTES
SERVES: 4

- 1 lb (455 g) turnips, peeled and cut into 1-inch (2.5 cm) pieces, or scrubbed baby turnips
- 1 tablespoon (15 g) butter
- 1 tablespoon extra-virgin olive oil
- ½ cup (120 ml) vegetable stock
- Salt and freshly ground black pepper
- 1 tablespoon fresh lemon juice
- 1 tablespoon chopped fresh parsley

Place the turnips in a saucepan big enough to hold them in a single layer. Cut a round of parchment paper that will fit inside the diameter of the saucepan. Cut a small hole in the center of the round. Set round aside.

Add the butter, olive oil, stock, ½ teaspoon salt, and ¼ teaspoon pepper to the pan and bring to a boil over high heat. Reduce to a simmer, place the parchment round directly on top of the turnips, and cook over medium-low heat until the liquid is almost all evaporated and the turnips are tender, about 20 minutes. Remove from the heat, discard the parchment, and stir in the lemon juice and parsley. Season to taste with salt and pepper.

BRAISED TURNIPS

MASHED WILD WAPATO

PREPARATION TIME: 10 MINUTES
COOKING TIME: 25 MINUTES
SERVES: 4

- 4 cups (1.2 kg) peeled wapato tubers
- 6 tablespoons (90 g) butter, melted
- ½ cup (120 ml) milk, warmed
- Salt

[Various wapato species are found across the United States in wetlands and marshes and along shallow lake edges. Their young, unfurled leaves and tender flower buds and stems are edible, although wapato is best known for its tubers. The explorers Meriwether Lewis and William Clark were invited by Native Americans to dine on wapato roasted in embers. They bought four bushels, about which Clark wrote: "an agreeable taste and answers verry [sic] well in place of bread." Wapato is also a good substitute for potatoes.]

In a pot of boiling water, cook the wapato tubers until fork-tender, about 15 minutes (this may vary depending on the size of the tubers). Drain and return to the pot over low heat. Flatten the cooked tubers with a potato masher and add the melted butter and warm milk. Mash until mixture is creamy. Season to taste with salt and serve.

BREADED ZUCCHINI

PREPARATION TIME: 25 MINUTES
COOKING TIME: 25 MINUTES
SERVES: 4

- 1 cup (130 g) all-purpose (plain) flour
- 3 eggs
- ½ cup (120 ml) milk
- 2 cups (225 g) panko breadcrumbs
- 4 tablespoons freshly grated Parmesan cheese
- 2 tablespoons chopped fresh parsley
- 2 lb (910 g) zucchini (courgettes), cut into ½-inch (1.25 cm) slices
- Vegetable oil, for shallow-frying
- Lemon wedges, for serving

Set up a dredging station: Place the flour in a wide shallow bowl. In a second bowl, whisk together the eggs and milk. In another bowl, whisk the panko, Parmesan, and parsley. Dredge each slice of zucchini (courgette) first in the flour, then the eggs, and finally the panko mixture and place on a baking sheet.

Pour ⅛ inch (3 mm) vegetable oil into a large frying pan over medium-high heat. Working in batches, cook the zucchini until golden brown, 2–3 minutes per side (between batches, add more oil to the frying pan as needed). Drain the zucchini on paper towels or a wire rack set over a baking sheet. Season to taste with salt. Serve with lemon wedges.

JAPANESE TEMPURA

PREPARATION TIME: 15 MINUTES
COOKING TIME: 5 MINUTES
SERVES: 4

- Vegetable oil, for deep-frying
- 1¼ cups (200 g) rice flour
- ¼ cup (30 g) cornstarch (cornflour)
- Salt
- 2 cups (475 ml) cold sparkling water
- ¾ lb (340 g) vegetables (such as carrots, broccoli, or green beans), cut into bite-size (¼-inch/6 mm) thick slices
- Freshly ground black pepper

Pour 3 inches (7.5 cm) oil into a large heavy pot or deep-fryer and heat to 360°F (182°C). Set up a wire rack over a baking sheet.

In a large bowl, whisk the rice flour, cornstarch (cornflour) together, and ½ teaspoon salt. Slowly whisk in the sparkling water.

Dip the vegetables into the batter one at a time, letting the excess batter drip off the end. Working in batches, cook the vegetables until lightly golden and crispy, about 2 minutes. As each piece is ready, transfer to the wire rack. Season to taste with salt and pepper. Serve hot.

REFRIED PINTO BEANS

PREPARATION TIME: 10 MINUTES, PLUS OVERNIGHT SOAKING AND COOLING TIME
COOKING TIME: 2 HOURS 40 MINUTES
SERVES: 4

- ½ lb (227 g) dried pinto beans, rinsed and picked over
- ¼ lb (112 g) salt pork, cut into 1-inch (2.5 cm) pieces
- 4 cloves garlic, smashed and peeled
- Salt
- ¼ cup (60 g) lard or bacon drippings

Place the beans in a large bowl and add cold water to cover by at least 2 inches (5 cm). Let soak for 8 hours or overnight.

Drain and rinse the beans, place in a large pot, and add fresh water to cover by 1 inch (2.5 cm). Place the pot over medium-high heat. Add the salt pork and garlic. Bring to a simmer over medium-high heat, skimming any foam from the surface. Reduce the heat to medium-low and simmer until the beans are still whole, but tender and very creamy, 1–1½ hours. If the level of water in the pot goes down to expose the beans, add 1 cup (240 ml) water at a time to replenish. Once the beans are tender, remove the salt pork (or leave in, if desired) and season to taste with salt. Let the beans cool in the cooking liquid so they will continue to soften and season. Cover and refrigerate.

Reserving the cooking liquid, drain the beans.

In a large frying pan, heat the lard or bacon drippings over medium heat. Add the beans and fry until beans are heated through, about 4 minutes. Remove from the heat and smash with a potato masher. Add the reserved bean cooking liquid to the beans, 1 tablespoonful at a time, as you continue to mash, until beans are smooth and easy to stir.

BLACK-EYED PEAS WITH SALT PORK AND GREENS

PREPARATION TIME: 15 MINUTES,
 PLUS OVERNIGHT SOAKING TIME
COOKING TIME: 2 HOURS 35 MINUTES
SERVES: 12

- 2 lb (910 g) dried black-eyed peas (beans), rinsed and picked over
- 1 lb (455 g) salt pork, cut into 1-inch (2.5 cm) pieces
- 1 large onion, peeled and quartered with the root end intact
- 1 bay leaf
- ½ teaspoon freshly ground black pepper
- ½ teaspoon ground allspice
- ¼ teaspoon ground cloves
- Kosher (coarse) salt
- 2 tablespoons vegetable oil
- 4 cloves garlic, minced
- ½ teaspoon crushed chili flakes
- 2 lb (910 g) collard greens, stems removed, cut into 2-inch (5 cm) pieces
- ¾ cup (115 g) sliced scallions (spring onions)

[This hearty dish, known as Hoppin' John, is a must on New Year's Day for Southerners, who say the distinctively marked dried beans bring luck, while greens symbolize money for the upcoming year. The combination is usually seasoned with a piece of cured pork (such as salt pork, used here), ham hock, or several slices of bacon. Serve alongside cornbread.]

Place the peas (beans) in a bowl with cold water to cover by at least 2 inches (5 cm). Soak overnight.

Drain the peas and transfer to a large Dutch oven (casserole) or heavy-bottomed soup pot. Add the salt pork, the onion quarters, bay leaf, pepper, allspice, and cloves. Add cold water to cover the peas by 3 inches (7.5 cm). Bring to a boil over high heat, then reduce to medium-low heat and cook at a gentle simmer until tender, 1½–2 hours, skimming off any foam that rises to the surface. While cooking, add 1 cup (240 ml) boiling water at a time, to keep the liquid above the surface of the peas. Remove from the heat and season to taste with salt. Measure out 1 cup (240 ml) of the cooking liquid and set aside.

In a large frying pan, heat the oil over medium-high heat. Add the garlic and chili flakes and cook for 1 minute. Add the collard greens and stir to coat. Season with 1 teaspoon kosher salt and add the reserved pea cooking liquid, stirring to help wilt the greens. Reduce the heat to medium, cover, and cook until the greens are soft, about 20 minutes.

To serve, divide the greens among shallow bowls, then ladle hot black-eyed peas and salt pork on top. Garnish with the scallions (spring onions) and season to taste with salt.

BLACK-EYED PEAS WITH SALT PORK AND GREENS

SOUTHERN-STYLE LIMA BEANS

PREPARATION TIME: 10 MINUTES
COOKING TIME: 45 MINUTES
SERVES: 10–12

- 8 slices bacon (streaky), cut into ½-inch (1.25 cm) pieces
- 1½ cups (240 g) diced yellow onion
- ½ cup (95 g) packed light brown sugar
- 1½ lb (690 g) lima beans (butter beans)
- 6 tablespoons (85 g) butter
- 4 cups (1 liter) vegetable stock
- 2 teaspoons salt
- 1 teaspoon cracked black pepper

[Lima beans, or butter beans, appear as a side vegetable on Southern tables everywhere. The shell beans are native to the Americas and are the beans to use when making succotash.]

Heat a large pot or Dutch oven (casserole) over medium heat. Add the bacon and cook until the bacon releases its fat, 4–5 minutes. Add the onion and cook until softened, 5–7 minutes. Stir in the brown sugar and cook for 2 minutes to melt the sugar. Add the beans and butter and stir well to coat. Add the vegetable stock and ½ cup (120 ml) water. Bring to a boil over high heat. Reduce the heat to low and simmer, stirring occasionally, until the beans are very tender, 35–45 minutes. Stir in the salt and pepper, adding more to taste.

LIMA BEAN BAKE

PREPARATION TIME: 5 MINUTES,
  PLUS 8 HOURS SOAKING TIME
COOKING TIME: 1 HOUR 40 MINUTES
SERVES: 8–10

- 1 lb (455 g) dried lima beans (butter beans), rinsed and picked over
- 1 tablespoon vegetable oil
- 1 lb (455 g) ground (minced) beef
- 1 large onion, diced
- 2 cans (15 oz/425 g each) tomato purée (passata)
- 1 tablespoon light brown sugar
- 2 teaspoons salt
- 1 teaspoon dried thyme

Place the beans in a bowl with cold water to cover by 2 inches (5 cm). Soak for 8 hours.

Drain the beans, place in a large pot, and add cold water to cover by at least 2 inches (5 cm). Bring to a boil over high heat, skimming any foam that rises to the surface. Reduce to a simmer and cook until tender, about 40 minutes. Reserve 1 cup (240 ml) of the cooking liquid, drain the beans, and set aside.

In a large pot, heat the oil over medium-high heat. Add the beef and cook, breaking it up with a wooden spoon, until browned, about 6 minutes. Add the onion and cook, stirring, until the beef and onions are cooked through, about 6 minutes. Add the tomato purée (passata), brown sugar, salt, and thyme. Stir in the cooked beans and reserved cooking liquid. Remove from the heat.

Preheat the oven to 350°F (180°C/Gas Mark 4). Grease a 9 x 13-inch (23 x 33 cm) baking dish.

Pour the bean mixture into the baking dish and bake until bubbling, 30–40 minutes. Serve hot.

SOUTHERN-STYLE LIMA BEANS

BOSTON BAKED BEANS

PREPARATION TIME: 10 MINUTES,
  PLUS OVERNIGHT SOAKING TIME
COOKING TIME: 8 HOURS
SERVES: 8

- 2 cups (430 g) dried small white beans, rinsed and picked over
- ¼ lb (115 g) salt pork, diced (optional)
- 1 large onion, chopped
- ¼ cup (85 g) molasses
- 2 tablespoons tomato paste (purée)
- 2 tablespoons light brown sugar
- 1 tablespoon mustard powder
- 1 teaspoon salt

[We have both Native American food traditions and the Pilgrims' Christian beliefs to thank for the evolution of Boston baked beans. Native people in the region baked beans sweetened with maple syrup in earthen pots, and taught white settlers to do the same. Because religious law prohibited working or cooking on the Sabbath, Pilgrims would often make beans on Saturday night and leave them in the oven for a warm meal on Sunday. Molasses replaced the maple syrup.]

Place the beans in a bowl with cold water to cover by several inches. Soak overnight.

If using salt pork, heat a cast-iron skillet until very hot. Without adding oil to the pan, sear the salt pork, cooking until dark and caramelized, about 3 minutes. Flip and caramelize the other side. Remove from the pan. When cool enough to handle, dice and set aside.

Preheat the oven to 250°F (120°C/Gas Mark ½).

Drain the beans and return to the bowl. Stir in the salt pork (if using), onion, molasses, tomato paste (purée), brown sugar, mustard powder, and salt. Transfer the mixture in a 2-quart (2 liter) baking dish (or bean pot) with a lid. Pour in enough water to cover the beans by 2 inches (5 cm).

Cover and bake until the beans are tender, 6–8 hours, checking periodically to make sure the beans haven't dried out, and adding water as needed.

TEPARY BEANS

PREPARATION TIME: 5 MINUTES,
  PLUS OVERNIGHT SOAKING TIME
COOKING TIME: 2 HOURS 45 MINUTES
SERVES: 8–10

- 1 lb (455 g) dried tepary beans, rinsed and picked over
- ½ lb (225 g) ham hock
- 8 cloves garlic, peeled but whole
- Salt

Place the beans in a bowl with cold water to cover by 4 inches (10 cm). Soak for 8 hours or overnight.

Drain and rinse the beans and transfer to a pot with fresh water to cover by 2 inches (5 cm). Add the ham hock and garlic. Bring to a simmer over medium-high heat, skimming any foam that rises to the surface. Reduce heat to medium-low and let simmer until the beans are firm-tender and still whole, 2–2½ hours. If the level of water in the pot goes down to expose the beans, add 1 cup (240 ml) boiling water at a time, to replenish. Remove the ham hock and season the beans to taste with salt. Let the beans cool in the cooking liquid to continue to soften and season. Reheat to serve, or cover and refrigerate, if not serving immediately.

COWBOY "CHARRO" BEANS

PREPARATION TIME: 15 MINUTES,
  PLUS OVERNIGHT SOAKING TIME
COOKING TIME: 3 HOURS 25 MINUTES
SERVES: 4–6

- 1 lb (455 g) dried pinto beans, rinsed and picked over
- ¾ lb (340 g) thick-cut bacon (streaky), cut crosswise into ¼-inch (6 mm) pieces
- 1 large yellow onion, chopped
- 1 head garlic (about 10 cloves), cloves separated, smashed, and peeled
- 2 jalapeño peppers, halved (ribs and seeds removed for less heat)
- 3–4 sprigs fresh thyme
- 2 sprigs fresh oregano
- 2 bay leaves
- Kosher (coarse) salt and freshly ground black pepper

[Here's a beloved soupy, porky alternative to refried pinto beans. If you forget to soak your beans overnight, bring a pot of beans and water to a boil, turn off the heat, and let stand, covered, for 1 hour. You could also make this dish in a slow cooker, keeping the same timing, if you prefer; simply sauté the ingredients as the first step and transfer to a 4-quart (4 liter) slow cooker.]

Place the beans in a bowl with water to cover by several inches and let soak overnight. Drain well.

Heat a Dutch oven (casserole) or other large heavy pot over medium heat. Add the bacon and cook, stirring, until it begins to release its fat and start to brown, about 5 minutes. Add the onion and cook, stirring, until tender and golden brown, 5–7 minutes.

Add 7 cups (1.7 liters) water, the beans, garlic, jalapeños, thyme, oregano, bay leaves, and 1 teaspoon salt. Bring to a boil over high heat, then reduce to a simmer and cook until the beans are very tender, 2–3 hours. Season to taste with salt and pepper. Before serving, remove the herbs and jalapeños.

BARBECUE BEANS

PREPARATION TIME: 5 MINUTES
COOKING TIME: 1 HOUR 10 MINUTES
SERVES: 8

- ½ lb (225 g) bacon (streaky), diced
- ½ lb (225 g) ground (minced) beef
- 1 medium onion, diced
- ½ cup (140 g) ketchup
- ½ cup (240 ml) barbecue sauce
- ¼ cup (60 ml) molasses
- 1 tablespoon yellow mustard
- ½ cup (95 g) packed light brown sugar
- 1 can (15 oz/425 g) red kidney beans, rinsed and drained
- 2 cans (15 oz/425 g each) pork and beans

In a large heavy-bottomed pot, cook the bacon over medium-high heat until some of the fat is rendered, about 3 minutes. Add the ground (minced) beef and onion and cook, stirring, until the bacon and beef are browned and the onions have wilted, 6–8 minutes. Stir in the ketchup, barbecue sauce, molasses, mustard, brown sugar, kidney beans, and pork and beans. Bring to a boil, then reduce the heat to very low and simmer for 1 hour, stirring occasionally.

CHEESE GRITS

COOKING TIME: 40 MINUTES
SERVES: 4

- 2 cups (475 ml) half-and-half (single cream)
- 2 teaspoons salt
- ½ teaspoon freshly ground black pepper
- 1 cup (140 g) coarsely ground grits
- 2 tablespoons (30 g) butter
- 1½ cups (170 g) shredded sharp cheddar cheese

[Plain grits are a hot breakfast cereal. Cheese grits elevate this dish to a side staple. They are often topped with shrimp, ham, sausage, or greens.]

In a medium saucepan, combine 3 cups (710 ml) water, the half-and-half (single) cream, salt, and pepper. Bring to a boil over medium-high heat. Whisking constantly, gradually add the grits and continue whisking until fully combined. Return to a boil, then reduce the heat to a bare simmer, cover, and cook, stirring frequently, until the grits are thickened and tender, 25–30 minutes. Remove from the heat and stir in the butter and cheddar. (If the grits get too thick, add more hot water as needed and return to a simmer.)

SPOONBREAD

PREPARATION TIME: 10 MINUTES,
    PLUS COOLING TIME
COOKING TIME: 30 MINUTES
SERVES: 4

- 1½ cups (355 ml) boiling water
- 1 cup (130 g) cornmeal
- 1 tablespoon (15 g) butter
- 1 egg
- 1 cup (240 ml) buttermilk
- 1 teaspoon baking soda (bicarbonate of soda)
- ½ teaspoon salt

[This is often served alongside roasted meats or thick stews.]

In a large heatproof bowl, pour the boiling water over the cornmeal. Stir in the butter and let cool to room temperature.

Meanwhile, preheat the oven to 350°F (180°C/Gas Mark 4). Butter an 8-inch (20 cm) round baking dish (such as a pie plate) and put in the oven to heat.

In a bowl, whisk together the egg, buttermilk, baking soda (bicarbonate of soda), and salt. Add the cornmeal mush and mix thoroughly. Pour the batter into the hot dish. Bake until golden brown and set, about 30 minutes.

ASIDA

PREPARATION TIME: 5 MINUTES
COOKING TIME: 25 MINUTES
SERVES: 4–6

- 2½ cups (300 g) millet flour
- Salt

[Omaha, Nebraska has welcomed many refugees from South Sudan. They brought with them their recipe for asida (also spelled aseeda, or aseda). Similar to thick polenta when made with cornmeal, it can also be made with teff, sorghum, millet, plantains, or cassava. It can be eaten for any meal and in Sudan is used as a "spoon" to scoop up stews, or served for breakfast as a porridge.]

In a large heavy pot, bring 2½ cups (590 ml) water to a boil over medium-high heat.

Meanwhile, pour 2½ cups (590 ml) water into a bowl and gradually whisk in the millet flour, whisking until smooth.

Whisking constantly, pour the millet mixture into the boiling water. Use a sturdy wooden spoon or paddle to stir from the bottom and sides of the pot. The mixture will bubble and thicken quickly. Keep stirring, quickly and thoroughly. Add salt to taste, reduce the heat to medium-low, and continue to cook, stirring constantly, until very thick, about 10 minutes. Test for doneness by removing a small spoonful, letting it cool slightly, and with wet fingers, picking it up. If the mixture doesn't stick to your fingers, it is done. Pour the asida onto a serving plate and let it cool before serving.

OYSTER DRESSING

PREPARATION TIME: 15 MINUTES
COOKING TIME: 1 HOUR
SERVES: 8–10

- 7 tablespoons (105 g) butter
- 16 oz (455 g) Cornbread (page 436), crumbled
- 8 oz (225 g) day-old French bread, torn into ½-inch (1.25 cm) pieces
- 1 cup (160 g) diced white onion
- 2 stalks celery, finely chopped
- ½ cup (120 ml) white wine
- 1 cup (240 ml) shellfish or chicken stock, plus more as needed
- 2 dozen freshly shucked oysters, chopped, liquor reserved
- 3 tablespoons fresh lemon juice
- 3 tablespoons chopped fresh parsley
- 2 teaspoons chopped fresh thyme
- 2 teaspoons Tabasco-style hot sauce
- 1 teaspoon salt
- ½ teaspoon freshly ground black pepper

Preheat the oven to 350°F (180°C/Gas Mark 4). Grease an 8-inch (20 cm) square baking dish with 1 tablespoon (15 g) of the butter.

In a large bowl, combine the cornbread and French bread.

In a large frying pan, melt 4 tablespoons (60 g) of the butter over medium heat. Add the onion and celery and cook until softened and translucent, 5–7 minutes. Add the wine and cook, scraping up any browned bits from the bottom of the pan. Cook until the wine reduces by half, 3–4 minutes, then pour over the bread mixture. Add the stock and stir gently to combine. Add the oysters and their liquor, the lemon juice, parsley, thyme, hot sauce, salt, and pepper. Toss gently to combine.

Arrange the dressing in an even layer in the buttered baking dish. Cut the remaining 2 tablespoons (30 g) butter into small pieces and scatter over the top of dressing. Bake until the top is lightly golden and the inside is still moist, 35–40 minutes. Let rest for 10 minutes, then serve.

DESSERTS

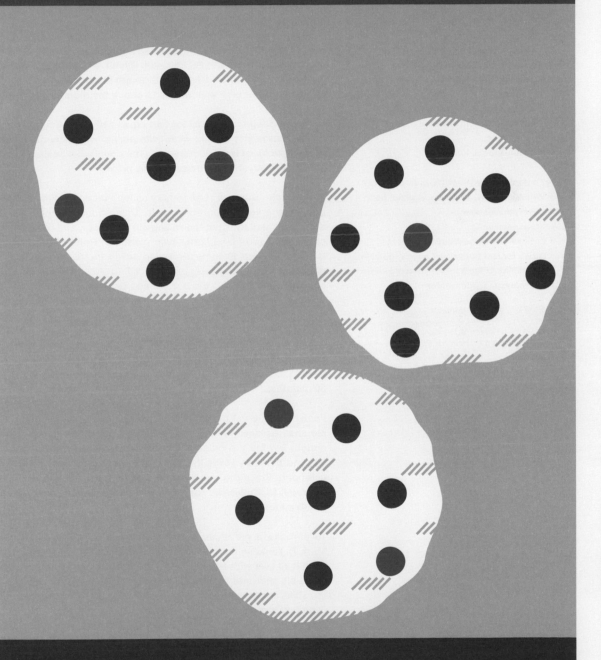

BASIC PIE DOUGH

PREPARATION TIME: 20 MINUTES,
  PLUS DOUGH CHILLING TIME
MAKES: ENOUGH FOR A SINGLE
  OR DOUBLE CRUST

For a single 8- or 9-inch (20 or 23 cm) crust:
- 1¼ cups (163 g) all-purpose (plain) flour
- 1 teaspoon sugar (omit if making a savory pie)
- ½ teaspoon salt
- 1 stick (115 g) cold unsalted butter, cut into cubes
- 3–4 tablespoons ice water

For a double 8- or 9-inch (20 or 23 cm) crust:
- 2½ cups (325 g) all-purpose (plain) flour
- 2 teaspoons sugar
- 1 teaspoon salt
- 2 sticks (225 g) cold butter, cut into cubes (or half butter, half solid vegetable shortening or lard)
- 7–8 tablespoons ice water

Hand method: In a large bowl, whisk together the flour, sugar, and salt. Cut in the butter (using a pastry/dough blender or your fingers) until the mixture resembles coarse cornmeal. Add just enough ice water to bring the dough together. Begin by adding the smaller amount, blend in, then add more only as necessary. It is helpful to take a handful of dough and squeeze it: The dough should be neither wet, nor dry and crumbly.

Mixer method: In a stand mixer fitted with the paddle attachment, combine the flour, sugar, and salt. Blend in the butter on low speed. Add the water gradually. Stop the mixer before the dough comes together (use your hands to check the moisture content).

Form the dough into a ball (or two equal balls if making a double crust), flatten into a disk, wrap with plastic wrap (clingfilm), and refrigerate for at least 30 minutes. (The dough can be made up to 24 hours in advance, or frozen at this point.)

For a single-crust pie shell (pastry case): Place the chilled disk of dough on a lightly floured surface. Using floured hands, flatten the dough slightly. Dust the rolling pin with flour, and roll from the center outward using light, even pressure. Roll until the dough is about ¼-inch (6 mm) thick and 10–11 inches (25–28 cm) in diameter. Drape the pastry over the rolling pin and place it in a pie plate. Press firmly into the bottom and sides of the pan. If you like you can trim at this point: use a paring knife to trim the dough, leaving at least ½ inch (1.25 cm) all around.

Crimp the edges using the side of your forefinger and thumb, or the tines of a fork to press down along the edge. Place the pie shell in the freezer for 10 minutes (or chill in the refrigerator for 30 minutes).

For a double-crust pie shell (pastry case) and top crust: Make the pie shell as described above, but don't crimp the edges of the dough. For the top crust, roll out the second disk of dough into a round that can cover the top of the pie plus 1 inch (2.5 cm) of overhang. Place the top crust on a plate. Place the pie shell and top crust in the freezer for 10 minutes (or chill in the refrigerator for 30 minutes).

To parbake a pie shell: Preheat the oven to 425°F (220°C/Gas Mark 7). Remove the pie shell from the freezer or refrigerator and prick it all over with a fork. Place a sheet of foil or parchment paper in the pie shell and fill with pie weights, dried beans, or rice. Place the shell in the oven and bake for 12 minutes. Remove from the oven and remove the foil or parchment and weights.

To blind bake a pie shell: Follow the directions above and after 12 minutes, remove the pie from the oven and reduce the oven temperature to 350°F (180°C/Gas Mark 4). Carefully remove the foil or parchment and weights. Return the shell to the oven and bake until golden brown, 10–12 minutes. Let cool before filling.

APPLE PIE

PREPARATION TIME: 1 HOUR,
  PLUS DOUGH CHILLING TIME
COOKING TIME: 1 HOUR
SERVES: 8

- Basic Pie Dough (page 280) for
  a double-crust pie
- 8 large tart crisp baking apples,
  such as Cortland or Swiss Gourmet
  (peeling optional), cut into ¼-inch
  (6 mm) thick slices
- 1 tablespoon fresh lemon juice
- ¾ cup (150 g) granulated sugar
- 1 teaspoon ground cinnamon
- ½ teaspoon freshly grated nutmeg
- ¼ teaspoon ground allspice
- ⅛ teaspoon ground cloves
- 4 tablespoons all-purpose (plain) flour
- 1 egg
- 3 tablespoons turbinado sugar
  (demerara)

Prepare the pie shell (pastry case) and top crust and chill as directed.

Preheat the oven to 375°F (190°C/Gas Mark 5). Line a baking sheet with parchment paper.

In a large bowl, gently toss together the apples, lemon juice, granulated sugar, cinnamon, nutmeg, allspice, and cloves. Let sit for 10 minutes or so until the sugar starts to bring out the juices in the apples. Toss again. Dust the apple mixture with 1 tablespoon flour at a time, mixing thoroughly after each addition. (This allows you to distribute the flour evenly in the mixture, which will thicken the pie filling, without creating clumps of flour.)

Remove the pie shell from the refrigerator or freezer and arrange the apple mixture in it. Whisk the egg with 1 teaspoon water, then brush some of the egg wash on the outer edge of dough. Place the top crust over the apples and with your thumb and forefinger, go around the edge of the pie just pinching the top crust and pie shell together. Place the crimped pie back in the refrigerator or freezer for 10 minutes.

Brush the entire top of the pie with the remaining egg wash, even the crimped edge, and sprinkle with turbinado (demerara) sugar. Using a paring knife, cut 4 slits into the top.

Place the pie on the lined baking sheet. Bake until the filling is bubbling and the crust is golden brown, about 1 hour. If the edges begin to brown before the pie is done, cover the edges lightly with foil. Let the pie cool for at least 1 hour to set before slicing.

APPLE-CRANBERRY PIE

PREPARATION TIME: 35 MINUTES,
  PLUS DOUGH CHILLING TIME
COOKING TIME: 1 HOUR
SERVES: 8

- Basic Pie Dough (page 280) for
  a double-crust pie
- ¾ cup (150 g) granulated sugar
- 4 tablespoons all-purpose (plain) flour
- 1 teaspoon ground cinnamon
- ½ teaspoon freshly grated nutmeg
- ¼ teaspoon ground allspice
- 4 large tart, firm apples, peeled and cut
  into ¼-inch (6 mm) slices
- 1 tablespoon fresh lemon juice
- 2 cups (200 g) fresh cranberries
- 1 egg
- 3 tablespoons turbinado
  (demerara) sugar

Prepare the pie shell (pastry case) and top crust and chill as directed.

Position a rack in the middle of the oven and preheat to 375°F (190°C/Gas Mark 5).

In a large bowl, whisk together the granulated sugar, flour, and spices. In a separate bowl, toss the apples with the lemon juice. Add the apples to the flour and sugar mixture and toss to combine. Stir in the cranberries.

Pour the filling into the pie shell, place the top crust over the filling and seal and crimp the edges. Whisk the egg with 1 teaspoon water, then brush the top crust with the egg wash and sprinkle with turbinado (demerara) sugar. Cut vents in the top. Bake until the top is browned and the filling is bubbling, about 1 hour.

APPLE PIE WITH HATCH GREEN CHILIES

PREPARATION TIME: 1 HOUR,
  PLUS DOUGH CHILLING TIME
COOKING TIME: 1 HOUR 15 MINUTES
SERVES: 8

- Basic Pie Dough (page 280) for
  a double-crust pie
- 8 tart apples, such as Granny Smith,
  peeled and sliced
- 2 Hatch green chilies, roasted and peeled
  (see Note, page 86), then chopped
- 1 tablespoon fresh lemon juice
- ¾ cup (150 g) granulated sugar
- ½ teaspoon ground cinnamon
- ¼ teaspoon ground allspice
- ⅛ teaspoon ground cloves
- 4 tablespoons all-purpose (plain) flour
- 1 egg
- 3 tablespoons turbinado (demerara)
  sugar

Prepare the pie shell (pastry case) and top crust and chill as directed.

Position a rack in the middle of the oven and preheat to 375°F (190°C/Gas Mark 5). Line a baking sheet with parchment paper.

In a large bowl, toss the apples, chilies, lemon juice, granulated sugar, and spices together. Let the mixture sit for about 10 minutes, until the juices in the apples start to release. Mix again. Mix in the flour, 1 tablespoon at a time, combining well.

Pour the apple mixture into the pie shell. Cover with the top crust, pinching the edges together. Crimp the edges with your fingers or a fork. Place the pie back in the freezer for 10 minutes.

Whisk the egg with 1 teaspoon water, then brush the top of the pie with the egg wash. Sprinkle with the turbinado (demerara) sugar. Using a paring knife, cut 4 vents in the top of the pie. Place the pie on the baking sheet and bake until the filling is bubbling and the crust is golden brown, about 1 hour. If the edges begin to brown before the pie is done, cover the edges lightly with foil. Let the pie cool for at least 1 hour before slicing.

APPLE-CRANBERRY PIE

CHEDDAR APPLE PIE

PREPARATION TIME: 40 MINUTES,
  PLUS DOUGH CHILLING TIME
COOKING TIME: 1 HOUR
SERVES: 8

For the dough:
- 2⅓ cups (303 g) all-purpose (plain) flour
- ½ teaspoon salt
- 1 stick plus 3 tablespoons (155 g) cold unsalted butter, diced
- ⅓ cup (40 g) grated sharp cheddar cheese
- ⅓ cup (80 ml) ice water
- 1 egg
- Cheddar cheese slices, for serving

For the filling:
- 8 large tart crisp baking apples (peeling optional), cut into ¼-inch (6 mm) slices
- 1 tablespoon fresh lemon juice
- ¾ cup (150 g) sugar
- 4 tablespoons all-purpose (plain) flour
- 1 teaspoon ground cinnamon
- ¼ teaspoon freshly grated nutmeg
- 2 tablespoons (30 g) butter

[There is an American saying that goes, "An apple pie without the cheese is like a kiss without a squeeze."]

For the dough: In a bowl, whisk together the flour and salt. Cut in the butter (using a pastry/dough blender or two knives) until the mixture resembles coarse meal. Toss in the cheddar. Add the ice water 1 tablespoon at a time until the dough comes together. Divide the dough in half, wrap, and refrigerate for at least 1 hour. (Dough may be made up to 24 hours in advance.)

Position a rack in the middle of the oven and preheat to 375°F (190°C/Gas Mark 5).

Remove the dough from the refrigerator and allow to soften slightly while preparing the filling.

For the filling: In a large bowl, toss the apples with the lemon juice. In a small bowl, whisk together the sugar, flour, cinnamon, and nutmeg. Add to the apples and toss.

Roll out one piece of the pie dough into a round that will line a 9-inch (23 cm) pie plate and have about 1 inch (2.5 cm) overhang all around. For the top crust, roll the other half of dough into a round that can cover the top of the pie plus 1 inch (2.5 cm) of overhang. Line the pie plate with the bottom crust and place the top crust on a plate.

Pour the filling into the pie shell (pastry case) and dot with butter. Whisk the egg with 1 teaspoon water. Place the top crust on, seal and crimp the edges, and brush with the egg wash. Cut vents in the top and bake until the pastry is deep golden brown and the filling is bubbling, about 1 hour.

Serve warm, with extra cheddar on the side.

PEACH PIE

PREPARATION TIME: 50 MINUTES,
   PLUS DOUGH CHILLING TIME
COOKING TIME: 1 HOUR 15 MINUTES
SERVES: 8

- Basic Pie Dough (page 280) for
  a double-crust pie
- 8 large peaches, peeled (see Note,
  page 364) and cut into ½-inch (1.25 cm)
  wedges
- 1 tablespoon fresh lemon juice
- 4 tablespoons all-purpose (plain) flour
- ⅓ cup (65 g) granulated sugar
- ⅓ cup (65 g) packed light brown sugar
- ¼ teaspoon ground cinnamon
- ¼ teaspoon freshly grated nutmeg
- Pinch of salt
- 1 egg
- 3 tablespoons turbinado (demerara)
  sugar

Prepare the pie shell (pastry case) and top crust and chill as directed.

Position a rack in the middle of the oven and preheat to 375°F (190°C/Gas Mark 5).

Place the peaches in a large bowl and toss with the lemon juice. In a medium bowl, whisk together the flour, both sugars, cinnamon, nutmeg, and salt. Add to the peaches and mix gently to combine. Pour the filling into the pie shell (pastry case). Cover with the top crust and seal and crimp the edges. Whisk the egg with 1 teaspoon water, then brush the top of the pie with the egg wash and sprinkle with the turbinado (demerara) sugar.

Cut vents in the top of the pie and bake until the filling is bubbling and the crust is golden brown, about 1 hour. Let the pie cool for at least 1 hour before slicing.

WILD BLUEBERRY PIE

PREPARATION TIME: 40 MINUTES,
  PLUS DOUGH CHILLING TIME
COOKING TIME: 1 HOUR
SERVES: 8

- Basic Pie Dough (page 280) for
  a double-crust pie
- 6 cups (890 g) wild blueberries,
  fresh or frozen (unthawed)
- Grated zest and juice of 1 lemon
- ¾ cup (150 g) granulated sugar
- ½ teaspoon ground cinnamon
- 4–5 tablespoons all-purpose (plain) flour
- 1 egg
- 3 tablespoons turbinado (demerara)
  sugar

[Big blueberries grow wild in Alaska. Some people wear "bear bells" when they go berry-picking, so the bears, which also love to feast on the wild fruit, won't be surprised.]

Prepare the pie shell (pastry case) and top crust and chill as directed.

Preheat the oven to 375°F (190°C/Gas Mark 5).

In a large bowl, mix together the blueberries, lemon zest and juice, granulated sugar, and cinnamon. Let the mixture sit for 10 minutes. Add the flour 1 tablespoon at a time, mixing well.

Pour the berries into the pie shell (pastry case). Cover with the top crust and seal and crimp the edges of the pie. Whisk the egg with 1 teaspoon water, then brush the top with the egg wash. Sprinkle with the turbinado (demerara) sugar. Cut vents in the top. Bake until the top is golden brown and the filling is bubbling, about 1 hour. Let the pie cool for at least 1 hour before serving.

HUCKLEBERRY PIE

PREPARATION TIME: 25 MINUTES,
  PLUS DOUGH CHILLING TIME
COOKING TIME: 1 HOUR 10 MINUTES
SERVES: 8

- Basic Pie Dough (page 280) for
  a double-crust pie
- 6 cups (890 g) huckleberries
- ¾ cup (150 g) granulated sugar
- 1 teaspoon grated lemon zest
- 1 tablespoon fresh lemon juice
- 5 tablespoons (60 g) instant tapioca
- 1 egg, beaten
- 2 tablespoons coarse sugar
- ½ teaspoon ground cinnamon

[The state fruit of Idaho, huckleberries have a flavor that is tart and distinct. Most ripen in late summer, ranging in color from red to blue to black. They're sometimes found in farmers' markets, but many people pick their own in the wild.]

Prepare the pie shell (pastry case) and top crust and chill as directed.

In a medium saucepan, combine 1 cup (150 g) of the huckleberries, the granulated sugar, lemon zest, and lemon juice. Bring to a simmer over medium heat, stirring, until the berries burst open, 6–8 minutes. Remove from the heat and let cool slightly.

In a large bowl, toss the remaining berries with the tapioca. Stir in the cooked berries. Set aside.

Position a rack in the middle of the oven and preheat to 375°F (190°C/Gas Mark 5).

Pour the filling into the pie shell (pastry case), cover with the top crust, and seal and crimp the edges. Brush the top with the beaten egg. Sprinkle with coarse sugar and cinnamon and cut vents in the top.

Bake until the crust is golden brown and the filling is bubbling, about 1 hour. Let the pie cool completely before serving.

SOUR CREAM RAISIN PIE

PREPARATION TIME: 40 MINUTES,
    PLUS DOUGH CHILLING TIME
COOKING TIME: 1 HOUR
SERVES: 8

- 1 baked pie shell (pastry case)
  (see Basic Pie Dough, page 280)
- 1 cup (165 g) raisins
- 3 tablespoons all-purpose (plain) flour
- ¾ cup (150 g) sugar
- ¼ teaspoon freshly grated nutmeg
- 2 eggs, separated
- 1 cup (240 ml) sour cream
- 2 tablespoons (30 g) butter
- 1 teaspoon pure vanilla extract
- Pinch of salt

Blind bake the pie shell (pastry case) as directed.

Place the raisins in a small saucepan, add water to cover, and bring to a boil. Remove from the heat and let sit for 10 minutes. Drain.

In a medium bowl, whisk together the flour, ½ cup (100 g) of the sugar, and the nutmeg. Whisk in the egg yolks and sour cream. Scrape the batter into a medium saucepan and cook over low heat, stirring constantly, until thickened, 10–15 minutes. Remove from the heat and stir in the butter, vanilla, and drained raisins.

Pour the filling into the baked pie shell (pastry case). (The pie can be assembled to this point in advance and refrigerated for up to several hours before making the meringue.)

Preheat the oven to 350°F (180°C/Gas Mark 4).

In a bowl, with an electric mixer, beat the egg whites with a pinch of salt on high speed until foamy, about 2 minutes. On medium-high speed, gradually add the remaining ¼ cup (50 g) sugar, beating until stiff peaks form and the meringue is shiny.

Spread the meringue over the top of the pie. Bake until the top is lightly browned, 10–12 minutes. Let the pie cool completely before serving.

RUM RAISIN PIE

PREPARATION TIME: 25 MINUTES,
    PLUS DOUGH CHILLING TIME
COOKING TIME: 55 MINUTES
SERVES: 8

- 1 parbaked pie shell (pastry case)
  (see Basic Pie Dough, page 280)
- 3 cups (710 ml) heavy (whipping) cream
- 4 eggs
- 2 egg yolks
- ¾ cup (150 g) sugar
- ¼ cup (60 ml) dark rum
- ¼ teaspoon freshly grated nutmeg
- ¼ teaspoon salt
- 1 cup (165 g) raisins

Parbake the pie shell (pastry case) as directed, then reduce the oven temperature to 350°F (180°C/Gas Mark 4).

In a medium saucepan, bring the cream just to a simmer over medium-low heat. Remove from the heat and set aside.

In a large bowl, whisk the whole eggs, egg yolks, and sugar until well combined. Whisking constantly, gradually pour the warm cream into the egg mixture. Pour the mixture back into the saucepan and cook over medium heat, stirring constantly, until it thickens and coats the back of the spoon, about 12 minutes. Remove from the heat and whisk in the rum, nutmeg, and salt.

Scatter the raisins over the bottom of the parbaked pie shell (pastry shell). Pour the custard over the raisins. Bake until set, about 30 minutes. Let the pie cool completely before slicing.

SOUR CHERRY PIE

PREPARATION TIME: 30 MINUTES,
  PLUS DOUGH CHILLING TIME
COOKING TIME: 1 HOUR
SERVES: 8

- Basic Pie Dough (page 280) for
  a double-crust pie
- 1 cup (200 g) granulated sugar
- 4 tablespoons cornstarch (cornflour)
- 5 cups (775 g) pitted sour cherries
- 1 teaspoon pure vanilla extract
- 2 tablespoons (30 g) butter
- 2 tablespoons heavy (whipping) cream
- 2 tablespoons coarse sugar

[Sour cherries are brilliantly red and very juicy. They're often known as pie cherries. Today many sodas and candies are "cherry-flavored," wishing to channel the hue and taste of this pie.]

Prepare the pie shell (pastry case) and top crust and chill as directed.

Position a rack in the middle of the oven and preheat to 375°F (190°C/Gas Mark 5).

In a large bowl, whisk together the granulated sugar and corn-starch (cornflour). Add the cherries and vanilla and mix well. Pour into the pie shell, dot with the butter, and place the top crust over the filling. Seal and crimp the edges. Brush the pie with the cream and sprinkle with the coarse sugar. Cut vents in the top.

Bake until the crust is golden brown and the filling is bubbling, 45 minutes to 1 hour. Allow the pie to cool to room temperature before serving.

MARIONBERRY PIE

PREPARATION TIME: 45 MINUTES,
  PLUS DOUGH CHILLING TIME
COOKING TIME: 1 HOUR
SERVES: 8

- Basic Pie Dough (page 280) for
  a double-crust pie
- 4 cups (575 g) marionberries
- ¾ cup (150 g) granulated sugar
- Grated zest and juice of 1 lemon
- 4 tablespoons all-purpose (plain) flour
- 1 egg
- 3 tablespoons turbinado (demerara)
  sugar

Prepare the pie shell (pastry case) and top crust and chill as directed.

Position a rack in the middle of the oven and preheat to 375°F (190°C/Gas Mark 5).

In a medium bowl, mix together the marionberries, granulated sugar, lemon zest, and lemon juice, smashing the berries slightly. Let stand for 10 minutes. Sprinkle the flour over the berries 1 tablespoon at a time, mixing well after each addition.

Pour the berry mixture into the pie shell (pastry case). Whisk the egg with 1 teaspoon water, then moisten the outer edge with some of the egg wash. Cover with the top pastry and seal and crimp the edges with your fingers or a fork.

Brush the top of the pie with the remaining egg wash and sprin-kle with the turbinado (demerara) sugar. Cut vents in the top of the pie.

Bake until the crust is golden brown and the filling is bubbling, about 1 hour. Let the pie cool to room temperature before serving.

SOUR CHERRY PIE

FIG TART

PREPARATION TIME: 30 MINUTES,
PLUS DOUGH CHILLING TIME
AND COOLING TIME
COOKING TIME: 25 MINUTES
SERVES: 8–10

- Basic Pie Dough (page 280) for
  a single-crust pie
- 1 cup (240 g) mascarpone cheese
- 18 fresh figs, halved lengthwise
- ¼ cup (85 g) honey
- ¼ teaspoon sea salt (optional)

Prepare the basic pie dough, but increase the amount of sugar in the dough to 1 tablespoon. On a floured surface, roll the dough into a round 12 inches (30 cm) in diameter. Transfer the dough to a 9–10-inch (23–25 cm) tart pan and gently press into the corners of the pan, all around. Trim the dough at the edge of the pan with a paring knife. Refrigerate for 30 minutes.

Preheat the oven to 425°F (220°C/Gas Mark 7).

Prick the tart shell (pastry case) 8–10 times, all over, with a fork. Line with parchment paper and fill with pie weights (baking beans). Bake for 12 minutes. Remove from the oven and remove the parchment and pie weights. Reduce the oven temperature to 350°F (180°C/Gas Mark 4), return to the oven, and bake until the crust is golden brown, 10–12 minutes. Let cool completely.

For the filling: In a medium bowl, whisk the mascarpone until smooth, about 2 minutes. Spread the whipped mascarpone in the cooled tart shell. Arrange the fresh figs over top. Drizzle with the honey and sprinkle with sea salt, if desired. Serve immediately or refrigerate for up to 6 hours and serve chilled.

BOILED CIDER PIE

PREPARATION TIME: 25 MINUTES,
PLUS DOUGH CHILLING TIME
COOKING TIME: 35 MINUTES
SERVES: 8

- Basic Pie Dough (page 280) for
  a single-crust pie
- 1 cup (240 ml) boiled cider
- 1 tablespoon (15 g) butter
- ⅓ cup (65 g) maple sugar or brown sugar
- ¼ (60 ml) cup heavy (whipping) cream
- ½ teaspoon salt
- ½ teaspoon freshly grated nutmeg
- 2 eggs, separated

[If you want to make your own boiled cider, gently boil 2 quarts (2 liters) apple cider in a saucepan until reduced to 1 cup (240 ml). As the amount of cider decreases, switch to a smaller pan so as not to burn the mixture.]

Prepare the single-crust pie shell (pastry case) and chill as directed.

Preheat the oven to 350°F (180°C/Gas Mark 4).

In a medium saucepan, combine the boiled cider, butter, maple sugar, cream, salt, and nutmeg and cook over medium-low heat until the butter is melted and the sugar has dissolved. Let cool slightly. Mix in the egg yolks.

In a medium bowl, with an electric mixer, beat the egg whites until soft peaks form. Fold the egg whites into the cider mixture.

Pour the filling into the prepared pie shell (pastry case) and bake until the custard is set, about 30 minutes. Let the pie cool completely before slicing.

FIG TART

LEMON CHESS PIE

PREPARATION TIME: 30 MINUTES,
  PLUS DOUGH CHILLING TIME
COOKING TIME: 1 HOUR
SERVES: 8

- Basic Pie Dough (page 280) for
  a single-crust pie
- 1 stick (115 g) unsalted butter, softened
- 1½ cups (300 g) sugar
- Grated zest of 2 lemons
- 4 eggs, at room temperature
- 4 tablespoons heavy (whipping) cream
- 6 tablespoons fresh lemon juice
- 2 tablespoons finely ground cornmeal
- 1 tablespoon all-purpose (plain) flour
- ½ teaspoon salt

Prepare the single-crust pie shell (pastry case) and chill as directed.

Position a rack in the middle of the oven and preheat to 350°F (180°C/Gas Mark 4).

In a large bowl, using an electric stand or hand-held mixer, cream the butter, sugar, and lemon zest until light and fluffy. Beat in the eggs, 1 at a time. Beat in the cream and lemon juice. Beat in the cornmeal, flour, and salt.

Pour the filling into the pie shell. Bake until the top is golden brown and the filling is set, 45 minutes to 1 hour.

SHAKER LEMON PIE

PREPARATION TIME: 30 MINUTES,
  PLUS CHILLING TIME AND OVERNIGHT
  MACERATING
COOKING TIME: 45 MINUTES
SERVES: 8

- 3 large lemons, preferably organic,
  washed
- 1 cup (200 g) granulated sugar
- ¼ teaspoon salt
- Basic Pie Dough (page 280) for
  a double-crust pie
- 4 eggs
- 4 tablespoons (60 g) butter, melted
- 3 tablespoons all-purpose (plain) flour
- 1 egg
- Coarse sugar, for sprinkling

Slice off and discard the two ends of each of the lemons. Slice the lemons paper thin, removing any seeds. Place the lemon slices, granulated sugar, and salt in a medium bowl and mix well. Cover and refrigerate overnight.

Prepare the pie shell (pastry case) and top crust and chill as directed.

Position a rack in the middle of the oven and preheat the oven to 375°F (190°C/Gas Mark 5).

Remove the lemons from the refrigerator. In a separate bowl, beat the eggs. Whisk the melted butter into the eggs and stir the mixture into the lemons. Stir in the flour, mixing well. Pour into the pie shell (pastry case). Cover with the top crust and seal and crimp the edges. Whisk the egg with 1 teaspoon water, then brush the top with the egg wash and sprinkle with the coarse sugar.

Bake until the filling is bubbling and the crust is golden brown, about 45 minutes. Let the pie cool for at least 1 hour before slicing.

LEMON CHESS PIE

PUMPKIN PIE

PREPARATION TIME: 25 MINUTES,
    PLUS DOUGH CHILLING TIME
COOKING TIME: 55 MINUTES
SERVES: 8

- 1 parbaked pie shell (see Basic Pie Dough, page 280)
- 1 can (15-oz/425 g) pumpkin purée
- 1½ cups (355 ml) heavy (whipping) cream
- 3 eggs, beaten
- ½ cup (95 g) packed light brown sugar
- ¼ cup (50 g) granulated sugar
- 1 teaspoon ground cinnamon
- ½ teaspoon ground ginger
- ½ teaspoon freshly grated nutmeg
- Pinch of ground cloves
- Pinch each of salt and finely ground black pepper

[Pumpkins are native to North America, but the custard element of this famous open-crust pie likely evolved from French and English pie traditions and came back across the Atlantic with 17th- and 18th-century settlers. Today, traditional pumpkin pie spices—cinnamon, ginger, nutmeg, and cloves—are a ubiquitous symbol of autumn and are labeled collectively as "pumpkin pie spice."]

Parbake the pie shell (pastry case) as directed then reduce the oven temperature to 375°F (190°C/Gas Mark 5).

In a large bowl, combine the pumpkin purée, cream, eggs, both sugars, and spices. Pour the mixture into the pie shell (pastry case) and bake until the center is just set, 35–40 minutes. Let the pie cool completely before slicing.

SWEET POTATO PIE

PREPARATION TIME: 50 MINUTES,
    PLUS DOUGH CHILLING TIME
COOKING TIME: 1 HOUR
SERVES: 8

- Basic Pie Dough (page 280) for a single-crust pie
- 3 large sweet potatoes
- ½ cup (100 g) granulated sugar
- ½ cup (95 g) packed light brown sugar
- 3 eggs
- 1 cup (240 ml) heavy (whipping) cream
- 3 tablespoons (45 g) butter, melted
- ½ teaspoon pure vanilla extract
- 1 teaspoon salt
- ½ teaspoon ground cinnamon
- ¼ teaspoon freshly grated nutmeg
- ¼ teaspoon ground allspice

Prepare the single-crust pie shell (pastry case) and chill as directed.

Preheat the oven to 425°F (220°C/Gas Mark 7). Roast the sweet potatoes until tender, about 30 minutes. Remove from the oven and reduce the temperature to 350°F (180°C/Gas Mark 4). Let the potatoes cool slightly, then peel and mash.

In a large bowl, whisk together the sweet potatoes, both sugars, the eggs, cream, melted butter, vanilla, salt, and spices. Pour into the pie shell (pastry case) and bake until the crust is golden brown and the filling is just set in the center, 50–60 minutes. Let the pie cool for at least 30 minutes before serving.

PUMPKIN PIE

PECAN PIE

PREPARATION TIME: 30 MINUTES,
   PLUS DOUGH CHILLING TIME
COOKING TIME: 55 MINUTES
SERVES: 8

- 1 parbaked pie shell (see Basic
  Pie Dough, page 282)
- 3 eggs
- ½ teaspoon salt
- ¾ cup (150 g) sugar
- 1 stick (115 g) butter, melted
- ¾ cup (180 ml) dark corn syrup
- 1½ cups (150 g) pecan halves

Parbake the pie shell (pastry case) as directed and leave the oven on.

In a medium bowl, beat the eggs with the salt and sugar until very light, 2–3 minutes. Drizzle in the melted butter, whisking constantly. Add the corn syrup and mix well.

Pour the mixture into the pie shell (pastry case) and arrange the pecan halves cut side down over the top. Bake for 10 minutes, then reduce the oven temperature to 325°F (160°C/Gas Mark 3) and bake until the crust is golden and the filling is set, about 30 minutes. Let the pie cool for at least 15 minutes and serve warm or chilled.

DERBY PIE

PREPARATION TIME: 20 MINUTES,
   PLUS DOUGH CHILLING TIME
COOKING TIME: 1 HOUR
SERVES: 8

- Basic Pie Dough (page 280) for a
  single-crust pie
- ½ cup (95 g) packed dark brown sugar
- ¼ cup (50 g) granulated sugar
- ⅓ cup (43 g) all-purpose (plain) flour
- ½ teaspoon salt
- ½ cup (120 ml) cane syrup
- 4 eggs
- 4 tablespoons (60 g) butter, melted
  and cooled
- 2 tablespoons bourbon
- 1 teaspoon pure vanilla extract
- 1⅓ cups (130 g) pecans, toasted and
  coarsely chopped
- ¾ cup (170 g) dark chocolate chips
- Whipped cream, for serving

[Named for Kentucky's famous annual horse race, this chocolate-pecan pie is spiked with bourbon, for which the state is celebrated.]

Prepare the single-crust pie shell (pastry case) and chill as directed.

Position a rack in the middle of the oven and preheat to 350°F (180°C/Gas Mark 4).

In a large bowl, whisk together both of the sugars, the flour, and salt. Whisk in the cane syrup, eggs, melted butter, bourbon, and vanilla until well combined. Stir in the walnuts and chocolate chips.

Pour the mixture into the pie shell (pastry case). Bake until the center is set, 50–60 minutes. Let cool for at least 30 minutes before serving. Serve warm or chilled, with whipped cream.

DERBY PIE

SHOOFLY PIE

PREPARATION TIME: 30 MINUTES,
   PLUS DOUGH CHILLING TIME
COOKING TIME: 50 MINUTES
SERVES: 8

- Basic Pie Dough (page 280) for
  a single-crust pie
- ½ teaspoon baking soda (bicarbonate
  of soda)
- ¾ cup (180 ml) boiling water
- ¾ cup (180 ml) molasses (treacle)
- 1½ cups (195 g) all-purpose (plain) flour
- ½ cup (95 g) packed light brown sugar
- 1 teaspoon ground cinnamon
- ½ teaspoon freshly grated nutmeg
- 1 stick (115 g) cold unsalted butter,
  cut into small cubes

Prepare the single-crust pie shell (pastry case) and chill as directed.

In a small bowl, dissolve the baking soda (bicarbonate of soda) in the boiling water and then stir in the molasses (treacle).

In a medium bowl, whisk together the flour, brown sugar, cinnamon, and nutmeg. Cut in the butter (using a pastry/dough blender or two knives) until the mixture resembles coarse cornmeal.

Pour one-third of the molasses mixture into the pie shell (pastry case). Then sprinkle one-third of the crumble mixture over the top, covering evenly. Continue alternating the layers, ending with crumble.

Bake until set, 30–40 minutes. Let the pie cool slightly before serving.

CHOCOLATE CREAM PIE

PREPARATION TIME: 20 MINUTES,
   PLUS OVERNIGHT CHILLING
COOKING TIME: 30 MINUTES
SERVES: 8

For the cookie crust:
- 1⅓ cups (150 g) chocolate wafer cookie
  crumbs
- ¼ cup (50 g) granulated sugar
- 6 tablespoons (85 g) unsalted butter,
  melted

For the filling:
- 7 oz (200 g) good-quality semisweet
  chocolate, finely chopped
- 3 cups (710 ml) heavy (whipping) cream
- 3½ tablespoons cornstarch (cornflour)
- 4 egg yolks
- ⅔ cup (130 g) granulated sugar
- 1 teaspoon pure vanilla extract

For the topping:
- 1½ cups (355 ml) heavy (whipping) cream
- 2 tablespoons powdered (icing) sugar

Preheat the oven to 375°F (190°C/Gas Mark 5).

For the cookie crust: In a medium bowl, combine the cookie crumbs, sugar, and melted butter. Press evenly into a 9-inch (23 cm) pie plate. Bake for 15 minutes. Let cool completely.

For the filling: In a heatproof bowl set over a pan of simmering water, melt the chocolate. Set aside.

In a medium saucepan, whisk the cream and cornstarch (cornflour) until smooth. Bring just to a simmer over medium heat. Remove from the heat.

In a bowl, whisk the egg yolks and granulated sugar. Whisking constantly, slowly pour the hot cream mixture into the egg mixture. Pour back into the saucepan. Cook over medium-low heat, whisking constantly, until very thick, about 10 minutes. Remove from the heat and whisk in the melted chocolate and vanilla. Pour into a bowl and cover with plastic wrap (clingfilm) so the plastic is touching the entire surface of the pudding. Refrigerate overnight to chill.

Spoon the pudding into the prepared crust, smoothing the top with a rubber spatula.

For the topping: In a bowl, with an electric mixer, whip the cream with the powdered (icing) sugar until stiff peaks form. Spread over the top of the pie.

MAPLE CREAM PIE

PREPARATION TIME: 20 MINUTES,
   PLUS DOUGH CHILLING TIME
COOKING TIME: 1 HOUR 10 MINUTES
SERVES: 8

- 1 parbaked pie shell (pastry case)
  (see Basic Pie Dough, page 280)
- 1 cup (240 ml) pure maple syrup
- 2 cups (475 ml) heavy (whipping) cream
- 1 egg
- 4 egg yolks
- 1 teaspoon pure vanilla extract

Parbake the pie shell (pastry case) as directed, then reduce the oven temperature to 350°F (180°C/Gas Mark 4).

In a medium saucepan, cook the maple syrup over medium heat until it is reduced by half, about 9 minutes. Reduce the heat and stir in the cream. Bring just to a simmer, remove from the heat, and set aside.

In a medium bowl, whisk together the whole egg and egg yolks. In a slow steady stream, and whisking constantly, add the warm cream to the eggs. Return the mixture to the saucepan. Cook over medium-low heat, stirring constantly, until mixture thickens enough to coat the back of the spoon, about 10 minutes. Add the vanilla and stir well to combine.

Pour the filling into the parbaked pie shell (pastry case). Bake until the center is set, 35–40 minutes. Let the pie cool completely before serving.

BUTTERSCOTCH PIE

PREPARATION TIME: 25 MINUTES,
   PLUS OVERNIGHT CHILLING
COOKING TIME: 1 HOUR
SERVES: 8

- 1 baked pie shell (pastry case) (see Basic
  Pie Dough, page 280)
- 4 tablespoons (60 g) butter
- 1 cup (190 g) packed light brown sugar
- 1 cup (240 ml) milk
- 4 tablespoons all-purpose (plain) flour
- 3 egg yolks
- 1 cup (240 ml) heavy (whipping) cream
- Pinch of salt
- ½ teaspoon pure vanilla extract
- 2 tablespoons Scotch whisky

Blind bake the pie shell (pastry case) as directed.

In a medium saucepan, combine the butter and brown sugar and cook over medium heat, stirring frequently, until the butter and sugar start to caramelize and brown, about 4 minutes. Remove from the heat and set aside.

In a large bowl, whisk together ½ cup (120 ml) of the milk and the flour. Whisk in the egg yolks, combining well. Whisk in the cream, salt, and remaining ½ cup (120 ml) milk. Whisking constantly, gradually pour in the reserved butter/brown sugar mixture. Whisk in the vanilla and Scotch whisky. Pour into a clean saucepan and cook over medium-low heat, stirring constantly, until thickened, about 30 minutes.

Pour the mixture into the baked pie shell (pastry case). Refrigerate overnight to chill.

MISSISSIPPI MUD PIE

PREPARATION TIME: 25 MINUTES,
 PLUS COOLING TIME
COOKING TIME: 35 MINUTES
SERVES: 8–10

For the crust:
- 16 chocolate graham crackers (250 g)
- ½ cup (60 g) chopped pecans
- 6 tablespoons (85 g) butter, melted

For the filling:
- 3 ounces (85 g) unsweetened chocolate
- 1 stick (115 g) butter, diced
- 2 tablespoons all-purpose (plain) flour
- ⅛ teaspoon salt
- 1¼ cups (250 g) granulated sugar
- 2 tablespoons light corn syrup
- 2 tablespoons brewed coffee
- 1½ teaspoons pure vanilla extract
- 3 eggs

For the topping:
- 1½ cups (355 ml) heavy (whipping) cream
- 1 tablespoon powdered (icing) sugar
- ½ teaspoon pure vanilla extract
- 3 tablespoons finely chopped pecans
- ¼ cup (60 ml) chocolate sauce

Position a rack in the middle of the oven and preheat to 350°F (180°C/Gas Mark 4).

For the crust: In a food processor, combine the graham crackers and pecans and process until finely ground. Add the melted butter and process just until moistened. Measure out 2 tablespoons of the crumb mixture and set aside for topping. Press the remaining mixture into the bottom and up the sides of a 9-inch (23 cm) pie plate. Bake until set, about 10 minutes. Transfer to a rack to cool. Increase the oven temperature to 375°F (190°C/Gas Mark 5).

For the filling: Chop the chocolate. In a medium saucepan, combine the butter and chocolate and stir frequently over medium heat until just melted. Remove from the heat, then stir in the flour and salt until smooth. Stir in the granulated sugar, corn syrup, coffee, and vanilla. Add the eggs, 1 at a time, stirring until smooth.

Pour the filling into the crust and bake until set and cracked on top (like a brownie), about 30 minutes. Transfer to a rack and let cool to room temperature.

For the topping: In a large chilled bowl, with an electric mixer, whip the cream, powdered (icing) sugar, and vanilla until soft peaks form.

Top the pie with the whipped cream, pecans, and reserved chocolate crumb mixture. Drizzle with the chocolate sauce and serve immediately.

BUTTERMILK PIE

PREPARATION TIME: 25 MINUTES,
 PLUS DOUGH CHILLING TIME
COOKING TIME: 50 MINUTES
SERVES: 8

- Basic Pie Dough (page 280) for a single-crust pie
- 1 cup (200 g) sugar
- 3 tablespoons all-purpose (plain) flour
- 3 eggs
- 1 cup (240 ml) buttermilk
- 1 stick (115 g) butter, melted
- 2 teaspoons grated lemon zest
- 2 tablespoons fresh lemon juice
- 1 teaspoon pure vanilla extract

Prepare the single-crust pie shell (pastry case) and chill as directed.

Position a rack in the middle of the oven and preheat to 350°F (180°C/Gas Mark 4).

In a medium bowl, whisk together the sugar and flour. Whisk in the eggs. Blend in the buttermilk, melted butter, lemon zest, lemon juice, and vanilla.

Pour the filling into the pie shell (pastry case). Bake until the filling is just set, 40–45 minutes. Let the pie cool to room temperature before serving.

COCONUT CREAM PIE

PREPARATION TIME: 30 MINUTES,
    PLUS DOUGH CHILLING TIME
COOKING TIME: 1 HOUR
SERVES: 8

- 1 parbaked pie shell (see Basic Pie Dough, page 280)
- 1⅓ cups (100 g) coconut flakes, sweetened or unsweetened
- 1½ cups (355 ml) coconut milk
- 1½ cups (355 ml) heavy (whipping) cream
- ¾ cup (150 g) sugar
- 4 egg yolks
- 1 whole egg
- Pinch of salt
- 1 teaspoon pure vanilla extract
- 1 cup (240 ml) heavy (whipping cream), whipped to soft peaks

Parbake the pie shell (pastry case) as directed, then reduce the oven temperature to 350°F (180°C/Gas Mark 4).

On a small rimmed baking sheet, toast ⅓ cup (25 g) coconut flakes in the oven until golden brown, about 5 minutes. Set aside.

In a medium saucepan, bring the coconut milk and cream just to a simmer over medium-high heat. Remove from the heat.

In a medium bowl, whisk together the sugar, egg yolks, and whole egg. Whisking constantly, pour the hot cream in a steady stream into the egg/sugar mixture. Pour back into the saucepan and cook over medium-low heat, stirring constantly, until slightly thickened, about 8 minutes. Remove from the heat and stir in the salt, untoasted coconut flakes, and vanilla.

Pour the filling into the prepared pie shell (pastry case) and bake until the center is set, 30–40 minutes. Let cool completely before topping.

Cover the top of the pie with the whipped cream and sprinkle with the toasted coconut.

MARGARITA PIE

PREPARATION TIME: 15 MINUTES,
    PLUS COOLING AND FREEZING TIME
COOKING TIME: 10 MINUTES
SERVES: 8

- 1 sleeve (about 8) graham cracker sheets (or 125 g digestive biscuits), broken into pieces
- ¼ cup (50 g) granulated sugar
- ¼ teaspoon kosher (coarse) salt
- 1 stick (115 g) unsalted butter, melted
- 2 cans (14 oz/395 g each) sweetened condensed milk
- 1 tablespoon finely grated lime zest
- ½ cup (120 ml) fresh lime juice
- ¼ cup (60 ml) tequila
- 1 tablespoon orange liqueur, such as Grand Marnier
- Whipped cream, for topping (optional)

[This pie is served frozen.]

Position a rack in the middle of the oven and preheat to 350°F (180°C/Gas Mark 4).

In a food processor, combine the crackers, sugar, salt, and melted butter and pulse until the mixture is the consistency of wet sand. Firmly press the crumbs into a 9-inch (23 cm) pie plate to form the crust. Bake until the crust is golden and puffs slightly, 8–10 minutes. Set aside to cool completely.

In a medium bowl, combine the condensed milk, lime zest, lime juice, tequila, and orange liqueur and let stand for 5 minutes to thicken. Pour into the prepared crust. Cover with plastic wrap (clingfilm) and freeze until the filling sets, at least 2 hours and up to overnight. When ready to serve, top with whipped cream, if desired.

APPLE TURNOVERS

PREPARATION TIME: 30 MINUTES,
   PLUS DOUGH CHILLING TIME
COOKING TIME: 35 MINUTES
SERVES: 4

For the dough:
- 1 cup (130 g) all-purpose (plain) flour
- ½ teaspoon salt
- 1 stick (115 g) cold unsalted butter
- 4 tablespoons ice water

For the filling:
- 2 cups (240 g) peeled and finely diced apples
- 2 teaspoons fresh lemon juice
- ¼ cup (50 g) granulated sugar
- 2 teaspoons cornstarch (cornflour)
- Dash each of cinnamon and freshly grated nutmeg

For the glaze:
- ⅓ cup (40 g) powdered (icing) sugar
- 1 tablespoon milk or water

For the dough: In a bowl, whisk together the flour and salt. Cut 4 tablespoons (60 g) of the butter into small pieces. Cut the butter into the flour (using a pastry/dough blender or two knives) until the mixture resembles small crumbs. Gradually add the ice water until the dough comes together. Turn out onto a lightly floured surface and roll the dough into a 12 x 6-inch (30 x 15 cm) rectangle.

Cut the remaining 4 tablespoons (60 g) butter into thin slices and place in the freezer for a few minutes if the butter softens. Arrange one-half of the sliced butter over two-thirds of the dough, starting at one short end, and leaving a ½-inch (1.25 cm) border at the edges. Fold the unbuttered third over the middle third, then fold the bottom buttered third over the middle. Roll out again to 12 x 6 inches (30 x 15 cm) and repeat the process with the remaining butter. Roll a third time to 12 x 6 inches (30 x 15 cm), then fold in half crosswise to make a 6-inch (15 cm) square. Wrap and refrigerate the dough for 1 hour.

For the filling: In a small saucepan, combine the apples, lemon juice, granulated sugar, cornstarch (cornflour), and spices and bring to a boil over medium heat, stirring constantly. Reduce to a simmer and cook, uncovered, until the apples are tender and the liquids have thickened, about 10 minutes. Remove from the heat and set aside to cool.

Position a rack in the middle of the oven and preheat to 375°F (190°C/Gas Mark 5). Line a baking sheet with parchment paper.

Roll the chilled dough to a 12-inch (30 cm) square. Cut into 4 squares. Dividing evenly, place the filling on one-half of each square. Moisten the edges with water and fold the other half of the dough over on the diagonal, to make a triangle. Use a fork or your fingers to seal the edges closed. Place the turnovers on the baking sheet and cut vents in the top of each. Bake until golden brown and bubbling, 20–25 minutes.

For the glaze: In a small bowl, mix the powdered (icing) sugar with the milk. Drizzle the glaze over the warm turnovers.

SWEET EMPANADAS

PREPARATION TIME: 30 MINUTES,
  PLUS DOUGH RESTING TIME
COOKING TIME: 35 MINUTES
MAKES: 16–20 EMPANADAS

For the dough:
- 2 cups (260 g) all-purpose (plain) flour
- 1 teaspoon baking powder
- 1 teaspoon ground cinnamon
- 1 teaspoon granulated sugar
- ½ cup (120 ml) vegetable oil
- 1 egg white

For the filling:
- 2 cups (300 g) fresh strawberries or peaches, diced
- ½ cup (95 g) packed light brown sugar
- 2 teaspoons ground cinnamon
- ½ teaspoon ground cloves
- ½ teaspoon freshly grated nutmeg

For the dough: In a large bowl, whisk together the flour, baking powder, cinnamon, and sugar. Whisk in the oil, then water, 1 tablespoon at a time, until the dough is moistened and begins to form a ball when stirred. Turn the dough onto a lightly floured surface and knead 8–10 times, until smooth. Cover with plastic wrap (clingfilm) and set aside for 30 minutes.

Meanwhile, for the filling: In a small pot, combine the fruit, brown sugar, cinnamon, cloves, and nutmeg. Cook over medium heat, stirring/mashing occasionally, until the fruit begins to break down, about 5 minutes. Simmer, stirring occasionally, until the mixture is slightly thickened, about 5 minutes longer. Set aside to cool.

Position a rack in the middle of the oven (see Note) and preheat to 350°F (180°C/Gas Mark 4). Line a baking sheet with parchment paper.

On a lightly floured surface, roll the dough into a large round ⅛-inch (3 mm) thick. Using a 4-inch (10 cm) round cutter, cut rounds from the dough and set aside. Re-roll the dough scraps one time to cut out more rounds.

For each empanada, place 1½ tablespoons of the fruit mixture on one side of an empanada dough round, leaving a ½-inch (1.25 cm) border. Fold the empty side over the fruit and press with a fork to bind the two sides. Fold the dough edges in small ½-inch (1.25 cm) pleats, over top of the fork marks, to seal the empanada.

Whisk the egg white with 2 tablespoons water. Arrange the empanadas on the baking sheet about 1 inch (2.5 cm) apart and brush evenly with the egg wash. Bake until the empanadas are lightly golden, 20–25 minutes. Transfer to a wire rack to rest for 10 minutes. Serve warm.

If baking 2 batches at a time, position racks in the upper and lower thirds of the oven and switch baking sheets halfway through baking.

PREPARATION TIME: 20 MINUTES,
   PLUS DOUGH CHILLING TIME
COOKING TIME: 20 MINUTES
SERVES: 8

For the dough:
- ⅔ cup (87 g) all-purpose (plain) flour
- Pinch of salt
- ⅓ cup (75 g) cold unsalted butter,
  cut into small pieces
- ⅓ cup (80 ml) sour cream

For the filling:
- 4 tablespoons (60 g) butter, softened
- ½ cup (95 g) packed light brown sugar
- ½ cup (60 g) chopped walnuts

For the glaze:
- ½ cup (60 g) powdered (icing) sugar
- 2 tablespoons milk
- ½ teaspoon pure vanilla extract

[Originally from Denmark, kringle is made in the Midwest with a dough base (yeasted dough, cake, puff pastry, or another rich flaky crust), often filled with nuts and fruit, that's shaped into a wreath and sometimes braided.]

For the dough: In a medium bowl, whisk together the flour and salt. Cut in the butter (using a pastry/dough blender or two knives) until the mixture resembles coarse crumbs. Stir in the sour cream. The dough will be sticky. Wrap the dough in plastic wrap (clingfilm) and refrigerate for 6 hours or overnight.

Position a rack in the middle of the oven and preheat to 375°F (190°C/Gas Mark 5).

For the filling: In a small bowl, stir the softened butter with the brown sugar. Stir in the nuts.

On a long sheet of parchment dusted with flour, pat the dough into a rough rectangle, then with a floured rolling pin, roll the dough to 6 x 20 inches (15 x 50 cm). Spoon the filling down the center the long way, bring the sides together, and pinch to seal, making a tube. Gently form the tube into a ring and seal the seam where the ends meet.

Slide the parchment with the kringle on it onto a baking sheet. Gently reform if necessary. Using a pastry brush, brush off any excess flour. Bake until light golden brown, about 20 minutes.

Meanwhile, for the glaze: Sift the powdered (icing) sugar into a bowl. Stir in the milk and vanilla to make a smooth pourable glaze.

While the kringle is still warm, but not too hot, use a spoon to drizzle the glaze evenly across the top.

YELLOW CAKE
WITH CHOCOLATE FROSTING

PREPARATION TIME: 20 MINUTES,
  PLUS COOLING TIME
COOKING TIME: 35 MINUTES
SERVES: 8–10

For the cake:
- 3 cups (410 g) all-purpose (plain) flour
- 1 tablespoon baking powder
- ½ teaspoon salt
- 2 sticks (225 g) unsalted butter, softened
- 1½ cups (300 g) granulated sugar
- 3 eggs, at room temperature
- 2 egg yolks, at room temperature
- 1 teaspoon pure vanilla extract
- 1½ cups (355 ml) buttermilk

For the frosting:
- 1 stick (115 g) unsalted butter, softened
- ½ cup (40 g) unsweetened cocoa powder
- 4 cups (480 g) powdered (icing) sugar
- ⅓ cup (80 ml) milk
- 1 teaspoon pure vanilla extract

[This is the classic American birthday cake.]

Position a rack in the middle of the oven and preheat to 350°F (180°C/Gas Mark 4). Butter and flour two 8-inch (20 cm) round cake pans.

For the cake: In a large bowl, whisk together the flour, baking powder and salt.

In another large bowl, with an electric mixer, cream the butter and sugar until light and fluffy. On medium-low speed, beat in the whole eggs and egg yolks, one at a time, beating well after each addition. Beat in the vanilla. Alternately add the flour mixture and buttermilk, beginning and ending with the flour.

Divide the batter between the prepared pans. Bake until a skewer inserted in the center of a cake comes out clean, 30–35 minutes. Let cool in the pans for 10 minutes, then invert onto a wire rack to cool completely before frosting.

Meanwhile, for the frosting: While the cake cools, in a bowl, with an electric mixer, beat together the butter, cocoa, and 2 cups (240 g) powdered (icing) sugar. Beat in the milk, remaining 2 cups (240 g) sugar, and the vanilla.

Spread the frosting between the layers and over the top and sides of the cake.

CLASSIC CARROT CAKE

PREPARATION TIME: 20 MINUTES,
  PLUS COOLING TIME
COOKING TIME: 40 MINUTES
SERVES: 10–12

For the cake:
- 2 cups (260 g) all-purpose (plain) flour
- 2 teaspoons baking soda (bicarbonate of soda)
- 1 teaspoon ground cinnamon
- ½ teaspoon salt
- 1 cup (240 ml) vegetable oil
- 4 eggs, at room temperature
- 1½ cups (300 g) granulated sugar
- 1 teaspoon pure vanilla extract
- 2 cups (220 g) peeled and coarsely grated carrots (about 5 medium)
- 1 cup stir-ins, such as raisins, sweetened shredded (desiccated) coconut, or canned crushed pineapple (optional)

For the frosting:
- 4 tablespoons (60 g) unsalted butter, softened
- 8 oz (225 g) cream cheese, at room temperature
- 1½ cups (180 g) powdered (icing) sugar
- 1 teaspoon pure vanilla extract

Position a rack in the middle of the oven and preheat to 350°F (180°C/Gas Mark 4). Butter and flour a 9 x 13-inch (23 x 33 cm) baking pan.

For the cake: In a medium bowl, whisk together flour, baking soda (bicarbonate of soda), cinnamon, and salt.

In a large bowl, whisk together the oil, eggs, and sugar until the eggs lighten in color and the mixture is thoroughly blended. Beat in the vanilla. Stir in the flour mixture, carrots, and a stir-in (if using).

Pour the batter into the prepared pan. Bake until a skewer inserted in the center of the cake comes out clean, 35–40 minutes. Let the cake cool completely in the pan on a wire rack before frosting.

Meanwhile, for the frosting: In a bowl, with an electric mixer, cream the butter, cream cheese, and about half the powdered (icing) sugar until well combined, then add the remaining sugar and the vanilla.

Frost the top of the cooled cake.

CLASSIC CARROT CAKE

DEVIL'S FOOD CAKE

PREPARATION TIME: 15 MINUTES,
  PLUS COOLING TIME
COOKING TIME: 50 MINUTES
SERVES: 10–12

For the cake:
- ½ cup (40 g) unsweetened cocoa powder, plus more for the pans
- ½ cup (120 ml) boiling water
- ½ cup (120 ml) milk
- 2 cups (275 g) all-purpose (plain) flour
- ¾ teaspoon baking soda (bicarbonate of soda)
- ½ teaspoon salt
- 2 sticks (225 g) unsalted butter, softened
- 2 cups (400 g) granulated sugar
- 3 eggs, at room temperature

For the frosting:
- 1½ cups (355 ml) heavy (whipping) cream
- 1 bag (12 oz/340 g) semisweet chocolate chips
- ½ cup (120 ml) sour cream

[Devil's food cake is rich, moist, and delicate. This chocolate frosting is almost like fudge.]

Position a rack in the middle of the oven and preheat to 350°F (180°C/Gas Mark 4). Butter two 8-inch (20 cm) round cake pans and dust with cocoa.

For the cake: In a medium bowl, combine the cocoa with the boiling water. Set aside to cool until mixture is just warm, then whisk in the milk.

Sift together the flour, baking soda (bicarbonate of soda), and salt into a large bowl.

In a bowl, with an electric mixer, cream the butter and sugar until light and fluffy. Add the eggs 1 at a time, pausing to scrape the mixer bowl between the additions. On medium-low speed, alternately add the flour mixture and cocoa mixture, beginning and ending with flour.

Divide the batter between the prepared pans. Bake until a skewer inserted in the center of a cake comes out clean, 35–45 minutes. Let the cakes cool in the pans for 10 minutes, then invert onto a wire rack to cool completely before frosting.

For the frosting: In a small saucepan, bring the cream just to a boil over medium heat. Remove it from the heat, then add the chocolate chips. Set aside for 5 minutes. Stir in the sour cream until the mixture is smooth. Transfer the warm chocolate mixture to a shallow bowl and set aside to cool at room temperature, stirring occasionally, until it thickens and cools. Once it has thickened, gently beat it with a whisk for about 30 seconds to make it slightly fluffy and spreadable.

Spread the frosting between the layers and over the top and sides of the cake.

DEVIL'S FOOD CAKE

RED VELVET CAKE

PREPARATION TIME: 40 MINUTES,
    PLUS COOLING TIME
COOKING TIME: 30 MINUTES
SERVES: 8–10

For the cake:
- 2½ cups (340 g) cake flour (see Note)
- 1 teaspoon baking soda (bicarbonate of soda)
- ½ teaspoon salt
- 2 tablespoons unsweetened cocoa powder
- 2 tablespoons red food coloring
- 1 stick (115 g) unsalted butter, softened
- 1½ cups (300 g) sugar
- 2 eggs
- 1 teaspoons pure vanilla extract
- 1 cup (240 ml) buttermilk
- 1 tablespoon fresh lemon juice

For the frosting:
- 6 tablespoons all-purpose (plain) flour
- 1¼ cups (295 ml) milk
- 1½ teaspoons pure vanilla extract
- 2 sticks plus 4 tablespoons (285 g) salted butter, softened
- 1¼ cups (250 g) sugar

Note:
    All-purpose (plain) flour can be used
    as a substitute for cake flour. To do so
    in this case, remove 2 tablespoons per
    1 cup (130 g) of flour, and replace with
    2 tablespoons cornstarch (cornflour).

[Essentially a red version of a devil's food cake, this dessert has been part of the Southern layer cake tradition since the 1940s.]

Position racks in the upper and lower thirds of the oven and preheat to 350°F (180°C/Gas Mark 4). Butter three 9-inch (23 cm) cake pans and line the bottoms with rounds of parchment paper.

For the cake: In a large bowl, whisk together the flour, baking soda (bicarbonate of soda), and salt. In a small bowl, mix together the cocoa powder and food coloring to make a paste.

In a large bowl, with an electric mixer, cream the butter and sugar until light and fluffy. Beat in the eggs, 1 at a time, beating well after each addition. Beat in the vanilla. On medium-high speed, beat in the cocoa mixture. Alternately add the flour mixture and the buttermilk and lemon juice, beginning and ending with the flour.

Divide the batter among the prepared pans and bake until a skewer inserted in the center of the cake comes out clean, 20–25 minutes, switching racks halfway through the baking. Let the cakes cool for 5 minutes in the pans, then turn out onto a wire rack to cool completely before frosting.

For the frosting: In a medium saucepan, whisk together the flour, milk, and vanilla. Whisking constantly, bring to a low boil over medium heat. Reduce the heat to low and continue to whisk until the mixture thickens, 2–3 minutes. Transfer the mixture to a bowl and let cool to room temperature, whisking occasionally as it cools to make it smooth.

In a large bowl, with an electric mixer, cream the butter and sugar until light and fluffy. Gradually beat in the milk mixture. On medium-high speed, beat until the icing is light and fluffy, 2–3 minutes.

Spread the frosting between the layers and over the top and sides.

RED VELVET CAKE

ANGEL FOOD CAKE

PREPARATION TIME: 15 MINUTES
COOKING TIME: 1 HOUR
SERVES: 8–10

- 2 cups (400 g) sugar
- 1 cup (140 g) cake flour, sifted (see Note, page 310)
- 1½ cups (355 ml) egg whites (from about 12 eggs)
- 2 teaspoons pure vanilla extract
- 1½ teaspoons cream of tartar
- ¼ teaspoon kosher (coarse) salt

[The white sponge cake recipe in *The Kentucky Housewife* cookbook published by Lettice Bryan in 1839 is the precursor to modern-day angel food cake. The soufflé-like combination of egg whites, sugar, and flour was stabilized with lemon juice and flavored with lemon zest. Today's angel food cakes call for cream of tartar to stabilize the egg whites — yes, a dozen of them. Save the twelve yolks for making ice cream. The finished cake is the color of a cloud, and light as air. Crown it with whipped cream and whatever berries are at their peak.]

Position a rack in the middle of the oven and preheat to 350°F (180°C/Gas Mark 4).

In a medium bowl, whisk together the sugar and flour. In a large bowl, with an electric mixer, beat the egg whites, vanilla, cream of tartar, and salt on high speed until stiff (but not dry) peaks form, 4–5 minutes. Using a rubber spatula, fold the flour mixture gently into the beaten egg whites (do not overmix).

Transfer the batter to an ungreased 10-inch (25 cm) tube pan and smooth the top. Bake until lightly browned and a skewer inserted halfway between the edge and center tube comes out clean, about 1 hour.

Place the tube pan upside down on a wire rack and let the cake cool completely. Using a long, serrated knife, run along the outer and inner edges of the cake to release. Invert the cake onto a plate and serve.

ANGEL FOOD CAKE

TEXAS SHEET CAKE

PREPARATION TIME: 10 MINUTES
COOKING TIME: 25 MINUTES
SERVES: 15–20

For the cake:
- 2 sticks (225 g) butter
- ½ cup (40 g) unsweetened cocoa powder
- ½ teaspoon salt
- 2 cups (260 g) all-purpose (plain) flour
- 1½ cups (300 g) granulated sugar
- 1 teaspoon baking soda (bicarbonate of soda)
- ½ cup (120 ml) buttermilk

For the frosting:
- 1 stick (115 g) butter
- ¼ cup (20 g) unsweetened cocoa powder
- ¼ cup (60 ml) milk
- 1 lb (455 g) powdered (icing) sugar
- ½ cup (50 g) pecans, finely chopped

[This cake is thin, flat, and spiked with two of Texans' culinary mainstays: pecans and buttermilk.]

Position a rack in the middle of the oven and preheat to 375°F (190°C/Gas Mark 5). Butter and flour a 13 x 18-inch (33 x 46 cm) rimmed sheet pan.

For the cake: In a medium saucepan, combine the butter, 1 cup (240 ml) water, cocoa, and salt and bring to a boil. Stir in the flour, granulated sugar, and baking soda (bicarbonate of soda), then stir in the buttermilk. Pour the batter into the prepared pan. Bake until the cake springs back when touched, 15–20 minutes.

Meanwhile, for the frosting: In a saucepan set over medium heat, combine the butter, cocoa, and milk and warm until the butter melts. Stir in the powdered (icing) sugar until smooth, then sprinkle the pecans on top.

Pour the warm frosting over the cake and let the cake cool completely before slicing.

BLUEBERRY CAKE

PREPARATION TIME: 15 MINUTES
COOKING TIME: 50 MINUTES
SERVES: 12–14

- 2½ cups (325 g) plus 2 tablespoons all-purpose (plain) flour
- 2 teaspoons baking powder
- 1 teaspoon salt
- 2 sticks (225 g) unsalted butter, softened
- 1¼ cups (250 g) sugar
- 4 eggs, at room temperature
- 1 tablespoon pure vanilla extract
- ⅔ cup (160 ml) milk
- 3 cups (445 g) Maine wild blueberries, fresh or frozen
- Cinnamon sugar: 3 tablespoons sugar mixed with 2 teaspoons ground cinnamon

Position a rack in the middle of the oven and preheat to 350°F (180°C/Gas Mark 4). Grease and flour a 9 x 13-inch (23 x 33 cm) baking pan.

In a large bowl, whisk together 2½ cups (325 g) of the flour, the baking powder, and salt. In another large bowl, with an electric mixer, cream the butter and sugar until light and fluffy. Beat in the eggs, 1 at a time, beating well after each addition. Beat in the vanilla. Alternately add the flour mixture and the milk, beginning and ending with the flour. Mix on medium-high speed for 60 seconds.

In a medium bowl, toss the berries with the remaining 2 tablespoons flour. Fold the berry mixture into the batter until just incorporated.

Scrape the batter into the prepared pan. Sprinkle the cake with the cinnamon sugar. Bake until the cake is golden brown and a skewer inserted in the center comes out clean, 40–50 minutes.

Let the cake cool in the pan before slicing.

TEXAS SHEET CAKE

BOSTON CREAM PIE

PREPARATION TIME: 25 MINUTES,
    PLUS COOLING AND CHILLING TIME
COOKING TIME: 40 MINUTES
SERVES: 8

For the pastry cream:
- ⅓ cup (65 g) sugar
- 2 tablespoons cornstarch (cornflour)
- Pinch of salt
- 1½ cups (355 ml) milk
- 3 egg yolks
- 2 teaspoons pure vanilla extract

For the cake:
- 1¼ cups (163 g) all-purpose (plain) flour
- 1½ teaspoons baking powder
- 1 teaspoon salt
- ⅓ cup (75 g) unsalted butter
- 1 cup (200 g) sugar
- 2 eggs
- ⅓ cup (80 ml) milk
- 1 teaspoon pure vanilla extract

For the chocolate glaze:
- 4 oz (115 g) bittersweet (dark) chocolate, chopped
- ½ cup (120 ml) heavy (whipping) cream

[Invented in the 1800s at Boston's Parker House hotel, this classic dessert isn't actually a pie; it's two moist layers of cake with a pastry-cream filling between, all dressed up in a chocolate glaze.]

For the pastry cream: In a small heavy-bottomed saucepan, whisk together the sugar, cornstarch (cornflour), and salt. In a bowl, whisk together the milk and egg yolks, then whisk the mixture into the saucepan. Cook over medium heat, whisking constantly, until the pastry cream thickens and bubbles, a few minutes. Reduce the heat to a simmer and continue whisking for several more minutes, until mixture is thick enough to coat the back of a spoon (a finger drawn across the spoon will leave a defined swipe), about 5 minutes. Remove from the heat and stir in the vanilla. Transfer to a bowl, cover and refrigerate until ready to use.

Position a rack in the middle of the oven and preheat to 350°F (180°C/Gas Mark 4). Butter and flour a 9-inch (23 cm) round cake pan.

For the cake: In a medium bowl, whisk together the flour, baking powder, and salt.

In a large bowl, with an electric mixer, cream the butter and sugar until light and fluffy. Beat in the eggs, 1 at a time. Alternately add the flour mixture and milk, beginning and ending with the flour. Beat in the vanilla.

Pour the batter into the prepared pan. Bake until a skewer inserted in the center comes out clean, 30–35 minutes. Let the cake cool in the pan for several minutes, then turn out of the pan onto a wire rack to cool completely. Halve the cooled cake horizontally.

For the chocolate glaze: Place the chocolate in a heatproof bowl. In a small saucepan, bring the cream to a boil. Pour over the chocolate, let sit 1 minute, then stir the cream and chocolate together until smooth.

To assemble: Place the bottom layer of cake on a cake plate and spread the pastry cream on top. Place the top layer (with the top of the cake facing up) over the pastry cream. Pour the chocolate glaze over the top, spreading it just to the edges and allowing it to drip down the sides.

HOT MILK CAKE

PREPARATION TIME: 20 MINUTES,
   PLUS COOLING TIME
COOKING TIME: 40 MINUTES
SERVES: 12–16

- 2½ cups (325 g) all-purpose (plain) flour
- 2 teaspoons baking powder
- 1 cup (240 ml) milk
- 4 sticks (455 g) unsalted butter, softened
- 2½ cups (500 g) granulated sugar
- 4 eggs
- 3 teaspoons pure vanilla extract
- 2 cups (240 g) powdered (icing) sugar
- 2 tablespoons heavy (whipping) cream

[This recipe can also be baked in two 9-inch (23 cm) round cake pans to make a layer cake.]

Position a rack in the middle of the oven and preheat to 350°F (180°C/Gas Mark 4). Butter and flour a 9 x 13-inch (23 x 33 cm) baking pan. In a bowl, whisk together the flour and baking powder.

In a medium saucepan over medium heat, warms the milk and 3 sticks (340 g) of the butter until the butter melts. Remove from the heat and set aside to cool to lukewarm.

In a bowl, with an electric mixer, beat the sugar and eggs on medium-high speed until the eggs are light yellow and thick, 3–5 minutes. Alternately add the flour mixture and lukewarm milk and butter, beginning and ending with the flour. Beat in 2 teaspoons of the vanilla. Pour the batter into the baking pan and bake until a skewer inserted in the center comes out clean, 30–35 minutes. Let cool completely in the pan.

In a bowl, with an electric mixer on low speed, beat together the remaining 1 stick (115 g) butter, the powdered sugar, cream, and remaining 1 teaspoon vanilla. Increase the speed to medium-high and beat until fluffy, about 2 minutes. Frost the cake and serve.

ALABAMA FRUITCAKE

PREPARATION TIME: 20 MINUTES
COOKING TIME: 1 HOUR 30 MINUTES
SERVES: 12

- 2 cups (260 g) all-purpose (plain) flour
- 1 teaspoon baking powder
- ½ teaspoon baking soda (bicarbonate of soda)
- ½ teaspoon salt
- 2 teaspoons ground cinnamon
- ½ teaspoon freshly grated nutmeg
- ¼ teaspoon ground cloves
- ⅔ cup (150 g) unsalted butter, softened
- ¾ cup (145 g) packed light brown sugar
- 2 eggs
- 1 cup (240 ml) apple juice
- 1 lb (455 g) candied maraschino cherries (red and green), halved
- 1 cup (165 g) raisins
- ⅔ cup (70 g) pecans or walnuts, chopped
- 1¼ cups (425 g) molasses (treacle)

Position a rack in the middle of the oven and preheat to 325°F (160°C/Gas Mark 3). Line a 9 x 5-inch (23 x 13 cm) loaf pan with parchment paper.

In a medium bowl, whisk together the flour, baking powder, baking soda (bicarbonate of soda), salt, cinnamon, nutmeg, and cloves.

In a large bowl, with an electric mixer, cream the butter and brown sugar until lightened in color and texture, about 5 minutes. Beat in the eggs, 1 at a time, until well combined. Alternately add the flour mixture and the apple juice, beginning and ending with the flour. Fold the fruits and nuts into the batter, then stir in the molasses (treacle) until well combined.

Scrape the batter into the prepared loaf pan. Bake until a skewer inserted in the center comes out clean, 1–1½ hours.

SMITH ISLAND CAKE

PREPARATION TIME: 25 MINUTES,
   PLUS COOLING TIME
COOKING TIME: 1 HOUR 15 MINUTES,
   PLUS COOLING TIME
SERVES: 8–10

For the cake:
- 3 cups (390 g) all-purpose (plain) flour
- 2 teaspoons baking powder
- 2 sticks (225 g) unsalted butter, softened
- 2 cups (400 g) sugar
- 5 eggs, at room temperature
- 1 tablespoon pure vanilla extract
- 1 can (12 oz/340 g) evaporated milk

For the frosting:
- 2 cups (400 g) sugar
- 1 can (12 oz/340 g) evaporated milk
- 1½ sticks (170 g) unsalted butter,
   cut into pieces
- 4 oz (115 g) unsweetened chocolate,
   chopped

[Maryland's state dessert, this is a dramatic dessert boasts ten carefully stacked vanilla layers sandwiched with fudge frosting. In order to make that number of layers with a standard kitchen setup, one pair of pans is reused – fortunately the layers are very thin, so the baking times are short. In the 1800s, the women of Smith Island (off the Chesapeake Bay) would make these cakes each fall for their husbands harvesting oysters.]

Position a rack in the middle of the oven and preheat to 375°F (190°C/Gas Mark 5). Butter and flour two 9-inch (23 cm) round cake pans.

For the cake: In a medium bowl, whisk together the flour, baking powder, and salt. In a large bowl, with an electric mixer, cream the butter and sugar until light and fluffy. Beat in the eggs, 1 at a time, beating well after each addition. Beat in the vanilla. Alternately add the flour mixture and evaporated milk, beginning and ending with the flour.

Spread ⅔ cup (155 ml) batter in each prepared pan. Bake until a skewer inserted in the center of a cake comes out clean, 10–15 minutes. Let the cakes cool in the pans for 10 minutes, then invert onto a wire rack to cool completely. Wash and dry the cake pans, butter and flour them, and repeat with the remaining batter—there will be 10 cake layers in total.

Meanwhile, for the frosting: In a medium saucepan, combine the sugar, evaporated milk, and butter. Cook over medium heat, stirring, until the sugar dissolves and the butter melts. Stir in the chocolate until melted. Bring to a simmer and cook, stirring occasionally, until the icing is the consistency of hot fudge, about 10 minutes. (The frosting will thicken as it cools.)

Place a cake layer on a cake stand and spread about 4 tablespoons of the frosting in the center of the layer. Repeat the process with the remaining cake layers (reheating the frosting over low heat if necessary), leaving the top layer bare. Pour the remaining frosting over the top and spread around the sides of the cake. (If the cake layers slip as they are stacked, readjust within a few minutes to avoid the frosting setting the cake askew.)

SMITH ISLAND CAKE

HUCKLEBERRY CAKE

PREPARATION TIME: 15 MINUTES
COOKING TIME: 40 MINUTES
SERVES: 8

- 1 cup (200 g) sugar
- 2 eggs
- 2½ cups (325 g) all-purpose (plain) flour
- ½ cup (50 g) almond flour (ground almonds)
- 1 tablespoon baking powder
- Pinch of salt
- 1½ cups (355 ml) milk
- 2 cups (300 g) huckleberries
- 1 tablespoon (15 g) butter, melted
- Whipped cream, for serving

[Black huckleberries were an important part of Native American diets, and were preserved by drying, being reconstituted for use in cakes, porridges, soups, and sauces. Use the fruit in any way you would a blueberry, such as in this cake.]

Position a rack in the middle of the oven and preheat to 375°F (190°C/Gas Mark 5). Grease an 8-inch (20 cm) springform pan.

In a large bowl, beat the sugar and eggs until creamy. In a medium bowl, whisk together the flour, almond flour (ground almonds), baking powder, and salt. Alternately add the flour mixture and the milk to the sugar mixture, beginning and ending with the flour. Add the huckleberries and melted butter and stir well.

Pour the batter into the pan. Bake until a skewer inserted in the center of the cake comes out clean, about 40 minutes. Turn out onto a wire rack to cool. Serve with whipped cream.

HUCKLEBERRY CAKE

PINEAPPLE UPSIDE-DOWN CAKE

PREPARATION TIME: 10 MINUTES
COOKING TIME: 1 HOUR 10 MINUTES
SERVES: 8–10

- 4 tablespoons (60 g) unsalted butter, softened
- ½ cup (95 g) packed dark brown sugar
- 6 slices (½ inch/1.25 cm thick) fresh pineapple
- 4 tablespoons (60 g) unsalted butter, melted
- 1 cup (240 ml) buttermilk
- 2 eggs
- ½ cup (100 g) granulated sugar
- 1½ cups (195 g) all-purpose (plain) flour
- ½ cup (65 g) cornmeal
- 1 teaspoon baking soda (bicarbonate of soda)
- ½ teaspoon salt

Position a rack in the middle of the oven and preheat to 350°F (180°C/Gas Mark 4).

Heavily butter a 9-inch (23 cm) round cake pan or ovenproof cast-iron skillet with the softened butter (use all of it). Sprinkle the brown sugar evenly over the bottom of the pan, then arrange the pineapple slices in a single layer.

In a medium bowl, whisk together the melted butter, buttermilk, eggs, and granulated sugar until foamy. In a large bowl, combine the flour, cornmeal, baking soda (bicarbonate of soda), and salt. Gradually add the egg mixture to the flour mixture and stir until well incorporated.

Carefully spread the batter over the pineapple in an even layer. Bake until cake is golden brown on top and a skewer inserted into the center comes out clean, 50–60 minutes. Let the cake cool in the pan for 5 minutes. Run a knife around the edges of the pan and cover with a dinner plate. Flip to turn the cake out of the pan. Let rest for 10 minutes before serving.

DATE CAKE

PREPARATION TIME: 30 MINUTES
COOKING TIME: 1 HOUR
SERVES: 8–10

- ½ cup (120 ml) brewed coffee
- ½ cup (170 g) honey
- ½ lb (227 g) dates, pitted
- 2 cups (260 g) all-purpose (plain) flour
- 1 teaspoon baking soda (bicarbonate of soda)
- ½ teaspoon ground cinnamon
- ⅛ teaspoon salt
- ¼ teaspoon apple pie spice (mixed spice)
- 2 eggs
- ½ cup (100 g) sugar
- 2 tablespoons (30 g) butter, melted
- 1 tablespoon grated orange zest

[California's date palm tree farmers cultivate dozens of varieties.]

Position a rack in the middle of the oven and preheat to 350°F (180°C/Gas Mark 4). Butter an 8-inch (20 cm) round cake pan.

In a small saucepan, combine the coffee and honey and bring to a low simmer over medium heat. Add the dates and simmer for 5 minutes, then remove from the heat, cover, and let rest for 15 minutes. Transfer to a blender and purée until smooth.

In a medium bowl, combine the flour, baking soda (bicarbonate of soda), cinnamon, salt, and spice blend. In a large bowl, with an electric mixer, beat the eggs and sugar until airy and light yellow in color. Beat in the date mixture, then the melted butter and orange zest. Gently fold in the flour mixture until just combined.

Pour the batter into the prepared pan and bake until a skewer inserted in the center comes out clean, 40–50 minutes. Let the cake cool in the pan for 5 minutes, then turn out onto a wire rack to cool completely (or serve warm).

TENNESSEE JAM CAKE

PREPARATION TIME: 30 MINUTES,
  PLUS COOLING TIME
COOKING TIME: 40 MINUTES
SERVES: 8–10

For the cake:
- 2 cups (260 g) all-purpose (plain) flour
- 1¼ teaspoons baking soda (bicarbonate of soda)
- 1 teaspoon freshly grated nutmeg
- 1 teaspoon ground cinnamon
- ½ teaspoon ground cloves
- ½ teaspoon salt
- 1 stick (115 g) unsalted butter, softened
- 1½ cups (300 g) granulated sugar
- 1 cup (320 g) jam or preserves (as smooth as possible, without large pieces of fruit)
- 4 eggs, at room temperature
- 1½ cups (355 ml) buttermilk
- 2 teaspoons pure vanilla extract

For the frosting:
- 1 stick (115 g) unsalted butter, softened
- 1 cup (190 g) packed light brown sugar
- ¼ cup (60 ml) milk
- 3 cups (360 g) powdered (icing) sugar

Position racks in the upper and lower thirds of the oven and preheat to 350°F (180°C/Gas Mark 4). Butter and flour three 8-inch (20 cm) round cake pans.

For the cake: In a medium bowl, whisk together the flour, baking soda (bicarbonate of soda), spices, and salt. In a large bowl, with an electric mixer, cream the butter and granulated sugar until light and fluffy. On medium-low speed, beat in the jam. Then beat in the eggs, 1 at a time, beating well after each addition. Alternately add the flour mixture and the buttermilk, beginning and ending with the flour. Stir in the vanilla.

Divide the batter among the prepared pans. Bake until a skewer inserted in the center of a cake comes out clean, 30–35 minutes, switching racks halfway through. Let cool in the pans for 10 minutes, then turn out onto a wire rack to cool completely before frosting.

For the frosting: In a saucepan, combine the butter, brown sugar, and milk and bring to a boil over medium heat. Set aside to cool completely, then transfer to a mixer bowl. With the mixer on low, beat in the powdered (icing) sugar until light and fluffy.

Spread the frosting/icing between the layers and over the top and sides of the cake.

HUMMINGBIRD CAKE

PREPARATION TIME: 25 MINUTES,
   PLUS COOLING TIME
COOKING TIME: 35 MINUTES
SERVES: 8–10

For the cake:
- Butter, for the cake pans
- 3 cups (390 g) all-purpose (plain) flour
- 1¾ cups (350 g) granulated sugar
- 1 teaspoon salt
- ½ teaspoon baking powder
- ½ teaspoon baking soda (bicarbonate of soda)
- 1½ teaspoons ground cinnamon
- 3 eggs, beaten
- 1½ cups (355 ml) vegetable oil
- 1½ teaspoons pure vanilla extract
- 1 can (8 oz/225 g) crushed pineapple, in its juice
- 2 cups (500 g) chopped bananas
- 1 cup (120 g) chopped toasted pecans

For the cream cheese frosting:
- 1 lb (455 g) cream cheese, at room temperature
- 2 sticks (225 g) butter, softened
- 2 lb (910 g) powdered (icing) sugar, sifted
- 2 teaspoon pure vanilla extract
- ½ cup (50 g) pecan halves, toasted

[Home baker L. H. Wiggin submitted her version of this Jamaican banana-pineapple spice cake to *Southern Living* magazine, where it appeared in 1978. It became the magazine's most-requested recipe among readers.]

Preheat the oven to 350°F (180°C/Gas Mark 4). Butter and flour three 9-inch (23 cm) round cake pans and line the bottoms with rounds of parchment paper.

For the cake: In a large bowl, whisk together the flour, granulated sugar, salt, baking powder, baking soda (bicarbonate of soda), and cinnamon. In a medium bowl, whisk together the eggs, oil, and vanilla. Add the egg mixture to the flour mixture and mix well to combine. Fold in the pineapple with its juices, bananas, and chopped pecans.

Divide the batter among the cake pans. Bake until a toothpick inserted in the center of the cake layers comes out clean, 25–30 minutes. Let the cakes cool in the pans on wire racks for 10 minutes, then turn out of the pans onto the racks to cool completely before frosting.

For the cream cheese frosting: In a large bowl, with an electric mixer, beat the cream cheese and butter until smooth. On low speed, gradually beat in the powdered (icing) sugar until fully blended. Beat in the vanilla. Increase the speed to medium-high and beat until fluffy, 1–2 minutes.

Spread the frosting between the layers and over the top and sides of the cake. Arrange the toasted pecan halves in a circular pattern over the top of the cake.

APPALACHIAN APPLE STACK CAKE

PREPARATION TIME: 25 MINUTES,
   PLUS 1–3 DAYS STANDING TIME
COOKING TIME: 1 HOUR 20 MINUTES
SERVES: 10–12

For the cake:
- 5 cups (650 g) all-purpose (plain) flour
- 1 teaspoon baking powder
- ½ teaspoon baking soda (bicarbonate of soda)
- 1 teaspoon salt
- 1 teaspoon ground cinnamon
- 2½ cups (480 g) packed light brown sugar
- 1 cup (225 g) solid vegetable shortening
- 2 eggs
- 2 teaspoons pure vanilla extract
- ½ cup (120 ml) buttermilk

For the apples:
- 1 lb (455 g) dried apples, chopped
- 2¼ cups (430 g) packed light brown sugar
- 2½ teaspoons ground cinnamon
- ½ teaspoon freshly grated nutmeg
- ¼ teaspoon ground cloves
- ½ teaspoon salt
- ⅔ cup (80 g) powdered (icing) sugar (optional)

[Spices and flavorings were rare and expensive for early 20th-century cooks in Appalachia, the mountainous region that covers all of West Virginia and reaches from southern New York to northern Alabama. That's why this cake's sole flavor components are molasses (in the cake) and dried apples (rehydrated and cooked into applesauce for the filling), two inexpensive, readily available ingredients. Traditionally, the layers were baked one at a time, in a cast-iron skillet.]

Position racks in the upper and lower thirds of the oven and preheat to 425°F (220°C/Gas Mark 7). Grease and flour six 9-inch (23 cm) round cake pans. (Or do this in multiple batches, depending on how many cake pans you have and what you can fit in your oven at one time.)

For the cake: In a large bowl, combine the flour, baking powder, baking soda (bicarbonate of soda), salt, and cinnamon. In another large bowl, with an electric mixer, cream the brown sugar and shortening until lightened in color and texture. Beat in the eggs, 1 at a time, beating well after each addition. Beat in the vanilla and buttermilk. On low speed, beat in the flour mixture.

Divide the dough into 6 equal portions. Working with one portion at a time (keep the remaining dough covered), use floured hands to pat the dough into an even layer in a cake pan. Bake until lightly browned, 10–12 minutes, switching racks halfway through. Remove the layers from the pans and transfer to a wire rack to cool completely.

For the apples: In a large Dutch oven (casserole) or heavy-bottomed pot, bring 5 cups (1.2 liters) water to a boil over high heat. Add the dried apples, reduce the heat to medium, and cook uncovered until almost all the water is absorbed, 20–25 minutes. Stir in the brown sugar, cinnamon, nutmeg, cloves, and salt and simmer, stirring frequently, until thickened, about 15 minutes.

Stack the cake layers, spreading an equal amount of hot filling between them as you go. Leave the top layer plain. Cover the cake well with plastic wrap (clingfilm) and let stand 1–3 days before serving. Dust with powdered (icing) sugar, if desired, just before serving.

HICKORY NUT CAKE

PREPARATION TIME: 30 MINUTES,
   PLUS COOLING TIME
COOKING TIME: 55 MINUTES
SERVES: 8–10

For the cake:
- 2½ cups (325 g) all-purpose (plain) flour
- 2 teaspoons baking powder
- ½ teaspoon salt
- 1½ sticks (170 g) unsalted butter, softened
- 2 cups (400 g) granulated sugar
- 3 eggs, at room temperature
- 1 cup (240 ml) milk
- 1 teaspoon pure vanilla extract
- 1 cup (5 oz/142 g) toasted hickory nuts, roughly chopped

For the frosting:
- 1 stick (115 g) butter
- 1 cup (190 g) packed light brown sugar
- ¼ cup (60 ml) heavy (whipping) cream
- ½ cup (60 g) powdered (icing) sugar
- ¾ cup (3½ oz/106 g) hickory nuts, toasted and finely chopped

[Hickory nuts can be found for sale at farmers markets in the Midwest. Use a nutcracker and a nut pick to extract the meat. Hazelnuts can be used as a substitute if hickory is not available.]

Position a rack in the middle of the oven and preheat to 350°F (180°C/Gas Mark 4). Butter and flour two 8-inch (20 cm) round cake pans.

For the cake: In a medium bowl, sift the flour, baking powder, and salt. Set aside.

In a large bowl, with an electric mixer, cream the butter and granulated sugar until light and fluffy. Beat in the eggs, 1 at a time, scraping down the bowl after each addition.

Alternately add the flour mixture and milk, in three additions, starting and ending with the flours. Stir in the vanilla and hickory nuts.

Pour the batter into the prepared pans and bake until a skewer inserted in the center of a cake comes out clean, 30–40 minutes. Let the cakes cool in the pans for 2 minutes, then invert the cakes onto a wire rack to cool completely before frosting.

For the frosting: In a medium saucepan, melt the butter over medium heat. Stir in the brown sugar, bring to a boil, and boil for 2 minutes. Add the cream and bring back to a boil. Remove from the heat. Pour into a large bowl and allow to cool to lukewarm, then sift the powdered (icing) sugar into the bowl and beat it in. Stir in the chopped nuts.

Spread the frosting between the layers and over the top and sides of the cake.

BLACK WALNUT CAKE

PREPARATION TIME: 20 MINUTES,
  PLUS COOLING TIME
COOKING TIME: 35 MINUTES
SERVES: 8–10

For the cake:
- 2 cups (260 g) all-purpose (plain) flour
- 1¼ teaspoons baking soda (bicarbonate of soda)
- ½ teaspoon salt
- 1 cup (120 g) black walnut pieces, plus more for decoration (optional)
- 2 sticks (225 g) unsalted butter, softened
- 1½ cups (300 g) granulated sugar
- 3 eggs, at room temperature
- 1 teaspoon pure vanilla extract
- 1½ cups (355 ml) buttermilk

For the frosting:
- 1 stick (115 g) unsalted butter, softened
- 8 oz (225 g) cream cheese, at room temperature
- 3 cups (360 g) powdered (icing) sugar
- 1 teaspoon pure vanilla extract

[Black walnuts have a wonderfully distinctive nutty flavor that's stronger than that of conventional supermarket walnuts. Most American-grown black walnuts come from Missouri.]

Position a rack in the middle of the oven and preheat to 350°F (180°C/Gas Mark 4). Butter and flour two 8-inch (20 cm) round cake pans.

For the cake: In a medium bowl, whisk together the flour, baking soda (bicarbonate of soda), salt, and walnuts.

In a large bowl, with an electric mixer, cream the butter and granulated sugar until light and fluffy. On medium-low speed, beat in the eggs, 1 at a time, beating well after each addition. Beat in the vanilla. Alternately add the flour mixture and buttermilk, beginning and ending with flour.

Divide the batter between the prepared pans. Bake until a skewer inserted in the center of a cake comes out clean, 30–35 minutes. Let the cakes cool in the pans for 10 minutes, then invert onto a wire rack to cool completely before frosting.

For the frosting: In a bowl, with an electric mixer, cream the butter, cream cheese, and about half the powdered (icing) sugar. Beat in the remaining sugar and the vanilla.

Spread the frosting between the layers and over the top and sides of the cake. If desired, press chopped walnuts into the sides of the cake.

COCONUT CAKE

PREPARATION TIME: 40 MINUTES,
   PLUS COOLING TIME
COOKING TIME: 40 MINUTES
SERVES: 8–10

For the cake:
- Butter, for the pan
- 2 cups (260 g) all-purpose (plain) flour
- 1½ teaspoons baking powder
- ¼ teaspoon salt
- ½ cup (120 ml) vegetable oil
- 1 cup (200 g) granulated sugar
- 4 eggs
- ⅓ cup (80 ml) milk
- 1 cup (120 g) sweetened shredded coconut (desiccated), finely chopped

For the frosting:
- ½ cup (65 g) all-purpose (plain) flour
- 2 cups (475 ml) milk
- 2 teaspoons pure vanilla extract
- 2 teaspoons pure coconut extract
- 1 lb (455 g) unsalted butter, softened
- 2 cups (240 g) powdered (icing) sugar
- 1 cup (80 g) toasted coconut flakes

Position a rack in the middle of the oven and preheat to 350°F (180°C/Gas Mark 4). Butter and flour two 8- or 9-inch (20 or 23 cm) round cake pans.

For the cake: In a medium bowl, combine the flour, baking powder, and salt. In a large bowl, with an electric mixer, combine the oil, granulated sugar, and eggs and beat for 4–5 minutes. Add the flour mixture in two additions. Add the milk and shredded coconut and mix well to combine.

Divide the batter between the cake pans. Bake until a skewer inserted in the center of the cakes comes out clean, 30–35 minutes. Let the cakes cool in the pans for 15 minutes, then turn onto a wire rack to cool completely before icing.

For the frosting: In a small saucepan, whisk together the flour, ½ cup (120 ml) of the milk, the vanilla, and coconut extract. Place the saucepan over medium heat and gradually whisk in the remaining 1½ cups (355 ml) milk. Cook, whisking constantly, until the mixture comes to a low boil. Reduce the heat to low and continue to whisk until the mixture thickens, 2–3 minutes. Let cool to room temperature, whisking occasionally as it cools to make it smooth.

In a large bowl, with an electric mixer, beat the butter until lightened in texture. On low speed, gradually beat in the powdered (icing) sugar, then increase the speed to high and beat until light and fluffy, 1–2 minutes. On low speed, gradually beat in the cooled milk mixture. Increase the speed to medium-high and beat until the buttercream is light and fluffy, 2–3 minutes.

Spread the frosting between the layers and over the top and sides of the cake. Garnish with toasted coconut flakes up the sides of the cake and sprinkled over the top. Serve.

COCONUT CAKE

CARAMEL CAKE

PREPARATION TIME: 40 MINUTES,
  PLUS COOLING AND CHILLING TIME
COOKING TIME: 15 MINUTES
SERVES: 8–10

For the cake:
- 1 cup (240 ml) sour cream
- ¼ cup (60 ml) milk
- 2¾ cups (358 g) all-purpose (plain) flour
- 2 teaspoons baking powder
- ½ teaspoon salt
- 2 sticks (225 g) butter, softened
- 2 cups (400 g) granulated sugar
- 4 eggs
- 1 teaspoon pure vanilla extract

For the frosting:
- ¾ cup (150 g) granulated sugar
- ¾ (180 ml) cup heavy (whipping) cream
- 2 teaspoons pure vanilla extract
- 2½ sticks (340 g) unsalted butter, softened
- 1½ teaspoons salt
- 3 cups (360 g) powdered (icing) sugar

[Caramel cake bakers often turned to brown sugar for caramel flavor, while "true" caramel, made by cooking white sugar to the caramel stage, was called "burnt sugar."]

Position a rack in the middle of the oven and preheat to 350°F (180°C/Gas Mark 4). Grease and flour two 9-inch (23 cm) round cake pans.

For the cake: In a small bowl, whisk together the sour cream and milk. In a medium bowl, combine the flour, baking powder, and salt.

In a large bowl, with an electric mixer, beat the butter until creamy. Gradually beat in the granulated sugar, beating until lightened in color and airy, about 5 minutes. Beat in the eggs, 1 at a time, beating well after each addition. Alternately beat in the flour mixture and the sour cream mixture, beginning and ending with the flour. Beat in the vanilla.

Pour the batter into the cake pans. Bake until a skewer inserted in the center of the cakes comes out clean, 30–35 minutes. Let the cakes cool in the pans on a wire rack for 10 minutes, then turn out of the pans onto the rack to cool completely before frosting.

For the frosting: In a small saucepan, combine the granulated sugar and 6 tablespoons water. Place over medium-high heat and bring to a boil. Cook, without stirring, until the mixture turns a dark amber color, 6–8 minutes. Remove from the heat and slowly whisk in the cream and vanilla. Whisk until smooth. Let the caramel cool for 15 for minutes.

In a large bowl, with an electric mixer, beat the butter and salt until light and fluffy. On low speed, beat in the powdered (icing) sugar. With the mixer running, slowly add the caramel to the butter mixture. Increase the speed to medium-high and beat until fluffy, 1–2 minutes. Refrigerate for 30 minutes.

Spread the frosting between the layers and over the top and sides of the cake.

MOLASSES SPICE CAKE

PREPARATION TIME: 15 MINUTES
COOKING TIME: 55 MINUTES
SERVES: 8–10

- 2 tablespoons (30 g) butter
- 1 tablespoon grated orange zest
- 1½ cups (195 g) all-purpose (plain) flour
- ½ cup (60 g) whole wheat (wholemeal) flour
- 1 teaspoon baking soda (bicarbonate of soda)
- ½ teaspoon ground cinnamon
- ⅛ teaspoon salt
- ¼ teaspoon apple pie spice (mixed spice)
- 2 eggs
- ½ cup (100 g) sugar
- ½ cup (120 ml) brewed coffee
- ½ cup (170 g) molasses (treacle)

[In the colonial days, Rhode Island produced a half-million gallons (almost 1,900 liters) of rum out of molasses every year.]

Position a rack in the middle of the oven and preheat to 350°F (180°C/Gas Mark 4). Butter a 9 x 5-inch (23 x 13 cm) loaf pan or an 8-inch (20 cm) round cake pan.

In a small pan, combine the butter and orange zest and cook over medium heat until bubbling. Let cool to room temperature.

In a medium bowl, combine both flours, the baking soda (bicarbonate of soda), cinnamon, salt, and apple pie spice (mixed spice). In a large bowl, with an electric mixer, beat the eggs and sugar until lightened in color and thickened. Beat in the coffee and molasses (treacle), then the melted butter and zest. Gently fold in the flour mixture until just combined. Do not overmix.

Pour the batter into the prepared pan and bake until a skewer inserted in the center of the cake comes out clean, 40–50 minutes. Let the cake cool in the pan for 5 minutes, then turn it out onto a wire rack to cool completely before slicing.

SHOOFLY CAKE

PREPARATION TIME: 5 MINUTES
COOKING TIME: 50 MINUTES
SERVES: 12–15

- 1 cup (240 ml) molasses (treacle)
- 1 teaspoon baking soda (bicarbonate of soda)
- 4 cups (520 g) all-purpose (plain) flour
- 2 cups (385 g) packed light brown sugar
- 1 teaspoon salt
- 1 cup (240 ml) vegetable oil or melted butter

[This cake is baked frequently by the Pennsylvania Dutch (a regional group including the Amish and Mennonites) and often found at Amish market stands.]

Position a rack in the middle of the oven and preheat to 350°F (180°C/Gas Mark 4). Grease a 9 x 13-inch (23 x 33 cm) baking pan.

In a medium saucepan, bring 2 cups (475 ml) water to a boil. Stir in the molasses (treacle) and baking soda (bicarbonate of soda). Remove from the heat and set aside.

In a large bowl, stir together the flour, brown sugar, salt, and oil until the mixture forms moist crumbs. Measure out 1½ cups (135 g) of the crumb mixture and set aside. Stir the molasses mixture into the remaining flour mixture (the batter will be thin).

Pour the batter into the prepared pan and scatter the reserved crumb mixture over the top. Bake until a skewer inserted in the center of the cake comes out clean, 40–45 minutes. Let the cake cool completely in the pan on a wire rack before slicing.

MORAVIAN SUGAR CAKE

PREPARATION TIME: 15 MINUTES,
   PLUS RISING TIME
COOKING TIME: 45 MINUTES
SERVES: 10–12

- 1 russet (baking) potato (8 oz/225 g), peeled and cut into 1-inch (2.5 cm) pieces
- 1 packet (7 g/2¼ tsp) active dry yeast
- 3 sticks (345 g) unsalted butter, softened
- 1 cup (200 g) granulated sugar
- 2 eggs
- 2 cups (260 g) all-purpose (plain) flour, plus more as needed
- 1 teaspoon ground cinnamon
- ½ cup (95 g) packed light brown sugar

[This cake is well known in North Carolina, where the Moravian Church was first settled in the United States long ago. The sweetened, leavened cake is now most often served as a coffee cake at Easter.]

In a medium saucepan of boiling water, cook the potato until very tender, about 15 minutes. Reserving the cooking water, drain the potato, transfer to a medium bowl, and finely mash. Measure out 1 cup (240 ml) of cooking water (discard the remainder) and place it in a small bowl to cool to lukewarm, then sprinkle the yeast over the surface.

In a bowl, with an electric mixer, cream 2 sticks (230 g) of the butter and the granulated sugar until light and fluffy. Beat in the eggs, 1 at a time, beating well after each addition. Beat in the mashed potatoes and yeast mixture. Add the flour gradually until the mixture forms a soft, firm dough (it should not stick to your fingers)—add more flour if needed. Gather the dough to form a ball at the bottom of the bowl. Cover with a tea towel and set aside until the dough is doubled in volume, about 1 hour.

Preheat the oven to 375°F (190°C/Gas Mark 5). Butter a 9 x 13-inch (23 x 33 cm) baking dish.

Stretch and roll the dough so it fits the baking dish, then use your fingers to form indentations across the top of the dough (be careful not to push all the way to the bottom of the dish). In a small saucepan, melt the remaining 1 stick (115 g) butter and stir in the cinnamon and brown sugar. Pour the butter-sugar mixture over the surface of the dough (taking care to fill the indentations).

Bake until evenly golden on top, about 25 minutes. Serve warm.

MISSISSIPPI MUD CAKE

PREPARATION TIME: 20 MINUTES
COOKING TIME: 40 MINUTES
SERVES: 12

For the cake:
- 2 sticks (225 g) unsalted butter, melted
- 2¼ cups (450 g) granulated sugar
- 4 eggs
- 1½ teaspoons pure vanilla extract
- 1⅔ cups (210 g) all-purpose (plain) flour
- ⅓ cup (25 g) plus 1 tablespoon
  unsweetened cocoa powder
- 1 cup (120 g) chopped toasted walnuts
- 1 jar (7 oz/200 g) marshmallow cream,
  such as Marshmallow Fluff

For the frosting:
- 1 stick (115 g) unsalted butter, melted
- 1½ teaspoons pure vanilla extract
- ⅓ cup (25 g) unsweetened cocoa powder
- 4 cups (480 g) powdered (icing) sugar

[Dense, gooey, and chocolate-y seem to be the only criteria for desserts that go by the name of Mississippi Mud Cake, though many recipes call for marshmallows or marshmallow fluff in the batter or icing. The cake's appearance — dark brown and mud-like — recalls famous muddy Mississippi River, which runs from northern Minnesota to southern Mississippi.]

Position a rack in the middle of the oven and preheat to 350°F (180°C/Gas Mark 4). Butter a 9 x 13-inch (23 x 33 cm) baking pan.

For the cake: In a medium bowl, with an electric mixer, combine the melted butter and granulated sugar and beat until well combined, about 1 minute. Beat in the eggs and vanilla.

In a large bowl, whisk together the flour and cocoa powder. Slowly add the butter and egg mixture and beat until well combined. Gently stir in the walnuts.

Pour the batter into the prepared pan. Bake until a skewer inserted in the center of the cake comes out clean, 25–28 minutes. While the cake is still warm, spread evenly with all of the Marshmallow Fluff.

Meanwhile, for the frosting: In a medium bowl, with an electric mixer, combine the melted butter and vanilla. Whisk in the cocoa powder. Add 2 cups (240 g) of the powdered (icing) sugar and whisk well to combine. Add 4 tablespoons of the milk and whisk well to combine. Add the remaining 2 cups (240 g) powdered (icing) sugar and whisk well to combine. Add more milk as necessary to reach the consistency you desire.

Top the cake with the chocolate frosting. Serve warm or let cool to room temperature to serve. Can be covered and refrigerated for up to 2 days.

HUGUENOT TORTE

PREPARATION TIME: 20 MINUTES
COOKING TIME: 45 MINUTES
SERVES: 6

- 1 tablespoon (15 g) butter, softened
- 2 eggs
- ½ teaspoon salt
- 1½ cups (300 g) sugar
- 1 teaspoon pure vanilla extract
- 1 cup (120 g) coarsely chopped pecans
- 1 Granny Smith apple, peeled and diced
- 4 tablespoons all-purpose (plain) flour
- 2½ teaspoons baking powder
- Lightly sweetened whipped cream, for serving

["Ozark Pudding" was the inspiration for this Charleston, South Carolina, recipe. Evelyn Anderson renamed the dessert while working as a cook at the Huguenot Tavern and it was one of the original contributions to the cookbook *Charleston Receipts*, which was published by the Junior League of Charleston in 1950.]

Position a rack in the middle of the oven and preheat to 325°F (160°C/Gas Mark 3). Grease a 9-inch (23 cm) square baking pan with the butter.

In a bowl, with an electric mixer, whisk the eggs and salt until light and lemon colored, about 1 minute. Gradually beat in the sugar and vanilla and continue to whisk on medium-high speed for 3 more minutes. With a spatula, gently fold the pecans and apple into the egg mixture. Then gently fold in the flour and baking powder.

Pour the batter into the prepared pan and bake until crusty on top and warm and moist underneath, about 45 minutes. Serve warm, with whipped cream.

ST. LOUIS GOOEY BUTTER CAKE

PREPARATION TIME: 10 MINUTES
COOKING TIME: 30 MINUTES
SERVES: 8–10

For the crust:
- 1 cup (130 g) all-purpose (plain) flour
- 4 tablespoons granulated sugar
- ½ teaspoon salt
- 1 stick (115 g) unsalted butter
- 1 egg

For the filling:
- 1½ sticks (170 g) butter, softened
- 1 cup (100 g) granulated sugar
- 1 egg
- 1 cup (130 g) all-purpose (plain) flour
- ⅔ cup (160 ml) evaporated milk
- ¼ cup (60 ml) light corn syrup
- 1½ teaspoons pure vanilla extract
- Powdered (icing) sugar, for dusting

[This cake was created in the 1930s by a German-American baker who accidentally mixed too much butter into a coffee cake recipe.]

Position a rack in the middle of the oven and preheat to 350°F (180°C/Gas Mark 4). Butter an 8-inch (20 cm) square baking pan.

For the crust: In a large bowl, whisk together the flour, granulated sugar, and salt. Cut in the butter (using a pastry/dough blender or two knives) until small crumbs form. Stir in the egg. Press into the bottom of the buttered pan and set aside.

For the filling: In a medium bowl, with an electric mixer, cream the butter and granulated sugar until light and fluffy. Add the egg and blend thoroughly. Alternately add the flour and evaporated milk. Beat in the corn syrup and vanilla.

Pour the batter over the crust. Bake until just set, 25–30 minutes. Let the cake cool in the pan and dust with powdered (icing) sugar before serving.

ST. LOUIS GOOEY BUTTER CAKE

CHEESECAKE

PREPARATION TIME: 20 MINUTES,
  PLUS CHILLING TIME
COOKING TIME: 2 HOURS 40 MINUTES
SERVES: 16

For the crust:
- 1¾ cups (180 g) graham cracker crumbs (or 180 g digestive biscuits ground to crumbs)
- 2 tablespoons sugar
- 4 tablespoons (60 g) butter, melted
- Pinch of salt

For the filling:
- 2 lb (910 g) cream cheese, at room temperature
- 1¼ cups (250 g) sugar
- Pinch of salt
- 4 eggs
- 2 teaspoons pure vanilla extract
- 2 teaspoons fresh lemon juice
- ⅔ cup (160 ml) sour cream
- ⅔ cup (160 ml) heavy (whipping) cream

[Italians, French, Russians, and Greeks all stir their soft cheeses into sweet cake batter. But New York cheesecake is born of a decidedly American ingredient: cream cheese. Despite having "Philadelphia" in its name, cream cheese was born in New York State in 1880. The Kraft company bought it in 1909. This cake debuted around 1928.]

Position a rack in the middle of the oven and preheat to 350°F (180°C/Gas Mark 4). Wrap the outside of a 10-inch (25 cm) spring-form pan with several layers of foil. Gently fold the foil up around the base of the pan and make sure there are no holes. (The cake will be baked in a water bath.)

For the crust: In a bowl, stir together the graham cracker crumbs, sugar, butter, and salt until well combined. Press into the bottom of the pan. Bake the crust for 10 minutes. Remove from the oven and set aside to cool. Reduce the oven temperature to 325°F (160°C/Gas Mark 3).

For the filling: In a medium bowl, with an electric mixer, beat the cream cheese until smooth and soft. Beat in the sugar and salt. Add the eggs, 1 at a time, beating well and scraping down the bowl after each addition. Beat in the vanilla, lemon juice, sour cream, and cream.

Bring a kettle of water to a boil. Place the foil-wrapped springform pan (with the prebaked crust) in a large roasting pan. Pour the cheesecake batter into the crust. Pour enough boiling water to reach halfway up the sides of the pan. Bake just until the center is set and the edges of the cake are golden brown, about 1 hour 30 minutes. Turn the oven off, crack the oven door a few inches, and let the cake cool in the oven for 1 hour. Remove from the oven and run a knife around the edge of the cake. Carefully remove the ring and refrigerate the cake until well chilled, at least 4 hours, before serving.

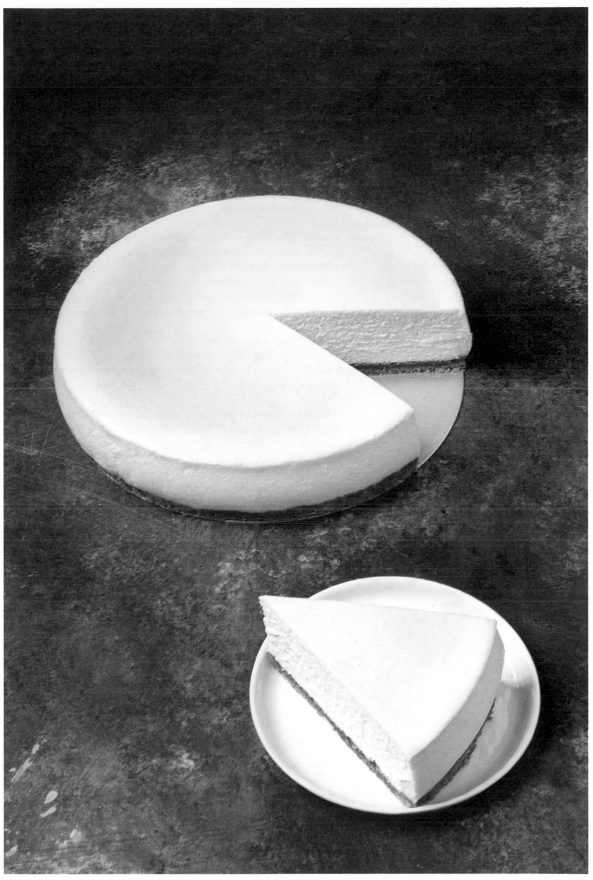

CHEESECAKE

WHOOPIE PIES

PREPARATION TIME: 20 MINUTES
COOKING TIME: 20 MINUTES
MAKES: 8–9 LARGE WHOOPIE PIES

For the cakes:
- 2 cups (260 g) all-purpose (plain) flour
- ½ cup (40 g) unsweetened cocoa powder
- 1 teaspoon baking soda (bicarbonate of soda)
- 1 teaspoon baking powder
- 1 teaspoon salt
- 1 stick (115 g) butter or ½ cup (115 g) solid vegetable shortening, at room temperature
- 1 cup (190 g) packed light brown sugar
- 1 egg
- 1 cup (240 ml) buttermilk
- 1 teaspoon pure vanilla extract

For the filling:
- 1 stick (115 g) butter or ½ cup (115 g) solid vegetable shortening, at room temperature
- 1 cup (120 g) powdered (icing) sugar
- 2 cups (190 g) marshmallow cream, such as Marshmallow Fluff
- 1 teaspoon pure vanilla extract

[This cake-like chocolate sandwich cookie started showing up in bakeries and lunchboxes in the 1920s, and both Maine and Pennsylvania claim it as their own. It gets its name from the reception it gets when it is served. A whoopie pie can be as big as a hamburger. Serve with a glass of cold milk.]

Position racks in the upper and lower thirds of the oven and preheat to 350°F (180°C/Gas Mark 4). Lightly grease two baking sheets or line with parchment paper.

For the cakes: In a mdium bowl, sift the flour, cocoa powder, baking soda (bicarbonate of soda), baking powder, and salt. In a large bowl, with an electric mixer, cream the butter and brown sugar until light and fluffy. Reduce the speed and beat in the egg. On very low speed, alternately add the flour mixture and the buttermilk, beginning and ending with the flour. Beat in the vanilla.

Drop ¼ cup (60 ml) batter 2 inches (5 cm) apart on the baking sheets. Bake until the top springs back when lightly touched, 15–20 minutes, switching racks halfway through. Transfer the cakes to wire racks to cool.

Meanwhile, for the filling: In a bowl, withan electric mixer, whisk the butter with the powdered (icing) sugar until smooth. Beat in the fluff and vanilla.

To fill the cakes, turn half the cakes upside down (flat side up) and spread with the filling. Top with the remaining cakes.

WHOOPIE PIES

KUCHEN

PREPARATION TIME: 20 MINUTES,
   PLUS RISING TIME
COOKING TIME: 40 MINUTES
MAKES: SERVES 24

For the dough:
- ¾ cup (180 ml) milk
- 2 tablespoons (30 g) unsalted butter
- ¼ cup (50 g) sugar
- ½ teaspoon salt
- 1 packet (¼ oz/7 g) active dry yeast
- 1 egg, beaten
- 2 cups (260 g) all-purpose (plain) flour

For the custard filling:
- 1 cup (240 ml) milk
- 1 cup (240 ml) heavy (whipping) cream
- ½ cup (100 g) sugar
- 1 heaping tablespoon all-purpose
  (plain) flour
- 2 eggs
- 1 teaspoon pure vanilla extract

For the topping:
- 1 cup (200 g) sugar
- 1 cup (130 g) all-purpose (plain) flour
- Pinch of salt
- 1 stick (115 g) unsalted butter, softened

For the fruit filling:
- 3 large apples, peeled, cored, and very
  thinly sliced

[The German word for cake, kuchen is the official state dessert of South Dakota. Variations call for different fillings such as fresh fruit, dried fruit, custard, or sweet cheese, while the cake base is made with either a yeasted dough or a simple dough using baking powder.]

For the dough: In a small saucepan, scald the milk over medium heat. Remove from the heat and stir in the butter, sugar, and salt. Transfer to a medium bowl and let cool to lukewarm. Stir in the yeast and beaten egg. Stir in the flour to form a sticky dough. With oiled hands, add the dough to a large oiled bowl and turn to coat. Cover with damp tea towel and let the dough rise in a warm draft-free area for 1 hour, until almost doubled in volume.

Grease four 8- or 9-inch (20 or 23 cm) pie plates. Divide the dough into 4 equal pieces and, on a floured surface, roll each to a round about ¼ inch (6 mm) thick. Fit each dough round into a pie plate or cake pan so it comes slightly up the sides. Let the dough rise, uncovered, for 20 minutes.

Position racks in the upper and lower thirds of the oven and preheat to 375°F (190°C/Gas Mark 5).

Meanwhile, for the custard filling: In a medium saucepan, heat the milk and cream until very hot but not boiling. In a bowl, whisk the sugar and flour together, then whisk in the eggs. Whisk some of the hot milk/cream into the egg mixture, then whisk the egg mixture back into the hot milk in the pan. Cook, stirring constantly, until thickened, about 8 minutes. Remove from the heat and stir in the vanilla. Set aside.

For the topping: In a bowl, mix together the sugar, flour, salt, and butter until the mixture just comes together (it is preferable if it is somewhat lumpy). Set aside.

For the fruit filling: Arrange the sliced apples over the top of the dough rounds. Pour ¾ cup (180 ml) custard filling over each kuchen. Sprinkle with the topping. Bake until the kuchens are golden brown around the edges and the filling is bubbling, about 30 minutes, switching racks halfway through baking. Let cool to room temperature before serving.

DIVINITY ICING

PREPARATION TIME: 10 MINUTES
COOKING TIME: 35 MINUTES
MAKES: ENOUGH TO FROST AN 8-INCH
  (20 CM) TWO-LAYER CAKE

- 2½ cups (500 g) sugar
- ½ teaspoon salt
- ½ cup (120 ml) light corn syrup
- 2 egg whites, at room temperature
- ⅛ teaspoon salt
- 1½ teaspoons pure vanilla extract
- ¾ cup (90 g) chopped pecans (optional)

[Also known as seven-minute frosting, divinity icing frosts ices many cakes across the south. The stiffly beaten egg whites become fluffy and light as a heavenly cloud—divinity indeed.]

In a medium saucepan, combine the sugar, salt, corn syrup, and ½ cup (120 ml) water. Cook over medium heat, stirring frequently, until the mixture comes to a boil and the sugar is dissolved. Continue cooking until the mixture reaches the soft ball stage: 240°F (115°C) on a candy (sugar) thermometer, 15-20 minutes. Measure out one-third of the hot syrup and set aside.

In a stand mixer fitted with the whisk attachment, beat the egg whites and salt at medium speed until soft peaks form. With the machine running at medium speed, gradually pour the reserved hot syrup into the egg whites.

Return the remaining sugar syrup to medium heat and cook to the firm ball stage: 248°F (120°C), about 10–15 minutes. With the mixer running at medium speed, slowly pour the remaining hot syrup into the egg white mixture. Increase the speed to high and continue beating until stiff peaks form and the frosting thickens. Stir in the vanilla and pecans (if using). Use immediately to frost a cooled cake.

CHOCOLATE CHIP COOKIES

PREPARATION TIME: 15 MINUTES
COOKING TIME: 1 HOUR
MAKES: 60 COOKIES

- 2¼ cups (293 g) all-purpose (plain) flour
- 1 teaspoon baking soda (bicarbonate of soda)
- 1 teaspoon salt
- 2 sticks (225 g) butter, softened
- ½ cup (100 g) granulated sugar
- ¾ cup (145 g) packed light brown sugar
- 1 teaspoon pure vanilla extract
- 2 eggs
- 1½ cups (335 g) semisweet chocolate chips
- 1 cup (130 g) chopped nuts (optional)

[Chocolate chip cookies were invented in the 1930s at the Toll House Inn in Whitman, Massachusetts.]

Position a rack in the middle of the oven and preheat to 375°F (190°C/Gas Mark 5).

Sift the flour, baking soda (bicarbonate of soda), and salt into a bowl.

In a stand mixer fitted with the paddle attachment, cream the butter and both sugars until light and creamy. Beat in the vanilla. Beat in the eggs, 1 at a time. On low speed, beat in the flour mixture. Fold in the chocolate chips and nuts (if using).

Drop the dough by rounded tablespoons onto an ungreased baking sheet, 2 inches (5 cm) apart. Bake until golden brown, 9–11 minutes. If baking 2 batches at a time, position the racks in the upper and lower thirds of the oven and switch racks halfway through baking. Let cool on the baking sheet for 2 minutes, then transfer to a wire rack to cool completely.

OATMEAL RAISIN COOKIES

PREPARATION TIME: 15 MINUTES
COOKING TIME: 25 MINUTES
MAKES: 36 COOKIES

- 1½ sticks (170 g) unsalted butter, softened
- ½ cup (100 g) granulated sugar
- ½ cup (95 g) packed light brown sugar
- 2 eggs
- 1½ cups (195 g) all-purpose (plain) flour
- 2 cups (160 g) rolled (porridge) oats
- 2 teaspoons baking powder
- 1 teaspoon ground cinnamon
- ½ teaspoon salt
- 1 teaspoon pure vanilla extract
- 1 cup (165 g) raisins

Position a rack in the middle of the oven and preheat to 375°F (190°C/Gas Mark 5).

In a stand mixer fitted with the paddle attachment, cream the butter and both sugars until light and fluffy. On medium speed, beat in the eggs, 1 at a time, beating well after each addition. In a separate bowl, whisk together the flour, oats, baking powder, cinnamon, and salt. With the mixer on low speed, add the flour mixture. Beat in the vanilla. Beat in the raisins.

Using a tablespoon as a scoop, drop walnut-size pieces of dough 3 inches (7.5 cm) apart on an ungreased baking sheet. Bake until the cookies are golden brown around the edges, about 12 minutes. If baking 2 batches at a time, position the racks in the upper and lower thirds of the oven and switch racks halfway through baking. Let the cookies cool on the pan for a few minutes, then transfer to a wire rack to cool completely.

CHOCOLATE CHIP COOKIES

SHORTBREAD

PREPARATION TIME: 15 MINUTES,
   PLUS DOUGH CHILLING TIME
COOKING TIME: 15 MINUTES
MAKES: 30 COOKIES

- 2 sticks (225 g) unsalted butter, softened
- 1 teaspoon salt (optional)
- ¾ cup (150 g) sugar
- 1 teaspoon pure vanilla extract (optional)
- 2 cups (260 g) all-purpose (plain) flour

In a stand mixer fitted with the paddle attachment, cream the butter, salt (if using), and sugar until light and fluffy. Beat in the vanilla (if using). On low speed, beat in the flour.

On a clean surface or parchment, roll the dough into 4 logs about 2 inches (5 cm) in diameter. Wrap and chill the dough in the freezer for at least 1 hour or until ready to bake.

Position a rack in the middle of the oven and preheat to 350°F (180°C/Gas Mark 4). Line a baking sheet with parchment paper.

Slice the dough logs into ¼-inch (6 mm) thick slices and arrange on the baking sheet. Bake until the cookies are just starting to brown on the edges, about 12 minutes. Let cool.

To make shortbread bars: After making the dough, press it into an ungreased 8-inch (20 cm) square baking pan. Bake at 325°F (160°C/Gas Mark 3) until set in the center and golden brown around the edges, 20–25 minutes. If baking 2 batches at a time, position the racks in the upper and lower thirds of the oven and switch racks halfway through baking. Cut into bars while the shortbread is warm.

CHEWY SUGAR COOKIES

PREPARATION TIME: 15 MINUTES
COOKING TIME: 30 MINUTES
MAKES: 36 COOKIES

- 2 sticks (225 g) unsalted butter, softened
- 1¼ cups (250 g) sugar
- 1 egg
- 2 teaspoons pure vanilla extract
- 2¼ cups (293 g) all-purpose (plain) flour
- ½ teaspoon baking powder
- ½ teaspoon salt
- ⅓ cup (65 g) sugar for rolling

Position a rack in the middle of the oven and preheat to 350°F (180°C/Gas Mark 4). Butter a baking sheet or line with parchment paper.

In a stand mixer fitted with the paddle attachment, cream the butter. Gradually add the sugar and mix on medium-high speed until light and fluffy, about 2 minutes. Add the egg and mix well. Beat in the vanilla. On low speed, beat in the flour, baking powder, and salt. Mix thoroughly, scraping down the bowl as necessary.

Scoop up roughly 1 tablespoon of cookie dough at a time and roll between your hands into balls. Toss the cookies in the sugar to coat lightly and place them on the baking sheet about 2 inches (5 cm) apart. Flatten each cookie slightly with the bottom of a glass dipped in sugar (as needed to prevent sticking). Bake until the cookies are light golden brown on the edges, about 8–10 minutes. Transfer to a wire rack to cool. If baking 2 batches at a time, position the racks in the upper and lower thirds of the oven and switch racks halfway through baking. Repeat to make more cookies.

PECAN SANDIES

PREPARATION TIME: 20 MINUTES
COOKING TIME: 50 MINUTES
MAKES: 36–48 COOKIES

- 2¼ cups (293 g) all-purpose (plain) flour
- ½ teaspoon salt
- ⅛ teaspoon baking soda (bicarbonate of soda)
- 7 tablespoons (100 g) butter, softened
- ⅔ cup (130 g) sugar
- 1 egg, at room temperature
- 2 teaspoons pure vanilla extract
- 1 cup (120 g)pecans, toasted and chopped

Position a rack in the middle of the oven and preheat to 325°F (160°C/Gas Mark 3).

In a medium bowl, whisk together the flour, salt, and baking soda (bicarbonate of soda). In a stand mixer fitted with the paddle attachment, cream the butter and sugar until lightened in color and texture, about 5 minutes. Beat in the egg, vanilla, and 1 teaspoon water. On low speed, beat in the flour mixture until just combined. Beat in the pecans.

Roll the dough into 1-inch (2.5 cm) balls and place on an ungreased baking sheet about 1½ inches (4 cm) apart. With your hands, gently flatten the balls into disks about ¼ inch (6 mm) thick and 1½ inches (4 cm) wide. Bake until lightly golden, 10–12 minutes. If baking 2 batches at a time, position the racks in the upper and lower thirds of the oven and switch racks halfway through baking. Let cookies cool on the pan for 1 minute, then transfer to a wire rack to cool completely.

MANZANITA BUTTER COOKIES

PREPARATION TIME: 15 MINUTES,
   PLUS DOUGH CHILLING TIME
COOKING TIME: 20 MINUTES
MAKES: 36 COOKIES

- 1 cup (67 g) dried manzanita berries
- 2 cups (260 g) all-purpose (plain) flour
- ½ teaspoon salt
- ¼ teaspoon baking powder
- 2 sticks (225 g) unsalted butter, softened
- ¾ cup (150 g) sugar
- 1 egg

[Native to the dry and mountainous parts of the Southwest and the Pacific Coast, the manzanita shrub bears berries that can be harvested in various stages of ripeness: tart in early summer, sweeter in fall.]

Grind the dried berries very briefly in a spice grinder, then sift to separate, discard the seeds, and grind again until fine.

In a bowl, whisk together the flour, salt, and baking powder. In a stand mixer fitted with the paddle attachment, cream the butter, sugar, and ground manzanita berries until light and fluffy. Beat in the egg. On low speed, slowly add the flour mixture, beating until a dough forms.

Divide the dough in two and shape each portion into a log 2 inches (5 cm) in diameter. Wrap in wax (greaseproof) paper and chill until firm, about 40 minutes.

Position racks in the upper and lower thirds of the oven and pre-heat to 350°F (180°C/Gas Mark 4). Butter 2 baking sheets.

Bake the cookies in batches. Cut the chilled dough logs into slices ⅛ inch (3 mm) thick and place on the baking sheets ¼ inch (6 mm) apart. Bake until golden, about 10 minutes. If baking 2 batches at a time, position the racks in the upper and lower thirds of the oven and switch racks halfway through baking. Transfer to a wire rack to cool.

BISCOCHITOS

PREPARATION TIME: 25 MINUTES,
  PLUS DOUGH CHILLING TIME
COOKING TIME: 50 MINUTES
MAKES: 36–48 COOKIES

- 3 cups (390 g) all-purpose (plain) flour
- 1½ teaspoons baking powder
- 1 tablespoon crushed anise seed
- ½ teaspoon salt
- 1¼ cups (255 g) lard
- 2¾ cups (550 g) sugar
- 1 teaspoon pure vanilla extract
- 1 egg
- 2 teaspoons ground cinnamon

[The official state cookie of New Mexico, these shortbread bites are aromatic with anise and cinnamon. They are especially popular at Christmas, served with hot chocolate.]

In a large bowl, whisk together the flour, baking powder, anise seed, and salt. In a stand mixer fitted with the paddle attachment, cream the lard and ¾ cup (150 g) of the sugar until light and fluffy, about 4 minutes. Beat in the vanilla and egg. On low speed, gradually beat in the flour mixture. Cover with plastic wrap (clingfilm) and refrigerate for 30 minutes.

Position a rack in the middle of the oven and preheat to 350°F (180°C/Gas Mark 4). Line a baking sheet with parchment paper.

In a large bowl, whisk together the remaining 2 cups (400 g) sugar and the cinnamon.

On a lightly floured surface, roll the dough to a rectangle ¼ inch (6 mm) thick. Using a 2-inch (5 cm) round cookie cutter, cut out cookies and place ½ inch (1.25 cm) apart on the lined baking sheet. If baking 2 batches at a time, position the racks in the upper and lower thirds of the oven and switch racks halfway through baking. Bake until just set, 10–12 minutes. Let the cookies cool for 1 minute on the baking sheet, then place all at once into the large bowl of cinnamon sugar. Toss very gently to cover the cookies with the mixture. Transfer to a wire rack to cool completely.

HERMIT COOKIES

PREPARATION TIME: 20 MINUTES
COOKING TIME: 45 MINUTES
MAKES: ABOUT 36 COOKIES

- 2¼ cups (293 g) all-purpose (plain) flour
- 1 teaspoon baking soda (bicarbonate of soda)
- ½ teaspoon salt
- ½ teaspoon ground cinnamon
- ½ teaspoon freshly grated nutmeg
- 1 stick (115 g) unsalted butter, softened
- 1 cup (190 g) packed light brown sugar
- 2 eggs
- 4 tablespoons molasses (treacle)
- 3 tablespoons buttermilk
- 1 cup (165 g) raisins
- 1 cup (160 g) dried currants

Position a rack in the middle of the oven and preheat to 350°F (180°C/Gas Mark 4). Lightly grease a baking sheet or line with parchment paper.

Sift the flour, baking soda (bicarbonate of soda), salt, cinnamon, and nutmeg into a bowl. In a stand mixer fitted with the paddle attachment, cream the butter and sugar until light and fluffy. Beat in the eggs, 1 at a time. Beat in the molasses (treacle) and buttermilk. On low speed, beat in the flour mixture and blend well. Stir in the raisins and currants.

Drop by spoonful onto the baking sheet, 2 inches (5 cm) apart. If baking 2 batches at a time, position the racks in the upper and lower thirds of the oven and switch racks halfway through baking. Bake until set around the edges, 12–15 minutes. Transfer to wire racks to cool.

BISCOCHITOS

SNICKERDOODLES

PREPARATION TIME: 15 MINUTES,
  PLUS DOUGH CHILLING TIME
COOKING TIME: 30 MINUTES
MAKES: 36 COOKIES

- 2½ cups (325 g) all-purpose (plain) flour
- 1½ teaspoons baking powder
- 1 teaspoon salt
- ¼ teaspoon freshly grated nutmeg
- 2 cups (400 g) sugar
- ¾ cup (170 g) fat (lard, vegetable oil,
  or shortening)
- 2 eggs
- 1 teaspoon pure vanilla extract
- 2 teaspoons ground cinnamon

Sift the flour, baking powder, salt, and nutmeg into a medium bowl. In a large bowl, stir 1 cup (200 g) of the sugar and the fat until well blended. Stir in the eggs and vanilla. Stir in the flour mixture and mix well. Cover the dough and refrigerate for 1 hour to chill (this makes the dough easier to handle).

Position a rack in the middle of the oven and preheat to 350°F (180°C/Gas Mark 4). Lightly grease a baking sheet or line with parchment paper.

In a medium bowl, whisk together the remaining 1 cup (200 g) sugar with the cinnamon.

Form the dough into 1½-inch (4 cm) balls and roll in the cinnamon sugar. Place the cookies 2 inches (5 cm) apart on the prepared baking sheets. Using the bottom of a glass dipped in cinnamon sugar, flatten the cookies slightly. Bake just until the edges of the cookies start to turn golden brown, about 10 minutes. If baking 2 batches at a time, position the racks in the upper and lower thirds of the oven and switch racks halfway through baking. Cool for a few minutes on the baking sheet, then transfer to wire racks to cool.

MOLASSES COOKIES

PREPARATION TIME: 15 MINUTES,
  PLUS DOUGH CHILLING TIME
COOKING TIME: 25 MINUTES
MAKES: 20 COOKIES

- 2 cups (260 g) all-purpose (plain) flour
- 1 teaspoon baking soda (bicarbonate
  of soda)
- 1½ teaspoons ground ginger
- 1 teaspoon ground cinnamon
- ½ teaspoon ground cloves
- ½ teaspoon salt
- ½ cup (100 g) lard or vegetable
  shortening
- ¾ cup (150 g) sugar, plus more for rolling
- 1 egg
- ¼ cup (85 g) unsulfured molasses
  (treacle)

In a medium bowl, sift the flour, baking soda (bicarbonate of soda), ginger, cinnamon, cloves, and salt. In a large bowl, with an electric mixer, cream the lard and sugar until light. Beat in the egg and molasses (treacle) and mix well. Stir in the flour mixture. Cover the dough and refrigerate for 1 hour.

Position a rack in the middle of the oven and preheat to 350°F (180°C/Gas Mark 4). Lightly grease a baking sheet or line with parchment paper.

Set out a dish of sugar for rolling the cookies. Form the dough into large balls, roughly 2 tablespoons of dough each. Roll the cookies in sugar to coat and place them 2 inches (5 cm) apart on the baking sheet. Using the bottom of a glass dipped in sugar, flatten the cookies a bit.

Bake until the cookies have flattened and the edges are just getting brown, 10–12 minutes. If baking 2 batches at a time, position the racks in the upper and lower thirds of the oven and switch racks halfway through baking. Let cool on the pan for a few minutes, then transfer to a wire rack to cool completely.

SNICKERDOODLES

SWEDISH GINGERSNAPS

PREPARATION TIME: 1 HOUR, PLUS AT
    LEAST 24 HOURS (AND UP TO 1 WEEK)
    DOUGH CHILLING TIME
COOKING TIME: 35 MINUTES
MAKES: 120 COOKIES

For the cookies:
- 1½ sticks (170 g) unsalted butter, plus extra for greasing
- 1 cup (200 g) granulated sugar
- ¼ cup (85 g) molasses (treacle)
- 1 tablespoon ground cinnamon
- 1 tablespoon ground ginger
- 2 teaspoons ground cardamom
- 1½ teaspoons ground cloves
- 2 teaspoons baking soda (bicarbonate of soda)
- 2 eggs
- 2½ cups (325 g) all-purpose (plain) flour

For the icing (optional):
- 1 egg white
- 1¾ cups (210 g) powdered (icing) sugar
- 1 teaspoon fresh lemon juice

[Also known as *pepparkakor*, these cookies are traditionally made at Christmas.]

For the cookies: In a large saucepan, melt the butter over low heat. Add the granulated sugar, molasses (treacle), and spices. Cook the mixture for 5 minutes, stirring constantly. Remove from the heat. Stir in the baking soda (bicarbonate of soda) and ¼ cup (60 ml) water. Add the eggs, whisking quickly to avoid cooking them. Stir in the flour. Pour the contents into a bowl, let cool, and cover tightly with plastic wrap (clingfilm). Refrigerate for at least 24 hours and up to 1 week. The flavor improves the longer the dough sits.

Position a rack in the middle of the oven and preheat to 400°F (200°C/Gas Mark 6). Grease a baking sheet with butter.

Work with one-fourth of the dough at a time, keeping the rest covered and refrigerated. On a floured surface, roll the dough to a thickness of about ¼ inch (6 mm). Cut into shapes using cookie cutters and place on the baking sheets, re-rolling scraps if needed.

Bake until golden, 5–6 minutes. If baking 2 batches at a time, position the racks in the upper and lower thirds of the oven and switch racks halfway through baking. Transfer the cookies to a wire rack to cool. Repeat with the remaining dough. (The cookies keep well and can be stored for up to 4 weeks in a tightly covered container.)

For the icing (optional): In a bowl, with an electric mixer fitted with the whisk attachment, whisk the egg white on high speed until foamy. Reduce the speed to medium and gradually whisk in the powdered (icing) sugar. Add the lemon juice and whisk on high speed until the icing is thick and thoroughly mixed, about 3 minutes. This icing works best if piped on (using a piping bag with a small plain tip) in simple designs.

SWEDISH GINGERSNAPS

GINGERSNAPS

PREPARATION TIME: 20 MINUTES
COOKING TIME: 50 MINUTES
MAKES: 65 SMALL COOKIES

- 2¼ cups (293 g) all-purpose (plain) flour
- 2 teaspoons baking soda (bicarbonate of soda)
- 2 teaspoons ground ginger
- 1 teaspoon ground cinnamon
- ½ teaspoon ground cloves
- ½ teaspoon salt
- 1½ sticks (170 g) unsalted butter (or ¾ cup/170 g shortening or lard), at room temperature
- 1 cup (200 g) sugar
- 1 egg
- ⅓ cup (110 g) molasses (treacle)

For the spiced sugar:
- ¾ cup (150 g) sugar
- 1 teaspoon ground cinnamon
- ¼ teaspoon ground ginger

Position a rack in the middle of the oven and preheat to 275°F (140°C/Gas Mark 1). Lightly grease a baking sheet or line with parchment paper.

Sift the flour, baking soda (bicarbonate of soda), ginger, cinnamon, cloves, and salt into a bowl. In a stand mixer fitted with the paddle attachment, cream the butter and sugar until light and fluffy. Beat in the egg. Beat in the molasses (treacle). On low speed, beat in the flour mixture.

For the spiced sugar: In a shallow dish, stir together the sugar, cinnamon, and ginger.

Roll the cookie dough into small balls, about 1 heaping teaspoon per cookie, and roll in the spiced sugar. Place about 2 inches (5 cm) apart on the baking sheet. Bake until golden brown and crispy, about 10 minutes. If baking 2 batches at a time, position the racks in the upper and lower thirds of the oven and switch racks halfway through baking. Let cookies cool slightly on the pan, then remove to a wire rack to cool completely.

MORAVIAN GINGERBREAD COOKIES

PREPARATION TIME: 15 MINUTES, PLUS OVERNIGHT CHILLING TIME
COOKING TIME: 35 MINUTES
MAKES: 48–60 COOKIES

- 1½ sticks (170 g) unsalted butter
- 1¼ cups (240 g) packed dark brown sugar
- 2 cups (670 g) molasses (treacle)
- 1 tablespoon baking soda (bicarbonate of soda)
- 1 tablespoon ground cinnamon
- 2 teaspoons ground ginger
- 1 teaspoon ground allspice
- ½ teaspoon salt
- 4½ cups (585 g) all-purpose (plain) flour

In a large saucepan, combine the butter, brown sugar, molasses (treacle), baking soda (bicarbonate of soda), cinnamon, ginger, allspice, and salt. Cook over medium heat, whisking to combine, until heated through. Remove from the heat and whisk in the flour. Transfer to a bowl, cover, and refrigerate overnight to chill.

Position a rack in the middle of the oven and preheat to 375°F (190°C/Gas Mark 5). Lightly butter a baking sheet.

On a lightly floured surface, roll the dough to a rectangle about ⅛ inch (3 mm) thick. Cut with 2- to 3-inch (5 to 7.5 cm) round cookie cutters. Transfer to the baking sheet.

Bake until lightly browned and crispy, 5–7 minutes. With a clean, dry pastry brush, brush off any excess flour and let cookies cool completely on the baking sheet. If baking 2 batches at a time, position the racks in the upper and lower thirds of the oven and switch racks halfway through baking. Serve or store airtight for up to 1 month.

DESSERTS

LEBKUCHEN

PREPARATION TIME: 20 MINUTES,
   PLUS AT LEAST 24 HOURS (AND UP TO
   1 WEEK) FOR THE DOUGH TO "RIPEN"
COOKING TIME: 35 MINUTES
MAKES: 36 COOKIES

For the cookies:
- ¾ cup (250 g) honey
- ½ cup (95 g) packed light brown sugar
- 1 egg
- ¼ cup (60 g) minced candied lemon peel
- 1 tablespoon ground cinnamon
- 2 teaspoons ground ginger
- ½ teaspoon ground anise
- ½ teaspoon ground cardamom
- ½ teaspoon ground cloves
- ½ teaspoon freshly grated nutmeg
- ¼ teaspoon baking soda (bicarbonate of soda)
- ½ cup almond flour (ground almonds)
- 2¼ cups (280 g) all-purpose (plain) flour

For the glaze:
- 1½ cups (180 g) powdered (icing) sugar
- ½ cup (120 ml) brandy

[Lebkuchen is a classic Christmas cookie from Germany, still baked by people of German ancestry across the Midwest.]

For the cookies: In a heavy-bottomed pan, combine the honey and brown sugar and cook over low heat just until the sugar melts. Remove from the heat and let cool.

In a large bowl, whisk together the cooled honey mixture and egg. Stir in the lemon peel, spices, baking soda (bicarbonate of soda), almond flour (ground almonds), and flour and mix to form a sticky dough. Place the dough in a clean bowl, cover tightly, and refrigerate for at least 24 hours and up to 1 week. The flavors will develop more the longer the dough sits.

Position a rack in the middle of the oven and preheat to 350°F (180°C/Gas Mark 4). Grease a baking sheet.

Form the dough into walnut-size balls and place on the baking sheet about 1½ inches (4 cm) apart. Flatten slightly with the palm of your hand. Bake until the cookies are fragrant and firm, about 15 minutes. If baking 2 batches at a time, position the racks in the upper and lower thirds of the oven and switch racks halfway through baking. Let cookies cool on wire racks.

For the glaze: Sift the powdered (icing) sugar into a bowl. Whisk in the brandy. Brush or spoon a small amount of the glaze onto each cookie.

These cookies store extremely well (up to 1 month, tightly covered, in a cool dark place); however, it is best to glaze them the day you plan to serve them, otherwise the glaze will discolor and crack.

BENNE SEED WAFERS

PREPARATION TIME: 20 MINUTES
COOKING TIME: 30 MINUTES
MAKES: 36 COOKIES

- 1½ cups (195 g) all-purpose (plain) flour
- ¼ teaspoon baking soda (bicarbonate of soda)
- 1½ cups (215 g) toasted sesame seeds
- 1½ sticks (170 g) salted butter, softened
- ½ cup (95 g) packed light brown sugar, firmly packed
- 1½ teaspoons pure vanilla extract
- 1 egg

[These savory wafers get their name from *beni*, the Nigerian word for sesame seeds. Enslaved Africans first brought sesame seeds to the New World and planted them wherever they could to use in their cooking.]

Position a rack in the middle of the oven and preheat to 350°F (180°C/Gas Mark 4). Line a baking sheet with parchment paper.

In a bowl, combine the flour, baking soda (bicarbonate of soda), and sesame seeds. In a stand mixer fitted with the paddle attachment, cream the butter and sugar until light and fluffy. Beat in the vanilla and egg and mix well to combine. Add the flour mixture in 3 additions and beat well.

Spoon the dough by the tablespoonful, ½ inch (1.25 cm) apart, onto the lined baking sheet. Bake until cookies are golden brown, 8–9 minutes. If baking 2 batches at a time, position the racks in the upper and lower thirds of the oven and switch racks halfway through baking. Let cool for 1 minute on the baking sheet, then transfer to a wire rack to cool completely.

APLETS

PREPARATION TIME: 10 MINUTES,
    PLUS 20 HOURS SETTING TIME
COOKING TIME: 20 MINUTES
MAKES: 32 SQUARE CANDIES

- ¾ cup (180 ml) apple cider
- 1 tablespoon fresh lemon juice
- 2 tablespoons unflavored gelatin powder
- 1 cup (120 g) chopped walnuts
- ½ cup (245 g) unsweetened applesauce
- 1½ cups (300 g) granulated sugar
- Powdered (icing) sugar, sifted, for coating

[These gelatin fruit candies are similar to Turkish delight. "Aplets" (made with apple) and "cotlets" (using apricots) are sold at fruit orchards throughout the western United States.]

In a small bowl, combine ¼ cup (60 ml) of the cider and the lemon juice. Sprinkle the gelatin over it and set aside. Lightly grease an 8-inch (20 cm) square glass baking dish. Sprinkle the walnuts over the bottom and set aside.

In a small heavy-bottomed saucepan, combine the remaining ½ cup (120 ml) cider, the applesauce, and sugar. Bring to a boil and cook until it reaches the soft ball stage: 234°F (112°C) on a candy (sugar) thermometer, about 10 minutes. Add the reserved gelatin mixture and bring back to a boil. Remove from the heat and pour over the walnuts. Let the candy sit at room temperature for at least 10 hours to set up.

Cut the candy into small squares and coat each piece with powdered (icing) sugar. Place the candy on a wire rack and let sit at room temperature for about 10 more hours before eating.

BENNE SEED WAFERS

SALT WATER TAFFY

PREPARATION TIME: 30 MINUTES,
  PLUS RESTING TIME
COOKING TIME: 15 MINUTES
MAKES: ABOUT 50 PIECES

- 1 tablespoon (15 g) butter, plus more for the pan, pulling, and cutting
- 1 cup (200 g) sugar
- 1 tablespoon cornstarch (cornflour)
- ⅔ cup (160 ml) light corn syrup
- ½ teaspoon salt
- 1 teaspoon pure vanilla extract (see Note)

Note:
  You can use any number of flavorings (and associated food coloring) in place of the vanilla, such as lemon, maple, banana, red licorice, watermelon, raspberry, or mint extracts.

[Legend has it that this iconic New Jersey confection was accidentally created when a beachfront candy shop was flooded. Whatever the true origin, this soft taffy has been made and sold in Atlantic City on the Atlantic Ocean boardwalk for over a century.]

Butter a large rimmed baking sheet.

In a heavy-bottomed medium saucepan, whisk the sugar and cornstarch (cornflour) together. Add the corn syrup, 1 tablespoon (15 g) butter, ½ cup (120 ml) water, and the salt. Cook over medium heat, stirring, until the sugar dissolves. Continue to cook, without stirring, until a candy (sugar) thermometer reads 255°F (124°C). As the mixture cooks, brush any crystals that form on the sides of the pan with a pastry brush dipped in water.

Remove from the heat, add the vanilla, and pour onto the buttered baking sheet. When the candy is cool enough to handle, butter your hands and pull the taffy until it is light and glossy, about 10 minutes. Roll the taffy into a long rope ½ inch (1.25 cm) in diameter. Using a buttered knife or scissors, cut the taffy into 1-inch (2.5 cm) pieces. Allow the taffy to sit for 30 minutes before wrapping the individual pieces in wax (greaseproof) paper.

BUTTER MOCHI

PREPARATION TIME: 10 MINUTES
COOKING TIME: 1 HOUR
SERVES: 10–12

- 1 lb (455 g) glutinous or sweet rice flour
- 2½ cups (500 g) sugar
- 1 teaspoon baking powder
- 1 stick (115 g) butter, melted
- 2 cups (475 ml) milk
- 1½ cups (355 ml) coconut milk
- 5 eggs
- 2 teaspoon pure vanilla extract

Preheat the oven to 350°F (180°C/Gas Mark 4). Butter a 9 x 13-inch (23 x 33 cm) baking pan.

In a large bowl, whisk together the rice flour, sugar, and baking powder. In a medium bowl, mix together the melted butter, milk, coconut milk, eggs, and vanilla. Pour the milk mixture into the flour mixture, stirring well to combine.

Pour the batter into the prepared pan and bake until set, about 1 hour. Let cool completely, then cut into squares to serve.

SUGAR ON SNOW

PREPARATION TIME: 10 MINUTES
COOKING TIME: 20 MINUTES
MAKES: AS MUCH AS YOU'D LIKE

- Fresh snow
- Pure maple syrup (Very Dark and Robust Flavor)

[This chewy maple candy is simply boiled maple syrup, chilled on fresh snow until it turns nearly solid. In Vermont, it is traditionally served with sour pickles and plain doughnuts.]

Gather clean fresh snow and pack it in a shallow pan. Put the pan of snow in the freezer while the syrup is cooking.

In a heavy-bottomed saucepan, bring the maple syrup to a boil. Cook until a candy (sugar) the thermometer reads 235°–240°F (113°–116°C).

Drizzle the syrup over the snow. Eat with a fork or fingers.

CANDIED YUCCA PETALS

PREPARATION TIME: 40 MINUTES
COOKING TIME: 1½ HOURS
MAKES: 2 CUPS (80 G)

- 2 egg whites
- 2 cups (80 g) yucca petals, separated
- Superfine (caster) sugar

[Yucca grows wild in the West and Southwest. (The large "yuca" tubers sold in some supermarkets do not belong to the plant known botanically as yucca—they are cassava, *Manihot esculenta*.) The edible parts of yucca are the tender, immature stems (resembling a giant asparagus), which can be peeled and eaten raw, or cooked; and the fresh flower petals and fruits, which are packed with edible seeds (the latter can be bitter unless all green parts are removed). Native Americans used the fruit's seeds extensively, in beverages, porridges, and baked breads and cakes. Collect flowers when they are in bud or just opening and remove the anthers before eating, as they can be slightly bitter. Use the pretty petals in candy or as cake decorations.]

Preheat the oven to 200°F (95°C). Line a baking sheet with wax (greaseproof) paper.

Beat the egg whites until they begin to form soft peaks. Dip each yucca petal into the egg white, covering the petal completely and allowing any excess to drip off. Gently dip each petal into superfine sugar, gently tossing some sugar onto hard-to-reach spots, to cover all surfaces. Place the petals on the baking sheet, making sure they do not touch one another. If the petals fold in on themselves, use a skewer to open them up. Dust any bare spots with extra sugar.

Dry the petals in the oven until the sugar hardens, 1–1½ hours. Let cool on wire racks spread with wax (greaseproof) paper and store in airtight containers with wax paper between layers of petals (they should not touch each other).

BUCKEYE CANDY

PREPARATION TIME: 1 HOUR,
  PLUS CHILLING TIME
COOKING TIME: 5 MINUTES
MAKES: 72

- 2 cups (510 g) smooth peanut butter
- 4 tablespoons (60 g) butter, softened
- 1 teaspoon salt
- 3¾ cups (450 g) powdered (icing) sugar
- 2 cups (450 g) semisweet chocolate chips
- 2 tablespoons (30 g) solid vegetable shortening

[These peanut butter balls are dipped in chocolate and resemble a buckeye—a type of horse chestnut so common in Ohio that it's become a nickname for people from the state.]

In a large bowl, with an electric mixer, cream the peanut butter, butter, and salt until the butter is thoroughly incorporated, about 2 minutes. On low speed, gradually beat in the powdered (icing) sugar, then increase to medium speed and beat until smooth, about 3 minutes.

Shape the mixture into 1-inch (2.5 cm) balls. Place them on tray lined with wax (greaseproof) paper or parchment. Refrigerate until firm, at least 30 minutes.

In a heatproof bowl set over a pan of simmering water, melt the chocolate chips and shortening. Using a toothpick (cocktail stick), dip each peanut butter ball into the chocolate, leaving the top of each ball uncovered so that it resembles a buckeye, and transfer to the lined tray.

After they have all been dipped, smooth over the holes left by the toothpick. Refrigerate, covered, until ready to serve.

BOURBON BALLS

PREPARATION TIME: 20 MINUTES,
  PLUS 2 DAYS CHILLING TIME
COOKING TIME: 5 MINUTES,
  PLUS 1 HOUR CHILLING TIME
MAKES: 25 BALLS

- 1 lb (455 g) powdered (icing) sugar
- ⅓ cup (80 ml) bourbon
- 4 tablespoons (60 g) butter, softened
- 50 pecan halves (about 1 cup)
- 1½ cups (335 g) semisweet chocolate chips
- 1 tablespoon heavy (whipping) cream

[These no-bake, truffle-shaped confections are especially popular across the South at Christmas and every May for Kentucky Derby parties. They are sometimes flavored with rum, though Kentucky's native spirit is the choice here.]

In a large bowl, blend together the powdered (icing) sugar, bourbon, and butter. Cover and refrigerate for 8 hours or overnight.

Shape the mixture into 25 (1-inch/2.5 cm) balls. Gently press 2 pecan halves into opposite sides of each ball. Refrigerate for 8 hours or overnight.

Line a baking sheet with wax (greaseproof) paper. In a saucepan, combine the chocolate and cream and melt over medium heat. Remove from the heat. Using a toothpick (cocktail stick), dip the bourbon balls into the chocolate and transfer to the baking sheet. Refrigerate for 1 hour to set the chocolate.

BUCKEYE CANDY

PRALINES

PREPARATION TIME: 10 MINUTES
COOKING TIME: 20 MINUTES
MAKES: 24 PRALINES

- 1¼ cups (250 g) granulated sugar
- 1 cup (190 g) packed light brown sugar
- ½ cup (120 ml) heavy (whipping) cream
- 6 tablespoons (85 g) butter
- ¾ teaspoon pure vanilla extract
- ½ cup (50 g) pecan halves

[The South is known for its towering pecan groves. When the crop is harvested in the fall, locals freeze the nuts for the holiday months, when they top sweet potatoes, appear in pie, or are simmered into these iconic caramel candies. Pecan-studded pralines used to be sold by strolling vendors in the French Quarter of New Orleans, Louisiana.]

Line a large baking sheet with parchment paper and set aside.

In a heavy-bottomed medium saucepan, combine both sugars, the cream, butter, vanilla, and pecans. Cook over medium heat, whisking frequently, until a candy (sugar) thermometer reads 236°F (113°C), 12–18 minutes. Remove from the heat and whisk until the mixture cools slightly and is opaque. (The mixture is at the correct temperature when the pecans do not sink to the bottom of the pot.) Place spoonfuls of the praline mixture onto the lined baking sheet. Let cool completely at room temperature before serving.

CANTALOUPE SORBET

PREPARATION TIME: 10 MINUTES,
    PLUS FREEZING TIME
SERVES: 4–6

- 4 cups (625 g) peeled, seeded, and diced melon, such as cantaloupe
- ½ cup (100 g) sugar
- 1 teaspoon finely grated lime zest
- 2 tablespoons fresh lime juice

[Cantaloupe, the common American name for muskmelon, is a cousin of squash and was cultivated by Native Americans. Colorado's Rocky Ford region produces spectacularly sweet cantaloupe.]

In a blender, working in batches, combine the melon, sugar, lime zest and lime juice and blend on high speed until very smooth, 1–2 minutes. Freeze in an ice cream maker according to the manufacturer's instructions. Transfer to the freezer for 1 hour before serving.

PRALINES

GRAPEFRUIT SORBET

PREPARATION TIME: 10 MINUTES,
  PLUS COOLING AND FREEZING TIME
COOKING TIME: 5 MINUTES
MAKES: 1 QUART (950 ML)

- ½ cup (100 g) sugar
- 1 teaspoon finely grated grapefruit zest
- ½ teaspoon grated fresh ginger
- 2 cups (475 ml) fresh grapefruit juice

[Grapefuit has been grown in South Texas since the 1890s. Today the area's sub-tropical climate, fertile soil, and abundant sunshine yield famous fruits, especially ruby red varieties. Look for grapefuits heavy for their — because they hold the most juice.]

In a small saucepan, combine the sugar and ½ cup (120 ml) water and bring almost to a boil, whisking until the sugar is dissolved. Remove from the heat and let cool completely.

Whisk in the grapefruit zest, ginger, and juice. Freeze in an ice cream maker according to the manufacturer's instructions. Transfer to the freezer to harden for 1 hour, then serve.

PEACH ICE CREAM

PREPARATION TIME: 25 MINUTES,
  PLUS CHILLING AND FREEZING TIME
MAKES: 1 QUART (950 ML)

- 1 lb (455 g) peaches, peeled and cut into chunks
- ¼ cup (50 g) sugar
- 1½ teaspoons fresh lemon juice
- ⅛ teaspoon salt
- 1 teaspoon pure vanilla extract
- 1 cup (240 ml) cold heavy (whipping) cream
- ½ cup (120 ml) cold milk

[Peaches have long been an important part of Delaware agriculture. The state was once the leading peach producer in the country and is still known for its gorgeous, flavorful fruit. Peach pie was named the official state dessert in 2009.]

In a large bowl, combine the peaches, sugar, lemon juice, salt, and vanilla. Crush the mixture (using your hands or a potato masher). Cover and refrigerate for at least 5 hours and up to overnight.

In a blender, purée the peach mixture, cream, and milk until smooth. Freeze in an ice cream maker according to the manufacturer's instructions.

WILD PAWPAW ICE CREAM

PREPARATION TIME: 30 MINUTES,
   PLUS CHILLING AND FREEZING TIME
MAKES: 1 QUART (950 ML)

- 2 cups (476 ml) heavy (whipping) cream
- ½ cup (95 g) superfino (caster) sugar
- 2 cups (525 g) fresh pawpaw pulp,
  seeds removed

[Pawpaws grow wild in the eastern United States, and Ohio holds an annual pawpaw festival. One of the least-known fruits of North America, even though it grows on the largest native fruit tree, pawpaw's brief season is from late summer into early fall. While pies, sweet breads, and muffins are common ways to cook with pawpaw, the fruit's flavor and aroma are best captured uncooked. Chiffon pie and ice cream also maintain pawpaw's floral character well.]

In a bowl, with an electric mixer, whip the cream until soft peaks form, sprinkling the sugar over as you whip. Slowly fold the pawpaw pulp into the whipped cream. Chill the mixture, and freeze in an ice cream maker according to the manufacturer's instructions.

BLACK WALNUT ICE CREAM

PREPARATION TIME: 10 MINUTES,
   PLUS STEEPING, COOLING,
   AND FREEZING TIME
COOKING TIME: 30 MINUTES
MAKES: 1 QUART (950 ML)

- 2½ cups (590 ml) heavy (whipping) cream
- 1½ cups (360 ml) milk
- ¾ cup (150 g) sugar
- ¾ cup (95 g) shelled black walnuts,
  roughly chopped
- 1 vanilla bean, split lengthwise
- 4 egg yolks

Note:
  Black walnut trees often grow like towering weeds around their native territory on the East Coast of North America, dropping what look like tennis balls each October. The nuts within are a delicacy — their haunting, distinctive taste is a far cry from the milder Carpathian varieties.

In a medium saucepan, combine the cream, milk, sugar, and walnut pieces and heat over medium heat, stirring occasionally, just until the sugar dissolves and steam rises off the top of the milk, 6–8 minutes (do not boil). Remove from the heat, scrape in the vanilla seeds and add the pod, stir well, and cover. Let steep in the refrigerator for at least 1 hour and up to 24 hours.

Strain the mixture to remove the vanilla pod and the walnut pieces, but reserve the walnut pieces in the refrigerator.

Return the milk mixture to a medium saucepan and cook over medium heat until steam rises off the top of the milk, 8–10 minutes. Remove from the heat. In a medium bowl, whisk the egg yolks to combine. Whisking constantly, gradually add ½ cup (120 ml) hot milk to the egg yolks to warm them. Whisk in a second ½ cup (120 ml) hot milk. Pour the warmed egg mixture into the saucepan of milk and whisk until fully combined. Return the saucepan to medium-low heat and cook gently, stirring frequently, until the mixture thickens enough to coat the back of a spoon (do not let simmer), 6–8 minutes.

Set up a bowl of ice and water. Place the saucepan in the ice bath and let the mixture cool to room temperature. Freeze in an ice cream maker according to the manufacturer's instructions. Fold in the reserved walnut pieces and harden in a freezer for 1 hour before serving.

WILD STRAWBERRY FREEZER CRISP

PREPARATION TIME: 10 MINUTES,
   PLUS MACERATING AND FREEZING
   TIME
SERVES: 4

- Butter, for the pan
- 1½ cups (155 g) graham cracker crumbs (or crushed digestive biscuits)
- ½ cup (100 g) sugar
- 1½ cups (250 g) wild strawberries, stemmed
- 1 egg white
- 1 cup (240 ml) cold heavy (whipping) cream

[Wild strawberries — especially widespread in the Pacific Northwest, New England, and the Midwest — are conventional strawberries in miniature, with a concentrated flavor that makes collecting them worthwhile.]

Butter an 8-inch (20 cm) springform pan. Line the sides with wax (greaseproof) paper. Spread half the graham cracker crumbs in the bottom and tamp down.

In a large bowl, sprinkle the sugar over the strawberries and lightly crush the fruit with a potato masher or metal spatula (fish slice). Let sit in the refrigerator for 30 minutes to macerate.

In a small bowl, whisk the egg white until soft peaks form. In another bowl, with an electric mixer, beat the cream until soft peaks form. Fold the cream into the strawberries, then fold in the beaten egg white. Spoon this strawberry mixture onto the layer of crumbs in the springform pan. Top with the rest of the crumbs, cover with plastic wrap (clingfilm), and freeze for at least 3 hours.

Release the sides of the springform and carefully remove. Peel off the wax paper. Place on a serving plate and cut in wedges to serve.

HAZELNUT CRUMBLE TOPPING

PREPARATION TIME: 10 MINUTES,
   PLUS DOUGH CHILLING TIME
COOKING TIME: 30 MINUTES
MAKES: ABOUT 2 CUPS (240 G)

- 4 tablespoons almond paste
- 4 tablespoons (60 g) butter
- ½ cup (95 g) packed light brown sugar
- ¾ cup (98 g) all-purpose (plain) flour
- ½ cup (60 g) chopped hazelnuts, skinned
- ½ teaspoon ground cinnamon
- ¼ teaspoon salt

[This crumble is best served over fresh fruit or ice cream.]

In a stand mixer fitted with the paddle attachment, beat the almond paste, butter, and brown sugar on medium-high speed until fluffy and lightened in color, about 3 minutes. On low speed, gradually beat in the flour, hazelnuts, cinnamon, and salt. Wrap the dough in plastic wrap (clingfilm) and refrigerate for 30 minutes to chill.

Preheat the oven to 350°F (180°C/Gas Mark 4). Grease a rimmed baking sheet.

Crumble the dough in an even layer onto the baking sheet. Bake until golden, about 30 minutes. Let cool completely before using.

MAPLE CUSTARD

NH

PREPARATION TIME: 15 MINUTES
COOKING TIME: 45 MINUTES
SERVES: 6

- 2 cups (475 ml) heavy (whipping) cream
- ½ cup (120 ml) milk
- ½ cup (120 ml) pure maple syrup (Very Dark and Robust Flavor)
- 2 tablespoons pure maple sugar
- 6 egg yolks
- Boiling water

Preheat the oven to 325°F (160°C/Gas Mark 3).

In a medium saucepan, combine the cream, milk, maple syrup, and maple sugar and bring to a simmer over medium-low heat. Do not allow to boil. In a large bowl, whisk the egg yolks. Whisk a ladle of the hot cream mixture into the yolks to warm them. Whisking constantly, add the remaining hot cream to the warmed yolks. Strain through a fine-mesh sieve into a bowl.

Place six 6-ounce (180 ml) ramekins or ovenproof coffee cups in a baking pan. Pour the custard into the ramekins. Pour boiling water into the pan to reach halfway up the cups. Cover the whole pan with a sheet of foil. Bake until the custard is just set (there should be a ¼-inch/6 mm thick area in the center that is still loose), 35–40 minutes. The custard will fully set as it cools. Serve warm or chilled.

HAUPIA

HI

PREPARATION TIME: 5 MINUTES,
   PLUS CHILLING TIME
COOKING TIME: 15 MINUTES
MAKES: SIXTEEN 2-INCH (5 CM) SQUARES

- ½ cup (100 g) sugar
- ⅔ cup (85 g) cornstarch (cornflour)
- 1 cup (240 ml) milk
- 1½ cups (355 ml) coconut milk
- Pinch of salt

[This Hawaiian pudding, served in little squares, is popular at luaus.]

In a bowl, whisk together the sugar and cornstarch (cornflour). Whisk in the dairy milk.

In a medium saucepan, bring the coconut milk to a simmer over medium heat. Whisk the dairy milk mixture into the simmering coconut milk. Add the salt. Whisking constantly, cook over medium-low heat until the mixture thickens, about 7 minutes.

Pour into an ungreased 8-inch (20 cm) square baking pan. Refrigerate for 2–3 hours to chill and set. Cut into 2-inch (5 cm) squares to serve.

CAJETA

PREPARATION TIME: 5 MINUTES
COOKING TIME: 1 HOUR 50 MINUTES
MAKES: ABOUT 1¼ CUPS (295 ML)

- 4½ cups (1 liter) goat milk
- 1 cup (200 g) sugar
- ¾ teaspoon baking soda (bicarbonate of soda)
- ⅛ teaspoon kosher (coarse) salt

[Serve this luscious Mexican-style goat caramel sauce on baked goods, churros (see page 452), or ice cream.]

In a medium pot, whisk together the goat milk, sugar, baking soda (bicarbonate of soda), and salt. Cook over medium heat, stirring occasionally, until the sugar and salt dissolve, 10–12 minutes. Using a silicone spatula, continue cooking, scraping the sides of the pot frequently, until the milk is thick, golden, and reduced by three-fourths, about 1½ hours. Cook, stirring constantly, until the cajeta becomes a thick layer at the bottom of the pot, about 5 more minutes. (There should be about 1¼ cups/295 ml.) Remove from the heat and transfer to a heatproof glass jar. Let cool completely, then cover and refrigerate.

BOILED CUSTARD

PREPARATION TIME: 5 MINUTES
COOKING TIME: 25 MINUTES
SERVES: 8

- ½ gallon (2 liters) milk or half-and-half (single cream)
- 1 cup (200 g) sugar
- 7 egg yolks
- 2 teaspoons pure vanilla extract
- Pinch of salt

[Boiled custard is the South's name for French crème anglaise, made using the same ingredients and technique, but often with a lot more vanilla extract. Dolley Madison, the United States' fourth First Lady in the early 1800s, served her boiled custard topped with dollops of meringue, as many Southern cooks do today. Some people also drink it warm.]

In a large pot, whisk together the milk and ⅓ cup (65 g) of the sugar. Cook over medium heat until a thin skin forms on the top (do not boil), 10–12 minutes. Remove from the heat.

In a medium bowl, whisk together the remaining ⅔ cup (135 g) sugar and the egg yolks until lightened in color and texture. Whisking constantly, slowly add 1 cup (240 ml) of the hot milk to the egg yolk mixture to warm it. Whisk in another 1 cup (240 ml) hot milk, then pour the warmed eggs into the pot of milk and whisk until fully combined. Return the pot to medium heat and continue to cook, stirring frequently, until the mixture thickens enough to coat the back of a spoon, 18–20 minutes (do not boil). Remove the pot from the heat and stir in the vanilla and salt. Let cool completely. Cover and keep refrigerated for up to 3 days.

CAJETA

CREOLE BREAD PUDDING WITH WHISKEY SAUCE

PREPARATION TIME: 25 MINUTES
COOKING TIME: 1 HOUR
SERVES: 8–10

For the bread pudding:
- 6 eggs
- 4 cups (950 ml) half-and-half (single cream)
- 16 oz (455 g) day-old French bread, cut into 1-inch (2.5 cm) cubes, lightly toasted
- 1½ cups (300 g) sugar
- 1 cup (165 g) raisins
- 1 cup (125 g) walnuts or pecans, chopped
- 5 teaspoons pure vanilla extract
- 4 tablespoons butter, cut into ½-inch (1.25 cm) cubes, at room temperature

For the whiskey sauce:
- 3 tablespoons (45 g) butter
- 1 tablespoon all-purpose (plain) flour
- 1 cup (240 ml) heavy (whipping) cream
- ½ cup (100 g) sugar
- 2 tablespoons bourbon or other whiskey
- 1 tablespoon pure vanilla extract
- 1 teaspoon freshly grated nutmeg

Preheat the oven to 350°F (180°C/Gas Mark 4). Butter a 9 x 13-inch (23 x 33 cm) baking dish.

For the bread pudding: In a large bowl, lightly beat the eggs, then whisk in the half-and-half (single cream). Add the toasted bread cubes, sugar, raisins, nuts, and vanilla, stirring gently to coat. Let rest for 15 minutes so the bread can absorb the custard mixture.

Transfer the bread mixture to the baking dish. Dot with the diced butter. Bake until the center is set and the top is golden, 35–40 minutes. Let stand for 5 minutes before serving.

Meanwhile, for the whiskey sauce: In a small saucepan, melt the butter over medium-low heat. Whisk in the flour and cook, whisking constantly, until mixture reaches a light brown color, about 5 minutes. Stir in the cream and sugar, whisking frequently, and cook until the mixture thickens and the sugar dissolves, 3–5 minutes. Stir in the whiskey, vanilla, and nutmeg and cook, whisking constantly, for 3 minutes to heat through. Do not allow to boil. Serve hot over warm bread pudding.

PERSIMMON PUDDING

PREPARATION TIME: 10 MINUTES
COOKING TIME: 1 HOUR
SERVES: 4–6

- 2 cups (500 g) American persimmon pulp, from 6–8 persimmons
- ½ cup (100 g) sugar
- 3 eggs
- 4 tablespoons pure maple syrup
- 1½ cups (195) all-purpose (plain) flour
- ½ cup (60 g) corn flour (very finely ground cornmeal)
- ½ teaspoon ground cinnamon
- ½ teaspoon ground allspice
- ¼ teaspoon salt
- 1 cup (240 ml) milk
- 1 teaspoon baking soda (bicarbonate of soda)
- 1 teaspoon baking powder
- 1 cup (240 ml) heavy (whipping) cream, whipped

[The American persimmon (which grows wild in the Midwest, Mid-Atlantic, and South regions) is a cousin of Hachiya and Fuyu persimmons. It is best to work with overripe persimmons to get the pulp, which can be added to puddings, cakes, and soufflés and makes a good fruit leather. A colander or food mill is useful to separate out the seeds.]

Position a rack in the middle of the oven and preheat to 325°F (160°C/Gas Mark 3). Grease an 8-inch (20 cm) springform pan.

In a large bowl, with an electric mixer, beat the persimmon pulp to even the pulp out. Add the sugar and the eggs and beat until lighter and smooth. Beat in the maple syrup, both flours, the cinnamon, allspice, and salt, adding some of the milk if the batter becomes too thick to mix easily. Add the baking soda (bicarbonate of soda) and baking powder and the remaining milk.

Scrape the batter into the prepared pan and bake until a skewer inserted in the center comes out clean, about 1 hour. Serve warm, with whipped cream.

WHEAT BERRY PUDDING

PREPARATION TIME: 5 MINUTES
COOKING TIME: 2 HOURS
SERVES: 4

- ¾ cup (145 g) wheat berries (whole grain)
- 3 eggs, beaten
- 2½ cups (590 ml) milk
- 2 teaspoons grated orange zest
- ⅓ cup (110 g) honey
- ½ teaspoon salt
- ¼ teaspoon ground cinnamon
- Freshly grated nutmeg
- Fresh berries or sliced fruit, for serving (optional)

Place the wheat berries in a medium saucepan. Cover with 3 cups (710 ml) water and bring to a boil. Reduce the heat, cover, and simmer until the berries are tender, about 1 hour.

Meanwhile, preheat the oven to 350°F (180°C/Gas Mark 4). Butter an 8-inch (20 cm) square baking dish.

In a bowl, stir together the wheat berries, eggs, milk, zest, honey, salt, cinnamon, and nutmeg. Pour into the buttered dish and bake until set, about 1 hour.

Serve warm or chilled, with fresh fruit, if desired.

STICKY DATE PUDDING

PREPARATION TIME: 30 MINUTES
COOKING TIME: 1 HOUR 30 MINUTES
SERVES: 8

For the cake:
- 1½ cups (220 g) chopped pitted dates
- 1¼ cups (295 ml) boiling water
- 1½ teaspoons baking soda (bicarbonate of soda)
- 1½ cups (195 g) all-purpose (plain) flour
- 1 teaspoon ground ginger
- ¼ teaspoon freshly grated nutmeg
- ½ teaspoon salt
- 1 stick (115 g) unsalted butter, softened
- 1 cup (200 g) granulated sugar
- 2 eggs

For the sauce:
- 1 stick (115 g) butter
- 1¼ cups (240 g) packed light brown sugar
- 1 cup (240 ml) heavy (whipping) cream
- 1 teaspoon pure vanilla extract

- Vanilla ice cream or whipped cream, for serving

[This date cake with caramel sauce, this is the signature dessert in Indiana's Amish community.]

Preheat the oven to 350°F (180°C/Gas Mark 4). Butter and flour an 8-inch (20 cm) square baking pan.

For the cake: Place the dates in a small saucepan and cover with the boiling water. Simmer for a few minutes. Remove from the heat and stir in the baking soda (bicarbonate of soda). Set aside for 15 minutes.

In a medium bowl, whisk together the flour, ginger, nutmeg, and salt.

In a large bowl, with an electric mixer, cream the butter and granulated sugar until light and fluffy. Beat in the eggs, 1 at a time. On low speed, beat in the flour mixture. Add the dates, with their soaking liquid, and mix well.

Scrape the batter into the prepared pan. Place the pan in a larger pan or roasting pan and fill the roasting pan with boiling water to reach halfway up the side of the baking pan. Bake until a skewer inserted in the center of the pudding comes out clean, about 1 hour 15 minutes.

Meanwhile, for the sauce: In a large saucepan, melt the butter over medium heat. Stir in the brown sugar and bring to a boil, stirring. Add the cream and simmer for 5 minutes. Remove from the heat and stir in the vanilla.

Serve both the pudding and the sauce warm, with vanilla ice cream or whipped cream.

STICKY DATE PUDDING

BANANA PUDDING

PREPARATION TIME: 20 MINUTES,
  PLUS CHILLING TIME
COOKING TIME: 15 MINUTES
SERVES: 8

- ¾ cup (150 g) granulated sugar
- 3 tablespoons all-purpose (plain) flour
- ¼ teaspoon salt
- 1 egg
- 3 egg yolks
- 2 cups (475 ml) half-and-half
  (single cream)
- ¾ teaspoon pure vanilla extract
- 2 tablespoons (30 g) butter, diced
- 1 box (16 oz/455 g) vanilla wafer cookies
- 4 bananas, cut crosswise into ¼ inch
  (6 mm) thick slices
- 1 cup (240 ml) heavy (whipping) cream
- ¼ cup (30 g) powdered (icing) sugar

[Southern home cooks continue to riff on this classic combination of bananas and vanilla pudding, turning it into elegant pies, cakes, ice creams, and soufflés. The way the flavor of sliced bananas permeates vanilla pudding in the traditional version is pure alchemy, whether the dessert is made with store-bought pudding and vanilla wafers, or assembled from scratch.]

In a medium saucepan, whisk together ½ cup (100 g) of the sugar, the flour, and salt. Whisk in the whole egg, egg yolks, and half-and-half (single cream). Cook over medium heat, stirring frequently, until the mixture comes to a low boil and thickens, 10–12 minutes. Remove from the heat and stir in the vanilla and butter. Transfer to a bowl, press plastic wrap (clingfilm) onto the entire surface of the pudding, and refrigerate until well chilled, 4–6 hours.

Whisk the vanilla pudding well until light and fluffy. In the bottom of an 8-inch (20 cm) wide trifle dish, place one-third of the vanilla pudding and spread into an even layer. Place half of the vanilla wafers in a single layer on top of the pudding. Arrange the bananas over the wafers in a single layer. Repeat the pudding and wafer layers once more, reserving 4–5 wafers, ending with a final layer of vanilla pudding. Refrigerate for at least 2 hours.

In a bowl, with an electric mixer, whip the cream with the powdered (icing) sugar until medium-stiff peaks form. Dollop whipped cream over the top of the banana pudding. Serve immediately sprinkled with 4–5 crushed vanilla wafers, if liked.

BANANA PUDDING

MAYPOP MOUSSE

PREPARATION TIME: 15 MINUTES,
   PLUS 30 MINUTES CHILLING TIME
COOKING TIME: 5 MINUTES, PLUS
   OVERNIGHT CHILLING
SERVES: 8

- 12 maypops
- 3 sheets (silver strength) gelatin
- 1¼ cups (295 ml) heavy (whipping) cream
- ⅓ cup (67 g) superfine (caster) sugar

[The maypop, or passion vine, is the state flower of Tennessee, and they grow wild in Southeast. Sliced in half and arranged on a platter, maypop fruits are a simple and pretty feast, to be eaten with a teaspoon. Their tropical tang has an exceptional affinity for wobbly and whipped desserts. Instead of using individual ramekins, you could serve from one larger mold or bowl.]

Cut 10 of the maypops in half and scoop the pulp into a food processor. Pulse to loosen the seeds, then strain the juice through a sieve into a bowl, pushing on the pulp (discard the seeds). Transfer the maypop juice to a pot and heat over medium heat (do not boil).

Soften the gelatin in a little hot water and whisk into the warm maypop juice (if lumps form, blend for half a minute in a blender while still warm). Refrigerate the juice for 30 minutes to chill and start to set up, stirring from time to time.

In a bowl, with an electric mixer, whip the cream with the sugar until soft peaks form. Fold the whipped cream into the chilled maypop juice.

Spoon the mixture into 8 (3-inch/7.5 cm) ramekins or panna cotta molds and chill until firm, 4 hours or overnight.

To serve, dip the underside of each ramekin into very hot water and invert onto a small plate with a brisk shake, before lifting off the ramekin. Remove the pulp from the remaining 2 maypops and drizzle it over the top of the mousses before serving.

CHILLED WATERMELON DESSERT SOUP

PREPARATION TIME: 35 MINUTES,
   PLUS CHILLING TIME
COOKING TIME: 5 MINUTES
SERVES: 4

- ¼ cup (50 g) sugar
- 6 sprigs fresh mint, plus mint leaves for garnish
- 8 cups (1.2 kg) diced watermelon
- ¼ cup (60 ml) white rum (optional)
- 2 tablespoons fresh lime juice
- Pinch of salt

In a small saucepan, bring the sugar and ¼ cup (60 ml) water to a boil, stirring to dissolve the sugar. Add the mint sprigs, cover, remove from the heat, and let steep for 20 minutes. Discard the mint. Refrigerate until completely chilled.

In a blender, combine three-fourths of the watermelon, the mint syrup, rum (if using), lime juice, and salt and purée on high speed for 2 minutes, until very smooth. (If desired, strain through a fine-mesh sieve lined with cheesecloth to remove some of the watermelon pulp.)

Serve in soup bowls, garnished with the remaining watermelon cubes and some mint leaves.

CHILLED WATERMELON DESSERT SOUP

CHILLED SOUR CHERRY SOUP

PREPARATION TIME: 20 MINUTES,
PLUS CHILLING TIME
COOKING TIME: 30 MINUTES
SERVES: 4

- 1 lb (455 g) sour cherries, pitted
- 1 teaspoon ground cinnamon
- Pinch of ground cloves
- ½ cup (100 g) sugar, or more to taste
- Pinch of salt
- 1 cup (240 ml) sour cream
- 1 tablespoon all-purpose (plain) flour
- ½ cup (120 ml) red wine (optional)

In a medium saucepan, combine the cherries, cinnamon, cloves, sugar, salt, and 1 quart (1 liter) water. Bring to a boil, reduce to a simmer, and cook for about 10 minutes.

Meanwhile, in a small bowl, combine the sour cream and flour and whisk until smooth.

Whisk a ladle of the hot liquid into the sour cream, then whisk the warmed sour cream into the soup. Add the red wine (if using). Bring back to a simmer and cook, whisking often, about 5 minutes, until the soup thickens slightly. Remove from the heat, let cool, and refrigerate for at least 4 hours to chill.

CHILLED PRICKLY PEARS

PREPARATION TIME: 1 MINUTE PER PEAR,
PLUS CHILLING TIME
SERVES: AS MANY AS YOU'D LIKE

- 2–3 prickly pears per person

[Prickly pears, also known as cactus pears, grow widely in the arid Southwest. Most parts are edible and the domesticated species produces especially large fruit. When ripe, they are also delicious raw.]

To safely peel a prickly pear, pick up the fruit between your thumb and middle finger, touching the two ends only. Place on a cutting board. Spear the fruit with a fork and use it to keep the fruit steady and pinned against the board. With your other hand, use a small sharp knife to make an incision lengthwise from the top to the bottom of the fruit. Holding the fruit firmly with the fork, loosen the outer thick skin along the incision with the knife held lengthwise, and gradually peel the skin down toward the board. When you have exposed the fruit, use the fork to spear the naked flesh, and continue rolling the fruit out of its skin. Rinse the fruit well under water, in case it has picked up any loose fine hairy spines (glochids) that may have dropped onto the board.

Once the pears are peeled, rinse the board well before cutting the fruit into thick slices. Place them in a bowl. Cover and chill for at least 1 hour. Serve cold.

BANANAS FOSTER

PREPARATION TIME: 5 MINUTES
COOKING TIME: 10 MINUTES
SERVES: 6

- 6 bananas
- ⅓ cup (75 g) butter
- 1½ cups (290 g) packed light brown sugar
- ¾ teaspoon ground cinnamon
- 1 teaspoon finely grated orange zest
- ½ cup (120 ml) dark rum
- Vanilla ice cream, for serving

[The most famous dessert in New Orleans, Louisiana was invented at Brennan's Restaurant in the 1950s and named for a frequent customer (and friend of owner Owen Brennan), Richard Foster. Flambéing the buttery, caramelized bananas with rum remains the restaurant's signature flourish.]

Halve the bananas lengthwise, then cut in half crosswise. Set aside.

Heat a large frying pan over medium-low heat. Add the butter to melt, then swirl to coat the pan. Add the brown sugar, cinnamon, and orange zest and stir well to combine with the butter. Add ¼ cup (60 ml) of the rum and stir to combine. Place the bananas cut side down in the pan. When the bananas begin to caramelize and soften, 3–4 minutes, remove from the heat, add the remaining ¼ cup (60 ml) rum, and return to the heat. Increase the heat to medium-high and cook for 1 minute to get the pan hot, then ignite the rum with a long match. When the flames die down, divide the bananas evenly among 6 bowls. Top with vanilla ice cream and spoon the sauce from the pan over top. Serve immediately.

GRILLED FIGS

PREPARATION TIME: 5 MINUTES
COOKING TIME: 3 MINUTES
SERVES: 6–8

- 2 dozen firm-ripe fresh figs
- ⅓ cup (80 ml) melted butter or vegetable oil
- 1 tablespoon sugar

[Figs are one of the oldest crops cultivated by humans, predating wheat and corn. Spanish missionaries brought them to California in the mid-1700s and they've been thriving in the sunshine ever since. Although we think of figs as fruit, botanically, they are inverted flowers.]

Preheat a gas or charcoal grill (barbecue) to medium-high heat.

Halve the figs lengthwise if figs are large. If they are small, they can be grilled whole). Brush the cut sides with butter and sprinkle lightly with sugar. Place the figs cut side down on the grill rack over direct heat. Cook until figs are slightly charred and easily pull away from the grill, 2–3 minutes. Serve hot.

POACHED PEARS

PREPARATION TIME: 10 MINUTES
COOKING TIME: 40 MINUTES
SERVES: 4

- 2 cups (400 g) sugar
- 1 vanilla bean, split lengthwise
- 1 cinnamon stick, broken in half
- 5 whole cloves
- 1 bottle (750 ml) white wine,
  such as Riesling
- 4 Bosc or Conference pears

In a medium saucepan (large enough to hold all of the pears in a single layer), combine the sugar, vanilla bean, cinnamon stick, cloves, wine, and 2 cups (475 ml) water. Place over high heat and stir until the sugar dissolves.

Peel the pears and place them in the pan of poaching liquid. Bring to a simmer, then reduce the heat to medium-low and simmer, rotating the pears frequently so that each side cooks evenly, until a paring knife inserted into a pear slides out easily, 25–30 minutes.

Remove the pears from the poaching liquid. Strain liquid through a sieve (discard the solids or keep them for garnish) and return to the saucepan. Cook the liquid over high heat until reduced to 1 cup syrup, about 6 minutes. Return the pears to the pot and reheat for 1–2 minutes. Serve the pears warm with a drizzle of syrup over top.

APPLE SLUMP

PREPARATION TIME: 15 MINUTES
COOKING TIME: 1 HOUR
SERVES: 6

- 4 cups (450 g) peeled sliced apples
- ½ cup (95 g) packed light brown sugar
- ½ teaspoon ground cinnamon
- ¼ teaspoon freshly grated nutmeg
- 1½ cups (195 g) all-purpose (plain) flour
- 2 teaspoons baking powder
- ½ teaspoon salt
- ½ cup (100 g) granulated sugar
- 1 egg
- ½ cup (120 ml) milk
- 1 stick (115 g) unsalted butter, melted

Position a rack in the middle of the oven and preheat to 350°F (180°C/Gas Mark 4). Butter an 8-inch (20 cm) square baking dish.

In a large bowl, toss together the apples, brown sugar, cinnamon, and nutmeg. Place in the buttered baking dish and bake until the apples are soft and releasing liquid, 20–25 minutes.

Meanwhile, sift the flour, baking powder, salt, and granulated sugar into a bowl. In a separate bowl, whisk together the egg, milk, and melted butter. Add to the flour mixture and stir well to combine.

Place spoonfuls of the batter on top of the hot apples. Return to the oven and bake until the topping is deep golden brown, 20–30 minutes.

DESSERTS

POACHED PEARS

APPLE DUMPLINGS

PREPARATION TIME: 30 MINUTES
COOKING TIME: 1 HOUR
SERVES: 16

For the syrup:
- 3 cups (600 g) sugar
- ½ teaspoon ground cinnamon
- ½ teaspoon freshly grated nutmeg
- 6 tablespoons (85 g) butter

For the dumplings:
- 5 cups (650 g) all-purpose (plain) flour
- 5 teaspoons baking powder
- 2¼ teaspoons salt
- 1⅔ cups (340 g) lard
- 1¼ cups (295 ml) milk
- 2 cups (400 g) sugar
- 1 teaspoon ground cinnamon
- 12 medium apples, peeled and cut into ½-inch (1.25 cm) thick slices
- Ice cream or whipped cream, for serving

[Although you can fill squares of pie dough that make the dumpling crust with just about any fruit, apple remains the preferred choice in the South. Serve with vanilla ice cream.]

For the syrup: In a saucepan, combine the sugar, cinnamon, nutmeg, and 3 cups (710 ml) water and bring to a boil over high heat. Reduce to a simmer and cook for 3 minutes, whisking until the sugar dissolves completely. Remove from the heat and whisk in the butter.

Preheat the oven to 350°F (180°C/Gas Mark 4). Grease two 9 x 13-inch (23 x 33 cm) baking pans.

For the dumplings: In a large bowl, mix together the flour, baking powder, and 2 teaspoons of the salt. Using your fingertips, work the lard into the flour mixture, until small clumps form. Stir in the milk. Transfer to a floured surface and gently knead the dough just until it comes together. Divide the dough into 4 balls. Divide each ball into 4 more balls to end up with 16 small balls. Roll each ball into a 7–8-inch (18–20 cm) round.

In a small bowl, combine the sugar, cinnamon, and remaining ¼ teaspoon salt. Place a handful of apples in the center of each dough round. Sprinkle with 2 tablespoons of the cinnamon-sugar. Fold the pastry over the apples and pinch to seal at the top. Place 8 dumplings in each of the baking pans. Dividing evenly, pour the syrup over the dumplings.

Bake until lightly golden, 45–50 minutes. Serve warm with ice cream or whipped cream.

APPLE PANDOWDY

PREPARATION TIME: 35 MINUTES,
 PLUS DOUGH CHILLING TIME
COOKING TIME: 1 HOUR 20 MINUTES
SERVES: 12

For the dough:
- 2½ cups (325 g) all-purpose (plain) flour
- 1 teaspoon salt
- 2 sticks (225 g) cold unsalted butter, lard, or solid vegetable shortening (cut the butter into small pieces)
- About ⅓ cup (80 ml) ice water

For the filling:
- 10 medium apples, peeled and thinly sliced
- 1 tablespoon fresh lemon juice, or more to taste (optional)
- ½ cup (95 g) packed light brown sugar
- ½ teaspoon ground cinnamon
- ¼ teaspoon freshly grated nutmeg
- Pinch of ground cloves
- Pinch of salt
- ½ cup (120 ml) pure maple syrup
- 4 tablespoons (60 g) butter
- ½ cup (120 ml) heavy (whipping) cream
- Granulated sugar, for topping (optional)

[Pandowdy is a juicy apple pie with the crust broken so it soaks up the juices. There are also versions that call for stove-top cooking in a frying pan. This one is baked in a deep-dish pie plate.]

For the dough: In a bowl, whisk together the flour and salt. Cut in the fat (using a pastry/dough blender or two knives) until the mixture is broken up, about the size of peas. Add ice water, 1 tablespoon at a time, until the dough comes together and can be formed. Turn the dough out onto a floured surface. Form the dough into 2 disks, one larger than the other (about two-thirds and one-third). Wrap the dough in plastic wrap (clingfilm) and chill for about 1 hour.

Position a rack in the middle of the oven and preheat to 425°F (220°C/Gas Mark 7).

For the filling: If the apples are not tart, toss them first with the lemon juice. Then add the brown sugar, cinnamon, nutmeg, cloves, and salt and toss well.

On a floured surface, roll the larger piece of dough big enough that it will fit in the bottom and up the sides of a 9-inch (23 cm) deep-dish pie plate. Place the bottom crust in the pan. Pour the apples over the crust. In a small bowl, mix together ¼ cup (60 ml) water and the maple syrup. Pour over the apples. Dot all over with the butter. Roll out the second crust to fit the top. Brush the edges of the bottom crust with some of the cream. Place the crust on top and seal the edges. Brush the top with the rest of the cream and sprinkle with granulated sugar, if desired.

Bake for 20 minutes. Reduce the oven temperature to 325°F (160°C/Gas Mark 3) and bake until the crust is browned and the filling is bubbling, 40 minutes to 1 hour. Let cool for a few minutes, then use a knife to cut the pandowdy, through the bottom crust, in a random pattern. Slightly lift the bottom crust in places, and push the top crust down a bit. The idea is to have the crust soaking in the liquid. Let cool slightly before serving.

APPLE CRUMBLE

PREPARATION TIME: 15 MINUTES
COOKING TIME: 1 HOUR
SERVES: 8–10

For the filling:
- 7 medium apples, peeled, cored and thinly sliced
- 1 tablespoon fresh lemon juice
- 1 tablespoon rum or brandy
- ½ cup (95 g) packed light brown sugar
- 1½ teaspoons ground cinnamon
- ¼ teaspoon freshly grated nutmeg
- Pinch of ground cloves
- 1 tablespoon all-purpose (plain) flour

For the topping:
- 1 stick plus 2 tablespoons (140 g) butter, softened
- ½ cup (95 g) packed light brown sugar
- ¾ cup (60 g) thick-cut rolled (porridge) oats
- ½ cup (65 g) all-purpose (plain) flour
- 1 teaspoon baking powder
- 1 teaspoon ground cinnamon
- ½ teaspoon salt

Preheat the oven to 350°F (180°C/Gas Mark 4).

For the filling: In a bowl, toss the apple slices with the lemon juice, rum, brown sugar, cinnamon, nutmeg, cloves, and flour.

Butter a 9-inch (23 cm) round cake pan liberally with 2 tablespoons (30 g) of the softened butter. Place the apples in the pan.

For the topping: In a bowl, stir together the remaining butter and brown sugar until well mixed. Stir in the oats, flour, baking powder, cinnamon, and salt. Scatter over the apples.

Bake until the topping is browned and the apples are bubbling, about 1 hour. Serve warm or at room temperature.

BLUEBERRY GRUNT

PREPARATION TIME: 10 MINUTES
COOKING TIME: 25 MINUTES
SERVES: 8

- 4 cups (595 g) blueberries
- 1 cup (200 g) sugar
- 2 cups (260 g) all-purpose (plain) flour (or 1 cup (130 g) flour with 1 cup (130 g) cornmeal)
- 1½ teaspoons baking powder
- ½ teaspoon baking soda (bicarbonate of soda)
- ½ teaspoon salt
- 6 tablespoons (85 g) cold butter, diced
- ¾ cup (180 ml) buttermilk

[Cooked in a frying pan on the stove top, rather than baked in the oven, this dish is named for the sound it makes while cooking.]

In a large deep frying pan, mix the berries with the sugar. Add ¾ cup (180 ml) water and bring to a simmer.

Meanwhile, in a bowl, whisk together the flour, baking powder, baking soda (bicarbonate of soda), and salt. Cut in the butter (using a pastry/dough blender or two knives) until coarse crumbs form. Stir in the buttermilk.

Drop the batter by the spoonful into the simmering berries. Cover and cook over low heat until the dumplings are cooked through, 15–20 minutes. Serve hot.

SALMONBERRY SUMMER PUDDING

PREPARATION TIME: 20 MINUTES,
   PLUS CHILLING TIME
COOKING TIME: 10 MINUTES
SERVES: 6

- 2 lb (910 g) salmonberries
- ⅓ cup (65 g) sugar (more if necessary)
- 1 tablespoon fresh lemon juice
- 8 slices firm white bread (square Pullman slices are easiest), crusts removed, plus more as needed
- Whipped cream, for serving

[The fruit of the salmonberry, which resembles glossy orange raspberries, ripens in early summer. The berries vary in flavor, so taste your cooked fruit and add more sugar if necessary.]

In a saucepan, bring the berries and sugar to a simmer over medium heat until juicy. Remove from the heat. Pour the fruit into a sieve set over a bowl. (Reserve the fruit and juice.)

Line a 4-cup (950 ml) pudding bowl with plastic wrap (clingfilm) to make the pudding easier to turn out.

Dip 1 side of a slice of bread in the berry juice. Then place the slice on the bottom of the pudding bowl with either side facing up. Set aside another whole slice for the top. Cut the remaining bread slices into 3 strips each. Dip the strips in the berry juice and line the sides of the pudding bowl. Cut extra bread to patch holes. Fill the lined bowl with the fruit. Top with the reserved whole remaining slice and patch any gaps with more bread. Trim any overhanging slices.

Fold the plastic wrap (clingfilm) loosely over the top of the pudding. Place the bowl on a plate to catch any overflow and then put a small plate on top of the pudding. Weight it down with a couple of cans. Refrigerate for at least 6 hours or overnight.

Just before serving, unfold the plastic wrap on the top, place a serving plate upside down over the pudding, and flip swiftly (wear an apron just in case). Serve with whipped cream.

PEACH COBBLER

PREPARATION TIME: 20 MINUTES
COOKING TIME: 40 MINUTES
SERVES: 6

- 4 cups (600 g) peeled (see Note, page 364) and sliced peaches
- 2 teaspoons fresh lemon juice
- 2 tablespoons brandy
- ½ cup (95 g) packed light brown sugar
- 1¼ cups (163 g) all-purpose (plain) flour
- 1 teaspoon baking powder
- ½ teaspoon salt
- 1 cup (200 g) granulated sugar
- 2 eggs
- 4 tablespoons (60 g) butter, melted
- 2 tablespoons milk
- 1 teaspoon pure vanilla extract

[Georgia's magnificent peaches are renowned nationwide, thanks to sweltering summer heat and humidity that produce high levels of sugar in the fruit.]

Position a rack in the middle of the oven and preheat to 375°F (190°C/Gas Mark 5). Grease a 9 x 13-inch (23 x 33 cm) baking dish.

In a large bowl, toss the peaches with the lemon juice, brandy, and brown sugar. Place in the baking dish.

In a medium bowl, whisk together the flour, baking powder, and salt. In a separate bowl, whisk together the granulated sugar and eggs, then whisk in the melted butter, milk, and vanilla. Add the flour mixture to the egg mixture and stir just until combined.

Pour the batter over the peaches and bake until golden, about 30 minutes. Serve warm.

BLACKBERRY BUCKLE

PREPARATION TIME: 15 MINUTES
COOKING TIME: 45 MINUTES
SERVES: 8–10

For the batter:
- 2 cups (260 g) all-purpose (plain) flour
- 1 teaspoon baking powder
- ½ teaspoon baking soda (bicarbonate of soda)
- ½ teaspoon salt
- ¼ teaspoon freshly grated nutmeg
- 1 stick (115 g) unsalted butter, softened
- ¾ cup (150 g) sugar
- 1 egg
- ½ cup (120 ml) buttermilk
- 2 cups (290 g) blackberries

For the topping:
- ½ cup (100 g) sugar
- ½ cup (65 g) all-purpose (plain) flour
- ½ teaspoon ground cinnamon
- ¼ teaspoon salt
- 4 tablespoons (60 g) butter, melted

Position a rack in the middle of the oven and preheat to 350°F (180°C/Gas Mark 4). Grease and flour a 9-inch (23 cm) cake pan.

For the batter: In a medium bowl, whisk together the flour, baking powder, baking soda (bicarbonate of soda), salt, and nutmeg. In a large bowl, with an electric mixer, cream the butter and sugar. Add the egg and mix well. Alternately add the flour mixture and buttermilk, beginning and ending with the flour. Stir well to combine. Fold in the blackberries. Scrape the batter into the cake pan.

For the topping: In a small bowl, whisk together the sugar, flour, cinnamon, and salt. Stir in the melted butter.

Sprinkle the topping over the batter. Bake until a skewer inserted in the center comes out clean, about 45 minutes. Serve warm.

BLUEBERRY CRISP

PREPARATION TIME: 10 MINUTES
COOKING TIME: 50 MINUTES
SERVES: 8

- 1 stick (115 g) plus 1 tablespoon unsalted butter, melted
- 1 cup (200 g) sugar
- 1½ cups (195 g) plus 4 tablespoons all-purpose (plain) flour
- 4 cups (590 g) blueberries
- ½ teaspoon salt
- 1 cup (120 g) chopped nuts (walnuts, pecans, or hazelnuts)
- Whipped cream or vanilla ice cream, for serving

[Blueberries are an indigenous crop in Maine, covering thousands of acres of open land and serving as an understory crop in forests. Their skins are too thin for fresh shipping, so they are usually sold frozen.]

Position a rack in the middle of the oven and preheat to 350°F (180°C/Gas Mark 4). Grease a 9-inch (23 cm) pie plate with 1 tablespoon of the melted butter.

In a large bowl, whisk ½ cup (100 g) sugar with 4 tablespoons of the flour. Toss berries in the mixture and pour into the pie plate.

In a medium bowl, mix together the remaining ½ cup (100 g) sugar, 1½ cups (195 g) flour, the remaining ½ cup (120 ml) melted butter, and salt. Add the nuts and sprinkle over the blueberries. Bake until golden brown and bubbling, 45–50 minutes.

Serve warm or at room temperature with whipped cream or vanilla ice cream.

BLACKBERRY BUCKLE

STRAWBERRY SHORTCAKE

PREPARATION TIME: 20 MINUTES,
   PLUS MACERATING TIME
COOKING TIME: 15 MINUTES
SERVES: 6

For the strawberries:
- 2 pints (165 g) strawberries, halved (or quartered if large)
- Sugar

For the shortcakes:
- 2 cups (260 g) all-purpose (plain) flour
- 2 tablespoons sugar
- 4 teaspoons baking powder
- 1 teaspoon salt
- 4 tablespoons (60 g) cold unsalted butter, cut into small cubes
- 1¼ (300 ml) heavy (whipping) cream
- ½ teaspoon pure vanilla extract

For the strawberries: In a bowl, toss the strawberries with sugar to taste. Cover and set aside to macerate at room temperature for at least 30 minutes and up to several hours. The berries will release juice and become more flavorful as they sit.

Position a rack in the middle of the oven and preheat to 425°F (220°C/Gas Mark 7). Grease a baking sheet.

Meanwhile, for the shortcakes: In a medium bowl, whisk together the flour, sugar, baking powder, and salt. Cut in the butter (using a pastry/dough blender or two knives) until the mixture resembles coarse cornmeal. Stir in 1 cup (240 ml) of the cream. Do not overmix.

Turn the dough out onto a floured surface and roll the dough about 2 inches (5 cm) thick. Using a 3-inch (7.5 cm) biscuit cutter, cut the dough into rounds and place on the baking sheet, re-rolling scraps as necessary. Bake until light golden around the edges, 10–12 minutes. Transfer to a wire rack. While the shortcakes are still warm, split them in half horizontally.

Meanwhile, in a bowl, with an electric mixer, beat the remaining 1½ cups (360 ml) cream with the vanilla until soft peaks form.

Serve the shortcakes with a generous scoop of berries and whipped cream.

STRAWBERRY SHORTCAKE

BAKED ALASKA

PREPARATION TIME: 30 MINUTES,
   PLUS FREEZING TIME
COOKING TIME: 25 MINUTES
SERVES: 8

- 2 pints (500 ml tubs) ice cream or sorbet (or a combination), softened slightly
- 3 eggs, at room temperature
- 1¼ cups (250 g) sugar
- Pinch of salt
- ½ cup (65 g) all-purpose (plain) flour
- 1 teaspoon pure vanilla extract
- 6 eggs whites, at room temperature
- ½ teaspoon cream of tartar

[The Baked Alaska was invented in New York, but is now beloved in the 49th state. The three common elements of the dish are a cake base, an ice cream (or sorbet) layer, and the baked meringue topping. Together they look like a delicious glacier.]

Brush a 7-inch (18 cm) diameter bowl with oil. Line with plastic wrap (clingfilm) so the wrap hangs off the bowl in all directions. Pack the ice cream into the bowl. Cover and freeze for at least 3 hours.

Meanwhile, preheat the oven to 350°F (180°C/Gas Mark 4). Grease and flour an 8-inch (20 cm) round cake pan.

In a bowl, with an electric mixer, whip the eggs until light and foamy, about 2 minutes. Beat in the ½ cup (100 g) sugar and salt and beat until light and increased in volume, about 3 minutes. Fold in the flour by hand. Stir in the vanilla.

Pour the batter into the cake pan. Bake until the center of the cake springs back when lightly pressed, about 20 minutes. Let the cake cool in the pan, then invert onto a baking sheet lined with parchment.

Remove the ice cream from the freezer. Invert the bowl over the cake layer and remove the bowl, but leave the plastic wrap (clingfilm). Cover the cake edges with the plastic and place in the freezer for another 30 minutes, or longer if necessary.

Preheat the oven to 450°F (230°C/Gas Mark 8).

In a bowl, with the electric mixer, whip the egg whites with the cream of tartar until foamy, about 3 minutes. Gradually beat in the remaining sugar and continue to whip until the meringue is glossy and holds stiff peaks, about 5 minutes.

Remove the ice cream cake from the freezer and discard the plastic wrap (clingfilm). Cover the whole top with a thick layer of meringue, making the domed top thicker than the sides. Use a spatula to make decorative swirls and peaks in the meringue. Bake just until the meringue is golden brown, about 5 minutes. Remove from the oven and let the baked alaska sit for another 5 minutes before serving.

BAKED ALASKA

BREAKFAST

AVENA CALIENTE

PREPARATION TIME: 5 MINUTES
COOKING TIME: 20 MINUTES
SERVES: 6

- ½ cup (40 g) rolled (porridge) oats
- ¾ cup (145 g) packed light brown sugar, or less to taste
- 6 cups (1.4 liters) milk
- 2 cinnamon sticks
- ½ teaspoon ground cloves
- ½ teaspoon freshly grated nutmeg
- Pinch of salt

[A warm delicious oatmeal-and-milk breakfast drink popular among Dominican Americans, nearly half of whom live in New York City, especially in the Washington Heights neighborhood.]

In a blender, combine the oats and 4 cups (1 liter) water and blend until smooth. Pour into a medium saucepan, add the brown sugar, milk, cinnamon, cloves, nutmeg, and salt, and cook over medium-high heat, stirring constantly, until the mixture comes to a boil. Reduce to a simmer and cook until thickened and reduced by one-fourth, about 15 minutes. Serve warm.

GRANOLA

PREPARATION TIME: 5 MINUTES
COOKING TIME: 50 MINUTES
SERVES: 16–20

- ½ cup (170 g) honey
- 1 stick (115 g) butter, melted
- ½ teaspoon ground cardamom
- ½ teaspoon ground cinnamon
- ¼ teaspoon salt
- 6 cups (480 g) rolled (porridge) oats
- 2 cups (185 g) sliced (flaked) almonds
- 1 cup (80 g) coconut flakes (desiccated)
- ½ cup (65 g) hulled pumpkin seeds
- 2 cups (255 g) chopped dried apricots

[Popularized in the 1960s by a Michigan company, granola got its start in the 1860s in New York. Developed as a spa health food by the inventor of the graham cracker, granola has always featured whole grains, crumbled and baked into crunchy clusters. Today, this breakfast favorite retains its healthy reputation, though many recipes are now rich with butter or oil and sweet with honey or maple syrup. Easy to make and endlessly customizable, granola can feature anything from nuts to seeds—as well as dried fruits. Store airtight at room temperature indefinitely, and enjoy by the bowl with milk or yogurt.]

Preheat the oven to 275°F (140°C/Gas Mark 1). Line a rimmed baking sheet with foil.

In a large bowl, whisk together the honey, butter, cardamom, cinnamon, and salt until well combined. Add the oats, almonds, coconut, and pumpkin seeds and mix with a rubber spatula to coat well.

Spread in a single layer on the baking sheet. Bake, stirring every 15 minutes, until medium-golden brown, 45–50 minutes. The granola will feel soft when you remove it from the oven, but will crisp up as it sits. Let cool completely; then fold in the apricots.

GRANOLA

BUTTERMILK BISCUITS WITH SAWMILL GRAVY

PREPARATION TIME: 25 MINUTES
COOKING TIME: 40 MINUTES
MAKES: 12 BISCUITS

[In this iconic Southern breakfast, feather-light, piping-hot split buttermilk biscuits are slathered with a sausage-laden white sauce, heavily spiked with black pepper. The roux for the white sauce is made with the drippings from the cooked sausage.]

For the biscuits:
- 2½ cups (325 g) all-purpose (plain) flour
- ½ teaspoon salt
- 1 tablespoon baking powder
- 1 teaspoon baking soda (bicarbonate of soda)
- 1 stick (115 g) cold unsalted butter, cut into ½-inch (1.25 cm) dice
- 1 cup (240 ml) cold buttermilk
- 2 tablespoons heavy (whipping) cream (optional)

For the gravy:
- ¾ lb (340 g) loose pork breakfast sausage
- 4 tablespoons all-purpose (plain) flour
- 2½ cups (590 ml) milk
- ½ teaspoon freshly ground black pepper
- ¼ teaspoon cayenne pepper
- Salt

For the biscuits: Preheat the oven to 450°F (230°C/Gas Mark 8).

In a medium bowl, combine the flour, salt, baking powder, and baking soda (bicarbonate of soda). Cut in the butter (using a pastry/dough blender or your fingertips) until small clumps form. Place the bowl in the freezer or refrigerator for 10 minutes to chill.

Add the cold buttermilk to the flour mixture and stir gently just until the dough comes together. Turn the dough onto a lightly floured surface and knead 5 or 6 times, until just combined. Lightly flour your hands and press the dough into a rectangle about ¾ inch (2 cm) thick. Cut into 2-inch (5 cm) rounds with a biscuit cutter or glass and place on an ungreased baking sheet. Gently reshape the scraps and cut out more biscuits.

Brush the tops of the biscuits with cream, if using. Bake until golden brown, 16–18 minutes.

For the gravy: While the biscuits are baking, in a large frying pan, cook the sausage over medium-high heat, breaking it up with a wooden spoon, until dark golden and crispy, 8–10 minutes. Reduce the heat to medium, stir in the flour, and cook for 3 minutes. Stir in the milk, black pepper, and cayenne. Bring to a simmer and cook over medium-low heat until thickened, 6–8 minutes. Season to taste with salt. Use immediately or cover and refrigerate for up to 3 days. If refrigerated, gently rewarm over low heat before serving.

BUTTERMILK BISCUITS WITH SAWMILL GRAVY

BLUEBERRY PANCAKES

PREPARATION TIME: 5 MINUTES
COOKING TIME: 20 MINUTES
MAKES: 12 (6-INCH/15 CM) PANCAKES

- 2 cups (260 g) all-purpose (plain) flour
- 1 tablespoon sugar
- 2 teaspoons baking powder
- ¼ teaspoon salt
- 2 eggs
- 1½ cups (355 ml) milk
- 2 tablespoons (30 g) butter, melted
  and cooled, plus 1–2 tablespoons
  (15–30 g) for the griddle
- ¾ cup (110 g) blueberries

In a large bowl, mix together the flour, sugar, baking powder, and salt. In a medium bowl, whisk together the eggs, milk, and melted butter. Gently stir the wet ingredients into the dry ingredients until just combined. Add the blueberries and gently fold to combine. Do not overmix; the batter should be lumpy.

Heat a griddle or large nonstick frying pan over medium heat. Melt 2 teaspoons butter until bubbling. Working in batches, spoon batter by the heaping ¼ cup (70 ml) onto the griddle. Cook until golden brown on the bottom and bubbles rise to the surface of the pancake, all around the edges, 3–4 minutes. Flip and continue to cook until cooked through, 3–4 minutes longer. Repeat with the remaining batter, adding more butter to the griddle as needed.

BLUE CORN AND PINE NUT PANCAKES

PREPARATION TIME: 5 MINUTES
COOKING TIME: 30 MINUTES
MAKES: 20 PANCAKES

- 1½ cups (195 g) all-purpose (plain) flour
- 1½ cups (210 g) blue cornmeal
- 1 tablespoon baking powder
- 3 tablespoons sugar
- 1 teaspoon sea salt
- 2 eggs
- 2½ cups (590 ml) milk
- ½ cup (120 ml) buttermilk
- 4 tablespoons (60 g) butter, melted and
  cooled, plus more for the griddle
- ½ cup (70 g) pine nuts

In a large bowl, whisk together the flour, blue cornmeal, baking powder, sugar, and salt. In a medium bowl, gently mix the eggs, milk, buttermilk, and melted butter. Pour the wet ingredients into the flour mixture and gently stir until just combined. Do not over-stir; the batter should be lumpy.

In a frying pan or griddle, melt 2 tablespoons (30 g) butter until bubbling. Working in batches, spoon the batter by the ⅓ cup (80 ml) onto the frying pan. Place about 8 pine nuts on each pancake. Cook until golden brown on the bottom and bubbles rise to the top all around the edges, about 3 minutes. Flip and continue to cook until cooked through, about 3 minutes. Repeat with the remaining batter, replenishing the butter as needed.

BLUEBERRY PANCAKES

DUTCH BABY PANCAKE

PREPARATION TIME: 5 MINUTES
COOKING TIME: 15 MINUTES
SERVES: 2

- 4 tablespoons (60 g) butter
- 3 eggs
- ½ cup (65 g) all-purpose (plain) flour
- 4 tablespoons sugar
- Pinch of salt
- Pinch of freshly grated nutmeg
- ½ teaspoon pure vanilla extract
- ½ lemon

[A descendant of a German *Pfannkuchen*, this puff pancake was first popularized by a café in Seattle, Washington, in the 1940s and is now a breakfast standard throughout the state and Pacific Northwest. The simple, eggy, rich pancake is baked in the oven, no flipping needed.]

Preheat the oven to 425°F (220°C/Gas Mark 7). Place 3 tablespoons (45 g) of the butter in a large ovenproof cast-iron skillet and place in the oven to preheat.

In a bowl, whisk together the eggs, flour, 3 tablespoons of the sugar, the salt, nutmeg, and vanilla. Whisk vigorously for 1 minute, until the mixture is foamy.

Pour the batter into the hot skillet, return to the oven, and bake until puffed up and lightly browned, 10–15 minutes. Remove from the oven, quickly dot the pancake with the remaining 1 tablespoon butter, and sprinkle with the remaining 1 tablespoon sugar. Squeeze the lemon over the top. Serve immediately.

JOHNNY CAKES

PREPARATION TIME: 5 MINUTES
COOKING TIME: 15 MINUTES
MAKES: 2 PANCAKES

- 1 cup (240 ml) water or milk
- 1 cup (130 g) cornmeal
- 1 teaspoon sugar
- Pinch of salt
- Fat (bacon drippings, lard, or vegetable oil), for frying
- Butter and pure maple syrup, for serving

[The Native American Pawtuxet of the Wampanoag tribe taught New England settlers to use corn and today cornmeal in their cooking, and the ingredients remain a staple across the region. The johnny cake, also known as ashcake, hoe cake, corn pone, or pone, is at essence a thinner, sturdier version of cornbread, cooked on a griddle like a pancake. It can also be served cold and can take the place of cornbread as a breakfast side. The volume of liquid needed to make the batter will vary with the type of cornmeal and the grind.]

In a small saucepan, bring the water to a boil. Remove from the heat. In a small bowl, whisk together the cornmeal, sugar, and salt. Using a wooden spoon, stir in 1 cup (240 ml) of hot water or milk. The mixture should be the consistency of moderately thick pancake batter.

In a large cast-iron griddle or skillet over medium-high heat, heat enough fat to barely cover the surface. When the griddle is very hot, add the batter by the spoonful (you can make the cakes big or small depending on your preference). With the back of the spoon, spread the batter to a thickness of about ¼ inch (6 mm). Reduce the heat to medium and cook until bubbles appear on the surface and the bottom is well browned, 3–4 minutes. Flip and cook for another 3 minutes. Serve hot with butter and maple syrup. Repeat with any remaining batter.

SCRAMBLED EGGS WITH MOREL MUSHROOMS

PREPARATION TIME: 5 MINUTES
COOKING TIME: 10 MINUTES
SERVES: 4

- 3 tablespoons (45 g) butter
- ½ lb (225 g) fresh morel mushrooms, cleaned and halved lengthwise
- Salt and freshly ground black pepper
- 8 eggs
- 3 tablespoons heavy (whipping) cream
- Minced fresh chives (optional)

In a large frying pan, melt the butter over medium-high heat. Add the mushrooms, season with salt and pepper, and cook just until cooked through, about 5 minutes.

Meanwhile, in a bowl, whisk the eggs with the cream.

Pour the eggs over the mushrooms and scramble just until the eggs are almost set. Garnish with chives, if desired.

GUAVA PASTELILLOS

PREPARATION TIME: 15 MINUTES,
   PLUS COOLING TIME
COOKING TIME: 20 MINUTES
MAKES: 8 PASTRIES

- 1 package (1 lb/455 g) frozen puff pastry sheets, thawed but chilled
- All-purpose (plain) flour, for rolling out
- 4 oz (115 g) guava paste, cut into 8 pieces
- 8 oz (225 g) cream cheese, cut into 8 pieces
- 1 egg
- ¼ cup (30 g) powdered (icing) sugar

[This is a favorite breakfast in Miami. To prepare at home, look for guava paste (also known as *guayabate* or *goiabada*) in the Hispanic food section of grocery stores or online; it is typically sold in short, wide cans.]

Position a rack in the middle of the oven and preheat to 400°F (200°C/Gas Mark 6). Line a large baking sheet with parchment paper.

On a lightly floured surface, roll a pastry sheet into about a 16-inch (40 cm) square. Cut the sheet into 4 squares and transfer the squares to the baking sheet. Near one corner of a square, place a piece of cream cheese and one of guava paste on top of each other. Whisk the egg with 1 tablespoon water. Brush the border of the pastry with the egg wash and fold the dough over the filling to form a triangle-shaped pocket. Use a fork to crimp the edges together. Repeat with the remaining pastry, cream cheese, and guava paste.

Bake the pastries until puffed and golden brown, 15–20 minutes. Transfer to a wire rack to cool completely.

Once cool, stir together the powdered (icing) sugar and 1 tablespoon water. Drizzle the cooled pastries with the glaze. Allow the glaze to set before serving.

HUEVOS RANCHEROS

PREPARATION TIME: 15 MINUTES
COOKING TIME: 15 MINUTES
SERVES: 4

- 2 cups (475 ml) Salsa Verde (page 458) or store-bought red chile sauce
- 2 cups (510 g) Refried Pinto Beans (page 269)
- Vegetable oil, for shallow-frying
- 8 corn tortillas
- 8 eggs
- 2 scallions (spring onions), thinly sliced
- ½ cup (55 g) crumbled Cotija cheese
- 2 tablespoons chopped fresh cilantro (coriander)
- Lime wedges, for serving (optional)

Place 4 heavy dinner plates in the oven and preheat to 200°F (95°C).

In a small saucepan, heat the salsa or sauce over low heat, covered. Place the beans in a small pot with 2 tablespoons water. Whisk well to combine. Warm over medium-low heat, stirring frequently. Cover and keep warm.

Pour ½ inch (1.25 cm) oil into a large frying pan and heat over medium heat to 350°F (180°C).

Remove the plates from the oven. Working in batches, fry the tortillas until lightly golden and crispy, 25–30 seconds per side. Drain against the side of the pan, then overlap 2 tortillas on each warm plate. Spoon 4 tablespoons salsa evenly over the tortillas on each plate.

Reduce the heat to medium-low. Add 4 eggs to the frying pan, gently spooning oil over the yolks to set them, about 2 minutes (for firm whites and runny yolks). Place 2 eggs on each of two plates. Repeat with the remaining 4 eggs. Spoon the remaining sauce evenly over each plate. (Place the plates in the oven at any point in the process, to keep warm.)

Dividing evenly, sprinkle the scallions (spring onions), Cotija, and cilantro (coriander) over the eggs. Spoon the refried beans alongside the eggs. Serve immediately.

WESTERN OMELET

PREPARATION TIME: 5 MINUTES
COOKING TIME: 10 MINUTES
SERVES: 2

- 6 eggs
- 3 tablespoons (45 g) butter
- 4 tablespoons diced onion
- 4 tablespoons diced green bell pepper
- ½ cup (165 g) diced ham
- Salt and freshly ground black pepper, for serving

[Unlike a traditional French omelet, here the filling is cooked with the eggs. Adding cheddar is not traditional, but has become popular.]

In a bowl, beat the eggs and set aside.

In a small frying pan, heat 1 tablespoon (15 g) of the butter over medium heat. Add the onion and bell pepper and cook until tender, about 4 minutes. Add the ham and heat through. Set the filling aside.

In a medium frying pan, heat 1 tablespoon (15 g) butter over medium heat. Add half the filling and half of the beaten eggs. Cook, stirring with a silicone spatula, until barely cooked, about 30 seconds. Remove from the heat, smooth the top of the omelet, let rest for a few seconds, then fold in half and transfer to a plate. Repeat with the remaining butter, filling, and eggs to make a second omelet. Serve hot.

HUEVOS RANCHEROS

POTATO, EGG, AND BACON BREAKFAST TACOS

PREPARATION TIME: 10 MINUTES
COOKING TIME: 25 MINUTES
SERVES: 4

- 4 slices thick-cut bacon (streaky)
- 1 russet (baking) potato or 8 fingerlings (about 8 oz/225 g), peeled and cut into ½-inch (1.25 cm) pieces
- Kosher (coarse) salt and freshly ground black pepper
- Large pinch of paprika (optional)
- 2 eggs, lightly beaten
- 4 corn or flour tortillas (6-inch/15 cm), warmed according to package directions
- Optional toppings: Salsa, diced onion, diced avocado, hot sauce, fresh cilantro (coriander)

[Breakfast tacos are beloved throughout Texas, especially in Central Texas and Austin, the state's capital. They are filled with anything that might be on a typical American breakfast table and crowned with salsa. Try with handmade tortillas (page 423).]

Heat a large cast-iron skillet over medium-high until hot. Add the bacon and cook, turning occasionally, until the fat is frothy and the bacon is crisp, 4–6 minutes. Drain the bacon on paper towels. (Reserve the skillet and 2 tablespoons bacon fat.) When cool enough to handle, crumble the bacon.

Return the skillet to heat, add the potato, and season with salt, pepper, and paprika (if using). Cook, partially covered, until golden brown and tender, 10–12 minutes. Transfer the potatoes to a bowl.

Return the pan to medium heat, add the eggs, and season with salt and pepper. Scramble the eggs, pushing them around with a spoon, until they are fluffy and the desired consistency, 1–2 minutes.

To serve, top each tortilla with bacon, eggs, and potatoes. Serve with toppings, if desired.

TAYLOR HAM BREAKFAST SANDWICH

PREPARATION TIME: 5 MINUTES
COOKING TIME: 4–6 MINUTES
SERVES: 1

- 2 tablespoons (30 g) butter
- 2 slices Taylor ham or pork roll
- 1 egg
- Salt and freshly ground black pepper
- 1 slice American cheese
- 1 hard roll, split
- Ketchup, for serving

[Popular in New Jersey delis, this semi-soft pork mixture is called Taylor ham or pork roll. It resembles a sweet sausage more than a ham, but is chewier. It is delicious on a hard roll with egg and cheese.]

Heat a large frying pan over medium heat. Add 1 tablespoon (15 g) of the butter and fry the Taylor ham until crispy and browned on the edges. Flip and cook on the other side. Remove from the pan and set aside to keep warm.

Heat the remaining 1 tablespoon (15 g) butter in the pan. Add the egg and cook as desired (scrambled, sunny-side up, over easy, etc.). Season to taste with salt and pepper.

To assemble, place the cheese on the bottom half of the roll. Top with the egg and cooked pork, then close up the sandwich. Serve with ketchup.

POTATO, EGG, AND BACON BREAKFAST TACOS

MIGAS WITH CHEESE

PREPARATION TIME: 5 MINUTES
COOKING TIME: 10 MINUTES
SERVES: 4

- Vegetable oil, for shallow-frying
- 4 corn tortillas, cut into ½-inch (1.25 cm) pieces
- 8 eggs
- 8 oz (225 g) Monterey Jack cheese (optional), grated
- Salsa and sliced fresh jalapeños, for serving (optional)

[A cousin to the breakfast taco, this Texas breakfast typically stars scrambled eggs and is often accompanied by onions, tomatoes, peppers, and cheese, served over warm corn tortillas. Beloved across Texas and beyond, it is sometimes embellished with cheese, salsa, jalapeños, and avocado.]

Pour 1 inch (2.5 cm) oil into a large cast-iron skillet and heat to 350°F (180°C). A piece of tortilla dropped in the oil will sizzle when it is ready. Working in batches, fry the tortillas until crisp, about 1 minute. Drain on paper towels.

Pour off all but 2 tablespoons oil (a thin pool at the bottom of the pan). Heat at medium-high heat. Add the eggs and tortillas (and cheese, if using) to the hot oil and cook, stirring, until everything is scrambled together and the eggs are the desired consistency, about 2 minutes. Serve with salsa, jalapeños, and cheese, if desired.

RED CHILI ENCHILADAS

PREPARATION TIME: 15 MINUTES
COOKING TIME: 35 MINUTES
SERVES: 4

- ½ cup (120 ml) vegetable oil
- 12 corn tortillas
- 2 cups (475 ml) New Mexico red chili sauce
- 1 cup (160 g) finely chopped onion
- 3 cups (345 g) shredded asadero or Monterey Jack cheese
- 4 eggs, cooked sunny-side up or over easy (optional)
- Chopped cilantro (coriander), tomato, and lettuce, for serving (optional)

In a medium frying pan, heat the oil over medium heat. Working with one tortilla at a time, fry the tortillas in the oil until very lightly golden, 45–60 seconds. Drain on paper towels.

Preheat the oven to 300°F (150°C/Gas Mark 2). Pour the chili sauce into a wide bowl. Dip the tortillas, one at a time, in the sauce to thinly coat each side, scraping each against the side of the bowl before removing. Place a dipped tortilla on an ovenproof plate. Top the tortilla with 1 tablespoon onion and 3 tablespoons cheese. Add another dipped tortilla and another layer of onion and cheese. Finish with a third tortilla. Make 3 more stacks on three more ovenproof plates in the same manner.

Place the plates in the oven and heat until the cheese is melted, about 20 minutes. Remove and serve (warning, plates will be very hot). Top with a sunny-side up or over-easy egg, cilantro (coriander), tomato, and/or lettuce, if desired.

MIGAS WITH CHEESE

RED FLANNEL HASH

PREPARATION TIME: 10 MINUTES
COOKING TIME: ABOUT 1 HOUR 20
  MINUTES
SERVES: 4

- 3 large beets (beetroots)
- 3 medium potatoes
- 4 tablespoons olive oil
- 1 large red onion, diced
- ½ cup (120 ml) heavy (whipping) cream or sour cream
- Salt and freshly ground black pepper
- 1 tablespoon chopped fresh parsley

[Named for the color of its beets, this dish is often served with poached eggs.]

In a large pot of boiling water, cook the beets (beetroots) and potatoes until the potatoes are tender, about 20 minutes. Using a slotted spoon, lift the potatoes out and set aside to cool. Continue cooking the beets until they are tender, about 40 minutes. Drain the beets. When the potatoes and beets are cool enough to handle, peel and dice them.

In a large cast-iron skillet, heat the olive oil over medium-high heat. Add the onion and cook, stirring, until it starts to soften, about 3 minutes. Add the potatoes, beets, and cook, stirring occasionally, until browned and crispy, about 15 minutes. Stir in the cream and season to taste with salt and pepper. Serve hot, garnished with the parsley.

HANGTOWN FRY

TIME: 10 MINUTES
COOKING TIME: 15 MINUTES
SERVES: 4

- ½ lb (225 g) bacon (streaky)
- ¾ cup (95 g) all-purpose (plain) flour
- ½ teaspoon salt
- 1 pint (495 g) freshly shucked oysters
- 4 tablespoons (60 g) butter
- 8 eggs, lightly beaten
- 2 tablespoons finely chopped fresh parsley

In a frying pan, cook the bacon over medium-high heat until crispy, about 6 minutes. Drain on paper towels. When cool enough to handle, crumble the bacon. Set aside.

In a shallow bowl, whisk together the flour and salt. Dredge each oyster in the seasoned flour. In a large frying pan, melt the butter over medium-high heat. Fry the oysters for about 30 seconds on each side. Add the bacon to the pan. Pour the eggs over the oysters and bacon and, using a silicone spatula, gently push the eggs toward the center of the pan. Cook just until the eggs are set, about 4 minutes. Remove from the heat and carefully invert the whole omelet onto a plate. Sprinkle with parsley and serve.

RED FLANNEL HASH

SCRAPPLE

PREPARATION TIME: 20 MINUTES,
PLUS CHILLING TIME
COOKING TIME: 2 HOURS 30 MINUTES
SERVES: 6

- 1½ lb (680 g) boneless pork shoulder
- ¼ lb (115 g) pork liver
- 1 cup (130 g) cornmeal
- 2 teaspoons salt
- 1 small onion, minced
- 1 teaspoon dried marjoram
- 1 teaspoon dried sage
- ¼ teaspoon dried thyme
- ½ teaspoon freshly ground black pepper
- ¼ teaspoon ground cloves
- All-purpose (plain) flour, for dusting
- 2 tablespoons oil or lard

[Scrapple is traditionally made with pork scraps, cornmeal, buckwheat, and spices, and other meats and grains are sometimes added. The result is similar to sausage and meatloaf, but with a higher grain content. Slices are usually pan-fried or broiled and served for breakfast. Delaware has held an annual Apple Scrapple Festival in Bridgeville since 1992.]

In a large pot, combine the pork shoulder, liver, and cold water to cover and bring to a boil. Reduce to a simmer and cook for 15 minutes. Remove the liver with tongs and set aside to cool. Cover and continue to cook the shoulder over low heat until the meat is tender, about 1½ hours. Remove the shoulder from the pot, reserving the broth. Allow the meat to cool, then chop it finely. Chop the liver finely.

In a large pot, combine the cornmeal, salt, and 3 cups (710 ml) of the reserved broth. Bring the mixture to a boil over medium heat, stirring constantly. Reduce to a simmer, stir in the meat, liver, onion, herbs, and spices. Cover and simmer gently for 1 hour.

Grease a 9 x 5-inch (23 x 13 cm) loaf pan. Pour the mixture into the pan. Let cool, cover, and refrigerate for at least 3 hours and up to overnight to chill.

When ready to serve, cut the scrapple into ½-inch (1.25 cm) slices and dust with flour. In a large frying pan, heat 2 tablespoons oil or lard over medium-high heat. Working in batches, fry the scrapple until it is browned and crisp, 2–3 minutes on each side. Serve piping hot.

PREPARATION TIME: 15 MINUTES
COOKING TIME: 35 MINUTES
SERVES: 4

- 4 green plantains
- 1 teaspoon salt
- 6 tablespoons olive oil or butter
- 2 medium red onions, halved and thinly sliced
- 1 tablespoon cider vinegar
- 8 slices salami
- 4 eggs

[This dish was brought to New York by the large population from the Dominican and is especially popular for breakfast. It is traditionally served with eggs, fried salami, and pickled onions.]

Peel the plantains and halve lengthwise. Place in a medium pot, cover with water, add the salt, and bring to a boil over high heat. Cook until tender, about 15 minutes.

Meanwhile, in a large frying pan, heat 2 tablespoons of the oil over medium-high heat. Add the onions and cook until they have softened, about 6 minutes. Pour the onions into a bowl and toss with the vinegar. Set aside.

Add 1 tablespoon oil to the frying pan and cook the salami until browned. Set aside. In the same frying pan, add another 1 tablespoon oil and cook the eggs according to preference (scrambled, fried, etc.).

Drain the plantains and return to the cooking pot. Add the remaining 2 tablespoons oil and mash the plantains.

To serve, divide the mashed plantain among 4 plates. Top with the onions, salami, and eggs.

BAKERY

CLASSIC AMERICAN WHITE BREAD

PREPARATION TIME: 20 MINUTES,
  PLUS RISING TIME
COOKING TIME: 1 HOUR 10 MINUTES
MAKES: 2 LOAVES

- 1½ cups (355 ml) milk
- ¼ cup (50 g) sugar
- 6 tablespoons (90 g) unsalted butter
- 1 packet (7 g/2¼ teaspoons) active dry yeast
- 2 eggs
- 1 tablespoon salt
- 6–6½ cups (780–845 g) all-purpose (plain) flour

In a small saucepan, scald the milk over medium heat. Remove from the heat and stir in the sugar and 3 tablespoons (45 g) of the butter. Pour into a large bowl and let cool to lukewarm, then stir in the yeast. Stir in the eggs. Add the salt and 4 cups (520 g) of the flour. Beat with a wooden spoon for about 2 minutes, until smooth. Add 2 more cups (260 g) flour. The dough will become too stiff to stir, but work in as much flour as possible.

Turn the dough out onto a floured surface and knead for 10 minutes, adding flour if necessary, to make a smooth and elastic dough. Add the dough to a large buttered bowl and turn to coat. Cover with a damp tea towel and let the dough rise in a warm draft-free area until doubled in volume, about 1½ hours.

Punch down the dough. Divide it in half and form each half into a loaf. Place each loaf in a buttered 9 x 5-inch (23 x 13) loaf pan. Cover with a damp tea towel and let rise until doubled, 45 minutes to 1 hour.

Position a rack in the middle of the oven and preheat to 350°F (180°C/Gas Mark 4).

Bake until the bread is browned and sounds hollow when tapped on the bottom, 45 minutes to 1 hour.

Remove the bread from the pans and place on a wire rack. Melt the remaining 3 tablespoons (45 g) butter and brush over the tops of the bread. Let cool completely before slicing.

**PREPARATION TIME: 40 MINUTES,
  PLUS RISING TIME
COOKING TIME: 1 HOUR
MAKES: 2 LOAVES**

- 1 packet (7 g/2¼ teaspoons) active dry yeast
- ⅓ cup warm water (110°F/43°C)
- 3 cups (710 ml) milk
- 2 tablespoons (30 g) butter
- 1 tablespoon honey
- 1 tablespoon molasses
- 1 tablespoon salt
- 7 cups (840 g) whole wheat (wholemeal) flour, plus more for kneading

[Wyoming's rich soil and semi-arid climate contribute to a high protein content in its wheat crop, making it especially great for bread baking.]

In a small bowl, mix the yeast in the warm water and let sit for 10 minutes.

Meanwhile, in a medium saucepan, scald the milk over medium heat. Remove from the heat and add the butter, honey, molasses, and salt. Pour into a large bowl and let cool until it is warm but not hot (about 110°F/43°C).

Stir in the yeast mixture and 6 cups (720 g) flour. Turn out onto a floured surface and knead in the remaining 1 cup (120 g) flour. Knead for 6–7 minutes until smooth. Add the dough to a large oiled bowl and turn to coat. Cover with a damp tea towel and let the dough rise in a warm draft-free area for 1 hour, until doubled.

Punch down the dough. Divide it in half and form each into a loaf. Place the loaves in two greased 9 x 5-inch (23 x 13 cm) loaf pans. Cover with a damp tea towel and let rise for 40 minutes.

Preheat the oven to 350°F (180°C/Gas Mark 4).

Bake until the bread is golden brown and the loaf sounds hollow when tapped on the bottom, about 1 hour. Remove from the pans and let cool on a wire rack.

PREPARATION TIME: 10 MINUTES,
  PLUS 12 HOURS STANDING TIME
COOKING TIME: 20 MINUTES
MAKES: 10 FLATBREADS

- 1¼ cups (163 g) all-purpose (plain) flour
- 1¼ cups (150 g) buckwheat flour
  (preferably silverskin buckwheat, which
  has a lighter flavor)
- ¼ teaspoon active dry yeast
- 1 teaspoon salt
- Fat (bacon grease, lard, butter, or olive
  oil), for frying

[Popular in northern Maine, ployes are a traditional Acadian flat-bread made with buckwheat flour and served with savory stews or with butter and maple syrup. Some home cooks now use baking powder, but this traditional version uses yeast and rises overnight before cooking.]

Whisk together both flours with the yeast and salt. Add 1¾ cups (415 ml) water and mix well. Cover and let sit at room temperature for 12 hours.

Stir in enough water (about 6 tablespoons) to make a thin batter.

Lightly grease a 6-inch (15 cm) frying pan and heat over medium-high heat. Pour about 3 tablespoons batter into the hot pan and tilt to distribute the batter. Cook until bubbles form and burst and the edges slightly curl up, about 2 minutes. Do not flip. Transfer to a plate and repeat with the remaining batter is used up, regreasing the pan each time.

SOURDOUGH STARTER

 AK

PREPARATION TIME: 2½–3 DAYS
MAKES: 1 STARTER (VOLUME
  AND WEIGHT WILL VARY)

- Rye, whole wheat (wholemeal),
  or unbleached all-purpose (plain) flour
- 1½ cups (350 ml) cool water
  (unchlorinated or filtered)

[This versatile starter is made by capturing wild yeasts in the environment. Alaskans love the sourdough tang; the starter can be used for everything from breads to crackers to pancakes and beyond.]

Combine ½ cup (50 g) flour with ½ cup (120 ml) water in a large nonreactive container (glass, ceramic, food-grade plastic, or wood). Stir well. Cover loosely with a tea towel and let stand for 24 hours at room temperature.

Stir in another ½ cup flour (50 g) and ½ cup (120 ml) water. Cover and let sit for 24 hours.

On the third day, the mixture should be starting to bubble and should smell fresh. Stir in another ½ cup (50 g) flour and ½ cup (120 ml) water. Cover and let sit for another 12 hours.

At this point the sourdough should be actively bubbling and still smell fresh but with a sour note. If your house is very cool, this pro cess could take another day. If it is warm, it may be ready sooner. The starter may now be used in recipes.

Store in a tightly covered nonreactive container in the refrigerator. If you use the starter often, it can sit out on the counter. If not using it regularly (and replenishing it), feed the starter once a week: Discard ½ cup (120 ml) starter and feed with ½ cup (50 g) flour and ½ cup (120 ml) water.

SOURDOUGH BAGUETTE

PREPARATION TIME: 30 MINUTES,
PLUS RISING TIME AND OVERNIGHT
RESTING TIME
COOKING TIME: 30 MINUTES
MAKES: 1 BAGUETTE

For the sponge:
- ⅓ cup (80 ml) Sourdough Starter (page 415)
- 1 cup (130 g) all-purpose (plain) flour

For the bread:
- ½ teaspoon active dry yeast
- 2 teaspoons sugar
- 1½ teaspoons salt
- 2½ cups (325 g) all-purpose (plain) flour
- Cornmeal

[This bread calls for sourdough starter (page 414), which needs to be made at least three days in advance. Then the initial sponge for this bread has to sit overnight. The rising times will vary with the ambient temperature and the vigor of the starter.]

For the sponge: In a large glass, ceramic, or wood bowl, combine the starter, flour, and 1 cup (240 ml) water. Stir vigorously. Scrape down the sides of the bowl. Cover with a tea towel and let sit at room temperature overnight.

For the bread: In a small bowl, combine the yeast, ¼ cup (60 ml) warm water, and the sugar and let sit for a few minutes until the yeast starts to bubble. Stir into the sponge. Add the salt and flour and stir to combine.

Turn the dough out onto a floured surface and knead, adding flour as necessary to make a soft dough. Do not add too much flour. The dough will be somewhat sticky at first. Knead the dough for 10 minutes. Add the dough to a large oiled bowl and turn to coat. Cover the bowl with the tea towel and let the dough rise in a warm draft-free area until doubled in volume, about 2 hours.

Punch down the dough and turn out onto a floured surface. Pat the dough into a rectangle, then roll and pinch together into a baguette. Sprinkle cornmeal on a baking sheet and place the baguette on the cornmeal. Cover and let rise until nearly doubled.

Preheat the oven to 400°F (200°C/Gas Mark 6).

With a razor, slash the top of the bread lengthwise down the center, or make 3 horizontal slashes diagonally. Bake the bread until browned and crusty, 20–30 minutes.

PREPARATION TIME: 45 MINUTES,
 PLUS RISING AND COOLING TIME
COOKING TIME: 50 MINUTES
MAKES: 2 LOAVES

- ½ cup (120 ml) plus ⅔ cup (155 ml) warm water (105°–115°F/40°–46°C)
- 2 tablespoons active dry yeast
- 1 tablespoon plus ¾ cup (150 g) sugar
- 5 eggs
- ¾ cup (180 ml) plus 1 tablespoon vegetable oil
- 1 teaspoon salt
- 7½ cups (195 g) all-purpose (plain) flour
- 1 egg yolk

[This eggy, yeasted, braided bread is essential in the Jewish kitchen. Thick slices make excellent French toast.]

In a medium bowl, combine ½ cup (120 ml) of the warm water, the yeast, and 1 tablespoon sugar and stir until the yeast dissolves. Let stand at room temperature until foamy, about 10 minutes.

In a large bowl (or in a stand mixer), whisk the eggs. Add ¾ cup (180 ml) of the oil, the salt, and the remaining ¾ cup (150 g) sugar and whisk well until pale yellow and slightly thickened, about 4 minutes. Whisk in the remaining ⅔ cup (155 ml) warm water. Add the yeast mixture and whisk until blended. Stirring with a wooden spoon (or the dough hook of a stand mixer), beat in the flour 1 cup (130 g) at a time until a smooth dough forms, beating well between additions. Turn the dough onto a floured surface and knead for 6–8 minutes, or until the dough is smooth. Add more flour by the tablespoon if sticky.

Add the dough to a large oiled bowl and turn to coat. Cover with plastic wrap (clingfilm) and then a clean tea towel and let the dough rise in a warm draft-free area until doubled in volume, about 1 hour.

Punch down the dough. Cover with plastic wrap (clingfilm) and a clean tea towel and let rise an additional 30 minutes.

Grease 2 large baking sheets with the remaining 1 tablespoon oil. Turn the dough out onto a lightly floured surface. Divide the dough into 2 equal portions. Divide each portion into 3 equal pieces. Roll each piece into a rope 10 inches (25 cm) long. Lay 3 of the ropes parallel to one another and braid (plait) together. Pinch the ends underneath the loaf to seal. Repeat with the remaining 3 dough pieces to make a second loaf. Place each loaf on a baking sheet. Cover with plastic wrap (clingfilm) and let rise in a warm area until almost doubled, 30–45 minutes.

Position racks in the upper and lower thirds of the oven and preheat to 400°F (200°C/Gas Mark 6).

Whisk the egg yolk with 1 tablespoon water. Brush the loaves with the egg wash. Bake for 10 minutes. Reduce the oven temperature to 350°F (180°C/Gas Mark 4) and bake until the bread is golden brown and sounds hollow when tapped on the bottom, about 35 minutes, switching the sheets from rack to rack halfway through. Transfer the loaves to a wire rack to cool completely.

CHALLAH

ANADAMA BREAD

PREPARATION TIME: 35 MINUTES,
  PLUS RISING TIME
COOKING TIME: 1 HOUR 10 MINUTES
MAKES: 1 LOAF

- ½ cup (65 g) cornmeal, preferably
  stone-ground
- 3 tablespoons (45 g) butter
- ¼ cup (85 g) molasses
- 1 packet (7 g/2¼ teaspoons) active
  dry yeast
- 2 teaspoons salt
- 3 cups (390 g) all-purpose (plain) flour

In a medium saucepan, bring 1 cup (240 ml) water to a boil. Slowly pour in the cornmeal and cook, stirring constantly, until thickened, about 5 minutes. Remove from the heat, stir in the butter and molasses, pour into a large bowl, and set aside to cool to lukewarm.

Stir in the yeast and let sit for 10 minutes. Stir in the salt and 2 cups (260 g) of the flour. Add the rest of the flour a little at a time, stirring to make a stiff dough. Turn out onto a floured surface and knead for 6–8 minutes, until the dough is smooth and elastic. Add the dough to a large buttered bowl. Cover with a damp tea towel and let the dough rise in a warm draft-free area until doubled in volume, about 1 hour.

Punch down the dough. Form into a loaf and transfer to a greased 9 x 5-inch (23 x 13 cm) loaf pan. Cover and let rise until doubled, about 45 minutes.

Meanwhile, position a rack in the middle of the oven and preheat to 350°F (180°C/Gas Mark 4).

Bake the bread until the loaf sounds hollow when tapped on the bottom, about 1 hour. Remove from the pan to a wire rack to cool.

SWEDISH LIMPA

PREPARATION TIME: 20 MINUTES,
  PLUS COOLING AND RISING TIME
COOKING TIME: 40 MINUTES
MAKES: 2 LOAVES

- 1¾ cups (415 ml) orange juice
- ¼ cup (60 ml) molasses
- ¼ cup (50 g) packed dark brown sugar
- 1½ teaspoons fennel seeds
- 1 teaspoon anise seeds
- 1 teaspoon caraway seeds
- 4 tablespoons (60 g) butter
- 1 packet (7 g/2¼ teaspoons) active
  dry yeast
- 2½ cups (255 g) rye flour
- 2 cups (270 g) bread (strong white) flour,
  plus more for kneading
- 2½ teaspoons salt
- 1 tablespoon grated orange zest

[Limpa is a staple on many Midwestern Scandinavian smorgasbord tables during Christmas. It's also known as *vortlimpa* ("wort loaf"), because it was originally made from the fermented brewer's wort left over from beer making.]

In a small saucepan, combine the orange juice, molasses, brown sugar, fennel seeds, anise seeds, and caraway seeds and bring to a boil. Reduce to a simmer and cook for 5 minutes. Remove from the heat, stir in the butter, and cool to lukewarm. Stir in the yeast.

In a large bowl, whisk together the rye and bread flours, salt, and orange zest. Add the liquid ingredients and stir to combine. The dough will be sticky. Turn out onto a floured surface and knead in more bread flour as needed to make a stiff, smooth dough. Knead for about 8 minutes. Add the dough to a large oiled bowl and turn to coat. Cover with a damp tea towel and let the dough rise in a warm draft-free area until doubled in volume, about 1 hour.

Punch down the dough and divide in half. Shape each into a round loaf and place on a lightly greased baking sheet. Cover with a damp tea towel until doubled in size, 45 minutes to 1 hour.

Position a rack in the middle of the oven and preheat to 375°F (190°C/Gas Mark 5). Bake until the bread is golden brown and sounds hollow when tapped on the bottom, about 30 minutes.

PREPARATION TIME: 10 MINUTES
COOKING TIME: 2 HOURS
MAKES: 1 (2 LB/910 G) LOAF
   OR 2 (1 LB/455 G) LOAVES

- About 2 tablespoons butter or lard, for greasing the mold
- 1 cup (130 g) cornmeal
- 1 cup (100 g) rye flour
- 1 cup (120 g) whole wheat (wholemeal) flour
- 1 teaspoon baking soda (bicarbonate of soda)
- 1 teaspoon salt
- 1 cup (165 g) raisins
- ¾ cup (180 ml) molasses
- 2 cups (475 ml) buttermilk
- Boiling water (enough to half-fill a large pot)

[This bread is steamed on top of the stove rather than baked in the oven. You can either use a 2-quart (2 liter) pudding mold with a lid or two 1-pound (455 g) cans, set in a large pot. If you are short on stove top space it can be steamed in the oven in a large roasting pan. It is traditionally served with baked beans.]

Liberally grease either a 2-quart (2-liter) pudding mold (steamer) with a tight-fitting lid or two clean 1-pound (455 g) cans (tins) with butter or lard. Place a trivet or metal pie plate upside down on the bottom of a large pot with a tight-fitting lid.

In a large bowl, mix together the cornmeal, both flours, the baking soda (bicarbonate of soda), and salt. Add the raisins. In a medium bowl, whisk together the molasses and buttermilk. Add the buttermilk mixture to the dry ingredients and stir well.

Pour the batter into the pudding mold or cans and cover the top with foil, then secure with kitchen twine. Place the mold or cans on the trivet in the large pot and pour boiling water into the pot to reach two-thirds of the way up. Cover the pot tightly and bring to a boil over high heat. Reduce the heat to medium-low and steam for 1½ to 2 hours, until the center is set and the edges are starting to pull away from the mold or cans. Check the level of the water as the bread steams, adding more if necessary.

If steaming in the oven, preheat the oven to 350°F (180°C/Gas Mark 4) with a rack positioned to allow for the roasting pan to fit. Place the prepared and filled molds on a trivet in the roasting pan and pour boiling water into the pan to reach two-thirds of the way up the molds. Cover the roasting pan tightly and steam for 1½ to 2 hours.

Remove the cans or mold from the pot and let the bread cool for 30 minutes before unmolding. Slice and serve.

PREPARATION TIME: 5 MINUTES, PLUS
   AT LEAST 1 DAY FERMENTING TIME
COOKING TIME: 30 MINUTES
MAKES: 4–6 INJERA

- 1½ cups (240 g) teff flour
- Pinch of salt
- Coconut oil, for cooking

[Washington, D.C. is home to a thriving Ethiopian community. Many residents have developed an appetite for the culture's traditional foods, which are often served atop injera. This traditional Ethiopian flatbread, made with fermented teff flour, is soft and spongy with a hint of sourness. The batter is fermented for one to three days according to taste (it will become more sour the longer it sits). Cooked into a giant pancake, injera is used both as a base on which to serve cooked meats and vegetables, and as an edible utensil, for scooping up mouthfuls a bite at a time.]

Place the flour in a glass or ceramic bowl. Add 2 cups (475 ml) unchlorinated or filtered water and stir well. Cover with a clean tea towel and let sit, undisturbed, for 24 hours. The batter should have risen and bubbles should be forming. At this point it may be used, or, if you prefer a more sour flavor, allow the batter to sit for another 1 to 2 days.

When ready to cook, stir a pinch of salt into the batter. Grease a 12-inch (30.5 cm) or larger diameter frying pan with a very small amount of coconut oil and heat over medium heat. Pour just enough batter into the pan to cover the bottom of the pan. Cover with a lid. Bubbles will form and the top will start to dry out. Continue steaming the bread until the top is completely dry and the edges begin to curl, about 5 minutes. Transfer to a plate and repeat with the remaining batter, separating the injera with pieces of parchment paper to keep them from sticking together.

PREPARATION TIME: 15 MINUTES,
PLUS DOUGH RESTING TIME
COOKING TIME: 15 MINUTES
MAKES: 20 TORTILLAS

- 2 cups (240 g) masa harina
- ½ teaspoon kosher (coarse) salt
- 1½ cups (355 ml) hot water
- Cooking spray

In a medium bowl, combine the masa harina and salt. Pour in the water and stir to combine. Knead the dough for 1–2 minutes in the bowl. The dough is ready when it's smooth, no longer sticky, and easily forms a ball in your hands. Cover with plastic wrap (clingfilm) and let rest for 30 minutes.

Pinch off 2–3 tablespoons of dough and roll it between your hands to form a ball roughly the size of a golf ball.

Cut 2 squares of parchment paper to fit the width of a tortilla press. Place one sheet on the base of the tortilla press and coat with cooking spray. Place a dough ball on the press. Spray one side of the second parchment sheet and place it sprayed side down on the dough ball. Press the tortilla press almost fully closed to spread the tortilla to ⅛–¼ inch (3–6 mm) thick. Remove from the press, peel away the top sheet of parchment, flip the tortilla over onto your palm, and peel off the back sheet of parchment (reserve the parchment to reuse). Repeat with the remaining dough.

Heat a comal, cast-iron skillet, or griddle over medium-high heat. Cook the tortillas one at a time (or in a single layer if your pan is big enough) for 60–90 seconds on each side, until toasted and spotted with brown. As the tortillas are cooked, stack them up and wrap them in a clean tea towel. The tortillas will be a bit dry and brittle just off the griddle, but will continue to steam and soften inside the towel as you finish cooking the rest of the batch. Serve immediately.

PREPARATION TIME: 30 MINUTES,
PLUS RISING TIME
COOKING TIME: 30 MINUTES
MAKES: 8 BAGELS

- 1¼ cups (300 ml) warm water
  (110°F/43°C)
- 1 tablespoon sugar
- 1 packet (7 g/2¼ teaspoons) active
  dry yeast
- 3½ cups (475 g) bread (strong white)
  flour, plus more for kneading
- 1½ teaspoons salt
- 1 egg, beaten (optional)
- Optional toppings: coarse salt, sesame
  seeds, poppy seeds, minced garlic and/
  or onion

[New York's iconic Jewish bagel is traditionally covered with a "schmear" of cream cheese and lox.]

Place ½ cup (120 ml) of the warm water in a small bowl. Stir in the sugar and yeast and let sit for 5 minutes.

In a large bowl, whisk the flour and salt together. Add the yeast mixture and the remaining ¾ cup (180 ml) warm water. Stir to combine as much as possible; the dough will be very stiff. Turn out onto a floured surface and knead for 10 minutes, or until the dough is firm and smooth. Add the dough to a large oiled bowl and turn to coat. Cover with a damp tea towel and let the dough rise in a warm draft-free area until doubled in volume, about 1 hour. Punch down the dough and let rest for another 30 minutes.

Turn the dough out of the bowl and divide into 8 pieces. Shape each piece into a smooth ball by rolling with the palm of your hand on the work surface to bring all of the dough together. Press a finger into the center of the ball and stretch the bagel to resemble a doughnut shape. Place the bagels on a parchment-lined baking sheet and cover with a damp tea towel. Let rest for 15 minutes.

Meanwhile, bring a large pot of water to a rolling boil. Position a rack in the middle of the oven and preheat to 400°F (200°C/Gas Mark 6).

Drop the bagels into the boiling water. After the bagels rise to the top, let them cook for 2 minutes, then flip them and cook for 2 more minutes. Remove them with a slotted spoon and place on a parchment-lined baking sheet. Lightly beat the egg, if using, and brush the bagels with the egg wash, if desired. At this point the bagels can be left plain or covered with toppings of your choice.

Bake until golden brown, about 20 minutes. Cool on a wire rack before serving.

PREPARATION TIME: 25 MINUTES,
   PLUS RISING TIME
COOKING TIME: 25 MINUTES
MAKES: ABOUT 18 ROLLS

- 1 cup (240 ml) milk
- 2 tablespoons sugar
- 10 tablespoons (140 g) unsalted butter
- 1 teaspoon salt
- 1 packet (7 g/2¼ teaspoons) active
  dry yeast
- 1 egg
- 3 cups (390 g) all-purpose (plain) flour,
  plus more for kneading

In a small saucepan, scald the milk over medium heat. Remove from the heat and stir in the sugar, 3 tablespoons (45 g) of the butter, and the salt. Pour into a large bowl. Stir in the egg and combine well. Stir in the flour. Turn the dough out onto a floured surface and knead for 10 minutes. The dough should be soft and smooth. Melt the remaining 7 tablespoons (95 g) butter and use 1 tablespoon to butter a large bowl. Place the dough in the bowl and turn to coat with the butter. Cover loosely with a tea towel and let rise in a warm draft-free place until the dough has doubled in volume, about 1 hour.

Brush a 9 x 13-inch (23 x 33 cm) baking dish with 2 tablespoons of the melted butter. Punch down the dough and turn out onto a lightly floured surface. Roll the dough to a thickness of ½ inch (1.25 cm). Cut into rounds with a 3-inch (7.5 cm) round biscuit cutter, re-rolling scraps as necessary. Brush the tops with 2 more tablespoons of the melted butter and fold the rounds in half. Slightly pinch the corners of the dough together. Place close together in rows in the buttered baking dish, slightly overlapping, with the folded side down. Cover loosely with a tea towel and let rise for 1 hour.

Preheat the oven to 350°F (180°C/Gas Mark 4).

Bake the rolls until golden brown, 20–25 minutes. Remove from the oven and brush with the remaining melted butter. Serve warm.

PREPARATION TIME: 30 MINUTES,
    PLUS RISING TIME
COOKING TIME: 1 HOUR 50 MINUTES
MAKES: 8 LARGE PRETZELS

- 2 teaspoons active dry yeast
- 1 cup (240 ml) warm water (110°F/43°C)
- 2 tablespoons granulated sugar
- 1½ teaspoons salt
- 2½–3 cups (325–390 g) all-purpose (plain) flour
- 4 tablespoons baking soda (bicarbonate of soda)
- 1 tablespoon dark brown sugar
- 1 egg
- Coarse salt, for sprinkling

[German immigrants introduced pretzels to Pennsylvania, and today the state still produces the most pretzels in the country, often twisted by hand by Amish women. Made with a basic white bread dough, Amish pretzels get their distinctive flavor by being dipped in a water-lye solution before baking (the home cook uses a baking soda solution). For a savory snack, serve with mustard and beer. For breakfast or dessert, dip in melted butter.]

In a large bowl, sprinkle the yeast over the water and let sit for 5 minutes. Stir in the sugar, salt, and 2 cups (260 g) of the flour. Stir well. Add another ½ cup (65 g) flour. Turn out onto a floured surface and knead the dough for 5–8 minutes, adding more flour if necessary, to make a smooth, soft, slightly tacky dough. Add the dough to a large oiled bowl and turn to coat. Cover with a damp tea towel and let the dough rise in a warm draft-free area until doubled in volume, about 1 hour.

Divide the dough into 8 pieces. Roll each piece into a rope about 20 inches (50 cm) long. Form a pretzel shape by first forming a U shape, then bringing the arms of the U down and crossing them, twisting the cross and pressing the ends over the bottom of the U. Pinch the ends to seal. Place the pretzels on parchment-lined baking sheets, cover with a damp tea towel, and let rise for at least 20 and up to 30 minutes.

Preheat the oven to 425°F (220°C/Gas Mark 7).

In a large, wide pot, combine 2 quarts (2 liters) water, the baking soda (bicarbonate of soda), and brown sugar and bring to a boil. Reduce to a simmer. Using a skimmer or a slotted spoon, and working in batches if necessary (so as not to crowd the pot), lower the pretzels one at a time into the simmering water. Cook for 2 minutes per side. Remove the pretzels and place them on the baking sheets.

Whisk the egg with 1 tablespoon warm water. Brush the pretzels with the egg wash and sprinkle with coarse salt. Bake until dark golden brown, 12–15 minutes. Cool on wire racks.

SOFT PRETZELS

For the dough:

- 2 packets (7 g/2¼ teaspoons each) active dry yeast
- 2 cups (475 ml) warm water (110°F/43°C)
- ½ cup (100 g) granulated sugar
- 2 teaspoons salt
- 6½–7 cups (845–910 g) all-purpose (plain) flour
- 2 eggs
- 4 tablespoons (60 g) unsalted butter, melted and cooled

For the filling:

- 1 stick (115 g) butter, softened
- ½ cup (95 g) packed light brown sugar
- ½ cup (100 g) granulated sugar
- 1 tablespoon ground cinnamon

For the dough: In a large bowl, dissolve the yeast in the warm water. Stir in the sugar, salt, and 3 cups (390 g) flour. Stir well to combine. Stir in the eggs, one at a time. Stir in the melted butter. Stir in 3½ cups (455 g) flour. Turn the dough out onto a floured surface and knead until the dough comes together and is smooth, adding flour as necessary. The dough should be soft, not stiff, so don't add too much flour. Add the dough to a large oiled bowl and turn to coat. Cover with a damp tea towel, place in the refrigerator, and let the dough rise overnight.

The next morning, remove the dough from the refrigerator and punch it down. Leave it in a warm place to rise until the dough has risen somewhat (doesn't need to double), 1 or more hours.

For the filling: Place the dough on a work surface and roll to a rectangle about 15 x 20 inches (38 x 50 cm). Spread the softened butter over the top and sprinkle with both sugars and the cinnamon. Beginning with a long side, roll the dough up into a log. Pinch the seam together to seal. Cut the log crosswise into twelve 2-inch (5 cm) thick rolls and place them in a buttered 9 x 13-inch (23 x 33 cm) baking pan. Cover with a tea damp towel and let rise for 30 minutes.

Position a rack in the middle of the oven and preheat to 375°F (190°C/Gas Mark 5). Bake until golden brown, 15–20 minutes.

CINNAMON ROLLS

PREPARATION TIME: 40 MINUTES,
   PLUS RISING TIME
COOKING TIME: 25 MINUTES
MAKES: 30 BUNS

- 3 cups (710 ml) milk
- ¾ cup (150 g) sugar
- ⅔ cup (150 g) unsalted butter
- 2 packets (7 g/2¼ teaspoons each) active
  dry yeast
- 2 eggs, lightly beaten
- 1 tablespoon salt
- 8 cups (1 kg) all-purpose (plain) flour, plus
  more for kneading

[Meaning "twice baked" in German, Zweiback were brought to the Western states by Russian Mennonites (and are also known as Mennonite Buns). They can refer to twice-baked sweet bread made with eggs, like this recipe, or a type of roll in which two pieces of dough are baked together.]

In a medium saucepan, scald the milk. Remove from the heat and stir in the sugar and butter. Pour into a bowl and let cool to about 110°F (43°C). Add the yeast and let sit for about 5 minutes. Stir in the eggs.

In a large bowl, whisk together the salt and flour. Stir in the milk mixture. Turn out onto a floured surface and knead for 8–10 minutes, until the dough is smooth and soft, adding flour as necessary. Add the dough to a large oiled bowl and turn to coat. Cover with a damp tea towel and let the dough rise in a warm draft-free area until doubled in volume, about 1 hour.

Punch down the dough. Divide about two-thirds of the dough into 30 egg-size pieces, the other one-third into 30 walnut-size pieces. Place each small piece on top of a larger piece and poke a finger all of the way through both dough balls (this insures that the dough balls remain together during baking). Place the buns on two parchment-lined baking sheets and cover with a damp tea towel. Allow to rise for 30 minutes.

Position a rack in the middle of the oven and preheat to 375°F (190°C/Gas Mark 5).

Bake the buns until golden brown, about 20 minutes, switching racks halfway through.

PREPARATION TIME: 20 MINUTES
COOKING TIME: 35 MINUTES
SERVES: 10–12

For the crumb topping:
- 4 tablespoons all-purpose (plain) flour
- 4 tablespoons sugar
- ½ teaspoon ground cinnamon
- 4 tablespoons (60 g) butter

For the cake:
- 1½ cups (195 g) all-purpose (plain) flour
- 1 teaspoon baking powder
- ½ teaspoon salt
- 1 stick (115 g) unsalted butter, softened
- 1 cup (200 g) sugar
- 2 eggs, at room temperature
- ¼ cup (60 ml) sour cream
- ¼ cup (60 ml) milk
- ½ teaspoon pure vanilla or
  almond extract
- 2 cups (270 g) berries, such as
  marionberries, blackberries, or
  raspberries

Position a rack in the middle of the oven and preheat to 350°F (180°C/Gas Mark 4). Butter and flour a 9 x 13-inch (23 x 33 cm) baking pan.

For the crumb topping: In a bowl, combine the flour, sugar, and cinnamon. Cut in the butter (using a pastry/dough blender or two knives) until the mixture resembles breadcrumbs. Set aside.

For the cake: In a medium bowl, whisk together the flour, baking powder, and salt. In a large bowl, with an electric mixer, cream the butter and sugar until light and fluffy. Add the eggs, one at a time, beating well after each addition. Beat in the sour cream. Beat in half of the flour mixture, then the milk, then the remaining flour mixture and vanilla.

Pour half of the batter into the prepared pan. Scatter the berries over the batter. Pour the remaining batter over the berries and top with the crumb topping. Bake until a skewer inserted in the center comes out clean, 30–35 minutes. Let cool completely in the pan on a wire rack.

PREPARATION TIME: 20 MINUTES
COOKING TIME: 40 MINUTES
SERVES: 10–12

For the crumb:
- 2 sticks (225 g) unsalted butter
- 1 cup (190 g) packed dark brown sugar
- 2 teaspoons ground cinnamon
- ½ teaspoon salt
- ½ teaspoon almond extract
- 2½ cups (325 g) all-purpose (plain) flour

For the cake:
- 2 cups (260 g) all-purpose (plain) flour
- 1 teaspoon baking powder
- ½ teaspoon baking soda (bicarbonate of soda)
- ½ teaspoon salt
- 1 stick (115 g) unsalted butter, softened
- 1 cup (200 g) granulated sugar
- 2 eggs
- 1 teaspoon pure vanilla extract
- 1 cup (240 ml) sour cream

Position a rack in the middle of the oven and preheat to 350°F (180°C/Gas Mark 4). Grease a 9- or 10-inch (23 or 25 cm) tube pan.

For the crumb: In a small saucepan, melt the butter and pour into a medium bowl. Stir in the brown sugar, cinnamon, salt, and almond extract. Stir in the flour until well mixed. Set aside.

For the cake: In a medium bowl, sift the flour, baking powder, baking soda (bicarbonate of soda), and salt.

In a large bowl, with an electric mixer, cream the butter and granulated sugar until light and fluffy. Add the eggs, one at a time, blending well after each addition. Beat in the vanilla and sour cream. On low speed, beat in the flour mixture until well combined.

Pour half of the batter into the tube pan. Sprinkle one-third of the crumb mixture evenly over the top. Pour the other half of the batter over the crumb mix. Spread with a rubber spatula and cover with the remaining two-thirds crumb mixture. Bake until the top is browning and a skewer inserted in the center comes out clean, 30–40 minutes. Let the cake cool slightly in the pan, then turn out of the pan onto a wire rack to cool thoroughly before serving.

CRUMB COFFEE CAKE

PREPARATION TIME: 20 MINUTES
COOKING TIME: 1 HOUR
MAKES: 1 LOAF

- 2½ cups (325 g) all-purpose (plain) flour
- 1 teaspoon baking powder
- 1 teaspoon baking soda (bicarbonate of soda)
- 1 teaspoon salt
- 1 teaspoon ground cinnamon
- 2 eggs
- 1 cup (200 g) sugar
- ¾ cup (180 ml) vegetable oil
- 1 teaspoon pure vanilla extract
- 1¼ cups (340 g) mashed ripe bananas with brown spots, from approximately 3 bananas
- 1 cup (240 ml) buttermilk
- ¾ cup (75 g) walnuts or pecans (optional), toasted and chopped

Position a rack in the middle of the oven and preheat to 350°F (180°C/Gas Mark 4). Grease and flour a 9 x 5-inch (23 x 13 cm) loaf pan or line the pan with parchment paper.

In a medium bowl, sift the flour, baking powder, baking soda (bicarbonate of soda), salt, and cinnamon into a bowl. In a separate large bowl, whisk together the eggs, sugar, oil, and vanilla. Stir in the mashed bananas. Add the flour mixture and stir briefly. Stir in the buttermilk. Combine all, being careful not to overmix. Stir in the nuts, if using.

Pour the batter into the loaf pan. Bake until a skewer inserted in the center comes out clean, about 1 hour. Let the bread cool in the pan for 10 minutes, then turn out onto a wire rack to cool.

BANANA BREAD

PREPARATION TIME: 30 MINUTES
COOKING TIME: 40 MINUTES
SERVES: 8–10

- 3 Sandia green chilies, roasted and peeled (see Note, page 86)
- 3 Big Jim green chilies, roasted and peeled (see Note, page 86)
- 1 stick (115 g) unsalted butter, melted and cooled
- 1½ cups (180 g) cornmeal mix (self-rising cornmeal)
- 1 cup (130 g) all-purpose (plain) flour
- ½ teaspoon baking powder
- ¼ cup (50 g) packed light brown sugar
- 2½ cups (590 ml) buttermilk
- 2 eggs, lightly beaten

Cut the roasted chilies into ½-inch (1.25 cm) pieces.

Position a rack in the middle of the oven and preheat to 425°F (220°C/Gas Mark 7). Place 4 tablespoons melted butter in a 9-inch (23 cm) cast-iron skillet and place in the oven for 4 minutes, until the butter is foamy and golden.

Meanwhile, in a large bowl, whisk together the cornmeal mix, flour, baking powder, and brown sugar. In a separate bowl, whisk together the buttermilk, eggs, and remaining 4 tablespoons melted butter. Stir in the chopped green chilies. Make a well in the center of the dry ingredients, add the wet ingredients, and stir just until moistened. Pour the batter into the hot skillet with melted butter.

Bake until golden brown, 25–30 minutes. Let cool for 5 minutes in the pan, then turn out onto a cutting board and serve.

GREEN CHILI CORNBREAD

PEPPERONI BREAD

PREPARATION TIME: 35 MINUTES,
 PLUS RISING TIME
COOKING TIME: 30 MINUTES
SERVES: 8–10

- 1 teaspoon honey
- ¼ cup (60 ml) warm water (110°F/43°C)
- 1 packet (7 g/2¼ teaspoons) active dry yeast
- 1 cup (240 ml) warm milk (110°F/43°C)
- 1 tablespoon sugar
- 1 teaspoon salt
- 2 tablespoons olive oil
- 3 cups (390 g) all-purpose (plain) flour, plus more for kneading
- 12 oz (340 g) pepperoni sticks, cut into slices ½ inch (1.25 cm) thick
- 2 cups (225 g) shredded mozzarella cheese
- 1 egg
- 2 tablespoons grated Parmesan cheese

In a large bowl, whisk together the honey and warm water. Sprinkle the yeast over and let stand for 10 minutes, until bubbly.

Stir in the milk, sugar, salt, and oil. Stir in 1 cup (130 g) of the flour. Stir in the remaining 2 cups (260 g) flour and mix to form a dough. Turn the dough onto a lightly floured surface and knead until smooth and elastic, 8–10 minutes. Add the dough to a large oiled bowl and turn to coat. Cover with a damp tea towel and let the dough rise in a warm draft-free area until doubled in volume, about 1½ hours.

Position a rack in the middle of the oven and preheat to 375°F (190°C/Gas Mark 5). Grease a baking sheet.

Punch down the dough, turn out onto a lightly floured surface, and divide in half. Stretch and press each half into a rectangle about 12 x 8 inches (30 x 20 cm). About 2 inches (5 cm) in from each of the long edges of the dough rectangles, lay out the pepperoni slices in a row spanning the length of the dough. Sprinkle all with the mozzarella cheese. Roll up each dough like a jelly (Swiss) roll, pinching the sides together. Place seam side down on the baking sheet.

Whisk the egg with 1 tablespoon water. Brush the pepperoni rolls with the egg wash and sprinkle with the Parmesan. Bake until golden brown, 25–30 minutes. Let rest for 15 minutes before slicing into 1-inch (2.5 cm) pieces.

WHOLE WHEAT MUFFINS

PREPARATION TIME: 10 MINUTES
COOKING TIME: 25 MINUTES
MAKES: 12 MUFFINS

- 2 cups (240 g) whole wheat (wholemeal) flour
- 1 teaspoon baking powder
- 1 teaspoon baking soda (bicarbonate of soda)
- 1 teaspoon salt
- 1 cup (240 ml) buttermilk
- 1 egg
- ⅓ cup (110 g) molasses
- 2 tablespoons (30 g) butter, melted

Position a rack in the middle of the oven and preheat to 350°F (180°C/Gas Mark 4). Grease 12 cups of a muffin tin or line with cupcake papers (cases).

In a large bowl, whisk together the flour, baking powder, baking soda (bicarbonate of soda), and salt. In a medium bowl, whisk the buttermilk, egg, molasses, and melted butter. Add the wet ingredients to the dry and stir just until combined. Do not overmix.

Spoon the batter into the muffin cups. Bake until the muffin tops spring back when lightly pressed, 20–25 minutes. Serve warm.

CORN MUFFINS

PREPARATION TIME: 10 MINUTES
COOKING TIME: 20 MINUTES
MAKES: 12 MUFFINS

- 1 cup (135 g) cornmeal
- 1 cup (130 g) all-purpose (plain) flour
- ½ cup (100 g) sugar
- 2 teaspoons baking powder
- ½ teaspoon salt
- 2 eggs
- 1 cup (240 ml) milk
- ⅓ cup (75 g) butter, melted and cooled

Position a rack in the middle of the oven and preheat to 350°F (180°C/Gas Mark 4). Grease 12 cups of a muffin tin or line with cupcake papers (cases).

In a large bowl, whisk together the cornmeal, flour, sugar, baking powder, and salt. In a medium bowl, whisk together the eggs, milk, and melted butter. Add the wet ingredients to the dry and blend well.

Spoon the batter into the muffin cups. Bake until the muffin tops are light golden brown and a skewer inserted in the center comes out clean, 15–20 minutes.

PREPARATION TIME: 20 MINUTES,
  PLUS CHILLING TIME
COOKING TIME: 20 MINUTES,
  PLUS SWEET POTATO BAKING TIME
MAKES: 12 BISCUITS

- 2¾ cups (358 g) all-purpose (plain) flour
- ¾ teaspoon salt
- 4 teaspoons baking powder
- 1 stick (115 g) cold butter, cut into ½-inch (1.25 cm) dice
- 1 cup mashed sweet potato (see Note), chilled
- ¾ cup (180 ml) cold buttermilk
- 2 tablespoons heavy (whipping) cream (optional)

Note:
  To get enough sweet potato for this recipe, bake 1 large (12 oz/340 g) sweet potato (see Sweet Potato Pie on page 296).

[Adding mashed sweet potatoes to biscuit dough can be traced to Caribbean influences on Southern cooking. Wheat, and therefore flour, was scarce in the islands, and so starchy vegetables were often used to make or fill out breads and other baked goods. Sweet potato biscuits are denser and richer than basic buttermilk biscuits and have a gorgeous sunset color.]

Preheat the oven to 450°F (230°C/Gas Mark 8).

In a medium bowl, combine the flour, salt, and baking powder. Add the cold butter and blend in quickly with your fingertips until small clumps form. Place the bowl in the freezer (or refrigerator) for 10 minutes to chill.

Gently stir the mashed sweet potato and buttermilk into the dough, just until the mixture comes together. Turn the dough onto a floured surface and knead 5–6 times, until just combined. Flour your hands and press the dough (or roll with a rolling pin) into a rectangle about ½ inch (1.25 cm) thick. Cut into 2-inch (5 cm) rounds with a biscuit cutter and place on an ungreased baking sheet. Gently reshape the remaining dough and cut out more biscuits.

If desired, brush the tops of biscuits with cream. Bake until lightly browned, 16–18 minutes. Serve warm.

SWEET POTATO BISCUITS

MORNING GLORY MUFFINS

PREPARATION TIME: 20 MINUTES
COOKING TIME: 30 MINUTES
MAKES: 12 MUFFINS

- 2 cups (260 g) all-purpose (plain) flour
- 1 cup (200 g) sugar
- 2 teaspoons baking soda (bicarbonate of soda)
- 2 teaspoons ground cinnamon
- ½ teaspoon salt
- 2 cups (220 g) peeled and grated carrots
- 1 large apple, grated
- 1 cup (150 g) pineapple chunks
- ½ cup (80 g) raisins
- ½ cup (50 g) unsweetened shredded coconut (desiccated)
- ½ cup (60 g) chopped walnuts or sunflower seeds
- 3 eggs
- ¾ cup (180 ml) vegetable oil
- 1 teaspoon pure vanilla extract

Position a rack in the middle of the oven and preheat to 350°F (180°C/Gas Mark 4). Grease 12 cups of a muffin tin or line with cupcake paper (cases).

In a large bowl, whisk together the flour, sugar, baking soda (bicarbonate of soda), cinnamon, and salt. Stir in the carrots, apple, pineapple, raisins, coconut, and walnuts. In a medium bowl, whisk together the eggs, oil, and vanilla. Add the egg mixture to the flour mixture and stir until combined.

Divide the batter among the muffin cups. They will be very full. Bake until the muffin tops are golden brown, about 30 minutes. Let cool in the pan until cool enough to handle, then transfer to a wire rack.

BLUEBERRY MUFFINS

PREPARATION TIME: 15 MINUTES
COOKING TIME: 25 MINUTES
MAKES: 12 MUFFINS

- 2 cups (260 g) all-purpose (plain) flour
- 1 teaspoon baking powder
- ½ teaspoon baking soda (bicarbonate of soda)
- ¼ teaspoon freshly grated nutmeg
- ½ teaspoon salt
- 1 stick (115 g) unsalted butter, melted
- ¾ cup (150 g) sugar
- 2 eggs
- 1 teaspoon pure vanilla extract
- ½ cup (120 ml) buttermilk
- 2¼ cups (335 g) blueberries
- Turbinado sugar, for topping

Position a rack in the middle of the oven and preheat to 375°F (190°C/Gas Mark 5). Grease 12 cups of a muffin tin or line with cupcake papers (cases).

In a large bowl, whisk together the flour, baking powder, baking soda (bicarbonate of soda), nutmeg, and salt.

In a separate bowl, whisk the melted butter with the sugar. Whisk in the eggs, one at a time, and combine well. Stir in the vanilla and buttermilk. Pour the wet ingredients into the flour mixture and stir well to combine. Fold in the blueberries.

Scoop the batter into the muffin cups. Sprinkle with turbinado sugar. Bake until the muffin tops are golden brown and a skewer inserted into the center comes out clean, 20–25 minutes. Let the muffins cool slightly in the pan, until they are cool enough to handle, then transfer to a wire rack.

CRANBERRY MUFFINS

PREPARATION TIME: 10 MINUTES
COOKING TIME: 30 MINUTES
MAKES: 12 MUFFINS

- 3 cups (390 g) all-purpose (plain) flour
- ½ cup (100 g) sugar
- ½ teaspoon salt
- 4 teaspoons baking powder
- 1 teaspoon grated lime zest
- 2 eggs
- 1 cup (240 ml) buttermilk
- 3 tablespoons (45 g) butter, melted and cooled
- 1 cup (100 g) fresh cranberries, roughly chopped

[Wisconsin is the country's leading cranberry producer.]

Position a rack in the middle of the oven and preheat to 400°F (200°C/Gas Mark 6). Line 12 cups of a muffin tin with cupcake papers (cases).

In a large bowl, combine the flour, sugar, salt, baking powder, and lime zest. In a medium bowl, combine the eggs, buttermilk, and melted butter. Add the wet ingredients to the dry and stir to combine, but do not overmix. Gently fold in the cranberries.

Divide the batter among the muffin cups, filling them about two-thirds full. Bake until the muffins are golden on top and a skewer inserted in the center of a muffin comes out clean, 22–26 minutes. Let the muffins cool in the pan for 5 minutes, then transfer to a wire rack.

SUNFLOWER SEED MUFFINS

PREPARATION TIME: 20 MINUTES
COOKING TIME: 20 MINUTES
MAKES: 12 MUFFINS

- 1¼ cups (175 g) sunflower seeds
- 1 cup (120 g) whole wheat (wholemeal) flour
- ½ teaspoon salt
- 1 teaspoon baking powder
- 1 teaspoon baking soda (bicarbonate of soda)
- ½ teaspoon ground cinnamon
- 2 tablespoons sugar
- 1 egg
- 3 tablespoons honey
- 3 tablespoons (45 g) butter, melted
- ¾ cup (180 ml) milk
- ¾ cup (125 g) raisins

[Sunflowers were one of the earliest cultivated crops in North America. After European settlement, they fell out of favor before being reintroduced. Today, sunflowers are grown primarily as a source of healthy, high-heat cooking oil, but they are also eaten whole as a snack, ground into spreads, and incorporated in breads, salads, and other dishes. North and South Dakota grow most of the sunflower seeds produced in this country.]

Position a rack in the middle of the oven and preheat to 375°F (190°C/Gas Mark 5). Grease 12 cups of a muffin tin or line with cupcake papers (cases).

Grind the sunflower seeds in a blender or food processor, using the pulse setting, until coarsely ground. Set aside.

In a large bowl, whisk together the flour, ground sunflower seeds, salt, baking powder, baking soda (bicarbonate of soda), cinnamon, and sugar. In a small bowl, whisk together the egg, honey, melted butter, and milk. Add the wet ingredients to the dry and stir to combine. Stir in the raisins.

Spoon the batter into the muffin cups. Bake until the muffin tops are golden brown and spring back when lightly touched, 15–20 minutes. Transfer to a wire rack to cool.

PREPARATION TIME: 10 MINUTES,
   PLUS CHILLING TIME
COOKING TIME: 50 MINUTES
MAKES: ABOUT 24 DOUGHNUTS

- 1 cup (240 ml) apple cider
- 3½ cups (455 g) all-purpose (plain) flour, plus more for rolling
- 1 teaspoon salt
- 2 teaspoons baking powder
- 1 teaspoon baking soda (bicarbonate of soda)
- 1 teaspoon ground cinnamon
- ½ teaspoon freshly grated nutmeg
- 4 tablespoons (60 g) butter, softened
- 1 cup (200 g) sugar
- 1 egg
- ½ cup (120 ml) buttermilk
- Vegetable oil, for deep-frying
- Cinnamon sugar (optional): 1¼ cups (250 g) sugar plus 2 teaspoons ground cinnamon

[Cider-flavored doughnuts are beloved in the Hudson Valley's bucolic orchards, where rural and urban New Yorkers alike swarm each fall to pick the fall crop, feast on these, warm from the fryer, and wash them down with cups of hot apple cider. They are often sold at farmers' markets throughout the Northeast, where children and adults enjoy them each weekend – offered with sugar and without.]

In a small saucepan, cook the apple cider over medium heat until reduced to ½ cup (120 ml), about 15 minutes. Remove from the heat and set aside.

Sift the flour, salt, baking powder, baking soda (bicarbonate of soda), cinnamon, and nutmeg into a large bowl.

In another large bowl, with an electric mixer, cream the butter and sugar. Add the egg and blend well. Add the reduced cider and the buttermilk. The mixture will look curdled, but that's normal. Add the flour mixture and blend just until mixed. Cover the dough well and chill for 1 hour.

Pour 3 inches (7.5 cm) oil into a large heavy pot or deep-fryer and heat to 375°F (190°C).

While the oil is heating, on a floured surface, roll the dough to ½–¾ inch (1.25–2 cm) thick. Cut with a 3-inch (7.5 cm) doughnut cutter or two biscuit cutters (one 3-inch/7.5 cm and one 1¼-inch /3.2 cm), re-rolling scraps as necessary.

Working in batches, add the doughnuts and doughnut holes to the hot oil (do not crowd the pot) and cook for 2–4 minutes per side (less for the holes), until dark golden brown. Drain on paper towels. Cool until just warm. Toss in cinnamon sugar, if desired.

PREPARATION TIME: 25 MINUTES,
  PLUS RISING TIME
COOKING TIME: 1 HOUR 15 MINUTES
MAKES: 48 DOUGHNUTS

- 1 lb (455 g) russet (baking) potatoes, peeled and cut into large chunks
- 1½ cups (355 ml) milk, warmed to 110°F (43°C)
- 2 packets (7 g/2¼ teaspoons each) active dry yeast
- ½ cup (120 ml) vegetable oil
- ½ cup (100 g) granulated sugar
- 2 eggs
- 2 teaspoons salt
- 7 cups (910 g) all-purpose (plain) flour
- Vegetable oil or lard, for deep-frying
- 3 cups (360 g) powdered (icing) sugar
- 2 teaspoons pure vanilla extract

Place the potato chunks in a medium saucepan and add cold water to cover. Bring to a boil, then reduce the heat to medium and cook until tender, 10–15 minutes. Reserving ½ cup (120 ml) of the cooking liquid, drain the potatoes. Mash well and set aside.

In a large bowl, combine the reserved potato water and milk. Add the yeast and stir to dissolve. Let sit for 5 minutes, until the yeast is bubbling. Stir in the oil, sugar, and eggs. Stir in the salt and enough flour to make a soft dough. Add the dough to a large oiled bowl and turn to coat. Cover with a clean tea towel and let the dough rise in a warm draft-free area until doubled in volume, about 1 hour or more.

Punch down the dough and let rise another 20 minutes. Turn the dough out onto a floured surface and roll to a thickness of ½ inch (1.25 cm). Cut out doughnuts using a 3-inch (7.5 cm) doughnut cutter or two biscuit cutters (one 3-inch/7.5 cm and one 1¼-inch/3.2 cm) dipped in flour.

Pour 6 inches (15 cm) oil into a large heavy pot or deep-fryer and heat to 375°F (190°C).

Working in batches, add a few doughnuts at a time to the hot oil (do not crowd the pot) and cook until they are golden, 1–2 minutes per side. Drain on paper towels.

To make a glaze, whisk together the powdered (icing) sugar, ¼ cup (60 ml) water, and the vanilla. Dip the doughnuts in the glaze while they're still warm.

BUTTERMILK DOUGHNUTS

PREPARATION TIME: 20 MINUTES,
　PLUS OVERNIGHT CHILLING
COOKING TIME: 25 MINUTES
MAKES: ABOUT 24 DOUGHNUTS
　PLUS HOLES

- 3¼ cups (423 g) all-purpose (plain) flour
- 2 teaspoons baking powder
- 1 teaspoon baking soda (bicarbonate of soda)
- 1 teaspoon salt
- ½ teaspoon freshly grated nutmeg
- 2 eggs
- ¾ cup (150 g) sugar
- 2 tablespoons lard or butter, melted
- ¾ cup (180 ml) buttermilk
- 1 teaspoon pure vanilla extract (optional)
- 2 quarts (2 liters) lard or vegetable oil, for deep-frying
- Sugar, cinnamon sugar, or powdered (icing) sugar, for coating (optional)

Sift the flour, baking powder, baking soda (bicarbonate of soda), salt, and nutmeg into a bowl.

In a separate large bowl, beat the eggs until foamy, whisk in the sugar gradually, and mix well. Whisk in the lard or butter, buttermilk and vanilla. Mix in the flour mixture a bit at a time, stirring well to combine. Scrape the dough into a clean container. Cover and chill in the refrigerator overnight.

Line a baking sheet with parchment and lightly dust with flour. Work with one half of the dough at a time (keep the other half chilled). On a very lightly floured surface (use as little flour as possible; the dough should be sticky), roll the dough to a thickness of about ⅓ inch (8 mm). Cut with a 3-inch (7.5 cm) doughnut cutter or two biscuit cutters (one 3-inch/7.5 cm and one 1¼-inch/3.2 cm). Place the doughnuts on the lined baking sheet. Repeat with the remaining dough while the oil is heating.

In a large heavy pot or deep-fryer, heat the lard or oil to 375°F (190°C).

Working in batches (do not crowd the pot), fry the doughnuts and the holes separately. The doughnuts will take about 2 minutes or a little less per side. The holes cook quickly; turn them as soon as you add them to the oil.

Drain the doughnuts on paper towels. Eat plain or tossed with sugar.

BUTTERMILK DOUGHNUTS

PREPARATION TIME: 20 MINUTES,
  PLUS RISING TIME
COOKING TIME: 40 MINUTES
MAKES: 12 DOUGHNUTS AND HOLES

For the doughnuts:
- 2½ cups (325 g) all-purpose (plain) flour
- ½ teaspoon salt
- 3 tablespoons granulated sugar
- 1 packet (7 g/2¼ teaspoons) active
  dry yeast
- 1 egg
- 1 egg yolk
- 1 cup (240 ml) milk
- 2 tablespoons (30 g) butter, melted
- ½ teaspoon pure vanilla extract
- Vegetable oil or lard, for deep-frying

For the glaze:
- 1¾ cups (210 g) powdered (icing) sugar
- 3 tablespoons milk
- ¼ teaspoon pure vanilla extract

For the doughnuts: In a large bowl, whisk together the flour, salt, sugar, and yeast. In a medium bowl, whisk together the whole egg, egg yolk, milk, melted butter, and vanilla. Stir the milk mixture into the flour mixture. Turn the dough out onto a floured surface and knead for about 5 minutes, until the dough is smooth. Do not add too much extra flour; the dough should be soft. Add the dough to a large oiled bowl and turn to coat. Cover with a damp tea towel and let the dough rise in a warm draft-free area until doubled in volume, about 1½ to 2 hours.

On a lightly floured surface, roll the dough to about ⅓ inch (8 mm) thick. Cut into doughnuts using a 3-inch (7.5 cm) doughnut cutter or biscuit cutters (one 3-inch/7.5 cm and one 1¼-inch/3.2 cm), re-rolling scraps as necessary. Lightly dust a baking sheet with flour. Set the doughnuts and holes on the baking sheet, leaving several inches (7–8 cm) between them. Cover and let rise for 20 minutes.

Pour 3 inches (7.5 cm) oil into a large heavy pot or deep-fryer and heat to 375°F (190°C).

Working in batches, fry the doughnuts until golden, about 1 minute per side (less for doughnut holes). Drain on paper towels.

For the glaze: Sift the powdered (icing) sugar into a medium bowl. Whisk in the milk and vanilla. While the doughnuts are still warm, dip them into the glaze. Transfer to a wire rack to cool.

PACZKI

PREPARATION TIME: 3 HOURS
COOKING TIME: 35 MINUTES
MAKES: 8 PACZKI

- 1 cup (240 ml) milk, warmed to 110°F (43°C)
- 1 packet (7 g/2¼ teaspoons) active dry yeast
- ⅓ cup (65 g) plus 1 teaspoon sugar, plus more for coating
- 2½ cups (325 g) all-purpose (plain) flour
- 1 egg
- 1 egg yolk
- 3 tablespoons (45 g) butter, melted
- ½ teaspoon salt
- Oil or lard, for deep-frying
- 1 cup (240 ml) jam

[These Polish jam-filled donuts are popular in Chicago, Illinois—home to the largest Polish community outside Poland.]

Pour the warmed milk into the bowl of a stand mixer fitted with the paddle attachment. Add the yeast and 1 teaspoon of the sugar. Stir to combine. Let sit for a few minutes, until foamy.

Add 1 cup (130 g) of the flour, mixing well on medium speed and scraping the bowl down. Shut off the mixer and let sit for 10 minutes. With the mixer on medium speed, add the whole egg, egg yolk, and melted butter. Add the salt and remaining ⅓ cup (65 g) sugar. Mix well. With the mixer on low speed, add the remaining 1½ cups (195 g) flour, a little at a time, beating until the dough is stiff. Transfer the dough to a floured surface and knead lightly until smooth.

Add the dough to a large oiled bowl and turn to coat. Cover with a damp tea towel and let the dough rise in a warm draft-free area for 1 hour; the dough will not quite double in size.

Punch down the dough and cut the dough into 8 pieces. Form into rolls, place on a greased baking sheet, and cover with a damp tea towel. Let rise for 1 hour.

Add 3 inches (7.5 cm) oil or lard to a large heavy pot or deep-fryer and heat to 375°F (190°C). Working in batches, add the *paczki* a few at a time, being careful not to crowd them, and fry to a deep golden brown, 2–3 minutes per side.

Drain on paper towels. When the *paczki* are cool enough to handle, using a pastry bag with a plain tip, pipe jam into the center of each one.

Toss in sugar to coat and serve.

MAINE POTATO DOUGHNUTS

PREPARATION TIME: 20 MINUTES
COOKING TIME: 25 MINUTES
MAKES: ABOUT 18 DOUGHNUTS

- 2¼ cups (293 g) all-purpose (plain) flour
- 1 teaspoon baking powder
- 1 teaspoon baking soda (bicarbonate of soda)
- ½ teaspoon salt
- ½ teaspoon freshly grated nutmeg
- 4 tablespoons (60 g) butter, softened
- ¾ cup (150 g) sugar
- 1 egg
- 1 cup (210 g) plain mashed potatoes (see page 256)
- ¼ cup (60 ml) buttermilk
- Sugar or cinnamon sugar, for coating (optional)
- Vegetable oil, for deep-frying

Sift the flour, baking powder, baking soda (bicarbonate of soda), salt, and nutmeg into a bowl.

In a stand mixer fitted with the paddle attachment, cream the butter and sugar until light and fluffy. Beat in the egg. On low speed, beat in the mashed potatoes and buttermilk. Blend just until combined. Beat in the flour mixture. Do not overmix. Turn the dough out onto a floured surface, cover, and let sit for 15 minutes.

Pour 3 inches (7.5 cm) oil into a large heavy pot or deep-fryer and heat to 375°F (190°C).

While the oil is heating, on a floured surface, roll out the dough to a thickness of ½ inch (1.25 cm). Cut the doughnuts using a 3-inch (7.5 cm) doughnut cutter or two biscuit cutters (one 3-inch/7.5 cm and one 1¼-inch/3.2 cm), re-rolling scraps as necessary. Working in batches of 3 or 4, add the doughnuts to the hot oil (do not crowd the pot) and cook until golden brown, 2–4 minutes per side. Drain on paper towels. If desired, toss the doughnuts in sugar or cinnamon sugar.

FUNNEL CAKES

PREPARATION TIME: 5 MINUTES
COOKING TIME: 20 MINUTES
MAKES: ABOUT 8 CAKES

- 2 cups (260 g) all-purpose (plain) flour
- 1 teaspoon baking powder
- ½ teaspoon ground cinnamon
- 1 teaspoon salt
- 2 eggs
- 1¼ cups (295 ml) milk
- 2 tablespoons granulated sugar
- Vegetable oil, for deep-frying
- Powdered (icing) sugar, for dusting

Sift the flour, baking powder, cinnamon, and salt into a large bowl. In a medium bowl, whisk together the eggs, milk, and sugar. Add the milk mixture to the flour mixture and mix well.

Pour 3 inches (7.5 cm) oil into a large heavy pot or deep-fryer and heat to 375°F (190°C).

Fill a funnel with a ½-inch (1.25 cm) wide opening with about ½ cup (120 ml) batter, keeping a finger over the hole. Hold the funnel over the hot oil and starting from the center, make overlapping concentric circles of batter in the hot oil, enough to make the cake about 6 inches (15 cm) in diameter. Fry on both sides until golden brown, about 2 minutes per side. Drain on paper towels. Dust with powdered (icing) sugar. Serve warm.

PREPARATION TIME: 35 MINUTES,
  PLUS RISING TIME
COOKING TIME: 1 HOUR
MAKES: 12 FRITTERS

For the fritters:
- Dough from Glazed Yeasted Doughnuts
  (page 446), made through the first rising
- 4 tart apples
- 1 tablespoon cider vinegar
- 4 tablespoons (60 g) butter
- 1 tablespoon ground cinnamon
- ½ teaspoon freshly grated nutmeg
- ½ cup (100 g) granulated sugar
- ¼ cup (60 ml) apple cider
- Vegetable oil, for deep-frying

For the glaze:
- 1¼ cups (150 g) powdered (icing) sugar
- 3 tablespoons milk
- 1½ teaspoons pure vanilla extract
- Pinch of salt

For the fritters: Make the doughnut dough through the first rising as directed.

Peel and dice the apples into ¼-inch (6 mm) pieces, tossing them in a bowl with the vinegar as you work.

In a large frying pan, melt the butter over medium-high heat. Add the apples, sprinkle with the cinnamon, nutmeg, and sugar, and add the cider. Cook, stirring, until the apples are tender and the juices are almost completely reduced, 10–12 minutes. Set aside to cool.

On a heavily floured surface, roll the doughnut dough to about a ½ inch (1.25 cm) thick. Spread the cooled apples over one-half of the dough and fold the other half of dough over. Pinch the edges together. With a sharp knife cut the filled dough on the diagonal one way and then the other in roughly ½-inch (1.25 cm) slices. Scoop the dough up and turn it over. Slice again, to roughly combine the apples with the dough. The combination will feel soft and slippery. Dust with more flour. Using floured hands, mold the cut dough and apples into 12 pieces. Flatten the pieces with the palm of your hand and place on a lightly floured tray. Cover the fritters with a tea towel and let rise for about 30 minutes.

Pour 5 inches (13 cm) oil into a large heavy pot or deep-fryer and heat to 375°F (190°C).

Working in batches of a few at a time, add the fritters to the hot oil (do not crowd the pot) and cook until golden brown, about 1 minute per side. Drain on paper towels.

For the glaze: Sift the powdered (icing) sugar into a bowl. Whisk in the milk, vanilla, and salt. While the fritters are still warm, dip them in the glaze. Cool on a wire rack.

CHURROS

PREPARATION TIME: 10 MINUTES
COOKING TIME: 15 MINUTES
MAKES: 36 CHURROS

- 1 stick plus 1 tablespoon (130 g) unsalted butter, melted
- 1½ teaspoons kosher (coarse) salt
- 5 teaspoons ground cinnamon
- 1½ teaspoons pure vanilla extract
- 3¼ cups (422 g) all-purpose (plain) flour
- 2 eggs
- 3 cups (600 g) sugar
- Vegetable oil, for deep-frying

In a medium saucepan, whisk together 3¼ cups (770 ml) water, the butter, salt, 1 teaspoon of the cinnamon, and vanilla and bring to a boil over medium-high heat. Remove from the heat and add the flour all at once. Return to low heat and mix well with a wooden spoon until a smooth dough forms. Continue to cook the dough to dry out, stirring constantly, another 5 minutes. Remove from the heat and beat in the eggs, one at a time, completely incorporating the first before adding the second. Place the dough in a 1-gallon (1.5-liter) piping bag (or a plastic food bag) fitted with a ³/₈-inch (9.5 mm) star tip and set aside.

In a large bowl, combine the sugar and remaining 4 teaspoons cinnamon.

Pour 2 inches (5 cm) oil into a large heavy pot or deep-fryer and heat to 400°F (200°C).

Working in 6 batches of 6, pipe 6-inch (15 cm) long strips of dough directly into the hot oil. Cook, turning once, until golden brown, about 2 minutes total. Remove each churro with tongs or a slotted spoon, and place directly into the large bowl of cinnamon sugar. Toss well to coat thoroughly. Shake excess sugar from the churro and set aside. Serve warm.

UTAH SCONES

PREPARATION TIME: 30 MINUTES, PLUS RISING TIME
COOKING TIME: 10 MINUTES
MAKES: 12 SCONES

- 1¼ cup (295 ml) warm water (110°F/43°C)
- ⅓ cup (65 g) sugar
- 2 packets active dry yeast (7 g/2¼ teaspoons each)
- 1 egg, beaten
- ⅓ cup (80 ml) vegetable oil
- 1½ teaspoons salt
- 3½ cups (455 g) all-purpose (plain) flour, plus more for kneading
- Vegetable oil or lard, for deep-frying

[The ubiquitous Utah scone bears little resemblance to the European pastry of the same name. Rather, this is a fry bread made with yeasted dough. Serve with butter and Utah honey drizzled over the top.]

Place the warm water in a large bowl. Stir in the sugar and yeast and let sit until bubbly, about 10 minutes.

Stir in the egg and oil. Add the salt and 2 cups (260 g) of the flour and beat with a wooden spoon for 2 minutes. Stir in the remaining 1½ cups (195 g) flour. Turn out onto a lightly floured surface and knead for about 5 minutes. The dough should be elastic and smooth. Add the dough to a large oiled bowl and turn to coat. Cover with a damp tea towel and let the dough rise in a warm draft-free area until doubled in volume, 30–40 minutes.

Punch down the dough and divide into 12 equal pieces. Roll each about ¼ inch (6 mm) thick.

Pour 2 inches (5 cm) oil or lard into a large deep frying pan and heat to 375°F (190°C).

Working in batches, fry the scones until puffed and golden, 1–2 minutes per side. Drain on paper towels.

CHURROS

BEIGNETS

PREPARATION TIME: 30 MINUTES,
   PLUS DOUGH CHILLING TIME
COOKING TIME: 30 MINUTES
MAKES: ABOUT 30 BEIGNETS

- 1 packet (7 g/2¼ teaspoons) active dry yeast
- 1½ cups (355 ml) warm water (110°F/43°C)
- ½ cup (100 g) granulated sugar
- 1 cup (240 ml) milk
- 2 eggs, lightly beaten
- 1 teaspoon salt
- 4 tablespoons (60 g) butter
- 6½–7 cups (910–980 g) bread (strong white) flour
- Vegetable oil, for deep-frying
- Powdered (icing) sugar, sifted, for dusting

[These deep-fried, sugar-dusted, and light-as-air beignets are popular in New Orleans, Louisiana, and served with chicory coffee.]

In a stand mixer fitted with a dough hook, combine the yeast, ½ cup (120 ml) of the warm water, and 1 teaspoon of the granulated sugar. Let stand for 10 minutes. Add the milk, eggs, salt, and remaining granulated sugar.

Add the butter to the remaining 1 cup (240 ml) warm water and stir to melt. Add to the yeast mixture. On low speed, slowly beat in 4 cups (540 g) of the flour until smooth, 3–4 minutes. Increase the speed to medium and slowly add the remaining 2½ cups (335 g) flour. Beat until a sticky dough forms, 3–4 minutes. If the dough is too sticky to handle, add the remaining ½ cup (65 g) flour. Transfer the dough to a lightly greased bowl and turn to grease the top. Cover with plastic wrap (clingfilm) and refrigerate for 4 hours.

Turn the dough out onto a floured surface. Roll out to a rectangle ¼–½ inch (6–12 mm) thick. Cut into 2-inch (5 cm) squares.

Pour 3 inches (7.5 cm) oil into a large heavy pot or deep-fryer and heat to 360°F (182°C).

Working in batches of 3 or 4, fry the beignets, turning, until golden brown, 4–6 minutes total. Drain on paper towels. Dust generously with powdered (icing) sugar and serve hot.

SOPAPILLAS

PREPARATION TIME: 40 MINUTES
COOKING TIME: 45 MINUTES
SERVES: ABOUT 24 SOPAPILLAS

- 4 cups (520 g) all-purpose (plain) flour
- 1 tablespoon baking powder
- 1 teaspoon salt
- ½ cup (100 g) lard, diced
- 1⅔ cups (395 ml) milk
- Vegetable oil, for deep-frying
- 1 cup (335 g) honey
- 1 cup (125 g) toasted and chopped pecans

In a large bowl, whisk together the flour, baking powder, and salt. Using your fingertips, work the lard into the flour mixture until it resembles coarse sand. Add the milk and mix until the dough roughly comes together in a ball. On a well-floured surface, knead the dough 10–12 times, adding more flour as needed, until a moist, yet smooth dough forms (dough should be soft but not sticky). Cover the dough with plastic wrap (clingfilm) and let rest for 15 minutes.

Cut the dough into quarters. Working with one piece at a time—keep the other 3 pieces covered with the plastic wrap (clingfilm)—roll out the dough on a well-floured surface into a rectangle about ⅛ inch (3 mm) thick. Cut the dough in 2-inch (5 cm) squares. (Discard any dough that cannot be used after the first roll.) Repeat with remaining 3 pieces of dough.

Pour 2 inches (5 cm) oil into a large heavy pot or Dutch oven (casserole) and heat to 360°F (182°C). Working in batches of 3–4, carefully slide squares of dough into the oil. They should puff up quickly. Let the sopapillas cook until lightly golden, about 2 minutes on each side. Drain on paper towels. Serve drizzled with honey and topped with pecans.

BEIGNETS

CHICAGO STEAKHOUSE RUB

PREPARATION TIME: 5 MINUTES
MAKES: 4 TABLESPOONS

- 1 tablespoon mustard powder
- 2 teaspoons garlic powder
- 2 teaspoons salt
- 2 teaspoons freshly ground black pepper
- 1 teaspoon smoked sweet Spanish paprika
- ½ teaspoon cayenne pepper
- ½ teaspoon dried thyme

[Allow seasoned steaks to rest for 15 minutes before grilling.]

Mix all together and store airtight, for up to 1 year.

ALABAMA DRY RUB

PREPARATION TIME: 5 MINUTES
MAKES: 5 TABLESPOONS

- 2 tablespoons plus 2 teaspoons salt
- 2 tablespoons dark brown sugar
- 1 tablespoon paprika
- 1 teaspoon garlic powder
- 1 teaspoon onion powder
- 1 teaspoon freshly ground black pepper
- ½ teaspoon mustard powder

Mix all together and store airtight, for up to 1 year.

'INAMONA

PREPARATION TIME: DEPENDS ON HOW
  MUCH YOU ARE MAKING
COOKING TIME: 2 HOURS 30 MINUTES
MAKES: AS MUCH AS YOU'D LIKE

- Kukui nuts (candlenuts)
- Hawaiian red sea salt

Preheat the oven to 325°F (160°C/Gas Mark 3).

Dump the kukui nuts into a deep basin of water and discard any that float. Drain the remaining nuts and arrange in an even layer on rimmed baking sheets. Bake for 1 hour 30 minutes. Let the nuts cool completely.

Now get cracking: Tap each nut hard with a hammer to break the covering and extract the nut meat inside, using a fork or skewer. Give each nut a sniff as you crack it: If it smells bad, discard. Once all the meats are removed, lay them on a clean baking sheet and bake for another hour at 325°F (160°C/Gas Mark 3) or until deep golden-brown. Set aside to cool.

Transfer the cooled nut meats to a food processor (or mortar and pestle) and pulse or crush until roughly ground. Add Hawaiian red salt to taste (the 'inamona should be quite salty). Store the 'inamona in small airtight jars or resealable plastic food bags and freeze for up to 6 months until needed (the high oil content of the nuts allows them to turn rancid quickly).

BOILED DRESSING

COOKING TIME: 5 MINUTES
MAKES: 2 CUPS (475 ML)

- 2 teaspoons mustard powder
- 2 tablespoons sugar
- 1 teaspoon salt
- 3 tablespoons all-purpose (plain) flour
- ½ teaspoon paprika
- ½ teaspoon celery seeds (optional)
- ¼ cup (60 ml) any type vinegar
- 2 eggs
- 4 tablespoons (60 g) butter or heavy
  (whipping) cream

[This dressing was commonly made (and preserved by canning) by home cooks who didn't have access to oils. Not actually boiled, the dressing is cooked in a double boiler and chilled. It's good on German potato salad and coleslaw.]

In a heatproof bowl set over a pan of simmering water, whisk the mustard powder, sugar, salt, flour, paprika, and celery seeds (if using). Whisk in ¾ cup (180 ml) cold water, the vinegar, and eggs and cook over medium heat, whisking constantly, until thick and smooth, about 4 minutes. Whisk in the butter or cream. Remove from the heat, let cool, and refrigerate to chill. Store in the refrigerator airtight for up to 3 days.

SALSA VERDE

PREPARATION TIME: 15 MINUTES
COOKING TIME: 25 MINUTES
MAKES: ABOUT 2 CUPS (475 ML)

- 1 lb (455 g) tomatillos, husked and rinsed
- 1 large onion, cut into eighths
- 2 poblano peppers
- 2 serrano chilies
- 2 tablespoons vegetable oil
- 2 cloves garlic, peeled but whole
- 1 teaspoon dried oregano
- ½ cup fresh cilantro (coriander), roughly chopped
- 2 tablespoons fresh lime juice
- 1 teaspoon salt
- ¼ teaspoon crushed chili flakes

Preheat the oven to 425°F (220°C/Gas Mark 7).

On a large rimmed baking sheet, arrange the tomatillos, onion, poblanos, and serranos. Toss with the oil. Roast until softened, 20–25 minutes.

When cool enough to handle, remove the stems, skins, and seeds from the poblanos and serranos. Place all the roasted vegetables in a blender with the garlic, oregano, cilantro (coriander), lime juice, salt, and chili flakes. Blend on high for 30–60 seconds to combine all. Serve at room temperature or refrigerate for up to 2 days.

FRESH CORN SALSA

PREPARATION TIME: 20 MINUTES
MAKES: ABOUT 2 CUPS (475 ML)

- 4 tablespoons finely chopped red onion
- 1 clove garlic, finely chopped
- 2 tablespoons fresh lime juice
- 3 ears of corn, kernels cut from cobs
- 1 jalapeño pepper, seeded and finely diced
- 4 tablespoons chopped fresh cilantro (coriander)
- Salt

In a medium bowl, combine the onion, garlic, and lime juice and let rest for 10 minutes. Add the corn, jalapeño, cilantro (coriander), and salt to taste. Serve immediately or refrigerate for up to 2 days.

SALSA VERDE

FRESH CHOLLA FRUIT SALSA

PREPARATION TIME: 5 MINUTES
SERVES: 6

- 1 cup (225 g) peeled and chopped fresh cholla fruit
- 1 cup (180 g) diced tomatoes
- ½ cup (80 g) finely chopped red onion
- 4 tablespoons chopped fresh cilantro (coriander)
- 1 jalapeño pepper, seeded and finely diced
- 2 teaspoons sugar
- ¼ teaspoon salt

[Cholla grows wild in the Southwest, in the deserts of New Mexico, Arizona, and western Texas, as well as California. Serve with crisped tortillas or chips, or stuffed into tacos.]

Combine all the ingredients in a bowl and stir very well. Chill before serving. Store in the refrigerator airtight for up to 2 days.

KETCHUP

PREPARATION TIME: 10 MINUTES
COOKING TIME: 1 HOUR 10 MINUTES
MAKES: 1 QUART (1 LITER)

- 2 tablespoons olive oil
- 1 red bell pepper, diced
- 1 large onion, roughly chopped
- 1 stalk celery, chopped
- 2 cloves garlic, peeled and smashed
- 3 tablespoons tomato paste (purée)
- ¼ teaspoon crushed chili flakes
- ½ teaspoon ground coriander
- ½ teaspoon mustard powder
- ¼ teaspoon freshly ground black pepper
- 1 teaspoon salt
- 2 cans (28 oz/795 g each) peeled whole tomatoes in juice
- ¼ cup (50 g) packed light brown sugar
- 2 tablespoons cider vinegar

[New Jersey, also known as the Garden State is famous for its Jersey tomatoes, and for its deep-fried foods. This recipe is for people who love both.]

In a large pot, heat the oil over medium-high heat. Add the bell pepper, onion, celery, and garlic and cook, stirring occasionally, until the onion is softened and translucent, about 7 minutes. Add the tomato paste (purée), chili flakes, coriander, mustard powder, black pepper, and salt. Cook until the tomato paste is evenly distributed among the vegetables and begins to darken. Add the whole tomatoes and juice, brown sugar, and vinegar. Cook, stirring occasionally, until slightly thickened, 50–55 minutes.

Let cool slightly and purée in a blender or food processor until smooth. Let cool completely, then store in the refrigerator for up to 6 months.

KETCHUP

BOURBON BARBECUE SAUCE

PREPARATION TIME: 5 MINUTES
COOKING TIME: 20 MINUTES
MAKES: ABOUT 2 CUPS (475 ML)

- 2 cups (545 g) ketchup
- ⅓ cup (80 ml) bourbon
- ¼ cup (60 ml) red wine vinegar
- 4 teaspoons Worcestershire sauce
- 4 teaspoons chipotle chili powder
- 1 clove garlic, finely chopped
- Salt and freshly ground black pepper

In a small saucepan, combine the ketchup, bourbon, vinegar, Worcestershire sauce, chili powder, and garlic. Cook over medium-low heat, stirring occasionally, until slightly thickened, 15–20 minutes. Season to taste with salt and pepper and store in the refrigerator for up to 1 month.

CHIPOTLE BARBECUE SAUCE

PREPARATION TIME: 10 MINUTES
COOKING TIME: 20 MINUTES
MAKES: ABOUT 2 CUPS (475 ML)

- 2 cups (545 g) ketchup
- 2 canned chipotle peppers in adobo sauce, minced
- ¼ cup (60 ml) red wine vinegar
- 4 teaspoons Worcestershire sauce
- 4 teaspoons chipotle chili powder
- 2 tablespoons finely chopped onion
- 2 cloves garlic, finely chopped
- Salt and freshly ground black pepper

In a medium saucepan, combine the ketchup, chipotles, vinegar, Worcestershire sauce, chili powder, onion, garlic, ⅓ cup (80 ml) water, and ½ teaspoon each salt and pepper. Cook over medium-low heat, stirring occasionally, for 15–20 minutes meld the flavors and thicken the sauce. Season to taste with salt and pepper. Use immediately or let cool, cover, and refrigerate for up to 1 week.

EASTERN BARBECUE SAUCE

PREPARATION TIME: 5 MINUTES,
PLUS 12 HOURS STANDING TIME
COOKING TIME: 5 MINUTES
MAKES: 8 CUPS (2 LITERS)

- 4 cups (950 ml) distilled white vinegar
- 4 cups (950 ml) cider vinegar
- 4 tablespoons Tabasco-style hot sauce
- ¼ cup (50 g) packed light brown sugar
- 4 tablespoons crushed chili flakes
- 4 teaspoons salt
- 2 teaspoons cayenne pepper
- 2 teaspoons freshly ground black pepper

[North Carolina is home to two distinct styles of barbecue: Eastern and Lexington. Each contains vinegar, but Eastern-style omits tomato. Serve alongside whole-hog barbecue or pork baby back or spareribs.]

In a large saucepan, combine both vinegars, the hot sauce, brown sugar, chili flakes, salt, cayenne, and black pepper. Cook over medium heat, whisking until the sugar and salt have dissolved. Remove from the heat immediately. Let the sauce cool, then pour into a glass jar or vinegar-style bottle. Allow the ingredients to sit for at least 12 hours for the flavors to blend. Store for up to 6 months in the refrigerator and shake occasionally.

KANSAS CITY–STYLE BARBECUE SAUCE

PREPARATION TIME: 10 MINUTES
COOKING TIME: 40 MINUTES
MAKES: ABOUT 1 QUART (950 ML)

- 2 tablespoons vegetable oil
- 1 small yellow onion, finely diced
- 3 cloves garlic, minced
- 2 cups (510 g) tomato paste (purée)
- 1 cup (275 g) ketchup
- ½ cup (95 g) packed dark brown sugar
- ½ cup (120 ml) cider vinegar
- 2 tablespoons yellow mustard
- 1 teaspoon freshly ground black pepper
- 1 teaspoon salt
- ½ teaspoon ground ginger
- ½–1 teaspoon cayenne pepper

[When many people think of barbecue sauce, they think of Kansas City style — a tomato-based sauce that is sweet, with just a hint of spice. It's delicious with chicken, beef, and pork.]

In a medium saucepan, heat the oil over medium heat. Add the onion and cook, stirring often, until softened, about 5 minutes. Add the garlic and cook for about 30 seconds. Stir in 1 cup (240 ml) water, the tomato paste (purée), ketchup, brown sugar, vinegar, mustard and spices. Bring to a boil, then reduce the heat to low and simmer, stirring frequently, until slightly thickened, about 30 minutes. Transfer the sauce to a blender and blend until smooth. Let cool to room temperature, transfer to a jar, and store in the refrigerator for up to 1 month.

MEMPHIS-STYLE BARBECUE SAUCE

PREPARATION TIME: 5 MINUTES
COOKING TIME: 45 MINUTES
MAKES: ABOUT 3 CUPS (710 ML)

- 1 tablespoon chili powder
- 1 tablespoon garlic powder
- 1 tablespoon onion powder
- 2 cups (545 g) ketchup
- ⅔ cup (160 ml) cider vinegar
- 3 tablespoons Worcestershire sauce
- ½ cup (95 g) packed light brown sugar
- ½ cup (170 g) molasses
- ½ cup (120 g) yellow mustard
- 1½ teaspoons freshly ground black pepper
- 1½ teaspoons salt

In a medium saucepan, combine the chili powder, garlic powder, onion powder, ketchup, vinegar, Worcestershire sauce, brown sugar, molasses, mustard, pepper, and salt. Simmer over medium heat, stirring frequently, for 45 minutes to let the flavors meld and thicken the sauce. Store in the refrigerator for up to 1 month.

TEXAS BARBECUE SAUCE

PREPARATION TIME: 10 MINUTES
COOKING TIME: 15 MINUTES
MAKES: 2 CUPS (475 ML)

- 2 cups (545 g) ketchup, store-bought or homemade (page 460)
- 1 small onion, finely chopped
- 3 cloves garlic, finely chopped
- ¼ cup (60 ml) Worcestershire sauce
- ¼ cup (60 ml) cider vinegar
- ¼ cup (50 g) packed dark brown sugar
- 1 tablespoon yellow mustard
- 2 teaspoons kosher (coarse) salt
- ¼ teaspoon cayenne pepper
- Tabasco-style hot sauce to taste

[Texas barbecue is really about the meat. Some argue that it needs no sauce at all. But in East Texas, this style of sweet, tomato-based sauce is used to baste and serve alongside slow-smoked meats that fall from the bone.]

In a medium saucepan, combine all the ingredients and bring to a boil. Reduce to a simmer and cook for 10 minutes to let the flavors meld and thicken the sauce. Transfer to a blender and purée until smooth. Store in the refrigerator for up to 1 week.

MEMPHIS-STYLE BARBECUE SAUCE

LEXINGTON BARBECUE SAUCE

PREPARATION TIME: 5 MINUTES
MAKES: ABOUT 2¾ CUPS (650 ML)

- 2 cups (475 ml) cider vinegar
- ½ cup (135 g) ketchup
- ¼ cup (50 g) packed dark brown sugar
- 2 tablespoons granulated sugar
- 1 tablespoon salt
- 1 tablespoon ground white pepper
- 2 teaspoons crushed chili flakes
- 1 teaspoon freshly ground black pepper

[People are passionate about barbecue in North Carolina, a state that has two distinct styles featuring different parts of the pig, and different sauces. Lexington recipes include tomato. Use this sauce with Smoked Pork Shoulder (page 141).]

In a large bowl, whisk together the vinegar, ketchup, both sugars, salt, white pepper, chili flakes, and black pepper. Store in the refrigerator for up to 1 month.

WHITE BARBECUE SAUCE

PREPARATION TIME: 5 MINUTES
MAKES: ABOUT 1 CUP (240 ML)

- 1 cup (210 g) mayonnaise (preferably Duke's)
- 1 tablespoon cider vinegar
- 1 teaspoon fresh lemon juice
- 1 teaspoon hot sauce, such as Tabasco or Crystal
- 1 teaspoon Worcestershire sauce
- 1 teaspoon Creole or Dijon mustard
- 4 teaspoons sugar
- ½ teaspoon garlic powder
- ½ teaspoon onion powder
- Kosher (coarse) salt and freshly ground black pepper

[Serve alongside smoked barbecue chicken.]

In a small bowl, whisk together the mayonnaise, vinegar, lemon juice, hot sauce, Worcestershire sauce, mustard, sugar, garlic powder, and onion powder until combined. Season to taste with salt and black pepper. Store in the refrigerator for up to 1 week.

COMEBACK SAUCE

PREPARATION TIME: 5 MINUTES,
  PLUS CHILLING TIME
MAKES: ABOUT 2¾ CUPS (650 ML)

- 2 cups (420 g) mayonnaise
- ½ cup (135 g) tomato-based chili sauce, such as Heinz
- ¼ cup (70 g) ketchup
- 2 tablespoons fresh lemon juice
- 1 tablespoon Worcestershire sauce
- 2 teaspoons Tabasco-style hot sauce
- 2 teaspoons smoked paprika
- 1 teaspoon garlic powder
- 1 teaspoon mustard powder
- 1 teaspoon kosher (coarse) salt
- ½ teaspoon freshly ground black pepper

[Mississippi's quintessential condiment, this pink-hued mayonnaise-based sauce is the South's answer to remoulade. First developed by Greek immigrants in Jackson, the sauce is often served with anything fried, from onion rings and French fries to oyster fritters and fried green tomatoes.]

In a large bowl, whisk together the mayonnaise, chili sauce, ketchup, lemon juice, Worcestershire sauce, hot sauce, smoked paprika, garlic powder, mustard powder, salt, and pepper. Cover and refrigerate for at least 30 minutes to chill before serving. The sauce will keep refrigerated for up to 1 week.

CHOCOLATE GRAVY

PREPARATION TIME: 5 MINUTES
COOKING TIME: 15 MINUTES
MAKES: ABOUT 3 CUPS (710 ML)

- 1 cup (200 g) sugar
- ½ cup (40 g) unsweetened cocoa powder
- ¼ cup (35 g) all-purpose (plain) flour
- 1 stick (115 g) unsalted butter
- 2 cups (475 ml) milk
- ½ teaspoon pure vanilla extract
- ⅛ teaspoon salt

[This chocolate "gravy" is eaten atop biscuits across the Ozark region, covering Arkansas, Missouri, and Oklahoma.]

In a bowl, whisk together the sugar, cocoa, and flour in a bowl. In a medium saucepan, melt the butter over medium-high heat. Add the cocoa mixture and whisk to combine well. Whisking constantly, slowly whisk in the milk until smooth. Bring to a simmer and cook until thick, 3–4 minutes. Whisk in the vanilla and salt. Store in the refrigerator for up to 1 week.

WOJAPI

PREPARATION TIME: 5 MINUTES
COOKING TIME: 20 MINUTES
MAKES: 4 CUPS (950 ML)

- 4 cups (525 g) berries or stone fruit: blueberries, huckleberries, raspberries, blackberries, serviceberries, or pitted cherries
- ¼ cup (85 g) honey
- 1 tablespoon cornstarch (cornflour)

[Serve this berry sauce hot or cold with biscuits, grits, waffles, or ice cream. For a savory option, pair with grilled meats.]

In a pot, combine the fruit, honey, and 1 cup (240 ml) water and bring to a boil over medium heat. When the fruit softens, mash slightly with a potato masher. Continue cooking until the mixture is slightly thickened, about 12 minutes.

In a small bowl, stir the cornstarch (cornflour) into a little cold water and add the slurry to the warm berry mixture, stirring well. Cook for another 2 minutes over medium heat.

Serve immediately or store in the frigerator for up to 1 week.

BEACH PLUM JELLY

PREPARATION TIME: 5 MINUTES
COOKING TIME: 1 HOUR
MAKES: FIVE 8 FL OZ (240 ML) JARS

- 8 cups (1.8 kg) beach plums
- 6 cups (1.2 kg) sugar
- 6 tablespoons liquid pectin

[Scrubby beach plums grow along the Atlantic Ocean shoreline, right into the beach sand, producing ripe purple fruit in the last days of summer. They are smaller than but as sweet as regular plums, and can be used any way you would use a plum.]

In a heavy pot, combine the beach plums and 1 cup (240 ml) water and cook over medium-high heat until soft, about 25 minutes. Strain the juice overnight through a jelly bag or 2 layers of super-fine cheesecloth over a bowl. Do not press the fruit as it will make the jelly cloudy.

Measure out 4 cups (950 ml) of the juice and place in a saucepan. Add the sugar and bring to a boil over medium-high heat, stirring until the sugar is dissolved. Add the pectin and boil for an additional minute. Remove from the heat and let cool slightly. Pour into 5 sterilized jars and process using standard canning methods. Store at room temperature for up to 1 year.

MAYAPPLE JELLY

PREPARATION TIME: 2 HOURS
COOKING TIME: 30 MINUTES
MAKES: FIVE 8 FL OZ (240 ML) JARS

- 8 cups (3.5 lb/1.6 kg) pulp from ripe mayapples, weighed
- Sugar, equal to half the weight of the mayapples
- 1 box (1.75 oz/50 g) powdered pectin
- ¼ cup (60 ml) fresh lemon juice

[Mayapple grows wild east of the Rocky Mountains, especially in Illinois. To enjoy the fruit raw, cut it in half and scoop out the flesh with a spoon. If you are lucky enough to have found many, make this clear yellow jelly.]

Place the mayapple pulp in a food processor and pulse for a few seconds to help separate the seeds from the pulp. Press through a fine sieve into a saucepan (discard the seeds).

Add 1 cup (240 ml) water to the saucepan, bring to a gentle simmer, and cook for 10 minutes. Let cool slightly and pour the juice through a strainer lined with cheesecloth and set over a bowl. Don't force or squeeze it through—let it drip (this will help the liquid to stay clear). Let cool.

In a large saucepan, mix the sugar and the pectin well, then add the cooled juice. Stir in the lemon juice. Bring to a boil, skimming off any foam, and cook until the temperature reaches 220°F (105°C).

Remove the jelly from the heat pour into hot, sterilized jars and process using standard canning methods. Store at room temperature for up to 1 year.

MOUNTAIN ASH JELLY

PREPARATION TIME: 5 MINUTES
COOKING TIME: 1 HOUR 40 MINUTES
MAKES: EIGHT 8 FL OZ (240 ML) JARS

- 3 lb (1.4 kg) mountain ash berries
- 1 lb (455 g) crabapples or other small tart apples, roughly chopped
- 3–4 lb (1.4–1.8 kg) sugar

Note:
  To test whether the jelly is set, chill a saucer in the freezer. Place 1 tablespoon of hot jelly onto the cold saucer. After 30 seconds, tip the saucer. The jelly should be a soft gel that barely moves. If it runs, the jelly is not set yet.

[Also known as rowan, mountain ash is a tree that likes cool air and plenty of moisture. Its pretty clusters of fruit ripen into fall, when they offer their tart berries to passing birds. The fruit makes good jellies and fruit sauces. This delicate jelly is delicious on bread or muffins, or served with game.]

Place the mountain ash berries and the chopped crabapples in a pot. Add water to just cover the fruit. Simmer until soft, about 1 hour. Let cool slightly, then use a food mill to separate seeds from the cooked fruit.

Transfer the fruit to a jelly bag and suspend the bag over a large pot to collect the juice. Allow the bag to drain for at least 4 hours and up to overnight. Do not be tempted to squeeze (this will make your jelly cloudy).

Weigh the liquid and return to the pot. Add an equal weight of sugar to the pot. Bring to a boil over high heat, stirring to dissolve the sugar and skimming off any scum that rises. Clip a candy (sugar) thermometer to the side of the pan and when the liquid reaches 220°F (104°C), about 30 minutes, until the jelly is set (see note). Remove from the heat. Transfer the jelly to the sterilized jars and process using standard canning methods. Store at room temperature for up to 1 year.

HOT PEPPER JELLY

PREPARATION TIME: 10 MINUTES
COOKING TIME: 10 MINUTES
MAKES: SIX 8 FL OZ (240 ML) JARS

- 4 cups (600 g) finely diced Hatch chilies (a mix of red and green, spicy and mild)
- 1 cup (240 ml) cider vinegar
- 4½ cups (900 g) sugar
- 2 tablespoons salt
- 1 box (1.75 oz/50 g) powdered pectin

In a medium saucepan, combine the chilies, vinegar, sugar, and salt. Stir over medium-high heat to dissolve the sugar and salt. Add the pectin and bring to a boil, cook for 1 minute, then remove immediately from the heat. Transfer to 6 hot sterilized jars. Store in the refrigerator or seal and process using standard canning methods. Store at room temperature for up to 1 year.

CRANBERRY CHUTNEY

PREPARATION TIME: 5 MINUTES
COOKING TIME: 30 MINUTES
MAKES: ABOUT 2 CUPS (475 ML)

- 2 cups (200 g) fresh cranberries
- ½ cup (80 g) dried cranberries or cherries
- 1½ tablespoons peeled and minced fresh ginger
- ½ teaspoon mustard powder
- ⅓ cup (80 ml) orange juice
- ⅓ cup (65 g) packed light brown sugar
- 1 tablespoon minced jalapeño pepper

In a small saucepan, combine the fresh and dried cranberries, ginger, mustard powder, orange juice, brown sugar, and jalapeño. Bring to a simmer over medium-high heat. Reduce the heat to medium-low and cook at a low simmer until the cranberries have broken down and the sauce is slightly thickened, 20–25 minutes. Serve warm or refrigerate to serve cold. Store in the refrigerator for up to 1 month.

CRANBERRY CHUTNEY

WILD NANNYBERRY BUTTER

PREPARATION TIME: 15 MINUTES
COOKING TIME: 1 HOUR
MAKES: ONE 16 FL OZ (475 ML) JAR

- 6 cups (660 g) nannyberries
- ¾ cup (150 g) sugar
- ½ teaspoon finely grated orange zest
- 2 teaspoons ground cinnamon
- 1 teaspoon ground ginger
- ½ teaspoon ground spicebush berries (see page 488)

[Nannyberry, also known as wild raisin, also makes good sauces, syrups, leather, butters, chutneys, and preserves.]

Place the nannyberries in a large pot with just enough water to cover the fruit. Bring to a boil over medium-high heat, then reduce to a simmer and cook until the fruit is soft, about 30 minutes. Pour the contents through a colander set over a bowl and press the fruit pulp into the bowl (or use a food mill). Store airtight in the refrigerator for up to 1 month.

Measure out 2 cups (475 ml) of the strained pulp and place in a small pot over medium heat. Add the sugar, orange zest, and spices. Simmer, stirring, until the mixture is thick, 10–15 minutes. Let cool, transfer to a sterilized 1-pint glass jar, and store in the refrigerator.

WILD ARONIA SYRUP

PREPARATION TIME: 10 MINUTES,
PLUS 2 WEEKS STEEPING TIME
MAKES: SCANT 1½ CUPS (350 ML)

- 1 lb (455 g) chokeberries
- 1 lb (455 g) sugar

[The black chokeberry contains high levels of antioxidants. Chokeberry syrup can be drizzled over yogurt, ice cream, or pound cake. It is also mixed into cocktails (pairing well with gin) and enjoyed simply with seltzer.]

Rinse the fruit. Pull off the stems and place the fruit in a clean glass jar. Cover with the sugar, put on the lid, and turn the jar back and forth until the sugar is as evenly distributed as possible. Place in a dark cupboard for about 2 weeks. Turn the jar daily as the juice begins to be extracted from the fruit. The syrup is ready when it covers the fruit. It can either be drained and strained to be kept in a smaller bottle, or left with the fruit and used. Store in the refrigerator for up to 6 months.

WILD MESQUITE "MOLASSES"

PREPARATION TIME: 10 MINUTES
COOKING TIME: 14 HOURS
MAKES: 1 GALLON (3.8 LITERS)

- 1½ lb (680 g) mesquite pods, crushed

[Native Americans have widely used mesquite (especially the variety known as honey mesquite)—cooked fresh and green as a vegetable; ground into flour for mushes, breads, and puddings; and as a fermented beverage and spice. Serve this "molasses" on hot buttered biscuits, use in a barbecue marinade or sweeten tea. Instead of making molasses, you can use the strained juice as an ingredient in mesquite jelly.]

In a large pot or in a slow cooker on low, combine 1 gallon (3.8 liters) water and the pods. If on the stove, use the lowest heat setting available and cook the mixture below a simmer for 12 hours. It should never reach a simmer. The lower the heat the fewer the tannins that are extracted from the pods, and the better the taste. Strain the liquid twice through cheesecloth.

Return the strained juice to a large pot and cook over medium heat at a very gentle simmer until it has the consistency of a thin syrup, about 2 hours. Cool and store in the refrigerator for up to 6 months.

DILL PICKLES

PREPARATION TIME: 25 MINUTES
COOKING TIME: 25 MINUTES
MAKES: 4 QUARTS (4 LITERS)

- 4 cups (1 liter) distilled white vinegar
- 4 tablespoons kosher (coarse) salt
- 4½ lb (2 kg) Kirby (pickling) cucumbers, quartered lengthwise into long spears (or keep whole, just have more jars on hand)

Per jar:
- 1 clove garlic
- 1 dill flower or 4–5 large sprigs fresh dill
- 1 tablespoon yellow mustard seeds
- 1 tablespoon brown mustard seeds
- 1 teaspoon dill seeds
- 1 teaspoon black peppercorns

[There are two ways to pickle fruits and vegetables: cover them in salt water brine to allow lacto fermentation or submerge them in acid, usually vinegar. Although there are many vegetables that could be pickled with dill, the term "dill pickle" always refers to pickled cucumbers, which are by far the most popular pickle in America.]

In a nonreactive pot, combine the vinegar, salt, and 2 cups (475 ml) water and bring to a boil. Give it a stir to make sure the salt is dissolved.

Sterilize four 1-quart (1-liter) mason jars. Into each hot jar, place the garlic, dill, mustard seeds, dill seeds, and peppercorns. Pack the cucumbers as tightly as possible without crushing. Pour the boiling brine over the cucumbers, leaving ½ inch (1.25 cm) headspace. Make sure the cucumbers are covered in liquid. Check for air bubbles, releasing any with a skewer or chopstick. Wipe the rims, seal, and process using standard canning methods. Store at room temperature for up to 1 year.

KOSHER PICKLES

PREPARATION TIME: 15 MINUTES,
  PLUS COOLING AND BRINING TIME
MAKES: 26–30 LARGE PICKLE HALVES

- ½ cup (67 g) kosher (coarse) salt
- 2 cups (475 ml) boiling water
- 2½ lb (1 kg) pickling cucumbers, such
  as Kirbys
- 6 cloves garlic, peeled and smashed
- 10 sprigs fresh dill, small stems only
- ½ teaspoon dill seeds

[As immigrants from Eastern Europe poured into New York City's Lower East Side during the 19th and early 20th centuries, the neighborhood was home to hundreds of pickle pushcarts.]

Place the salt in a large heatproof bowl. Pour the boiling water over the salt and whisk well until all of the salt is dissolved. Let cool to room temperature.

Halve the cucumbers lengthwise. Add the cucumbers, garlic, dill, and dill seeds to the salt water solution. Add enough cold water to completely cover the cucumbers. Set a plate over the top to keep the pickles submerged. Let rest at room temperature for 12–48 hours, or until the cucumbers have pickled to personal preference. Store in the refrigerator for up to 1 week.

PICKLED RAMPS

PREPARATION TIME: 15 MINUTES
COOKING TIME: 5 MINUTES
MAKES: FIVE 1-PINT (475 ML) JARS

- 3 cups (710 ml) cider vinegar
- 3 tablespoons kosher (coarse) salt
- 3 tablespoons sugar
- 5 lb (2.3 kg) ramps, bulb and purple
  stem only (green tops reserved for
  another use)

Per jar:
- 1 clove garlic
- 1 fresh bay leaf
- ¼ teaspoon brown mustard seeds
- ¼ teaspoon yellow mustard seeds
- ¼ teaspoon black peppercorns
- ¼ teaspoon coriander seeds
- ¼ teaspoon cayenne pepper
  or chili flakes

[These "wild leeks" herald spring's arrival each year in the forest, where they pop up looking like tiny lilies. Recently discovered by upscale chefs, they've long been a local favorite and are celebrated in annual mountain festivals.]

In a medium nonreactive pot, combine the vinegar, 2 cups (475 ml) water, salt, and sugar and bring to a boil, stirring occasionally to make sure the salt and sugar are dissolved.

Divide the garlic and spices among 5 hot sterilized jars. Pack the jars tightly with ramps, being careful not to smash them. Pour the boiling brine over the ramps, leaving ½ inch (1.25 cm) headspace. Make sure ramps are submerged in liquid. Seal and process using standard canning methods. Store at room temperature for up to 1 year.

PICKLED CHERRIES

PREPARATION TIME: 5 MINUTES,
  PLUS 24 HOURS PICKLING TIME
COOKING TIME: 20 MINUTES
MAKES: 1 QUART (1 LITER)

- 2 cups (475 ml) cider vinegar
- 1 cup (200 g) sugar
- 1 cinnamon stick
- ½ teaspoon whole allspice berries
- 4 whole cloves
- Pinch of salt
- 4 cups (550 g) dark sweet cherries

[These are delicious with fatty meats, pâté, or ham.]

In a nonreactive medium saucepan, combine ¾ cup (180 ml) water, the vinegar, sugar, cinnamon stick, allspice, cloves, and salt and bring to a boil over medium-high heat. Reduce to a simmer and cook for 10 minutes. Add the cherries and simmer for 5 minutes. Remove from the heat and let cool to room temperature. Pour the cherries and liquid into a large 1-quart (1 liter) jar, cover, and refrigerate for at least 24 hours before serving. These will keep in the refrigerator for up to 1 month.

BISON OR BEEF JERKY

PREPARATION TIME: 7 HOURS,
  PLUS FREEZING AND MARINATING TIME
MAKES: 1 LB (455 G)

- 2 lb (910 g) bison top round (topside), trimmed
- 1½ cups (355 ml) soy sauce
- 1 tablespoon honey
- 2 teaspoons freshly ground black pepper
- 1½ teaspoons smoked paprika
- 1 teaspoon crushed chili flakes

[Wyoming's Yellowstone National Park is home to one of America's largest buffalo herds. This spicy bison jerky might be a bit more flavorful than the version cowboys chewed on 150 years ago – but it's a delicious descendant.]

Cut the meat into 3 or 4 pieces and place in the freezer for at least 1 hour and up to 2 hours to make it firm enough to thinly slice. Slice the meat, with the grain, as thinly as possible (about ⅛ inch/ 3 mm thick).

In a saucepan, combine the soy sauce, honey, pepper, paprika, and chili flakes. Bring to a boil, then remove from the heat and let cool to room temperature.

In the same pan, toss the meat slices in the marinade, then cover and refrigerate for at least 3 hours and up to 6 hours, stirring once or twice during the marinating time. Remove the meat from the marinade and pat dry with paper towels.

Dehydrator method: Spread the meat on dehydrator trays and dehydrate according to the manufacturer's instructions.

Oven method: Remove the racks from the oven. Preheat the oven to 170°F (75°C). Hang the meat from one of the racks so that it hangs down. Place the rack on the highest shelf in the oven and prop the door open very slightly, so the steam escapes. Dry the meat until it is stiff, dry, and leathery, 6–7 hours.

The jerky will keep for about 1 month in an airtight container at room temperature.

CHOW-CHOW

PREPARATION TIME: 30 MINUTES
COOKING TIME: 40 MINUTES
MAKES: SIX 1-PINT (475 ML) JARS

- 1 lb (455 g) green beans, cut into 1-inch (2.5 cm) pieces
- 1 medium head cauliflower, separated into florets
- 1½ cups (235 g) shelled fresh lima (butter beans)
- 1½ cups (200 g) corn kernels
- 2 cups (320 g) chopped onions
- 6 cups (1.4 liters) cider vinegar
- 2 cups (400 g) sugar
- ¼ cup (65 g) sea salt
- 1 tablespoon celery seeds
- 1 tablespoon yellow mustard seeds
- 1 tablespoon mustard powder
- 2 teaspoons ground turmeric
- 4 cups (720 g) chopped green tomatoes
- 3 red bell peppers, chopped

[This tangy, sweet-and-sour pickled relish is a common way to preserve summer harvests. It's especially popular on hot dogs and with pinto beans.]

Set up a large bowl of ice and water. Bring a large pot of water to a boil. Add the green beans and cauliflower and blanch until they are just barely cooked, about 5 minutes. Scoop out the beans and cauliflower with a sieve and plunge them into the ice bath.

Add the lima (butter) beans, corn, and onions to the same boiling water and bring the water back to a boil. Pour the vegetables into a colander or sieve to drain well. Drain the green beans and cauliflower.

In the pot that was used to boil the water, combine the vinegar, sugar, salt, celery seeds, mustard seeds, mustard powder, and turmeric and bring to a boil. Add the blanched vegetables, green tomatoes, and bell peppers. Bring to a boil, reduce the heat, and simmer for 10 minutes. Ladle the chow-chow into 6 hot sterilized jars. Seal and process using standard canning methods. Store at room temperature for up to 1 year.

DILLY BEANS

PREPARATION TIME: 14 MINUTES, PLUS 2 WEEKS PICKLING TIME
COOKING TIME: 10 MINUTES
MAKES: FOUR 1-PINT (475 ML) JARS

- 12 sprigs fresh dill or 4 dill seedheads
- 8 cloves garlic, peeled but whole
- 4 teaspoons yellow mustard seeds
- 2 teaspoons brown mustard seeds
- 1 teaspoon black peppercorns
- 4 lb (1.8 kg) green beans, trimmed to fit into 1-pint (475 ml) mason jars
- 4 cups (950 ml) distilled white vinegar
- 3 tablespoons kosher (coarse) salt

Dividing evenly, place the dill, garlic, mustard seeds, and peppercorns in 4 sterilized mason jars. Pack the green beans in tightly.

In a medium nonreactive pot, combine 2 cups (475 ml) water, the vinegar, and salt and bring to a boil, stirring to dissolve the salt. Pour the boiling brine over the beans, leaving ½ inch (1.25 cm) headspace and making sure the beans are covered in liquid. Process using standard canning methods. Allow to sit for 2 weeks before eating. Store at room temperature for up to 1 year.

CHOW-CHOW

CORN RELISH

PREPARATION TIME: 20 MINUTES
COOKING TIME: 30 MINUTES
MAKES: EIGHT 1-PINT (475 ML) JARS

- 10 ears of corn, kernels cut from the cob
- 2 large red bell peppers, diced
- 2 large green bell peppers, diced
- 6 stalks celery, diced
- 1 large onion, diced
- 4 cups (950 ml) cider vinegar
- 2 cups (400 g) sugar
- 1 tablespoon yellow mustard seeds
- 1 tablespoon ground turmeric
- 1 tablespoon salt
- 2 teaspoons celery seeds

[This sweet-and-sour condiment is commonly paired with pork.]

In a large pot, combine the corn, bell peppers, celery, onions, vinegar, sugar, mustard seeds, turmeric, salt, and celery seeds. Bring to a boil over high heat, stirring constantly, until the sugar has dissolved. Reduce the heat and simmer until all of the vegetables are tender, about 20 minutes.

Ladle the hot relish into 8 hot sterilized jars. Seal and process using standard canning methods. Store at room temperature for up to 1 year.

GREEN CHILI ENCHILADA SAUCE

PREPARATION TIME: 25 MINUTES
COOKING TIME: 50 MINUTES
MAKES: ABOUT 6 CUPS (1.4 LITERS)

- 12 Hatch green chilies, roasted and peeled (see Note, page 86)
- ¼ cup (50 g) lard
- 1 large onion, chopped
- 2 large cloves garlic, minced
- 4 tablespoons all-purpose (plain) flour
- 4 cups (950 ml) chicken stock
- 1 teaspoon salt
- 1 teaspoon ground cumin

Finely chop the chilies and set aside.

In a large pot, melt the lard over medium heat. Add the onion and cook until softened and translucent, 5–7 minutes. Add the garlic and cook for 2 minutes. Add the flour and cook until lightly golden, 2–3 minutes. Add the stock, salt, and cumin and whisk well until all lumps are removed. Add the green chilies and bring to a simmer over medium-high heat, then reduce to medium-low and cook for 15–20 minutes to meld the flavors and thicken the sauce. Store in the refrigerator for up to 3 days.

CORN RELISH

GREEN GODDESS DRESSING

PREPARATION TIME: 15 MINUTES,
   PLUS CHILLING TIME
MAKES: ABOUT 1¼ CUPS (300 ML)

- ½ cup (105 g) mayonnaise
- ½ cup (120 ml) buttermilk
- 3 tablespoons finely chopped fresh parsley
- 2 tablespoons finely chopped fresh tarragon
- 2 tablespoons finely chopped fresh chives
- 1 tablespoon fresh lemon juice
- 2 anchovy fillets, minced
- 1 clove garlic, minced
- Salt and freshly ground black pepper

Either purée all of the ingredients in a blender or whisk them together. Season to taste with salt and pepper. Refrigerate for 1 hour to chill before serving. Store airtight in the refrigerator for up to 3 days.

RANCH DRESSING

PREPARATION TIME: 10 MINUTES
MAKES: ABOUT 2 CUPS (475 ML)

- 1 clove garlic, minced
- 3 tablespoons finely minced fresh parsley
- 2 tablespoons finely chopped fresh chives
- 1 tablespoon finely chopped fresh dill
- 1 cup (210 g) mayonnaise
- ½ cup (120 ml) sour cream
- ½ cup (120 ml) buttermilk
- 1 tablespoon cider vinegar
- Salt, freshly ground black pepper, and cayenne pepper to taste
- Worcestershire sauce to taste (optional)

Mix all the ingredients together. Store in the refrigerator until ready to use. Store in the refrigerator airtight for up to 3 days.

SCUPPERNONG JELLY

PREPARATION TIME: 5 MINUTES,
PLUS OVERNIGHT DRAINING
COOKING TIME: 1 HOUR 15 MINUTES
MAKES: TEN TO TWELVE 4-OUNCE
(120 ML) JELLY JARS

- 5 lb (2.3 kg) just-ripe scuppernong grapes
- 2 lb (910 g) sugar
- Juice of 1 lemon

[Scuppernongs are a favorite grape in the South. The harvests are made into wine or jelly, or just eaten off the vine.]

In a stainless-steel pot, bring all the ingredients to a boil over high heat, stirring often. Mash the fruit with a spoon and be sure it is not sticking to the bottom of the pan. Cook down until the grape skins split and the flesh is soft and breaking down, about 40 minutes.

Remove from the heat and transfer to a jelly bag. Suspend the bag over a bowl and let drain overnight. Do not squeeze the bag.

The next day, return the grape juice to the pot and bring to a boil over high heat. Cook until it reaches 220°F (104°C) on a candy (sugar) thermometer and is thick enough to coat the back of a spoon.

Pour the hot jelly into 10–12 hot sterilized jelly jars. Seal and process using standard canning methods. Store at room temperature for up to 1 year.

PENNSYLVANIA DUTCH APPLE BUTTER

PREPARATION TIME: 25 MINUTES
COOKING TIME: 7–10 HOURS
MAKES: 2 QUARTS (2 LITERS)

- 12 lb (5.5 kg) apples (use an assortment of varieties for more flavor)
- 1 cup (190 g) packed dark brown sugar
- 1 tablespoon ground cinnamon
- 2 teaspoons ground ginger
- 1 teaspoon freshly grated nutmeg
- ½ teaspoon ground cloves
- 2 teaspoons ground allspice
- 2 cups (475 ml) apple cider

Peel, core, and chop the apples. Place them in a large heavy-bottomed pot. Add the brown sugar, spices, and cider. Cook over medium heat until the apples soften and fall apart, stirring frequently, and making sure to scrape the bottom of the pot so the apples don't burn. This will take about 1 hour.

Reduce the heat to low and continue to cook the apples, stirring frequently, until the sauce is very thick and all the liquid has evaporated (the sauce will become thicker and darker in color). This will take anywhere from 6 to 10 hours, depending on the apple varieties used (how dry or juicy they are), and the cooking temperature. When the apple butter is finished, spoon it into quart (liter) jars and store in the refrigerator for up to 1 month. For longer storage, spoon into hot sterilized quart (1 liter) jars and process using standard canning methods. Store at room temperature for up to 1 year.

DRINKS

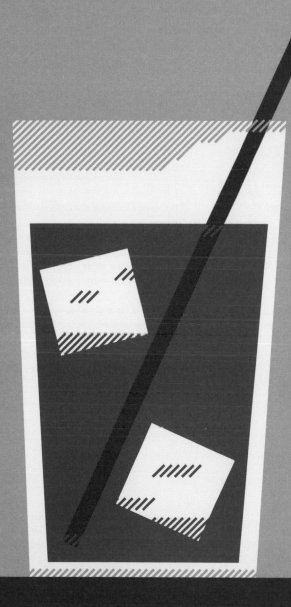

CHICORY COFFEE

PREPARATION TIME: 5 MINUTES
COOKING TIME: 20 MINUTES
SERVES: 4

- 4 tablespoons ground dried chicory root
- 4 tablespoons ground coffee

[The Café du Monde in New Orleans, Louisiana, has been serving its signature café au lait made with chicory-laced coffee—alongside beignets—for over a century. The chicory root lends a strong, rich, almost nutty flavor to the coffee and turns it a dark mahogany color. The café ships its cans of ground coffee all over the world.]

In a saucepan, bring 4 cups (950 ml) water to a simmer. Add the chicory and coffee, cover, and simmer for 15 minutes. Strain and divide among 4 cups.

To make Chicory Café au Lait: In a saucepan, bring 2 cups (475 ml) water to a simmer and brew the chicory coffee as directed. Steam 2 cups (475 ml) milk. Divide the strained chicory coffee among 4 cups and top with steamed milk.

CAFÉ CON LECHE

PREPARATION TIME: 5 MINUTES
COOKING TIME: 10 MINUTES
SERVES: 1

- 1–2 tablespoons Cuban coffee (such as Bustelo or Pilon), to taste
- 1 cup (240 ml) milk
- 4–6 teaspoons sugar, to taste

[This recipe calls for the coffee to be made in an individual percolator.]

Fill the bottom portion of an individual percolator with cold water. Fill the metal filter portion with coffee and screw the pieces together. Place over medium heat until the water boils and fills the top portion with brewed coffee. Remove from the heat.

Meanwhile, in a small saucepan, heat the milk over medium heat until warmed through but not boiling, about 5 minutes.

Place the sugar in a coffee cup and stir in a few drops of hot coffee to dissolve. Add the remaining coffee and heated milk.

COFFEE SYRUP

PREPARATION TIME: 10 MINUTES
COOKING TIME: 20 MINUTES
MAKES: 1 CUP (240 ML), ENOUGH TO
    SERVE 8

- 1 cup (240 ml) strong coffee
- ¾ cup (150 g) sugar

In a small heavy-bottomed saucepan, bring the coffee and sugar just to a boil, stirring constantly. Reduce to a simmer and cook, stirring occasionally, for 15 minutes. Store in the refrigerator for up to 1 month.

COFFEE MILK

RI

PREPARATION TIME: 5 MINUTES
SERVES: 1

- 1 cup (240 ml) milk
- 4 tablespoons Coffee Syrup (opposite page)

Sweeten a glass of milk with 2 tablespoons coffee syrup.

COFFEE CABINET

RI

PREPARATION TIME: 5 MINUTES
SERVES: 2

- 1 pint (473 ml) coffee ice cream
- ¼ cup (60 ml) milk, or more to taste
- 2 tablespoons Coffee Syrup (page 484)
- 1 shot espresso (optional)

[What is commonly known as a "milkshake" to most of the country (ice cream and milk), Rhode Islanders call a "cabinet."]

Blend all the ingredients in a blender. Pour into 2 chilled glasses and serve.

HORCHATA

NY

PREPARATION TIME: 5 MINUTES,
  PLUS CHILLING AND OVERNIGHT
  STEEPING TIME
COOKING TIME: 5 MINUTES
SERVES: 4–6

- ⅓ cup (65 g) rice
- ⅓ cup (75 g) blanched almonds, toasted and chopped
- 1 cinnamon stick
- 3 cups (710 ml) hot water
- ¼ cup (60 ml) simple syrup

[New York City's Latino community has added many culinary traditions to the metropolitan area, including this thick, sweet drink, reminiscent of a puréed, chilled, rice pudding.]

In a blender, grind the rice to a fine powder. Transfer the ground rice to a jar and add the almonds, cinnamon stick, and hot water. Let cool to room temperature, then cover and let steep at room temperature for 3 hours.

Transfer the mixture to a blender, add 2 cups (475 ml) cold water, and blend until very smooth, 1–2 minutes. Strain the liquid through a fine-mesh sieve lined with a double layer of cheesecloth. Transfer to a pitcher (jug), stir in the simple syrup, and refrigerate to chill until ready to serve.

MALTED MILK

PREPARATION TIME: 5 MINUTES
SERVES: 2

- 2½ cups (270 g) vanilla or chocolate ice cream
- ½ cup (55 g) malted milk powder
- 1 cup (240 ml) milk

[Malted milk powder, trademarked by the Horlick brothers in 1887 as a nutritional supplement for infants, was manufactured in Racine, Wisconsin. It later became popular with explorers, who carried it on expeditions. It eventually found its way to soda fountains, where it was mixed with ice cream as "malted." Some people still call it Horlicks.]

Place all the ingredients in a blender and blend on high speed for 1 minute. Pour into 2 tall glasses and serve right away.

SOUTHERN SWEET TEA

PREPARATION TIME: 5 MINUTES,
    PLUS CHILLING TIME
COOKING TIME: 20 MINUTES
MAKES: 2 QUARTS (2 LITERS)

- ½ cup (100 g) sugar
- 16 black tea bags
- ⅛ teaspoon baking soda (bicarbonate of soda)
- 1½ quarts (1.4 liters) ice cubes
- Lemon wedges and mint sprigs, for serving (optional)

In a small saucepan, bring the sugar and ½ cup (120 ml) water to a low simmer over medium-high heat, stirring to dissolve the sugar. Remove the simple syrup from the heat, let cool, and refrigerate to chill completely.

Place the tea bags and baking soda (bicarbonate of soda) in a large (4-quart/3.8-liter) heatproof glass container. Bring 1½ quarts (1.4 liters) water to a boil. Pour over the tea bags to submerge completely. Cover and steep for 7 minutes. Discard the tea bags.

Add the ice and stir until it melts. Stir in the chilled simple syrup and serve in ice-filled glasses, with lemon wedges and mint sprigs, if desired.

WATERMELON LEMONADE

PREPARATION TIME: 10 MINUTES,
    PLUS CHILLING TIME
COOKING TIME: 5 MINUTES
SERVES: 8–10

- ¾ cup (150 g) sugar
- 6 cups (910 g) diced watermelon
- 1¼ cups (295 ml) fresh lemon juice
- Crushed ice
- Mint sprigs, for garnish

In a small saucepan, combine 1 cup (240 ml) water and the sugar. Heat over medium-low heat, stirring well to dissolve the sugar. Once dissolved, remove the simple syrup from the heat and refrigerate until chilled.

Working in batches, purée the watermelon and lemon juice in a blender until smooth. Transfer to a large pitcher (jug). Stir in 5 cups (1.2 liters) cold water and the chilled simple syrup.

Serve in tall ice-filled glasses. Garnish with mint.

WATERMELON LEMONADE

MULLED CIDER WITH BOURBON AND WILD SPICEBUSH

PREPARATION TIME: 5 MINUTES
COOKING TIME: 30 MINUTES
SERVES: 6

- 6 cups (1.4 liters) apple cider
- 1 orange, sliced
- 1 tablespoon fresh lemon juice
- 3 cinnamon sticks
- 1 tablespoon spicebush berries
- 1 cup (240 ml) bourbon

[Spicebush has long been used by Native Americans as a seasoning and a tea. The dried berries are the strongest-tasting part of the plant and can be dried and finely ground if using for baking for use in savory or sweet dishes.]

In a pot, warm the apple cider over medium heat. Add the orange slices, lemon juice, cinnamon sticks, and spicebush berries. Bring to a boil, then reduce the heat and simmer for 15 minutes. Add the bourbon and bring back to a simmer. Serve hot.

TOM COLLINS

PREPARATION TIME: 5 MINUTES
SERVES: 1

- 2 tablespoons fresh lemon juice
- 4 tablespoons London dry gin
- 1 teaspoon superfine (caster) sugar
- ½ cup (120 ml) club soda (soda water), chilled
- Lemon wedge, for garnish

In an ice-filled cocktail shaker, shake the lemon juice, gin, and sugar vigorously for 30 seconds to chill. Strain over ice in a tall glass and top with club soda. Garnish with a lemon wedge.

MOJITO

PREPARATION TIME: 5 MINUTES
SERVES: 1

- ½ small bunch mint
- 2 tablespoons fresh lime juice
- 2 teaspoons superfine (caster) sugar
- ¼ cup (60 ml) white rum
- Club soda (soda water)
- 1 lime slice, for garnish

Place all but 1 sprig of the mint in a Collins glass. Add the lime juice and sugar and muddle well.

In an ice-filled cocktail shaker, add the mint-lime mixture and the rum and shake vigorously for 30 seconds to chill. Strain over ice in a Collins glass. Top with a splash of club soda and garnish with a lime slice and a mint sprig.

SALTY DOG

.FL

PREPARATION TIME: 15 MINUTES
SERVES: 2

- ¾ cup (180 ml) fresh grapefruit juice
- Coarse salt
- ½ cup (120 ml) vodka or gin

Note:
   Start with the best, freshest grapefruit
   you can find and juice it yourself.

Moisten the rims of 2 highball glasses with a little grapefruit juice. Spread salt on a small plate and dip the rims in the salt to coat. Fill the glasses with ice, then add ¼ cup (60 ml) vodka to each glass. Divide the grapefruit juice between glasses and serve.

MAI TAI

.CA

PREPARATION TIME: 5 MINUTES
SERVES: 2

- ¼ cup (60 ml) amber rum
- ¼ cup (60 ml) dark rum
- 2 tablespoons Curaçao or triple sec
- ¼ cup (60 ml) pineapple juice
- 2 tablespoons orange juice
- 2 tablespoons fresh lime juice
- 1 teaspoon sugar
- Dash of grenadine
- Orange slices, for garnish

[The original tiki cocktail, this California invention co-starred with Elvis in the film *Blue Hawaii*.]

In an ice-filled cocktail shaker, shake the rums, liqueur, fruit juices, sugar, and grenadine vigorously for 30 seconds to chill. Strain into 2 glasses and garnish with orange slices.

MANHATTAN

.NY

PREPARATION TIME: 5 MINUTES
SERVES: 1

- 2 dashes of Angostura bitters
- 2 tablespoons Italian vermouth
- 5 tablespoons rye whiskey
- 1 maraschino cherry

[Invented in the 1870s in the place for which it was named.]

Half-fill a short glass with ice. Add the bitters, vermouth, and whiskey. Add the cherry and crush it against the side of the glass with a spoon. Stir.

BLOODY MARY

PREPARATION TIME: 15 MINUTES,
PLUS CHILLING TIME

SERVES: 6

- 1½ cups (355 ml) tomato juice
- 2 teaspoons prepared or grated fresh horseradish
- 1 teaspoon grated yellow onion
- Juice of 1 lemon
- 2 teaspoons Worcestershire sauce
- ½ teaspoon celery salt
- ¼ teaspoon kosher (coarse) salt
- Hot sauce
- Freshly ground black pepper
- 1½ cups (355 ml) vodka
- 6 stalks celery or lovage, including leaves

[This is a tomato salad turned into a cocktail.]

In a large pitcher, combine the tomato juice, horseradish, onion, lemon juice, Worcestershire, celery salt, kosher (coarse) salt, and hot sauce and black pepper to taste. Stir well to combine. Add the vodka and refrigerate to chill. Serve in tall glasses over ice, garnished with a stalk of celery (or use the lovage as a straw).

SAZERAC

PREPARATION TIME: 5 MINUTES,
PLUS CHILLING TIME

SERVES: 1

- 1 teaspoon sugar
- 3 dashes of Peychaud's bitters
- ¼ cup (60 ml) rye whiskey
- 1 teaspoon Herbsaint, Pernod, or absinthe
- Lemon peel, for garnish

Place a small tumbler in the freezer to chill.

In a mixing glass, combine the sugar, bitters, whiskey, and a handful of ice and stir well.

Pour the Herbsaint down the side of the chilled tumbler and turn to coat. Pour out any excess. Strain the mixing glass contents into the tumbler. Twist the lemon peel over the drink.

BLOODY MARY

COSMOPOLITAN

PREPARATION TIME: 5 MINUTES
SERVES: 2

- ¼ cup (60 ml) cranberry juice
- 2 tablespoons fresh lime juice
- ½ cup (120 ml) vodka
- ¼ cup (60 ml) triple sec

In an ice-filled cocktail shaker, shake the juices, vodka, and triple sec vigorously for 30 seconds to chill. Strain into 2 martini glasses.

TEQUILA SUNRISE

PREPARATION TIME: 5 MINUTES
SERVES: 2

- 6 tablespoons tequila
- 1½ cups (355 ml) orange juice
- 3 tablespoons grenadine
- Orange slices, for garnish
- Maraschino cherries, for garnish

Fill 2 highball glasses with ice. Divide the tequila and orange juice between the glasses. Drizzle the grenadine down the side of each glass. Garnish with orange slices and maraschino cherries.

MINT JULEP

PREPARATION TIME: 5 MINUTES
SERVES: 1

- 1½ teaspoons superfine (caster) sugar
- 1 bunch fresh mint
- 5 tablespoons bourbon

[This drink is especially beloved on the day of the Kentucky Derby, in the state synonymous with bourbon, just when mint is springing up.]

In the bottom of a silver julep cup, combine the sugar with a small handful of mint leaves. Muddle until the leaves release their fragrance. Fill the cup three-fourths full with finely cracked ice, then add the bourbon. Stir and garnish with fresh mint.

DAIQUIRI

PREPARATION TIME: 5 MINUTES
SERVES: 1

- ¼ cup (60 ml) light rum
- 2 tablespoons fresh lime juice
- 1 tablespoon simple syrup

Half-fill a cocktail shaker with ice. Add the rum, lime juice, and simple syrup and shake vigorously for 30 seconds to chill. Strain into a chilled glass.

PIÑA COLADA

PREPARATION TIME: 5 MINUTES
SERVES: 2

- 1 cup ice cubes
- ¼ cup (60 ml) pineapple juice
- ¼ cup (60 ml) coconut cream
- 3 tablespoons white rum
- 2 tablespoons dark rum
- Pineapple wedges, for garnish

[The national drink of Puerto Rico is widely beloved across the country.]

In a blender, combine the ice, pineapple juice, coconut cream, and rums. Blend until smooth. Divide between 2 glasses and garnish with pineapple wedges.

MARGARITA

PREPARATION TIME: 10 MINUTES
SERVES: 1

- ¼ cup (60 ml) tequila
- 2 tablespoons fresh lime juice
- 2 tablespoons Cointreau or other orange liqueur

In an ice-filled cocktail shaker, shake the tequila, lime juice, and liqueur vigorously for 30 seconds to chill. Strain into an ice-filled rocks glass.

RAMOS GIN FIZZ

PREPARATION TIME: 5 MINUTES
SERVES: 1

- ¼ cup (60 ml) London dry gin
- 1 egg white
- 1 tablespoon simple syrup
- 1 tablespoon fresh lemon juice
- 1 tablespoon fresh lime juice
- 1 tablespoon half-and-half (single cream)
- 2 dashes of orange blossom water
- ¼ cup (60 ml) club soda (soda water)
- Orange slice, for garnish

In a cocktail shaker half-filled with ice, shake the gin, egg white, simple syrup, lemon juice, lime juice, half-and-half (single) cream, and orange blossom water vigorously for 30 seconds, until chilled and frothy. Strain into a Collins glass. Finish with the club soda and garnish with orange slice.

LONG ISLAND ICED TEA

PREPARATION TIME: 5 MINUTES
SERVES: 2

- 2 tablespoons vodka
- 2 tablespoons gin
- 2 tablespoons white rum
- 2 tablespoons white tequila
- 1 tablespoon triple sec
- 2 tablespoons fresh lemon juice
- ½ cup (120 ml) cola
- Lemon wedges, for garnish

In an ice-filled cocktail shaker, shake the vodka, gin, rum, tequila, triple sec, and lemon juice vigorously for 30 seconds to chill. Strain into 2 ice-filled glasses. Top each with ¼ cup (60 ml) of the cola and garnish with lemon wedges.

GUEST CONTRIBUTIONS: ESSAYS & RECIPES BY STATE

Scott Peacock was named Best Chef: Southeast by the James Beard Foundation and lives in his native state of Alabama.

When I left Alabama, I was never coming back. I'd grown up in Hartford, a farming town of two thousand tucked in the southeast corner of the state, near the Florida border. The road in town terminated sixty-seven miles away in the Gulf of Mexico.

I grew up with hot water cornbread often on the table, made from Pollard's white cornmeal ground in town, baked or fried into a cornbread with an ivory cream interior. I ate chicken and dumplings, and chicken and rice—which I recall as the best tastes of my life—made by my uneducated, impoverished Grandmaw Peacock, who lived deep in the country down a gravel road in a house that had no indoor bathroom until I was in first grade.

When I left for college in 1981, I was not interested in cornbread—or in anything my mother had cooked. I was never going back.

I didn't consider food a way to make a living—but I was always cooking. One night I was helping at a fundraiser for the Georgia governor. Two cooks didn't show up, so I was sent to help in the kitchen. Soon I was working for the caterer, then I got a job in a French restaurant, and eventually a call came asking me to be the chef at the Georgia Governor's Mansion.

There I baked cornbread every night—but inside I was interested in "real" food, in French food. I was saving my money, and in my mind I was on my way to Italy—because that food was on the cover of every magazine.

While cooking for the Governor I read that Miss Edna Lewis was coming to town, and I wanted to meet her. I had seen her image in a magazine and something just told me: *Get there.* We talked, and I told her I wanted to move to Italy to learn about cooking.

She said, "Before you go off and learn about someone else's food, you should learn about your own." It knocked me down. I didn't understand her reaction.

A year later Miss Lewis came back, and I was asked to help her cook Southern food, the past I was trying to leave far behind.

Working with her, reading her book *The Taste of Country Cooking*, and learning the foods she knew from Virginia—the similarity but also the tremendous difference from what I knew—I began to see how incredibly special the food that I'd grown up on really was. With that discovery came my appreciation of Pollard's cornmeal.

Pollard's is white, not yellow—a point of debate that causes Southerners to get emotional. And Pollard's is so finely ground—to nearly a powder—that it can absorb more liquid, which yields an amazingly crispy, crunchy hoecake or that hot water cornbread, which calls for no egg or buttermilk. Some compare it to cake, even without a trace of sugar.

My favorite way to use cornmeal became to bake it into corn muffins. They're very light, slightly tangy with a fine, creamy texture, and much easier to make than a batch of biscuits.

So I set out to learn about my past. I knew that my great-grandmother on my mother's side—an incredibly stylish woman, much resented by members of my family for having good taste and loving fine things—had during the

Depression run a tearoom with a black cook. I asked my mother if anyone might remember it and she suggested Eloise Hause. At 107, she still remembered me—and still lived at home. I drove four hours to see her and, over three days, she told me where her father hid his whiskey in the corn crib, and she described in perfect detail every step of how her mother had made chicken pie a hundred years before.

I interviewed Ollie Glass, a woman who had worked for twenty years in the cafeteria at the black high school—and she was still driving at age 100. She told me that when she was growing up, a minister's daughter in a poor area at a poor time, flour had been a luxury because it was something you had to *buy*. But you could *grow* corn, and even if you had no money, you could take it to the gristmill, which would grind it in exchange for a portion. Each morning, they'd eat leftover cornbread to fill them up before they ate biscuits, because they couldn't afford much flour.

Speaking with those women opened a new portal for me. I began going back to Alabama, interviewing the oldest people I could find about their childhood food memories. Because when you get Southerners to talk about food, you're talking about everything—the connections between people and place and everything they reveal. Cornmeal, especially for people of a certain age, represents something that sustained many through very difficult times.

I soon realized that I hadn't understood the food—and that I also hadn't understood the place or the people. Over time I discovered an Alabama that I hadn't known about, and that I fell in love with.

I didn't come back intending to live here. But it was clear to my internal compass. I needed to honor that experience. There were things I knew could happen here that could never happen in Atlanta or New York. So I bought an old house and now grow wheat and indigo.

Cornbread is central to many people's identity here—but not everyone's. I teach a class at the Honors College at the University of Alabama. And when I brought my students cornbread muffins—made with Pollard's incredibly rare, finely ground cornmeal—it didn't have any of those associations for them. They had no memories of a grandmother or mother making it, or of cornmeal being sustenance or even a staple. Their parents are my age or younger, and their cornbread came out of a box of Jiffy mix.

I wouldn't be in Alabama if it hadn't been for Miss Lewis. She opened my eyes to something I didn't know existed—and to a *me* I didn't know existed. When I began to see the food of my childhood in a different way, I also began to see my parents and grandparents and the place I was from—I began to see *myself* differently. And to see life differently.

The old expression says: There are as many recipes for cornbread as there are cooks in the South. And it's really true. But my recipe is for corn muffins, made with Pollard's cornmeal. I bake them fast in a well-buttered tin and they emerge thin, not quite crunchy, well browned, golden from the buttermilk and egg. They are exquisite, especially with a large pat of good, warm butter and a good gush of honey. You may think they're excessive, but they're not, I promise you—I've been doing this a long time.

ALABAMA GUEST MENU RECIPES

Frank Stitt, an Alabama native, opened Highlands Bar and Grill, Chez Fonfon, and Bottega Dining Room and Café—all in Birmingham. He was named Best Chef: Southeast by the James Beard Foundation and received the Craig Claiborne Lifetime Achievement Award from the Southern Foodways Alliance.

LADY PEA SALAD

PREPARATION TIME: 20 MINUTES,
  PLUS RESTING AND COOLING TIME
COOKING TIME: 30 MINUTES
SERVES: 4

For the peas:
- 2 cups (300 g) shelled fresh or frozen peas, such as lady peas, white acre, or butter peas
- 1 onion, peeled and quartered
- 1 carrot, peeled and quartered
- 4 sprigs fresh thyme, or a pinch of dried thyme
- 4 bay leaves
- ½ tablespoon kosher (coarse) salt

For the salad:
- 1 red bell pepper, cut into small dice
- 1 yellow bell pepper, cut into small dice
- 3 scallions (spring onions), finely sliced
- 1 small jalapeño pepper, finely diced
- 1 tablespoon sherry vinegar
- 1 tablespoon cider vinegar
- ½ teaspoon honey
- Salt and freshly ground black pepper

Note:
  The pea broth can be reserved and used for soups.

For the peas: Place the peas in a pot and add water to cover by 2 inches (5 cm). Add the onion, carrot, thyme, bay leaves, and salt and bring to a boil. Skim, reduce the heat to a simmer, and cook until tender, 20–25 minutes. Taste and adjust seasonings if necessary. Let the peas rest in their liquid for 30 minutes. Drain (see Note) and set the peas aside to cool (discard the other vegetables and any remaining hulls).

For the salad: In a bowl, combine the bell peppers, scallions (spring onions), jalapeño, vinegar, and honey. Add the lady peas and toss. Season to taste with salt and pepper.

ALABAMA . FRANK STITT

GRILLED HEAD-ON SHRIMP

PREPARATION TIME: 25 MINUTES
COOKING TIME: 35 MINUTES
SERVES: 4

- 20 large (U-10) head-on shrimp (prawns), ideally from the Gulf Coast
- Olive oil, for drizzling
- ¼ cup (60 ml) good-quality extra-virgin olive oil, divided
- 1 teaspoon salt
- ½ teaspoon freshly ground black pepper
- Leaves from 1 small bunch basil, finely chopped
- Juice and finely grated zest of 1 lemon

Note:
 As an alternative to charcoal, you can also use a grill (griddle) pan over medium-high heat. The cooking time will be the same.

[We use wild-caught shrimp from Bayou La Batre. This is best served with Lady Pea Salad (opposite page).]

Prepare a charcoal fire (see Note) in a grill (barbecue). Drizzle the shrimp (prawns) with 2 tablespoons of the extra-virgin olive oil, season with the salt and pepper, and cook for about 3 minutes per side, until just done. Remove from the grill.

In a bowl, toss the shrimp with the remaining 2 tablespoons extra-virgin olive oil, the lemon juice, and half of the basil. Garnish with lemon zest and the remaining basil.

PEACH GALETTES

PREPARATION TIME: 30 MINUTES, PLUS FREEZING AND DOUGH CHILLING TIME
COOKING TIME: 15 MINUTES
MAKES: 6 INDIVIDUAL GALETTES

For the pastry dough:
- 1 cup (130 g) all-purpose (plain) flour
- 2 teaspoons granulated sugar
- ¼ teaspoon salt
- 6 tablespoons (85 g) unsalted butter, cut into 1-inch (2.5 cm) cubes and placed in the freezer for 20 minutes
- 3–4 tablespoons ice water

For the topping:
- 6 medium firm-ripe peaches, peeled and sliced about 1 inch (2.5 cm) thick, in perfectly even wedges
- 6 tablespoons (85 g) butter, cut into 4 thin slices per tablespoon (15 g)—very little pats
- 6 tablespoons turbinado (demerara) sugar

[Chilton County, just south of Birmingham, is Alabama's epicenter for peaches. From May until September, an array of varieties come to market and onto our menu. We recommend enjoying the galette with buttermilk ice cream and a glass of Beaumes de Venise or Sauternes.]

For the pastry dough: In a stand mixer fitted with the paddle attachment, combine the flour, sugar, and salt. Add the chilled butter and mix until chunky. Add 3 tablespoons of the ice water and mix until the dough just comes together. Gather the dough and shape into a disk, wrap with plastic (clingfilm), and refrigerate for 1 hour or overnight.

Preheat the oven to 400°F (200°C/Gas Mark 6). Line a baking sheet with a silicone baking mat.

For the topping: Roll out the dough until ¹⁄₁₆ inch (1.6 mm) thick and cut into six 4-inch (10 cm) squares. Transfer to the baking sheet. Place even rows of peaches onto each square of pastry and place pats of butter over the peaches. Sprinkle with the turbinado (demerara) sugar.

Bake until golden, about 20 minutes. Let cool on a wire rack until warm or at room temperature before serving.

Christopher Nicolson is a fifth-generation Alaskan sockeye salmon fisherman and the resident winemaker at the Red Hook Winery in Brooklyn, New York.

Alaska is vast. It is indisputable and terrifying and beautiful. It's a place where humans like me are transient, tentative additions to the land and sea. I am dwarfed by jagged peaks, endless green tundra, a fearsome, open sky, and wide, howling seas. My tiny Alaskan nook, a nestled speck of transience in the immensity, is a fisherman's cabin overlooking the sea.

My mother's family has been fishing in and around Bristol Bay, in southwestern Alaska, about 300 miles (483 km) west and south of Anchorage, for hundreds of years. In our little skiffs, we gillnet wild sockeye, by hand, as they migrate from the chill, blue-gray sea, up the long miles of the winding Kvichak River, and finally to the clear, deep water of Lake Iliamna.

My mother was raised on the shores of Iliamna, the largest freshwater lake in Alaska, in a log cabin. The quality of her family's life, during the long winters on the cabin by the lake, was built upon the bounty (or suffered from the dearth) of the summer salmon catch. In the same way, the quality of my family's life, during our winters in my adopted "off-season" home in New York, remains tied to the outcome of our summer catch.

About 70 miles (113 km) downriver from Lake Iliamna—where the salty ocean water begins to marry with the fresh water of the mighty Kvichak—is our family's "fish camp." Our cabins, built by my grandparents, are situated just above the beach line of a stark little arm of alder-dotted tundra called Graveyard Point. Together with my brothers and cousins, we make Graveyard Point our home for six weeks every summer.

I spent my first summer in fish camp at age six, playing on the beach and watching my mother and father and extended family work: catching, selling, cutting, and preserving fish. I saw the bright silver bodies of sockeye in the gray water, the startling blood, and their black pupils, set amidst gold retinas, as they expired. In the distance, range upon range of rugged, snow-capped mountains encroached upon the tundra and the sea. I smelled the summer tundra, crushed underfoot—the tiny fragrant wildflowers balanced atop the green expanse—and the savory alder wood of the smoldering smokehouse fires, where we preserved fish for the winter months. And, always, we heard the ocean, and judged its mood, to prepare ourselves for clear weather or for storms.

When I was thirteen years old, instead of playing on the beach, I began to fish to make a living. Every summer since then, I've returned to Bristol Bay, even though my adult winter home in New York is far away. In my transience, I copy the migration of salmon, as they wander far away in the cold, black depths of the Arctic, only to return to Bristol Bay to see the solstice light. While the salmon return to make love, to reproduce, and to die, I return so that I might live.

Christopher Nicolson

BROILED SALMON

PREPARATION TIME: 10 MINUTES
COOKING TIME: 10 MINUTES
SERVES: 4

- 1½ lb (680 g) wild Alaskan sockeye salmon fillet, pin bones removed
- 1 tablespoon tamari or soy sauce
- 2 teaspoons kosher (coarse) salt
- 2 tablespoons unsalted butter, softened
- Freshly cracked black pepper

Note:
Prepare and bake the dessert first, then prepare and cook the potatoes. Cook the sockeye last—so it's crispy and hot when you sit down to eat.

[This recipe and those on the next page make up an Alaskan fish camp menu. Together they are an example of the simple way we eat when working in "fish camp," our temporary home during the summer salmon season in Bristol Bay. We stock our pantry with ingredients that can survive in a cool, dark root cellar (since we have no electricity and only highly limited refrigeration) and augment it with fresh things that are available to us, like wild salmon and blueberries.]

Preheat the broiler (grill). Pat the fillet until completely dry and tacky. Rub the tamari onto the flesh side of the fillet and sprinkle with half the salt. Place the fillet, skin side up, on a baking sheet and sprinkle with the remaining salt. Broil until the fish is beginning to crisp and lightly char in places, 5–6 minutes. Remove from the oven and use your fingers to paint the softened butter onto the skin side. Don't rush. Return to the broiler and cook until the butter has melted completely and the skin has crisped and charred (lightly) in places, 2–4 minutes. To serve, break the salmon (do not cut) into portions and generously apply freshly cracked pepper. Serve on warmed plates.

STUFFED BAKED POTATOES

PREPARATION TIME: 20 MINUTES
COOKING TIME: 1 HOUR
SERVES: 4

- 4 russet (baking) potatoes (8–10 oz/ 225–285 g each)
- 2 tablespoons olive oil
- Kosher (coarse) salt
- 4 teaspoons Dijon mustard
- 4 tablespoons sour cream
- 1 stick (115 g) unsalted butter

Preheat the oven to 400°F (200°C/Gas Mark 6).

Scrub, rinse, and completely dry the potatoes. Rub with the oil and season all over with 1 teaspoon salt. Roast until the flesh is tender and the skin is crisp, about 45 minutes. Let cool slightly (about 5 minutes), then use a fork to split the top of each potato, scoop out the flesh into a bowl, and reserve the 4 skins. Fold the mustard and sour cream into the potato flesh and season the mixture to taste with salt. Mash with a fork until almost smooth, then pack the mixture back into the skins. Dot with the butter and bake until the tops are golden, 10–15 minutes. Keep warm until ready to serve.

HUCKLEBERRY COBBLER

PREPARATION TIME: 10 MINUTES
COOKING TIME: 40 MINUTES
SERVES: 4

- 1 stick (115 g) butter, melted
- 1 cup (130 g) all-purpose (plain) flour
- ½ cup (100 g) sugar
- 2 teaspoons baking powder
- 1 teaspoon salt
- ⅔ cup (160 ml) milk
- 1 lb (455 g) huckleberries or Alaskan tundral blueberries
- Whipped cream, for serving

Preheat the oven to 400°F (200°C/Gas Mark 6).

Pour the melted butter into an 8-inch (20 cm) square baking dish or pan. In a bowl, mix together the flour, sugar, baking powder, and salt. Gently stir in the milk (do not overmix). Arrange the berries in the baking dish and pour the batter into the center without stirring.

Bake until the cake portion is lightly golden, 30–40 minutes. Serve warm or at room temperature, with whipped cream.

Gary Paul Nabhan is an Ecumenical Franciscan brother. He has been honored as a pioneer in the local food movement and is the endowed chair at The University of Arizona Southwest Center.

What does the American desert taste like?

It bites like the essential oils of Sonoran oregano, the thymol and carvacrol that bead on the leaves of this spindly desert shrub, growing ever more fragrant and flavorful with each subsequent drought.

It pricks like the prickly pear cactus pad that sends its stickers into your fingers as you try to de-thorn it to make nopalitos, but then its mucilaginous goo heals your cuts and soothes your skin, just like it soothes the scars and wound of the cactus itself.

It offers the fleetingly sweet, smoky aroma of fire-roasted mesquite pod flour, as if the smoke of a mesquite wood fire and the gummy sugars of a carob pod had merged through some hostile takeover of one by the other.

It burns like the incendiary madness of a wild chiltepin pepper no larger than a pea, but with a lot of debilitating pungency in each minute fruit.

It has the oily texture and grassy flavors of range-fed beef cut from the carcass of a Criollo cow that never got near any alfalfa hay.

You don't bite into the traditional fare of Sonoran or Chihuahuan deserts. No, they bite into you, chomping down on your flesh, unwilling to let you go back to whatever you knew as "comfort food" before. These deserts have no room for comfort food or comfortable people either, for that matter. These deserts exact their price from you, as you sweat through heat and drought, and as you greet the cactus and critters.

As one herder once told me, "Everything in the desert either sticks, stinks, or stings." That's what desert terroir is all about.

Its pungency and perspicacity teach you how to be a survivor.

Gary Paul Nabhan

CARNE MACHACA CON CHILTEPINS Y QUELITES

PREPARATION TIME: 15 MINUTES
COOKING TIME: 30 MINUTES
SERVES: 6

- 1 lb (455 g) sun-dried tasajo strips of carne seca deshebrada or machacada (see Note)
- 2 tablespoons lard or olive oil
- 2 white onions, diced
- 5 fresh green chiltepin chilies, thinly sliced
- 1 clove garlic, mashed
- 8 cups (280 g) wild greens (such as purslane, lambsquarter, watercress, or amaranth), roughly chopped
- Salt
- 18 Sonoran sobaquera white flour tortillas

Note:
This is the softly jerked meat of range-fed Corriente cattle.

[Before the United States–Mexico border existed, *carne con chile*, not chili con carne, was the on-the-spot, make-do-with-what-you-have dinner of choice when strangers arrived at your gate. And before kale was king, wild purslane (*verdolagas*), lambsquarter (*chuales*), watercress (*berros*), or wild amaranths (*quelites de las aguas*) were half the meal, while rehydrated jerked meat, chiltepins, and wild onions were the other half of the mix.]

Place the carne seca in a medium saucepan. Cover with 1 inch (2.5 cm) water and place over medium-high heat. Simmer until soft, about 15 minutes.

Meanwhile, in a large frying pan, heat the lard over medium-high heat. Add the onions, chilies, garlic, and greens and cook for 10 minutes.

Drain the meat and return it to the saucepan. Add the sautéed vegetables and cook over medium heat for 5 minutes so the greens make their own potlikker for the meat. Season to taste with salt.

Serve with 3 tortillas per plate.

GUACAVAQUI

PREPARATION TIME: 25 MINUTES,
   PLUS OVERNIGHT BEAN SOAKING TIME
COOKING TIME: 3 HOURS 45 MINUTES
SERVES: 6

- 6 beef or venison ribs, or all the backstrap meat from a deer or cow
- 1 lb (455 g) dried chickpeas, soaked overnight
- 1 young calabaza de las aguas or green-striped cushaw squash, peeled, seeded, and roughly chopped
- 3 Texas yellow onions or 8 shallots, diced
- 3 wild saiya roots or 5 carrots, coarsely chopped
- 2 lb (910 g) fresh green kernels from Mexican June white corn
- 2 cups (450 g) chopped quelites (amaranth greens)
- 5 dried red chiltepin chilies
- A handful of dried Mexican oregano leaves
- 5 cloves rose-colored Sonoran garlic, peeled and smashed
- Sea salt (ideally from the Gulf of California)
- Freshly ground black pepper
- Lime slices and chopped cilantro (coriander), for serving

[This is Venison Cocido of the Binational Yaqui People. In the indigenous Cahitan dialects of the Yaqui and Mayo languages, *guaca* or *huaca* means "*carne*," or "meat," whether of deer or the Spanish-introduced Criollo Corriente cattle, while *vaqui* refers to a "*cocido*," or simmered stew of any vegetables, wild or cultivated. Traditionally boiled in a clay *olla* (you can use a large pot), this is the food of seasonally sacred feasts where Yaqui deer dancers and *pascola* clowns keep you awake and wondrous all night long.]

Place the ribs or backstrap meat in a large soup pot. Cover with 1 inch (2.5 cm) water. Bring to a boil, then reduce to a simmer. Cover and cook until the meat is tender and easily falls off the bone, about 3 hours. Remove the bones and add the squash, onions, and saiya roots and simmer for 30 minutes.

Fifteen minutes before serving, add the corn, quelites, chilies, oregano, garlic, and a pinch of salt. Remove the pot from the heat. Season to taste with salt and black pepper. Serve in bowls, topped with lime slices and chopped cilantro.

P. Allen Smith comes from a long line of Southern farmers and cooks. He is an author and television host and he lives at Moss Mountain Farm, near Little Rock, Arkansas.

When I was growing up, the table was a place to share family wisdom, gossip, laughter, and lore. Not infrequently there were four if not five generations present around the turnip greens, chicken and dumplings, and coconut cake.

I grew up hearing stories about the food— who grew it or caught it or cooked it—but also my grandparents' and great-grandparents' stories from the Civil War, the World Wars, the Great Mississippi Flood of 1927, and the Great Depression.

My great-grandmother Josephine Foster was a preacher's daughter, who during the Depression raised eight children, including my grandmother, whom I called Kee Kee. Times had been hard for everyone then, but they used to say with pride that Arkansas was the only state in the nation that could be truly self-sufficient, because of all its natural resources. There were diamonds, timber, gas, and oil and, just as valuable, alluvial soil, lakes, bayous, and rivers that produced edible riches and abundant game.

Those hard years from the '27 flood, through the Great Depression, and on through the Second World War, had been difficult for everybody. But my family laughingly recalled that when they were young, they hadn't even known times were hard. They would reminisce about how Papa Joe would slice the ham so thinly you could read the newspaper through it. But more of their memories were about eating well through the bounty of the gardens, the wild, and the community.

People lived modestly, but they helped one another, particularly when it came to food. Many would plant large patches of greens or peas and invite friends and neighbors to pick all they wanted "on the halves"—meaning you shared half of what you picked with the landowner. Fresh field peas—such as crowder peas, black-eyed peas, whippoorwill peas, red zipper peas, purple-hulled peas, and the little cream-colored lady peas—are an important part of Arkansas's culinary heritage, and taste absolutely divine. Some of my favorite meals were those field peas, with fried okra and sliced fresh tomatoes.

Wild foods were on the table, too. My great-grandmother showed me how to gather poke salat early in the spring, and how to blanch the shoots and cook them for breakfast with eggs—almost how we add chard and kale today to scrambled eggs. Dandelions made salad, and wild blackberries, muscadines, and mayhaw made delicious jams and jellies.

By summer, the Arkansas heat and humidity are relentless, but many plants love that heat —tomatoes, okra, peaches, and of course watermelon. It was a prize to have a watermelon from Cave City; something about the soil there gives the watermelon such a delectable fresh, crisp, rich flavor. We also feasted on peaches from Crowley's Ridge. There were Bradley pink tomatoes from Bradley County, those fresh field peas, and okra.

Everything in the South is fried, and I do love fried okra, as my granddad did. But Kee Kee also liked her okra boiled, with a teaspoon of vinegar to cut the slipperiness, slow-cooked with tomatoes and onions, and served on Arkansas-grown rice with her famous cornbread. Her cast-iron skillet was something hallowed, in that she never washed it—it was "seasoned" after decades of preparing corn pone or hot water cornbread.

Granddad was notorious for growing, or gathering from friends, small hot peppers, and in late summer he'd make his vinegar-based hot pepper sauce, which he loved to put on peas and greens. When Kee Kee would cook a big pot of turnip and collard greens, yielding plenty of potlikker for the cornbread, my granddad would say they tasted so good, they'd make a bulldog break his chain.

Wild hogs (or razorbacks) and domestic pigs have been central to Southern fare since the Spanish first brought them in the 1500s, and in fall, we used to joke that we ate every part of the pig except the squeal. Fall also brought the Arkansas Red sweet potato, which doesn't keep as well as the Beauregard, but the flavor made it my family's favorite.

My granddad was a legendary hunter who would walk our legs off when we'd go quail hunting. He kept a kennel of dogs, pointers and setters, that were obedient and as skilled as he was at bringing in the quail. He'd bag quite a lot of quail, which we would help dress, and Kee Kee was very adept at preparing them. The thought of her quail and gravy makes my mouth water. Granddad also shot dove, and later in the season friends shared duck and we feasted on duck gumbo over rice.

The Fosters also kept a flock of Silver-Laced Wyandottes in Lonoke County. This was their favorite breed of chicken because of their eggs and meat and beauty. Chickens brought thrift to the household economy. The extra roosters went into my great-grandmother's amazing chicken and dumplings.

Come winter, every dessert featured pecans, which grow abundantly in much of the South. I cannot recall a Thanksgiving or Christmas when there weren't at least a couple of pecan pies amongst the desserts—with my great-aunts fishing for compliments about a particular recipe or the quality of their crust.

Everyone seemed to have a version of the Karo syrup pecan pie recipe. One of my great-uncles said it was so sweet it would make your teeth hurt. He and I preferred the family recipe made with buttermilk. It cut the sweetness and made for a more delicious experience—something only buttermilk can do.

Sitting there as a child, I shared these foods, and also the lore and wisdom and laughter behind them. At the table, I learned that no matter how much money is in your bank account, when the land is as generous as it is in Arkansas, everyone can live well through gardening, hunting, cooking, and sharing.

But the richness of that multigenerational experience has grown less prevalent today—and it's not until it's gone that you really appreciate it. It's lovely when suddenly you're in the midst of that great commune, of being together.

Today at Moss Mountain Farm, we still hold the Foster Family Reunion and an annual Christmas party. We still grow greens, field peas, and sweet potatoes, and still raise Silver-Laced Wyandottes. And when we sit down, talking about the past and the present and the future, we are communing. As we share food together, a constellation of memories, aromas, and flavors occurs, and it's magical.

Matthew McClure was born and raised in Little Rock, Arkansas. In Bentonville, he is chef at The Hive, where he focuses on local ingredients and was named a *Food & Wine* People's Best New Chef.

BRAISED COLLARD GREENS

PREPARATION TIME: 15 MINUTES
COOKING TIME: 2 HOURS
SERVES: 4–6

- 2 cups (450 g) diced tesa (pancetta)
- 1 yellow onion, peeled and diced
- 3 cloves garlic, peeled and finely chopped
- 1 tablespoon mustard seeds
- 1 teaspoon crushed chili flakes
- 1 quart (1 liter) chicken stock
- ½ cup (95 g) packed light brown sugar
- 2–3 large bunches collard greens, center stems discarded, leaves sliced 2-inch (5 cm) thick
- Salt
- Cider vinegar

In a large pot cook the tesa over medium heat, to render the fat, about 15 minutes. Add the onion and garlic and cook until caramelized, about 10 more minutes.

Meanwhile, heat a small skillet over medium heat. Add the mustard seeds and chili flakes and toast, stirring occasionally, about 3 minutes, or until aromatic.

Add the chicken stock to the pot slowly, deglazing the pan. Add the brown sugar and toasted spices. Increase heat to medium-high and bring to a simmer. Working in batches, fold in the collard greens, stirring until wilted. Cover and bring to a boil. Once boiling, reduce the heat to medium-low, cover, and simmer until the greens are tender, 1½–2 hours. Season to taste with salt and vinegar.

SORGHUM ROAST DUCK

PREPARATION TIME: 10 MINUTES, PLUS 2
  DAYS FOR SALTING AND HANGING
COOKING TIME: 50 MINUTES
SERVES: 4

- 1 Peking duck, about 3.5 lb (1.5 kg)
- 1.5 lb (675 g) kosher (coarse) salt
- 2 cups (670 g) sorghum syrup or sorghum
  molasses (treacle)

Place the duck on a rimmed baking sheet. Cover evenly and generously with salt and refrigerate, uncovered, overnight. Rinse the duck with water to remove the salt, and place on a rack set over a rimmed baking sheet or roasting pan. Refrigerate, uncovered, overnight.

Preheat the oven to 400°F (200°C/Gas Mark 6).

In a large pot, combine the sorghum and 1½ gallons (5.7 liters) water and bring to a boil over high heat. Reduce the heat to medium-low. Carefully submerge the duck, breast side down, in the water, and simmer for 7 minutes. Remove the duck from the poaching liquid and return to the rack set over a roasting pan. Pat dry with paper towels and place in the oven. Roast until the leg is easily pulled loose from the body, about 50 minutes.

GNOCCHI DUMPLINGS

PREPARATION TIME: 25 MINUTES
COOKING TIME: 5 MINUTES
SERVES: 4–6

- 1½ lb (680 g) russet (baking) potatoes,
  about 4
- 2 eggs
- 1 scant cup (125 g) bread (strong white)
  flour
- 2 teaspoons kosher (coarse) salt,
  plus additional for ice bath
- 2 tablespoons olive oil, divided

Preheat the oven to 350°F (180°C/Gas Mark 4).

Bake the potatoes until tender, about 1 hour. When just cool enough to handle, peel and run the potatoes through a ricer into a bowl. Quickly stir the eggs into the hot potato. Stir in the flour and salt and mix until the dough just comes together. Divide into 4 portions and roll each into a ball. On a floured surface roll each ball into a "snake" ½ inch (1.25 cm) thick. Cut the snakes crosswise into ½-inch (1.25 cm) lengths. Transfer to a floured baking sheet so they don't stick together.

Set up a large bowl of salted ice water. Bring a large pot of water to a simmer. Working in two batches, add the dumplings to the simmering water. Once the dumplings float, cook for 45 seconds, then quickly transfer to the salted ice water to cool for 2–3 minutes. Using a slotted spoon, scoop the dumplings out of the ice bath, transfer to a bowl, and toss with 1 tablespoon of the olive oil. Repeat with the second batch and set aside to dry.

RABBIT AND DUMPLINGS

PREPARATION TIME: 2 HOURS
COOKING TIME: 1½ HOURS
SERVES: 4–5

For the rabbit brine:
- 6 tablespoons kosher (coarse) salt
- 6 tablespoons sugar
- 1 cinnamon stick
- 1 bay leaf
- 10 black peppercorns
- 1 (3 lb/1.4 kg) rabbit, cut into 6 pieces, 2 front legs, 2 hind legs, and cage in half

For the braise:
- 2 tablespoons olive oil
- 4 stalks celery, cut into large dice
- 2 carrots, peeled and cut into large dice
- 1 onion, peeled and cut into large dice
- 3 cloves garlic, sliced
- 1 tablespoon tomato paste (purée)
- 8 sprigs fresh thyme
- 2 oz (50 g) pancetta, coarsely diced
- 1 quart (1 liter) chicken stock

For assembling the dish:
- 2 tablespoons olive oil
- 2 tablespoons finely diced shallot
- ¼ cup finely diced carrot
- ¼ cup finely diced celery
- ½ lb (230 g) hen of the woods (maitake) mushrooms
- 2 cups (475 ml) braising liquid
- Gnocchi Dumplings (page 511)
- 2 tablespoons chopped fresh parsley
- Grated zest and juice of 1 lemon
- 2 tablespoons unsalted butter
- 2 tablespoons chopped, toasted almonds
- Salt
- Aleppo pepper, for garnish

[This is a refined take on the way my mother used to prepare the rabbits my father hunted. The basic idea is simple: Slow-cook tough meat to make it tender and delicious.]

For the rabbit brine: In a saucepan, combine the salt, sugar, cinnamon stick, bay leaf, peppercorns, and 1 quart (1 liter) water and heat over medium until the salt and sugar are dissolved. Allow the brine to cool. Place the rabbit in a container (of a size that will allow the rabbit to be completely submerged), add the brine, and brine for 1 hour 30 minutes.

Remove the rabbit from the brine and arrange on a towel-lined baking sheet. Pat dry and refrigerate until ready to braise.

For the braise: Preheat the oven to 350°F (180°C/Gas Mark 4).

In a large sauté pan, heat the olive oil over medium heat. Add the celery, carrots, and onion and cook until nice and soft but not browned, about 8 minutes. Add the garlic and cook for 2 minutes. Stir in the tomato paste (purée) and cook for another 2 minutes. Remove from the heat.

Arrange the rabbit, thyme, and pancetta, evenly spaced, in a small roasting pan. Pour the sautéed vegetables evenly over the rabbit and cover with chicken stock. Cover the pan with the lid or foil and roast until the meat is tender, about 1 hour 30 minutes. Let the rabbit cool in the liquid. Pick the meat off the skin and bones and set aside. Warm the cooking juices in the pan and strain; reserve the braising liquid.

To assemble the dish: In a large sauté pan, warm the olive oil over medium heat. Add the shallot, carrot, celery, and mushrooms and cook until very soft, about 10 minutes. Add the 2 cups (475 ml) reserved braising liquid and the meat. Bring to a simmer over medium-high heat, and cook until the sauce has reduced and thickened slightly, about 6 minutes. Add the gnocchi, parsley, lemon zest and juice, butter, and almonds. Season with salt to taste. Garnish with Aleppo pepper.

ARKANSAS . MATTHEW MCCLURE

RICE GRITS PUDDING WITH BLACKBERRIES

PREPARATION TIME: 45 MINUTES
COOKING TIME: 20 MINUTES
SERVES: 6–8

For the rice:
- 1 quart (1 liter) heavy (whipping) cream
- 1 vanilla bean, split lengthwise
- ½ cup (100 g) sugar
- 2 cups (280 g) milled rice, also known as rice grits
- 1 tablespoon mascarpone

For the custard:
- 8 egg yolks
- ¼ cup (50 g) sugar
- 1 vanilla bean, split lengthwise
- 1 quart (1 liter) heavy (whipping) cream

For the blackberries:
- 2 cups (290 g) blackberries, halved
- ½ cup (100 g) sugar
- ¼ cup (60 ml) Moscato
- Juice of 1 lemon
- Pinch of salt
- 1 tablespoon torn fresh mint

For the rice: In a large saucepan, combine the cream and 1 quart (1 liter) water and bring to a boil. Scrape in the vanilla seeds and add the pot. Add the sugar, then slowly stir in the rice, trying to maintain the boil. Reduce to a simmer and cook until the rice is softened and thickened considerably, 5–7 minutes. Stir in the mascarpone.

For the custard: Set up a large bowl of ice and water. In a medium bowl, whisk together the egg yolks and sugar. Scrape in the vanilla seeds. In a saucepan, scald the cream over medium heat. Slowly whisk the hot cream into the yolks, whisking constantly, making sure not to scramble. Return the custard to the saucepan over medium heat. Stir frequently, scraping the bottom and corners of the pan, until the mixture thickens or reaches 180°F (82°C). Remove from the heat and transfer to a clean bowl set over the ice bath.

For the blackberries: In a bowl, gently toss together the berries, sugar, Moscato, lemon juice, salt, and mint and let sit for 30 minutes.

Divide the pudding among serving bowls. Top with the custard and blackberries.

CALIFORNIA

Jonathan Gold is the Pulitzer Prize–winning restaurant critic for the *Los Angeles Times*.

The first time I visited New York, the entrance of the most fashionable French restaurant in town was lined with crates of tired vegetables, with labels I associated with second-tier food stores back home. The produce at the carriage trade shops I'd dreamed of visiting was haggard (although the meat was nice). The Union Square Greenmarket was bare of almost everything but onions and apples. I hadn't yet made it to Chez Panisse, and my student budget didn't extend to as many trips to Spago and Michael's as I would have liked, but for the first time it occurred to me: California may really have the best food in the United States.

To me, California is unsurpassed as a center of agriculture, with some of the world's best wine, splendid growing regions, 840 miles (about 1,300 km) of coastline, and for a good part of the year not just America's best—but America's *only*—vegetables, as any Easterner who has ever craved a February avocado can attest. The tradition of grilled meats and minimally altered vegetables, stretching from the *rancho* days through the *Sunset*-magazine ideal of back-porch barbecue (and on to Spago), turned out to be exactly the way you would want such lovely produce to be treated.

California is a place of almost unimaginable cultural diversity—a locus of 21st-century immigration, as well as the world's center of entertainment and technology, astrophysics and art, urban innovation and inconceivable wealth. The cuisines and ingredients of a hundred civilizations are available here in something close to their ideal forms. It is the first American state tied more closely to Asia than to Europe, and a dish that becomes popular in Chengdu, Hanoi, or Seoul may be on Los Angeles or Oakland menus within

a month. It could be correct to think of great swaths of Southern California less as influenced by Mexico than as spiritually part of Mexico. It may be easier to find a great Afghan meal in California's Bay Area than in Kabul.

And it is not an accident that the first restaurant to serve salad as a first course was in Los Angeles, or that the concept of casual fine dining started in California. The wrestling match between earty naturalism and technical rigor that informs so many of the world's best menus was likely first expressed by the contrast between Chez Panisse in Berkeley and French Laundry in Yountville.

To taste California is to taste the world, but more than anything, it's about the taste of California. Because when you encounter the word "California" on a menu, anywhere from Tokyo to Rome, it doesn't refer to a specific dish, flavor, or technique, but rather to the idea of freshness, simplicity, and vegetables allowed to taste of themselves.

Alice Waters is a chef, author, food activist, founder of the Edible Schoolyard Project, and founder/owner of Chez Panisse restaurant, which opened in Berkeley, California, in 1971. She was awarded the National Humanities Medal by President Barack Obama.

CROUTONS

MAKES: 8–10 CROUTONS

- 8–10 slices country-style bread
- Olive oil, for brushing
- 1 clove garlic, peeled

Preheat the oven to 375°F (190°C/Gas Mark 5).

Brush the bread with the oil. Lay the oiled bread on a baking sheet and toast until golden brown, about 10 minutes. Rub the croutons with the garlic.

Serve with Rockfish Soup with Aïoli and Croutons (page 516).

AÏOLI (GARLIC MAYONNAISE)

MAKES: ABOUT 1 CUP (210 G)

- 2 or 3 small cloves garlic, peeled
- A pinch of salt
- 1 egg yolk
- 1 cup (240 ml) olive oil

Pound the garlic until smooth with a mortar and pestle, along with the salt. Place the yolk in a bowl and add about half the garlic and ½ teaspoon water. Mix well with a whisk.

Measure the oil into a cup with a pour spout. Slowly dribble the oil into the egg yolk mixture, whisking constantly. As the egg yolk absorbs the oil, the sauce will thicken, lighten in color, and become opaque. This will happen rather quickly. Then you can add the oil a little faster, whisking all the while. If the sauce is thicker than you like, thin it with a few drops of water. Taste and add more salt and garlic, as desired.

Serve with Rockfish Soup with Aïoli and Croutons (page 516).

ROCKFISH SOUP
WITH AÏOLI AND CROUTONS

PREPARATION TIME: 45 MINUTES
COOKING TIME: 1 HOUR 50 MINUTES
SERVES: 8–10

For the fish stock:
- 3 lb (1.35 kg) fish bones and heads (gills removed), white-fleshed fish only
- Olive oil
- 1 onion, sliced
- 1 small carrot, sliced
- 1 small bulb fennel, trimmed and sliced
- 3 medium tomatoes, coarsely chopped
- 1 head garlic, halved horizontally
- ¼ teaspoon black peppercorns
- ¼ teaspoon fennel seeds
- ¼ teaspoon coriander seeds
- A few sprigs of fresh herbs (such as fennel tops, wild fennel, savory, thyme, or parsley)
- 1 bay leaf
- Pinch of saffron threads
- Scant 2 cups (450 ml) dry white wine
- Salt

For the fish:
- 2 lb (910 g) California rockfish fillets
- Extra-virgin olive oil
- 2 tablespoons chopped fennel tops, wild fennel, or parsley
- 4 cloves garlic, smashed and coarsely chopped
- Salt

For the soup base:
- 3 tablespoons olive oil
- 1 medium onion, finely diced
- 1 leek, white part only, rinsed and diced
- 1 medium bulb fennel, trimmed and diced
- Pinch of saffron threads
- Salt
- 4–5 medium tomatoes (about ¾ lb/ 350 g), peeled, seeded, and diced

For finishing the soup:
- Croutons (page 515)
- Aïoli (page 515)

For the fish stock: Rinse and clean the fish bones and heads. If necessary, chop the bones so they will fit in a large heavy pot.

Heat a large heavy pot over medium-high heat and pour in enough olive oil to cover the bottom of the pan. Add the fish bones and sauté for 2 minutes. Add the onion, carrot, fennel, tomatoes, garlic, peppercorns, fennel seeds, coriander seeds, fresh herbs, bay leaf, and saffron. Cook for a few more minutes, until the vegetables start to soften. Pour in the wine, bring to a boil, and cook for a couple of minutes. Add about 6 cups (1.5 liters) water and season with salt. Bring to a boil and immediately reduce heat to a simmer. Skim off the foam that rises to the surface. Simmer for 45 minutes, then strain.

Meanwhile, for the fish: Trim away any bones from the fillets and add them to the simmering fish stock.

Cut the fillets into 2- or 3-inch (5 or 7.5 cm) pieces and toss them in a bowl with enough olive oil to just coat. Add the fennel tops, garlic, and salt to taste.

For the soup base: Heat a heavy soup pot over medium heat. Add the olive oil and when hot, add the onion and cook for 5 minutes. Add the leek, fennel, and saffron and cook, stirring now and then, until soft, about 7 minutes; do not brown. Season with salt, add the tomatoes, and cook for another 3–4 minutes. Pour in the strained fish stock and bring to a boil. Reduce to a simmer and cook for 5 minutes. Taste for salt and adjust. (This can be done ahead of time and in fact, it tastes better if this soup base has had a chance to sit for a while before you add the fish.)

When ready to finish and serve the soup, bring the soup base to a simmer and add the fish. Simmer for another 5 minutes. Serve topped with the croutons and an a scoop of aïoli.

SLOW-ROASTED ALMONDS WITH SAGE LEAVES

PREPARATION TIME: 5 MINUTES
COOKING TIME: 35 MINUTES
MAKES: 3½ CUPS (470 G)

- 3 cups (430 g) almonds (or equal amounts of almonds, walnuts, and pecans)
- 1½ cups (40 g) loosely packed sage leaves
- 3 tablespoons extra-virgin olive oil
- 1 teaspoon sea salt
- Thin strips of peel from 1 lemon or orange (optional)
- 2 tablespoons fennel seeds (optional)

[I love these slow-roasted almonds rich with the flavor of fresh herbs. I put them in beautiful bowls around the house whenever I have people over. Slow-roasting is a wonderful method for mixed nuts that normally have different cooking times. The delightfully crisped sage leaves are as satisfying as the roasted nuts themselves. Thin strips of lemon or orange peel and a sprinkling of fennel seed add extra flavor and brightness.]

Preheat the oven to 275°F (140°C/Gas Mark 1). Line a rimmed baking sheet with parchment paper.

In a medium bowl, mix together the nuts and sage leaves. Add the oil and salt, as well as citrus rind and fennel seed, if using, and toss gently until the nuts and sage are evenly coated.

Spread the nuts and sage on the baking sheet and bake for 20 minutes. Stir the nuts and return them to the oven for 10 more minutes. Remove the pan from the oven and break a few nuts open. If their centers are golden brown they are done; if the nuts still need more time, stir them and return them to the oven, checking every 5 minutes or so. You want them to roast fully, though not to burn—usually 35 minutes is about right.

FALL CHICORY SALAD WITH FUYU PERSIMMONS

PREPARATION TIME: 15 MINUTES
SERVES: 4

- 4 generous handfuls of chicories (radicchio, escarole, Belgian endive, and frisée or curly endive)
- 1 clove garlic, pounded to a fine paste
- 1 tablespoon red wine vinegar
- Salt and freshly ground black pepper
- 3–4 tablespoons olive oil
- 2 Fuyu persimmons, thinly sliced

Carefully wash and dry the greens. In a small bowl, mix together the garlic, vinegar, and salt and pepper to taste. Stir to dissolve the salt, taste, and adjust if needed. Whisk in the olive oil. Use a lettuce leaf to taste the vinaigrette as you add the oil.

Put the greens in a large bowl, add about three-fourths of the vinaigrette, then toss, and taste. Add more dressing as needed. Plate immediately.

In a small bowl, toss the persimmon slices with 1 teaspoon of vinaigrette. Spread on top of the plated chicories.

MEYER LEMON SHERBET

PREPARATION TIME: 10 MINUTES,
    PLUS CHILLING AND FREEZING TIME
COOKING TIME: 10 MINUTES
MAKES: 1 QUART (1 LITER)

- 1½ cups (300 g) sugar
- 1 cup (240 ml) Meyer lemon juice
- 1 tablespoon finely chopped Meyer lemon zest
- ¾ cup (180 ml) milk
- 1 teaspoon plain unflavored gelatin

In a small saucepan, combine the sugar and 1½ cups (355 ml) water and gently heat until the sugar is dissolved. Pour this syrup into a bowl with the lemon juice. Stir in the zest and milk. In the same saucepan, combine the gelatin with 2 tablespoons water and let sit for 5 minutes. Once the gelatin has plumped up, heat it gently until there is no graininess. Add the melted gelatin to the lemon mixture and refrigerate until thoroughly chilled.

When the sherbet base is cold, freeze in an ice cream maker according to the manufacturer's instructions.

HUCKLEBERRY ICE CREAM

PREPARATION TIME: 15 MINUTES,
    PLUS CHILLING AND FREEZING TIME
COOKING TIME: 15 MINUTES
MAKES: 1 QUART (1 LITER)

- 6 egg yolks
- 1 cup (240 ml) half-and-half (single cream)
- 1¼ cups (250 g) sugar
- 2 cups (475 ml) heavy (whipping) cream, chilled
- 2 cups (275 g) huckleberries
- 4 teaspoons fresh lemon juice
- 2 teaspoons kirsch (optional)

[Wear an apron: Huckleberry stains are difficult to remove.]

In a bowl, whisk the egg yolks just enough to break them up.

In a nonreactive saucepan, combine the half-and-half (single cream) and ¾ cup (150 g) of the sugar and gently heat over low heat, stirring slowly, until the half-and-half is steaming and the sugar is dissolved. Drizzle the warm mixture into the egg yolks, whisking constantly as you pour. Pour the mixture out of the bowl and back into the saucepan. Measure the heavy (whipping) cream into the bowl and set aside.

Place the saucepan over low heat and cook, stirring slowly and scraping the bottom of the pan with a wooden spoon or silicone spatula, until the mixture thickens enough to coat the spoon. Immediately remove the mixture from the heat and strain through a fine-mesh sieve into the bowl, whisking it into the cold heavy cream. Cover and refrigerate until thoroughly chilled.

In a saucepan, stir together the berries and the remaining ½ cup (100 g) sugar. Cook over medium heat until the sugar is dissolved and the berries have released their juices. Pass the berries through a food mill. Stir the berry purée into the chilled ice cream base. Stir in the lemon juice and kirsch (if using) and freeze in an ice cream maker according to the manufacturer's instructions.

COLORADO

Eugenia Bone is a food journalist and the author of five books, including *At Mesa's Edge: Cooking and Ranching in Colorado's North Fork Valley*.

When I first arrived in western Colorado from the verdant East Coast, all I saw was brown grass and tangled barbed-wire fences. After a few months, I noticed sturdy peach orchards and a network of cold ditches that circulated across the land like blue veins. After a year, I really saw Colorado: the dense, green alfalfa meadows filled with grazing cattle; farms wedged between the rocks exploding with corn, potatoes, and melons; and towering mountains that changed color every minute. Colorado is an agricultural state like no other, because while it takes time to appreciate its abundance, the grand landscape is what truly nourishes.

Think about what it took to settle Colorado. Native Coloradans made a living by hunting bison, elk, and deer on the perennial grass-lands of the valleys, the flat-topped mountains, and the eastern prairie. In the semiarid south, the Puebloans farmed beans, squash, and corn in the ancient practice of companion planting. It was Hispanic immigrants from New Mexico who trans-planted their communal irrigation tradition to Colorado. Their *acequias*, a system of engineered ditches that used gravity to move river water to distant fields and pastures, has expanded throughout the state. Water is on every Coloradan's mind, always. Hope for rain and snow, battles over shares of runoff. At any diner, you'll hear creaky ranchers and sunburned farmers argue about water rights over their black coffees and cinnamon buns. Hispanic ranchers brought their horses, cattle, and cowboy culture too, and they were followed by waves of immigrants, who utilized the vast lands.

When I imagine Colorado, I think of peach orchards along riffling gravelly rivers, melon patches hot as biscuits, and fields of sweet corn ripening between the pink adobe hills. These represent the traditional specialty crops of Colorado. New markets have opened up for grass-fed beef and lamb.

In Colorado, wilderness is never far away. I know farmers whose frosty pastures are colonized by huge herds of winter elk, orchard-ists whose trees shelter flocks of turkeys, and ranchers whose llamas are tormented by prowling mountain lions. There are fires on the mountains in the summer, blizzards in the winter, and floods in the arroyos in the spring. Grand nature, in all her cruelty and beauty, is constantly on display.

We make our lives among the red rocks because of this divine landscape, and because sometimes nature gives up her treasures, fat porcini erupt throughout the alpine forests, and storm clouds darken with the hymn of water.

Holly Arnold Kinney is the owner of her family's The Fort Restaurant in Morrison, Colorado, where she houses her 3,000-volume library of rare cookbooks and Western history.

BOWL OF THE WIFE OF KIT CARSON

PREPARATION TIME: 25 MINUTES
COOKING TIME: 25 MINUTES
SERVES: 6

- 2 lb (910 g) boneless, skinless chicken breasts
- 6 cups (1.4 liters) chicken broth
- ¼ teaspoon dried Mexican leaf oregano, crumbled
- 1 cup (160 g) cooked rice
- 1 cup (165 g) cooked chickpeas or canned, rinsed and well drained
- 1 canned chipotle chile in adobo sauce, minced
- 6 oz (170 g) Monterey Jack or Havarti cheese, diced
- 2 avocados, sliced
- 6 sprigs fresh cilantro (coriander), optional
- 1 lime, cut into 6 wedges
- 12 hot corn tortillas, for serving

[In the spring of 1961, two years before opening The Fort, my family and I took a road trip to Mexico. When we reached Durango, some six hundred miles south of the border, we were told that the best place to eat was the drugstore. The next morning, we watched as a stream of young children came in from the fields to fill family lunch buckets with a special soup sold at the store. It smelled so good, we knew we had to try it. The bowls we were served held a heady, spicy broth of chicken with white meat, nutty chickpeas, rice, a touch of oregano, chunks of avocado, and bite-size pieces of soft white cheese. The secret of the amazing flavor, though, was the chipotle chile. This smoked jalapeño gave the soup a distinctive and delicious smokiness. *Caldo tlalpeño* is the soup's proper name and when The Fort opened, it was on the menu. No one could pronounce its name or knew what it meant, and despite its innate deliciousness, the soup did not sell. One day Leona Wood, the septuagenarian who ran our gift shop/trade room on weekends, told us that she remembered her grandmother serving this dish. Miss Wood happened to be the last granddaughter of the American frontiersman Kit Carson (who at one time took command in Colorado, where he died). With a little genealogical figuring, we dubbed the soup Bowl of the Wife of Kit Carson.]

In a large saucepan, combine the chicken and broth. Bring to a boil over medium-high heat, skimming off any foam that rises to the top. Remove from the heat, cover, and let the chicken poach gently for 12 minutes. Remove the chicken from the pot and cut into strips about 1½ inches (4 cm) long. Return the chicken strips to the broth and add the oregano, rice, chickpeas, and chipotle. Return to a simmer over medium heat.

To serve, divide the cheese among 6 deep soup bowls. Then divide the soup evenly among the bowls. Garnish each portion with avocado slices, cilantro (coriander; if using), and a wedge of lime. Serve with hot tortillas.

SPOTTED DOG SAVORY BREAD PUDDING (CAPIROTADA)

PREPARATION TIME: 25 MINUTES
COOKING TIME: 1 HOUR 30 MINUTES
SERVES: 4–6

- ¾ cup (95 g) raisins
- 1½ cups (290 g) crushed piloncillo or brown sugar
- ½ medium sweet onion, finely chopped
- 3 eggs
- 1½ cups (355 ml) half-and-half (single cream) or milk
- 4 cups toasted bread pieces (cut or torn, about 1½ inches/4 cm)
- 1 Gala or Granny Smith apple, peeled, quartered, and sliced
- 4 tablespoons unsalted butter, cut into pieces
- 1½ teaspoons ground cinnamon
- ½ teaspoon freshly grated nutmeg
- 4 ounces (115 g) yellow cheddar cheese, grated (about 1 cup)
- Cold heavy (whipping) cream, for pouring on top

Note:

Capirotada may be baked ahead of time, except for the cheese topping. Thirty minutes before serving, preheat the oven to 350°F (180°C/Gas Mark 4). Cover the capirotada and heat for 20 minutes. Top with the cheese and return to the oven, uncovered, for 5 minutes to allow the cheese to melt and begin to brown.

[This bread pudding evolved from the old Spanish dish called *capirotada*, which, according to *Libro del Arte Cozina,* a cookbook compiled by Spanish chef Diego Granado in the late 1500s, began as a savory dish of layered bread, onions, and cheese, with meat or poultry. It was topped with sweet meringue, an odd flourish to our modern sensibilities.]

Preheat the oven to 350°F (180°C/Gas Mark 4).

In a small saucepan, bring 2 cups (475 ml) water to a boil set over high heat. Add the raisins, cover, and remove from the heat. Let sit for 10 minutes to reconstitute. Drain and reserve the plumped raisins.

In a small saucepan, combine the brown sugar and 1 cup (240 ml) water. Cook over medium-high heat until the mixture is the consistency of maple syrup, about 10 minutes. Add the onion and continue to boil for 5 minutes.

In a medium bowl, gently stir together the eggs and half-and-half (light cream). Don't beat them.

In a shallow 3-quart (3-liter) baking dish, layer the bread, raisins, apple, butter, cinnamon, and nutmeg. Pour the syrup-onion mixture on top, then the egg-cream mixture. Push down the filling with a spoon to make sure all the ingredients get wet.

Bake for 40 minutes, remove from the oven, and spread the grated cheese on top. Return the pudding to the oven and bake until the cheese is melted, the pudding has absorbed all the liquid, and the top is well browned, about 10 minutes. Serve hot, with a bit of cold heavy (whipping) cream poured over each serving.

CONNECTICUT

Michael Stern lived in Connecticut for more than four decades and is a multiple James Beard journalism award winner. He is the author of many books with Jane Stern and the co-creator of Roadfood.com.

When I recently moved to South Carolina after more than forty years in Connecticut, I knew I would be trading clam shacks and Deco diners for barbecue parlors and meat-and-three cafes. I anticipated missing my old home state's hot lobster rolls as well as New Haven pizza (like Neapolitan with buff crust). What I did not expect to pine for is a steamed cheeseburger.

I never realized how much I liked this strange style of hamburg (Yankee for hamburger), which is so geographically pinpointed in central Connecticut around Meriden that many enthusiastic eaters as close as New Haven and Hartford have never heard of it. As a culinary explorer, I did very much appreciate its extreme regionality. My heart goes pitta-pat when I come across such extremely local specialties as ployes along the US–Canadian International Boundary in Maine, bierocks in Nebraska, turkey Devonshire in Pittsburgh, and the St. Pauls sandwich in St. Louis. If the bedrock definition of Roadfood is a unique dish found nowhere else, the steamed cheeseburger is quintessential.

What locals know as a steamer was conceived in the 1920s as health food. At the time, steaming things was a popular nostrum as an alternative to frying them. A steamed cheeseburger is made by placing individual portions of ground beef topped with blocks of cheddar cheese in their own separate small metal trays inside a steam cabinet, where they are vapor-cooked. The meat loses all its pink, but its placement in the tray and generous fat content insure that it is outlandishly juicy. The cheese becomes a pearlescent mass just viscous enough to seep into every crevice of the meat below, but not so runny that it escapes the sandwich. The cheese-crowned meat is placed into a hard roll (usually accompanied by lettuce, tomato, pickle, and onion), the whole edifice becoming an oozing package of precarious succulence. A steamer sometimes is accompanied by steamed cheese-topped potatoes, and it might even be followed by a slice of apple pie topped with steamed cheese.

For those who like burgers with crusty black-ened edges shoring in juicy red meat, a gray steamed cheeseburger is not an immediately lovable proposition. At its worst, it has all the appeal of a gravy-sopped sponge, with none of the textural delight of a patty that has been grilled. Yes, crunch is lacking, but a proper steamed cheeseburger can be a juicy orgy of maximum umami, delivering more flavor per bite than any other food. Local restaurants gleefully riff on the principle, offering steamers made with different cheeses and topped with guacamole, bacon, or baked beans. At Meriden's Lunch Box, you can start the day with a steamed cheeseburger omelet.

Steamers never went the way of Buffalo chicken wings, Chicago deep-dish pizza, or Nashville hot chicken. They are strictly local and too plumb weird to go national. For me, now that I am in the South, they are a case of not missing something until it's gone. I do love living in a land of fried chicken, shrimp 'n' grits, and pig pickin' cake, and there's even a spot nearby that makes New Haven–style pizza. But when the craving for a steamed cheeseburger strikes, Connecticut is the only place to be.

Gabe McMackin grew up in Connecticut and is chef/owner of the Michelin-starred restaurant The Finch in Brooklyn, New York.

SUMAC PUNCH

COOKING TIME: 20 MINUTES
MAKES: 3 QUARTS (3 LITERS)

- 3 ripe sumac clusters (best in late summer)
- Sugar (optional)
- Handful of lemon thyme or basil (optional)

[Cooking the sumac will release lots of tannins. It can also help you get a powerful concentrate that you can dilute with a spirit such as gin, if you want.]

In a saucepan, bring 3 quarts (3 liters) water to a boil. Add the sumac and return to a simmer. Remove from the heat, cover, and steep for 20 minutes. Taste it. For a stronger flavor, continue cooking. When the desired strength is reached, strain through a fine-mesh sieve lined with cheesecloth.

Alternatively, place the sumac in a large glass jar and cover with 3 quarts (3 liters) room-temperature water. Crush up the berries a bit, swirl them around, and leave for a few hours. Taste occasionally. When it's as strong as you'd like, strain it.

You may wish to sweeten the punch by adding a bit of sugar to your taste. You can also give it a bit of fresh lemon thyme leaves, or basil.

GRILLED BLUEFISH WITH CORN, SUN GOLD TOMATOES, AND LITTLENECK CLAMS

PREPARATION TIME: 1 HOUR,
  PLUS SOAKING TIME
COOKING TIME: 20 MINUTES
SERVES: 4

- Wood chips
- 10 ears of corn, husked
- Sea salt and freshly ground black pepper
- ¾ cup (180 ml) light beer or sparkling wine
- 20 littleneck clams, soaked and scrubbed
- 2 lb (910 g) side bluefish, skinned, belly and loin separated, and bloodline removed entirely
- Extra-virgin olive oil
- 2 fresh ají dulce peppers or other sweet, not-too-hot chilies, sliced (or 1 teaspoon crushed chili flakes)
- A fistful of basil leaves, torn
- 4 cups (595 g) Sun Gold tomatoes, halved
- Finely grated zest and juice of 2 lemons

[The bluefish should smell clean and not fishy. It should also be dense and firm. You can make this dish with hake, monkfish, or fluke. Ask your fishmonger to keep the fillet flat, not folded.]

Set up a gas or charcoal grill (barbecue) for indirect cooking. If using a gas grill, heat one side to about 500°F (260°C). If using hardwood charcoal, build a fire on one side of your grill. Let it get hot, and don't shake it out. Put some wood chips in a small foil pan, light them (with a blowtorch, if you have one) just until they're smoking a bit (you don't want a big fire, just smoking and smoldering).

Season the corn with salt and pepper and place on the grill for about 5 minutes (less if your grill is very hot). You want it to pick up some grill marks, but it should have that bright fresh mid-season corn flavor with just a hint of char and smoke. When the corn is cool enough to handle, cut the kernels off the cobs into a large bowl lined with a tea towel.

Put an open pan on one side of the grill. Add the beer, then add the clams. Cook the clams until they open; then remove them from the pan (strain and reserve the broth for another use, such as pasta sauce). When the clams are cool enough to handle, pull the meat from the shells.

Your chips should still be smoldering and smoking. If not, torch them or add some more chips and torch them, then let them burn off for a moment. Turn off the heat on one side if you can, or reduce the heat to medium-low—275°F (140°C)—and let it build up some smoke.

Cut the bluefish into reasonable portions (4–5 oz/115–140 g). Season well with salt and pepper.

Put the bluefish on a wire rack lined with parchment or on a silicone baking mat, evenly spaced. Dress with a little olive oil, then put the rack or baking mat on the grill. (This is so you'll be able to cleanly remove the fish, which will be delicate when it's cooked. If you try to get a spatula under it, it's going to tear up the fish.) Cover the grill and cook until the fish is at 225°F (107°C). After 10 minutes, the proteins should be starting to set on the outside and the fish should be taking on some smoke flavor, but still be rare in the center. Cook 5 minutes longer and it will be soft and luscious and just cooked through. It should flake if you push it, without being tough.

To assemble the dish, in a large bowl, combine the corn, chilies, clams, basil, and Sun Gold tomatoes. Taste it. Season with salt, pepper, and olive oil. Stir in the lemon zest and lemon juice.

Serve a generous few scoops of corn, making sure to get some clams on each plate. Carefully top with a piece of fish and drizzle with olive oil.

CHICKEN WITH MAPLE SAP, APPLES, AND POLENTA

PREPARATION TIME: 15 MINUTES
COOKING TIME: 13 HOURS, INCLUDING
  OVERNIGHT POLENTA COOKING
SERVES: 4

- 2 cups (280 g) polenta
- 6–8 cups (1.4–2 liters) milk
- 4 quarts (4 liters) maple sap
- Sea salt
- 1 lemon, halved
- 4 crisp apples
- 1 whole chicken, cut into 8 pieces, carcass reserved
- Freshly ground black pepper
- 1 sprig fresh rosemary

[Maple sap, fresh out of the tree, looks and tastes like water, with just a hint of sweetness. In late winter, farmers simmer it into syrup, but the straight sap is also wonderful to cook with. Tapping trees is very easy to do, but if you don't have trees of your own, ask a maple "sugar maker" for some sap in late winter or early spring.]

In a slow cooker, combine the polenta, 6 cups (1.4 liters) milk, and 2 cups (475 ml) of the maple sap, plus a good glug of sea salt. Cook on medium for 12 hours (overnight). When it's done, give it a stir. It should be loose and thin but creamy. Set aside to cool.

Set up a bowl of water and squeeze the lemon juice into the water. Peel and core the apples and cut them into large wedges, adding them to the lemon water as you work. Reserve the cores and peels.

In an 8-quart (7.6-liter) pot set over medium heat, bring the remaining 3½ quarts (3.3 liters) maple sap to a simmer. Add the apple cores and peels and the chicken carcass.

Season the chicken pieces with salt and pepper. Add them to the simmering maple sap in the following order (each cut takes a different amount of time to cook): Add the drumsticks and wings. After 8 minutes, add the thighs. After 10 minutes, add the breasts. Cook until the meat is just set, about 10 more minutes. It shouldn't get hard, but become firmer to the touch. Transfer the cooked chicken to a platter. Reserve the broth in the pot.

Transfer the polenta to a large pot and bring to a simmer over medium-low heat to thicken it to the desired consistency. Whisking constantly so the bottom doesn't scorch, let the polenta thicken slightly, about 10 minutes. It should taste sweet, clean, and a lot like corn. Add a few rosemary leaves and season to taste with salt and pepper. If the polenta is too thick, thin it out with some more of the milk. If it's too chewy, or you prefer to cook it more, let it keep going slowly, over low heat. Whisk regularly.

Drain the apples. Add the rest of the rosemary and the apple wedges to the broth and cook gently until a skewer easily pierces the apples (but before they become mushy), about 10 minutes.

Preheat the oven to 475°F (250°C/Gas Mark 9). Pat the chicken completely dry and arrange it on a rimmed baking sheet, skin side up. Season it again with salt and pepper and roast until it turns golden. You're not looking to cook the chicken more, just to warm it through and brown the skin a bit. Serve the polenta topped with the chicken pieces and the apples.

DELAWARE

Sam Calagione opened Dogfish Head brewpub in Rehoboth Beach, Delaware, in 1995 and now also owns restaurants, a distillery, and a hotel in the area.

Punkin Chunkin is a legendary local event in beautiful coastal Delaware that signifies fall is in full swing. It began in the late 1980s, when some Southern Delawareans decided a beer-fueled backyard wager must settle the debate of who could throw a pumpkin the farthest. In subsequent years, the technological ante was upped and the MacGyveresque evolution of pumpkin-throwing devices was profound: from slingshots, to trebuchets, to, eventually, pneumatic cannons. In recent years, over a hundred teams from across the country have competed in the World Championship Punkin Chunkin, and now the biggest machines hurl pumpkins almost 5,000 feet—roughly a mile (1.6 km)!

In 1994, I made a homebrew, as I was working on the business plan to open our little brewery, just as the craft-brewing renaissance was gaining momentum. I knew that in addition to the pumpkin-throwing contest that is the centerpiece of Punkin Chunkin, there would also be an annual baking competition with very loose rules. Any food or beverage made with pumpkins could be entered to be judged. I entered my first-ever batch of Punkin Ale, which we made (and still make today) with real pumpkin meat, brown sugar, and freshly crushed spices. Most other entries were in the pie or cake categories. Proud mothers, and mothers of mothers, stood stoically behind their respected homemade dessert items. My future wife and business partner, Mariah, poured alongside me and helped me navigate the social awkwardness I had created.

Our pumpkin-laced beer won best in show.

Here is one way to enjoy it: Pour a 12-ounce (355 ml) bottle of pumpkin beer into a saucepan, add 2 tablespoons of brown sugar, then simmer and stir until the volume is reduced to roughly 6 oz (180 ml). Toast pumpkin seeds in a baking pan and coat with salt and cinnamon. Put two scoops of vanilla ice cream in a pint glass. Drizzle with the pumpkin beer reduction sauce and top with toasted and coated pumpkin seeds. Pair this dessert with a pint of your favorite dark and roasty beer. And there you have it, the most awesome autumnal dessert ever.

Hari Cameron is the chef/owner of a(MUSE.) in Rehoboth Beach, Delaware. He has been nominated by the James Beard Foundation for Rising Star Chef and Best Chef: Mid-Atlantic.

CUCUMBER SALAD

PREPARATION TIME: 30 MINUTES
COOKING TIME: 2 MINUTES
SERVES: 6

- 3 stalks celery, thinly sliced
- 1 large white onion, halved and thinly sliced
- 1½ tablespoons sea salt
- 4 tablespoons sugar
- ¼ teaspoon celery seeds
- ¼ teaspoon yellow mustard seeds
- ¼ teaspoon dill seeds
- 3 large cucumbers
- ½ cup (120 ml) distilled white vinegar
- ½ cup (120 ml) champagne vinegar or rice vinegar
- ½ bunch fresh dill, finely chopped

[This is my mom's summertime garden salad.]

In a large bowl, combine the celery, onion, salt, and sugar. Let sit for 10 minutes while the salt and sugar draw moisture from the celery and onions.

Meanwhile, in a small dry skillet, toast the seeds over medium heat, keeping them moving for 2 minutes, until fragrant, and making sure that they don't burn.

With a sharp knife or on a mandoline, slice the unpeeled cucumbers into very thin slices (1/16 inch/1.6 mm).

Pour the two vinegars over the salt-macerated vegetables. Add the toasted seeds. Let sit 10 minutes. Add the cucumbers and dill and toss to combine.

CHICKEN AND SLIPPERY DUMPLINGS

PREPARATION TIME: 30 MINUTES,
  PLUS COOLING TIME
COOKING TIME: 1 HOUR 50 MINUTES
SERVES: 4–6

For the chicken and broth:
- 1 heritage-breed chicken (3–5 lb/
  1.4–2.3 kg), such as an Indian River,
  Jersey White Giant, or Poulet Rouge
- Salt and freshly ground black pepper
- 3½ quarts (3.3 liters) chicken stock,
  to fortify the broth
- ¾ cup (180 ml) white soy sauce
- 1 bunch celery, coarsely diced, reserving
  inner light green leaves for garnish
- 1 celeriac (1¼ lb/565 g), peeled and
  roughly chopped
- 1 Spanish onion (1 lb/455 g), quartered
- 2 sheets kombu seaweed
- 15 dried shiitake mushrooms
- 1 bunch thyme
- 3 bay leaves
- 25 black peppercorns

For the slippery dumplings:
- 4 cups (520 g) stone-ground hard wheat
  flour (I like Castle Valley Mill) or all-
  purpose (plain) flour
- 2 teaspoons baking powder
- ½ teaspoon salt
- 6 tablespoons chicken fat, duck fat, lard,
  or vegetable shortening

For the garnishes:
- 1 lb (455 g) chicken of the woods or hen
  of the woods (maitake) mushrooms
- 2 tablespoons grapeseed oil
- Salt and freshly ground black pepper
- 1 tablespoon sherry vinegar or cider
  vinegar
- 3 cups (1 lb/455 g) fresh lima beans (butter
  beans), such as Dr. Martins heirloom

For the chicken and broth: Preheat the oven to 450°F (230°C/Gas Mark 8).

Season the bird with salt and pepper. Roast until the skin is nicely browned, about 30 minutes. (It will cook further in the broth.) Let cool for 30 minutes, then remove the meat from the carcass and reserve, skin-on and covered, in the refrigerator. Reserve the carcass for the broth.

To make the broth: Place the chicken carcass, stock, soy sauce, celery, celeriac, onion, kombu, shiitakes, thyme, bay leaves, and peppercorns into an 8-quart (8-liter) pressure cooker. Secure the lid and set a timer for 45 minutes—it will take 15 minutes for the pressure cooker to come up to the right pressure. Once it's up to temperature, turn down to medium for the remainder of the time. Let the pressure naturally dissipate. Strain the broth through a fine sieve (discard the solids). Transfer the broth to a 4-gallon (15-liter) stockpot and return to a simmer. Season to taste with salt.

Remove the skin from the chicken and add the meat to the simmering broth. Lightly simmer until the chicken is tender, about 25 minutes. It will naturally break into pieces but should not completely fall apart. Once cooked, scoop the chicken out of the broth and set aside (it will be added back after the dumplings are cooked).

Meanwhile, for the slippery dumplings: Measure out 1 cup (240 ml) of the hot chicken broth. Pile the flour on a work surface, mix in the baking powder and salt, and cut in the fat with a pastry (dough) blender. Gradually add enough hot broth to make a firm dough. Make sure to not overwork the dough, as it will become tough. Once a smooth dough forms, cover it in plastic wrap (clingfilm) and let rest for 15–30 minutes. On a floured surface, roll the dough to ¹⁄₁₆ inch (1.6 mm) thickness and cut into 2-inch (5 cm) squares.

For the garnishes: Preheat the oven to 425°F (220°C/Gas Mark 7).

Remove any hard or woody pieces from the mushrooms. Toss the mushrooms with the oil, season to taste with salt and pepper, spread on a rimmed baking sheet, and roast until lightly browned, 10–15 minutes. Season with the vinegar.

In a small pot of boiling water, blanch the lima beans until tender, about 3 minutes. Drain.

With the broth at a light boil, drop in the dumplings and then reduce the heat to medium. Cook the dumplings, uncovered, until tender, 10–15 minutes. Add the chicken to heat through. Serve garnished with black pepper, blanched lima beans, roasted mushrooms, and celery leaves.

DELAWARE POTATO PIE

PREPARATION TIME: 20 MINUTES,
   PLUS CHILLING AND COOLING TIME
COOKING TIME: 2 HOURS
SERVES: 8

For the potato custard:
- 3 medium russet (baking) potatoes
  (about 7 oz/170 g each)
- 1 cup (240 ml) heavy (whipping) cream
- 1¼ cups (250 g) sugar
- ½ teaspoon salt
- 3 fresh bay leaves
- 1 vanilla bean, split lengthwise
- ¾ teaspoon freshly grated nutmeg
- 3½ tablespoons (50 g) butter
- 4 tablespoons sour cream
- ½ teaspoon fresh lemon juice
- 3 egg whites

For the pie dough:
- 3 egg yolks
- ¼ cup (60 ml) heavy (whipping) cream
- ½ cup (100 g) plus 1½ tablespoons sugar
- 1 teaspoon salt
- 1 cup (120 g) graham flour or whole
  wheat (wholemeal) flour
- 1 cup (135 g) bread (strong white) flour
- ½ lb (230 g) rendered leaf lard or butter,
  well chilled

[This unusual custard dessert is like a russet's answer to sweet potato pie, without the wintry spices. With deep roots in Delaware and neighboring states, this potato pie is a wonderful way to use a bumper crop of potatoes. We serve it at the restaurant with a scoop of peach ice cream.]

For the potato custard: In a medium pot, combine the potatoes with cold water to cover. Bring to a boil, reduce to a simmer, and cook until tender, about 25 minutes. Peel the potatoes and pass through a food mill into a medium bowl, discarding the skins. Let cool.

In a medium saucepan, combine the cream, sugar, salt, bay leaves, vanilla bean, and nutmeg. Bring to a simmer and cook for 15 minutes. Remove from the heat and let the cream mixture cool for 15 minutes; strain through a fine-mesh sieve. Whisk in the butter, sour cream, and lemon juice. Whisk the cream mixture into the mashed potato.

In a large bowl, with an electric mixer, beat the egg whites to stiff peaks. Gently fold the potato mixture into the whites.

For the pie dough: In a small bowl, whisk together the egg yolks and cream and set aside.

Keep all the dough ingredients very cold. In a food processor, pulse together the sugar, salt, flours, and lard or butter until the mixture resembles coarse crumbs, 15–20 seconds. Slowly add the cream/egg yolk mixture. Pulse for another 10 seconds, just to incorporate. Be careful not to overwork. Form into a dough disk and refrigerate until firm, at least 1 hour and up to 24 hours.

On a floured surface, roll the dough out to a ⅛-inch (3 mm) thickness. Fit the dough into a pie plate, crimping the edges. Top with a sheet of parchment and pie weights (baking beans) and refrigerate for 1 hour.

Preheat the oven to 425°F (220°C/Gas Mark 7).

Bake the pie shell (pastry case) until the bottom is golden brown, 15–20 minutes. Let the crust cool slightly. Leave the oven on but reduce the temperature to 350°F (180°C/Gas Mark 4).

Once the crust is cool, fill with the potato custard. Return to the oven and bake until the filling is set and lightly browed, 45 minutes to 1 hour.

Norman Van Aken is the founder of Norman's at The Ritz-Carlton Orlando and 1921 by Norman Van Aken in Mount Dora. He is the only Floridian in the James Beard Foundation's "Who's Who of Food & Beverage in America."

There was a defining moment in my decision to become the chef that I am today; it was one morning in 1987, as I sat on the wooden deck overlooking the gently rocking waters behind Louie's Backyard, the restaurant where I'd become chef two years before, on the island of Key West, Florida. At that point I'd cooked in a lot of joints, and I use that word purposefully. I'd been frying eggs and barbecuing ribs, even as I was venturing into the Cuban and Bahamian shacks and cafés around Key West for lunch or a café con leche. By the '80s, I had become a chef and was running Louie's, long considered one of the best restaurants in Key West. It is situated in a spot where the Gulf of Mexico meets the Atlantic Ocean. I was studying a stack of cookbooks—French, Middle Eastern, Southwestern, Italian—in pursuit of dishes for my menus, when I looked up to see a sailboat drifting southward. I too drifted with it for some time, wondering where it might be going and what the sailors would see, touch, and taste when they got there.

And just like that, I realized it was time for me to put away my books on the dishes of other places. It was one of those moments of complete clarity: As much as I had drawn from the wisdom and artistry of hundreds of years of European cuisine, it was now time for me to express where and what I was living, and that was Florida.

I thought about how North America's music had evolved, how its literature, architecture, and dance were amalgamations of cultures bumping up against one another. Florida was a place where Spanish, African, and Anglo influences converged, yet the foods we were eating (including those at the restaurant I was helming) seemed almost frozen in time.

No one had yet imagined what kind of "fusion cuisine" might result if those cultures were expressed in food the way the cuisines of New Orleans, California, and the American Southwest were products of the different peoples who have inhabited them.

My moment of clarity then became one of resolve. I could feel Cuba just 90 miles (145 km) away. The answer had been around me all along. I ate it and drank it almost every day. My new teachers were going to be in the cafés and homes of Florida. In the next weeks and months I went back to some of the same joints I'd eaten in many times. I sat on stools at counters and ordered the very local fare. I pestered cops and fishermen and housepainters and housewives about what they were having.

We added a second story to Louie's Backyard called The Café and made a sign that read Nuevo Latino Cuisine. Inspired by the Café at Chez Panisse in Berkeley, California, I wanted an informal restaurant. I offered then-unheard-of constructions such as Mojo Marinated and Roasted Chicken with Saffron Rice and Rioja Essence, Seared Tenderloin of Beef on a Bed of Crispy Vaca Frita, and Grilled Florida Snapper with Mojo Verde and Plantain Curls. Diners at Louie's would come up when they heard I was now cooking at The Café, eye the menu, and often head down the stairs to the more "cosmopolitan" food I had created in the original restaurant. That was then, and we not only survived, but we prevailed.

Norman Van Aken

HOT FRIED CHICKEN SALAD

PREPARATION TIME: 35 MINUTES,
  PLUS MARINATING TIME
COOKING TIME: 15 MINUTES
SERVES: 4

For the marinade and chicken:
- 3 eggs, beaten
- 1 cup (240 ml) heavy (whipping) cream
- 1 jalapeño pepper, seeded and thinly sliced
- 2¼ teaspoons cayenne pepper
- 2¼ teaspoons crushed chili flakes
- 2¼ teaspoons paprika
- Salt and freshly ground black pepper
- 4 boneless chicken breasts (skinless
  if desired), sliced into "finger" shapes

For the "hot fry flour":
- 1½ cups (195 g) all-purpose (plain) flour
- 3 tablespoons crushed chili flakes
- 2 tablespoons freshly ground black pepper
- 2¼ teaspoons cayenne pepper
- 2¼ teaspoons salt

To finish the dish:
- Peanut (groundnut) oil, for frying
- 2 heads inner romaine leaves, torn or
  chopped into bite-size pieces
- Honey Mustard Dressing (page 532)
- ½ red onion, thinly sliced into rings

[I created this salad upon taking the reins at Louie's Backyard in Key West. One of the restaurant owners was dubious of the notion. It remained on the menu for the next seventeen years.]

For the marinade and chicken: In a large bowl, beat the eggs with the cream. Mix in the jalapeño, cayenne, chili flakes, paprika, and salt and black pepper to taste. Add the chicken and stir to coat. Cover and marinate for at least 4 hours and up to overnight.

For the "hot fry flour": Mix together the flour, chili flakes, black pepper, cayenne, and salt and keep in a sealed container until ready to use.

To finish the dish: Lift the chicken fingers out of the marinade and roll in the flour mixture.

Preheat the oven to 200°F (95°C). Place a large skillet over medium-high heat. Add ½ inch (1.25 cm) peanut (groundnut) oil to the skillet and heat to 350°F (180°C). Working in 2 batches to avoid crowding the pan, carefully place half of the chicken in the hot oil. Cook until golden, turning once, about 6 minutes total. Remove from the oil, drain on paper towels, and keep warm in the oven. Clean out the pan between batches.

In a large bowl, toss the lettuce with dressing to taste, reserving any extra dressing for another use. Divide the lettuce among serving bowls. Cut the chicken into bite-size pieces. Top the greens with the hot chicken and red onion and serve immediately.

HONEY MUSTARD DRESSING

PREPARATION TIME: 15 MINUTES
MAKES: 1 CUP (240 ML)

Place the egg yolk, honey, and mustard in a stand blender. Blend on medium speed until pale yellow. Reduce the speed to low and gradually add the 3 oils, in order. Add the vinegar, Sriracha, lemon juice, and salt and/or pepper to taste. Refrigerate until ready to use.

- 1 egg yolk
- 1½ teaspoons honey
- 2 tablespoons Creole mustard
- ½ cup (120 ml) canola (rapeseed) oil
- 3 tablespoons extra-virgin olive oil
- 1 tablespoon sesame oil
- 2 tablespoons sherry wine vinegar or balsamic vinegar
- 1½ teaspoons Sriracha sauce
- 2 tablespoons fresh lemon juice
- Kosher (coarse) salt and/or freshly ground black pepper

BLACK BEAN AND SHRIMP FRITTERS

PREPARATION TIME: 1 HOUR 30 MINUTES
COOKING TIME: 20 MINUTES
MAKES: 30–36 FRITTERS

[Slaves from Africa brought to the New World their religion, music, and cooking. They were very experienced in frying various delicious foods. These fritters can be served with sour cream spiked with lime juice and cayenne, if you like.]

In a large bowl, beat the egg. Beat in the milk, then stir in the flour, baking powder, salt, onion, jalapeño, bell pepper, black beans, beer, cumin, and Tabasco and whisk thoroughly. Fold in the shrimp (prawns). Cover and refrigerate for 1 hour.

Pour 2 inches (5 cm) oil into a large heavy pot or deep-fryer and heat to 350°F (180°C).

Working in 4 batches, use 2 soup spoons to scoop a small ball of shrimp fritter batter with 1 and scrape it carefully into the hot fat with the other. Cook the fritters about 4 minutes total, turning them over from time to time to brown evenly. Then transfer to paper towels to drain.

Serve hot, garnished with lemon and lime wedges.

- 1 small egg
- ⅓ cup (80 ml) milk
- 1 cup (130 g) sifted all-purpose (plain) flour
- 1¼ tablespoons baking powder
- ½ teaspoon kosher (coarse) salt
- ¾ cup (120 g) minced red onion
- ½ jalapeño pepper, seeded and minced
- ½ red bell pepper, minced
- 1 cup (170 g) cooked black beans (if canned, rinse well)
- 3 tablespoons light beer
- ¾ cup (45 g) minced cilantro (coriander)
- ½ teaspoon ground cumin
- 1 tablespoon Tabasco sauce
- 1½ cups (500 g) chopped peeled shrimp (prawns)
- Canola (rapeseed) or peanut (groundnut) oil, for deep-frying
- Lemon and lime wedges, for garnish

PLANTAIN SOUP WITH SMOKED HAM AND SOUR CREAM

PREPARATION TIME: 25 MINUTES
COOKING TIME: 50 MINUTES
SERVES: 6–8

For the soup:
- 5 tablespoons blended vegetable oil
- 2 tablespoons (30 g) butter
- 2 very ripe plantains, peeled and cut crosswise into slices ½ inch (1.25 cm) thick
- Pinch each of salt, sugar, and cayenne pepper
- ½ teaspoon ground turmeric
- 2 leeks, white part only, cleaned and finely diced
- 1 large carrot, finely diced
- 1 sweet onion, finely diced
- 3 cloves garlic, thinly sliced
- 1 Scotch Bonnet chili, seeded and minced
- 1 small bunch cilantro (coriander), minced
- 1 cup (240 ml) orange juice (fresh if possible)
- 1 quart (1 liter) chicken stock
- 2 cups (475 ml) heavy (whipping) cream
- Kosher (coarse) salt and freshly cracked black pepper

For the garnish:
- ½ cup (70 g) diced or shredded cooked ham
- ½ cup (120 ml) sour cream

[My first love of an ingredient was the plantain. I was in a café in 1971 and ordered roast pork. It came with black beans, yellow rice, and some cooked "bananas" that were so dark I thought the cook had burned them. What I came to realize was the black edge was a kind of "banana candy" that gave whatever it was served with a sweet harmony.]

For the soup: Heat a large saucepan over medium-high heat. Add the oil and butter. When hot, add the plantains and season them with the salt, sugar, and cayenne. Cook, stirring occasionally, until nicely browned, about 10 minutes. Stir in the turmeric, leeks, carrot, onion, garlic, and chili. When the vegetables are nicely caramelized, about 10 minutes, stir in the cilantro (coriander) and orange juice and cook for 2 minutes.

Stir in the chicken stock and bring to a boil. Reduce the heat to a high simmer and cook until the liquid is quite reduced, about 12 minutes. Add the cream. Increase the heat and cook to reduce the soup for 5 minutes. Remove from the heat. Purée the soup with a hand blender or in a stand blender until smooth. (I do not strain it, but feel free if you like.) Season to taste with salt and pepper. Return the soup to the pan to keep warm.

For the garnish: Stir the ham into the soup to warm it up. Ladle the soup into cups or bowls. Serve with sour cream spooned on top.

FLORIDA LOBSTER WITH CAPERS, CROUTONS, AND LEMON

PREPARATION TIME: 15 MINUTES
COOKING TIME: 30 MINUTES
SERVES: 2 (4 AS AN APPETIZER)

For the lobster:
- 2 spiny lobsters (about 4 oz/115 g each), halved lengthwise
- Kosher (coarse) salt and freshly ground black pepper
- 4 tablespoons (60 g) clarified butter
- 1 tablespoon (15 g) butter
- 1 shallot, diced
- 1 bay leaf, broken
- ½ cup (120 ml) Chardonnay

For the sauce:
- 1 lemon
- 3 tablespoons (45 g) unsalted butter
- 1 tablespoon small capers, drained and briefly rinsed
- 1 tablespoon coarsely chopped fresh flat-leaf parsley leaves
- 1 cup (30 g) small croutons

[Grenobloise is a sauce I learned to make from a fellow line cook, "The Irish Angel," Danny McHugh, in my early days at the Pier House in Key West. How he learned about it is unknown. This is a great all-purpose sauce for many shellfish and even chicken breast.]

For the lobster: Preheat the oven to 350°F (180°C/Gas Mark 4).

Season the lobster meat side with salt and pepper. Set aside.

Heat the clarified butter in a large nonstick skillet over medium-high heat. Add the lobsters and cook about 6 minutes, until golden brown, turning once. Transfer to an ovenproof pan, meat side up.

Melt the butter in the skillet over medium heat. Add the shallots and cook until golden brown, about 4 minutes. Add the bay leaf and wine and reduce it until syrupy, about 4 minutes. Pour the butter–wine mixture over the lobster tails. Reserve the skillet.

Place the pan of lobsters in the oven and bake until the tails are cooked through, 7–9 minutes, basting the lobsters with the pan juices one time.

For the sauce: Cut the skin and white pith away from the lemon. Remove the segments by slicing between the membranes. Cut the segments into ½-inch (1.25 cm) pieces.

Add the butter to the reserved skillet and cook over medium-high heat, stirring, until it turns a deep brown and smells nutty, about 3 minutes. Remove from the heat and stir in the lemon pieces, capers, and parsley, swirling the skillet to combine. Transfer to a bowl and keep warm (or use immediately).

To assemble the dish, remove the lobsters from the oven and place them on warm plates. Spoon the sauce over the cooked lobster halves. Scatter the small croutons on top. Serve immediately.

Nicole A. Taylor is the author of *The Up South Cookbook,* the founder of *The Modern Travelers' Green Zine,* and an editor for the biannual magazine *Crop Stories.* She grew up in Georgia and lives in Brooklyn, New York.

In 1996, right after the Summer Olympics, I moseyed up Interstate 85 North—from Athens, Georgia, to Clark Atlanta University—for my freshman orientation at Paschal's, a now-defunct 120-room motel, restaurant, and lounge in Atlanta. My new dorm stood on a lush college campus, but I was as drawn to what could be found a few blocks away: ribs from historic Aleck's Barbecue Heaven, Busy Bee's blackberry cobbler, and a street marker for the Yates and Milton Drugstore soda fountain, where a generation before a protest movement had been born.

In the early 1960s, young people had grabbed cafeteria-style fried chicken from large silver pans and drafted a strategic plan to use cafe sit-ins and the media to chop down segregation in the capital of the South. Students from Morehouse College, Clark Atlanta University, Spelman College, Morris Brown College, and The Interdenominational Theological Center met over food and cooked up social change.

"One day," said my Miami-raised roommate with Jamaican roots, "I want you to teach me how to make fried chicken." She loved the afternoons when I'd whip up golden fowl in our suite's small brown kitchen. It shocked me that there were black people unskilled at frying protein, because it seemed everyone knew a master maker of it.

On Sunday, all the dining halls served chicken dinner with classic vegetable sides, and I'd glide over to Busy Bee. There, sitting between the who's who and the blue-collar backbone of the city, my mainstay was fried chicken with fresh skillet corn, smoky collard greens, cornbread muffins, and a large plastic cup of sweetened-just-right lemonade.

Two decades later, Atlanta has transformed. Shiny new towers scrape the sky. The old Paschal's Restaurant and Motor Hotel is vacant and the quaint storefronts of Atlanta's Southwest neighborhoods have yet to be reborn. A street name honors the Atlanta Student Movement, but African American–owned Southern culinary spots are vanishing.

The hope lies in the people and the stove. A new generation must look beyond the pines and make the dishes—cook the food. Stories of progress and equality are waiting for an open door.

Hugh Acheson is a chef, food writer, and restaurateur who lives in Athens, Georgia. He is chef-partner of Athens-based restaurants 5&10 and The National, Atlanta-based Empire State South and Spiller Park Coffee, and The Florence in Savannah.

BUTTERMILK DRESSING

PREPARATION TIME: 5 MINUTES
MAKES: 1 CUP

- ½ cup (120 ml) buttermilk
- 1 tablespoon Dijon mustard
- 1 tablespoon fresh lemon juice
- ¼ cup (50 g) mayonnaise
- 2 tablespoons crème fraîche
- ½ teaspoon kosher (coarse) salt
- Freshly ground black pepper

[Simple salads are the secret to a long life and a happy existence. You can use this dressing in a hundred ways, so make some extra.]

In a small bowl, whisk together the buttermilk, mustard, lemon juice, mayonnaise, crème fraîche, salt, and pepper to taste. The dressing will keep in the refrigerator for 5 days.

FRIED OKRA WITH RÉMOULADE

PREPARATION TIME: 20 MINUTES
COOKING TIME: 5 MINUTES
SERVE: 4 AS A SIDE OR SNACK

- 2 quarts (2 liters) canola (rapeseed) oil
- 2 lb (910 g) okra, halved lengthwise
- Sea salt
- 2 cups (475 ml) buttermilk
- 1 cup (210 g) mayonnaise
- ¼ cup (60 g) Creole mustard
- 1 tablespoon Worcestershire sauce
- 1 teaspoon Louisiana-style hot sauce
- 1 teaspoon finely grated lemon zest
- 1 tablespoon fresh lemon juice
- 1 shallot, minced
- 6 scallions (spring onions), white and
  light green parts only, thinly sliced
- 2 teaspoons cayenne pepper
- 1 cup (130 g) all-purpose (plain) flour
- 2 cups (260 g) cornmeal
- 1 teaspoon freshly ground black pepper

[Fried okra is a Southern classic for a good reason: It is addictively great. People love crispy foods, especially when it comes to okra.]

Pour the oil into a large heavy pot or deep-fryer and heat to 350°F (180°C) over medium heat.

While the oil is heating, place the cut okra in a bowl, season it with 2 teaspoons sea salt, and let it sit for 10 minutes. Then add the buttermilk to the bowl and let it sit for an additional 5 minutes.

Meanwhile, make the rémoulade: In a small bowl, combine the mayo, mustard, Worcestershire, hot sauce, lemon zest, lemon juice, shallot, scallions (spring onions), and 1 teaspoon of the cayenne. Adjust the seasoning with sea salt and hot sauce if needed, and set aside.

In a large bowl, combine the flour, cornmeal, 1 tablespoon sea salt, the remaining 1 teaspoon cayenne, and the black pepper. Drain the okra and toss it in the cornmeal mixture. Working quickly, and with one half-pod at a time, add the okra to the hot oil and cook until it is golden brown, 3–4 minutes. Drain on paper towels.

Season the okra with sea salt and serve with the rémoulade for dipping.

FIELD PEAS
WITH FATBACK AND HERBS

PREPARATION TIME: 10 MINUTES,
  PLUS SOAKING TIME
COOKING TIME: 1 HOUR 15 MINUTES
SERVES: 4–8

- 1 cup (165 g) dried field peas or beans
  (of recent harvest and good pedigree,
  like Sea Island red peas)
- ¼ lb (115 g) salted fatback
- ½ yellow onion, sliced
- 1 bay leaf
- 1 quart (1 liter) chicken stock (or water
  in a pinch)
- ½ teaspoon crushed chili flakes
- 1 tablespoon chopped fresh flat-leaf
  parsley leaves
- 1 teaspoon chopped fresh thyme leaves
- 1½ teaspoons kosher (coarse) salt

[Simple and proven, beans feed our Southern souls.]

Put the peas in a bowl, add cold water to cover, and let sit at room temperature for 5–6 hours.

Rinse the fatback really well under cold running water, then cut into ½-inch (1.25 cm) thick slices. Place a large heavy pot over medium heat, add the sliced fatback, and cook for 5 minutes, until it starts to render. Add the onion and bay leaf and cook for 10 minutes, so the onion and fatback get to know each other really well. Pour the stock into the pot.

Drain the soaked peas and add them to the pot. Increase the heat to high and bring to a boil. Reduce to a low simmer and cook the peas until tender to the bite—the skin should not be bursting or broken—about 1 hour (depending on the peas or beans, this can vary a lot).

Remove from the heat and stir in the chili flakes, parsley, thyme, and salt. Stir well and serve. The lucky person gets the bay leaf.

Rachel Laudan lived in Hawaii for ten years and is the author of *The Food of Paradise: Exploring Hawaii's Culinary Heritage*.

When I fly to Hawaii, I ask for a window seat. For the last five hours of the journey, I glance at the gray ocean, the swells crosshatched on the surface, and the occasional ship. When the islands finally come into view, tiny green fragments surrounded by the vast ocean moat, I ponder again the miracle that humans not only made it to Hawaii but managed to turn it into a culinary paradise.

The first human colonizers, now called the Hawaiians, sailed from the south Pacific perhaps fifteen hundred years ago. Their joy at sighting cloud-capped mountains that promised plentiful fresh drinking water must have been tempered when they discovered that, fish, seaweed, and flightless birds aside, the islands offered nothing to eat. Only because they had laden their catamarans with edible plants, including slips of taro, coconuts, and sugarcane, as well as chicken, pigs, and dogs, were they able to survive and flourish.

For centuries, Hawaiians remained isolated from the rest of the world, until a second diaspora, this time of English and Americans, sailed around Cape Horn at the beginning of the 19th century. On the decks of their sailing ships cattle were tethered, and in the holds were stocks of wheat for bread, bread ovens, and iron ranges. Each successive sailing brought new plants to acclimatize in botanic gardens, including varieties of sugar and pineapple to be grown commercially.

To work the sugar and pineapple crops, the planters recruited the third major group of settlers, mainly Chinese, Japanese, Koreans, and Filipinos, but also others including Portuguese. These arrivals too wanted their own food, so they introduced rice and woks, set up noodle factories, and opened small groceries and restaurants.

I step out into the warm plumeria-scented air and make my way into Honolulu to sample again the local food that I grew to love when I lived there. Some is grown locally, but what makes it local is that it is the food of the different settlers. The madcap diversity—the chestnut-y taste of freshly cooked taro, creamy-coconutty haupia, Japanese rice that lifts easily on chopsticks, fresh hot malasadas, and sweet-salty Spam musubi—makes me chuckle.

More than that, though, it brings home the hard work, ingenuity, and courage it took to turn what had been the emptiest of food deserts into a culinary heritage drawn from the far ends of the earth.

Martha Cheng is a Honolulu-based food writer and cookbook author. Her writing has appeared in the *Wall Street Journal* and Eater, among other media outlets.

POKE WITH NORI CHIPS

PREPARATION TIME: 15 MINUTES
COOKING TIME: 30 MINUTES
SERVES: 4

For the nori chips:
- 4 sheets nori
- 3 tablespoons cornstarch (cornflour)
- 1 cup (240 ml) canola (rapeseed) oil
- Salt

For the poke:
- 1 lb (455 g) sushi-grade tuna, cut into ½-inch (1.25 cm) cubes
- 1 medium avocado, diced
- ½ cup (80 g) finely diced yellow onion
- ½ cup (50 g) thinly sliced scallions (spring onions), dark green parts only
- ½ cup chopped fresh cilantro (coriander)
- 4 tablespoons ikura (salmon roe)
- 3 tablespoons soy sauce, or more to taste
- 2 teaspoons sesame oil
- ½ teaspoon Sriracha sauce

For the nori chips: Halve each nori sheet lengthwise. Then cut each half sheet into thirds crosswise.

Line a baking sheet with paper towels. In a small bowl, whisk together the cornstarch (cornflour) and 1 cup (240 ml) water. Set aside.

In a small saucepan, heat the oil over medium heat to 375°F (190°C). If the cornstarch has settled, whisk the cornstarch mixture. Dip each nori rectangle into the cornstarch mixture and immediately transfer to the hot oil, frying three rectangles at a time. Using tongs, flip the nori, and when the bubbling subsides, about 2 minutes, remove the nori and set on the baking sheet. Sprinkle with salt. Repeat with the remaining nori.

For the poke: In a medium bowl, combine the tuna, avocado, onion, scallions (spring onions), cilantro (coriander), ikura, soy sauce, sesame oil, and Sriracha and mix gently to combine.

To serve, lay the nori chips on a plate and spread the poke on top. Serve immediately.

LILIKOI CHIFFON PIE

PREPARATION TIME: 20 MINUTES,
  PLUS CHILLING TIME
COOKING TIME: 10 MINUTES
SERVES: 8

- 1 tablespoon unflavored gelatin
- 4 large eggs, separated
- 1 cup (200 g) sugar
- ½ cup (120 ml) strained passion fruit juice (from about 8 passion fruits)
- ½ teaspoon salt
- Finely grated zest of 1 lemon
- One 9-inch (23 cm) baked and cooled pie shell (pastry case) (page 280)
- ½ cup (120 ml) heavy (whipping) cream
- ½ cup (40 g) large-flake coconut (desiccated)

In a small bowl, sprinkle the gelatin over ¼ cup (60 ml) cold water and let stand for a few minutes to soften.

Set up a large bowl of ice and water. In a medium saucepan, bring 2 inches (5 cm) water to a simmer over medium heat. In a metal bowl that can stack snugly on top of the saucepan, whisk together the egg yolks, ½ cup (100 g) of the sugar, the passion fruit juice, and salt. Set the bowl over the saucepan and whisk constantly until the mixture is hot to the touch, about 5 minutes. Remove the bowl from over the hot water and whisk in the softened gelatin until dissolved. Add the lemon zest. Nest the bowl in the ice bath and whisk until the mixture is just slightly thickened and cool to the touch.

In a large bowl, with an electric mixer, beat the egg whites until foamy. Continue whisking while gradually adding the remaining ½ cup (100 g) sugar. Beat until stiff peaks form. Gently fold the egg whites into the gelatin mixture until combined and no streaks remain. Pour the mixture into the pie shell (pastry case) and chill in the refrigerator until firm, about 2 hours.

When the pie is set, whip the cream to soft peaks in a medium bowl. Spread the whipped cream over the pie and sprinkle with the coconut.

Serve the pie cold. It will keep in the refrigerator for up to 3 days (the gelatin will continue to stiffen the filling, so it will be firmer the longer it sits).

IDAHO

Kevin Huelsmann cooks at State & Lemp in Boise, Idaho.

Idaho food is hard to pin down. So often the state is cast in stereotypes, namely, potatoes. High-volume agriculture is an integral part of Idaho's identity and a multibillion-dollar part of our state's economy. It's an industry that creates some high-quality products and feeds millions. But there's so much more to our food and the culture that surrounds it.

Here in Boise, there is a growing network of young cooks and farmers who are putting down roots and trying to push boundaries. They're taking a fresh approach to the surrounding landscape, foraging new ingredients, and testing what might grow in our high desert climate. For instance, a short hike into the foothills surrounding the city can yield huckleberries, currants, chamomile, elderflower, hyssop, yarrow, and lomatium, among other wild ingredients.

Farmers throughout the state are finding innovative ways to turn their crops into ingredients that are both sustainable and profitable. In central Idaho, farmers are breeding and raising catfish and sturgeon, selling caviar to influential restaurants on both coasts, using UV light to sustain crops year-round in harsh climates, milling heritage strains of corn and wheat, and even growing tropical fruit.

It's an exciting time to dig into what's around us. We're learning more about our landscape and what makes it special. There are young, talented, and creative cooks, bakers, servers, brewers, winemakers, coffee roasters, and many others who want to push Idaho forward. There's also a growing international community that's added greatly to the city's diversity and culture.

We're the rural state that's just beyond the reach of the Pacific Northwest, above the Rockies, and not quite a part of the Great Plains or Midwestern states. That might seem a little isolating, but most often it feels more freeing. We're not bound to a certain identity or forced to chase trends. Instead, we're able to create our food on our terms.

Kris Komori is head chef at State & Lemp restaurant in Boise, Idaho, and has twice been nominated for the James Beard Foundation's Best Chef: Northwest award.

SMOKED TROUT MORELS

MAKES: 18 STUFFED MORELS

- 18 medium morel mushrooms, stems trimmed and reserved
- 3½ tablespoons Cedar Oil (recipe below) or mild olive oil
- 2½ oz (75 g) diced yellow onion
- 1 teaspoon minced garlic
- Finely grated zest of 1 lemon
- 2 egg whites
- 1 teaspoon kosher (coarse) salt
- 4 oz (110 g) smoked trout

Wash the mushrooms by gently tossing in a bowl of cold water, letting the morels sit so the debris sinks to the bottom. Carefully transfer the morels to fresh water, without stirring up the debris from the bottom. Repeat until the water runs clear. Spin in a salad spinner and lay out on a baking sheet, cut sides down, to dry. Measure out 2 ounces (50 g) of morel trim.

In a medium frying pan, heat the cedar oil over medium heat. Add the morel trim, onion, and garlic and cook until softened but not browned, 9–10 minutes. Let cool. Transfer to a food processor. Add the lemon zest, egg whites, salt, and smoked trout. Purée and check the seasoning. Transfer to a piping bag and pipe the filling into the empty centers of the cleaned morels.

CEDAR OIL

MAKES: 2 CUPS (475 ML)

- 1 lb (450 g) untreated cedar plank, broken into 2-inch (5 cm) pieces
- 2 cups (475 ml) canola (rapeseed) oil

In a large saucepan, combine the cedar and oil and bring the oil to 140°F (60°C). Steep at that temperature for 2 hours. Strain the oil through a fine-mesh sieve lined with cheesecloth (muslin).

PINE PESTO

MAKES: 2 CUPS (475 ML)

- ½ cup plus 1 tablespoon (80 g) black sesame seeds
- ¾ cup (100 g) pine nuts
- 2½ ounces (75 g) Parmesan cheese, finely grated
- ½ cup plus 2 tablespoons (100 g) minced shallots
- 3½ ounces (100 g) pine tips (see Note), minced
- 1 cup (240 ml) pine oil
- Salt

Note:

Use only the fresh, young tips of pine or spruce trees. These are the bright-green, soft little shoots that grow from the ends of the branches in May or June, before they darken and become rigid.

In a dry frying pan, toast the sesame seeds and pine nuts over low heat until fragrant and the pine nuts are golden brown. Immediately transfer to a food processor and add the Parmesan cheese, shallot, and pine tips. Pulse to combine. With the food processor running, drizzle in the pine oil until combined. Season to taste with salt.

CEDAR-ASH AÏOLI

MAKES: 1 CUP (240 ML)

- 2 egg yolks
- 1 clove garlic, minced
- 1 teaspoon Dijon mustard
- 1 teaspoon yellow miso
- 1 teaspoon fresh lemon juice
- ½ cup (120 ml) Cedar Oil (page 542) or mild olive oil
- ½ cup (120 ml) canola (rapeseed) oil
- Kosher (coarse) salt
- ½ teaspoon ash

In a bowl, whisk together the egg yolks, garlic, mustard, miso, and lemon juice. Slowly drizzle in the cedar oil, followed by the canola (rapeseed) oil, maintaining the emulsion. Season to taste with salt and add the ash. Adjust the acidity with lemon juice if necessary. (You can also make the aïoli in a food processor.)

TROUT WITH FINGERLING POTATOES

PREPARATION TIME: 2 HOURS
COOKING TIME: 1 HOUR
SERVES: 6

- ¼ cup (60 g) kosher (coarse) salt, plus more as needed
- One 2-lb (900 g) whole trout, scaled, gutted, and divided into six (3 oz/85 g) pieces
- 1½ lb (680 g) fingerling potatoes
- 6 tablespoons Cedar Oil (page 542)
- 2 tablespoons olive oil
- 1 lb (455 g) green garlic or scallions (spring onions), charred (see Note)
- 18 Smoked Trout Morels (page 542)
- Canola (rapeseed) oil, for deep-frying
- ¾ cup (180 ml) Cedar-Ash Aioli (page 543)
- ¾ cup (180 ml) Pine Pesto (page 543)

Note:
The restaurant uses fresh trout trim, brined and smoked over applewood chips, but you can substitute good-quality smoked trout.

Dissolve the salt in 2½ cups (600 ml) boiling water. Let cool completely. Meanwhile, score the trout skin. Brine the trout in the salt water for 10 minutes. Pat dry and transfer to a baking sheet with the skin side up to dry slightly.

Preheat the oven to 400°F (200°C/Gas Mark 6).

Toss the potatoes in 2 tablespoons of the cedar oil and salt lightly. Roast until tender, 25–30 minutes. Let cool, then halve. Heat the olive oil in a skillet over high heat. Sear the potato halves, in batches, cut side down, until crispy, about 5 minutes per batch.

Preheat the broiler (grill) on high heat. Toss the green garlic with 2 tablespoons cedar oil and season to taste with salt. Place the garlic under the broiler until charred, turning once, about 8 minutes total.

When ready to serve, pour 2 inches (5 cm) canola (rapeseed) oil into a large heavy pot or deep-fryer and heat to 375°F (190°C). Working in batches, fry the stuffed morels until golden and crispy, about 3 minutes. Season to taste with salt.

In a sauté pan, heat the remaining 2 tablespoons cedar oil over medium heat. Add the brined trout and cook for 3 minutes per side.

To serve, drizzle each plate with 2 tablespoons aïoli. Scatter the fingerling potatoes, green garlic, and morels on the plate. Place the trout skin side up. Drizzle each plate with 2 tablespoons pine pesto.

WHITE CURRANT GRANITÉ

PREPARATION TIME: 5 MINUTES, PLUS CHILLING TIME
COOKING TIME: 1 HOUR 15 MINUTES
SERVES: 4

- 2½ cups (360 g) white currants
- 1⅓ cups (280 g) sugar
- 2¼ sheets gelatin (or 2¼ teaspoons powdered gelatin)

[This granité was developed by our pastry chef Michelle Kwak.]

In a large saucepan, combine the currants, sugar, with 3¾ cups (890 ml) water and bring to a boil. Simmer for 1 hour, occasionally crushing the currants with a ladle. Strain the syrup through a cheesecloth-lined sieve into a large bowl.

Bloom the gelatin according to package directions. In a large saucepan, bring 1 cup (240 ml) of the syrup to a simmer and add the bloomed gelatin. While stirring, slowly add the remaining syrup. Remove from the heat, strain through a fine-mesh sieve, and let cool to room temperature.

Pour the syrup into a wide pan or baking dish and freeze for at least 1 hour until mostly frozen. Remove from the freezer, scrape with a spoon or fork, and serve.

ILLINOIS

Paul Kahan is the executive chef-partner of One Off Hospitality Group, including Blackbird, avec, and The Publican. The James Beard Foundation named him Best Chef: Midwest and Outstanding Chef.

When I was growing up, my dad owned a little old-fashioned smokehouse called the Village Fishery, in Rogers Park, the northernmost area of Chicago, Illinois and much of the fish came out of Lake Michigan.

To earn some pocket change as a kid, I would ride along in the van to pick up chub. In the herring family, ranging from four to twelve inches long, chub was indigenous to the Great Lakes but would later be virtually eliminated due to the introduction of an invasive species called alewives. Back then we'd pick up chub by the barrel.

I went with my dad a few times, but after that I'd ride along with the drivers, leaving very early in the morning. We would meet the chub boats, throw the fish in the van, and drive back to Chicago to brine it in enormous vats before smoking.

At the smokehouse we'd pull the fish from the brine and skewer them on long rods, each rack holding hundreds of chub. My dad would light a fire of old wooden boxes, we'd roll the racks in and close the door, and they'd smolder all night.

One of the first times I was there working as a kid, my dad pulled me aside and took a hot smoked fish right off the rack, fresh out of the smoker. He tore the head off, pulled the skin back, scraped the warm flesh off the bone, and shoved the flesh in my mouth.

Smoked chub is wonderfully briny, and the meat is very high in fat, wonderfully rich. It's good cold. But when it's hot, there's nothing like it.

Maybe it was my level of naïveté—I wasn't jaded yet from many meals in fine restaurants, so those early tastes were more influential. But that remains my seminal food memory. From then on we had a ritual. My dad had a toaster in his office and we'd toast poppy seed or onion bagels and top them with some cream cheese, a little red onion, and hot smoked chub.

To try to re-create the memory, at a number of my restaurants we've tried smoking fish à la minute. We're fairly successful, but to my mind it always falls a little short. To this day, in the kitchen, when I come over to taste a dish, I often say things like, "It needs more acidity." But the cooks joke that I'll say, "It needs gratuitous red onion." Because nothing will ever quite match the incredible depth of flavor of a toasted bagel with my dad's smoked chub.

Stephanie Izard was born in Chicago, Illinois, and her restaurants there are Girl and the Goat, Little Goat Diner, and Duck Duck Goat. She won the James Beard Award for Best Chef: Great Lakes, and is a *Food & Wine* magazine Best New Chef.

SWEET CORN ELOTES

PREPARATION TIME: 20 MINUTES
COOKING TIME: 10 MINUTES
SERVES: 4–6

- 4 tablespoons (60 g) unsalted butter, softened
- ⅛ teaspoon cayenne pepper
- Salt
- Vegetable oil
- 6 cups (875 g) corn kernels
- ⅓ cup (80 ml) fresh lime juice
- ⅓ cup (30 g) freshly grated Parmesan cheese
- 4 tablespoons roughly chopped cilantro (coriander)

In a small bowl, use a fork to smash the butter. Add the cayenne and ¼ teaspoon salt and mix well. The butter should be slightly red hued. Set aside.

In a large frying pan, heat a small amount of oil over medium-high heat. Add the corn and a sprinkle of salt and toss to coat. Cook for 3 minutes. Add the cayenne butter, let melt, and toss to coat. Add the lime juice and toss. Season with another pinch of salt. Add almost all of the Parmesan, reserving a small amount for garnish. Add the cilantro (coriander), toss once more, and transfer to a large bowl. Sprinkle with the remaining Parmesan and serve hot.

CORN PIEROGI

PREPARATION TIME: 1 HOUR 30 MINUTES
COOKING TIME: 1 HOUR 5 MINUTES
SERVES: 6–8

For the filling:
- 1 lb (450 g) Yukon Gold potatoes
- 4 ears sweet corn, husked and grilled (see Note)
- 2 cups (475 ml) heavy (whipping) cream
- 4 tablespoons (60 g) unsalted butter
- ½ lb (225 g) sharp cheddar cheese, grated
- Salt

For the dough:
- 2 cups (260 g) all-purpose (plain) flour
- 1 teaspoon salt
- 1 egg
- ½ cup (120 ml) sour cream
- 4 tablespoons (60 g) butter, softened

To serve:
- 8 tablespoons (115 g) butter

Note:
The grilled corn should be slightly charred.

For the filling: In a large pot of boiling salted water, cook the potatoes until fork-tender, about 40 minutes.

Meanwhile, cut the kernels off the cobs. Transfer one-third of the kernels and the cobs to a pot and add the cream and butter. (Set aside the remaining kernels.) Simmer the corn–cream mixture for 20 minutes. Discard the cobs and buzz the mixture in a blender until smooth. Strain the liquid into a bowl.

Transfer the cooked, unpeeled potatoes to a separate bowl. Add some of the strained corn cream and mash and mix slowly until you have a smooth, creamy consistency that is not too loose (you may not need all the cream). Fold in the reserved corn kernels and the cheese. Season to taste with salt. Let cool fully before filling the pierogis.

For the dough: In a stand mixer fitted with the dough hook, mix together the flour, salt, egg, sour cream, and butter until a dough forms. Wrap the dough in plastic wrap (clingfilm). Refrigerate until well chilled (or freeze for later).

Roll out chilled pierogi dough to approximately ⅛-inch (3 mm) thickness. Cut out round circles from the dough using a 2-inch (5 cm) round cookie cutter, glass or measuring cup. Pack a measuring tablespoon tightly with the filling and place in the middle of a dough circle. Using an egg wash, lightly brush the edges of the dough and fold into half-moon shapes. Press the edges together to seal. Repeat with remaining filling and dough.

To serve: working in 4 batches, place a large sauté pan over medium-high heat. Melt 2 tablespoons (30 g) of the butter (do not brown). Cook the pierogis until golden brown, approximately 2–3 minutes on each side. Serve immediately.

Jonathan Brooks grew up in Indiana. In Indianapolis, he is chef of Milktooth, which he owns with his wife Ashley and for which *Food & Wine* named him a Best New Chef.

The most vivid food memory from my Indiana childhood is the scent of the fried golden cornmeal bits that popped and scattered and remained sprawled across my mother's gas oven top, like some sort of fatty galaxy after she'd been frying orange roughy in her cast-iron pans. This greasy incense filled our home and lured me into the kitchen to steal bites of the fillets that were being drained and kept warm on the comics section of old newspapers in the oven. I was lucky enough to have the kind of mother who would not exile me from the kitchen, wooden spoon in hand, but encouraged my behavior by enthusiastically partaking of the greedy treat herself.

Last Christmas, my mother and I were hunting through old shoe boxes of family photos for pictures of me when I was my son's age, when we found one that always makes us both laugh. In black and white, standing in the backyard, surrounded by thin raspberry bushes and smiling ear to ear in my blond bowl cut, dress shirt, and clip-on tie, my four-year-old self is proudly holding the large pumpkin we had spent the summer growing. It could easily fool most people as being a picture of my own son. What makes us laugh is the fact that, seconds after this photo was taken, I dropped the pumpkin and it exploded onto our lawn, spilling out its sweet golden guts.

Like most chefs, my formative food memories are based on visual and olfactory snapshots. I can't remember the moment I knew I wanted to become a chef. I wasn't struck by culinary lightning during some particular meal at Restaurant X. But without a doubt I can still feel the butter coating my lips as I ate grilled sweet corn at the Indiana State Fair or taste the cold rock salt on my fingertips as I hand-cranked peach ice cream on the back steps during many a wonderful humid summer afternoon. I can still see my mulberry-stained hands as I reached for the fruit that bent the limbs of our neighbor's tree, close enough that I could reach them from the top of my birdshit-stained swing set.

After high school, I left home as soon as I could. I wanted to get far away and see what my dreams looked like. I honestly didn't think I'd ever want to come back. But from Montana via Chicago I returned, partially against my will. What I found was something I never knew before—the most wonderful produce, dairy, meat, and local bounty I've ever seen. Childhood and family friends were now passionate young farmers working with pride alongside their neighbors and relatives to hold Indiana's crops into the sunlight, much like I held that pumpkin high, for everyone to see. Several middle school and high school friends were now servers and bartenders and chefs, working in the kind of restaurants that didn't emulate other places around the country, but were confident in just doing things right for their city.

I immediately felt back at home. I was glad I'd left, but felt even luckier that I had been brought back. I was inspired and confident to, through food, tell my story of this place that grew me. I was learning new things about the Midwest and my hometown and all its weird and hidden culinary habits and customs. And I was able to take those stories, meals, and food experiences and look at them in a new way through the lens of the local harvest. And it's all become my Indiana food.

Jonathan Brooks

INDIANA WILD MUSHROOMS

PREPARATION TIME: 25 MINUTES
COOKING TIME: 10 MINUTES
SERVES: 4

- 1 cup (140 g) glutinous (sweet) rice flour
- 1 cup (130 g) cornstarch (corn flour)
- 1 teaspoon smoked paprika
- 1 teaspoon ground ginger
- ½ teaspoon celery salt
- ½ teaspoon onion salt
- ½ teaspoon garlic powder
- ½ teaspoon chili powder (we use ground dried white habaneros) or scorpion peppers)
- ½ teaspoon ground allspice
- ½ teaspoon freshly ground black pepper, plus more for the mushrooms
- ½ teaspoon dried basil
- ½ teaspoon dried marjoram
- ½ teaspoon dried oregano
- 1½ cups (355 ml) cold sparkling water plus a few ice cubes
- Canola (rapeseed) oil, for deep-frying
- 1–1½ lb (455–680 g) wild mushrooms (my favorite are Indiana lions mane, hen of the woods (maitake), or shiitakes), trimmed and cut into ⅓–½-inch (8 mm–1.25 cm) slices
- Salt
- 1 cup (240 ml) Nam Prik Green Goddess Dressing (page 551)

In a metal bowl, whisk together the rice flour, cornstarch (corn-flour), all the herbs and spices, and the sparkling water and ice cubes. As the cubes melt, adjust with a little cold tap water if necessary to reach a thin pancake batter consistency. Keep cold until ready to cook.

Pour 3 inches (7.6 cm) of oil into a large heavy pot or deep-fryer and heat to 350°F (180°C).

Toss the mushrooms in the batter until evenly coated. Working in 3 batches, deep-fry until light golden brown and very crispy, about 3 minutes. Season with salt and pepper. Serve on paper towels, with the green goddess dressing for dipping.

MARINATED SLOW-ROASTED WATERMELON

PREPARATION TIME: 35 MINUTES
COOKING TIME: 12 HOURS
MAKES: 4 CUPS

- 1 (20 lb/9 kg) watermelon
- 1 sweet onion, peeled and thinly sliced
- 3 jalapeño peppers, sliced into thin rings
- 2 cups (475 ml) smoked soy sauce (we use BLiS brand)
- ½ cup (120 ml) best-quality extra-virgin olive oil

[This recipe exploits roasted watermelon's tuna-like texture and marries it with soy and jalapeños.]

Preheat the oven to 175°F (80°C). Place a whole watermelon (about 20 lb/9 kg) on a rack set in a large roasting pan. Roast until wilted, about 12 hours. Let cool to room temperature, then refrigerate for 12 hours.

Quarter the watermelon; reserve a quarter and save the rest for another use. Remove and discard the watermelon rind, and slice the flesh like you would slice sashimi.

In a large bowl, gently combine the watermelon, onion, jalapeños, soy sauce, and olive oil. Marinate for at least 20 minutes before serving.

TOMATOES WITH ROASTED WATERMELON, AVOCADO, AND COTTAGE CHEESE

PREPARATION TIME: 40 MINUTES
COOKING TIME: 12 HOURS
SERVES: 4

- 3 cups (680 g) local or best-quality cottage cheese
- 2 barely ripe avocados, sliced
- 2 very ripe local or best-quality heirloom tomatoes, sliced
- Coarse salt and freshly ground black pepper
- About ½ cup (100 g) Marinated Slow-Roasted Watermelon (page 550)
- 4 teaspoons toasted sesame seeds

Divide the cottage cheese among 4 bowls. Top with avocado and tomatoes and season very lightly with salt and pepper. Spoon the marinated watermelon and some of the marinade around and over the avocado and tomatoes. Garnish with toasted sesame seeds.

PREPARATION TIME: 15 MINUTES
MAKES: ABOUT 5 CUPS (ABOUT
    1.2 LITERS)

- 2 cups (475 ml) mayonnaise
- 1 cup (240 ml) sour cream
- ½ cup (120 ml) buttermilk
- ½ cup (120 ml) barrel-aged fish sauce
  (we use BLiS brand)
- 2 cloves garlic, peeled and left whole
- Finely grated zest of 2 limes
- ¼ cup (60 ml) fresh lime juice
- Finely grated zest of 2 lemons
- ¼ cup (60 ml) fresh lemon juice
- 1 shallot, peeled and finely diced
- 2 jalapeño peppers, stemmed
- 2 serrano peppers, stemmed
- 2 bunches cilantro (coriander),
  stems and all
- 1 bunch parsley, stems and all
- 1 cup (10 g) fresh dill
- ½ cup (5 g) fresh tarragon leaves
- 10 basil leaves

[There are so many uses for this condiment, but serving it along-side the Indiana Fried Mushrooms (page 549) is my favorite.]

In a blender, combine all the ingredients and blend on high until bright green and very smooth. Refrigerate until ready to use.

BRAISED PORK CHEEKS OVER GRITS WITH KUMQUATS AND CRISPY COLLARDS

PREPARATION TIME: 20 MINUTES,
   PLUS OVERNIGHT REFRIGERATION,
   SOAKING, AND PICKLING
COOKING TIME: 4 HOURS 30 MINUTES
SERVES: 6

For the braised cheeks:
- 12 pork cheeks, trimmed of silver skin
- Salt and freshly ground black pepper
- ¼ cup (60 ml) Canola (rapeseed) oil
- 1 bottle (750 ml) dark beer, such as porter
- 2 quarts (2 liters) strong veal stock or other dark stock
- 6 celery ribs, coarsely diced
- 4 carrots, coarsely diced
- 2 onions, coarsely diced
- 2 heads garlic, halved horizontally
- 1 large bunch fresh thyme
- 4 bay leaves
- 3 dried ancho chilies
- 1 (3-inch/7.5 cm) cinnamon stick
- 2 vanilla beans, split lengthwise
- 3 tablespoons (45 g) butter

For the crispy collard greens:
- 6 large collard leaves, center rib removed, cut into 4-inch (10 cm) pieces
- 3 tablespoons olive oil
- ½ tablespoon salt
- ½ tablespoon freshly ground black pepper
- ½ tablespoon annatto powder (optional)

For serving:
- 8 cups (2 liters) Heirloom Grits (page 553)
- 12 Pickled Kumquats (page 553), sliced

For the braised cheeks: Preheat the oven to 275°F (140°C/Gas Mark 1).

Season the pork cheeks generously with salt and pepper. Heat a large skillet over medium-high heat. Add the canola (rapeseed) oil and, working in two batches, sear the pork cheeks on both sides, until a dark, golden crust forms, about 6 minutes per side. Transfer to a large roasting pan. Pour the fat out of the skillet. Deglaze with the beer, scraping up the browned bits with a wooden spoon, and pour the juices over the pork.

Add the stock, vegetables, herbs, chilies, and cinnamon to the roasting pan. Scrape the vanilla seeds in (reserve the pods). Bring to a boil on the stove top. Carefully and tightly cover the pan with two layers of foil and transfer to the oven. Braise until the pork is very tender but not falling apart, about 4 hours. Let cool in the liquid. Cover and refrigerate overnight.

For the crispy collard greens: Preheat the oven to 350°F (180°C/Gas Mark 4).

Rub the leaves with the oil and spices. Bake until crispy, about 20 minutes, flipping once during cooking time.

Meanwhile, remove the pork cheeks from the refrigerator and scrape any fat off the surface of the braising liquid and the pork cheeks. Remove the pork cheeks from the liquid and set aside. Bring the roasting liquid to a boil and strain through a fine-mesh sieve into a large saucepan. Cook over medium-high heat to reduce the liquid by two-thirds, about 15 minutes. Reduce heat to medium-low and return the cheeks to the saucepan to rewarm. Swirl in 3 tablespoons (45 g) butter until melted and remove from the heat.

To serve, divide the grits among 6 bowls. Top each bowl with 2 cheeks and evenly ladle sauce over the top. Garnish with sliced pickled kumquats and crispy collards.

HEIRLOOM GRITS

PREPARATION TIME: 5 MINUTES,
  PLUS OVERNIGHT SOAKING TIME
COOKING TIME: 45 MINUTES
SERVES: 6

- 1½ cups (210 g) heirloom corn grits
- 6 cups (1.4 liters) whey or water
- 4 tablespoons (60 g) butter
- Salt

In a bowl, soak the grits overnight in 2 quarts (2 liters) water. Drain.

In a large pot, bring the whey (or water) to a boil and whisk in the grits. Reduce the heat to very low and cover. Whisking every 5 minutes, being careful not to scorch the bottom, cook until the grits are nice and soft, about 40 minutes. Whisk in the butter and season to taste with salt.

PICKLED KUMQUATS

PREPARATION TIME: 5 MINUTES,
  PLUS OVERNIGHT PICKLING
COOKING TIME: 10 MINUTES
MAKES: 12 KUMQUATS

- 1 cup (240 ml) champagne vinegar
- 2 tablespoons pickling spice
- 1 tablespoon kosher (coarse) salt
- 1 tablespoon sugar
- 1 clove garlic, smashed
- ½ serrano pepper
- 2 sprigs fresh thyme
- 12 kumquats

In a saucepan, combine ½ cup (120 ml) water, the vinegar, pickling spice, salt, sugar, garlic, serrano, and thyme. Bring to a boil and simmer for 3–4 minutes. Add the kumquats and let cool to room temperature. Let pickle in the refrigerator at least overnight before serving. They will keep refrigerated for up to 1 year.

Jeremy Jackson was raised on a small farm and is a novelist and cookbook author. He lives in Iowa City, Iowa.

Every August, the corn of Iowa has grown so dense and in such profusion that you can walk atop it across the breadth of the state. Most of this hard, starchy field corn is grown for livestock and, in the form of ethanol, for cars and trucks. But I'm here to talk about food in Iowa.

Some years ago, about a block away from my little house in Iowa City, my then-girlfriend, now-wife, Kelly, and I found a sour cherry tree loaded with fruit. If you listened carefully, you could hear the branches groaning under the burden. No one was picking the cherries. They were just falling to the sidewalk when they ripened. On two occasions, I knocked on the door to the house, to ask permission to pick the cherries. But no one answered. More cherries fell each day, a tragedy of ripeness, neglect, and gravity.

We went to the farmers' market early in hopes of buying some sour cherries of our own. There were vendors selling cat paintings, mystery sauces, and gourmet buffalo jerky, but no cherries. It was disheartening. We bought some scrappy-looking strawberries— a minor coup even though they were in the early stages of rotting. The local strawberry crop had been hit hard by a late frost.

From the market we drove west out of town, into the rolling countryside north of the town of Kalona. We stopped at Stringtown Grocery, run by Mennonites, which sells bulk foods—nuts, pasta, cereals, and such—and a smattering of local produce, baked goods, and preserves. In the store's back room I saw locally grown strawberries that were prettier than anything I'd seen all year.

We drove into the woodsy hills surrounding Coralville Reservoir and hiked into the woods. There were gooseberry bushes and black raspberry vines, and we started picking. There is nothing quite like that little plop of a berry dropping into your berry pail.

For dinner, Kelly stuffed her farmers' market squash blossoms with ricotta and basil and fried them. For dessert we made strawberry shortcake (with biscuits, not cake). The next day I sprinkled the little black raspberries into some pancake batter and the result was delightful. The gooseberries made it into a rectangular tart with a cinnamon-spiced pastry crust—a rare treat.

All this is to say that there is much more to Iowa than corn. As for those sour cherries growing near our house, we did get them.

Andy Schumacher, a graduate of The University of Iowa, and Carrie Schumacher, an Iowa native, opened their restaurant Cobble Hill Eatery & Dispensary in Cedar Rapids, Iowa. He is the chef and she is the general manager.

CORN-MANCHEGO TORTELLINI

PREPARATION TIME: 1 HOUR 30 MINUTES
COOKING TIME: 1 HOUR
MAKES: 16 TORTELLINI

For the pasta dough:
- 2¾ oz (80 g) egg yolks (about 5 egg yolks)
- 1 egg
- 1½ teaspoons olive oil
- 2¼ cups (300 g) bread (strong white) flour, plus additional for rolling

For the filling:
- 4 tablespoons (60 g) butter
- 3½ oz (100 g) onion, diced
- Salt
- 1½ cups (220 g) sweet corn kernels (from 2 ears of corn), cobs reserved for corn stock (see Note)
- 3½ oz (100 g) Manchego cheese, cut into small chunks
- 2½ tablespoons all-purpose (plain) flour

Note:
To make corn stock, in a saucepan, add enough water to the corn cobs to cover by ½ inch (1.25 cm) and bring to a boil. Simmer for 30 minutes, then strain through a fine-mesh sieve.

For the pasta dough: In a stand mixer fitted with a dough hook, combine the egg yolks, whole egg, oil, and 2 oz (60 grams) water. Add the flour and mix on low speed for 15 minutes, to fully develop the gluten. Wrap the dough with plastic wrap (clingfilm) and let rest for 30 minutes before using.

For the filling: In a saucepan, warm the butter over medium-low heat. Add the onion and a pinch of salt and cook until softened but not browned, 10–12 minutes. Add the corn and continue to sweat until the corn is tender, about 15 minutes. The goal is to release (and cook off) as much moisture from the vegetables as possible so they are not too wet when you purée them.

Transfer the corn/onion mixture to a food processor and purée to a fine paste, about 3–4 minutes, scraping down the bowl as needed. Transfer to a bowl and set aside.

In a food processor, process the Manchego and flour for 1 minute, until the texture resembles fine sand (the flour coats the cheese and allows you to grind it finer; it will also absorb any extra moisture when you add it to the corn mixture). Stir the cheese into the corn mixture and season with salt. If the mixture seems a little too wet, stir in some extra flour; the final consistency should be like ricotta cheese.

Roll out the pasta dough in a pasta roller to make one (1/16-inch/ 1.5 mm) thin sheet, and cut the sheet into 3-inch (7.5 cm) rounds. Place about 2 teaspoons of the filling in each round and form into a tortellini shape. If not cooking right away, the tortellini can be frozen.

TORTELLINI WITH MAITAKE MUSHROOMS AND SUN GOLD TOMATOES

COOKING TIME: 15 MINUTES
SERVES: 2

- Salt
- 4 tablespoons (60 g) butter, divided
- 1 hen of the woods (maitake) mushroom cluster (3–4 oz/85–115 g), separated into 1-inch (2.5 cm) pieces
- ⅓ cup (50 g) sweet corn kernels
- 16 Corn-Manchego Tortellini (page 555)
- 6 tablespoons corn stock (see Note, page 555)
- 12 Sun Gold or cherry tomatoes
- 1 tablespoon chopped fresh tarragon
- 1 tablespoon chopped fresh chives

Bring a large pot of salted water to a boil.

Heat a medium frying pan over medium-high heat. Add 2 tablespoons (30 g) of the butter, then the mushrooms and corn. Cook until lightly browned and tender, about 5 minutes.

Meanwhile, boil the tortellini until they float to the top of the water, 2–3 minutes.

Remove the pasta from the water and place directly in the frying pan with the mushroom-corn mixture. Add the corn stock and tomatoes and bring to a simmer. Swirl in the remaining 2 tablespoons (30 g) butter and the herbs. If the sauce is too dry, add more corn stock. If it's too watery, boil to thicken.

To serve, divide pasta evenly between 2 bowls.

HILLJACK COCKTAIL

PREPARATION TIME: 10 MINUTES, PLUS FREEZING TIME AND 12 HOURS INFUSING TIME
COOKING TIME: 1 HOUR
MAKES: ABOUT 15 DRINKS

- 3 cups (450 g) sweet corn kernels (from about 5 ears of corn), cobs and husks reserved
- 3¾ cups (890 ml) Flor de Caña (or comparable) white rum
- 2½ cups (590 ml) simple syrup
- 1¼ cups (295 ml) fresh lemon juice
- ¼ teaspoon cayenne pepper
- Lemon peel, for garnish

Place the corn cobs in a medium soup pot with just enough water to cover. Simmer over low heat for 1 hour. Strain the corn broth through a fine-mesh sieve and let cool. Pour the broth into a silicone ice cube mold that makes at least 2-inch (5 cm) cubes. Freeze. (Make sure to keep the ice cubes extra cold; they can melt quickly because of the sugar from the corn.)

In a high-powered blender, combine 3¾ cups (890 ml) water, the corn kernels, rum, simple syrup, lemon juice, and cayenne and purée until very smooth. Strain through a fine-mesh sieve. Allow the infusion to sit 12 hours, then stir and taste for spice level. Adjust to taste.

Rub a lemon peel on the rim of an old-fashioned glass. Place a corn ice cube in the glass, pour over the cocktail, and garnish with a lightly charred corn husk.

SWEET CORN ICE CREAM WITH BLACKBERRY ICE

PREPARATION TIME: 1 HOUR, PLUS
  REFRIGERATING AND FREEZING TIME
COOKING TIME: 30 MINUTES
SERVES: 8

For the sweet corn ice cream:
- 3 corn cobs, kernels removed
  and reserved for another use
- ½ cup (60 g) nonfat milk powder
- ½ cup (100 g) plus 3 tablespoons sugar
- ⅛ oz (3 g) ice cream stabilizer
- 1 oz (30 g) glucose powder
- 2 cups (475 ml) milk
- ¾ cup (180 ml) heavy (whipping) cream
- 3 oz (90 g) egg yolks (about 5 egg yolks),
  whisked until smooth
- ½ teaspoon salt

For the blackberry ice:
- 2¼ cups (325 g) blackberries
- ½ cup (100 g) sugar
- 1 teaspoon salt
- 1 cinnamon stick
- 1½ teaspoons fresh lemon juice

To serve:
- 1 cup (145 g) blackberries, sliced in half
- ½ cup (65 g) raw sweet corn kernels
- 12 lemon basil leaves

For the sweet corn ice cream: Preheat the oven to 350°F (180°C/ Gas Mark 4). Arrange the corn cobs in a pan and roast until caramelized, about 20 minutes.

In a medium bowl, whisk together the milk powder, sugar, stabilizer, and glucose powder. In a large saucepan, combine the milk and cream and bring to a simmer. Whisk all the dry ingredients into the simmering milk mixture until dissolved. Slowly add the egg yolks and gently whisk until the custard thickens slightly (or reaches 180°F/82°C on a thermometer).

Scrape the cobs with a spoon to get any remaining pulp into the custard and add the charred corn cobs to the pot. Steep in a warm spot off the stove for 3 hours. Season with salt (this ice cream is best savory-sweet). Strain the ice cream base through a sieve and chill well. Freeze in an ice cream maker according to the manufacturer's instructions.

For the blackberry ice: In a saucepan, combine 1⅓ cups (315 ml) water, the blackberries, sugar, salt, cinnamon, and lemon juice and simmer over low heat for 10 minutes. Purée on low in a blender for 2 minutes. Strain through a sieve and place in an 8-inch (20 cm) square shallow baking dish. Place in the freezer and stir with a fork every 20 minutes until ice crystals form, about 3-4 hours.

To serve: Chill dessert bowls in the freezer. Divide the blackberry ice evenly among the bowls and top each with a scoop of ice cream. Garnish with blackberries, corn kernels, and basil.

Carl Thorne-Thomsen attended Wichita State University in Kansas. He opened the restaurant Story in Prairie Village in 2011. He was named a *Food & Wine* People's Best New Chef.

The mushrooms begin in April with morels—conical, honeycombed, and delicately flavored. Morels are the most prized of our local mushrooms, costing more than 50 dollars per pound at farmers' markets. Our forager, Mike, finds them at the beginning of the season in Texas and Arkansas, then he follows them, as the weather warms, up through Missouri, then Kansas, Iowa, and lastly, Minnesota.

Then we have chanterelle season in July and August. Beautiful orange-gold mushrooms with delicate ruffled caps flaring out of long stems, they smell faintly of flowers and, at times, taste almost fruity. They're found in forests, meadows, and sometimes backyards.

In September, the forests offer up the giant hen of the woods. Some clusters are larger than basketballs and weigh more than five pounds (2.3 kg), tasting of shade, damp earth, and fallen leaves. Dark tan to brown on the outside and creamy white underneath, they literally bring the forest into our kitchen—releasing small leaves, pine needles, spiders, and roly polies, as the restaurant cooks pull them apart, wipe them clean with damp towels, and spread them out on sheet pans.

Our dishes with wild mushrooms have the ability to transport us to the fields and forests where they were foraged, and like all great ingredients, they compel us to respect them and to create something as beautiful as they are.

Carl Thorne-Thomsen

MUSTARD VINAIGRETTE

PREPARATION TIME: 10 MINUTES
MAKES: ½ CUP (120 ML)

- 2 tablespoons Dijon mustard
- 2 tablespoons white wine vinegar
- ¼ cup (60 ml) olive oil
- 1 teaspoon minced fresh dill
- Pinch of salt

In a small bowl, whisk together the mustard and vinegar. While continuing to whisk, slowly pour in the olive oil to create an emulsion. The final consistency should be thick, almost like a condiment. Stir in the dill and salt. Use on Beet Salad with Apples, Burrata, and Smoked Walleye (page 560).

BEET SALAD WITH APPLES, BURRATA, AND SMOKED WALLEYE

PREPARATION TIME: 40 MINUTES, PLUS
  REFRIGERATION TIME
COOKING TIME: 2 HOURS
SERVES: 4

For the walleye:
- 2 tablespoons kosher (coarse) salt
- 1 tablespoon sugar
- Finely grated zest of 1 lemon
- 6 sprigs fresh thyme, roughly chopped
- 6 oz (170 g) walleye fillet, skin on
- 4 handfuls applewood chips

For the beets:
- 3 medium red beets, well washed
- 2 tablespoons grapeseed or canola
  (rapeseed) oil
- 1 tablespoon kosher (coarse) salt
- 1 teaspoon sugar

For the salad assembly:
- 4 oz (115 g) burrata cheese
- 2 tablespoons Mustard Vinaigrette
  (page 559)
- 1 tablespoon minced fresh chives
- Kosher (coarse) salt
- Extra-virgin olive oil
- 1 cup (120 g) peeled diced (¼ inch/6 mm)
  apple, tossed with the juice of 1 lemon
- 1 teaspoon minced fresh dill
- 16 medium spinach leaves

[Good-quality smoked salmon, purchased or smoked at home, is a fine substitution for walleye if the latter is not available.]

For the walleye: In a small bowl, mix together the salt, sugar, lemon zest, and thyme. With a sharp knife, score the walleye skin 5 or 6 times, then rub the entire fillet with the salt mixture. Place the seasoned fish in a small pan, cover with plastic wrap (cling-film), and refrigerate for 3 hours.

Line a stainless-steel baking pan with foil and arrange the wood chips in a single layer on the bottom. Have another sheet of foil ready to cover the pan. Choose a rack that will fit in the baking pan. Rinse the walleye, pat dry, place it skin side down on the rack, and set aside.

Turn on the stove's exhaust hood and set the pan of chips on a hot burner. To ignite them, light a match and, from a distance of 2 feet (½ meter), toss the match into the pan. Let the chips burn until they turn black and begin to smolder, about 3 minutes. Carefully drop the walleye on the rack directly into the fire. Cover the pan with the second sheet of foil, taking care to seal the edges well. Reduce the heat beneath the pan and leave on the burner until the fish is cooked through, about 15 minutes.

Remove the top foil and let the fish cool to room temperature. Break into ½-inch (1.25 cm) flakes, discarding the skin and any bones. Refrigerate until ready to use.

For the beets: Preheat the oven to 325°F (160°C/Gas Mark 3).

Place the beets in a large bowl and toss them with the oil, salt, and sugar. Transfer to a small roasting pan and cover with foil. Bake until a paring knife slips easily into the largest beet, about 1 hour 30 minutes. Uncover the beets and when cool enough to handle, peel and cut each beet into 8 wedges. Cover and refrigerate until ready to use.

To assemble the salads: In a small bowl, break the burrata with a spoon, releasing the creamy interior. Mix the two textures, then divide among 4 plates. With the back of a spoon, flatten and spread the cheese into an elongated oval.

In a separate bowl, dress the flakes of walleye with the vinaigrette and stir in the chives and a pinch of salt. Distribute the walleye over the surface of the cheese.

In another bowl, toss the beets with 1 tablespoon olive oil and a large pinch of salt. Arrange 6 beet wedges on each plate. Add the minced dill to the apples and spoon the apples over the beets.

Lightly dress the spinach leaves with olive oil. Season them with salt. Finish the salad by arranging 4 spinach leaves on each plate, on top of the beets and apples. Drizzle additional olive oil over the entire salad.

MUSHROOM RISOTTO WITH POACHED EGG, PANCETTA, AND SALSA VERDE

PREPARATION TIME: 20 MINUTES
COOKING TIME: 1 HOUR
SERVES 4

For the garnishes:
- 4 oz (115 g) pancetta or (streaky) bacon, minced
- Leaves from 1 bunch flat-leaf parsley, minced
- 1 shallot, minced
- 2 dried chiltepin chilies, crushed
- Finely grated zest and juice of 1 lemon
- ¼ cup (60 ml) extra-virgin olive oil
- Salt and freshly ground black pepper

For the risotto:
- 5 tablespoons (75 g) unsalted butter
- 3 tablespoons extra-virgin olive oil
- 1 lb (455 g) wild mushrooms, such as morels, chanterelles, or hen of the woods (maitake), roughly chopped
- Salt and freshly ground black pepper
- 4 tablespoons minced onion
- 3 cloves garlic, minced
- 1 cup (195 g) Arborio rice
- ½ cup (120 ml) white wine
- 6 cups (1.4 liters) chicken or vegetable stock, at a simmer
- ½ cup (45 g) freshly grated Parmesan cheese

For the poached eggs:
- 1 teaspoon red wine vinegar
- 4 eggs

For the garnishes: In a medium frying pan, cook the pancetta slowly over low heat until it renders its fat, begins to caramelize, and reaches a texture we call in the kitchen "crispy-chewy," about 12 minutes. Drain the contents of the pan in a fine-mesh sieve set over a bowl (discard the fat). Set the pancetta crumbs aside at room temperature until ready to use.

In a small glass or stainless-steel bowl, combine the parsley, shallot, crushed chilies, lemon zest, and olive oil. Season to taste with salt and pepper. This salsa verde can be made to this point 3–4 hours in advance and held at room temperature. When ready to serve, stir in the lemon juice.

For the risotto: In a large saucepan, combine 1 tablespoon (15 g) of the butter and 2 tablespoons of the olive oil. Heat over low to medium heat to melt the butter. Add the mushrooms and season with salt and pepper. Cook until the mushrooms have softened and released much of their moisture, about 12 minutes. Add the onion and garlic and cook until softened but not browned, about 5 minutes. Stir in the rice to coat. Increase the heat to medium-high and stir the rice and mushrooms without interruption for 3 minutes. Reduce the heat to medium and stir in the wine, then ladle in enough stock to cover the rice and mushrooms. Add 2 pinches of salt and cook the rice in the stock. Stirring frequently, continue adding hot stock as needed to keep the rice covered, cooking until the risotto is loose—wet, creamy—but not soupy, about 15 minutes. Toward the end, regulate the amount of liquid that is added in order to attain proper consistency.

Meanwhile, poach the eggs. Fill a 4-quart (4-liter) saucepan with water and add the vinegar. Bring to a simmer and hold at a simmer while the risotto cooks. As the risotto nears its completion, crack the eggs into 4 small bowls or cups. Add them to the saucepan by touching the lip of each bowl to the simmering water and sliding the egg in. Poach until the whites have set but the yolks have not, about 4 minutes.

Remove the risotto from the heat and stir in the remaining 4 tablespoons (60 g) butter, remaining 1 tablespoon olive oil, and most of the Parmesan (reserve some for garnish). Season to taste with salt and pepper.

Divide the risotto among 4 bowls. Top each with a poached egg, crumbled pancetta, salsa verde, and reserved Parmesan.

Adam Sachs is the editor-in-chief of *Saveur* magazine and grew up in Louisville, Kentucky.

Once, in the course of a genteel dinner held by a group called the Kentuckians of New York, I made the error of cracking a small joke.

We, the Bluegrass Diaspora of Manhattan, had gathered in the swank dining room of a celebrated private club on Fifth Avenue to share stories and many bottles of decent bourbon. A wireless microphone was passed around. We took turns declaring our longstanding affiliation with, and undying fealty to, the Commonwealth. Some of us were natives, long ago displaced by marriage, work, or wanderlust. Many had spent only a few months or years there but testified nonetheless that the experience had marked them permanently: "It was a long time ago— *but it feels like it was just yesterday!*"

Feeling the bourbon a bit, and feeling a little like the kid I'd been for most of my time there (aged six months until I left home for college), I announced: "I only lived in Louisville for eighteen years—*but it felt like much longer!*" The quip didn't kill with the mostly older crowd. In point of fact, they hissed. In rep ties and pastel dresses, they scowled and hissed.

And I *get it*. Looking back, I might've hissed too. Or at least murmured heavily. Because though we are scattered and displaced, we who have lived there are—proudly, deeply, occasionally defensively, and especially when we're comparing aged country hams or approaching the first Saturday in May (Derby Day, for noninitiates)—Kentuckians for life. We drink bourbon not just because it softens all of life's hard edges but to feel, as the novelist Walker Percy described it, that "little explosion of Kentucky U.S.A. sunshine in the cavity of the nasopharynx."

We read the Kentucky poet-farmer Wendell Berry's dictum that "eating is an agricultural act" and we nod with home-state pride and feel a tingle of distant longing, a nostalgia for a rural, earthy connection to our food that we might never have actually experienced.

Like many Louisvillians, I didn't grow up around horses. The grass always looked green to me, and there was a lot of it in our lovely Frederick Law Olmsted-designed parks and the rolling fields and pastures outside of town. I've eaten precisely one pot of burgoo and I couldn't swear there was squirrel in it. What I'm trying to say is that I'm not exactly a poster boy for the pastoral Kentucky culinary experience. But I come from this place and am shaped by its contours and sense-memories and feel a connection and warmth toward it that grows the longer I'm away. It makes me happy to see its foodstuffs and homegrown flavors cycle into fashion and receive the regard they deserve.

Is Kentucky food familiar to you? (Please, do not mention Colonels or buckets. We will hiss.) It may offer fewer name-brand dishes than some better-known Southern foodways, but in the suddenly au courant Appalachian ingredients and traditions and River City's restaurant scene, you can find the proof of a true, distinct, evolving American regional cuisine: Things taste different here. There's an approach to food that's rooted in geography, informed by memory, and receptive to new ideas. And I'm getting hungry and homesick thinking about it.

Edward Lee is chef/owner of 610 Magnolia, MilkWood, and Whiskey Dry in Louisville, where he lives, plus Succotash in Maryland and Washington, D.C. A James Beard finalist, he is author of *Smoke & Pickles*.

STEAK TARTARE DEVILED EGG WITH SPOONBILL CAVIAR

PREPARATION TIME: 35 MINUTES
COOKING TIME: 15 MINUTES
MAKES: 24 CANAPÉS

For the deviled eggs:
- 12 eggs
- 2 cloves garlic, halved
- ⅓ cup (70 g) mayonnaise
- 1 tablespoon Dijon mustard
- ¼ teaspoon smoked paprika
- Salt and freshly ground black pepper

For the steak tartare:
- 4 oz (115 g) beef ribeye
- 2 tablespoons olive oil
- 2 tablespoons minced shallots
- 1 clove garlic, finely chopped
- 2 teaspoons finely grated fresh horseradish
- 1 tablespoon chopped fresh parsley
- Finely grated zest of 1 lemon
- 1 teaspoon Dijon mustard
- ½ teaspoon anchovy paste
- ⅛ teaspoon Worcestershire sauce

To serve:
- 2 oz (57 g) spoonbill caviar
- ½ teaspoon togarashi

For the deviled eggs: In a medium pot, cover the eggs with cold water and bring to a boil. Simmer for 6 minutes. Remove from the heat and let stand for 5 minutes. Drain the eggs and cool them under cold running water. Gently crack each egg and peel. Halve the eggs lengthwise. Remove the yolks and transfer to a bowl. Set the whites aside.

Grate the garlic on a zester into the yolks. Stir in the mayonnaise, mustard, paprika, and salt and pepper to taste until smooth. Transfer to a piping bag and set aside.

For the steak tartare: Chop the beef very finely by hand. Transfer to a bowl and mix in the olive oil, shallots, garlic, horseradish, parsley, lemon zest, mustard, anchovy paste, and Worcestershire sauce.

To serve: Arrange the hollow egg whites on a platter. Fill the holes with the steak tartare and smooth out. Pipe a little of the egg yolk filling over the top of the beef tartare. Spoon a little spoonbill caviar over the egg yolk mixture. Dust with a little togarashi.

FRIED QUAIL WITH WHITE KIMCHI

PREPARATION TIME: 10 MINUTES,
PLUS 5 DAYS FOR THE KIMCHI
COOKING TIME: 20 MINUTES
SERVES: 4

- 2 tablespoons sea salt
- 2 teaspoons ground Sichuan peppercorns
- 1 teaspoon Chinese 5-spice powder
- 2 teaspoons fish sauce
- 1 clove garlic, peeled and smashed
- 4 whole semi-boneless quail (back and rib bones removed, but wing and leg bones intact)
- Peanut (groundnut) oil, for deep-frying
- White Kimchi (recipe below)

In a small bowl, mix together the salt, Sichuan peppercorns, and 5-spice powder.

In a medium pot, bring 4 cups (1 liter) water, the fish sauce, and garlic to a boil. Add 1 teaspoon of the spiced salt. Working in two batches if necessary, add 2 quail to the water and boil for 2 minutes. Drain on paper towels until thoroughly dry and leave on a plate at room temperature, until ready to fry.

Pour 2 inches (5 cm) of peanut oil into a large heavy pot or deep-fryer and heat over medium-high to 375°F (190°C).

Working with one at a time, deep-fry the quail for 1 minute. Flip and fry for another 30 seconds. It will crisp up very quickly and turn a dark shiny shade of amber. Drain and pat dry with paper towels. Immediately sprinkle more of the spiced salt over the quail.

Serve the quail over a bed of white kimchi.

WHITE KIMCHI

PREPARATION TIME: 1 HOUR 20 MINUTES,
PLUS 5 DAYS FERMENTATION TIME
MAKES: 2 QUARTS (2 LITERS)

- 1 lb (455 g) napa cabbage
- 5 tablespoons kosher (coarse) salt
- 1 tablespoon sugar
- 4 oz (115 g) Asian pear, peeled and finely diced
- 2 oz (55 g) grated daikon radish
- 2 tablespoons grated fresh ginger
- 1 clove garlic, chopped
- ½ teaspoon ground coriander
- ½ teaspoon ground fennel
- 1 serrano pepper, thinly sliced

Slice the cabbage into thin ribbons and toss well in a bowl with 4 tablespoons of the salt and the sugar. Let sit at room temperature for 1 hour. Rinse in cold water, drain, and place in a clean bowl.

In a food processor, combine the Asian pear, daikon, ginger, garlic, coriander, fennel, and remaining 1 tablespoon salt and purée on high until well blended. Fold this mixture into the cabbage. Add the serrano pepper and thoroughly mix.

Transfer to a clean 64-oz (2-liter) glass jar or airtight plastic container with a tight-fitting lid. Leave at room temperature for 24 hours, then refrigerate. It will be ready to eat in 4–5 days and will keep for another 2 weeks.

BOURBON AFICIONADO

PREPARATION TIME: 15 MINUTES,
  PLUS COOLING TIME
COOKING TIME: 1 HOUR
SERVES: 12

For the fruit nut cake:
- ¼ cup (35 g) chopped dates
- ¼ cup (35 g) raisins
- ¾ cup (180 ml) bourbon
- 1½ cups (195 g) all-purpose (plain) flour
- 1 teaspoon baking powder
- ½ teaspoon baking soda (bicarbonate of soda)
- ¾ teaspoon ground cinnamon
- ¼ teaspoon ground cloves
- 1 cup (200 g) granulated sugar
- ½ teaspoon salt
- 2 eggs
- ½ cup (120 ml) vegetable oil
- 1 teaspoon pure vanilla extract
- 1 cup (270 g) mashed ripe bananas, from about 2 bananas
- ½ cup (50 g) pecans, toasted and finely chopped

For the butterscotch sauce:
- 4 tablespoons (60 g) butter
- 1½ cups (290 g) packed dark brown sugar
- 1 teaspoon sea salt
- 2 cups (475 ml) heavy (whipping) cream
- 1 cup (240 ml) milk
- 2 tablespoons bourbon
- 2 teaspoons pure vanilla extract
- 2 sheets gelatin

[Serve this bourbon cake and butterscotch sauce with fine vanilla ice cream. At my restaurant, the cake is paired with brown butter ice cream and finished with freeze-dried corn, dehydrated chocolate, and bourbon-barrel-aged maple syrup.]

Preheat the oven to 350°F (180°C/Gas Mark 4). Grease a 9 x 13-inch (23 x 33 cm) cake pan and line with parchment paper.

For the fruit nut cake: In a small saucepan, combine the dates, raisins, and ½ cup (120 ml) of the bourbon and cook until almost all the liquid is boiled off, about 10 minutes.

Sift the flour with the baking powder, baking soda (bicarbonate of soda), cinnamon, and cloves into a large bowl. Stir in the granulated sugar and salt.

In a medium bowl, whisk together the eggs, oil, and vanilla extract. Place the bananas, and cooked dates and raisins in a food processor. Process until combined, then add to the egg mixture.

Gently fold the banana mixture into the flour mixture until smooth. Gently fold in the pecans.

Transfer the batter to the cake pan and bake until risen and golden, about 30 minutes.

While still hot right out of the oven, brush the cake with the remaining ¼ cup (60 ml) bourbon. Run a knife around the edges, then leave to cool for 10 minutes before transferring to a wire rack. Let cool completely, about 1 hour, and cut into cubes.

For the butterscotch sauce: In a saucepan, melt the butter over medium heat and let it brown slightly, about 8 minutes. Add the brown sugar and salt and stir to dissolve. Add the cream, milk, bourbon, and vanilla and bring to a simmer. Add the gelatin and cook until slightly thickened, about 8 more minutes. Let cool.

Transfer the butterscotch to the canister of an iSi siphon, charge twice, and siphon. Pour on top of the cake.

Brett Anderson is a two-time James Beard Award winner and has been the restaurant critic and a features writer for the *Times-Picayune* in New Orleans, Louisiana, since 2000.

Many southernmost residents of Louisiana believe you have to travel north to get to the South. The longleaf pine forests appear to reside on different planets than the cypress swamps, even when they are across the highway from each other. People from Monroe don't sound like people from Lafayette, neither of whom sound like people from New Orleans. Louisiana is a state, but it is not one place.

New Orleans is not representative of Louisiana as a whole, but when people think about the state's food, they're often thinking about the food served in its most famous city, which has, by and large, done the state incredibly proud. The folks in Acadiana, the Cajun country around Lafayette, roughly two hours west of New Orleans, could justifiably take issue with this statement. Cajun cuisine is well worth exploring for its one-pot stews and jambalayas alone. But no one can argue with the fact that it is the chefs and cooks of New Orleans who brought Louisiana food to the attention of the world, even if they didn't happen to be from there. New Orleans is home to Louisiana's melting pot.

It is home to Creole cooking, the French-based, seafood-and-butter-intensive cooking you'll find in historic, upper-crust temples like Galatoire's and Antoine's. And it is also home to the equally refined, soul-influenced dishes found on the buffet and menu at Dooky Chase's, a monument to the contributions, culinary and otherwise, that African-Americans have made to the city's culture.

Embedded in all of this are, depending on the cook or restaurant in question, influences from Spain, the Caribbean, Vietnam, Native Americans, and the broader South. In recent years, Mexican moles and Middle Eastern tahini have inched their way toward becoming local staples.

Cajun food is a rural expression historically distinct from urban Creole cooking, but is part of the New Orleans swirl as well. Andouille sausage, a ubiquitous ingredient in New Orleans today, didn't start showing up in city gumbos until the Cajun chef Paul Prudhomme carried it from the country to the city in the late 1970s. In the process, he helped create a fusion cuisine that doesn't cross the state line.

This is a story outsiders should know and is a source of pride for those close to it, but it shouldn't bewilder you at the stove or table. Louisiana cooks across generations have turned their heritage into something tasteful and tasty. This happened in large part because the cooks built an audience that wouldn't settle for less. Once you get a taste, you won't either.

John Besh owns restaurants in New Orleans, was named a *Food & Wine* Best New Chef, and won the James Beard Award for Best Chef: Southeast. He is also an author and television host. The John Besh Foundation preserves the culinary heritage of New Orleans and the Gulf Coast.

MAMMA'S SEAFOOD GUMBO

PREPARATION TIME: 40 MINUTES
COOKING TIME: 2 HOURS 10 MINUTES
SERVES: 10

- ¾ cup (180 ml) canola (rapeseed) oil
- ¾ cup (100 g) all-purpose (plain) flour
- 2 large onions, chopped
- 6 blue crabs, quartered
- 1 stalk celery, chopped
- 4 cloves garlic, minced
- 3 quarts (3 liters) shrimp (prawn) or shellfish stock
- 2 cups (200 g) sliced okra
- 1 tablespoon fresh or dried thyme
- 2 bay leaves
- 1 lb (455 g) smoked sausage, cut into ½-inch (1.25 cm) thick slices
- 4 scallions (green onions), chopped
- 2 tablespoons Creole spice mixture
- Salt and freshly ground black pepper
- Tabasco sauce
- 1 lb (455 g) medium wild American shrimp (prawns), peeled and deveined
- 1 pint (500 g) shucked oysters and their liquor
- 1 cup (165 g) lump crabmeat, picked over for shells and cartilage
- 6 cups (960 g) cooked white rice

In a large heavy-bottomed pot, heat the oil over high heat. Whisk the flour into the hot oil. It will immediately begin to sizzle. Reduce the heat to medium and continue whisking until the roux turns a deep brown color, about 15 minutes. Add the onions, stirring them into the roux with a wooden spoon. Reduce the heat to medium-low and continue stirring until the roux turns a glossy dark brown, about 10 minutes.

Add the blue crabs and stir for a minute to toast the shells, then add the celery and garlic. Increase the heat to medium and cook, stirring, for 3 minutes. Add the stock, okra, thyme, and bay leaves. Bring the gumbo to a boil, stirring occasionally.

Reduce the heat to medium-low and simmer for 45 minutes. Stir occasionally and skim off the fat from the surface (moving the pot half off the burner helps collect the impurities).

Add the sausage and scallions (spring onions) to the pot and cook for 15 minutes. Season with the Creole spice mixture and salt, black pepper, and Tabasco to taste. Add the shrimp, oysters and their liquor, and crabmeat to the pot and cook for about 5 minutes. Serve with the rice.

COURT-BOUILLON

PREPARATION TIME: 45 MINUTES
COOKING TIME: 1 HOUR 50 MINUTES
SERVES: 8

- 1 whole redfish (5 lb/2.3 kg)
- Juice of 1 lemon
- Salt and freshly ground black pepper
- ½ cup (120 ml) canola (rapeseed) oil
- ½ cup (65 g) all-purpose (plain) flour
- 2 onions, chopped
- 2 blue crabs, quartered
- 1 green bell pepper, chopped
- 2 stalks celery, chopped
- 4 cloves garlic, minced
- 6 tomatoes, peeled and diced
- Leaves from 1 sprig fresh tarragon, minced
- 1 teaspoon crushed chili flakes
- ¼ teaspoon ground allspice
- ¼ teaspoon ground coriander
- 3 bay leaves
- 2 cups (475 ml) shrimp or fish stock
- 1 lb (455 g) medium Louisiana or wild American shrimp (prawns), peeled and deveined
- 1 cup (250 g) shucked oysters
- 1 lb (455 g) jumbo lump crabmeat, picked over for shells and cartilage
- 3 scallions (spring onions), chopped
- 3 dashes of Worcestershire sauce
- Tabasco sauce
- 4 cups (640 g) cooked white rice

Preheat the oven to 300°F (150°C/Gas Mark 2).

To keep the fish from curling up in the roasting pan while cooking, score both sides of the redfish about ¾ inch (2 cm) deep in a couple of places between the pectoral fins and the tail and along both sides of the dorsal fin. Put the fish in a roasting pan just large enough for it to lie flat. Season the fish all over with the lemon juice, season with salt and pepper, and set aside.

In large heavy-bottomed saucepan, stir together the oil and flour. Cook over medium heat, stirring constantly, until the roux becomes a deep brown and has a nutty aroma, about 15 minutes. Add the onions and blue crab to the roux and cook, stirring frequently, for 5 minutes. Add the bell pepper, celery, garlic, and tomatoes. Increase the heat to medium-high and bring to a boil, stirring every so often. Add the tarragon, chili flakes, allspice, coriander, bay leaves, and shrimp stock and bring to a boil, stirring frequently. Season to taste with salt and pepper.

Pour the mixture over the redfish in the roasting pan, cover the pan with foil, and bake the fish for 40 minutes. Uncover and scatter the shrimp (prawns), oysters, crabmeat, and scallions (spring onions) around the fish. Bake the fish, uncovered, until it begins to flake from the bone, about 15 minutes more.

Add the Worcestershire, a little Tabasco, and salt and pepper to the tomato-shellfish gravy in the roasting pan. Use a large spoon and fork to portion the fish, serving it with the gravy over the rice.

SHRIMP ÉTOUFFÉE

PREPARATION TIME: 30 MINUTES
COOKING TIME: 50 MINUTES
SERVES: 2

- ¼ cup (60 ml) canola (rapeseed) oil
- ¼ cup (33 g) all-purpose (plain) flour
- 1 onion, chopped
- 1 stalk celery, chopped
- 4 cloves garlic, minced
- Pinch of ground allspice
- Pinch of cayenne pepper
- ½ cup (90 g) chopped tomatoes
- 2½ cups (600 ml) shrimp or fish stock
- 1 lb (455 g) medium wild American shrimp
  (prawns), peeled and deveined
- 1 scallion (spring onion), minced
- Tabasco sauce
- Salt and freshly ground black pepper
- 3 tablespoons (45 g) butter, diced
- 4 cups (640 g) cooked white rice

In a large heavy-bottomed pot, heat the oil over high heat. Whisk the flour into the hot oil. It will immediately begin to sizzle. Reduce the heat to medium and continue whisking until the roux turns a deep brown color, about 15 minutes. Add the onions, stirring them into the roux with a wooden spoon. Reduce the heat to medium-low and continue stirring until the roux turns a glossy dark brown, about 10 minutes. Add the celery, garlic, allspice, and cayenne. Cook for 5 minutes. Add the tomatoes and stock, increase the heat to high, and bring to a boil. Reduce the heat to medium and simmer for 5–7 minutes, until slightly thickened, stirring often to make sure the sauce doesn't burn or stick to the pan.

Reduce the heat to medium-low. Add the shrimp and scallion (spring onion). Cook for 3–4 minutes, just until the shrimp turn pink and are heated through. Season to taste with Tabasco, salt, and pepper. Remove the pot from the heat and stir in the butter just until melted. Serve over rice.

BANANAS FOSTER

PREPARATION TIME: 5 MINUTES
COOKING TIME: 15 MINUTES
SERVES: 6

- 1 stick (115 g) butter
- ½ cup (95 g) packed light brown sugar
- 1 teaspoon ground cinnamon
- Pinch of freshly grated nutmeg
- 3 tablespoons fresh orange juice
- 6 bananas, halved lengthwise and
  then crosswise
- ½ cup (120 ml) dark rum

In a large frying pan, warm the butter and brown sugar over high heat, stirring until they have melted into a caramel. Cook 3 minutes more, stirring constantly. Stir in the cinnamon, nutmeg, and orange juice. Add the bananas and cook for 3 minutes, stirring gently to coat the bananas and spooning the sauce over them.

Remove the pan from the heat and, holding the skillet away from you, carefully add the rum. Return the skillet to the heat and cook for another 3 minutes. Be aware that the alcohol may ignite if you're cooking over an open flame. If you're into pyrotechnics, use a long match to burn off the alcohol. Serve immediately on individual plates, spooning the sauce over the bananas.

Andrew Taylor and Mike Wiley, co-owners and co-chefs of Big Tree Hospitality in Portland, have earned acclaim for Hugo's, Eventide Oyster Co., and The Honey Paw. They've been named Best Chef: Northeast by the James Beard Foundation.

When people think of Maine, they think of two foods well-known by everybody and their brother: lobster rolls and blueberry pie. But those aren't the only items on the state's menu. When we were opening our restaurants we did a lot of research, and Maine's mainstream culinary sensibility provided our kitchens' backbone. The driving force for us has been—what do people in Maine actually eat, and why?

So we humbly present our heartfelt thoughts on four iconic Maine dishes—what they mean, and why they matter.

BAKED BEANS: Bostonians like to claim baked beans as their own, and that's fine. Beantown has a nice ring and Boston Baked Beans has some fine alliteration. But Mainers will argue that baked beans really originated in logging camps in northern Maine. Furthermore, we can certainly count "bean hole beans" as a Maine original. Traditionally, in logging camps, beans were soaked overnight and then, while the loggers were working, cooked all day in massive wood-fired pits where cauldrons of beans were effectively buried, to be unearthed when the loggers returned to camp. While rare today, you still see reader-board signs in rural Maine outside churches and grange halls advertising "bean hole suppers"—a Maine tradition.

CLAM CHOWDER: Much ink has been spilled on the topic of New England clam chowder. There is no need to further discuss the significance or origin of this regional delicacy or how it differs from its Rhode Island or Manhattan counterparts—except to say it's the best type of chowder there is. Our recipe is about as classic as it gets and is what we've always envisioned Little Sal and Jane eating after their action-packed morning of digging

clams in the quintessential Robert McCloskey children's book, *One Morning in Maine*. Only use high-quality clams that were harvested in the past day or two. This is the most important step to the whole process. Old clams will yield old chowder.

CRAB ROLL: There is no doubt that the lobster roll is king in Maine. Certainly the state's most iconic dish, lightly dressed lobster meat on a butter-griddled split-top hot dog bun can be found in most restaurants there and especially the small lobster and clam shacks that dot the coast. While tourists and Mainers alike argue about the various merits of each version of the lobster roll, lost in this discussion is the menu item that invariably sits directly below the lobster roll and usually in a smaller font— the crab roll. Many Mainers argue that if the lobster roll is for tourists, the crab roll is for us. The reason the crab roll has wedged itself into cultural significance is simple—it's cheaper. Rock crab and Jonah crab, the two species picked for Maine crab rolls, are often found in lobster traps as by-catch. While fishermen would pick and sell lobster meat at a high price, the crab would be picked and either eaten at home or sold at a lower price to earn a few extra bucks.

HOME FRIES: Home fries are often the sad heap parked on the corner of the griddle at your local breakfast diner and then on the side of your plate, where they are scarcely touched while you focus on the bacon, eggs, and toast. Barely a second of attention is paid to them by the owner, the cook, and the customer before they are whisked into the trash can next to the dish slide. Such a shame too, because when proper care is taken with home fries, with just three to five ingredients, they can be not only a spectacular side dish, but a meal—a really good, wholesome, rewarding meal. And this is what they have been in northern Maine for a century and a half.

Aroostook County—simply called "The County"—represents the northern third of the state. Sparsely populated, it is divided between the western waterways and wilderness, as well as the eastern plains, which border Canada. In the plains of The County, the primary occupation is potato farming and the primary export are potatoes, which cause the tubers to have the same cultural significance to this landlocked section of Maine as lobsters have for the coastal areas. That is not to say they have the same cachet.

Our method for cooking home fries gives a huge nod to John Thorne, a culinary writer, whose musings on the subject inform ours. You likely don't own the traditional tool for cooking them—a wood-burning cook-stove, which doubles as the only heat source for the house—because it is so antiquated and have been replaced in most of the country. Care, though, is required and attention to details need be paid, because then you will be rewarded.

Andrew Taylor and Mike Wiley

BAKED BEANS

PREPARATION TIME: 10 MINUTES,
PLUS OVERNIGHT SOAKING
COOKING TIME: 1 HOUR, PLUS
OVERNIGHT BAKING
MAKES: 2 QUARTS (2 LITERS)

- 1 lb (455 g) dried Swedish brown beans
- ½ medium sweet onion
- ¼ cup (60 ml) molasses
- ½ cup (120 ml) pure maple syrup
- 2 tablespoons mustard powder
- ½ teaspoon baking powder (particularly important if your water is acidic)
- Salt
- ½ jalapeño pepper
- Generous chunk of salt pork or slab bacon (optional, but highly recommended)

Rinse and pick over the beans to remove any pebbles or sticks. Place in a container and cover with water triple the volume of the beans. They will swell dramatically. Let soak overnight or at least 8 hours.

Drain the beans, place in a pot, and add cold water to cover by 1 inch (2.5 cm). Bring to a high simmer, then reduce to a bare simmer and cook until the beans are completely tender. This is important. You don't want them all totally split, but they must be tender. Should take 45 minutes to 1 hour.

Meanwhile, heat a skillet over high heat and char the half onion, cut side down, for 8 minutes. Set aside.

Preheat the oven to 200°F (95°C).

Stir the molasses, maple syrup, mustard, and baking powder into the beans. Add a pinch of salt—not too much at this stage.

In the bottom of a bean pot, Dutch oven (casserole), or heavy cast-iron pot, place the charred onion, jalapeño, and salt pork (if using). Pour the hot beans into the pot, adding enough of the cooking liquid, to just barely cover the beans. Cover and bake overnight or at least 8 hours.

When done, uncover and season to taste with salt. If the liquid is too thin, smash a few beans against the side of the pot and stir in to thicken.

MAINE CRAB ROLLS

PREPARATION TIME: 10 MINUTES
COOKING TIME: 5 MINUTES
SERVES: 2

- 2 tablespoons (30 g) butter
- 2 split-top hot dog buns
- 5 tablespoons mayonnaise (Kewpie brand if you can find it)
- Finely grated zest of 1 lemon plus ½ teaspoon juice
- Finely grated zest of 1 lime plus ½ teaspoon juice
- Pinch of cayenne
- Pinch of salt
- ½ lb (225 g) lump crabmeat, picked over for shells and cartilage

[It is always better to pick over your own crabmeat if you can.]

In a frying pan, melt the butter over medium heat until nice and foamy. Toast the hot dog buns until golden brown on each side.

In a small bowl, combine the mayonnaise, lemon zest and juice, lime zest and juice, cayenne, and salt. Taste to make sure it's seasoned to your liking.

Pick over the crabmeat again. Wring out the excess water from the crabmeat—you don't want a watery crab roll. In a medium bowl, flake the crabmeat with a fork. Stir in the mayonnaise mixture and taste. It may need another pinch of salt.

Snugly spoon the crab salad into the toasted hot dog buns, and pity the tourists clamoring for their lobster rolls.

HOME FRIES

PREPARATION TIME: 5 MINUTES
COOKING TIME: 20 MINUTES
MAKES: AS MUCH AS YOU'D LIKE

- Fat (bacon grease, pork lard, beef tallow, vegetable oil, or canola (rapeseed) oil)
- Medium-starch potatoes (Green Mountain, Bintje, Kennebec, Shepody, or Yukon Gold; enough to fill the pan in a single layer–see directions), peeled or unpeeled
- Salt and freshly ground black pepper
- Diced onion (optional)

Heat a cast-iron pan until hot: in a 300°F (150°C/Gas Mark 2) oven for 10 minutes or on the stove top over medium-low heat for 5 minutes. Move the pan around the burner to ensure even heat. In the pan, melt the fat to a depth between ⅛ and ¼ inch (3 and 6 mm), so the potatoes get browned, but not greasy.

Cube enough potatoes to fill the pan in a single layer. The size is less important than making all the cubes consistent. Place the cubes in the pan, comfortably snug but not stacked on each other. Season lightly with salt and toss.

Cover the pan and cook over medium-low heat, shaking the covered pan periodically, until fork-tender, 15–30 minutes depending on the size of the cut. This is the most critical period: to steam the potatoes with their own moisture, saturate the exterior with the fat, and draw out and convert the starches. If the heat is too high, the potatoes will start to brown too much and develop a crust. If the heat is too low, the potatoes will take forever to cook. When you remove the lid to check for doneness, tilt the lid so the condensation drips back into the pan.

When the potatoes are fork-tender, remove the lid and increase the heat to medium. Add onions, if using. Now is the time to brown: you want to get a good crust. Then toss the potatoes to get a crust on another side. If the heat is going too fast, turn it down; too slow, turn it up. Season the potatoes liberally with salt and pepper. Turn the potatoes out onto a plate and enjoy with eggs and bacon.

John Shields is a television host, cookbook author, and chef at Gertrude's at the Baltimore Museum of Art in Maryland.

It was a humid August day in 1958 on the Chesapeake Bay. Scattered clouds drifted along the brightly lit summer sky as our 14-foot (4.3 m) wooden skiff workboat gently bobbed up and down on the brackish green waves. My uncles, cousin, and I had been out trotline crabbing the whole morning, just off Bowley's Quarters near the mouth of Middle River.

This motley crew of metal workers and their kids from Baltimore were not official Chesapeake watermen, but rather a resourceful band of "chicken neckers," which in the 1950s and '60s did not have the same negative connotation as today. On the eastern shore of the bay, the locals call any outsiders, or folks from the western shore, "chicken neckers." They are not real fond of newcomers who stay. But in the olden days the chicken-necker term simply described a method of catching crabs, normally employed by weekend boaters.

The pros spend lots of money on crab pots, which are placed in various locations and baited. The watermen then check their pots regularly to retrieve the crabs. Trotlining is a much more skilled method of plying the blue crabs from the water. Long lines are baited (sometimes with bull lips) and stretched out on the water, held up by buoys. A very cool contraption on the bow of a small motorboat raises the lines slowly from the water and the watermen can use nets to snag the crabs.

We chicken neckers would tie pieces of chicken necks to the lines and dangle them in the water, hoping to lure crabs. When they bite, you slowly pull up the line, scoop the crab tangling there with your net, and plop it into a bushel basket. It's not real complicated, and if you hit the right stretch of water, a number of crabs can be harvested. And that is key to living in the Chesapeake region. We love our blue crabs.

During our boat trip that summer day, we had a banner day of crabbing, with, as I recall, a bushel of nice-size crabs. You want the crabs to be large and heavy. That means you will be able to pick ample amounts of lumps from the cooked crustaceans. We were heading into Galloway Creek, just a skootch east of Middle River, when Uncle Willie noticed a dorsal fin off the bow of the boat. As the fish swam closer it was apparent that we had a sandbar shark getting in position to follow us. I don't know whether he was just trying to scare the bejesus out of me (he succeeded) or if he wanted the bushel of crabs, but I do know that boat ride seemed to take forever to get us back to shore.

The rivers outside the confined city limits of Baltimore became the working-class families' getaway from the oppressive heat and humidity of the city. Most of the dwellings along the banks were shacks, with outhouses and outdoor summer kitchens. Ours was no grander, but to a kid my age it seemed the most amazing shore home one could imagine. Right up from the makeshift pier were "picnic tables" that had been fashioned out of sawhorses and plywood and adorned with old newspaper, sometimes taped down to keep from blowing away.

When we docked the boat and hauled the crabs up to the summer kitchen, the assembled aunts, uncles, cousins, and grandparents were in high gear. With crabs in hand the ▶

◄ party was on. The family had a huge steel pot with a lid on the fire getting the flat, stale beer and vinegar up to a rolling boil. The feisty crabs were placed in the pot in layers— one at a time. As each layer was complete, a good handful of Old Bay seafood season-ing was applied, followed by another layer of crabs. When the pot was full the lid went back on, and within a half hour it was time for a crab feast.

The crab feast of the Chesapeake Bay is a traditional gathering. It's not so much a dinner per se, but rather an opportunity for family and friends to have a culinary celebration and get-together, not that we had a clue what "culinary" meant at the time. But the crab feast was definitely always a party, with steamed crabs unceremoniously dumped and piled high right on the news-paper-covered table. The beer flowed freely and the aroma of spicy crab seasoning wafted through the humid air. The kids had ginger ale or iced tea to wash down the crabs, unless the adults were otherwise occupied, affording us the opportunity to sneak a sip of beer. Or at least we thought we were sneaking a taste—they knew.

Skilled crab picking is handed down from generation to generation. People from outside the Chesapeake region sometimes think it is genetic, or a morphic resonance that enables us to tear apart a tightly compacted crustacean damn quick. When I was a wee child, my grand-mother would pick crab for me, explaining the process as she went. It was like a mother bird feeding the baby birds. But after not too long, just as the mother bird pushes the baby out of the nest, I was on my own amidst a tribe of proficient pickers, paring knife and mallet in

hand. We didn't know jumbo lump from backfin in those days. The only mission was to get the meat out of the crab in the biggest, most intact lumps possible.

Talking and spinning tales are the main ingre-dients of a successful feast, and a favorite subject is former crab feasts, especially tales of heroism and adventure. "Back in '48 all the crabs were at least 10 inches (25 cm) across and heavy as horses.... Your uncle Elmer could pick a crab clean as a whistle with one hand, while drinking down a mug of beer with the other without taking a breath.... Remember the time when that crab got hold of Sis's toe, and she ran round the backyard, crab clamped onto her toe, like a bat outta hell?" The National Bohemian beer encouraged a bit of exaggera-tion, but we kids loved the stories.

Besides sippin' beer and cracking crabs, we would take a break from picking by eating steaming ears of sweet summer corn, dripping with butter. Gigantic ripe summer tomatoes would be sliced and laid out on platters with just a touch of salt. A couple of bowls of potato salad and coleslaw often were brought down to the shore in coolers. We generally had fruit pies or cobblers for dessert, and never ice cream. It was a well-known fact in Chesapeake family circles that eating ice cream immediately following crabs could result in death. I believe that, according to Aunt Minnie, the ice cream would turn to stone in your stomach, resulting with your demise. We never dared to put Minnie's ice cream hypothesis to the test. Many of us are still alive.

Jeremiah Stone is chef-owner of Contra and Wildair restaurants in New York City. He grew up in Montgomery County, Maryland.

MARYLAND-STYLE CRAB CAKES

PREPARATION TIME: 15 MINUTES,
  PLUS CHILLING TIME
COOKING TIME: 10 MINUTES
MAKES: 6 CAKES

- 1 egg
- ½ cup (35 g) crushed oyster crackers
- 1 tablespoon grainy mustard
- 1 teaspoon fresh lemon juice
- 1 teaspoon Worcestershire sauce
- ½ lb (225 g) Maryland blue crab jumbo lump backfin meat
- ½ lb (225 g) Maryland blue crab backfin meat
- 2 teaspoons Old Bay seasoning
- Pinch of celery salt
- Salt and freshly ground black pepper
- ½ cup (105 g) mayonnaise
- ¼ cup (15 g) chopped fresh flat-leaf parsley and celery leaves mixed
- 4 tablespoons (60 g) butter, melted
- 2 tablespoons smooth mustard

[Every summer weekend, I would enjoy a bushel of crabs with my family, and we turned the leftover meat into crab cakes.]

In a small bowl, stir together the egg and cracker crumbs. In a cup or another small bowl, mix together the grainy mustard, lemon juice, and Worcestershire sauce.

In a large bowl, season the crab with the Old Bay, celery salt, and salt and pepper to taste. Fold in the mayonnaise and the parsley/celery leaves, then the egg mixture, and finally the lemon/mustard mixture. Divide the mixture into 6 even cakes. Pack gently to hold together and refrigerate for 1 hour.

Preheat the broiler (grill) and place an oven rack 9 inches (23 cm) from the broiler element. Stir together the melted butter and smooth mustard mixture. Brush the crab cakes with this and broil for 10 minutes, until golden on top and heated through.

CONGEE WITH MARYLAND BLUE CRABS

PREPARATION TIME: 15 MINUTES
COOKING TIME: 3 HOURS
SERVES: 8

- 3 medium Maryland blue crabs
- 1 lb (455 g) butter, melted
- 2 cups (400 g) jasmine or medium-grain white rice
- 2 cloves garlic, grated
- 1 (2-inch/5 cm) knob fresh ginger, finely grated
- 1 bunch scallions (spring onions), thinly sliced, whites and greens kept separate
- 1 teaspoon soy sauce
- 1 tablespoon fish sauce
- Pinch of celery salt
- Pinch of ground white pepper
- Safflower or sunflower oil, for deep-frying
- 10 wonton wrappers, cut into ¼-inch (6 mm) squares
- Old Bay seasoning
- 1 bunch cilantro (coriander), thinly sliced

Preheat the oven to 300°F (150°C/Gas Mark 2).

In a steamer, cook the crabs for 14 minutes. When cool enough to handle, pick out the backfin meat and set aside. Take a cleaver and crack the crab carcass. Break the shells into small pieces. Toss the crab carcasses with the melted butter and place in a medium roasting pan. Roast for 25 minutes. Strain the butter into a bowl and set aside. Discard the solids.

In a large soup pot, combine the rice, 3¼ cups (760 ml) water, garlic, and ginger. Cook over medium-low heat at a low simmer for 2 hours, stirring frequently. Add the scallion (spring onion) whites, soy sauce, fish sauce, celery salt, and white pepper. Mix the reserved crab butter into the rice.

In a separate large heavy-bottomed pot or deep-fryer, heat 1 inch (2.5 cm) oil to 365°F (185°C). Add the wonton squares and deep-fry until they float, about 1 minute. Toss with a liberal amount of Old Bay.

Serve bowls of congee topped with crabmeat, wonton wrappers, scallion (spring onion) greens, and cilantro (coriander).

Corby Kummer, a five-time James Beard Award winner for food writing, lives in Massachusetts. He is a senior editor at *The Atlantic* and author of *The Joy of Coffee* and *The Pleasures of Slow Food*.

Like many New England Jews, my family made an exception for lobster.

My mother had grown up in a kosher home, already an exception in her generation of assimilated New England farmers/businessmen in the Connecticut River Valley, about fifteen miles to Hartford one way and the Massachusetts border the other. To please my less-assimilated father, whose parents had immigrated as children and come to Connecticut early in their marriage, she kept kosher. But that didn't stop her from bringing home lobster rolls from our local seafood market. She would open the long white wax paper bundles on thick brown layers of grocery bags from the supermarket and tuck into her occasional illicit lunch.

She would carefully fold away the evidence afterward, dedicate a separate heavy green trash bag to it, tie it securely, and bring it to the garage to await the week's pickup. My father, I think, never knew that the barrier had been crossed in the confines of the kitchen table. But we crossed it whenever we ate out—standard operating procedure for a family that wanted to maintain cultural identity in a town where some years we were the only Jewish kids in our class. We could eat whatever we wanted at a restaurant—and that was, very often, baked stuffed lobster, a fancy New England restaurant dish with seasoned breadcrumbs and stuffing.

Lobster is the best shellfish: the sweetest and most silken. Soft-shelled clams are a Massachusetts-to-Maine obsession. Lobster is king. And a lobster roll is New England in a bun: the sheer luxury of meat someone else has picked for you, soaked in butter and mixed with perhaps some chopped celery and put in a toasted hot dog bun. To achieve the ideal, first there is the weight of the meat, then there's the bun. If it isn't lightly buttered and griddled on both sides—so it's warm with a shatteringly crisp outside and moist, pliant but not mealy crumb within—the whole experience is thrown off. There are in fact two schools of lobster roll production: a warm one with butter or binding, and a cool one with mayo. Both require an expertly toasted bun with crustless sides. And if the lobster isn't fresh or well handled, if it has been toughened by over-cooking or hardened by storage of more than a few hours after picking, much of the point is lost.

In Massachusetts, where I have lived since after college, the search for a great lobster roll is a constant activity. Seldom do a few months go by without a visiting friend texting urgently, seeking *the* place to find a lobster roll in Boston. If foreigners come to visit, I make sure they have one. Though Boston doesn't have seafood shacks, it has two rock-solid places to go. The first is Neptune Oyster, in the North End, in Boston's traditional Little Italy. It is a seafood bar with a wide selection of oysters—including Island Creek from Duxbury, and other oysters farmed off of the coastal towns south of Boston toward Cape Cod—displayed on ice in deep wooden trays. But people really come for the lobster rolls, with warm and fresh lobster meat gently tossed in butter and seasoned with both salt and black pepper, which is untraditional but works. The brioche bun is thin-walled enough not to overwhelm the lobster, as most brioche buns do. Neptune doesn't take reservations, is tiny, and there's always a long line. ▶

◄ So that leaves Legal Seafood, the place I always take first-timers for a true taste of Boston—and what gives glory to the whole state of Massachusetts and particularly the East Coast's fish and shellfish. Legal has many locations around Boston and in several other states, which makes people assume it isn't local and doesn't have real ties to Boston. It does.

George Berkowitz began selling seafood in Cambridge to Julia Child, and after his early days of picnic tables and mostly self-service, opened a series of simple but satisfying restaurants that have placed an emphasis on service and quality. Whenever my expat first cousin comes from California, he demands to go to Legal for boiled lobster. And it's where I take people for lobster rolls. The preparation is mayonnaise, not butter, and Massachusetts history is on the paper place mats. I feel sure that my mother would be very pleased that the current head of the restaurant group, who makes sure the buns stay meaty, is named Roger Berkowitz.

Barbara Lynch is a native of Boston, Massachusetts, and the chef/owner of Barbara Lynch Gruppo, which includes No. 9 Park and B&G Oysters. She is a two-time James Beard Award winner, was named a *Food & Wine* Best New Chef, and is an author.

LOBSTER BLT

PREPARATION TIME: 1 HOUR,
  PLUS SITTING AND COOLING TIME
COOKING TIME: 1 HOUR 45 MINUTES
SERVES: 4

- 4 whole lobsters (about 1¼ lb/565 g each)
- 1 cup (210 g) mayonnaise, preferably Hellmann's
- 1 teaspoon fresh lemon juice
- ½ cup (50 g) finely diced celery
- Salt and freshly ground black pepper
- 4 tomatoes, plum or heirloom, cut into ½-inch (1.25 cm) thick slices
- 6 cloves garlic, roughly chopped
- 1 sprig fresh thyme, roughly chopped
- ¼ cup (60 ml) olive oil
- 16 slices smoked bacon (streaky)
- 4 ciabatta rolls, split horizontally
- 1 tablespoon finely chopped fresh chives
- 1 tablespoon finely chopped fresh parsley
- 1 head Bibb (round) lettuce, washed and dried
- Coleslaw (page 582)
- Pickles (page 582)

[Few foods are more sought after, or argued about, in Boston than a proper lobster roll. At B&G Oysters, we've been serving one unchanged for years, overflowing with freshly steamed lobster meat. This recipe is a slight variation on the classic lobster roll, combining it with a BLT. Since tomatoes are only perfect for a few weeks in summer, we confit tomatoes year-round to intensify their flavor and sweetness. With the coleslaw and pickles, this is one of my all-time favorite sandwiches.]

Set up a large container of ice water. Bring a large pot of water to a gentle boil. Boil the lobsters for 8–10 minutes, then plunge into the ice water to stop the cooking process. Clean the lobsters, removing the meat from the tail, claws, and knuckles. Cut into bite-size pieces.

In a bowl, toss together the lobster meat, mayonnaise, lemon juice, celery, and salt and pepper to taste. Refrigerate until ready to use.

Preheat the oven to 225°F (110°C/Gas Mark ¼). Line a baking sheet with parchment paper.

Arrange the tomato slices on the baking sheet. Sprinkle with the garlic and thyme. Gently season with salt and pepper. Drizzle the olive oil evenly over the tomatoes. Bake the tomatoes until sweet and roasted, 45 minutes to 1 hour. Let the confit tomatoes cool on the baking sheet until ready to use.

In a frying pan, cook the bacon until crisp, about 10 minutes. Drain on paper towels. Pour all but 2–3 tablespoons of bacon fat from the pan. Return the pan to medium heat. Once hot, add the rolls, cut side down, and toast evenly in the fat, about 2 minutes. Drain on paper towels.

On each roll make a layer of confit tomatoes, lobster salad, chopped chives, parsley, and 2 lettuce leaves. Top each with 4 slices of bacon. Serve with coleslaw and pickles.

COLESLAW

PREPARATION TIME: 20 MINUTES,
PLUS SITTING TIME
SERVES: 6

- Salt
- 1 medium head napa cabbage, julienned
- 1 carrot, grated
- 1 red onion, thinly sliced
- 1 cup (210 g) mayonnaise, preferably Hellmann's
- 3 tablespoons cider vinegar
- 1 teaspoon fresh lemon juice
- 1 tablespoon sugar
- 1 teaspoon Dijon mustard
- Freshly ground black pepper

Gently salt the julienned cabbage in a large bowl. Let sit for at least 1 hour. Gently squeeze the cabbage to remove any excess water.

Transfer the cabbage to a clean bowl and add the carrot and onion. In a small bowl, mix together the mayonnaise, vinegar, lemon juice, sugar, and mustard. Season to taste with salt and pepper, remembering that the cabbage has been seasoned lightly already. Toss the vegetables with the dressing and taste for seasoning.

PICKLES

PREPARATION TIME: 10 MINUTES,
PLUS COOLING TIME
COOKING TIME: 10 MINUTES
MAKES: 1 QUART (1 LITER)

- 4 pickling cucumbers, cut into ⅛-inch (3 mm) thick slices
- 1 quart (1 liter) rice vinegar
- ⅓ cup (66 g) sugar
- 2 tablespoons salt
- 2 sprigs fresh dill
- 6 cloves garlic, peeled

Place the cucumbers in a large heatproof bowl.

In a 2-quart (2-liter) pot, combine the vinegar, 1⅓ cups (315 ml) water, the sugar, salt, dill, and garlic and bring to a boil.

Pour the hot pickling liquid over the cucumbers. Use a small plate to keep the cucumbers fully submerged. Let sit until cool. Refrigerate in an airtight container in the pickling liquid.

CLAM CHOWDER

PREPARATION TIME: 20 MINUTES,
    PLUS SOAKING TIME
COOKING TIME: 1 HOUR
SERVES: 4–8

For the clams:
- 50 fresh littleneck clams
- 1 cup (240 ml) white wine
- 1 sprig fresh thyme
- 1 shallot, chopped

For the chowder:
- 4 oz (115 g) thick-cut bacon (streaky), cut into large chunks
- 2 cups (225 g) medium-diced Yukon Gold potatoes (save the scraps)
- 4 tablespoons (60 g) unsalted butter
- 1½ cups (240 g) medium diced white onion
- ¾ cup (75 g) medium diced celery
- ¾ cup (70 g) medium diced leeks, cleaned
- ½ cup (120 ml) white wine
- 2 cups (475 ml) heavy (whipping) cream
- 1 cup (240 ml) milk
- Salt and freshly cracked black pepper

[This is a classic New England clam chowder that we have been serving at B&G Oysters since it opened, and it continues to be the best-selling item on the menu. The two keys are: 1. Steaming your own clams. Nothing beats fresh steamed clams, and you can use their liquid to fortify your chowder. 2. Adding potato purée to the chowder to thicken it. It is crucial that the chowder have the proper thickness, so we use all the trimmings from dicing the potatoes to make a quick purée. I like to cut my bacon thick, giving the soup great bacon lardons to bite into. But no matter what size you cut it, be sure to use a delicious smoky bacon—my favorite is Niman Ranch Applewood Smoked Bacon.]

For the clams: Place the clams in a large bowl and fill with cold water. Let sit for at least 20 minutes to clean out any sand.

Heat a large pot over high heat until hot. Drain the clams and transfer them to the pot. Add the wine, thyme, and shallot. Tightly cover the pot, reduce the heat to medium, and cook until all the clams open, 10–15 minutes. Pour the clams and cooking liquid into a sieve set over a bowl to catch the liquid. Reserve the liquid. Once the clams are cool, remove them from the shells. If you like, discard the belly (the dark, soft part of the clam).

For the chowder: In a frying pan set over medium-high heat, cook the bacon until crispy, 10 minutes. Drain on paper towels and set aside.

In a small pot, combine the potato scraps with cold water to cover and bring to a boil. Reduce to a simmer and cook until the potatoes are very soft. Transfer the potato and some of the cooking liquid to a blender and purée until smooth.

In a large pot set over medium heat, melt the butter until it begins to bubble. Add the onion, celery, and leeks. Cook until soft, stirring frequently, about 10 minutes. Add the wine and cook to reduce by half. Measure out 2 cups (475 ml) of the clam cooking liquid and add to the pan. Add the diced potatoes, cream, and milk. Bring to a simmer and cook until the potatoes are tender. Reduce the heat to low and add the potato purée.

Add the bacon and clams to the chowder and warm through. Season to taste with salt and pepper.

CASSOULET-STYLE BAKED BEANS

PREPARATION TIME: 15 MINUTES,
  PLUS OVERNIGHT SOAKING TIME
COOKING TIME: 2 HOURS 30 MINUTES
SERVES: 4–6

For the beans:
- 2½ cups (520 g) dried Tarbais beans,
  or other suitable white bean, soaked in
  water overnight
- 8 cups (2 liters) chicken stock, or more
  as needed
- Salt
- ⅔ cup (150 g) finely diced bacon (streaky)
- 1 cup (160 g) finely diced onion
- ½ cup (65 g) finely diced carrot
- ½ cup (50 g) finely diced celery
- 2 tablespoons light brown sugar
- ½ teaspoon ground cloves
- 1 tablespoon Dijon mustard
- 4 tablespoons (60 g) butter
- 3 bay leaves
- 1 sprig fresh thyme
- Boudin Blanc, cut into 3-inch (7.5 cm)
  segments

For the crumb topping:
- 2 cups (225 g) dried breadcrumbs
- 4 tablespoons (60 g) butter, melted
- Salt and freshly ground black pepper

[Everyone associates Boston with baked beans. My favorite variation is a French cassoulet, made with white Tarbais beans, sausage, duck confit, and breadcrumbs. Here we take the flavors of Boston baked beans—brown sugar, Dijon, and bacon—and combine them with the cassoulet technique. Snuggled down in the beans is the French sausage *boudin blanc*. After making this, you may never want to go back to regular old franks 'n' beans.]

For the beans: Drain the soaked beans, add to a large pot with the chicken stock, and salt to taste. Bring to a simmer and cook until the beans are just tender, about 2 hours. Let cool in the cooking liquid. Drain the cooked beans in a sieve set over a bowl and reserve 2 cups (475 ml) of the cooking liquid.

Meanwhile, preheat the oven to 350°F (180°C/Gas Mark 4).

In a Dutch oven (casserole) or heavy-bottomed pot large enough to hold the beans and boudin blanc, cook the bacon to render the fat. Remove the bacon but leave the bacon fat in the pot. Heat the pot over low heat. Add the onion, carrot, and celery and cook for about 10 minutes or until soft. Return the bacon to the pan and add the brown sugar, cloves, mustard, butter, bay leaves, thyme, and reserved bean cooking liquid. Bring to a simmer. Add the cooked beans and mix. Taste for seasoning. Add more stock or water if needed so that the mixture is saucy.

Remove the pot from the heat. Snuggle the boudin blanc sections into the beans, though do not fully submerge them.

For the crumb topping: Mix the breadcrumbs and melted butter. Season to taste with salt and pepper. Sprinkle the mixture over the beans and boudin blanc.

Cover the Dutch oven (casserole), transfer to the oven, and bake for about 20 minutes. Uncover and bake until the breadcrumbs are golden brown, 10–15 minutes.

Ari Weinzweig is CEO and co-founding partner of Zingerman's Community of Businesses in Ann Arbor, Michigan.

Wild rice is ancient, an original food of this region that has been highly cherished by the Ojibwe peoples who lived here for centuries, before any European ever set foot in the Great Lakes (and who still, though little recognized, live here today). Nutritionally, wild rice was the staple food that kept people fed much of the year. In summer it was cooked into soups and stews with fish and game; in winter it was often the only food available. Up until the first half of the 19th century, wild rice was used by Native Americans in the area as a medium of exchange in place of coins. It was one of the only nonperishable staple foods for European settlers in the Midwest that wouldn't have required weeks of transit to ship in from the Atlantic coast. It used to grow, wildly and abundantly, in lakes and rivers all across the upper Midwest, including much of what shows up on the American map as Michigan.

Real wild rice cooks quickly. It's an enormous amount of work to gather and get ready to eat, but it's naturally fast food once you get it into the kitchen. Just drop it into lightly salted boiling water and simmer for fifteen to twenty minutes (the time varies depending on the lake and the vintage), drain, and eat. Maybe with a touch of salt. It's nutty, it's nice. It's subtly earthy. It's on the specials list at Zingerman's Roadhouse with Great Lakes whitefish—if you'd come to this part of the world three or four or fourteen centuries ago you might have had much the same meal. I hope increased awareness will help protect this natural culinary treasure.

Cream cheese comes at the other end of the historical spectrum from wild rice. Handmade cream cheese from Zingerman's Creamery is a food that I hope and believe will lead Ann Arbor, Michigan, to be recognized as the place that brought back great American cream cheese.

It's an American original, historically made by taking fresh "curd," breaking it very fine, draining it, lightly salting it, then adding back cream to enrich the original cheese. One William Lawrence gets credit for developing it in the 1870s. His partner, Alvah Reynolds, came up with the "Philadelphia" moniker later, not because it was made there, but because "Philadelphia" in the 19th century carried a connotation of quality.

We started to make handmade cream cheese at Zingerman's Creamery in 1999, and every week we sell hundreds of pounds. Twenty years later, kids are growing up eating handmade cream cheese. To them this is cream cheese in the same way it would have been for their great-grandparents. My belief is that a century from now, this part of the world—Ann Arbor—will be known as the source for handmade cream cheese.

Iconic foods have to originate somewhere. Thanks to a generation or two of food-loving Ann Arbor kids, tens of thousands of travelers, and mail order customers, this cream cheese is now their norm—cheese that's never mechanically extruded, and that actually tastes like cheese, cream cheese from Ann Arbor, Michigan!

Anita Lo grew up in Michigan and was chef/owner of Annisa for over fifteen years. She is the author of *Cooking Without Borders* and was the first female chef invited to the White House to cook a state dinner.

RABBIT POT PIE WITH MORELS, FAVA BEANS, AND JERUSALEM ARTICHOKES

PREPARATION TIME: 20 MINUTES
COOKING TIME: 55 MINUTES
SERVES: 4–6

- 1 stick (115 g) butter
- 1 small onion, peeled and diced
- 6 rabbit legs, bones removed and cut into 1-inch (2.5 cm) pieces
- Salt and freshly ground black pepper
- ½ cup (65 g) all-purpose (plain) flour
- 1 quart (1 liter) chicken stock
- 1 cup (80 g) fresh morels, cleaned and cut into 1-inch (2.5 cm) pieces
- 6 oz (170 g) Jerusalem artichokes, cleaned and cut into ½-inch (1.25 cm) dice
- 2 tablespoons chopped fresh chives
- Pinch of chopped fresh tarragon
- Pinch of chopped fresh thyme
- Pinch of finely grated lemon zest
- 1 cup (125 g) blanched and peeled fresh fava (broad) beans
- 1 sheet (8 x 8 inches/20 x 20 cm) frozen all-butter puff pastry, thawed

Preheat the oven to 375°F (190°C/Gas Mark 5).

In a large pot or Dutch oven (casserole) over medium heat, melt the butter. Add the onion and stir until soft and translucent without browning, about 6 minutes. Season the rabbit pieces with salt and pepper and add to the pot. Stir in the flour and cook, stirring occasionally, for 5 minutes. While stirring, slowly add the chicken stock and cook to form a thick sauce, about 8 minutes. Stir in the morels and Jerusalem artichokes and bring to a boil. Remove from the heat and add the herbs, lemon zest, favas, and salt and pepper to taste.

Transfer to an 8-inch (20 cm) square baking dish, about 2 inches (5 cm) deep, and top with the puff pastry. Prick the pastry with a fork and slash it in the center to allow steam to escape. Bake until the top is browned and cooked through, about 30 minutes.

Let cool slightly before serving.

DUCK BREAST WITH ZA'ATAR AND DRIED CHERRIES

PREPARATION TIME: 5 MINUTES
COOKING TIME: 30 MINUTES
SERVES: 2

- 2 boneless, skin-on Peking duck breasts (about 1 lb/455 g) skin scored
- Salt and freshly ground black pepper
- 1 teaspoon za'atar spice mix
- 4 tablespoons (60 g) butter
- 16 dried Michigan cherries
- 1 tablespoon red wine vinegar

[This dish is inspired by Michigan's vibrant Middle Eastern communities and features Michigan's most famous fruit: cherries.]

Heat a sauté pan over high heat. Season the duck breasts on both sides with salt and pepper and place in the dry pan, skin side down. Immediately reduce the heat to the lowest setting. As the fat renders and accumulates in the pan, pour it off, reserving 2 tablespoons in the pan throughout the cooking process. Continue cooking until the skin is deep brown and has rendered most of its fat, about 15 minutes.

Sprinkle the flesh of the duck breast with half of the za'atar. Flip the breasts, increase the heat to high, and sprinkle the duck skin with the remaining za'atar. Place the butter in the pan and melt until bubbling. With a large spoon, baste the duck with the melted butter and cook until medium-rare—the internal temperature should reach 135°F (57°C). Transfer the duck from the pan to a warm plate and pour off the fat. Let rest 10 minutes.

Add the cherries and vinegar to the pan and cook until syrupy.

Serve the duck, sliced, and topped with the sauce.

Winona LaDuke is an activist and author who lives on the White Earth reservation. Her White Earth Land Recovery Project won the International Slow Food Award for Biodiversity and she was also *Ms.* Woman of the Year.

In the land where the food grows on the water; the mushrooms, berries, and fiddlehead ferns are in abundance; and a sugar comes from trees, this is indeed the good life and good food. The pleasure we take from drinking sap from a tree, or eating smoked fish with wild rice cannot be overstated. Nor should the pleasure of agrobiodiversity—a multitude of corn varieties, pumpkins, squash, and the lure of new vegetables—ever be taken for granted in this life.

Our ancestors understood it and lived by the seasons. Since the earliest times, the Anishinaabe people have taken to the woods for Iskigamizige-giizis—month of the Maple Syrup Moon in Ojibwe. The month that follows is the time to harvest the morel mushrooms. The following months, Ode'min-giizis and Miin-giizis (Strawberry Moon and Blueberry Moon), honor the foods of this place. August is the moon of the ripening of wild rice, our most sacred food. Wild rice is considered the first food served a baby coming into this world, and the last food served to the elders on their way out. To remember time based on the seasons of plenty is a gift. That gift is honored in feast and ceremony, and in the Northcountry, thanksgiving is frankly held throughout the year, reaffirmed in the kitchens and the campfires.

I eat and I love to cook (perhaps more than anything else except riding horses and writing), and my gratitude for food extends beyond wild rice, maple syrup, and smoked fish. I am a woman who enjoys fusion cooking. My love of Thai food and Mexican food has prompted many a Thai venison curry and a beaver tamale. Wild-harvested nettles make an excellent core to a pesto sauce, and the

mushrooms of the north move into many of my dishes, whether Italian or Ojibwe.

Care for the land and water. Care for the plants—do not take more than you will need—and be grateful, and they will return to feed and nourish you.

Andrew Zimmern is a James Beard Award-winning television personality, chef, writer, and teacher who has explored more than 150 countries. He has lived in Minnesota for twenty-five years.

SCANDINAVIAN GRAVLAX

PREPARATION TIME: 25 MINUTES,
   PLUS 2 DAYS CURING TIME
SERVES: 12–14 AS A PLATED APPETIZER
   OR AS PART OF A DINNER PARTY
   BUFFET

- 1 cup (50 g) minced fresh dill
- ½ cup (30 g) minced fresh parsley
- ¼ oup (40 g) minced shallots
- 3 tablespoons crushed juniper berries
- 1 tablespoon finely grated lime zest
- ¼ cup (60 ml) aquavit or gin
- 7 tablespoons light brown sugar
- 4½ tablespoons granulated sugar
- 2½ oz (70 g) kosher (coarse) salt
- 3–4 lb (1.4–1.8 kg) salmon fillet, trimmed and pin bones removed

[Our Nordic roots are strong here in Minnesota, and at holiday time, there isn't a Swedish, Norwegian, or Finnish home without a cured salmon fillet on the table. Serve it with bowls of toasts and sour cream, lemons, capers, and minced red onion on the side. If you can get a local steelhead in season, use it.]

In a bowl, combine the dill, parsley, shallots, juniper berries, lime zest, aquavit, both sugars, and salt.

Cut the bottom 3 inches (7.5 cm) off the tail end of the salmon and save for another use. Place the salmon, skin side down, in a nonreactive pan. Spread the curing mixture, without applying any pressure, to cover the salmon evenly. Wrap the pan carefully with plastic wrap (clingfilm) and refrigerate for 48 hours.

Lift the salmon out of the liquid (discard the liquid) and gently wipe away the cure with a moist towel. Then gently blot the salmon dry with a piece of paper towel. Very thinly slice across the grain from one end to the other.

DUCK WITH APPLE CIDER AND ROOT VEGETABLES

PREPARATION TIME: 20 MINUTES
COOKING TIME: 1 HOUR 50 MINUTES
SERVES: 4

- 1 tablespoon vegetable oil
- 4 duck legs with thighs
- 2 oz (55 g) pancetta, cut into small batons
- 2 carrots, diced
- 1 onion, diced
- 1 leek, diced
- 1 stalk celery, diced
- 2 medium parsnips, halved lengthwise and sliced into ½-inch (1.25 cm) slices
- 1 cup (140 g) cubed rutabaga (swede)
- Bouquet garni: several sprigs rosemary, thyme, and a bay leaf, tied with kitchen twine
- 1 cup (240 ml) Beaujolais or other light red wine
- 2 cups (475 ml) apple cider
- Wild Rice (page 593)

[Native American culture is the bedrock of how we in Minnesota define ourselves, but we also love the immigrant icing on our cultural cake. French and Italian influences and techniques merge in this recipe, which includes many of our state's finest ingredients. Duck, wild rice, cider, wine, and root vegetables have sustained Minnesotans since at least the 17th century. In the 1800s, soldiers at Fort Snelling lived off meager rations and supplemented their meals with wild game, especially ducks, which were plentiful along the Mississippi and Minnesota River flyways. The French and Italian cultures have been represented in our state for centuries, so while this dish has been updated for today's home cook, I'd like to think our pioneering ancestors would recognize every bit of it. And Minnesotans invented the Haralson, Honeycrisp, and Sweetango apples.]

Preheat a large Dutch oven (casserole) over medium heat. Add the oil and swirl. Add the duck legs and brown on both sides. Remove from the pot and set aside.

Add the pancetta and cook briefly until lightly browned. Add the carrots, onion, leek, celery, parsnip, and rutabaga. Stir and cook for several minutes. Add the bouquet garni. Return the duck to the pot and add the wine. Cook until the liquid is reduced by half, then add the cider.

Bring to a boil, cover, reduce to a simmer, and cook until fork tender, about 1 hour 15 minutes. Remove the duck legs and set aside. Discard the bouquet garni. Skim the fat from the sauce.

Reduce the sauce until it lightly coats a spoon. Return the duck to the sauce to heat through. Serve the duck with the wild rice.

TURKEY POT PIE

PREPARATION TIME: 35 MINUTES,
   PLUS COOLING AND CHILLING TIME
COOKING TIME: 2 HOURS 15 MINUTES
SERVES: 8–10

For the filling:
- 1 whole young turkey (8–10 lb/3.6–4.5 kg), cut into 8–10 pieces (see Note)
- Salt and freshly ground black pepper
- 2 cups (260 g) all-purpose (plain) flour
- 1 stick (115 g) salted butter
- 1 onion, diced
- 4 carrots, diced
- 3 stalks celery, diced
- 5 cloves garlic, sliced
- Bouquet garni: 3 fresh bay leaves, 3 sprigs fresh thyme, 1 sprig rosemary, 2 sprigs sage tied in cheesecloth
- 3 cups (710 ml) dry white wine
- 1 quart (1 liter) chicken stock
- 1 cup (240 ml) heavy (whipping) cream
- 2 cups (270 g) blanched fresh peas or thawed frozen

For the crust:
- 2½ cups (325 g) all-purpose (plain) flour
- 1 teaspoon salt
- ¾ cup plus 2 tablespoons (180 g) rendered lard or vegetable shortening, chilled
- 6–8 tablespoons ice water

Note:
   Cut the turkey into 2 wings, 2 drumsticks, 2 thighs, and 2 breasts. If the breasts are large, cut them in half (for a total of 10 pieces).

[Minnesota is the nation's largest producer of turkey, and local farms are raising beautiful all-natural, small, plump birds. This pot pie is a Zimmern family favorite.]

For the filling: Season the turkey pieces well with salt and pepper. Place the flour in a paper bag and season well with salt and pepper. Add the turkey, close the top, and shake. Remove the turkey and discard the flour.

Heat a very large soup pot or roasting pan with high sides over medium-high heat and add the butter. Working in batches if necessary (so you don't crowd the pan), add the turkey pieces skin side down and brown. Transfer to a plate.

Add the onion, carrots, celery, garlic, and bouquet garni and cook until slightly browned, about 10 minutes. Pour in the wine, stirring to incorporate any browned bits stuck to the bottom of the pan. Return the turkey to the pan. Bring to a boil, then reduce to a simmer and cook until the wine is reduced by half, about 10 minutes. Add the stock and bring to a boil. Reduce the heat to a bare simmer, cover, and cook for 30 minutes. Remove the white meat pieces and continue to cook the dark meat for an additional 20–25 minutes.

Transfer all the turkey to a cutting board or plate. Remove the meat from the bones and discard the bones or save for stock. Cut the meat into large pieces, but none bigger than a golf ball. (Refrigerate half the meat for turkey salad, sandwiches, or other uses.)

Skim the fat from the cooking liquid and cook over medium heat for about 5 minutes to reduce. Add the cream and cook until the liquid coats the back of a spoon, 7–8 minutes. Taste the gravy and season with salt and pepper if needed. Stir in the peas and the turkey meat. Remove from the heat and season with salt and pepper. Discard the bouquet garni.

Spoon the turkey mixture into a large high-sided roasting pan and let cool while you make the crust (but for at least 15 minutes).

For the crust: In a medium bowl, combine the flour and salt. Cut the lard into small pieces and work it into the flour with your fingertips or a pastry (dough) blender until the mixture resembles coarse meal, with pea-size pieces of fat remaining. Toss with 6 tablespoons of ice water and, with your fingertips, draw together into a ball, sprinkling with remaining water, as needed to gather together. Flatten into a small rectangle. Wrap in plastic wrap (clingfilm) and refrigerate for 1 hour to firm.

Preheat the oven to 350°F (180°C/Gas Mark 4). On a well-floured work surface, roll out the dough until it's 1–2 inches (2.5–5 cm) bigger on all sides than the baking pan you are using. Lay the crust across the entire pan, being sure to tuck the edges inside the pan, with the dough resting on the warm filling. Make a few attractive slashes in the dough with a very sharp knife or box cutter. Bake until the crust is golden brown, about 35 minutes.

FRIED WALLEYE AND WHITEFISH SHORE LUNCH

PREPARATION TIME: 40 MINUTES, PLUS
   DRAINING AND CHILLING TIME
COOKING TIME: 10 MINUTES
SERVES: 4

For the coleslaw:
- 5 cups (350 g) thinly shaved cabbage (about 1 small head)
- 2 tablespoons kosher (coarse) salt
- 2 carrots, julienned
- 2 stalks celery, thinly sliced
- 4 tablespoons minced fresh parsley
- 1 shallot, finely minced
- 1 tablespoon ground caraway seed
- 2 teaspoons mustard powder
- ½ cup (105 g) mayonnaise
- 2 tablespoons sugar
- 3 tablespoons distilled white vinegar
- Freshly ground black pepper
- Fresh lemon juice

For the tartar sauce:
- 3 egg yolks
- 1 teaspoon Dijon mustard
- 1 tablespoon distilled white vinegar
- 1 cup (240 ml) canola (rapeseed) oil
- 1 cup (240 ml) olive oil
- Finely grated zest and juice of 1 lemon
- 3 tablespoons capers, minced
- 3 tablespoons minced sweet pickle
- 3 tablespoons minced fresh parsley
- 2 tablespoons fresh tarragon leaves, minced

For the fish:
- 2 quarts (2 liters) vegetable oil
- 2 cups (260 g) all-purpose (plain) flour
- Salt and freshly ground black pepper
- 3 eggs, beaten
- 3 cups (210 g) Ritz cracker crumbs (pulsed in a food processor)
- 2 lb (910 g) mixed Lake Superior whitefish and walleye fillets, cut into pieces the size of your palm
- Sea salt
- Lemon wedges, for serving

[The ultimate Minnesota meal just might be the shore lunch: fried lake fish served with coleslaw and tartar sauce, oftentimes with oversized soft Parker House rolls for making sandwiches. Each spring when the fishing opener comes around, almost all the families across the state experience a true taste of our Land of 1,000 Lakes. It's a cultural obsession. If you don't have walleye or whitefish available, cod, hake, haddock, dogfish, snapper, grouper, buffalo fish, or almost any firm white-fleshed fish will do.]

For the coleslaw: In a bowl, combine the cabbage and salt, tossing well. Place in a colander and let sit/drain for 6 hours.

Gently squeeze the cabbage dry, discarding the liquid. Transfer the cabbage to a bowl and add the carrots, celery, parsley, shallot, caraway, mustard, mayonnaise, sugar, and vinegar. Refrigerate for several hours. Season to taste with pepper and a little lemon juice.

For the tartar sauce: In a food processor, pulse together the yolks, mustard, and vinegar. With the machine running, in a thin stream, emulsify the canola (rapeseed) and olive oils into this mixture. Transfer to a stainless-steel bowl and stir in the lemon zest, lemon juice, capers, pickle, parsley, and tarragon. Refrigerate until ready to serve.

For the fish: Pour the oil into a large heavy pot over an open fire or on your stove or a deep-fryer and heat to 375°F (190°C).

Set up a dredging station: In a wide shallow bowl, season the flour well with salt and pepper. Place the eggs in a second bowl and the cracker crumbs in a third. Dredge the fish in the flour, then dip in the egg, coating well, then into the cracker crumbs, being sure to get total coverage.

Fry the fish pieces until golden brown, about 5 minutes. Season with sea salt and serve with the coleslaw, cut lemons, and tartar sauce.

TATER TOT HOT DISH

PREPARATION TIME: 5 MINUTES
COOKING TIME: 1 HOUR
SERVES: 4–6

- 1 tablespoon vegetable oil
- 1 lb (455 g) ground beef
- 1 lb (455 g) ground turkey
- 1 onion, minced
- Sea salt and freshly ground black pepper
- 1 bag (16 oz/455 g) frozen cut green beans
- 2 cans (10.7 oz/305 g each) condensed cream of mushroom soup
- 20 oz (565 g) frozen tater tots (potato croquettes), such as Ore-Ida
- Sea salt, for serving

[This recipe is from my mother-in-law, whom I believe got it from her sister. It was served throughout my wife's childhood and we eat it twice a month. It's a Minnesota classic. Minnesota is a hot-dish-and-casserole state, dating back to the farmhouse rush of the 19th century, when treaty rights allowed for large land tracts to be purchased from the state and immigration here grew. Farmhouse cooks would serve one-pan meals to feed a hungry army. My family though has always called this a hot dish. This is comfort food at its finest. And yes, I eat this with ketchup.]

Preheat the oven to 400°F (200°C/Gas Mark 6).

In a large Dutch oven (casserole) over medium-high heat, warm the oil and brown the beef, turkey, and onion. Season the meat with salt and pepper while it browns. When cooked and nicely browned, and the juices have collected and evaporated, remove the pot from the heat. Remove the meat and onions and set aside.

Place the beans at the bottom of the pot and season. Spread the meat mixture evenly over the beans. Pour the soup over the meat and, using a spatula, spread evenly over the meat. Spread the tater tots evenly on top.

Cover and bake for 25 minutes. Uncover and bake until the potatoes are well crisped, 20–30 minutes. Sprinkle sea salt on top and serve.

WILD RICE

PREPARATION TIME: 10 MINUTES
COOKING TIME: 1 HOUR 15 MINUTES
SERVES: 4

- ½ lb (225 g) Minnesota wild rice
- 1 stick (115 g) salted butter
- 3 cups (250 g) sliced mushrooms (I prefer a mix of wild local mushrooms, but any will do)
- 1 cup (160 g) minced shallots
- 1 cup (100 g) minced celery
- ½ cup (120 ml) high-quality imported dry Spanish sherry
- Salt and freshly ground black pepper

In a large pot, bring 3 quarts (about 3 liters) water to a boil.

Add the rice and cook until the grains start to pop open, 35–45 minutes. Drain immediately and set rice aside.

In the same pot, melt the butter over high heat. Add the mushrooms and shallots, reduce the heat to medium, and cook until browned. Add the celery and cook for a few minutes, stirring. Add the sherry and cook until the pot is almost dry and the sherry has reduced by about three-fourths. Return the rice to the pot and cook for 5 minutes, stirring occasionally. Season well with salt and pepper.

Martha Foose is the author of the James Beard Award winner *Screen Doors and Sweet Tea* and *A Southerly Course*. She lives in the Mississippi Delta.

There is a long-standing joke about the Arkansas state motto: "At Least We Are Not Mississippi." Our state tends to end up at the bottom of lists, often coming in fiftieth out of fifty on many measurements of progress. We have gotten used to it over the years. It hasn't dampened our spirits though. It actually seems to have inspired our residents and municipalities across the state to exhibit a bit of self-aggrandizement. If we grow it, love to eat it, or cook it, we tend to celebrate our foods with regal flair.

Up north in the hills, the town of Vardaman has dubbed itself "The Sweet Potato Capital of the World." The town covers less than one and a half square miles. All along Highway 8, sheds overflowing with sweet potatoes line the road. In November, the town hosts a week-long festival culminating in the crowning of the Sweet Potato Queen and the auction of a lovingly crafted sweet potato–themed quilt. I judged the Sweet Potato Pie Eating Contest and it was one of the finest examples of civic pride I've ever witnessed. The competition was tough. Cash prizes were awarded for first place in each division. Seeing dozens of folks, young and old, diving face first (no hands) into the orange-colored pie filling and emerging with crumb-coated smiles was terrific.

Up Highway 45, the town of Corinth celebrates with the Slugburger Festival. The locals proclaim their town as the slugburger capital of the world. You wouldn't think there would be much competition for the title, but a neighboring municipality is putting up a fight. A slugburger is a deep-fried patty composed of meat mixed with cornmeal or soybean meal, served on a bun, then slathered with mustard, and topped with thick chopped white onions

and a few pickles. The off-putting name may derive from the fact that the sandwich used to cost a nickel, or a "slug." Others, however, say a fake coin is called a slug, and since the slugburger is a fake hamburger, the name fits. And, yes, there is a Slugburger Queen.

Farther south and over in the fertile Delta flatlands, the tiny town of Belzoni, Mississippi, has taken on the mantel of "Catfish Capital of the World." There, too, a festival honors the area's most notable industry, with the World Catfish Festival, where Little Miss and Miss Catfish are crowned. A public art project features forty-two five-foot-tall statues of catfish, which are on display throughout the town. And of course, there is the Catfish Eating Contest.

On the Mississippi River, the town of Greenville recently bestowed upon itself the title of "Hot Tamale Capital of the World." The related festival involves the crowning of Miss Hot Tamale, in which contestants vying for the title must fashion a formal gown out of corn husks. As expected, the festival stages the Hot Tamale Eating Contest.

Natchez, one of the state's earliest towns, assumed the "Biscuit Capital of the World" moniker. Each year, the Natchez Biscuit Festival sets up on a street named Biscuit Alley with a cook-off for biscuit makers, both amateur and professional, as a main attraction. The Natchez crowd picks the Biscuit Queen, with entrants ranging in age from five to ninety-five.

Although truck farming has fallen by the wayside, Long Beach holds its claim to the title of "Radish Capital of the World." Crystal

Springs residents still tout their town as the "Tomatopolis of the World" and they host a tomato festival to celebrate the crop that helped put the town on the map (even though there hasn't been much large-scale tomato farming in the area for decades). But we Mississippians tend to hold on to the past.

Gulfport proudly claims to be the "Root Beer Capital of the World," for it was here that the Barq family began bottling the soft drink in 1889. Gulfport's sister city along the Gulf Coast, Biloxi, announces itself as "The Seafood Capital of the World." The night before the Blessing of the Fleet, a Shrimp King and Queen are crowned at a *fais do-do* street dance and shrimp feast. The King is picked from gentlemen with long ties to the seafood industry and the Queen is selected from young ladies in a pageant that awards college scholarships. At a reunion of Shrimp Queens at the Slavonian Lodge, the older queens, many of Polish and Croatian descent, warmly greet the younger queens. The Shrimp King and Queen stand with the priest and bishop on the stationary "Blessing Boat" as members of the local St. Michael's Catholic Church and Vietnamese Martyrs Catholic Church sail by in boats, with names such as *Viet Pride* and *Southern Belle*, each indicative of the owner's heritage.

This penchant of ours to proclaim our towns as world capitals might come off as a bit silly to some folks. To me, it is a sign of how proud we are of the people who built the communities across our great state and work to show off what about them is unique. So, if you visit, and I sincerely hope you will, take some time and have a slice of sweet potato pie, try a greasy slugburger at a drugstore soda fountain, dance to some blues, eat hot tamales, smile at Little Miss Catfish, try some fluffy Natchez biscuits, and gobble up some shrimp spring rolls, washed down with an ice-cold root beer as the sun sets on the Gulf of Mexico. Mississippians know in our heart of hearts that we will always have room for one more at our table.

John Currence opened City Grocery in Oxford, Mississippi, in 1992. He is the recipient of a James Beard Award for Best Chef: South and the Guardians of the Tradition Award from the Southern Foodways Alliance. He is also a cookbook author.

CHICKEN AND DUMPLINGS

PREPARATION TIME: 30 MINUTES
COOKING TIME: 55 MINUTES
SERVES: 4–6

For the chicken:
- 1 whole chicken (3–4 lb/1.4–1.8 kg), cut into 8 pieces
- Salt and freshly ground black pepper
- 2 tablespoons olive oil
- 2 tablespoons bacon fat
- 1½ cups (240 g) finely diced yellow onion
- 2 tablespoons minced garlic
- 1 cup (100 g) finely diced celery
- 1 cup (130 g) finely diced carrot
- 2 tablespoons fresh thyme
- 2¼ teaspoons chopped fresh rosemary
- ½ tablespoon chopped fresh oregano
- Finely grated zest of 2 lemons
- 3 tablespoons dry white vermouth
- ½ cup (120 ml) white wine
- 10 cups (2.4 liters) chicken stock

For the dumplings:
- 1 stick (115 g) cold butter, diced and chilled
- 2 cups (260 g) self-rising flour
- 3 tablespoons mixed chopped fresh herbs
- 1 tablespoon sugar
- 1 tablespoon freshly ground black pepper
- 1¼ cups (300 ml) whole buttermilk

For the chicken: Sprinkle liberally with salt and pepper. In a soup pot over medium-high heat, warm the oil and bacon fat. Add the chicken pieces and brown on all sides, about 10 minutes. Remove and set aside.

Reduce the heat to medium. Add the onion, garlic, celery, and carrot to the same pot and sauté until tender, about 8 minutes. Stir in the herbs and zest. Return the chicken to the pot and deglaze with the vermouth and wine. Stir in the stock, increase the heat to high, and bring to a boil. Reduce the heat to medium-low, cover, and simmer until the chicken is tender, about 30 minutes. Remove the chicken and pull the meat from the bones (discard the skin and bones). Set the chicken meat aside.

Strain the stock and return to the pot. Bring to a simmer over medium-high heat while you make the dumplings.

For the dumplings: In a food processor, pulse together the butter, flour, herbs, sugar, and pepper until the mixture resembles a coarse meal. Transfer to a bowl and stir in the buttermilk until combined.

Drop the dumplings by the spoonfuls into the simmering stock. Do not stir until the top of the pot is covered with dumplings. Reduce the heat to medium and simmer for 15 minutes. Slowly stir the dumplings very gently. Carefully stir in the chicken meat to reheat and season to taste with salt and pepper.

SMOKED MUSHROOM TAMALES

PREPARATION TIME: 40 MINUTES,
  PLUS SOAKING AND COOLING TIME
COOKING TIME: 1 HOUR
SERVES: 4

For the mushroom filling:
- 4 oz (110 g) medium white mushrooms, quartered
- 4 oz (110 g) stemmed large shiitake mushrooms, sliced
- 4 oz (110 g) medium cremini (chestnut) mushrooms, quartered
- 1 shallot, sliced
- 4 cloves garlic, sliced
- ½ cup (120 ml) sherry vinegar
- ¼ cup (60 ml) fresh lime juice
- 1 teaspoon ground cumin
- 1½ teaspoons salt
- 1 teaspoon freshly ground black pepper
- 2 large handfuls hickory wood chips, soaked in water for 30 minutes

For the tamale dough:
- ½ cup (75 g) roasted corn kernels
- ½ cup (80 g) finely diced red onion
- 2 teaspoons minced garlic
- ¼ cup (60 ml) good-quality dark chicken stock
- 1 cup (120 g) masa harina
- 1 teaspoon sugar
- 1 teaspoon salt
- 2 teaspoons crushed black peppercorns
- 1 teaspoon ground cumin
- 4 tablespoons (60 g) cold unsalted butter
- 2 tablespoons (30 g) lard
- ¼ cup (40 g) fresh goat cheese

For the assembly:
- 8 dried corn husks, soaked in warm water for at least 30 minutes

[Tamales have roots in the Mississippi kitchen. They came along with Latin migrant workers after the Civil War, as the makeup of the agricultural workforce was changing. Tamales were an enormously stable food item in the field. They could spend a hot summer morning in the shade of a tree. They are full of carbohydrates and an excellent clearinghouse for whatever cooked protein you have lying around. All the ingredients for making them are indigenous to the Mississippi Delta, so it is no surprise that locals picked up on them when the workers moved on. Tamales have, as a result, become positively Mississippi. We have made dozens of versions of them, with everything from meat and seafood fillings to chocolate and nuts. They require a little bit of labor but are the kind of thing that, when you set up to start making them, is as easy to make enough for twenty-five people as for five. After they are steamed, they freeze beautifully.]

For the mushroom filling: In a large saucepan, combine 3 cups (710 ml) water, the mushrooms, shallot, garlic, vinegar, lime juice, cumin, salt, and pepper and bring to a boil over medium heat. Simmer for 4 minutes, then let the mushrooms cool in the liquid. Drain the mushrooms.

Prepare a stove-top smoker with the soaked wood chips and place on the stove over medium heat. As soon as the chips begin to smoke, place the mushroom mixture in the smoker and close the top tightly. Let the mushrooms smoke for about 5 minutes. Remove from the heat and continue to smoke, covered, for an additional 5 minutes.

Transfer the mushrooms to a food processor and pulse until they are finely chopped but not puréed. Set aside while making the tamale dough.

For the tamale dough: In a food processor, purée the corn kernels, onions, garlic, and stock until smooth. In a large mixing bowl, combine the masa harina, sugar, salt, crushed pepper, and cumin. Add the cold butter and lard and cut in until the dough resembles cornmeal. Cut in the goat cheese. Stir in the corn mixture until there are no lumps.

To assemble the tamales: Lay a large soaked corn husk (about 3 x 5 inches/7.5 x 13 cm) on a flat surface. In the center, place 5 tablespoons dough and spread into a rectangle about 2 x 4 inches (5 x 10 cm). Make a line of mushroom filling (2 to 3 tablespoons) lengthwise down the center. Grasp one long edge of a corn husk and role the tamale into a tube, encasing the filling with the dough. Fold the corn husk ends over the seam and rest the tamale on top of the folded ends so its weight holds the tamale together. Place the rolled tamale into a steamer insert. Repeat for all the tamales. Place the steamer insert over a pan of simmering water, cover, and steam for about 45 minutes. Remove from the steamer and serve hot.

Danny Meyer was born and raised in St. Louis, Missouri, and is the CEO of Union Square Hospitality Group. His restaurants and chefs have earned an unprecedented twenty-eight James Beard Awards and he is author of *Setting the Table*.

I was born in St. Louis, Missouri, in 1958. Coming of age in the middle of the country, as a middle child of three, and in the middle of the 20th century, I grew up amidst a confluence of communities, culinary traditions, and cultural developments: Vietnam, the antiwar movement, civil rights, Watergate, and the St. Louis Cardinals play-by-play blaring from my transistor radio and our family television. In elementary school, I navigated the subtle nuances of my diverse surroundings by observing what other kids brought to lunch; condiments were like windows into my classmates' souls (Hellmann's vs. Miracle Whip, Heinz vs. Hunt's, Wonder Bread vs. Pepperidge Farm, Skippy vs. Jif, and so on).

Tasting food was—and still is—my primary means of understanding the world around me, and I was a curious kid. My own family melded all kinds of culinary traditions, which is how we ended up eating roast beef with matzo balls, and mashed potatoes topped with frizzled onions. In "The Hill," St. Louis's Italian neighborhood, I downed toasted ravioli and the singular St. Louis–style pizza topped with Provel, a processed blend of several different kinds of cheese, the whole of which bears no resemblance to any of its parts. Over in the Lafayette Square area in Downtown St. Louis, where a small community of Chinese immigrants had settled, I learned about St. Paul sandwiches, an only-in-St.-Louis concoction of fried chopped suey patties topped with mayonnaise and a pickle, sandwiched between two slices of white bread. Everywhere, I was surrounded by the flavors of the American Midwest: curbside burgers, crinkle-cut fries, and root beer from Fitz's; frozen custard at Ted Drewes, and malts at the Crown Candy Kitchen.

And throughout all this, I was fortified with authentic soul food, prepared lovingly by my childhood housekeeper, Mary Smith. The day I turned sixteen and got my driver's license was probably the best day of my life, because it meant I could take myself across town to visit Mary for a home-cooked meal. No one needed to wonder where I'd been, as I always came home smelling like fried chicken—a hug that lingered long after I had been fed.

These experiences satisfied my voracious appetite, but more important, they laid the groundwork for what would become a lifelong pursuit: my effort to understand—and connect with—people through food. Looking back, I know now that not all the food I enjoyed as a child was earth-shattering cuisine, but it was a delicious-enough vehicle for something more meaningful: hospitality. The chicken and dumplings at Kreis' Restaurant was completely satisfying, but what really stuck with me was that the host had always remembered where I liked to sit—below the cuckoo clock. I loved the cheeseburgers and milkshakes at Straub's deli, but the really memorable part of the experience was that the woman behind the counter always offered me the extra "dividend" of getting my milkshake in the stainless-steel mixing cup. The hospitality, maybe even more than the food itself, was what nourished and nurtured me.

I moved to New York City after college and opened my first restaurant, Union Square Cafe, in 1985, when I was twenty-seven years old. Over the past thirty years, I've never stopped drawing new inspiration from my childhood in St. Louis. The roadside burger stands and malted milkshake counters inspired the heart of the menu at Shake Shack.

The flavors I remembered from The Hill, coupled with my love of St. Louis barbecue, were the basis for our toasted ravioli filled with pulled pork at Blue Smoke. I brought Fitz's Root Beer to New York City because I couldn't imagine serving any other kind of root beer alongside barbecue. My grandmother's roast beef and matzo balls inspired our similarly multicultural "Matzoh Polenta" dish at Union Square Cafe.

But most significantly, my inspiration is rooted in the way that those restaurants from my childhood made me feel. Everyone has a different interpretation of why Missouri is the "Show Me State." I think that Missourians care a lot about the authenticity of a gesture— what you show, more so than what you say. Growing up in St. Louis, I learned that no matter how good the food tasted, the way a restaurant made me feel left a far more lasting impression. "Show Me" might more pointedly have meant "Show Me the Love."

Colby Garrelts is a James Beard Award winner for Best Chef: Midwest and a *Food & Wine* Best New Chef. Megan Garrelts is a James Beard Semifinalist for Outstanding Pastry Chef. They are chef-owners of Bluestem in Kansas City, Missouri and Rye, in Leawood, Kansas.

BBQ DRY RUB

PREPARATION TIME: 10 MINUTES
MAKES: 4 CUPS (ABOUT 700 G)

- 1¾ cups (235 g) kosher (coarse) salt
- 1 cup (190 g) packed light brown sugar
- 1 cup (200 g) granulated sugar
- ¼ cup (30 g) onion powder
- ¼ cup (40 g) garlic powder
- 2 tablespoons smoked paprika
- 1 tablespoon crushed chili flakes
- 1 tablespoon mustard powder
- 1½ teaspoons chili powder
- 1 teaspoon freshly ground white pepper
- 1 teaspoon freshly ground black pepper

[BBQ rub is as central to Midwestern cooking as cumin and chilies are in South America or as curry is in Southeast Asia: It defines our culture. If you're lucky enough, you have your very own. Mine has evolved over the years. It started as some brown sugar, salt, and chili seasoning and has progressed into something more complex. When I started cooking professionally I began to understand what I need to look (or taste) for when making a good seasoning. When you're trained as a professional chef you're taught very specific disciplines, and in Western European cooking you rely on salt and pepper as the dry ingredients to put on proteins unless you're curing something. Some of the same qualities and flavors used in quick-curing something like salmon translate well to rubbing meat to smoke. It's salty, sweet, and herbaceous. The base of my rub came from the base of my salmon cure. Just tweak the flavoring and it's perfect. — Colby Garrelts]

In a large bowl, combine the salt, brown sugar, granulated sugar, onion powder, garlic powder, paprika, chili flakes, mustard powder, chili powder, white pepper, and black pepper and mix well. Transfer to an airtight container and store at room temperature for up to 1 month.

PAN-FRIED PORK CHOPS WITH TOMATO-HORSERADISH SAUCE

PREPARATION TIME: 20 MINUTES,
   PLUS OVERNIGHT CHILLING TIME
COOKING TIME: 50 MINUTES
SERVES: 4

For the sauce:
- 2 jars (14 oz/395 g each) home-preserved tomatoes or good-quality canned tomatoes
- 1 cup (240 ml) sherry vinegar
- 4 tablespoons prepared horseradish
- 4 tablespoons honey
- 4 cloves garlic, peeled and chopped
- 2 fresh bay leaves

For the pork chops:
- 4 pork loin chops (6 oz/170 g each)
- 4 tablespoons BBQ Dry Rub (page 600)
- 4 tablespoons vegetable oil
- 4 tablespoons (60 g) unsalted butter, softened
- 4 small shallots, sliced
- 8 cloves garlic, peeled
- 8 sprigs fresh thyme

[Pork chops are the go-to Midwestern dish for an easy, inexpensive, and satisfying meal. My mom often cooked pork chops with apples and sauerkraut in the fall and with preserved tomatoes and rice in the late winter. School nights and hectic evenings slowed down around the table, where my family recounted the day's activities, my dad checked on homework assignments, and my older brother took a break from annoying me so we could all enjoy Mom's cooking. Now my mom's pork chop recipe, combined with Colby's barbecue roots, creates new memories for our kids at the dinner table. Note that the sauce needs to be refrigerated overnight in order to bring all the flavors together.—Megan Garrelts]

For the sauce: In a small saucepan, combine the tomatoes, vinegar, horseradish, honey, garlic, and bay leaves and bring to a simmer over medium-high heat. Cook until reduced by half, about 20 minutes. Let cool, uncovered, then refrigerate overnight. Bring to room temperature before making the pork chops.

For the pork chops: Rub them all over with the dry rub. In a medium cast-iron skillet, heat the oil over medium-high heat. Add the seasoned pork chops and brown on each side, about 4 minutes total. Add the butter, shallots, garlic, and thyme and cook, basting the chops frequently with the butter and herb mixture, until the internal temperature reads 140°F (60°C), 2–3 minutes longer. Remove the chops from the pan, discard the butter, shallots, garlic, and thyme and serve alongside the tomato-horseradish sauce.

CIDER-BRAISED BRISKET

PREPARATION TIME: 20 MINUTES,
  PLUS OVERNIGHT CHILLING
COOKING TIME: 5 HOURS
SERVES: 6

- ⅓ cup (80 ml) vegetable oil
- 5 lb (2.3 kg) brisket, trimmed (see Note)
- 2 large yellow onions, cut into slices
  ¼ inch (6 mm) thick
- 6 cloves garlic, chopped
- 1 tablespoon tomato paste (purée)
- 2 tablespoons unbleached all-purpose
  (plain) flour
- 1 quart (1 liter) hard cider
- 2 cups (475 ml) chicken stock
- 2 sprigs fresh thyme
- 1 bay leaf

Note:
  Ask your butcher to trim the brisket for
  braising, but be sure a little fat is left on
  for flavor.

[I miss my favorite barbecue dishes in the colder months, so I like to braise tougher cuts of meat in the Dutch oven. Ribs, brisket, or pork shoulder take on such a different flavor and texture when they come out of the oven—they're softer, more tender, and comforting. This brisket recipe gets a nice fermented kick from the hard cider and the flavors are intensified by being refrigerated overnight.—Colby Garrelts]

Preheat the oven to 300°F (150°C/Gas Mark 2).

In a 4- to 6-quart (3.8- to 5.7-liter) Dutch oven (casserole), heat the oil over medium-high heat. Add the brisket and sear on all sides until golden, about 5 minutes per side. Remove the brisket and set it on a plate. Pour off all but 1 tablespoon fat from the Dutch oven. Add the onions, garlic, and tomato paste (purée) and cook over medium-high heat, stirring occasionally, until the onions are softened and golden, 10–12 minutes. Sprinkle the flour over the onions and cook, stirring constantly, until well combined, about 2 minutes. Add the cider, stock, thyme, and bay leaf, stirring to scrape up the browned bits from the pan. Bring to a simmer and cook for about 5 minutes to fully thicken.

Cook in the oven until the brisket is fork-tender, about 4 hours. Transfer the brisket to a large bowl. Set a mesh sieve over the bowl and strain the sauce over the brisket. Discard the bay leaf and thyme sprigs and place the onions in a small bowl. Cover both bowls with plastic wrap (clingfilm), poke holes in the plastic to vent, and refrigerate overnight.

To serve, preheat the oven to 350°F (180°C/Gas Mark 4).

Remove any hardened fat from the top of the sauce and brisket. Place the brisket on a carving board and cut into ¼-inch (6 mm) slices. Arrange the slices in a 9 x 13-inch (23 x 33 cm) baking dish. Reserving ½ cup (120 ml) of the sauce, pour the remaining sauce over the brisket, cover the dish with foil, and bake to heat through, 20–30 minutes.

Meanwhile, in a small saucepot, combine the onions and reserved ½ cup (120 ml) sauce and simmer for about 6 minutes.

Serve the brisket slices with spoonfuls of onions and sauce alongside.

BANANA CREAM PIE

PREPARATION TIME: 55 MINUTES,
PLUS OVERNIGHT CHILLING
COOKING TIME: 50 MINUTES
MAKES: ONE 9-INCH (23 CM) PIE

- Classic Pie Crust (page 604) for a single crust
- ½ cup (115 g) bittersweet chocolate chips, melted
- 2 cups (475 ml) milk
- 1 teaspoon pure vanilla extract
- 1 vanilla bean, split lengthwise
- ½ cup (100 g) sugar
- ¼ cup (30 g) cornstarch (cornflour), sifted
- 4 egg yolks
- ½ teaspoon kosher (coarse) salt
- 4 tablespoons (60 g) unsalted butter, softened
- 3 very ripe bananas, cut into slices ⅛ inch (3 mm) thick
- 1½ cups (355 ml) heavy (whipping) cream, whipped to stiff peaks
- ½ cup (75 g) ground Salted Toffee (page 605)

[On chilly winter nights, my mom would sometimes whip up a batch of warm vanilla or butterscotch pudding and top it with Nilla wafers and sliced ripe bananas. She would often serve these perfect puddings in little glass ramekins, which made dinner seem very fancy. Now at home with my little ones, I always make sure we have a box of Nilla wafers in the pantry as you never know when pudding, bananas, and Nillas will be needed as a treat! My recipe for banana cream pie is an ode to the creamy banana memories of my childhood. I coat the pie shell with a thin layer of dark chocolate to help the crust stay crispy under the pastry cream. If you prefer, a graham cracker crust can be substituted for the traditional pie crust here. —Megan Garrelts]

Blind bake the pie crust (pastry case) as directed.

Using a pastry brush, evenly coat the bottom and sides of the pie shell with the melted chocolate, and refrigerate to set the chocolate.

In a medium saucepan, combine the milk and vanilla extract. Scrape in the vanilla seeds and add the pod. Bring the mixture to just below boiling over medium heat, about 3 minutes.

Meanwhile, in a large bowl, whisk together the sugar, cornstarch (cornflour), egg yolks, and salt.

Slowly whisk the hot milk into the cornstarch mixture in three additions so not to curdle the egg yolks. Return the mixture to the saucepan and whisk constantly until the pastry cream is thickened, about 4 minutes. Whisk in the soft butter. Remove the pastry cream from the heat and discard the vanilla pod. Fold in the sliced bananas. Transfer the pastry cream to a bowl and cover with plastic wrap (clingfilm), pressing the wrap directly onto the pastry cream surface. Chill the pastry cream for about 15 minutes so it is cool enough to not melt the chocolate when it is added to the pie shell.

Fill the prepared pie shell and cover the top with plastic wrap (clingfilm), pressing it directly onto the pastry cream surface. Chill for at least 1 hour or overnight.

To serve, slice the pie into 8 even wedges, dollop each slice with whipped cream, and sprinkle the pie slices with salted toffee. (Alternatively, if taking the pie to an event or for a dramatic presentation, top the entire pie with the whipped cream and ground salted toffee. Keep the pie refrigerated for up to 3 days.)

CLASSIC PIE CRUST

PREPARATION TIME: 20 MINUTES,
   PLUS OVERNIGHT CHILLING
   AND FREEZING
COOKING TIME: 30 MINUTES
MAKES: ENOUGH FOR ONE 9-INCH
   (23 CM) DOUBLE CRUST OR TWO
   9-INCH
   (23 CM) SINGLE CRUSTS

- 2⅓ cups (303 g) unbleached all-purpose (plain) flour
- 1 tablespoon sugar
- ¾ teaspoon kosher (coarse) salt
- 1 stick (115 g) cold unsalted butter, cubed
- 8 tablespoons (115 g) lard, cubed
- 8 tablespoons ice water
- 1 egg, lightly beaten

[The pie crust scares some people, but it was my favorite pastry to master. In my early days in the bakeshop, I always had so much fun mixing, kneading, and rolling out the dough—even if the crust did not turn out right. This recipe was developed over time and after many attempts to find the right balance between good butter flavor and the delicate texture that lard creates, plus the perfect mix of sugar and salt. With very few ingredients in a crust, it's important to use the highest-quality ingredients possible. I recommend using good-quality butter high in butterfat, such as Plugra, to ensure the crust will form properly, and a delicate salt like kosher or sea salt. Remember: patience and practice are the key to making pie.—Megan Garrelts]

In a food processor, combine the flour, sugar, and salt and set the processor bowl in the freezer for 30 minutes; you want all the components to be very cold in order to get the flakiest crust possible. Place the cubed butter and lard on a baking sheet and set in the freezer to chill.

Return the bowl with the dry ingredients to the food processor. Add the cold butter and lard to the dry ingredients in 2 additions, pulsing to combine after each addition. Slowly add the ice water to the mixture, pulsing to combine until a dough forms. As soon as the dough holds together in the food processor, quickly transfer the dough to a cold work surface. Knead the dough just until smooth, working the fat into streaks and being careful not to overwork the pie dough. Divide the dough in half and flatten each piece into a disk. Wrap the disks in plastic wrap (clingfilm) and chill for at least 2 hours and preferably overnight.

To form the crust, dust a work surface and a rolling pin with flour. Place a dough disk on the floured work surface and press the dough down in the center with the palm of your hand to flatten slightly. Then pound the dough flat with the rolling pin. Roll the dough in one full pass, then rotate the dough a few inches and roll again. Continue rotating the dough and rolling, dusting slightly with flour only if needed, until the dough is large enough to fit the pie plate and is about ⅛ inch (3 mm) thick. Gently cut the dough to the desired pan size using a pot lid or bowl as a guide.

Gently slide both hands under the dough and hold the dough with your palms and forearms. Quickly slide the dough into the pie plate and gently press the dough into the pan. Crimp the dough around the edge and set in the freezer until needed, at least 30 minutes. The pie shell (pastry case) and pie plate can be double-wrapped in plastic and frozen for up to 1 month.

Bake the crust before adding the pie filling. To blind bake, preheat the oven to 375°F (190°C/Gas Mark 5).

Line the frozen pie shell (pastry case) with a coffee filter and fill the liner with pie weights (baking beans) or uncooked pinto beans. Press the weights lightly into the shell to ensure that the edges are weighed down. Bake until the outer edge of the crimp looks dry and golden brown, about 20 minutes, rotating 180 degrees halfway through the baking time. Remove from the oven and carefully remove the coffee filter and beans. If the filter sticks to the pastry, return to the oven to dry out for about 3 minutes and then try to remove the filter. Reduce the oven temperature to 350°F (180°C/Gas Mark 4). Brush the crimped edge and the bottom of the shell with the egg wash and then prick the bottom all over with a fork. Return to the oven and continue to bake until golden brown, 8–10 minutes longer. Set the baked shell aside until needed for final pie preparation.

SALTED TOFFEE

PREPARATION TIME: 5 MINUTES,
    PLUS COOLING TIME
COOKING TIME: 20 MINUTES
MAKES: ABOUT 2 CUPS (370 G)

- 1½ sticks (170 g) unsalted butter, melted
- 1 cup (200 g) sugar
- 1½ tablespoons light corn syrup
- 1 teaspoon kosher (coarse) salt

Line a baking sheet with a silicone baking mat and set aside. In a large saucepan, stir together the butter, sugar, corn syrup, and 2 tablespoons water. Set over medium heat and cook, without stirring, until the sugar mixture reaches 300°F (150°C). Carefully pour the caramelized sugar onto the prepared baking sheet. Let the toffee cool to room temperature so it can be handled and is not sticky.

Break the toffee into pieces and transfer to a food processor. Add the kosher (coarse) salt and pulse to grind the toffee to a fine crumb. Store in a dry airtight container at room temperature for up to 1 week.

Seabring Davis is a journalist who has lived in Montana since 1990. She is editor-in-chief of *Big Sky Journal* and author of five books, including *A Taste of Montana* and *A Montana Table*.

Venison embodies Montana. Harvested in autumn, it encapsulates the honeyed sunlight, these vast open spaces shadowed by mountains, and the wild ruggedness of this place.

The autumn ritual of hunting marks the turn of the year for our family like no other moment. There's a short conversation with our two daughters about hunting plans, which involves a curt briefing on the fact that they had better be ready to go when their father wakes them an hour before dawn. He'll go alone if they dally.

It's our older daughter who rallies every year. She and my husband leave at dark in the old Ford pickup, driving to a friend's property in nearby Paradise Valley. They arrive before sunup to find a position in the dry grass hills, when the Montana Fish, Wildlife & Parks rules declare it is legal to stalk and shoot animals. The cattle ranch where they hunt is private and access to it is a privilege. There, the land rolls in waves of hay and natural grass for a thousand acres at the base of the Absaroka Mountains.

My husband doesn't hunt at any other point throughout the year. We don't have a ranch of our own. We live in a modest house in town with a white picket fence around the yard. We are not card-toting members of the National Rifle Association. Our ethical stance is simple: We eat what we kill and we don't take trophies.

It started more than a decade ago. My husband came home with a whitetail doe, freshly harvested and field dressed, slung in the bed of the truck. Because the processor who butchers wild game was closed, he

wrapped the deer's hind legs with rope and strung it up in our garage to cure.

The girls were little, only six and one. I brought them to see the deer in the garage. It was dark outside and cold enough to see our breath. Both girls stroked its fur like a pet, awed that the animal did not leap from their touches and bound out through the open door. Enthralled, our oldest daughter asked where the deer lived, whether it was running when her dad took the shot, how old it was. She touched the doe's glazed eyes, her ears, the cloven hooves. Unfazed by the gore, she watched her father deftly use his knife, removing the skin to prevent the meat from spoiling overnight. With the tissue exposed, the muscles, veins, fat, and skeletal structure visible, there were more questions. Patiently, her dad answered each query, musing that she would either be a butcher or a physician someday. Finally, she asked one last question: What is her name? Without pause, my husband said that her name was Eleanor. Satisfied, our six-year-old, whispered in the ear of the deer: "Thank you, Eleanor." That started our tradition of naming the harvest. It's a way to honor the animal and the hunters. It's a way to give reverence to nature's bounty.

Later, when our older girl turned ten, she and her dad went on their first early morning hunt. The fields were crisp with frost. They hiked for hours before he shot another whitetail. She helped gut and haul the animal back to the truck without complaint. That sparked her love for hunting. By the time she was twelve she had shot her own mule deer buck.

Our younger daughter ventured out with her dad once, too. They drank cocoa in the cab of the truck until the sun crested over the high peaks. There was a lot of talking, too, which, my husband says, is not a good tactic for hunting. This duo didn't come home with any meat. They did have a lovely day outside, holding hands and walking in the October sun.

Since then, there have been other hunts. There have been many empty-handed mornings. But there are always stories. The flush faces of my husband and daughter have burst through the back door, ravenous for breakfast and excited with tales of the miles they've covered, the wondrous clear skies and open country. They have gushed about harrowing brushes with a grizzly bear one late day and a wolf sighting on another still morning.

The season's first meal of venison is always the most memorable. I rub the tenderloin with a mixture of crushed juniper berries picked from the bush in the alley, the last fresh herbs from our garden, olive oil, sea salt, and pepper. It's cooked rare over a grill with medium-hot coals, grassy and lean, touched with char from the fire. We let it rest before slicing.

We gather at the kitchen table. Immediately , my younger daughter asks what we are eating. I tell her it's the first deer of the season. "Oh," she'll exclaim, "it's so good to have Eleanor over for dinner!"

It's a family joke that never fails to elicit smiles. The names of the deer change. The children grow older. We sit as a family and say thank you—to the hunters at the table, to the animal that feeds us, to the place that makes it possible. We share a meal and listen, again, to the stories of the hunt.

Andy Blanton is chef-owner of Cafe Kandahar at Whitefish Mountain Resort in Montana. He has been a semifinalist for the James Beard Award Best Chef: Northwest.

ELK STROGANOFF WITH SHIITAKE MUSHROOMS

PREPARATION TIME: 20 MINUTES
COOKING TIME: 40 MINUTES
SERVES: 4

- 2 tablespoons olive oil
- ½ lb (225 g) shiitake mushrooms, stems discarded, caps thinly sliced
- 4 tablespoons finely chopped shallots
- 2 tablespoons minced garlic
- Kosher (coarse) salt and freshly ground black pepper
- ½ cup (50 g) finely chopped scallions (spring onions)
- 2 tablespoons capers
- 1 tablespoon finely chopped fresh rosemary
- ½ cup (120 ml) red wine
- ½ cup (120 ml) veal or beef stock
- ¼ cup (60 ml) heavy (whipping) cream, plus additional as needed
- ½ cup (115 g) crème fraîche
- 1 lb (455 g) elk meat (sirloin works well, as do other tender cuts), thinly sliced
- 1 lb (455 g) penne pasta, cooked according to package directions

In a large frying pan or sauté pan, heat the olive oil over medium-high heat until it begins to smoke. Carefully add the shiitakes and cook, stirring frequently, until the mushrooms start to caramelize slightly (to a light brown), about 3 minutes. Add the shallots, garlic, a good pinch of salt, and a smaller pinch of black pepper and cook for about 1 minute, stirring constantly. Stir in the scallions (spring onions), capers, and rosemary, then stir in the wine. Reduce the heat to medium and cook until the wine is almost evaporated and the mixture is thick and reduced, stirring occasionally to ensure the mixture does not stick to the pan, about 5 minutes. Add the stock and cook until the liquid reduces by about half, about 5 more minutes. Stir in the heavy whipping cream and cook 2 more minutes.

Add the crème fraîche, elk meat, and pasta. Stir to combine all the ingredients and cook over medium-high heat until the elk is cooked through and the sauce is thick enough to coat the pasta, about 3 minutes. Add more heavy cream if needed to ensure proper consistency. Serve immediately.

STEELHEAD TROUT WITH YELLOWSTONE CAVIAR, FIDDLEHEAD FERNS, AND BABY BEETS

PREPARATION TIME: 15 MINUTES,
  PLUS COOLING TIME
COOKING TIME: 2 HOURS 5 MINUTES
SERVES: 6

For the salt-roasted beets:
- 1 box (3 lb/1.4 kg) kosher (coarse) salt
- 1 bunch baby beets (1½–2 lb/680–910 g), trimmed

For the pickled vegetables:
- 1 teaspoon olive oil
- 1 teaspoon mustard seeds
- 1 teaspoon coriander seeds
- 3 tablespoons soy sauce
- ¾ cup (180 ml) rice vinegar
- ⅓ cup (70 g) turbinado (demerara) sugar
- 1 lb (455 g) fiddlehead ferns
- ½ lb (225 g) spring onions (salad onions), white part of bulbs only, halved or quartered for equal sizes

For the beurre blanc:
- 1 cup (240 ml) cava
- 1 shallot, minced
- 1 bay leaf
- 2 tablespoons heavy (whipping) cream
- 4 sticks (455 g) unsalted butter, cubed
- Dash of fresh lemon juice
- Pinch of fennel pollen
- Salt and freshly ground black pepper

For the trout:
- 2 lb (910 g) steelhead trout fillets (or salmon), cut into 6 equal portions
- Chef Paul Prudhomme's Seafood Magic seasoning blend
- Olive oil
- ½ oz (15 g) Yellowstone caviar (see Note)

Note:
  Yellowstone caviar is harvested in Montana from the Yellowstone Paddlefish. But just about any variety of caviar will work.

For the salt-roasted beets: Preheat the oven to 375°F (190°C/Gas Mark 5).

Pour the entire box of kosher (coarse) salt into a casserole dish and submerge the beets in the salt. Roast until tender, about 1½ hours. As soon as you can smell the beets cooking, check their doneness by piercing one with a small sharp knife. If it enters the beet easily with no resistance, the beets are ready. Let cool slightly, then remove the beets from the salt. While still warm, peel the beets by rubbing them with a tea towel or paper towel between your hands. (This salt can be reused the next time you salt-roast beets.)

For the pickled vegetables: In a frying pan, heat the oil over medium-high heat. Add the mustard and coriander seeds and heat, stirring, until the mustard seeds pop, about 25 seconds. Add the soy sauce, vinegar, sugar, and ¾ cup (180 ml) water and bring to a boil. Reduce the heat and simmer for about 5 minutes, so the seeds can infuse the marinade. Remove from the heat and let cool for 5 minutes. Strain, discarding the seeds, and return the liquid to the pan. Add the fiddleheads and onions, bring to a boil, then simmer until the fiddleheads begin to shrink and uncurl slightly, 2–3 minutes. Add water as needed to ensure that the fiddleheads and onions remain submerged. Remove from the heat and let the vegetables cool in the liquid. If making in advance, refrigerate until ready to use. The vegetables will keep for several weeks, or months if properly canned or stored. The longer they soak, the more flavorful they become.

For the beurre blanc: In a nonreactive saucepan, combine the cava, shallot, and bay leaf and cook over medium-low heat until almost all the liquid has evaporated, about 8 minutes. Reduce the heat if you notice the cava beginning to brown. Once the liquid is almost evaporated, stir in the cream. Whisking continuously over medium-low heat, add the butter, 1 or 2 pieces at a time, stirring each piece as it emulsifies, until fully incorporated. Season with the lemon juice, fennel pollen, and salt and pepper to taste. Cover and keep in a fairly warm place (not too hot).

For the trout: Preheat a grill (barbecue) to medium-high heat. Very lightly season the fillets all over with the seasoning blend Seafood Magic. Rub the grill racks with a little olive oil so the fish won't stick. Grill the fish to medium, evenly cooking on each side, 3–5 minutes per side, depending on the thickness of the fillets. (Alternatively, you can sear the fish in a cast-iron skillet with olive oil over medium-high heat.)

To serve, warm the beets and the fiddleheads and spring onions together in a little bit of the pickling marinade, then place on a plate. Set the steelhead on top of the vegetables on each plate, or to the side, spooning some of the warm beurre blanc over the fish. Garnish with the caviar.

BISON TENDERLOIN WITH HUCKLEBERRIES AND FINGERLING POTATOES

PREPARATION TIME: 20 MINUTES,
  PLUS STANDING TIME
COOKING TIME: 45 MINUTES
SERVES: 4

- 1 tablespoon olive oil
- ½ cup (80 g) finely chopped shallots
- Kosher (coarse) salt and freshly ground black pepper
- 1 cup (135 g) huckleberries (fresh or frozen)
- 1 bay leaf
- 2 tablespoons turbinado (demerara) sugar
- ½ cup (120 ml) port
- 2 tablespoons cider vinegar
- 2 cups (475 ml) demi-glace
- 2 lb (910 g) fingerling potatoes
- ¼ cup (10 g) spruce tips
- 1½ lb (680 g) bison tenderloin, cut into 4 steaks (6 oz/170 g each)
- 2 tablespoons extra-virgin olive oil
- 3 cloves garlic, sliced

In a large frying pan, warm the olive oil over medium heat. Add the shallots and cook, stirring often, until they turn translucent but do not brown, 2–4 minutes. Reduce the heat if they begin to turn color. Season with a little salt and pepper.

Add three-fourths of the huckleberries, the bay leaf, and the sugar to the pan. Increase the heat to medium-high and as soon as the mixture comes to a boil add the port and vinegar. Cook, stirring often, until the sauce begins to thicken, making sure the sauce does not stick to the pan, about 5 minutes. Stir in the demi-glace, transfer to a saucepan, and cook over medium heat until reduced by half, about 7 minutes. Add the reserved huckleberries and check the seasoning. Keep the sauce hot until ready to use.

Set up a bowl of ice and water. In a saucepan, combine the potatoes and cold water to cover and bring to just below a boil. During this step, quickly blanch the spruce tips by submerging them in the bubbling potato water for about 10–15 seconds, then set aside to cool. Cook the potatoes at a gentle simmer until tender, about 20 minutes. Drain the potatoes and transfer to the ice bath to stop the cooking. When cool, pat dry with paper towels. Halve the potatoes horizontally. Lightly chop the spruce tips to resemble rosemary.

At least 20 minutes before cooking, season the bison steaks on all sides with salt and pepper.

In a frying pan, heat the extra-virgin olive oil over medium heat. Carefully place the potatoes, cut side down, in the hot oil and cook until they develop a golden brown hue, about 5 minutes. Add a decent pinch of salt, a tiny pinch of black pepper, and the garlic. As soon as the garlic begins to turn color, add the spruce tips, remove from the heat, and keep warm (making sure neither the garlic nor spruce tips burn, transferring if necessary).

Cook the bison to desired doneness on a grill (barbecue), under the broiler (grill), or in a cast-iron skillet, preferably grilling to medium-rare to medium.

To serve, place a bison steak over the spruce-tip-infused potatoes. Spoon the huckleberry sauce over the bison or at the base of the plate.

HUCKLEBERRY TART WITH LEMON CRÈME FRAÎCHE AND CANDIED MINT

PREPARATION TIME: 1 HOUR,
  PLUS DRYING TIME
COOKING TIME: 45 MINUTES
MAKES: 1 TART

For the candied mint:
- 1 egg white
- Fresh mint leaves
- Superfine (caster) sugar (see Note)

For the vanilla pastry cream:
- 3 egg yolks
- 1 cup (240 ml) milk
- 3½ tablespoons all-purpose (plain) flour
- 7 tablespoons granulated sugar
- ¼ vanilla bean, split
- 1 tablespoon (15 g) unsalted butter

For the lemon crème fraîche:
- 1½ teaspoons powdered (icing) sugar
- Finely grated zest and juice of 1 lemon
- ½ cup (115 g) crème fraîche

For the filling:
- 1 cup (135 g) huckleberries
- 2 tablespoons granulated sugar
- Dash of fresh lemon juice

For the tart shell:
- 1 single-crust recipe Basic Pie Dough, (page 282)

Note:
  You can make superfine sugar by pulsing granulated sugar in a food processor.

For the candied mint: Use a pastry brush to gently paint an even, thin coat of egg white onto mint leaves. Sprinkle the sugar over the brushed mint leaves until slightly frosted. Add more sugar as needed to create a frosted appearance. Let dry at room temperature (these will keep for at least 1 week).

For the vanilla pastry cream: In a medium bowl, combine the egg yolks and ½ cup (120 ml) of the milk. Sift the flour and sugar together, then add to the bowl and whisk until smooth.

In a nonreactive saucepan, bring the remaining ½ cup (120 ml) milk and vanilla bean to a boil. Slowly whisk the hot milk into the egg mixture to temper it, whisking constantly until fully combined. Return the mixture to the saucepan and cook over medium-low heat, stirring constantly with a wooden spoon, until the custard begins to thicken. Quickly switch to a whisk, increase the heat to medium, and whisk until the custard thickens noticeably and pulls away from the sides of the pan, 1–2 minutes. Remove from the heat and immediately transfer to a cool container, such as a clean saucepan, and quickly stir in the butter while still hot. Continue stirring to cool and ensure the mixture does not overcook.

For the lemon crème fraîche: In a nonreactive bowl, stir together the powdered (icing) sugar, lemon zest, and lemon juice. Whisk in the crème fraîche and whip with a whisk or electric mixer until soft peaks form.

For the filling: In a frying pan, combine the berries, granulated sugar, and 2 tablespoons water and bring to a boil. Drain the berries in a mesh strainer set over a bowl and return the juices to the pan. Cook over medium-low heat until it becomes syrupy, then return the berries and season with the lemon juice, stirring to combine. Remove from the heat and set aside. (This will keep for several days in the refrigerator.)

For the tart shell: Roll the dough out to ¼-inch (6 mm) thickness and press into the bottom of a 9-inch (23 cm) tart pan. Prick the bottom with the fork and chill for at least 1 hour.

Preheat the oven to 375°F (190°C/Gas Mark 5). Line the shell with foil or parchment and fill with pie weights. Bake for about 12 minutes, until the shell is just beginning to turn golden brown around the edges and the bottom is set. Remove the shell from the oven, remove the foil and weights, and let the shell cool slightly.

Fill the tart shell about one-third full with the pastry cream. Top with the huckleberry filling. I like to use a few circular motions with a spoon to make a swirl design with the filling. Bake until the crust is golden and the pastry cream begins to rise, 15–20 minutes.

Serve immediately or let cool slightly and rewarm when ready to serve. (If making in advance, remove the tart from the oven just before it appears finished and let it finish cooking during the rewarming process.) Serve garnished with the lemon crème fraîche and candied mint.

Clayton Chapman is a native of Omaha, Nebraska. He is the chef-owner of The Grey Plume and Provisions by The Grey Plume in Omaha, as well as a five-time James Beard Award nominee.

We eagerly anticipate our first annual delivery of golden morels. They are beauties. The Nebraska morel season is fickle and fast and mushroom hunting is famously one of the most mysterious, secretive, and ancient activities.

How these treasures end up at our door is a bit of a mystery every year. Mushroom hunters appear: from arborists, farmers, and professional foragers who live in the wilderness and move with the seasons, to recreational hunters, basically anyone who likes the thrill of a hunt. Foraging is serious business.

By law, state inspection is required to sell wild edibles. Rules and regulations tend to be hard to interpret and vary from state to state. Nebraska didn't have a state mushroom inspector, so medical students moonlighting as foragers took a class at Iowa State University and became Nebraska's first certified state inspectors.

Morels are one of the easiest mushrooms to identify due to the shape of the cap and the crater-like appearance. (True morels have a hollow stem, false morels do not.) Morels love the rainy and damp weather, followed by a sunny day, and they can be found in the hills of shaded forests or on the riverbanks of waterways. Hill mushrooms tend to be cleaner than river mushrooms, which are sandy and more often than not have aphids. In Nebraska, morels emerge right after the asparagus season. When we are lucky, the two seasons overlap. Nature provides the pairing.

For me, cooking with morels is rooted in simplicity. In order to highlight the natural nutty flavor and meatiness of the mushroom, we sear them in foaming brown butter, salt, and pickled garlic. The mushrooms have enough natural water content so that when they sear, they purge their water and the mushroom-seasoned liquid forms its own sauce. The morels are best cooked within hours after being foraged.

It doesn't get any better, fresher, more local, seasonal, or exciting than this. The morel is an invitation to experience spring in all its glory, and by understanding its journey to the plate, you truly realize that you've struck gold.

Clayton Chapman

BUTTERNUT SQUASH WITH COFFEE AND CINNAMON

PREPARATION TIME: 25 MINUTES
COOKING TIME: 1 HOUR 30 MINUTES
SERVES: 4

- 2 small butternut squash
- ¼ oz (7 g) finely ground coffee beans
- 1 scant tablespoon ground cinnamon
- 4 tablespoons (60 g) unsalted butter
- 4 sprigs fresh thyme
- Kosher (coarse) salt and freshly cracked black pepper
- 6 tablespoons neutral cooking oil
- 2 tablespoons dark honey

Preheat the oven to 350°F (180°C/Gas Mark 4).

Cut the bulbs of the butternut squash away from the necks. Scrape the seeds out of the bulbs and peel the necks. Halve the necks lengthwise and then cut crosswise into ¼-inch (6 mm) half-moons. Sprinkle the inside of the bulbs with the ground coffee and cinnamon. Put 2 tablespoons (30 g) butter and 2 sprigs of thyme in each. Season with salt and pepper. Wrap the bulbs in foil and bake until they are completely tender, 1 to 1½ hours.

Meanwhile, in a frying pan or saucepan, heat the oil over medium heat. Add the squash slices, season with salt and pepper, and cook until tender but not browned, about 15 minutes. If the squash starts to develop any color, add teaspoonfuls of water in stages to help the cooking process. Transfer to a bowl.

When the bulbs are cooked, unwrap the foil and discard the thyme. Scrape the flesh out of the bulbs and into the bowl, making sure you get all the butter and liquid from the roasted squash.

For a rustic mash, add the honey and mash with a fork. For a very smooth purée, transfer the squash and honey to a blender and blend until smooth. Season to taste with salt and pepper.

COFFEE-MARINATED BOBWHITE QUAIL

PREPARATION TIME: 50 MINUTES,
  PLUS MARINATING TIME
COOKING TIME: 30 MINUTES
SERVES: 4

- 4 bobwhite quail
- 4 cups (1 liter) brewed coffee
- Kosher (coarse) salt and freshly ground black pepper
- 2 oz (55 g) finely ground coffee beans
- 6 tablespoons neutral cooking oil
- 8 sprigs fresh thyme
- 4 tablespoons (60 g) unsalted butter
- 1 tablespoon red wine vinegar
- 2 teaspoons dark honey
- Finely grated zest of 1 lemon
- Butternut Squash with Coffee and Cinnamon (page 613)
- Fall Apples (page 615)

[To me, quail is the perfect fall bird. It stands up to winter spices and is able to take on many flavors. Farmers Dave and Lori Sanders of Sanders Specialty Meats and Produce, just east of Lincoln, Nebraska, raise quail, rabbits, and bees and cure a variety of local meats for nearby chefs. The bobwhite species in this recipe has been successfully cultivated in Nebraska for many years. ShadowBrook Farm, also just east of Lincoln, is another breath of fresh air for us during the late fall and winter as produce becomes scarce.]

Place the whole quail in a baking pan, bowl, or any medium container. Pour the brewed coffee over the quail and let sit for at least 1 hour and up to 24 hours. Pull the quail out of the coffee and pat dry. Reserve the coffee marinating liquid for the sauce in another bowl.

Preheat the oven to 350°F (180°C/Gas Mark 4). Season the quail with salt, pepper, and ground coffee. Heat a medium frying pan over medium heat. Add the oil and when hot, add the quail to the pan and cook until golden brown on all sides. Transfer the quail to a baking sheet (reserve the frying pan) and place a thyme sprig on top of each bird. Bake until the internal temperature of the thigh reads 160°F (71°C), 10–15 minutes.

Meanwhile, to the reserved frying pan, add the butter and remaining thyme. Once the butter is hot, add the reserved coffee marinating liquid and cook until the sauce is as thick as ketchup or thick enough to coat the back of a spoon, about 10 minutes. Add the vinegar and honey. Discard the thyme sprigs and season to taste with salt and pepper. Set aside until the quail are done.

Once the birds come out of the oven, brush them with the sauce and sprinkle with the lemon zest. Divide the butternut squash evenly among 4 plates. Spoon the fall apples on top of the squash and place a quail on top of the apples. If you have any of the coffee sauce left, you can serve it with the quail.

FALL APPLES

PREPARATION TIME: 10 MINUTES
COOKING TIME: 10 MINUTES
SERVES: 4

- 4 tablespoons (60 g) unsalted butter
- 2 fall apples, unpeeled and cut into wedges ¼ inch (6 mm) thick
- 2 tablespoons white wine vinegar
- 1 tablespoon dark honey
- Kosher (coarse) salt and freshly cracked black pepper
- 2 tablespoons minced fresh chives or parsley

In a frying pan over medium-high heat, melt the butter until it foams. Add the apples and cook until they are crisp on the outside and tender on the inside, about 6 minutes. Add the vinegar and honey and season to taste with salt and pepper. When you are ready to serve, stir in the chives.

CRÈME FRAÎCHE SPÄTZLE

PREPARATION TIME: 10 MINUTES
COOKING TIME: 20 MINUTES
SERVES: 8

- 2 cups (475 ml) crème fraîche or sour cream
- 5 eggs
- 2⅔ cups (350 g) all-purpose (plain) flour
- Kosher (coarse) salt or sea salt
- Grated zest and juice of 2 Meyer lemons
- ¼ cup (60 ml) neutral cooking oil, such as grapeseed, divided
- 2 tablespoons chopped fresh parsley

[Crème fraîche is like a French sour cream, only a little more acidic, typically cultured with buttermilk. Spätzle literally translates as "tiny sparrow." These are tiny little dumplings that can be served soft or crispy. They are first poached in a water bath and then, for this recipe, seared for a crunchy texture. Feel free to add fresh herbs, mustard, or shaved hard cheese to the batter. This is typically a side dish, but can be served as an entrée.]

In a bowl or food processor, blend together 1 cup (240 ml) plus 2 tablespoons crème fraîche, the eggs, flour, salt to taste, and half of the lemon zest. Whisk until the batter is smooth and free of lumps. If not cooking right away, the batter will hold for 1 day in the refrigerator.

Bring a large pot of salted water to a boil.

Set up a bowl of ice and water. Set a heatproof colander over the pot of boiling water and pour half of the batter in. Push through with a rubber spatula. The batter will fall into the boiling water as little dumplings. Once the spätzle float to the surface, use a slotted spoon to scoop them out of the water and into the ice bath to stop the cooking. Repeat this process with the remaining batter.

In a large frying pan over high heat, warm 2 tablespoons of the oil. Add half of the spätzle, season to taste with salt, and sear until golden brown, about 4 minutes. Remove from the pan and set aside. Repeat with the remaining spätzle. Return the reserved spätzle to the pan, add the remaining ¾ cup (180 ml) plus 2 tablespoons crème fraîche and cook to reduce by half. Fold in the lemon juice and parsley. Serve garnished with the remaining lemon zest.

WAGYU BEEF RIBEYE WITH MORELS AND RADISH-ASPARAGUS SALAD

PREPARATION TIME: 20 MINUTES,
   PLUS OVERNIGHT REFRIGERATION
COOKING TIME: 25 MINUTES
SERVES: 4–6

- 12 French breakfast radishes, with tops attached
- 1 cup (240 ml) red wine vinegar
- Kosher (coarse) salt or sea salt
- 2 sprigs fresh thyme
- 8–12 spears asparagus (2 per person), woody ends trimmed
- Finely grated zest and juice of 1 Meyer or Eureka lemon
- 1 tablespoon chopped fresh parsley
- 1 tablespoon raw honey
- 4 tablespoons olive oil or neutral cooking oil
- Freshly ground black pepper
- 4–6 portions local wagyu ribeye (4 oz/ 115 g each)
- 2½ tablespoons (40 g) butter
- 2 cups (135 g) morel mushrooms, rinsed and patted dry
- Coarse sea salt

[You can change up the protein and the cooking technique if, for example, you would like to grill outdoors or make this with seafood. We pride ourselves on our beef in the heartland, so I wanted to feature a wagyu ribeye.]

Remove the radish tops and set aside for later. Cut 8 of the radishes in half and transfer to a heatproof bowl. Thinly shave the remaining radishes and set aside for later. In a saucepan, bring the vinegar to a boil and stir in 1 tablespoon salt and 1 sprig of thyme. Pour over the radishes and refrigerate the radishes overnight.

Set up a bowl of ice and water. In a saucepan, bring 8 cups (2 liters) water to a boil and season with 2 tablespoons salt. Add the asparagus and blanch until tender. Drain and shock in the ice bath. Cut the asparagus on the diagonal into 2-inch (5 cm) pieces.

Reserving the pickling liquid, drain the radishes and transfer to a bowl. Add the blanched asparagus, shaved radishes, three-quarters of the lemon zest, the parsley, honey, a splash of the radish pickling liquid, and 2 tablespoons of the olive oil and toss together. Season to taste with salt and pepper and set aside until ready to serve.

Season the ribeye with salt and pepper. Heat a cast-iron or other sauté pan over medium-high heat and add the remaining 2 tablespoons oil. Sear the steaks on all sides until golden brown, about 10 minutes. Drain off any excess oil. Add the remaining sprig of thyme and 2 tablespoons (30 g) of the butter. Once the butter foams, baste the steaks with the butter and cook until the internal temperature reads 140°F (60°C). Allow the steaks to rest while you prepare the morels.

In the same pan that the beef was seared in, cook the morels while the fat is still hot. Sear until golden brown and cooked through. Add the lemon juice and remove from the heat. Add the remaining ½ tablespoon (10 g) butter and the radish tops to the pan. Season to taste with salt and pepper.

When ready to serve, slice the steak across the grain and season with salt and the remaining one-fourth of the lemon zest.

To serve, place a bed of morels on each plate. Place a spoonful or so of the cold vegetable salad on top and add the sliced ribeye, and finish with a sprinking of coarse sea salt.

NEVADA GUEST ESSAY

Alicia Barber is an award-winning writer and historian and the founder of Stories in Place. She lives in Reno, Nevada.

There is a Nevada that demands the world's attention, a whirling spectacle of flashing lights, 24-hour poker, all-you-can-eat buffets, and big-name restaurants.

But outside the Las Vegas casino doors are landscapes of snow-capped peaks and sage-strewn valleys, vast expanses of desert stillness and fragrant pine, and towns and cities born of mining, ranching, and the shrill call of the locomotive. A land of contrasts, Nevada's culinary heritage is similarly diverse, a testament both to its unique, often forbidding landscape and to the myriad backgrounds of those who have moved across it.

The powerful influences of land and culture combine in one of the state's most beloved cuisines, the food of the Basque tradition. Basques set their sights on the American West from the time of the California Gold Rush, entering northern Nevada in large numbers after 1900. Many found work as sheepherders, tending flocks of sheep for months at a time, visited sporadically by a "camp tender" armed with food and other supplies.

Many of these men were single and young, intent on earning money and returning to the Basque Country, which straddles the border of northern Spain and southwestern France. In Nevada, Basque hotels and boarding houses known as *ostatuak* sprang up near railroad stations to house off-duty sheepherders alongside new arrivals and other workers. To their patrons, the *ostatuak* offered not just food and lodging but community, a welcome antidote to the isolation of the Sierra foothills, the Ruby Mountains, and the high reaches of the Toiyabe and Jarbidge ranges.

Today, dinner at a Basque restaurant continues that legacy of communal dining—some, like the Star Hotel in Elko, in the very same historic hotels. Shared dishes are passed around the table—steaming soup, salad, bread, stew, or vegetables, Basque beans, and French fries, accompanied by carafes of house red wine.

The Basque cuisine of the American West differs somewhat from its Old World counterpart, yet many influences persist. From the Spanish side of the Basque Country comes paella, and from the coast, salt cod. Befitting Nevada's heritage, lamb and beef play a central role. Sweetbreads and oxtails grace the menus of Nevada's Basque eateries, with tripe and tongue less common than they once were, a result of shifting tastes. Peppers, tomatoes, and, most of all, garlic layer on the flavor in many Basque dishes, adding warmth and kick to chicken, stew, and *solomo*, a boneless pork loin specialty.

Basque American fare is incomplete without a nod to the famous Picon Punch. An American invention, the cocktail is a heady blend of the bitter, herbal Torani Amer (a substitute for the increasingly rare Amer Picon), grenadine, and brandy, with optional club soda and a lemon twist. Longtime Reno restaurateurs Louis and Lorraine Erreguible were fond of cautioning patrons: "The first two are the Picon and the third is the punch." The aperitif is meant to whet the appetite for food as well as conversation, both of which Nevada's Basque restaurants have been supplying in abundance for more than a century.

Alicia Barber

PICON PUNCH

PREPARATION TIME: 3 MINUTES
MAKES: 1 COCKTAIL

- Ice
- A few dashes (or 1 bar spoon) grenadine
- ¼ cup (60 ml) Amer Picon or Torani Amer
- 2–4 tablespoons club soda (optional)
- 1 tablespoon brandy
- Lemon twist, for garnish

Fill a 6½-ounce (190 ml) glass with ice. Add the grenadine, Amer, and club soda (if desired) and stir. Top with a float of brandy. Garnish with the lemon twist.

LAMB SHANK BRAISED IN RED WINE

PREPARATION TIME: 10 MINUTES
COOKING TIME: 3 HOURS
SERVES: 4

- 4 lamb shanks (12 oz/340 g each)
- 1 tablespoon salt
- ½ tablespoon freshly ground black pepper
- 1 sprig fresh rosemary
- 1 sprig fresh thyme
- 1 tablespoon plus 2 teaspoons minced garlic, divided
- 1½ cups (355 ml) chicken stock
- 1 cup (240 ml) Carlo Rossi Paisano or other light-bodied red wine
- 1 cup (335 g) mint jelly, for serving

[The historic Martin Hotel in Winnemucca, Nevada, has been serving traditional Basque dishes, such as this wine-braised lamb shank, to area ranchers for over a century.]

Preheat the oven to 350°F (180°C/Gas Mark 4).

Place the lamb shanks in a large roasting pan and season with the salt and pepper. Bake uncovered for 1 hour. Add the rosemary, thyme, 2 teaspoons of the garlic, the stock, and the wine, cover tightly with foil, and cook for 2 more hours. Garnish with the remaining garlic and serve with the mint jelly on the side.

Susan Laughlin has been food editor for *New Hampshire Magazine* for more than fifteen years.

I consider poutine the perfect dish to represent New Hampshire. It's rustic in concept, rich in character, and a thing of beauty when its three basic components sing in perfect harmony. Live Free with Fries and Fat could be our new state motto. The correct pronunciation is poo-ten or poo-tsen. Asking for poo-teen earmarks you as a neophyte.

The dish is a cultural gift from French Canadians, beginning with their migration across our northern border to work in the woolen mills lining arterial rivers of the state. It's in these mill towns that the dish was kept alive by local cafés—Chez Vachon in Manchester for one. The poutine here has always been on the menu and is considered to be the most authentic around. I went on a pilgrimage to see what the fuss was about.

At Chez Vachon, teens pound down huge platters of the stuff. Those who can devour The Grand Poutine—five pounds of fries coated with gravy and studded with curds—get their names on the wall and a Chez Vachon T-shirt. I discovered the beauty of cheese curds and Chez Vachon had nailed the cheese quotient with fresh curds, barely melted, with plenty of tooth feel. I realized that the fries have to be tasty and crisp; the gravy, rich and with depth of flavor, and most important, the cheese has to be fresh curds that "squeak" as your teeth dig in. Curds are a very young cheese—almost flavorless. It's their rubbery texture when whole, and stringy character when melted, that makes the meal.

Chef Matt Provencher at The Foundry Restaurant in Manchester features a veal demi-glace-based gravy on house-cut fries served with caramelized onions and braised oxtail.

I also went to the New England's Tap House Grille in Hooksett. Owner Dan Laqueux was born in Quebec and authenticity was not his concern; he wanted to up the ante. The Tap House rendition features a peppercorn demi-glace, heavily sauced with sherry, atop hand-cut fries and fresh curds melted to the stringy stage. Then it's scented with truffle oil and rosemary.

Every pub in the state worth its salt has poutine on the bar menu. When the trinity of components is given careful attention, the dish is heavenly, and worth every calorie. If even just one element is lacking, it's a sin instead of sublime.

At home, in a cast-iron skillet, I fried local, organic potatoes, starting with cold oil. The gravy was easy, since it was just after Thanksgiving and a nice homemade turkey gravy was on hand. A touch of vinegar added a nod to "authenticity." Finally, fresh curds melded perfectly with the hot fries and glistening gravy. It was proclaimed a "wow" by two folks of French Canadian descent.

I'm happy that poutine has evolved with the gastronomic times—the sum can be far tastier than the parts. If you can't find a good one at a local bar or café, get into the kitchen. All things are possible when starring ingredients align in the pantry.

Alison Ladman owns and operates The Crust and Crumb Baking Company in Concord, New Hampshire. She ran the Associated Press test kitchen for ten years.

CLASSIC ROAST TURKEY

PREPARATION TIME: 15 MINUTES,
  PLUS STANDING TIME
COOKING TIME: 2 HOURS 45 MINUTES
SERVES: 12–14

- 5 lb (2.3 kg) onions, quartered
- 1 whole turkey (12–14 lb/5.4–6.4 kg), giblets removed
- 1 stick (115 g) unsalted butter, softened
- Kosher (coarse) salt and freshly ground black pepper
- 3 sprigs fresh rosemary
- 4 sprigs fresh thyme
- 6 sprigs fresh sage
- ½ cup (120 ml) dry white wine
- 2 cups (475 ml) unsalted turkey stock
- 3 tablespoons quick-mixing flour, such as Wondra

Note:
To keep this recipe even more basic, you can skip the onions and herbs, but they do keep moisture in the oven and flavor the gravy. If feeling adventurous, start your turkey breast side down, cook it for 1½ hours, then flip it over to finish breast side up—this makes for extra moist breast meat. To flip: check that the bird is not stuck on the rack, then use a long-handled wooden spoon shoved into the neck of the bird and a pair of sturdy tongs holding onto the cavity from the other end. Then flip the bird in one smooth motion.

[Creating recipes for the Associated Press, it was a repeated task to come up with new ways to make turkey every year for Thanksgiving. Most people just want a nice basic turkey that doesn't take fifty ingredients, a trip out of state, and four days to cook.]

Preheat the oven to 350°F (180°C/Gas Mark 4).

Place two-thirds of the onions in the bottom of a roasting pan. Coat a roasting rack with cooking spray and set in the pan. Pat the turkey dry all over with paper towels, then rub inside and out with the butter. Sprinkle liberally, inside and out, with salt and pepper. Place the remaining onions, rosemary, thyme, and half of the sage in the cavity. Chop the remaining sage and set aside. Arrange the turkey, breast side up, on the rack. Cover loosely with foil and roast for 1 hour. Remove the foil and baste all over with some fat drained down into the roasting pan. Roast until the internal temperature of the breast reads 160°F (71°C) and the thigh reads 170°F (77°C), 1 to 1½ hours.

Transfer the turkey to a serving platter and wrap it with a layer of foil and then a couple of layers of tea towels to keep warm while you prepare the gravy. Remove the rack from the roasting pan. Using a slotted spoon, remove and discard the onions. Place the roasting pan over medium heat and bring the juices to a simmer. Add the white wine and scrape any browned bits in the pan. Pour the stock into the pan, whisking constantly. Add the flour and whisk to combine. Simmer for 5 minutes, while continuing to stir. Stir in the reserved sage and season with salt and pepper. Strain if desired and serve alongside the turkey.

BOURBON APPLE SHORTCAKES

PREPARATION TIME: 15 MINUTES
COOKING TIME: 35 MINUTES
SERVES: 8

For the shortcakes:
- 2¾ cups (360 g) all-purpose (plain) flour
- ⅓ cup (65 g) granulated sugar
- 4 teaspoons baking powder
- ¼ teaspoon salt
- 10 tablespoons (145 g) butter, melted
- 1 cup (240 ml) heavy (whipping) cream
- ¼ cup (60 ml) sour cream
- 1 teaspoon pure vanilla extract
- Coarse sugar

For the fruit topping:
- 6 tart apples, such as Gala or Fuji
- 3 tablespoons (45 g) butter
- 3 tablespoons light brown sugar
- 1 teaspoon ground cinnamon
- ½ teaspoon freshly grated nutmeg
- 3 tablespoons bourbon
- Whipped cream or vanilla ice cream, for serving

[This recipe is a New England riff on the classic strawberry short-cake. You can use any fruit on hand, macerating fresh berries with a little sugar until juicy, or tossing stone fruit like peaches or plums with a little sugar in a skillet over medium heat for a few minutes. Citrus segments would also be delicious, with some toasted shaved coconut or bittersweet chocolate.]

For the shortcakes: Preheat the oven to 375°F (190°C/Gas Mark 5). Line a baking sheet with parchment paper.

In a medium bowl, whisk together the flour, granulated sugar, baking powder, and salt. Add the butter and stir together until the mixture resembles crumbs with some pieces as big as peas. In a small bowl, whisk together the cream, sour cream, and vanilla. Stir into the dry mixture just until the mixture is moistened. It should look a little rough, with bits and chunks of buttery crumbs.

Turn the dough out onto a lightly floured counter and pat into a rectangle about 1 inch (2.5 cm) thick. Halve the rectangle length-wise, then in four crosswise, so you have 8 pieces. It is not important that they be perfect squares, just even thickness and size. Arrange the pieces on the baking sheet and sprinkle liberally with coarse sugar. Bake until lightly golden and just slightly springy-firm, 20–25 minutes.

Meanwhile, for the fruit topping: Peel, core, and cut the apples into slices ¼ inch (6 mm) thick. In a large frying pan, melt the butter over medium heat. Add the brown sugar, cinnamon, nutmeg, and apples and cook until the apples are tender, about 8 minutes. Add the bourbon and stir to combine.

To serve, split the shortcakes horizontally. Top with the apples and whipped cream or ice cream. Enjoy warm.

Ian Knauer is a chef, author, television personality, and founder of The Farm Cooking School in Stockton, New Jersey.

The alarm screams to life just after 4:00 in the morning. It is still very dark outside, even at this time of year, when the nights are the shortest they will be. The truck is loaded and the coffee is poured in to-go cups with lids. The country air still feels cool before the sunrise. By 6:30 in the morning, seven hundred pounds of heirloom tomatoes, twenty-five bushels of sweet corn, baskets of berries, and bouquets of the greenest herbs are careening through the tunnel, headed to the farmers' markets of New York City.

This fresh food, grown by hand on small farms, is the stuff we would pay a pretty penny for in the test kitchens of *Gourmet* magazine, where I spent nearly a decade developing recipes. And it came from New Jersey, home to the world's finest tomatoes, sweet corn, and blueberries.

Pick up one of those tomatoes and close your eyes. Hold it to your face and breathe it in. There is no more intoxicating perfume on Earth than the scent of a ripe Garden State tomato. Pop one ripe blueberry in your mouth. Your body's response to the perfect balance of sweet and tart is to salivate. Just-picked sweet summer corn is so sweet there is no need to cook it. The kernels explode with sugary juice.

New Jersey has, well, a bad rap. And sure, there is the undeniable and unidentifiable stank of Port Newark, and that exaggerated Jersey Shore culture. But this is still the Garden State, and that is no exaggeration.

After *Gourmet* closed, I had to follow those tomatoes back across the river. I now have a cooking school, on a working organic produce farm in New Jersey. I can count eight more small farms, off the top of my head, within a fifteen-minute drive. This place is crawling with farmers. I know them all by name. I even live with one.

In the summer we walk out the doors of the cooking school, into the fields, and pick exactly what we need. We cook together with our students, then sit down to eat. Without exception, eyebrows go up. And, it's not that hard to figure out why it all tastes so good. When you start with really good stuff (the world's best tomato, for instance), you end up with really good stuff.

Ian Knauer

TOMATO-CHORIZO AND MANY HERB SALAD

PREPARATION TIME: 15 MINUTES
COOKING TIME: 5 MINUTES
SERVES: 6

- ¼ cup (60 ml) extra-virgin olive oil
- ½ lb (225 g) cured Spanish-style chorizo, skin removed and sliced
- 2 cloves garlic, thinly sliced
- 2 tablespoons red wine vinegar
- 3 medium heirloom tomatoes, cut into large wedges
- 3 scallions (spring onions), sliced
- Salt and freshly ground black pepper
- 2 cups (80 g) packed fresh herb leaves, such as parsley, cilantro (coriander), dill, marjoram, and chives
- Warm crusty bread, for serving

In a frying pan, heat the oil over medium-low heat. Add the chorizo and garlic and cook until the chorizo is warmed through and the garlic is fragrant, about 4 minutes. Add the vinegar, swirling it once or twice, then transfer it all to a large bowl.

Stir in the tomatoes and scallions (spring onions) and season with salt and pepper to taste. Toss in the herbs and serve with crusty bread.

SQUARE SPAGHETTI WITH CHERRY TOMATOES, GROUND CHERRIES, CORN, AND CHANTERELLES

PREPARATION TIME: 50 MINUTES,
   PLUS DOUGH RESTING TIME
COOKING TIME: 20 MINUTES
SERVES: 6–10

- Whole Egg Pasta (recipe follows)
- 2 tablespoons extra-virgin olive oil
- 2 cups (160 g) small chanterelle mushrooms, halved
- 4 ears of very fresh corn, kernels cut from the cob
- Kosher (coarse) salt and freshly ground black pepper
- 1 dry pint (300 g) very ripe cherry tomatoes, halved
- 1 dry pint (150 g) ground cherries (also called Cape gooseberries), husked and halved
- 2 large shallots, finely chopped
- ½ cup (120 ml) white wine vinegar
- ½ cup (120 ml) dry white wine
- ¼ cup (60 ml) heavy (whipping) cream
- 2 sticks (225 g) chilled unsalted butter, cut into bits
- ¼ cup (2 g) fresh dill fronds

[This dish is only worth making in July and August, when cherry tomatoes, ground cherries—also called Cape gooseberries—and corn are perfectly sweet and ripe and chanterelle mushrooms dot the woods with their bright-orange scatter. When we combine an Italian pasta technique with a French technique of a beurre blanc sauce, tying together the summer's freshest produce, the result is amazing.]

Make the pasta dough up to the point of wrapping it in plastic wrap (clingfilm) and letting it rest. If you're lucky enough to have a *chitarra* pasta cutter at home, now is the time to break it out. If you don't (we don't), then cut the dough into 4 pieces and dust each with flour. Using a pasta roller, put 1 piece of dough through the widest setting 7 or 8 times, folding and dusting lightly with flour as needed between each pass. Adjust the width of the rollers to the next-narrowest setting and pass the dough through the rollers once without folding. Continue thinning the dough once on each smaller setting without folding, but dusting with flour as needed if the dough feels tacky to the touch, until it is about ¹⁄₁₆ inch (1.6 mm) thick (to #5 on a KitchenAid pasta roller attachment). This thickness mimics the famous *alla chitarra* pasta. Cut the sheets into thin noodles, about ¹⁄₁₆ inch (1.6 mm) wide, using a thin pasta cutter, then toss the pasta with flour and reserve on a baking sheet.

In a large heavy frying pan, heat the oil over medium-high heat until hot. Stir in the mushrooms and cook, stirring occasionally, until they are golden in places, 6–8 minutes. Remove from the heat and stir in the corn, 1 teaspoon salt, and ½ teaspoon pepper and stir until the corn is just not raw any more, 30 seconds if you have really fresh corn, 1 minute if it's a little older. Transfer the mushrooms and corn to a large bowl. Add the cherry tomatoes and ground cherries.

In a heavy medium saucepan, combine the shallots, vinegar, and wine. Bring to a boil and boil until all the liquid is reduced and the only thing left is the shallots, 8–10 minutes. This may seem like it's going too far, but it's not: Reduce the liquid completely. Whisk in the cream and ½ teaspoon salt and bring to a boil. Reduce the heat to low and whisk in the butter, a few bits at a time, until it is completely melted and incorporated. Pour this sauce over the vegetables in the bowl and season to taste with salt and pepper.

In a pot of boiling salted water, cook the pasta until it is al dente, 2–3 minutes. Reserving 1 cup (240 ml) of the pasta water, drain the pasta and add it immediately to the bowl with the sauce. Toss the pasta with the sauce and let it stand for about 1 minute. The pasta will start to suck up the sauce. Stir the pasta to see if the sauce has become too thick and, if so, stir in some of the pasta water to thin it. Transfer the pasta to plates, then spoon the remaining sauce and vegetables over the pasta. Scatter the dill fronds over the plates and serve hot.

WHOLE EGG PASTA

PREPARATION TIME: 15 MINUTES,
  PLUS RESTING TIME
MAKES: ENOUGH TO SERVE 6 AS A MAIN
  COURSE OR 10 AS A STARTER

- 2⅔ cups (345 g) all-purpose (plain) flour
- 4 eggs
- 2 tablespoons extra-virgin olive oil
- Kosher (coarse) salt

[We used to make this recipe for simple egg pasta the way Nonna would have: by forming a well of flour on the work surface and cracking the eggs into it. But it's much easier, we've found, to work in a bowl. It prevents the liquid from breaking out of the flour-formed well, causing you to have to chase it across the table. You can easily halve or double the quantites of these ingredients depending on how many mouths you have to feed.]

Place the flour in a large bowl and make a well in the center. Add the eggs, oil, and ½ teaspoon salt to the well and work the flour into the liquid with a fork until a dough forms. Depending on the size of your eggs, you may not need all the flour, or you may need a little more if the dough is sticky. Turn the dough out of the bowl onto a work surface, and knead it until it is an elastic ball, about 8 minutes. (Alternatively, you can blend the ingredients in a food processor until the dough forms a ball.) Wrap the dough in plastic wrap (clingfilm) and let stand at room temperature for 1 hour.

Cut the dough into quarters and dust each with flour. Using a pasta machine or a floured rolling pin, roll each piece of dough into a thin sheet, dusting it with flour if it feels tacky at all. Cut the pasta into the desired shape, tossing it with additional flour to prevent it from sticking.

If not cooking the pasta right away, hang it to dry over a pole such as a clean broom handle. The dried pasta keeps well at room temperature until you're ready to use it.

BLUEBERRY–DULCE DE LECHE GRATINS

PREPARATION TIME: 5 MINUTES
COOKING TIME: 5 MINUTES
SERVES: 8

- 3 cups (445 g) blueberries
- 1 cup (305 g) dulce de leche
- 4 tablespoons chopped hickory nuts or hazelnuts
- Vanilla ice cream, for serving

Preheat the broiler (grill). Divide the blueberries among 8 broiler-proof gratin dishes. Drizzle the dulce de leche over the blueberries, then scatter the hickory nuts over the top. Broil the gratins about 5 inches (13 cm) from the heat until the blueberries have just started to burst and the dulce de leche is melted, about 2 minutes. Serve the gratins warm, with vanilla ice cream.

NEW MEXICO GUEST ESSAY

Freddie J. Bitsoie (Diné/Navajo) is executive chef at Mitsitam Café at the Smithsonian National Museum of the American Indian in Washington, D.C. He is owner of FJBits Concepts, which specializes in Native American foodways.

I am not that crazy about aluminum foil. I fear that metal reaction in my mouth that foil gives when I accidentally chew it, and even just the sound of it tearing drives me crazy.

In the early 1980s, I used to love to spend time with my grandmother, Mary. She only spoke Navajo and I did not speak any Navajo. I was five or six years old and she lived on the Navajo Reservation. My mom used to take me and my brothers and sisters to see her as often as she could. I saw humor in her from a very young age. We may not have communicated very well verbally, but our actions spoke clearly.

She lived on Cajon Mesa just south of Hovenweep National Monument, a very rural area that at the time had no electricity or running water. One cold autumn afternoon my grandmother took a pan out of her wood-burning oven. I cringed as I heard that foil rip. I remember her silhouette removing something from a roasting pan, placing it on the sheet of foil, and wrapping it. (I also noticed a coffee pot steaming away on the woodstove.) She put it in a large paper bag that clearly had been used many times. She rolled the top of the bag and asked me if I wanted to come along with her. I enthusiastically jumped into her pickup and we drove down the unpaved road, all while a wonderful aroma emanated from the rolled paper sack.

We approached a small community with a few dozen homes, a preschool, and a gas station with an attached post office. Across from the gas station stood a home. My grandmother wrapped a silk scarf around her head, got out of the truck, and knocked on the door. She laid a towel on the steps and placed the

steam-filled bag on top. It puffed a bit and when she unrolled the bag, a burst of aroma shot out, making me hungry. She pulled out a can of Shasta soda. She had a thermos of coffee that she poured into a white Styrofoam cup. She pulled out some scallions, a bag of potato chips, and a pickle. Then out came the mysterious foil-wrapped package, with the simple but delicious aroma that had filled the truck as we drove. She unwrapped it. It was a perfectly roasted chicken.

I grabbed a scallion and started to crunch on it. She pulled off a leg and handed it to me. Her other chicken-grease-filmed fingers reached for the miniature Morton's salt shaker. The chicken lay in the middle and the foil was open and all four corners were visible, resembling a flower. She shook the salt above my piece. As the grains fell on the foil, it sang a song to me, a culinary song that I would hear again later in life.

Many years later, in the late '90s, I was living in New Mexico. I was driving with my mother, father, and younger brother and sister to Utah. We had stopped in Shiprock in New Mexico, at a Navajo food stand at the local community open market. I ordered a grilled lamb leg with New Mexico green chile and fry bread. My parents ordered a bowl of mutton and Navajo corn soup with fry bread, and my younger brother and sister each ordered an Indian taco. We sat at the makeshift dining area under a portable canopy. Our food arrived and mine was the only order that came wrapped in foil. I feared that pieces of it would break off into my food and that I'd bite into them.

Unwrapping my food, I tore off a piece of bread and ate it and decided it needed salt. ▶

◄ As I reached for the metal saltshaker, a gust of wind swooped and the grains of salt hit the foil. The song that I'd heard many years before while eating the roast chicken with my grandma came back. The weather was almost the same as the day on the steps of the people I'll never know. I believe this was my true romantic experience of nostalgia.

As a cook, I still don't like many things about aluminum foil. But in order for my memories to have a high-definition quality, I need an element that I don't have in abundance: foil. Hearing many grains of salt hit foil and seeing them dance brings back the most memorable meal I've had. I believe it was the only meal I had alone with my grandmother. Every once in a while, people will witness me sprinkling salt on a sheet of foil. And when they do, they are witnessing my temporary truce with foil only to hear if the culinary song still sounds the same.

Jonathan Perno is from New Mexico and is the executive chef at Los Poblanos Historic Inn & Organic Farm in Albuquerque, New Mexico.

POBLANO STEW

PREPARATION TIME: 25 MINUTES
COOKING TIME: 1 HOUR
SERVES: 8

- 3 tablespoons olive oil
- 1 large onion, diced
- 3 large potatoes, peeled and cubed
- 4–6 medium carrots, cut into coins
- 3 bay leaves
- 2 teaspoons coriander seeds, toasted
- 2 teaspoons cumin seeds, toasted
- 1 teaspoon caraway seeds, toasted
- 2 cups (475 ml) white wine
- 12 poblano peppers, roasted (see page 86 on how to roast chilies), peeled, seeded, and chopped
- 2 quarts (2 liters) vegetable stock

In a large frying pan over medium-high heat, warm the oil. Add the onion, potatoes, and carrots and cook, stirring, until the onion has softened, 10–12 minutes. Add the bay leaves and toasted spices. Deglaze the pan with the wine and reduce by half. Add the poblano peppers and vegetable stock. Bring to a boil and simmer until the flavors have developed and the vegetables are tender, 30–40 minutes. Adjust the seasonings to taste.

NEW MEXICAN GREEN CHILIES

PREPARATION TIME: 30 MINUTES
COOKING TIME: 1 HOUR 15 MINUTES
MAKES: 4 QUARTS (3.8 LITERS)

- ¼ cup (60 ml) olive oil
- 4 medium onions, diced
- 6 cloves garlic, sliced
- 2 cups (475 ml) white wine
- 5 lb (2.3 kg) New Mexico green chilies, roasted, peeled, seeded, stemmed, and chopped (see page 86 on how to roast chilies)
- 2 tablespoons dried oregano
- 1 tablespoon salt
- 20–30 turns of freshly cracked pepper
- 3 bay leaves
- 6 large tomatoes, seeded and diced

In a large soup pot over medium heat, warm the olive oil. Add the onions and garlic and cook until translucent, 12–15 minutes. Deglaze the pot with the wine and cook to reduce by half. Stir in the green chilies, oregano, salt, pepper, and bay leaves. Bring to a boil, then reduce to a simmer and cook for 30 minutes. Stir in the tomatoes and cook for 20 minutes. Adjust the seasoning with salt. Meanwhile, set up a large bowl of ice and water. Transfer the mixture to a medium bowl and let cool in the ice bath. Then pour into zip-seal plastic food bags and freeze. Pull out as you need. The green chiles will last in the freezer up to 6 months.

NEW MEXICAN RED CHILIES

PREPARATION TIME: 35 MINUTES,
    PLUS 20 MINUTES SOAKING
COOKING TIME: 1 HOUR 20 MINUTES
MAKES: 4 QUARTS (3.8 LITERS)

- 2 lb (910 g) dried hot New Mexico red chilies, stemmed and seeded
- 1½ large onions, minced
- 4 cloves garlic, minced
- 3 bay leaves
- 1½ tablespoons dried oregano
- 2 teaspoons unsweetened cocoa powder
- 1 tablespoon salt
- Juice of ½ lemon

Preheat the oven to 350°F (180°C/Gas Mark 4).

Rinse the chilies. Drain and place on a rimmed baking sheet. Roast the pods until slightly toasted, about 20 minutes. Transfer to a large bowl, add water to cover, and soak for 20 minutes. Reserving the soaking liquid, drain the chilies. Working in batches, purée in a blender until smooth, adding soaking liquid as needed. Strain into a large soup pot, pressing all the liquid out of the chili pulp. Transfer the pulp to another bowl. Continue this process until all the pods have been blended. Heat the same pot over medium-high heat. Place the pulp back in the blender with a little of the soaking liquid purée and strain that mixture into the soup pot. (Save the pulp in a zip-seal plastic food bag and freeze. This can be added to refried beans or used for marinating meat.)

Stir the onions, garlic, bay leaves, oregano, cocoa, salt, and lemon juice into the pot. Bring to a boil, then simmer for 30–40 minutes. Adjust the seasoning. Meanwhile, set up a large bowl of ice and water. Transfer the mixture to a medium bowl and let cool in the ice bath. Pour into zip-seal plastic food bags and freeze. This will last for up to 6 months.

ARROZ CON POLLO Y CALABACITA INVIERNO

PREPARATION TIME: 35 MINUTES
COOKING TIME: 1 HOUR
SERVES: 4–6

- Olive oil
- 1 whole chicken (4–5 lb/1.8–2.3 kg), cut into 8 pieces
- Salt and freshly ground black pepper
- 1 cup (160 g) finely diced yellow onion
- 2 tablespoons minced garlic
- 4 cups (455 g) peeled cubed hard winter squash
- 4 tablespoons New Mexico chili powder
- 4 cups (800 g) brown rice
- 1 cup (240 ml) dry white wine
- Finely grated zest and juice of 1 lime
- 1 bay leaf
- 2 quarts (2 liters) chicken stock

[A delicious dish of rice with chicken and winter squash.]

Preheat the oven to 325°–350°F (160°–180°C/Gas Mark 3–4).

Cover the bottom of a deep heavy pot or Dutch oven (casserole) with olive oil. Heat until the olive oil begins to smoke. Season the chicken liberally with salt and pepper. Sear the chicken until golden on all sides. Set aside. Leaving the fat in the pan, add the onion and garlic and cook until softened but not browned. Add the squash and chili powder and stir until aromatic. Stir in the rice, making sure to coat it with the fat. Add the wine, lime zest and juice, and bay leaf and reduce for 1 minute. Add the stock and chicken pieces in 1 layer. Add salt to taste. Cover with a lid, bring to a boil, and transfer to the oven. Bake until the rice is tender and the chicken is cooked through, about 45 minutes.

Remove from the oven and let rest for 10 minutes before serving. Check the seasoning and adjust to taste.

Adam Gopnik is the author of several books, including *The Table Comes First*. He is a staff writer for the *New Yorker.*

Here is a gastronomical-heretical thought: Only small towns are true terroirs, only stagnant rural places truly deep reservoirs of unchanging tastes. Really interesting places to eat are all crossroads, intersections of many roads—market towns, before they are deep ingrown terroirs. So when I think about the food of New York state or city, or the many smaller subsidiary cities that fill it, I try to think crosswise, and what I taste are trips and sensory worlds in motion. This makes me recall a short trip I made in New York City not too long ago.

On that recent Friday I treated myself to a detour from the subway downtown to steal inside and eat my single favorite of all New York dishes, at my single favorite of all Manhattan restaurants: an oyster pan roast at the Oyster Bar in Grand Central Terminal, a dish that I have eaten at the counter there regularly for thirty-five years. A simple thing on the surface—oysters, heavy cream, toast, Worcestershire sauce, a little hot sauce—it is one of the great city dishes inasmuch as it travels across both space and time. A final lingering echo of the now forbidden cooking of the 19th century—all that cream! all that bread!—It is also a perfect expression of a remarkably unchanging place, our own.

For the oysters, the right ones are usually the delicious bluepoints of Long Island, about which true oyster lovers (of which I wish I could count myself one but can't quite, loving them all equally) can be very sniffy. Bluepoints have become an overly generic catch-shell for any local oyster, and in any case, have been rendered bland and fat by time and over-cultivation, the Wonder Bread of the oyster universe. But this lover of the

pan roast delights in them exactly because this most New York of dishes, like all great dishes, depends on contradiction—in this case between the sweet simplicity of the oysters and the heat and fat (and foundational starch) of the soup around them. It arrives on your palate with a shock of delight, the briny secret of a summer voyage and the rich abundance of the local Manhattan style, which, in every era, does tend to press inexorably toward luxury. (Even French food, in its Manhattan adaptations, used to turn to even more butter and cream and Pernod than the French allowed, blurring the space between rustic and city cuisine into one smear of "Gallic" richness.)

Oysters more refined in flavor would be less delightful in stew. When I eat oysters in that beautiful below-ground (not underground) space, I think of the countless intersections not only of city and country, but also of kinds and peoples: the basket-woven tile all around me made by the legendary Guastavino brothers, Basque artisans with a New York legacy. When I taste my pan roast, not only do I taste bounty that just a short time before was locked deep in salt water, bivalve mouth shut tight around its treasures, but I also taste a piece of history. I think I can taste something of the old 19th century cooking, the terrapin soups, and canvasback ducks with cherries that one sees listed on banquet menus from Delmonico's and the original Luchow's. They too partook of the same marriage of wild and rich—of elements that, even when they're cultivated, can never quite be industrialized, and are at their best when they're brought into beautiful dialogue with the perpetual overabundance of the local larder. Wild things in cream—it isn't a bad formula for city life.

And then I'm back on the subway and one short stop on the Lexington Avenue Express took me to my original destination—to 14th Street, and our local miracle, the Greenmarket in Union Square, where the same basic ritual of city and country is played out, with its ongoing connection to outlying farms and farmers of the "hinterland," with the incomparably dense and diverse population of the city. Green (and brown and eggplant-purple) arriving in gray and white Manhattan, and with it the intersection of two cultures, slow and fast, hypercompetitive consumers and permanently watchful producers. For there is as much pleasure to be had from looking as from tasting: the farmers taking a break on the backs of the trucks parked in a square around them, watching evenly but (can it be?) just a little mockingly at the crowds of foodies competing for the sweet winter spinach, or offering competitive recipes for the suddenly fashionable ramp risotto.

Meanwhile, the statue of Abraham Lincoln looks out warily toward Cooper Union, where one speech made him President of the United States. It was as though he was considering what an all-American union might mean. One can imagine as much, at such intersections and crossings, and collisions of city and country, space and time, oysters and cream, unions of varied makers and eaters, circles magically squared by appetite. This is the true terroir that our town and state and country constructed.

Melissa Clark is a staff reporter for the *New York Times* Food section, has written dozens of cookbooks, and received countless honors. She lives in her native Brooklyn, New York.

RAW KALE SALAD
WITH ANCHOVY-DATE DRESSING

PREPARATION TIME: 20 MINUTES
SERVES: 6

- 6–8 large Medjool dates, pitted, smashed, and finely chopped
- 6 anchovy fillets, finely chopped
- 3 cloves garlic, finely chopped
- Finely grated zest of 2 oranges
- Finely grated zest of 2 lemons
- ½ cup (120 ml) extra-virgin olive oil
- 1 tablespoon plus 1 teaspoon red wine vinegar, more to taste
- 2 large or 3 small bunches Tuscan kale (cavolo nero), ribs removed (or substitute red Russian kale)
- Coarse sea salt (optional)

[A few years ago I made a raw kale salad, a recipe I adapted from Franny's restaurant in Brooklyn and subsequently published in my column in the *New York Times*. Filled with tangy pecorino, loads of pungent garlic, and salty crisp breadcrumbs, it became one of my favorite things to eat—and I ate it as often as I could.

Kale salad is ideal for entertaining. I could make it a few hours in advance and it would hold up during the whole party, wilting a little but getting even tastier as it sat. One day, while I was making a date-citrus-anchovy dressing to toss with arugula for a friend's party, I got the idea to use kale instead. The slightly sticky, pungent date dressing was delicious, but it always wilted the arugula minutes after being dressed. Kale, however, would stand up to the dressing.

It worked beautifully, with the sweetness of the dates and salty, funky tang of the anchovies mitigating the assertive, green flavor of the kale. The salad was wonderful from the moment it graced the table, and then proceeded to get better as the evening wore on, softening, deepening, and becoming even interesting and complex with the passing hours—the perfect guest at any party.]

In a medium bowl, stir together the dates (use more dates if you like a sweeter salad, and fewer if you prefer a less sweet salad), anchovies, garlic, orange zest, and lemon zest. Stir in the olive oil and vinegar.

Wash and dry the kale leaves. Stack the leaves and slice them thinly crosswise. Transfer the greens to a large salad bowl. Add the vinaigrette and toss gently to combine. Add salt and more vinegar if needed.

CLASSIC CHICKEN PARM

PREPARATION TIME: 20 MINUTES
COOKING TIME: 50 MINUTES
SERVES: 6

- 2 lb (910 g) boneless, skinless chicken thighs
- ½ cup (65 g) all-purpose (plain) flour
- 3 large eggs, lightly beaten
- 2 cups (225 g) dried breadcrumbs, as needed
- 1 teaspoon dried oregano
- Kosher (coarse) salt and freshly ground black pepper
- Olive oil, for frying
- 5 cups (1.2 liters) marinara sauce
- ¾ cup (70 g) finely grated Parmesan cheese, preferably Parmigiano-Reggiano
- 10 oz (285 g) fresh mozzarella cheese, torn into bite-size pieces

Preheat the oven to 400°F (200°C/Gas Mark 6).

Place the chicken between two pieces of parchment or plastic wrap (clingfilm). Using a kitchen mallet or rolling pin, pound the meat to an even ¼-inch (6 mm) thickness.

Set up a dredging station: In three separate wide, shallow bowls, place the flour, eggs, and breadcrumbs. Stir the oregano into the flour.

Season the chicken generously with salt and pepper. Dip each piece in the flour-oregano mixture, then the eggs, then coat with breadcrumbs.

Pour ½ inch (1.25 cm) oil into a large frying pan and heat over medium-high heat. Working in batches, fry the chicken, turning halfway through, until golden brown, about 10 minutes. Transfer to a plate lined with paper towels.

Spoon a thin layer of marinara sauce over the bottom of a 9 x 13-inch (23 x 33 cm) baking pan. Sprinkle one-third of the Parmesan over the sauce. Place half of the fried meat over the Parmesan and top with half of the mozzarella pieces. Cover with half of the remaining sauce and repeat the layering, ending with a final layer of sauce and Parmesan.

Transfer the pan to the oven and bake until the cheese is golden and the casserole is bubbling, about 40 minutes. Let cool a few minutes before serving.

Rachel Wharton grew up in North Carolina and is a James Beard Award–winning food writer.

It may be sacrilege to some, but it is never North Carolina barbecue that I crave after too many nights away from the Old North State, even though I love it. It's our seafood. Not a specific species (I have universal affection for our small brown shrimp, bay scallops, flat-faced flounders, and mild-mannered oysters), but a specific technique: They must be fried in the style of Calabash.

I imagine I am not the only one. When I was growing up in Raleigh, "Calabash-style" was a billboard-worthy enticement throughout many South Atlantic states, a draw at restaurants hundreds of miles from any salt water. This "style" is a laughably straightforward one: a dredge of cornmeal or flour, very fresh seafood, and hot oil—originally lard, then peanut (groundnut) oil, now often soybean—and little else. Though some cooks do deviate into the exotic (for North Carolina). This means self-rising flour, salt and pepper, and evaporated milk; or maybe an egg dip, if you're frying shrimp or oysters.

But I know Calabash is really a place, albeit a little one. It's a Brunswick County fishing community of about 1,700 along the Calabash River, named after the bottle-shaped African gourd. (I've heard three theories as to why, one being that the waterway looks like the squash, another that they were once grown there, the third that the fruits were once dried and hung from local wells.) Many wrongly associate Calabash with South Carolina, as the town abuts the states' border and is little more than thirty minutes from Myrtle Beach.

Calabash is less than four square miles, and closer to three, if you limit yourself to dry land. The business end of things used to be (and

happily still is) a handful of Christmas stores like St. Nick Nacks and a clutter of seafood restaurants on River Road—a sandy, sort-of cul de sac lined with scrub oaks that ends at the river. It's home to places like the Calabash Seafood Hut, with a simple takeout window that appeals to me now as an adult, with its "we do only one thing, and we do it well" aesthetic. It is an homage to the first Calabash fish camps of the 1930s, where tables laden with steamed and roasted oysters became a draw for those visiting the county.

As a kid, though, I was more impressed with the "fancier" places like Ella's of Calabash, Dockside Seafood House, or Captain Nance's Seafood, all opened in the 1950s. In the 1990s, the Dockside's matriarch still lived in a house hidden in the shrubbery just off the parking lot, where she could watch the crowds and Calabash's small fleet of bobbing shrimp trawlers, with shrimp available to buy right there.

The Dockside, like the rest, had everything a grade-schooler could want in a seafood restaurant, like wooden ship's wheels, netting laced with starfish, whole baked potatoes wrapped in foil, and an iceberg lettuce salad with bright orange French dressing and Captain's Wafers from the Charlotte cracker company Lance. And that's all before the tidal wave of seafood, because a hallmark of the Calabash style has always been its quantity. A typical combo platter would consist of a mountain of small shrimp, foot-long slabs of whiting, a fistful of fat oysters, and a deviled crab, its belly bulging with seasoned breadcrumbs. The latter was served always with North Carolina's vinegar-heavy coleslaw—the best there is—and hush puppies sweet with milk and onion.

Sadly, Calabash is a long drive from my hometown, especially in the summer. Luckily, at Raleigh's state-run farmers' market, where seafood is shipped two hours up the interstate from the coast, a whole wing exists just for N.C. Seafood, a Calabash-style restaurant that uses only fresh Carolina catch.

When I worked close enough, I'd speed there on my lunch break, my eyes always bigger than my stomach. I'd get shrimp and oysters piled high on subdivided Styrofoam over steak fries, coleslaw, and hush puppies. (These are best with honey-butter that's even better dappled with a dribble of Texas Pete, which is a home-grown product.) Then I'd rush back to my cubicle, where I'd try to hide my fried seafood smell and the *parfum de* fry oil wafting up from the leftovers I'd stashed in a drawer.

Since those days, I have had fried seafood Cajun-spiced, tempura-battered, paprika-dredged, Sriracha-mayoed, and so on. But I still fall for the simplicity of Calabash, simplicity, after all, being the culinary hallmark of my state. Consider our Dixie White butter beans and crowder peas, our Champion collards, our pimiento cheese and pork chop sandwiches, our biscuits with bright pink sausage links or country-style steak, or even our pulled pork, with its minor shifts in marinade as you move west across the state. At their best, they're no more than a handful of excellent ingredients left to speak for themselves, just like the shrimp in Calabash. When good things are battered with heart and fried with integrity, after all, what more do you need?

Ashley Christensen is chef-owner of Poole's Diner, Beasley's Chicken + Honey, Chuck's, Fox Liquor Bar, Death & Taxes, and Bridge Club—in Raleigh, North Carolina. She won the James Beard Award for Best Chef: Southeast and is author of *Poole's*.

BANYULS VINAIGRETTE

PREPARATION TIME: 20 MINUTES
MAKES: 1⅓ CUPS (315 ML)

- 1 tablespoon minced shallot
- ⅓ cup (80 ml) Banyuls vinegar
- 1½ teaspoons Dijon mustard
- 1½ teaspoons honey
- Sea salt
- 1 cup (240 ml) neutral vegetable oil

In a bowl, cover the shallots with the vinegar. Let marinate for 15 minutes.

Whisk the mustard, honey, and a pinch of salt into the shallot and vinegar mixture. Slowly drizzle in the oil in a thin, steady stream, aiming it at the side of the bowl so it is taken up into the current of the vinegar whirlpool. Whisk constantly until all the oil is added. Taste for salt and season to your preference. Store the vinaigrette in a lidded container with a lid in the refrigerator for up to 2 weeks.

SWEET POTATOES WITH ROASTED POBLANOS AND CHÈVRE

PREPARATION TIME: 30 MINUTES,
  PLUS COOLING TIME
COOKING TIME: 1 HOUR 20 MINUTES
SERVES: 6–8

- 6 medium sweet potatoes (about 10 oz/ 285 g each), well washed and dried
- 2 poblano peppers (about 4 oz/115 g each)
- Sea salt
- Vegetable oil
- 1 medium red onion
- ¾ cup (180 ml) Banyuls Vinaigrette (page 638)
- Freshly cracked black pepper
- 4 oz (115 g) chèvre

Preheat a convection (fan-assisted) oven to 350°F (180°C/Gas Mark 4) or a regular oven to 375°F (190°C/Gas Mark 5). Line a baking sheet with foil.

Using a fork, poke each potato 10 times, evenly distributed. Place the potatoes on the baking sheet and bake until fork-tender, 50–60 minutes. Let cool for 20 minutes and then, using your hands, carefully peel the potatoes, keeping the potatoes whole.

Meanwhile, place the peppers directly over a high gas flame. Using metal tongs to safely rotate the peppers, char the entire surface of each pepper. My final step in this process is to balance the pepper on its curvy stem end on the grate of the burner to char that part. This ensures the best yield. (If you don't have a gas stove, roast the peppers under the broiler [grill] set on high, rotating them with metal tongs so they char evenly.)

Transfer the roasted peppers to a metal bowl and cover tightly with plastic wrap (clingfilm). Let sit for 15 minutes. Use a kitchen towel to gently rub off the skins of the peppers; don't run them under water as this will wash away some of the flavor. It's careful work, but it's worth it. Next, tear the peppers in half and remove the stems and seeds. Cut the peppers into ¼-inch (6 mm) squares. Place the peppers in a bowl, season with ¼ teaspoon sea salt, and set aside.

Place a cast-iron skillet over medium-high heat and use a paper towel to rub the interior of the pan with a fine layer of vegetable oil. Slice the red onion across the equator into slabs ½ inch (1.25 cm) thick. Season the face of each slab generously with sea salt and place the seasoned side down in the preheated skillet. Cook until the face of each onion slab is charred, 5–6 minutes. Remove the onion slabs from the pan and let them rest with the charred side up. Once they cool to room temperature, slice each slab from top to bottom and then from left to right (imagine a tic-tac-toe grid) into ¼-inch (6 mm) squares. Add to the bowl of roasted poblanos along with ¼ cup (60 ml) of the vinaigrette and thoroughly mix together.

Slice the sweet potatoes into coins ¾ inch (2 cm) thick and lay flat on a serving dish. Season the face of the potatoes with sea salt and freshly cracked pepper. Scatter the poblano and onion mixture over the sweet potatoes, covering as much of the surface as you can. Crumble the chèvre over the top. Drizzle the remaining ½ cup (120 ml) vinaigrette evenly over the surface of the dish and serve.

STEWED TOMATOES

PREPARATION TIME: 15 MINUTES,
   PLUS COOLING AND STANDING TIME
COOKING TIME: 30 MINUTES
SERVES: 12 AS A SIDE DISH

- 5 lb (2.3 kg) Roma (plum) tomatoes
  (about 20 medium)
- Sea salt
- 8 sprigs fresh thyme
- 1 bay leaf
- 2 cloves garlic, peeled but whole
- 2 teaspoons black peppercorns
- 2 tablespoons neutral vegetable oil
- 1½ lb (680 g) yellow onions (about
  2 large), minced

Fill a large pot three-fourths full with water and bring to a boil. While the water is coming up, core the tomatoes and, using a sharp knife, carve a shallow X on the bottom of each, doing your best to cut just the skin and not into the flesh.

Set up a large bowl of ice and water and place it within easy reach of the stove. Working in batches, place the tomatoes into the boiling water and cook until the cut skin at the bottom of the tomato begins to stretch and peel away, 45–90 seconds. As this happens, transfer the tomatoes one by one to the ice bath. Once the tomatoes are cool, peel them and set in a colander in the sink to drain off any excess liquid. Cut the tomatoes into ¾-inch (2 cm) cubes, then place them in a large bowl with 2 teaspoons salt and stir with your hands to combine. Let sit for 20 minutes to let the tomatoes bleed their juices.

Meanwhile, cut a medium square of cheesecloth. Place the thyme, bay leaf, garlic, and peppercorns in the center and tie into a bundle.

In a large heavy-bottomed pot, heat the oil over medium heat until it shimmers. Add the onions and cook until they have softened, about 5 minutes. Stir in the tomatoes and their liquid and add the herb bundle. Bring to a simmer and cook until the liquid has mostly evaporated, about 25 minutes. Taste and adjust the seasoning to your liking. Remove and discard the herb bundle and serve. The stewed tomatoes will keep for up to 1 week in the refrigerator or 3 months in the freezer.

CHARRED OKRA AND STEWED TOMATOES

PREPARATION TIME: 10 MINUTES
COOKING TIME: 15 MINUTES
SERVES: 6–8

- Neutral vegetable oil
- 1 lb (455 g) okra, cut into coins ½ inch (1.25 cm) thick
- Sea salt
- 4 cups (1 kg) Stewed Tomatoes (page 641)
- 2 tablespoons (30 g) unsalted butter, cut into cubes
- Freshly ground black pepper (optional)

Line a plate with a paper towel. Use a paper towel and tongs to wipe the surface of a cast-iron skillet with a thin layer of neutral vegetable oil. Heat over high heat for 5 minutes. When the skillet is very hot, add the okra. Let it sear undisturbed for 2 minutes, then stir for 1 minute more to char evenly. Transfer to the paper towel and season with salt.

In a saucepan, bring the stewed tomatoes to a simmer over medium heat. Fold in the okra. Add the butter, remove from the heat, and stir until the butter is completely melted. Season to taste with additional salt and with pepper if desired.

BUTTERMILK FRIED CHICKEN
WITH HOT HONEY

PREPARATION TIME: 20 MINUTES,
   PLUS 8 HOURS BRINING
COOKING TIME: 30 MINUTES
SERVES: 4

For the chicken:
- Kosher (coarse) salt
- 3 tablespoons sugar
- 1 whole chicken, cut into 8 pieces
  (see Note)
- Neutral vegetable oil, for deep-frying
- 4 cups (520 g) all-purpose (plain) flour
- 4 cups (1 liter) whole buttermilk

For the hot honey:
- ½ cup (170 g) honey
- 1 clove garlic, peeled and smashed
- 5 small sprigs fresh thyme
- 1 sprig fresh rosemary
- 3 dried pequín or árbol chilies
- 1 tablespoon (15 g) unsalted butter

Note:
   Cut the chicken into 2 drumsticks,
   2 thighs, and 2 breasts cut in half.

For the chicken: In a large pot, combine 6 tablespoons salt, the sugar, and 4 cups (1 liter) water and stir until the salt and sugar dissolve. Add another 4 cups (1 liter) cold water. Add the chicken pieces. Cover and refrigerate for at least 8 hours and up to 12 hours. Remove the chicken from the brine, discard the brine, and pat the chicken pieces dry.

Pour oil to come halfway up the sides of a large cast-iron skillet and heat to 325°F (163°C).

Meanwhile, put the flour and 1 teaspoon salt in a paper bag, fold closed, and shake to combine. Fill a large bowl with the buttermilk. Line a baking sheet with paper towels.

One by one, dip the chicken pieces in the buttermilk, lift to drain the excess back into the bowl, then place in the paper bag with the flour mixture. When all the chicken is in the bag, fold the bag closed and shake for about 30 seconds to coat the chicken thoroughly with the flour mixture.

Lift the chicken pieces from the bag and shake off the excess flour. Add the pieces to the skillet, making sure not to crowd the pan and adjusting the heat of the oil as necessary to maintain 325°F (163°C). Fry the pieces, turning once, until done 155°F (68°C) on the interior for white meat, 165°F (74°C) on the interior for dark meat), about 9 minutes for wings and drumsticks, 11–12 minutes for thighs and breasts. Transfer the chicken to the lined baking sheet and let rest for at least 10 minutes.

Meanwhile, for the hot honey: In a small saucepan, warm the honey, garlic, thyme, rosemary, and chilies over low heat for 5 minutes; the honey will begin to foam slightly. Remove from the heat and add the butter, gently swirling until it's completely melted.

Arrange the chicken on a platter and spoon some hot honey and herbs over the chicken. The remaining honey can be served at the table.

OYSTER STEW WITH TWICE-FRIED SALTINES AND CHARRED TURNIP RELISH

PREPARATION TIME: 25 MINUTES
COOKING TIME: 45 MINUTES
SERVES: 8

For the charred turnip relish:
- 1 tablespoon neutral vegetable oil
- 4 oz (115 g) turnip greens
- Sea salt
- 1 tablespoon minced shallot
- Finely grated zest of ½ lemon
- ¾ cup (180 ml) extra-virgin olive oil

For the oyster stew:
- 3 cups (745 g) shucked oysters (about 30 oysters) and their liquor
- 2 tablespoons neutral vegetable oil
- 2 cups (230 g) thinly sliced yellow onion (about 1 medium)
- 2 cups (175 g) thinly sliced fennel (about 1 bulb)
- 2 cups (200 g) diced turnips (about 2 small)
- 2 cloves garlic, peeled and smashed
- 8 medium sprigs fresh thyme
- 1 bay leaf
- 2 teaspoons black peppercorns
- 1 tablespoon sea salt
- 1 cup (240 ml) white wine
- 1 cup (240 ml) dry vermouth
- 6 cups (1.4 liters) heavy (whipping) cream
- 1 cup (240 ml) Dijon mustard

For the twice-fried saltines:
- Neutral vegetable oil, for frying
- 1 sleeve saltines

For the charred turnip relish: In a large cast-iron skillet, heat the oil over medium heat. Add the greens and cook, flipping the leaves occasionally, until they have a nice sear on them, about 3 minutes. Season with salt and transfer to a cutting board or baking sheet to cool. Once cool, finely chop the greens and place in a medium bowl. Fold in the shallot and lemon zest, then mix in the olive oil. Refrigerate until ready to use.

For the oyster stew: Place the oysters in a fine-mesh sieve set over a bowl and drain well. Reserve the oyster juices.

In a large soup pot or Dutch oven (casserole), heat the oil over medium heat until shimmering. Add the onion, fennel, turnips, and garlic. Reduce the heat and sweat until tender, about 8 minutes. Meanwhile, cut a medium square of cheesecloth. Place the thyme, bay leaf, and peppercorns in the center and tie into a bundle. Add the bundle and the salt to the pan and stir until you can smell the herbs.

Add the white wine and vermouth and bring to a boil. Reduce to a simmer and cook until the liquid is reduced by half, about 12 minutes. Add 1 cup of the drained oysters, the juices that were collected in the bowl, the cream, and mustard. Bring to a simmer and cook for 10 minutes. Discard the herb bundle.

Meanwhile, for the saltines: Line a plate with paper towels. Pour ½ inch (1.25 cm) oil into a frying pan and heat over high heat to 325°F (163°C). Working in batches of 6, add the saltines to the oil and fry, turning frequently, until tanned, 1–2 minutes. Transfer to the plate and reserve.

Using a hand blender or food processor, purée the stew mixture until smooth. Strain through a fine-mesh sieve and return the liquid to the pot. (You can prepare the stew to this point up to 1 day ahead.) Place over medium heat, stir in the remaining drained oysters, and cook for 1–2 just minutes to warm the oysters. Ladle into bowls and serve with the twice-fried saltines broken up over the top and a dollop of relish.

Laura Shunk is a food writer and editor whose work has appeared in *Denver Westword*, the *Village Voice*, and Food52. She spent her childhood summers in North Dakota.

When I was a kid, summer didn't start until my mom would open the sliding door of her maroon Dodge Caravan and let my brother and me loose upon New Rockford, North Dakota.

For a couple of suburban-dwellers whose after-school hours were filled with supervised activities like piano lessons and soccer practice, New Rockford, population just over one thousand, held a sort of special magic. No adult trailed us here, so we were free to do terrifying things, like watch my five-year-old cousin and throw firecrackers that he would pinch between his tiny thumb and forefinger.

Sometimes we'd see our mom only if we ran into her. But we were also related to a fair number of people in town: grandparents, great-aunts, second cousins, and vaguely distant relatives. We spent days at the community pool, nights on screened-in porches, and were fed by anyone who happened to be setting out a meal.

My grandparents grew up in New Rockford and returned there when they retired. To Grandma Judy, there were no strangers— only friends she hasn't met yet. In my grandma's hometown, everyone seems to live by the creed. Mealtimes spin into massive gatherings, with neighbors dropping by for a quick hello and staying until the wee hours of the morning. Food is potluck style—hot dishes (or casseroles) and dessert bars (dense meditations on brownies or cookies), and every dish with a secret shortcut that includes sour cream, canned soup, or whipped cream.

Breaking bread together is more important than what we actually eat. Perhaps that's why, despite the constant socializing, New Rockford has a hard time sustaining a restaurant: My grandpa holes up with friends at the doughnut shop and golf club, while my grandma frequents the theater cafe, but all real dining is done in people's homes, where you can keep a conversation rolling for hours.

Underlying that fierce sense of community is equally fierce dogged independence and hardiness, a legacy from Scandinavian and German ancestors who learned to brave sub-zero winters that stretch for half the year.

People in North Dakota hunt and fish for their food. They pickle pike caught in a nearby lake as their Swedish ancestors preserved herring, eating it on buttery Club crackers paired with cold beer. The pheasants we ate at Christmas came from hunting trips as memorable for the stories as the game they produced. We finished holiday meals with *lefse*, a Norwegian flatbread rolled with cinnamon sugar that my brother and I learned to griddle and flip using a special stick, before we could even reach the top of the counter. My grandma claims to be allergic to cooking, but still makes and cans her own apple butter from her apple trees every year.

There is evidence of these family traditions on every smorgasbord in New Rockford, at every card table hauled out to keep friends around until late in the night, and in every home refrigerator, next to store-bought condiments. The best food memories of my time in North Dakota tie the legacy of self-sufficiency to communal dining. It reminds me that it's always worth lingering around the dinner table for another story, another laugh, another snack.

Laura Shunk

PICKLING SPICE

PREPARATION TIME: 5 MINUTES
MAKES: ABOUT 6 TABLESPOONS

- 2 bay leaves, crumbled
- 1 cinnamon stick, broken into pieces
- 2 tablespoons coriander seeds
- 2 tablespoons mustard seeds
- 1 tablespoon whole peppercorns (any color)
- 2 teaspoons allspice berries
- 2 whole cloves
- 1 green cardamom pod
- 1 teaspoon crushed chili flakes
- ¼ teaspoon ground ginger
- ¼ teaspoon ground mace

[The crucial pieces of this pickling spice are the bay leaves, mustard seeds, and peppercorns, so even if you have just those three ingredients, your fish should turn out fine. You can adjust the rest of the aromatics to your taste.]

Combine and store at room temperature in an airtight container for up to 6 months.

UNCLE BOB'S PICKLED NORTHERN PIKE

PREPARATION TIME: 15 MINUTES,
  PLUS 10 DAYS BRINING, SOAKING,
  AND PICKLING TIME
COOKING TIME: 5 MINUTES
MAKES: 2 QUARTS (2 LITERS)

For the fish:
- 1 cup (225 g) kosher (coarse) salt
- 2 lb (910 g) northern pike, filleted, skinned, and cut into bite-size pieces
- Distilled white vinegar (enough to cover the fish)

For the pickle:
- 3 cups (710 ml) distilled white vinegar
- 2½ cups (500 g) sugar
- 4 tablespoons Pickling Spice (page 645)
- 1 cup (240 ml) white wine
- 1 cup (115 g) sliced white onions

Note:
  Some food safety experts recommend freezing pike for 48 hours before pickling.

[Northern pike is plentiful in the lake near my grandparents' house, which means pickled pike appears on just about every smorgasbord in the area. My great-uncle pickles the best version I've had and we eat it on Club crackers paired with light beer. Don't worry about boning it, the bones dissolve in the brine.]

For the fish: In a large bowl, dissolve the salt in 1 quart (1 liter) water. Cover the fish, refrigerate, and soak for exactly 2 days. Drain. Do not rinse the fish. In a large nonreactive bowl, cover the fish in vinegar, refrigerate, and soak for 24 hours. Drain. Do not rinse the fish.

For the pickle: In a saucepan, combine the vinegar, sugar, and pickling spice. Warm to dissolve the sugar and then let cool. Add the wine. In a container, layer the onions with the fish and add the pickling liquid to cover. Cover and refrigerate for at least 1 week before eating. Pickles last for several months refrigerated.

PHEASANT TETRAZZINI

PREPARATION TIME: 15 MINUTES
COOKING TIME: 1 HOUR
SERVES: 4

- 2 lb (910 g) bone-in, skin-on pheasant parts (breasts, legs, thighs)
- Salt and freshly ground black pepper
- ¼ cup (60 ml) canola (rapeseed) or coconut oil
- ½ yellow onion, chopped
- 2 cloves garlic, minced
- 7 cups (560 g) mushrooms (such as shiitake or button), trimmed and roughly chopped
- ¾ cup (180 ml) plus 2 tablespoons dry sherry
- 1 bay leaf
- 8 sprigs fresh thyme, leaves picked and chopped
- 1 teaspoon sugar
- Dash of freshly grated nutmeg
- Dash of cayenne pepper
- 1⅓ cups (315 ml) heavy (whipping) cream
- 18 oz (510 g) linguine
- Grated lemon zest and minced fresh
- Parsley, for garnish

Note:
 You can make this dish as a true casserole by removing the pheasant from the bone and cutting it into strips after cooking. Follow the same method through combining the chunks of pheasant with the sauce, but do not add pasta. Then, in a 9 x 13-inch (23 x 33 cm) glass baking dish, add a layer of sauce, the noodles, and then another layer of sauce. Sprinkle the lemon zest and parsley over the top, plus a thin coating of panko breadcrumbs. Cover with foil and bake at 375°F (190°C/Gas Mark 5) for 30 minutes.

[Casseroles and "hot dishes" crowd buffet tables across North Dakota, and they are usually made with cream of mushroom soup from a can. During hunting season, my family uses wild pheasant interchangeably with chicken, from brining and roasting whole birds, to cutting the meat into strips for stir-fry over rice. You could go the other way and substitute chicken for pheasant here.]

Preheat the oven to 450°F (230°C/Gas Mark 8).

Pat the pheasant dry and season generously with salt and pepper. In a large ovenproof sauté pan, heat the oil over medium-high heat until it shimmers. Working in batches so as not to crowd the pan, add the pheasant pieces skin side down and cook, flipping once, until the skin crisps and browns, about 3 minutes per side. Repeat with the remaining pieces.

Return all the browned pheasant pieces to the pan and transfer to the oven. Roast until the juices run clear and the internal temperature reads 155°–165°F (68°–74°C), about 15 minutes, depending on the size of your pieces. Remove and set the cooked poultry aside until cool enough to handle, reserving the juices in the pan. Remove all meat from the skin and bones, and reserve. Discard the skin and bones.

Return the pan to medium-high heat. Add the onion and cook until translucent, 3–5 minutes. Add the garlic and cook until fragrant, about 30 seconds. Add the mushrooms and cook, stirring frequently, until they darken, about 5 minutes. Increase the heat to high and add the sherry, scraping up the browned bits from the bottom of the pan. Add the bay leaf, thyme, sugar, nutmeg, and cayenne. Bring to a boil and reduce the liquid by two-thirds. Add the cream and stir to combine. Let simmer for about 2 minutes to thicken. Taste and season with salt and pepper. Add the pheasant meat to the sauce to warm.

In a large pot of boiling water, cook the pasta to al dente, according to package directions. Reserving some of the cooking water, drain the pasta. Add the pasta to the sauce and add some of the cooking water if the sauce seems dry or needs thinning. Divide evenly among plates and garnish with lemon zest and parsley.

Jeni Britton Bauer founded Jeni's Splendid Ice Creams based in Columbus, Ohio and is a James Beard Award–winning author.

I spent eight years making and selling my ice creams daily at the North Market, a bustling 180-year-old public market just north of downtown Columbus, Ohio. The forty-plus merchants—a cast of characters as unique as the exotic spices, chocolates, and cheeses they sold—provided countless inspiration for new flavors. I used every ingredient in the market, from wines and baked goods to meats and cracklings. It's here that I learned everything I know about seasonality of ingredients from the farmers who came to share their bounty each weekend, as they have for nearly two centuries, handing over berries, basil, or bunches of flowers. I learned that growth is good—that when you can buy one flat of strawberries from a farmer, that's "nice," but when you grow to the point where you can buy an entire field, that's "game-changing." I learned how to build and nurture a community of growers and makers. In truth, I learned how to do everything I do today from the people at the North Market.

Even today, during off hours, I walk within the walls of this wonderful old building, studying the offerings of every merchant. And I make discoveries, rediscoveries, and never go an hour without inspiration. The market is my church, you could say.

Ohio's food culture is practically defined by our public markets. At the center of each of our major cities—Cleveland, Columbus, and Cincinnati—is a very old public market. The iconic West Side Market in Cleveland is where Eastern European foods tell stories of the city's immigrant history, while the Findlay Market points to Cincinnati's Southern influences. And the North Market reflects the diversity of our city with its Palestinian, Indian, and Italian prepared foods and so much more. Each market not only mirrors the varied food history of its city, but the fact that Ohio is at the crossroads of at least three distinct food and cultural regions in America: the Midwest, the North and Northeast, and the South.

These historic markets are perhaps the greatest reflection of the breadth of Ohio food culture, and one that so many people grew up with. The tastes and aromas active in each market are ingrained in our scent memories, and the vibrancy and community at the markets informs our way of life and our deepest food cravings. If you want to know something about Ohio, especially what we eat, start at our public markets.

Michael Anthony grew up in Ohio. He is executive chef of Gramercy Tavern and Untitled in New York. He has been honored by the James Beard Foundation as both Best Chef: New York City and Outstanding Chef.

CHILLED CORN SOUP WITH COCONUT MILK

PREPARATION TIME: 20 MINUTES, PLUS
  CHILLING TIME
COOKING TIME: 40 MINUTES
SERVES: 4 AS A STARTER OR
  2 AS A MAIN COURSE

- 4 tablespoons olive oil, plus more for garnish
- 1 leek, white and pale green parts only, halved lengthwise and sliced crosswise
- 2 cloves garlic, minced
- ½-inch (1.25 cm) piece fresh ginger, minced
- 5 ears of corn, kernels cut from cobs, 3 cobs reserved for corn stock
- Corn Stock (page 650)
- ½ cup (120 ml) coconut milk
- Salt
- ½ avocado, cubed
- ½ cup (75 g) sautéed corn

In a medium saucepan, heat 2 tablespoons of the oil over medium heat. Add the leek, garlic, and ginger and cook until softened but not browned, about 5 minutes. Add the corn, corn stock, coconut milk, and salt to taste and simmer for 10 minutes. Transfer the soup to a blender and process with the remaining 2 tablespoons oil until satiny smooth. Check the seasonings and adjust as necessary. Refrigerate until cold. Serve garnished with the avocado, sautéed corn, and a drizzle of olive oil.

CORN STOCK

PREPARATION TIME: 10 MINUTES
COOKING TIME: 20 MINUTES
MAKES: 3 CUPS (710 ML)

In a medium saucepan, combine the cobs, leek, lemongrass, ginger, garlic, and 3 cups (710 ml) water and simmer for 20 minutes. Stir in salt to taste. Strain the stock. It will keep, covered, for 5 days in the refrigerator or 3 months in the freezer.

- 3 corn cobs, cut into pieces
- 1 leek, white part only, halved lengthwise
- 1 stalk lemongrass, halved
- 3 thin slices fresh ginger
- 1 clove garlic, sliced
- Salt

GRANMAW HARTLE'S POTATO DUMPLINGS

PREPARATION TIME: 25 MINUTES
COOKING TIME: 1 HOUR 10 MINUTES
SERVES: 2

- ¾ lb (340 g) Yukon Gold potatoes, unpeeled
- Olive oil
- Salt and freshly ground black pepper
- 5 cups (1.2 liters) chicken stock
- 2 carrots, diced
- 1 salsify root, peeled and diced
- 1 leek, white and pale green parts only, halved lengthwise and thickly sliced crosswise
- 1 boneless, skinless chicken breast, cut into large cubes
- ½ cup (65 g) all-purpose (plain) flour
- ½ teaspoon baking powder
- 2 tablespoons grated Gruyère cheese
- 1 egg, whisked
- Small handful of roughly chopped fresh dill

Preheat the oven to 375°F (190°C/Gas Mark 5).

Lightly coat the potatoes with oil, sprinkle with salt and pepper, then wrap in foil. Bake until tender, about 45 minutes.

Meanwhile, in a medium saucepan, bring the stock to a boil. Add the carrots and salsify and season with salt and pepper. Simmer until carrots are just tender, about 10 minutes. Add the leek and simmer for a couple of minutes, then add the chicken and poach until just cooked through, about 5 minutes. Remove from the heat. Remove the chicken from the broth and set aside.

Peel the baked potatoes, then pass them through a ricer or food mill into a large bowl. Stir in the flour, baking powder, Gruyère, egg, and salt and pepper to taste. If the mixture is too dry to form a dough, add a couple of drops of water. Turn the dough onto a floured work surface and knead for 1 to 2 minutes, then roll out and fold it onto itself a couple of times to give it a little body. Roll out the dough to a rectangle about ¼ inch (6 mm) thick and cut into rough squares.

Return the broth to a brisk simmer, add the dumplings, and cook until they float, about 3 minutes. Return the poached chicken to the pan and add the dill and salt and pepper to taste. Serve in shallow bowls.

Lucas Dunn is a writer and fishmonger from Oklahoma City. He writes for *Edible Oklahoma City* and *Munch Magazine*.

Thick gray clouds roiled under the sun, leaking light and then passing to make the sky alternate between luminescent and hazy. Partygoers clad in simple button-up shirts and sundresses gathered in a lovely and well-manicured backyard in uptown Oklahoma City. Near an old shed by the wooden picket fence, a man and woman about to be bride and groom stood facing each other, holding hands. The guests watched eagerly, clutching cans of craft beer or plastic cups of box wine, cheeks rosy from the sun and booze, some with gentle and joyful tears arcing down their faces.

A close friend of the couple wore a suit and spoke of the bonds of love and commitment. Dainty drops of rain sprinkled from the sky, but the crowd stood firm, enthralled by the ceremony. The officiant continued his speech, and midsentence a bleak wailing sound cried from above—the ubiquitous Oklahoma tornado siren, a sound we hear when the threat of a very serious storm is near (and also every Saturday at noon sharp, when the city tests the system).

The officiator paused for a moment, a few people in the crowd chuckled, and the service continued. He spoke louder over the howl, and the bride and groom became one. Aside from a wedding, the party was also enjoying a backyard cookout, and no storm would stop it.

Throughout that afternoon, the Klaxon would continue to sound and the rain would shower intermittently, but there was little concern. The grill was on a covered patio, after all, so we were safe to congregate, as a few members of the party who were the designated Grill Masters took turns flipping hamburgers and portobello mushrooms.

Of the few things Oklahoma is famous for, extreme weather is near the top of the list. Every spring, destructive tornadoes and thunderstorms rip through the state. Day to day, it may alternate from hot and muggy, cold and dry, severe winds, to the rare and eerie occasion of a perfectly nice and comfortable afternoon. None of this stops Oklahomans from cooking or eating outside.

As long as it's above fifty degrees, people will be dining or drinking alfresco, even if twenty-mile-per-hour gusts are sweeping down the plains. Barbecue season never ends, whether it's a sweltering summer day or the most bone-chilling winter night.

When I worked at a grocery seafood counter I would often ask my patrons how they planned to cook their fish. My first winter there, I was constantly surprised, when wrapping up their Gulf shrimp or swordfish steaks the common reply was that they would grill it. Regardless of subfreezing temperatures and impending snow or ice storms, it's not uncommon for Okies to want to be outdoors and cooking meat over flame and smoke.

That same hardscrabble DNA made chicken-fried steak—a tough piece of beef that's been tenderized and deep-fried—part of our state meal. Give us a poor piece of meat, and we will make do. Okra, which is as heat and drought tolerant as a vegetable gets, is also part of that meal (after it's been deep-fried, naturally). The summer crop could turn out awful, but there will always be okra in the backyard. No matter what happens with the weather, Okies will survive, even if it's in blatant defiance of a freezing blizzard or a wrath-of-God F5 tornado.

Judy Allen and Valarie Carter
are lifelong Okies and culinarians
who collaborate on the project
The Can Do Kitchen.

FRIED OKRA SALAD

PREPARATION TIME: 15 MINUTES
COOKING TIME: 15 MINUTES
SERVES: 6–8

- Peanut oil, for deep-frying
- 1 lb (455 g) okra, washed and dried well, stem ends removed, cut into ½-inch (1.25 cm) pieces (about 3 cups)
- Salt and freshly ground black pepper
- ½ cup (65 g) all-purpose (plain) flour
- ¼–⅓ cup (60–80 ml) buttermilk
- 1 cup (130 g) stoneground cornmeal
- ⅓ cup (80 ml) red wine vinegar
- 2 heaping tablespoons whole-grain mustard
- 1 cup (240 ml) olive oil or local pecan oil
- 1 cup (180 g) sliced, diced, or chopped tomatoes or whole pear or grape tomatoes
- 2 tablespoons capers
- ¼ cup (40 g) finely diced red onion
- 1 tablespoon chopped fresh oregano or other herbs of your choice
- ½ cup (45 g) feta cheese

Pour 2 inches (5 cm) peanut oil into a large heavy pot or deep-fryer and heat over medium-high heat to 350°F (177°C).

In a large bowl, season the okra well with salt and pepper. Lightly dust with flour to absorb any moisture and toss well. Add enough buttermilk to coat the okra and toss well. Add the cornmeal and toss well to coat.

Working in batches so as not to crowd the pot, fry the breaded okra until golden brown, 12–15 minutes. Drain on a wire rack or on paper towels. Sprinkle with salt. Set aside.

In a bowl or jar with a screwtop lid, combine the vinegar, mustard, olive oil, and a heavy pinch of salt and pepper. Whisk or shake to combine.

In a large bowl, combine the tomatoes, capers, onion, and oregano. Add the fried okra and feta and toss well. Drizzle with the vinaigrette, toss well, and serve.

GRAN JAN'S REFRIGERATOR PICKLES

PREPARATION TIME: 20 MINUTES,
  PLUS DRAINING AND PICKLING TIME
COOKING TIME: 5 MINUTES
MAKES: ABOUT 4 QUARTS (3.9 LITERS)

- A dozen or so small pickling cucumbers
- 1 medium Vidalia or other sweet white onion
- 2 jalapeño peppers
- Kosher (coarse) salt
- 2 cups (400 g) sugar
- 1 quart (1 liter) cider vinegar
- 2 tablespoons soy sauce
- 1–2 teaspoons crushed chili flakes

[These pickles will last for several months if kept refrigerated, or process using standard canning methods to keep them longer at room temperature.]

Line a colander with paper towels. Using a mandoline or sharp knife, very thinly slice the cucumbers, onion, and jalapeños. They should be 1/16–1/8 inch (1.6–3 mm) thick. Transfer the vegetables to the colander, salt liberally, and let sit for at least 30 minutes to allow any liquid to drain off. Rinse well and set aside to drain again.

In a saucepan, heat 2 cups (475 ml) water, the sugar, vinegar, soy sauce, and chili flakes, stirring until the sugar has dissolved. Set aside to cool slightly.

Divide the vegetables among four 1-quart (1 liter) containers (glass canning jars if you're going to process them). Pour the vinegar mixture over them and refrigerate for at least a couple of hours before eating.

BRAISED BEEF RIBS

PREPARATION TIME: 15 MINUTES
COOKING TIME: 3 HOURS 30 MINUTES
SERVES: 4

- 3 tablespoons olive oil, plus more as needed
- 4 lb (1.8 kg) beef short ribs
- Salt and freshly cracked black pepper
- 1 medium white or yellow onion, cut into medium dice
- 4 cloves garlic, chopped
- 1 tablespoon juniper berries
- 2 tablespoons herbes de Provence
- 2 teaspoons black peppercorns
- 1 bottle (750 ml) dry red wine
- 1 quart (1 liter) beef stock
- 3 tablespoons (45 g) butter
- 1 cup (130 g) frozen pearl onions, thawed
- 1 lb (455 g) cremini (chestnut) mushrooms, sliced or quartered

In a 6-quart Dutch oven (casserole), heat the oil over medium-high heat. Season the ribs well with salt and freshly cracked pepper. Working in batches if necessary, add the ribs in a single layer and brown well on both sides. Remove the ribs and set aside.

Reduce the heat to medium and add the onion (if the pan seems dry, add a little olive oil). Cook until almost translucent. Add the garlic, juniper berries, herbs, and peppercorns. Cook for about 1 minute. Return the ribs to the pan. Add the wine, bring to a simmer, and cook for 2–3 minutes. Add the stock and bring to a simmer. Reduce the heat to a bare bubble. Partially cover and cook at a slow, lazy bubble until the ribs are fork-tender, about 3 hours.

Remove the ribs from the braising liquid and set aside. Strain the liquid through a fine-mesh sieve into a bowl (discard the solids). Return the liquid to the pan and cook to reduce it to desired sauce consistency. We like ours the consistency of thin gravy. Return the ribs to the sauce and heat through.

In a frying pan, melt 1 tablespoon (15 g) of the butter. Add the pearl onions and cook until golden brown, about 5 minutes. Remove and set aside. Add the remaining 2 tablespoons (30 g) butter to the pan and heat over medium-high until foamy. Add half of the mushrooms and sauté until golden brown, about 5 minutes. Add the remaining mushrooms and sauté until golden.

Add the pearl onions and mushrooms to the sauce. Season to taste with salt and pepper. Serve immediately or refrigerate and serve within 3 days.

Mike Thelin is co-founder of the food festival Feast Portland. He is a fourth-generation Oregonian.

If you're looking for a regional cuisine in Oregon, you won't find one. At least you won't find a regional cuisine in a traditional sense. Some folks will toss out a recipe for grilled salmon and try to tell you otherwise, but don't believe them. They're wrong.

In Oregon there are no grandma recipes shared for millennia, no universally approved methods of seafood stews made with briny local oysters, nor any special time-tested formulas for Columbia River Chinook salmon chowder. You won't find an ancient method for bread making with Oregon's prized wheat. Sure, native culture goes back far, but European settlers haven't been around too long. And even today, Oregon is big and empty—the size of England with the population of Kuwait. At the end of the trail through the American West, Oregon was the last stop. Oregon never had a gold rush or a gold rush mentality. It's where those who sought a better life landed. It's where America's refugees still land.

What you will find in Oregon is a regional food culture—one that dislikes conformity and is full of contradictions ("Keep Portland Weird"), one so new it rewrites rules every day. That's what you get at the end of the Oregon Trail. The pioneers wouldn't have it any other way.

Need proof? Portland's most famous restaurant is Pok Pok—a place that serves America's most obsessively authentic Thai food. It's owned not by a Southeast Asian immigrant, but by Andy Ricker, a serial traveler from Vermont who became so obsessed with Thai food that he spent every winter in Chiang Mai learning the recipes. When he decided to create a restaurant that looked like the inside

of his head, Pok Pok was born. There's Biwa, a Japanese *izakaya* that would not feel out of place in Roppongi, owned and operated by a studious Jewish kid from Michigan. There's Ben Jacobson of Netarts who, like Lewis and Clark before him, took the business of boiling seawater to make salt and has built an empire from a hobby. There are still farmers who cart vegetables to the back doors of neighborhood restaurants, winemakers who sell bottles of prized Pinot Noir from the trunks of Subarus, and coffee roasters who roast in their basements and deliver by bicycle. This is all normal here, because no one goes to Oregon to live by the rules from which they escaped. Here creativity is currency and ideas still carry the most weight. Oregon is a place that makes it up as it goes. Oregon is a place where bartenders have more social capital than investment bankers. Oregon is the place where the weirdos won.

You will also find a landscape that produces the best ingredients in the world: an ocean teaming with Dungeness crab and albacore tuna, and forests so full of morels and chanterelles that neighbors trade paper sacks of priceless fungi for bushels of carrots and flats of strawberries.

There are native truffles—both black and white, growing around the base of hazelnut trees and Douglas firs. There are blackberries with an unrivaled sweetness and fennel that shoots up wild between sidewalk cracks. There are hops growing in the valleys, and that explains why Portland is home to more breweries than any other city in the world. Pinot Noir vines snake across hillsides, and the weekly Portland Farmers Market in Downtown Portland draws in excess of twenty thousand visitors a week. Here, carrots are as big a draw as a basketball game.

It's also a culture that everyone is in on. Local and seasonal isn't just what a few lauded chefs do in their restaurants. It's what everyone does in their kitchens. Here you might talk beekeeping with your barber, trade tips on backyard chicken keeping with the mailman, and discuss where to find the best chanterelles with the governor-elect. No one will care to debate you on how to make the perfect gumbo. No one cares. That's because rules don't matter in Oregon, because Oregon hasn't been around long enough to have any rules. And even so, Oregonians like to live outside of them.

So when you go to Oregon, look for the stories, love the landscape, taste the berries, and breathe the air. Like the state motto says, "She flies with her own wings."

Naomi Pomeroy, a native Oregonian, cooks produce-forward food at Beast in Portland, Oregon. She won the James Beard Foundation Best Chef: Northwest award and is author of *Taste and Technique*, winner of an International Association of Culinary Professionals award.

CHANTERELLE MUSHROOM AND HAZELNUT VELOUTÉ

PREPARATION TIME: 40 MINUTES
COOKING TIME: 1 HOUR
SERVES: 6

For the velouté:
- 2 tablespoons unsalted butter
- 2 tablespoons olive oil
- 2½ cups (400 g) finely diced yellow onions
- 2 tablespoons thinly sliced garlic (about 8 cloves)
- ½ lb (225 g) chanterelles or other wild mushrooms (weighed after cleaning), sliced
- ½ lb (225 g) button mushrooms (weighed after cleaning), sliced
- 2¼ teaspoons salt
- ½ teaspoon freshly ground black pepper
- ½ cup (120 ml) dry sherry
- ¾ cup (100 g) chopped toasted organic hazelnuts
- 2 cups (475 ml) milk
- ½ cup (120 ml) heavy (whipping) cream

For the hazelnut sauce verte:
- 3 tablespoons toasted hazelnut oil
- 2 tablespoons finely minced fresh parsley
- 1 tablespoon finely minced fresh chives
- 2 teaspoons finely minced fresh tarragon
- 1 tablespoon finely minced shallot
- 1 tablespoon red wine vinegar
- ¼ teaspoon salt
- 2 tablespoons roughly chopped toasted organic hazelnuts

For the velouté: In a Dutch oven (casserole) or large saucepan, melt the butter and olive oil over medium heat. Add the onions and sweat until translucent, 6–7 minutes. Add the garlic and sweat for 2 minutes. Add the mushrooms, salt, and pepper and cook until quite soft and tender, 15–20 minutes. If the mushrooms stick, add a little water. Reduce the heat if the onions and garlic are sticking. Deglaze with the sherry and simmer for 1 minute. Add the chopped hazelnuts.

Add 2½ cups (590 ml) water, the milk, and cream and bring to a simmer over medium-low heat. Cover and cook at a bare simmer over low heat for 20 minutes. (Do not boil or the soup will curdle.) Remove from the heat and let cool enough to handle, 20 minutes. Working in two batches, purée in a high-powered blender (like a Vitamix) on low until just blended, about 30 seconds. Increase the speed and blend until completely smooth, about 1 minute. A good test is to pour some from a wooden spoon: it should run easily down the back of the spoon, but pour in one steady stream. (If you don't have a high-powered blender, use a small ladle to push the soup through a chinois. Add a splash of cold cream or milk as needed to help thin out the soup if necessary, making sure to adjust the seasoning as you thin.)

For the hazelnut sauce verte: Place the oil in a small bowl (about 4 inches/10 cm across). As you chop the parsley, chives, and tarragon, add them immediately to the oil to prevent browning. In a separate bowl, cover the shallot with the vinegar and add the salt.

About 15 minutes prior to serving, mix together the herb/oil mixture and the macerated shallots with their liquid. Immediately before serving, add the chopped hazelnuts (to retain their crunch).

Reheat the soup gently and thin as needed, whisking to prevent any scorching. Ladle the soup into warm bowls. Top with a generous swoop of the hazelnut sauce verte and serve immediately.

UPDATED OYSTERS ROCKEFELLER

PREPARATION TIME: 30 MINUTES,
  PLUS OYSTER SHUCKING TIME
COOKING TIME: 5 MINUTES
SERVES: 8–10

- 3 dozen oysters of your choice
  (large to medium, but avoid small)
- Salt
- 1 bunch spinach, well washed (to yield
  ½ lb/230 g cooked and squeezed)
- 4 oz (115 g) streaky bacon, cut into
  wide lardons
- 1 tablespoon olive oil
- 4 oz (115 g) wild mushrooms, cleaned
  and very finely minced
- 4 oz (115 g) onion, very finely minced
- 2 large cloves garlic, very finely minced
- 1 cup (240 ml) milk
- ¾ cup (180 ml) heavy (whipping) cream
- 2 tablespoons (30 g) butter
- 2 tablespoons all-purpose (plain) flour
- ½ teaspoon freshly ground black pepper
  (12 turns of a mill)
- 2 tablespoons dry sherry
- ⅛ teaspoon freshly grated nutmeg
- 2 dashes of Tabasco sauce
- ½ teaspoon fennel pollen
- 5 tablespoons finely grated pecorino
  romano cheese

For the topping:
- ½ cup (55 g) panko breadcrumbs
- 4 tablespoons grated cheese blend
- 1 small clove garlic mashed with
  ¼ teaspoon salt into a smooth paste
- 4 tablespoons (60 g) butter, softened
- 1 lemon, cut into wedges and seeded

Open the oysters and check for any shell fragments. Discard the top shells. Store the bottom shells and the oyster meat with their liquid separately in the fridge.

Set up a large bowl of ice and water. In a large pot of well-salted boiling water, blanch the spinach until wilted, about 30 seconds. Scoop into the ice bath to cool, then drain and squeeze out all the liquid. Finely chop.

In a frying pan, cook the bacon until the fat is rendered and the bacon is crisp. Drain the bacon on paper towels. Discard the fat or reserve for another use.

In a separate frying pan, heat the oil over medium heat. Add the mushrooms and cook until soft and tender, about 2 minutes. Add the onion and garlic paste and cook for another minute. Add salt to taste if needed. Set the mushroom mixture aside.

In a measuring cup or small bowl, mix together the milk and cream and have at the ready. In a small saucepan, melt the butter over medium-low heat. Add the flour, 1 teaspoon salt, and the pepper and cook until the mixture turns a light golden blond, 2–3 minutes. Whisking constantly, slowly add the sherry, then do the same with the milk/cream mix, allowing no lumps to form. Grate in the nutmeg and allow the béchamel sauce to simmer over low heat for 8 minutes. Add a small splash of milk to thin if needed. Remove from the heat and stir in the Tabasco, fennel pollen, and cheese. Add the cooked mushroom mix and adjust the seasoning.

For the topping: In a bowl, mix together the panko, cheese, and garlic paste with the tips of your fingers until very well blended.

Preheat the broiler (grill) to medium or a convection (fan-assisted) oven to 425°F (220°C/Gas Mark 7).

Pull out 2 feet (60 cm) of foil and crumple it onto a baking sheet to create craters that will hold the bottom shells of the oysters completely level.

To the bottom of each shell, add a layer of chopped spinach, a few lardons of crispy bacon, then one oyster and a little juice. Spoon some of the mushroom béchamel onto each oyster, then top with panko topping and finish with a dot (¼–½ teaspoon) of butter.

Broil for 4–6 minutes depending on the size of the oysters. Feel gently for oyster firmness to check doneness. The crumbs should be golden brown. Serve immediately, with lemon wedges.

Aimee Olexy is a Pennsylvania native and owner-founder of Talula's Garden and Talula's Daily in Philadelphia, as well as Talula's Table in Kennett Square.

If you are looking for mushrooms, follow your nose. You will land near me in southern Chester County, Pennsylvania. Specifically, in my early-rising town of Kennett Square. Any kindergarten student at Greenwood Elementary school will tell you about the smell. Pinch your nose at the bus stop if you see a compost truck. It will only give you a little relief. As a grown-up, you learn to love it. It's a diaphanous reminder of history and invention, of earth and diversity, agriculture and education.

Half of all of the mushrooms cultivated in America come from Kennett Square: population six thousand. Over a million pounds of mushrooms are produced, packaged, and shipped each week. Pennsylvania gets the bragging rights to this terrific industry, which rose not from climate or terroir, but from the ingenuity of two Quakers in 1885.

At the time, two Quaker flower growers were aspiring to do more business. They observed more room for growing in their carnation greenhouse. Beneath the cypress-wood benches, which held colorful carnations, were dark, moist stretches of flat space bringing no profit. They thought of growing mushrooms there. Influence likely came from gardening journals of France, where it was believed that Louis XIV had mushrooms growing near his Palace of Versailles and in caves around Paris.

Into the 1900s, more mushroom entrepreneurs took root in Kennett Square. Large Italian families were employing experienced Mexican immigrant farmworkers. The mycelia and spores were everywhere. Abundant horse manure, compost, and corn cobs from Amish farms and apple orchards were a bonus.

Putting up cool, dark cement blockhouses was inexpensive and comprehensible for family businesses learning from one another.

Mushrooms are on every dinner table in town and in every neighborly "newcomer basket." They are in the mulch and the ice cream. Exotics and wild foraging have organically proliferated. The Kennett Square mushroom festival tallied 100,000 visitors in 2016. The community is now 50 percent Hispanic and is 100 percent growing. Recent health discoveries add to mushroom economics: Naturally low in calories, and rich in B vitamins, selenium, and iron; and when treated with sunlight they have high levels of vitamin D.

I eat and develop recipes every day for this flavor-loaded, healthy, and entirely sustainable ingredient. I live and own a restaurant steps away from the original Quaker crossroads. The mushroom traverses every cooking method and every type of cuisine. Name another food that can do that.

There is no more timeless treat than freshly harvested sherry-glazed mushrooms on toast. As an individual, a mother, and a restaurateur whose mission is promoting seasonal, local, and sustainable eating, I know that the all-season, affordable, delicious Kennett Square Mushroom possesses all the magic.

Greg Vernick is chef-owner of Vernick Food & Drink in Philadelphia. He is a James Beard Foundation winner for Best Chef: Mid-Atlantic and Chef of the Year by the *Philadelphia Inquirer*.

VEAL FLANK AND FARRO BOWL

PREPARATION TIME: 10 MINUTES,
   PLUS OVERNIGHT MARINATING TIME
COOKING TIME: 45 MINUTES
SERVES: 2

For the marinated steaks:
- 3 cloves garlic, thinly sliced
- 1 shallot, thinly sliced
- 1 jalapeno pepper, thinly sliced
- 2 fresh bay leaves
- 4 sprigs fresh thyme
- 2 sprigs fresh rosemary
- Finely grated zest of 1 lemon
- 2 tablespoons soy sauce
- 1 teaspoon fish sauce
- 3 tablespoons Dijon mustard
- 3 tablespoons olive oil
- 2 veal flank steaks

For the farro:
- 2 cups (315 g) farro
- 5 cups (1.2 liters) chicken stock
- 1 tablespoon kosher (coarse) salt
- 1 teaspoon crushed chili flakes
- 1 fresh bay leaf
- 1 teaspoon red wine vinegar
- 1 tablespoon olive oil

For the vinaigrette:
- 1 tablespoon Dijon mustard
- 1 tablespoon fresh lemon juice
- 3½ tablespoons vegetable oil
- 1 teaspoon green Tabasco sauce
- Salt

[Lancaster, Pennsylvania, is home to a large veal-farming community. Many people have misconceptions about veal and don't realize these animals can be some of the most humanely raised. Consider garnishing this bowl with pickles, sliced avocados, poached egg, fresh sprouts, lime wedges, thinly shaved cabbage, or your favorite hot sauce.]

For the marinated steaks: In a bowl, combine the garlic, shallot, jalapeño, herbs, lemon zest, soy sauce, fish sauce, mustard, and oil. Wearing gloves, mash up to combine well. Pour over and under the flank steaks, cover, and marinate in the refrigerator overnight.

For the farro: Preheat the oven to 350°F (180°C/Gas Mark 4). Spread the farro on a rimmed baking sheet and bake until farro is a deep golden brown and smells like popcorn, about 20 minutes, stirring every 5 minutes.

Transfer the farro to a pot and add the stock, salt, chili flakes, and bay leaf. Cook, covered, over low heat (slow to medium bubble) until the farro is tender, about 25 minutes. Drain any excess liquid and transfer the farro to a bowl. While still warm, stir in the vinegar and oil and allow to cool. Taste for seasoning and adjust as necessary.

For the vinaigrette: In a bowl, whisk together the mustard, lemon juice, oil, Tabasco, and salt to taste.

Preheat a gas or charcoal grill (barbecue) to high heat. Make sure the grill rack is properly oiled.

Scrape off any excess marinade from the steaks and lightly season the meat with kosher (coarse) salt. Grill the steaks for 4–5 minutes per side for a nice medium-rare or medium. Let rest be-fore thinly slicing across the grain.

To serve, spoon a mound of the farro into a bowl and drape 4–6 slices of the steak over the farro. Drizzle with some vinaigrette.

HONEY-RUBBED ROAST PORK SANDWICH

PREPARATION TIME: 35 MINUTES,
   PLUS OVERNIGHT MARINATING TIME
COOKING TIME: 5 HOURS
MAKES: 8–10 SANDWICHES

[In a sandwich-loving state, Philadelphia is one of the best sandwich places in the country. Maybe this is because it's traditionally a blue-collar town. When visitors come asking for a cheese steak, I often take them for a roast pork sandwich instead—it's so much better and more satisfying.]

For the roast pork:
- 8 cloves garlic, minced
- 2 shallots, minced
- 1 cup (90 g) freshly grated Parmesan cheese
- 2½ tablespoons kosher (coarse) salt
- 2 teaspoons cayenne pepper
- 2 teaspoons paprika
- 2 tablespoons soy sauce
- 3 tablespoons Tabasco sauce
- 3 sprigs fresh rosemary, leaves picked and lightly chopped
- 4 sprigs fresh thyme, leaves picked
- 4 sprigs fresh parsley, leaves picked and lightly chopped
- 1 cup (335 g) honey
- 4 lb (1.8 kg) boneless pork loin, fat cap on
- 2 onions, thinly sliced

For the broccoli rabe:
- 1 tablespoon olive oil
- 1 teaspoon chopped garlic
- 2 bunches broccoli rabe (rapini), stems and florets, cut into 2-inch (5 cm) pieces
- Pinch of salt
- Pinch of crushed chili flakes (preferably Italian style)
- 1 teaspoon red wine vinegar

For assembling:
- 8–10 Portuguese rolls or kaiser rolls (or baps)
- Baby arugula
- Sliced vine tomatoes
- Sliced avocado
- Salt

For the roast pork: In a bowl, combine the garlic, shallots, Parmesan, salt, cayenne, paprika, soy sauce, Tabasco, herbs, and honey. With gloves on, mash and mix to combine well. Rub the mixture all over the pork loin and transfer to a plastic container. Cover and refrigerate overnight.

Preheat the oven to 300°F (150°C/Gas Mark 2).

Scatter the sliced onions in a roasting pan and place the coated pork over top, fat cap up. Bake uncovered until fork-tender, about 4½ hours. Remove the loin and strain the cooking juices.

Break up the cooked pork in a bowl and mix with the strained juices. Keep warm until ready to assemble sandwiches.

For the broccoli rabe: In a large sauté pan, heat the olive oil over medium heat. Add the garlic and toast until golden brown. Add the broccoli rabe (rapini), salt, and chili flakes and sauté until the stems start to become tender, about 2 minutes. Add the vinegar to the pan, then quickly remove to cool. Cool to room temperate until ready to assemble sandwiches.

For assembling: Split the rolls horizontally. If they are fresh, do not toast. Place a small mound of fresh arugula on the bottom half. Add a pile of the braised pork with as much of the juices as you desire. Top the pork with a few slices of tomato and avocado. Place some broccoli rabe on top. Season with a pinch of salt. Place the top bun on, apply a little pressure, wrap in foil, then slice in half.

Chris Cosentino grew up in Rhode Island, where he clammed and fished. He graduated from Johnson & Wales University and is a chef in California.

My home is Rhode Island, the "biggest little state in the union." It's a place rooted in rich culinary history and brings a unique meeting of cultures, from English to Italian and Portuguese. Rhode Islanders are fiercely loyal—to their state, childhood friends, grandmothers' Sunday gravy recipe. What sticks with me most and makes me feel proud, too, is the shared dedication to keeping Rhode Island's iconic eateries and dishes alive.

It would be nearly impossible to pick one Rhode Island food memory as my favorite to wax poetic about, and it's possible many have never even heard of the Autocrat Coffee Syrup or Del's Frozen Lemonade. My earliest and fondest memories involve coffee milk with school lunch and sheet pans of Caserta pizza, cut into cheesy squares at almost every kid's birthday party. A little sharper are the memories of packing with my friends into our cars to hit Olneyville New York System, a place so special that David Byrne served dogs there while he attended the Rhode Island School of Design. We would order as many gaggers as we could eat, cooked in Narragansett beer and served on steamed buns with chopped onions and plenty of mustard. The dogs were so good you could hear the snap of the casing from the bite your friend took next to you. As I got older, late nights would end at Haven Brothers Diner in downtown Providence, where we filled up on burgers and subs before heading home.

My tastes eventually evolved and I learned to appreciate, more than anything, Rhode Island seafood: a classic lobster boil cooked in the ground, sandy clam cakes on the beach, steamers on the half shell with a cold beer at my grandmother's, a fried belly clam roll from Matunuck Oyster Bar in Narragansett, and fresh scup and flounder. We ate chowder the real Rhode Island way with beer, never cream, and full of the freshest clams. We made stuffies at home with huge quahogs, chopping the clams and cooking them with tons of butter, herbs, garlic, and crumbled Ritz crackers, to serve the mixture straight from the shell if we were having company. One of the first dishes I learned to cook was fresh-caught bluefish on the grill, with red onion and slices of tomato.

Sure, Rhode Island is best known for those summer staples, but even the fall and winter would bring quintessential dishes like my grandmother's homemade johnny cakes made with bacon fat in the morning, *malasadas* at the Portuguese American festival, and *pizza fritta* at the holiday fairs on Columbus Day.

Being from Rhode Island means I'm from the littlest state, but it also means I get to live with the biggest food memories, and that makes me proud.

Champe Speidel is chef-owner of Persimmon Restaurant in Providence, and Persimmon Provisions Butchery and Artisanal Foods in Barrington. He is a six-time semifinalist for the James Beard Foundation Best Chef: Northeast award.

QUAHOG CLAM CHOWDER WITH CHORIZO-CLAM FRITTERS

PREPARATION TIME: 20 MINUTES
COOKING TIME: 40 MINUTES
SERVES: 4

For the chowder:
- 2 teaspoons rendered bacon fat
- ⅓ cup (40 g) chopped celery
- ¼ cup (40 g) chopped shallot
- 8 quahog (hardshell) clams
- 2 fresh bay leaves
- 1 cup (240 ml) Sauvignon Blanc
- 2 tablespoons diced potato
- ½ cup (120 ml) heavy (whipping) cream
- Salt and freshly ground black pepper

For the fritters:
- 1¾ cups (230 g) plus 3 tablespoons all-purpose (plain) flour
- ½ cup (65 g) plus 2 tablespoons stone-ground cornmeal
- 1 teaspoon baking powder
- Salt and freshly ground black pepper
- 2 large eggs
- 1 scant cup (220 ml) milk
- 2 tablespoons minced dried chorizo
- 2 tablespoons minced celery
- 2 tablespoons minced scallions (spring onions)
- 1 tablespoon minced shallot
- 2 tablespoons minced fresh parsley
- 2 tablespoons minced fresh chives
- 2 teaspoons minced fresh tarragon
- Neutral oil, for deep-frying
- Malt vinegar powder

[New England is known for its clam chowders. This is our take on the Rhode Island favorite: chowder and clam cakes. We like to garnish it with petite celery, parsley leaves, and mustard flowers.]

For the chowder: In a soup pot, heat the bacon fat over low heat. Add the celery and shallot and sweat without browning, 5–7 minutes. Add the clams, bay leaves, and white wine, increase the heat, and cover. When the clams begin to open, after several minutes, remove them one by one, reducing the heat to a simmer. Shuck the clams and chop the clam meats into small pieces, removing any sand sacs. Set aside.

Strain the cooking juices and return to the pot. Add the potato and cream and simmer about 15 minutes. Season with salt and pepper. Remove from the heat. Discard the bay leaves and transfer the soup to a blender. Blend on high speed for at least 1 minute. Strain through a fine-mesh sieve and keep warm.

For the fritters: In a bowl, combine the chopped clams, flour, cornmeal, baking powder, ¼ teaspoon salt, pepper to taste, the eggs, milk, chorizo, celery, scallions, shallot, and herbs. Check for proper seasoning. Add more flour if the batter seems too wet and clam juice if the batter seems too dry.

Pour 3 inches (7.5 cm) oil into a large heavy pot or deep-fryer and heat to 375°F (190°C).

Using a small ice cream scoop or 2 spoons dipped in water, make fritters about 1½ inches (4 cm) across. Working in batches, fry until browned on the outside and cooked through, about 4 minutes. If the outside browns too quickly and the inside still raw, lower the oil temperature to 350°F (177°C) and use fresh oil. Remove the fritters from the oil and season with salt and malt vinegar powder. Serve the chowder in bowls with the fritters on the side.

CHARCOAL-GRILLED POINT JUDITH SQUID WITH PETITE VEGETABLE ESCABECHE

PREPARATION TIME: 20 MINUTES
COOKING TIME: 10 MINUTES
SERVES: 4

- ½ lb (225 g) cleaned squid
- 3 petite carrots, shaved
- 3 petite red radishes and 3 French breakfast radishes
- 12 baby Swiss chard and/or kohlrabi leaves
- Salt and freshly ground black pepper
- Extra-virgin olive oil
- ½ cup Escabeche Liquid (recipe follows)
- Fennel shoots, petite cilantro (coriander) leaves and flowers, blue basil buds and flowers, yellow chrysanthemum petals, for garnish

[Rhode Island residents love local squid. This and the recipe on page 664 are two of our favorite ways to prepare it.]

Preheat a charcoal grill (barbecue) to high heat.

Grill the squid until the bodies become an opaque white, about 3 minutes. Slice the bodies into very thin rings and slice the tentacles into pieces. Keep warm.

In a small bowl, combine the squid, carrots, radishes, and Swiss chard leaves. Season the mixture to taste with salt and pepper, olive oil, and a touch of the escabeche liquid without using all of it.

To serve, divide the squid mixture among shallow bowls. Garnish with the herbs, flowers, and fennel shoots. Spoon enough escabeche liquid to create a shallow pool around the squid. Serve warm.

ESCABECHE LIQUID

PREPARATION TIME: 20 MINUTES
COOKING TIME: 5 MINUTES
MAKES: ABOUT 2 CUPS (475 ML)

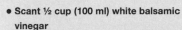

- Scant ½ cup (100 ml) white balsamic vinegar
- Scant ½ cup (100 ml) red wine vinegar
- Scant ½ cup (100 ml) sherry vinegar
- Scant ½ cup (100 ml) rice vinegar
- 1½ tablespoons sugar
- 2½ teaspoons coriander seeds
- 2 fresh bay leaves
- 5 g (¼ oz) fresh basil buds and flowers
- 10 parsley stems
- 1 pinch xanthan gum

In a saucepan, combine the vinegars and sugar and bring to a boil. Skim the surface and add the coriander seeds, bay leaves, basil, and parsley. Cover the pot, remove from the heat, and infuse for about 15 minutes. Strain into a blender and blend on low, adding the xanthan gum slowly and blending for about 45 seconds. Strain through a fine-mesh sieve and chill. Store the unused liquid in the refrigerator for up to 1 month.

SQUID INK MAYONNAISE

PREPARATION TIME: 5 MINUTES
MAKES: A GENEROUS 1 CUP (240 ML)

- 2 egg yolks, at room temperature
- 1 tablespoon miso paste
- ½ teaspoon squid ink
- ½ lemon
- 1 generous cup (250 ml) grapeseed
  or canola (rapeseed) oil
- 1 teaspoon sesame oil
- Salt

In a bowl, whisk together the egg yolks, miso, squid ink, and a squeeze of lemon juice. Whisking constantly, slowly add the grapeseed oil in a steady stream, whisking to form an emulsion. Add the sesame oil and more salt and lemon juice to taste. If the mayonnaise is too thick, add a touch of water to achieve a desired consistency.

FERMENTED BANANA PEPPERS

PREPARATION TIME: 15 MINUTES,
   PLUS 5 DAYS FERMENTING TIME
SERVES: 4

- 3 lb (1.4 kg) banana peppers
- Salt

[This process needs to be started 4 to 5 days ahead of time for the fermentation to occur. As an alternative, you can simply use the fresh peppers, unfermented.]

Slice the peppers into 1-inch (2.5 cm) rings, discarding the seeds. Place the peppers in a nonreactive container and cover with water by 2 inches (5 cm). Pour the water off into a bowl and weigh the water in grams. Multiply the weight of the water by .05 and then measure that weight in salt: This will be a 5 percent salt solution. Dissolve the salt in the water and return the peppers to the liquid. Cover the container with cheesecloth, place in a warm spot and let sit for at least 4 days. Do not allow the peppers to float or they may become moldy, in which case they will need to be discarded. When ready, the peppers should have a nice lactic acid tang to them. Leave them in the brine and transfer to the refrigerator.

CONFIT POINT JUDITH SQUID AND BANANA PEPPERS

PREPARATION TIME: 30 MINUTES
COOKING TIME: 1 HOUR 45 MINUTES
SERVES: 4

For the squid:
- 1 lb (455 g) cleaned squid, bodies cut into rings and tentacles trimmed and quartered
- Olive oil
- 1 lemon, halved across
- 3 fresh bay leaves
- 1 head garlic, halved through the equator
- ½ teaspoon salt

For the crispy banana peppers:
- 1¼ cups (200 g) rice flour
- ¼ cup (35 g) plus 2 tablespoons cornstarch (cornflour)
- ¾ teaspoon baking soda (bicarbonate of soda)
- ¼ teaspoon salt
- 1 liter (1 quart) club soda (soda water) or beer
- Canola (rapeseed) oil, for deep-frying
- Fermented Banana Peppers (page 664)
- Fine sea salt

For assembling:
- Salt
- 1 tablespoon chopped parsley
- Fresh lemon juice
- Squid Ink Mayonnaise (page 664)
- Fresh oregano, for garnish

[This is a take on the Rhode Island classic fried squid and peppers. But we reverse the dish by cooking the squid to a tender consistency via confit and frying the peppers.]

For the squid: Preheat the oven to 250°F (120°C/Gas Mark ½).

Place the cleaned squid in a large ovenproof pot and add enough olive oil to cover by 2 inches (5 cm). Squeeze the lemon lightly to release some juice, then add it and the bay leaves, garlic, and salt. Transfer to the oven and bake, uncovered, for at least 1½ hours. When the squid swells and is tender, remove from the oven and allow to cool in the oil to room temperature. (You can prepare the recipe to this point 1 day ahead. Keep the squid in the cooking liquid in the refrigerator until needed.)

For the crispy banana peppers: In a bowl, thoroughly mix together the flour, cornstarch, baking soda (bicarbonate of soda), and salt. When ready to batter and fry, add enough club soda (soda water) to make a thick, but smooth batter. It should be the consistency of heavy cream.

Pour 3 inches (7.5 cm) oil into a large heavy pot or deep-fryer and heat to 375°F (190°C).

Dip the peppers into the tempura batter to coat. Working in batches, fry until the batter turns crispy and golden brown, about 4 minutes. Season with a touch of fine salt and keep warm.

In a small saucepan, warm the drained confit squid. Season with salt. Add the parsley, lemon juice, and a few tablespoons of the confit oil, for flavor. Toss the fried peppers with the confit squid and arrange nicely on a plate. Add dollops of the squid ink mayonnaise and garnish with fresh oregano.

Matt Lee and Ted Lee, raised in Charleston, write about food, wine, and travel for national publications. They have won six awards from the James Beard Foundation and International Association of Culinary Professionals.

Boiled peanuts, perhaps more than any other snack, inspire intense cultural loyalty in South Carolina, crossing lines of class and race. That may be why we missed them when we moved away from Charleston to colleges in Massachusetts, and it's why, when we began to sell Southern foods by mail order, we used the boiled peanut as the keystone product in our little business, which we named "The Lee Bros. Boiled Peanuts Catalogue." Typically associated with the outdoors, boiled peanuts can be purchased by the roadside, in vacant lots, at gas stations, at the ballpark, and in the fairground parking lot. Serendipity is part of the formula. They are prepared in homes as well but are rarely seen in a restaurant setting.

That is primarily because, besides the inelegant name, the damp boiled peanut presents a few obstacles to universal enjoyment. Not everyone appreciates their distinctive earthy-beany flavor or the clammy wetness on the fingers as one pulls the kernels free from their shells—and they achieve some exclusivity by being challenging in that respect. Be aware that the salty, woody shells must be discarded somehow and are not even fit for compost. Judged on flavor alone, however, with an objective mind-set, boiled peanuts are incomparably divine. (They couldn't be simpler to prepare. Here's the recipe: Boil raw, unshelled peanuts in salty water for a long time.)

And the smell of peanuts boiling is, to us, part of the pleasure of the process. Our late grandmother's late landlady, Elizabeth Jenkins Young, once commented (in her perky Edisto Island accent) that the fragrance of our peanuts boiling on Gran's stove reminded her of a "yam gone rotten." Not that Liz Young didn't like them; she proudly displayed her I BRAKE FOR BOILED PEANUTS bumper sticker in the back window of the blue Volkswagen that she won at the 1983 Spoleto Festival auction. But the earthy quality of the peanut, which grows underground and is full of minerals, and the sweetness of it, does in fact suggest the soul of a sweet potato or yam.

The peanut plant, like the yam—and okra, guinea fowl, sesame, field peas, and many other important foodstuffs—represents a direct connection between South Carolina and West Africa. Slaves are universally credited with introducing the peanut to North America, and the written record shows that they, and their descendants, used the nutritious legume extensively in the pre-Revolutionary period and thereafter, gradually popularizing and mainstreaming peanuts by the early 20th century.

When peanuts are freshly dug, and refrigerated like a fresh vegetable rather than dried, they are called "green" peanuts; and these, when available (the South Carolina harvest begins in the latest summer and runs into the fall), are worth seeking out for their tenderness and subtlety of flavor. Some green peanuts will be slightly immature, and, like a soft-shell crab, may be eaten whole, shell and all.

There's a certain anti-commercial, anti-establishment spirit—an esoteric pride—surrounding the boiled peanut that is hard to articulate. But here's one example: When Act Number 270 was passed in the South Carolina legislature in 2006 declaring boiled peanuts "The State Snack," those of us who love them were more disappointed than elated.

Robert Stehling is chef-owner of the widely acclaimed Hominy Grill in Charleston, South Carolina.

RED RICE

PREPARATION TIME: 20 MINUTES
COOKING TIME: 2 HOURS
SERVES: 8

- 3 slices bacon (streaky), diced
- 1 cup (160 g) cubed ham
- ½ lb (225 g) smoked sausage, sliced
- ¼ lb (115 g) loose Italian sausage
- 3 tablespoons peanut (groundnut) oil, divided
- 2 cups (320 g) diced onions
- 1 cup (100 g) diced celery
- 1 cup (150 g) diced green bell pepper
- 1 cup (150 g) diced red bell pepper
- 1 tablespoon minced garlic
- 1 cup (80 g) peeled and diced eggplant (about ½ small eggplant)
- 2 cups (400 g) long-grain white rice
- 2 cups (200 g) sliced okra
- ½ cup (120 ml) red wine
- 2 cups (475 ml) chicken stock
- 1 can (14.5 oz/410 g) tomato purée (passata) or crushed tomatoes
- 2 bay leaves
- 2½ teaspoons kosher (coarse) salt, plus additional as needed
- ½ teaspoon dried basil
- ½ teaspoon dried thyme
- ½ teaspoon freshly ground black pepper
- Tabasco or similar hot sauce (optional)

[Red rice, also known locally as purloo, is the Lowcountry's rice casserole. A close cousin of jambalaya and paella, its origins reach back to Persian pilafs of almond milk, rice, and dates. This is a dish with endless iterations. You're limited only by your imagination and what's in the refrigerator.]

Preheat the oven to 375°F (190°C/Gas Mark 5).

In a large frying pan, cook the bacon over medium-high heat until browned, stirring occasionally, about 8 minutes. Set the bacon aside and reserve the fat in the pan. Add the ham, smoked sausage, and Italian sausage and cook, stirring occasionally, until the meats are well browned, about 10 minutes. Remove from the pan and set aside.

Add 1 tablespoon of the peanut (groundnut) oil, the onions, celery, and peppers and cook over medium heat, stirring occasionally, until the vegetables are just tender, about 6 minutes. Add the garlic and continue cooking, stirring occasionally, for 2 minutes. Add the eggplant and cook until tender, about 5 minutes. Transfer the vegetables to a 9 x 13-inch (23 x 33 cm) or other similar size baking dish. Spread evenly on the bottom of the dish.

Add 1 tablespoon peanut (groundnut) oil to the frying pan and return to the heat. Add the rice and cook, stirring occasionally, until the rice is fragrant and lightly golden, about 3 minutes. Cover the vegetable mixture with the toasted rice. Lay the reserved meats over the rice.

Return the skillet to medium-high heat. Add the remaining 1 tablespoon peanut (groundnut) oil. Sauté the okra until lightly browned, about 4 minutes. Add the wine and reduce until almost gone. Add the chicken stock, tomato purée (passata or crushed tomatoes), bay leaves, salt, basil, thyme, and pepper and bring to a boil. Pour over the vegetable, rice, and meat mixture.

Cover tightly with foil and bake until the rice is tender, about 1 hour and 15 minutes. Remove the bay leaves and season with additional salt to taste. Serve with Tabasco, if desired.

SWEET POTATO SPOONBREAD

PREPARATION TIME: 20 MINUTES
COOKING TIME: 45 MINUTES
SERVES: 6

- 1½ cups (200 g) cornmeal, preferably stone-ground
- 1 tablespoon sugar
- 1 teaspoon baking soda (bicarbonate of soda)
- ½ teaspoon salt
- 1 tablespoon (15 g) butter
- ¾ cup (245 g) mashed cooked sweet potato
- 1 cup (240 ml) buttermilk
- 2 eggs, separated
- 1 tablespoon honey
- ⅛ teaspoon ground cloves
- ⅛ teaspoon ground cumin
- ⅛ teaspoon ground white pepper
- Pinch of cayenne pepper

[Spoonbread is a light and fluffy soufflé version of cornbread—so light, in fact, that you'll need a spoon to pick it up.]

Preheat the oven to 425°F (220°C/Gas Mark 7). Grease a 2-quart (2-liter) baking dish and dust with cornmeal.

In a medium bowl, sift together the cornmeal, sugar, baking soda (bicarbonate of soda), and salt. Set aside.

In a small saucepan, bring 2 cups (475 ml) water to a boil over high heat. Stir in the butter until melted. Remove from the heat and mix with the dry ingredients. Allow the mixture to cool slightly.

In a large bowl, combine the sweet potato, buttermilk, egg yolks, honey, cloves, cumin, white pepper, and cayenne. Add the cornmeal mixture to the sweet potato mixture and stir until combined. In a bowl, with an electric mixer, beat the egg whites to stiff peaks. Gently fold the egg whites into the cornmeal/sweet potato mixture.

Pour the mixture into the prepared baking dish and bake until gently browned, puffed, and set, 35–40 minutes.

SHRIMP BURGERS

PREPARATION TIME: 35 MINUTES
COOKING TIME: 30 MINUTES
MAKES: 8 BURGERS

- 1 lb (455 g) shrimp (prawns), cooked, peeled, and chopped
- 3 tablespoons diced celery
- 2 tablespoons chopped fresh parsley
- 2 tablespoons thinly sliced scallions (spring onions)
- 1½ tablespoons grated lemon zest
- 3 tablespoons mayonnaise
- 1 cup (75 g) cornbread crumbs
- Salt and freshly ground black pepper
- Tabasco
- 1 egg, beaten
- 2 tablespoons peanut (groundnut) oil, divided
- 8 hamburger rolls
- Lettuce, tomato, and tartar sauce, for serving

[Shrimp are the star of Lowcountry waters. In early spring, the season opens and I can't help ordering more shrimp than we can possibly sell. These burgers are a great way to use extra shrimp.]

In a large bowl, mix the shrimp (prawns) with the celery, parsley, scallions (spring onions), and lemon zest. Stir in the mayonnaise and cornbread crumbs. Season to taste with salt, pepper, and Tabasco. Add the egg and beat with a whisk or wooden spoon until evenly distributed. Form the mixture into 8 patties.

In a 12-inch (30 cm) frying pan or sauté pan, heat 1 tablespoon peanut (groundnut) oil over medium-high heat. Add half the patties and cook until both sides are nicely browned, 3–4 minutes per side. Repeat with the remaining 1 tablespoon oil and patties. Drain on paper towels.

Serve on hamburger rolls with lettuce, tomato, and tartar sauce.

Emily Elsen co-owns Four & Twenty Blackbirds pie shop in New York City with her sister, Melissa Elsen. They were born and raised in the rural farm town of Hecla, South Dakota.

Like so many small-town restaurants in America, the Calico Kitchen, on Main Street in Hecla, South Dakota (population 225), was more than a place to eat. It was the hearth of a rural community in a time and place and will forever remain in the memories of those who knew and loved it. Founded, owned, and operated by our mother, Mary, with her sisters, Susan and Anne, the Calico, as we called it for short, was our second home as children.

It was a playground for our developing culinary minds, our venue for breakfasts of eggs and toast on the weekends, burgers and fries on high school lunch breaks, and after-school hangouts with milkshakes, chips, and pop (the de facto Midwestern term for anything you might call "soda").

If you were a lucky kid like we were, some extra sour cream lemon pudding pie filling from Grandma Liz's weekly pie-baking sessions would be there, too. And yes, her pies were famous. Rhubarb, coconut cream, sour cream raisin, peach, apple, pumpkin— always something right for the season. For us and my siblings and cousins, and many of our friends, it was also the site of our first job (dishwasher), second job (waitress), and third job (cook): and the backbone of our extended family life.

We welcomed the region's farmers during busy and social lunch hours—where you might enjoy a Roast Beef Combo and a side of creamy coleslaw—and the local bowling league for their evening banquets of fried chicken and potato salad. Wild game hunters traveled from afar for the abundant local pheasant - and deer - hunting seasons, and they were served early morning breakfasts of fresh cinnamon or caramel rolls and eggs fried any way they liked, with hash browns and fried onions crisped to perfection. From coffee to the after-church crowd to annual prom banquets to the high school students, the Calico Kitchen defined what a local restaurant should be—a place for community. It was the norm to be surrounded by hardworking women in white aprons simultaneously handling the grill, the oven, or the fryer; washing the dishes; prepping the potatoes; carving the meat; baking the pies; and humbly feeding their customers with food that was not only hearty but heartfelt.

MJ Adams is a chef, culinary consultant, and host of *Savor Dakota* on South Dakota public television.

PEAR AND ZUCCHINI SOUP

PREPARATION TIME: 25 MINUTES
COOKING TIME: 1 HOUR
SERVES: 6

- 2 tablespoons good olive oil
- 1 tablespoon (15 g) butter, plus more for finishing
- 1 small red onion or 3 shallots, cut into medium dice
- 2 stalks celery, peeled and cut into medium dice
- 2 carrots, cut into medium dice
- 6 medium zucchini (courgettes), cut into medium dice
- 2 cups (250 g) sliced leeks, white parts and about 1 inch (2.5 cm) of pale green, cleaned
- 2 medium pears (I like Forelle or Anjou), peeled, cored, and cut into medium dice
- 1 tablespoon chiffonaded fresh sage or finely chopped fresh thyme
- 5 medium potatoes, peeled and cut into medium dice (store in water until ready)
- Salt
- ¼ cup (60 ml) heavy (whipping) cream (optional)
- Homemade croutons, for serving

Note:
Chicken stock or vegetable stock can be substituted for the 5 cups (1.2 liters) water, but I prefer water. The soup tends to have a longer shelf life when made with it.

In a medium pot with a lid, warm the olive oil with 1 tablespoon (15 g) of the butter over medium-heat until sizzling. Add the onions, celery, and carrots and cook until the carrots have browned a little, about 10 minutes. Toss in the zucchini (courgettes) and leeks. Cover and cook until the leeks and zucchini soften and become translucent, about 10 minutes (lower the heat if necessary). Add the pears and sage, cover, and cook, stirring occasionally, for 7 minutes.

Add 5 cups (1.2 liters) cold water (see Note). Drain the potatoes and add to the pot along with 1 tablespoon salt. Cover and simmer until you can mash the vegetables easily with a fork, about 30 minutes.

Purée the soup with a hand blender until smooth. If the soup is too thick, add a little more water to create the desired thickness. Stir in the cream and bring to a simmer. Taste for additional seasoning. Add an extra knob of butter for flavor at the end. Serve in bowls, topped with croutons.

PHEASANT DUMPLINGS WITH LIME DIPPING SAUCE

PREPARATION TIME: 4½ HOURS,
  INCLUDING CHILLING TIME
COOKING TIME: 40 MINUTES
MAKES: 34 DUMPLINGS

- ½ cup (115 g) thinly sliced salt pork
- 2 cups (385 g) thin strips of pheasant breast
- 3 cloves garlic, peeled
- 1 (1-inch/2.5 cm) knob fresh ginger, peeled and halved
- 2 shallots, peeled and halved
- ½ cup (50 g) thinly sliced scallions (spring onions)
- 3 tablespoons sesame oil
- 2 tablespoons mirin
- 3 tablespoons fish sauce
- 1 tablespoon five-spice powder
- ½ teaspoon ground white pepper
- 1 (12-oz/340 g) package round gyoza wrappers
- 1¼ cups (300 ml) peanut (groundnut), safflower, or sunflower oil, for pan-frying
- Lime Dipping Sauce (recipe follows)

Place a large bowl under a meat grinder. Working quickly, and in this order, grind the pork, pheasant, garlic, ginger, and shallots.

Add the scallions, sesame oil, mirin, fish sauce, five-spice powder, and white pepper and mix well. Place plastic wrap (clingfilm) directly on the mixture, covering with a lid, to keep the mixture color. Refrigerate for at least 2 hours and up to overnight. This mixture will keep in the refrigerator for up to 1 week.

To make dumplings, take 1 tablespoon of the mixture and place in the center of a gyoza wrapper. Brush half of the outside of the rim of each wrapper with a little water, then fold and seal the edges and crimp. Set on a tray. When the tray is filled, cover with plastic wrap (clingfilm) and refrigerate for 1 hour.

To cook the dumplings, bring a large pot of water to a boil. Meanwhile, line a baking sheet with parchment paper that has been oiled lightly. Add the dumplings to the pot and cook until they float, about 3 minutes. Set on the baking sheet. Chill for at least 30 minutes.

Preheat the oven to 300°F (150°C/Gas Mark 2).

Pour the oil into a nonstick skillet at least 2 inches (5 cm) high and 10 inches (25 cm) wide, and heat to 350°F (177°C). Working in batches of 4–5, add the dumplings and cook until golden brown, then gently flip to the other side to brown. Drain on paper towels for a few seconds. Place the cooked dumplings on a parchment-lined sheet pan and keep warm in the oven while you finish cooking.

Serve with the dipping sauce on the side.

LIME DIPPING SAUCE

PREPARATION TIME: 5 MINUTES
MAKES: ABOUT ¾ CUP (180 ML)

- 6 tablespoons fresh lime juice
- 3 tablespoons mirin
- 1½ teaspoons tamari or soy sauce
- 1 teaspoon finely minced fresh ginger
- 1½ tablespoons light brown sugar
- ½ tablespoons finely diced fresh Thai green chili, seeded

Mix all the ingredients together with 3 tablespoons cold water and refrigerate until ready to serve. It will keep well in the refrigerator for up to 4 days.

BUFFALO–PORCINI BOLOGNESE WITH FIRE-ROASTED TOMATOES

PREPARATION TIME: 30 MINUTES,
 PLUS SOAKING TIME
COOKING TIME: 1 HOUR
MAKES: 4½ CUPS (ABOUT 1 LITER)
SERVES 8–10

- 1 oz (30 g) dried porcini mushrooms
- 3 tablespoons olive oil
- 2 carrots, finely diced
- 2 peeled stalks celery, finely diced
- ½ medium yellow onion, finely diced
- 2 teaspoons kosher (coarse) salt,
  plus additional as needed
- 3 cloves garlic, minced
- 1 lb (455 g) ground buffalo meat,
  broken up
- 1 tablespoon fresh oregano, minced
- 1 (14.5 oz/410 g) can diced fire-roasted
  tomatoes
- 1 cup (240 ml) strained tomato sauce
  (passata)
- ½ cup (30 g) chopped fresh parsley
- 1 teaspoon crushed chili flakes
- ¼ cup (60 ml) heavy (whipping) cream
  (optional)
- Cooked pasta, for serving

[This South Dakota riff on the classic pasta sauce combines two of our most prized ingredients: buffalo meat and porcini mushrooms. Serve over pasta, thinning the Bolognese with pasta cooking water if desired. Toss your pasta with the Bolognese well and serve on a big platter family style, or serve the pasta and sauce separately. Garnish with grated sheep-milk cheese such as Manchego or Fiore Sardo. The Bolognese freezes well for up to a month. You could also use in it lasagna.]

In a bowl, combine the dried porcini and 1 cup (240 ml) hot water and set aside to soften.

Preheat a large sauté pan over medium heat and add the olive oil. When the pan starts to smoke slightly, add the carrots, celery, and onion and cook until softened and beginning to caramelize, 8–10 minutes.

Lower the heat to medium-low and sprinkle 1 of the teaspoons of salt over the vegetables. Add the garlic and cook for another 4 minutes. Add the buffalo meat and season with the remaining 1 teaspoon salt. Add the chopped oregano. Cook until all the ground meat is only a little pink, 5–6 minutes, stirring occasionally.

Meanwhile, lift the porcini from the water and roughly chop. Strain the liquid through a fine-mesh sieve lined with a paper towel and set aside. Add the chopped porcini and porcini juice to the buffalo mixture and cook for 4 minutes. Add the fire-roasted tomatoes, strained tomato sauce (passata), chopped parsley, and chili flakes. Simmer on low heat for 20 minutes. Add the heavy (whipping) cream, if using. Taste for seasoning. Serve with large rigatoni, pappardelle, or tagliatelle pasta cooked according to package instructions.

Kevin West is the author of *Saving the Season* and co-author of *Truffle Boy* and *The Grand Central Market Cookbook*. He is from Blount County, Tennessee, and lives in Los Angeles and western Massachusetts.

The Martins and the Wests, the two sides of my family, come from Tennessee. To be precise, they come from east Tennessee, an Appalachian territory apart from the plateaus of middle Tennessee and the delta bottoms of west Tennessee, three cultural subregions united, if not unified, by a thread-thin state line. In the 1980s we followed my mother throughout the South for her job. Whenever we could, we'd drive to Blount County, at the foot of the Great Smoky Mountains, climbing out to hug relatives and say, "It's good to be home."

"Home" in this sense meant a familiar landscape of memory and taste. While the Wests and the Martins differed within the nuances of east Tennessee identity—farmers versus hillbillies, Presbyterian versus Baptist, "you all" versus "you'uns"—we all knew the same mountain views around Townsend. And we all would make the Sunday pilgrimage to Cades Cove, where we invariably stopped at the 1879 Becky Cable House to stick our heads in the smokehouse and marvel at the ghostly incense of hams cured and eaten decades before. I can't remember that anyone ever had to explain that smell to me. My West grandparents would have thought the pantry bare without supplies of cornmeal, sorghum, home-canned half-runner beans, and a leather-skinned country ham streaked inside like oiled red cedar.

Pappaw cured and sold his own hams, slaughtering and "working up" as many as twenty-five hogs at a time with Gran's help. Pappaw let his pigs roam the farm and wallow piggishly, the way that Iberian hogs destined for Spanish *pata negra* forage in the open oak woodlands of the *dehesa*. A storage shed near the barn, half-filled with junk by the time I first

poked inside, retained a permanent smell of smoky, greasy cured meat. Strands of baling twine hung from the rafters where the aged hams had been cut down.

Gran sliced her country ham a quarter-inch (6 mm) thick and scorched it brown in a frying pan. The muscle meat, bound by its band of fat, cupped as it fried. The flavor was intensely salty and feral, an adult taste on par with coffee and whiskey. "Your Gran thought there was no food as good as country ham," my dad told me. The frying smell stayed in her clothes.

Pigs first came to the New World on Christopher Columbus's second voyage. More arrived with the settlement of St. Augustine (1565) and Jamestown (1607). Hardy, clever, social, and omnivorous, their descendants proliferated throughout the Southeast. Pork became the cornerstone domesticated protein of the Southern diet, especially in isolated settlements such as Cades Cove, because pigs were cheap to keep, a minor investment that yielded a hundred-fold profit in ham, bacon, jowls, lard, and fresh loins. Unlike cattle, hogs were sized for single-family use and suited to the limitations of frontier food storage. Salting, smoking, and drying were simple but effective preservation techniques. Muggy Southern summers required a heavy cure, although some families cut the salt with sugar, which provided the same effect. Hogs slaughtered at the first cold snap yielded hams that would be ready the following Christmas.

Fully aged, and trimmed a few slices at a time, a ham would season a month's worth of braised greens, beans, and breakfast gravy. Boiled whole and sliced onto lard biscuits, a single ham supplied quantities ▶

◄ of food commensurate with life ceremonies requiring lavish hospitality—weddings, funerals, and family reunions. In the vernacular semiotics of east Tennessee, the country ham took on complex significations of kinship, communion, regional belonging, yeoman self-sufficiency, gracious welcome, "the good old days," neighborliness, continuity across the generations, and so on. Country ham provided nourishment beyond food.

After Gran died, Pappaw stopped making hams, and after he died, the home place was sold. My father never bothered with hogs on his farm, although every year he would buy a country ham to fry for his Christmas Day breakfast, which reliably brought in fifty or more neighbors. Uncle David didn't keep hogs either, and he had to stop eating country ham on doctor's orders. Even so, he allowed himself one piece at Christmas, and for that he drove down to a smokehouse he'd known for years in Madisonville, not twenty miles from the site of Gran and Pappaw's farm.

The Madisonville smokehouse belonged to Allan Benton, the maker of what are arguably the most esteemed hams in America. Benton's Smoky Mountain Country Hams, founded in 1973, first achieved wider recognition after chef John Fleer championed them at Blackberry Farm, a luxury resort on the road up to Cades Cove that brought to an apotheosis the farmstead self-sufficiency Pappaw practiced. In 2005, young New York chef David Chang started to use Benton's country ham in his dashi at Momofuku, and the next year writer John T. Edge accompanied Allan Benton on a trip to New York for *Gourmet* magazine. Edge described the visit as the triumphal procession of a self-effacing

country artisan astonished and amused by the genuflecting chefs who welcomed him. Humble Tennessee country ham had somehow become urbane luxury food. By analogy with *pata negra* and prosciutto, it was being shaved and served raw as "charcuterie." Gran would have been horrified.

When I read the press about Benton's, I called my dad to confirm it was where Uncle David went for his Christmas ham. My dad added a detail that pleased me immensely. Allan Benton remembered Pappaw. He told Uncle David once, "I knew John West, and your daddy cured hams just like I do."

After hearing that, I had to make the pilgrimage. Benton's Smoky Mountain Country Hams was a modest roadside shop off the 411 highway, but the air inside and the very building itself were infused with pork grease and smoke, the frankincense and myrrh of east Tennessee. It was an atmosphere of history, the physical presence of three centuries of culinary knowledge that spanned from Cades Cove to Gran and Pappaw's farm to today. Of course I bought a country ham for Christmas. It was good to be home.

Kevin West

WATERMELON RIND PICKLES

PREPARATION TIME: 30 MINUTES,
  PLUS OVERNIGHT BRINING
  AND 1 WEEK CURING TIME
COOKING TIME: 25 MINUTES
MAKES: FOUR 1-PINT (500 ML) JARS

- 3½ lb (1.5 kg) prepped watermelon rind from a 12–14 lb (5.4–6.4 kg) watermelon (see Note)
- 4 tablespoons kosher (coarse) salt
- 2½ cups (590 ml) red wine vinegar
- 1½ cups (300 g) sugar
- 2 tablespoons molasses
- ½ teaspoon allspice berries
- ½ teaspoon black peppercorns
- 5 whole cloves
- 3–5 dried red chilies
- 1-inch (2.5 cm) cinnamon stick

Note:
  To prep the rind, cut the melon in half, then into quarters. Cut each quarter in half and cut the resulting chunk into 1-inch (2.5 cm) slices. Using a sharp knife, slice the rind away from the flesh. (Save the flesh to eat.) Use a vegetable peeler to remove the outermost dark-green layer (discard the peelings). What is left to use for the recipe is the pale-green inner rind.

[People have often asked me about "those watermelon pickles from the South," so I developed a recipe. They are a picnic pickle to serve with cold fried chicken, sliced ham, and creamy church-supper dishes like macaroni salad and squash casserole. Traditional watermelon rind pickles are almost candied: Mine are less sweet, and I use red wine vinegar as the base.]

Cut each piece of rind into 1½-inch (4 cm) pieces and place in a large bowl. Make a brine of the salt and 6 cups (1.4 liters) water and pour over the rinds. Weight them with a plate and set aside overnight.

The next day, drain the rinds and rinse with fresh water. In a large saucepan, bring the vinegar, sugar, and molasses to a boil. Crush the spices in a mortar and add them to the pan. When the vinegar syrup boils, add the rinds to the pan and cook gently, turning them over regularly, until the rinds are translucent, about 10 minutes. Lift out the rinds with a slotted spoon and pack them into 4 sterilized 1-pint (500 ml) jars, leaving a generous ½ inch (1.25 cm) of headspace.

Bring the syrup back to a boil and pour it over the rinds to cover, leaving ½ inch (1.25 cm) of headspace. Run a skewer or other thin implement around the inside edge of the jars to release any air pockets and top up with more syrup as necessary. If you run short of syrup, top up the jars with straight red wine vinegar. Wipe the rims, seal the jars, and process in a boiling water bath for 10 minutes. Wait 1 to 2 weeks before eating.

CHERRY 'SHINE

PREPARATION TIME: 15 MINUTES,
   PLUS 1 MONTH MACERATING TIME
MAKES: 1 QUART (1 LITER)

- 1–1½ lb (455–680 g) firm dark cherries
- 2 cups (475 ml) 80-proof alcohol

[The English once knew cherry brandy by the name Cherry Bounce. This recipe is my down-home version, prepared with moonshine. Unaged corn liquor is legally sold by a few distilleries, sometimes under the trade name of "white dog." Another type of alcohol, such as vodka, rye, or bourbon, could also be used, provided it is 80 proof or higher. After a few months in the jar together, the cherries and liquor exchange their best parts. The cherries are delicious and the liquid itself is sublime. Serve Cherry 'Shine in tiny cordial glasses on nights when you want to sit by the fire and read thick books. Either sour or sweet cherries can be preserved this way. With sour cherries, you may want to add a modest amount of sugar. Start with ¼ cup (50 g) per quart (1 liter), and adjust to taste.]

Rinse the cherries and trim their stems to ½ inch (1.25 cm). Pack them snugly into a sterilized 1-quart (1 liter) jar. Cover the fruits completely with alcohol and seal the jar. Set aside to age for at least 1 month. The jar does not need to be refrigerated, but the cherries and alcohol are best if used within 7 months.

ZUCCHINI DILL SPEARS

PREPARATION TIME: 20 MINUTES,
   PLUS BRINING TIME
COOKING TIME: 20 MINUTES
MAKES: FOUR 1-PINT (500 ML) JARS

- 3 lb (1.4 kg) small zucchini (courgettes)
- 5 tablespoons kosher (coarse) salt
- 12 fronds fresh dill
- 2 teaspoons dill seeds
- 2 teaspoons mustard seeds
- 1 teaspoon coriander seeds
- ¼ teaspoon saffron threads
- 4 cloves garlic, halved
- 4 small dried chili peppers, split lengthwise
- 2½ cups (600 ml) white wine vinegar
- ¼ cup (50 g) sugar

[The zucchini (courgette) plant is tireless, and down South people compete for new ways to describe how fast zucchini grow. It's impossible to eat so many, and once the garden gets up to speed you literally cannot give them away. When they're small, zucchini make delicious pickles. Choose the smallest ones you can find, less than 4 inches (10 cm), to fit into 1-pint (500 ml) jars. Large zucchini can be cut into spears. Soaking them in cold brine will firm their texture.]

Scrub the zucchini well and trim the ends. If they're small enough to fit into the jar, halve them lengthwise. Otherwise, cut them into 4-inch (10 cm) spears. Toss the trimmed zucchini in a bowl with 4 tablespoons of the salt, the dill fronds, and a double handful of ice cubes. Add cold water to cover and weight the zucchini with a plate. Leave for 2 hours.

Drain the zucchini in a colander and rinse. Distribute the dill fronds and all the remaining aromatics among 4 sterilized 1-pint (500 ml) jars.

In a saucepan, combine 1 cup (240 ml) water, the vinegar, sugar, and remaining 1 tablespoon salt and bring to a boil. Working in batches, cook the zucchini for 2 minutes, until khaki colored and pliable. Pack them snugly into the jars.

Once all the zucchini are cooked, ladle the hot syrup into the jars, leaving ½ inch (1.25 cm) of headspace. Seal and process in a boiling water bath for 10 minutes. For a firmer texture, you can process in a hot water bath (180°–185°F/82°–85°C) for 30 minutes.

TEXAS GUEST ESSAY

Robb Walsh is a three-time James Beard Award winner, an author, a partner of El Real Tex-Mex Café in Houston, and co-founder of the non-profit organizations Galveston Eats and Foodways Texas.

Frito pie, Tex-Mex breakfast tacos, and barbecue brisket are emblematic Texas foods. But when you mention Southern classics like fried chicken, cornbread, fresh field peas, okra, yams baked in cane syrup, homemade biscuits, and chocolate sheet cake, Texas is not the place that springs to most people's minds. There's a reason for that.

Texas was a slave state, and part of the Confederacy, so it would seem its Southern-ness was a given. But at the time of the Civil War, only East Texas was settled. After the Civil War, when the buffalo were killed off and the Comanche were moved to reservations, West Texas became an open range and the cattle-drive era began. Thanks to "dime novels" and Hollywood Westerns, Texas in the popular culture became synonymous with cowboys.

In the late 1920s, a New York advertising executive gave a speech in which he challenged Texas to take advantage of its mythic reputation. Everybody in the rest of the country thought all Texans wore cowboy hats—so why not live up to their expecta-tions? The ad man presented a plan for state leaders to use the Texas Centennial in 1936, a World's Fair–style extravaganza, to rebrand the entire state of Texas.

As part of a national marketing campaign leading up to the event, the governor donned cowboy boots and a ten-gallon hat and took the University of Texas Longhorn marching band, a Texas Ranger on his horse, and a bevy of beauties in cowboy costumes on a railroad train that toured the country. The Ranger rode his horse into hotel lobbies, the governor gave Stetsons to Hollywood starlets and New York politicians, and the cowgirls posed for the newspaper photographers. It was quite a show.

After the Texas Centennial, Texas embraced its new cowboy image so enthusiastically that most people forgot the state was ever Southern at all. If not for Texans' undying love of fried chicken, their passion for chicken-fried steak, and the comfort they found in hot biscuits, the culinary connection to the Old South might have flickered out. But now, it looks like a revival is starting to take place.

Food folkways organizations like the Southern Foodways Alliance at the University of Mississippi and Foodways Texas at the University of Texas have brought us back to our roots by documenting and celebrating our Southern-ness and our diversity. On their websites, you can watch short films about Texas folk food heroes like Robert Patillo and his African American beef links, and Nathan "Mama Sugar" Sanders, who grew up in rural East Texas and became a famous chuck wagon cook.

At newly launched community gatherings like the Texas Purple Hull Pea Festival in the East Texas freedmen's town of Shankleville, old Southern food traditions are coming back to life. Fried chicken is a new obsession. Modern Southern restaurants are becoming more and more popular in Houston and Dallas.

I know, I know—it's a little greedy for the state that excels at Tex-Mex and barbecue to lay claim to outstanding Southern cooking too. But as we say around here: It ain't bragging if it's true.

Dean Fearing is chef-owner, in Dallas, Texas, of Fearing's Restaurant, which *Esquire* named Restaurant of the Year. He was awarded Best Chef: Southwest by the James Beard Foundation, as well Pioneer of American Cuisine by the Culinary Institute of America.

DEAN'S TORTILLA SOUP

PREPARATION TIME: 20 MINUTES
COOKING TIME: 1 HOUR
SERVES: 6–8

- 3 tablespoons olive oil
- 8 cloves garlic, peeled but whole
- 4 corn tortillas, cut into long strips
- 2 cups (220 g) fresh onion purée
- 6 cups (1.4 liters) chicken stock, more as needed
- 1 quart (1 liter) fresh tomato purée (passata)
- 5 dried ancho chilies, fire-roasted, stemmed, and seeded
- 2 jalapeño peppers, seeded and chopped
- 1 tablespoon chopped epazote or 2 tablespoons chopped cilantro (coriander)
- 1 tablespoon ground cumin
- 1 teaspoon ground coriander
- 1 large bay leaf
- Salt

In a large saucepan, heat the oil over medium heat. Add the garlic and tortilla strips and fry, stirring frequently, until the tortillas are crisp, about 5 minutes. Add the onion purée, bring to a simmer, and cook, stirring occasionally, for 10 minutes. Stir in the chicken stock, tomato purée, anchos, jalapeños, epazote, cumin, coriander, bay leaf, and salt to taste. Increase the heat and bring to a boil. Reduce to a gentle simmer and cook for 40 minutes, skimming off any fat that rises to the surface.

Transfer to a blender and process to a smooth purée. If too thick, add chicken stock, a bit at a time, to reach a smooth soup consistency. (The soup may be made up to this point and stored, covered and refrigerated, for up to 3 days or frozen for up to 3 months.)

SOUTH TEXAS ANTELOPE
WITH PRICKLY PEAR GLAZE

PREPARATION TIME: 20 MINUTES
COOKING TIME: 30 MINUTES
SERVES: 4

- 2 cups (475 ml) prickly pear (cactus) juice
- 1 tablespoon dark rum
- 1 teaspoon grated fresh ginger
- 1 tablespoon cornstarch (cornflour) dissolved in 1 tablespoon cold water
- 1 tablespoon pure maple syrup
- Fresh lime juice
- Salt
- 4 antelope sirloin steaks (6 oz/170 g each), trimmed of all fat and silverskin
- 2 tablespoons Garlic Powder (page 680)
- Freshly ground black pepper
- Jicama-Carrot Slaw (page 680)
- 4 cilantro (coriander) sprigs, optional garnish

In a small saucepan, combine the prickly pear juice, rum, and ginger and bring to a boil over medium-high heat. Immediately reduce to a simmer and cook until reduced by half, about 15 minutes. Whisking constantly, add the cornstarch mixture in a slow, steady stream. Continue to simmer until thickened, about 5 minutes. Remove from the heat and whisk in the maple syrup. Season to taste with lime juice and salt and set the glaze aside.

Preheat a gas or charcoal grill (barbecue) to medium-high heat, taking care that the rack is very clean and heavily brushed with oil.

Generously season the antelope with the garlic powder, and pepper. Grill on the first side just long enough to mark the meat, about 3 minutes. Flip and grill until the second side is marked and the steaks are rare (130°–135°F/54°–57°C), about 2 minutes. Generously brush both sides of the steaks with the reserved glaze and grill, turning once, for an additional minute or just long enough to set the glaze. Remove from the grill.

Divide steaks and slaw evenly among plates. Garnish with a sprig of cilantro.

GARLIC POWDER

PREPARATION TIME: 10 MINUTES
COOKING TIME: 4 HOURS 20 MINUTES
MAKES: 4 TABLESPOONS

- 24 cloves garlic, peeled

Note:
To make garlic salt, add ½ cup
(105 g) coarse sea salt when blending.

Preheat the oven to 200°F (95°C).

Fill a medium saucepan about two-thirds full with cold water. Add the garlic and bring to a boil over medium-high heat. Reduce to a simmer and cook until the garlic is very soft but not falling apart, about 15 minutes. Drain well. Transfer to a blender or food processer and process to a smooth purée.

Coat a 17 x 13-inch (43 x 33 cm) pan with cooking spray. Scrape the garlic purée onto the pan and spread it in an even layer about ¼ inch (6 mm) thick. Transfer to the oven and bake until the garlic has dried out completely and has hardened, about 4 hours. Set aside to cool completely.

When cool, place in a blender and process to a powder. Sift in a fine-mesh sieve set over a bowl to remove any large pieces remaining. Store, tightly covered, in a cool, dark spot for up to 3 months.

JICAMA-CARROT SLAW

PREPARATION TIME: 10 MINUTES
SERVES: 4

- ½ cup (45 g) thinly julienned red bell pepper
- ½ cup (50 g) julienned jicama
- ½ cup (50 g) julienned carrot
- 4 tablespoons julienned jalapeño pepper (seeded)
- 4 tablespoons fried julienned tortilla strips
- 4 tablespoons finely sliced cilantro (coriander)
- ⅓ cup (80 ml) extra-virgin olive oil
- 3 tablespoons fresh lime juice
- Salt

In a medium bowl, combine the bell pepper, jicama, carrot, jalapeño, tortilla strips, and cilantro (coriander). Add the olive oil and lime juice and toss to coat. Season to taste with salt.

BANANA PUDDING

PREPARATION TIME: 30 MINUTES, PLUS
   COOLING TIME
COOKING TIME: 40 MINUTES
SERVES: 6

- 1¼ cups (300 ml) heavy (whipping) cream
- 1 vanilla bean, split lengthwise
- 15 egg yolks, at room temperature
- ¾ cup (150 g) sugar
- 2 ripe bananas, thinly sliced crosswise
- ½ cup (120 ml) Caramel Sauce (recipe follows)

In a medium saucepan, combine the cream and vanilla bean and bring to a gentle simmer over medium-low heat.

In a heatproof bowl (preferably stainless steel), whisk together the egg yolks and sugar. Pour about ¼ inch (6 mm) water into a medium saucepan that is large enough to hold the bowl without the bottom of the bowl touching the water. Place the pan over medium heat and then set the bowl into it. Whisking constantly, cook until the mixture forms a ribbon when lifted from the bowl, about 5 minutes. At this point, increase the heat under the cream and bring it to a boil.

Remove the vanilla bean from the cream and, whisking constantly, slowly pour the hot cream into the egg yolk mixture. Cook, still whisking constantly, until the mixture begins to thicken. Remove the bowl from the saucepan.

Pour the pudding through a fine-mesh sieve into a clean container. Transfer to the refrigerator to cool completely. Once cool, the pudding can be covered and refrigerated for up to 3 days.

When ready to serve, remove the pudding from the refrigerator and fold the bananas into it.

Spoon an equal portion of the pudding into each of 6 small bowls. Lightly drizzle over with the caramel sauce.

CARAMEL SAUCE

PREPARATION TIME: 5 MINUTES
COOKING TIME: 10 MINUTES
MAKES: ¾ CUP (180 ML)

- ¾ cup (150 g) sugar
- ½ teaspoon fresh lemon juice
- ½ cup (120 ml) heavy (whipping) cream
- 2–4 tablespoons milk

In a medium saucepan, combine the sugar, lemon juice, and 2 tablespoons cold water and cook over medium-high heat, stirring, until the sugar has dissolved completely, about 2 minutes. Without stirring, bring the mixture to a boil and boil, still without stirring, until the mixture is golden brown in color, about 3 minutes. Watch carefully as it can burn very easily. If it begins to burn, lift the pan from the heat for a few seconds.

With the mixture still at a boil, carefully add the cream in a slow, steady stream, whisking to blend; the mixture may splatter when the cream is added. When all of the cream has been added, remove the pan from the heat.

Whisk 2 tablespoons of milk, then whisk in just enough more to make a thin sauce. The caramel will thicken as it cools. Set aside to cool. Use immediately or store tightly covered in the refrigerator for up to 1 week. Bring to room temperature before using.

DEAN'S SIGNATURE MARGARITA

PREPARATION TIME: 5 MINUTES
MAKES: 1 COCKTAIL

- 3 tablespoons tequila
- ½ tablespoon fresh lime juice
- ½ tablespoon damiana liqueur
- 1 teaspoon organic agave syrup
- Lime juice and salt, for rimming the glass

In an ice-filled cocktail shaker, combine the tequila, lime juice, liqueur, and syrup and shake vigorously until the cup is frosted and beaded with sweat. Serve in an ice-filled rocks glass rimmed with lime and salt.

Blake Spalding and Jen Castle are chef-owners of Hell's Backbone Grill and Blaker's Acres Farm in Boulder, Utah. They are the authors of *With a Measure of Grace* and *This Immeasurable Place*, both books about food.

Our longest power outage lasted four days. During these hard and hilarious days, we continued to serve breakfast, lunch, and dinner to frantic and stranded tourists. Fortunately, it happened during a freak snowstorm, so at least we didn't worry about the food in the freezers and refrigerators: We simply opened our outdoor walk-ins and let the storm rage in. Unfortunately, it was the week before Thanksgiving, and we were hosting a few hundred people for our annual "bounty from the farm" feast. Needless to say, we got behind on prep, but the twenty-six turkeys brining in buttermilk, sage, and Utah salt stayed good and cold.

The power goes out in our tiny southern Utah town a lot—so we require our servers and cooks to bring headlamps to work, along with their wine keys and knives. When there's an outage, we just light the candles and cook in the dark. Our restaurant is the only one open for many miles, and the people must be fed.

When we moved to Boulder, Utah, in 1999 to open our restaurant, people thought we were crazy. Boulder, population two hundred, is one of the most remote towns in the lower forty-eight states. But we were former Grand Canyon river cooks, confident in our ability to turn out reasonable food from unreasonable settings. A building with a roof, electricity (albeit unreliable), and running water could only up our game. Also, in 1996, the Grand Staircase-Escalante National Monument—almost two million acres of public lands—was declared protected land by President Clinton, and we had a strong sense that in making a restaurant here, we could bring happiness to the intrepid and inevitable tourists, while also living and working in one of the most beautiful places on planet Earth.

There were few iconic Utah foods back then, unless you count deep-fried offerings heaped in red plastic baskets and served with a side of "fry sauce" (a mixture of mayonnaise, ketchup, and pickle relish); or green Jell-O salad, the kind with pineapple and marshmallows; or cheesy Dutch oven "funeral potatoes" topped with crushed corn flakes and yes, served at all funerals; or the ubiquitous Postum—a caffeine-free instant beverage made of roasted wheat, bran, and molasses that is, in our opinions, a truly sad replacement for a cup of coffee.

The *real* Utah foods, however, the ones we could actually relate to, we found in our new community, which was largely populated by ranchers and Mormons. There was local lamb, grass-finished beef, beautiful heirloom apples, grapes, stone fruit, and of course (because Utah is the Beehive State), lots of good honey. And since the Latter Day Saints' "Word of Wisdom" eschews the use of any type of poison, the food in our verdant little valley was largely organic by default.

Utah's food history is inseparable from Mormon history. When the pioneers settled Utah in the 1840s, one of the first things the religious leaders did was create an "agricultural corridor" of sorts that ran the length of the state, with different communities focusing on specific productions. Certain towns were to concentrate on dairy, for instance, while others grew apples or raised pigs. Feeding the people was a key priority of the Church. And though we came from a much different place, it was a priority for us, too. ▶

◄ From the outset, we were eager to honor the prolific bounty of Utah farms and create a menu that represented a distillation of the state's food history. We ended up with what we came to call "Four Corners Food," wherein we married Mormon pioneer grandmother recipes, Western range cowboy fare, Pueblo Indian and indigenous foods, and humble farm dishes made with whatever we could manifest from our small organic gardens, or buy from local ranchers, or forage from the surrounding high desert. We wanted to showcase and elevate the foods that were the history of this magnificent wild landscape. In order to do that right, we had to grow our own food.

All members of the Mormon Church are encouraged to have a garden and to put up a minimum of three months' to a year's worth of food for the family. It's a virtue known as "preparedness." When you grow your own produce, you do as the grandmothers did, out of necessity and pragmatism. Faced with nine hundred pounds of freshly harvested and extremely fragile apricots or six hundred pounds of perfect tiny cucumbers, you get busy and hone your food preservation skills in a hurry. Foods you harvest are precious; they represent so much effort that wasting a single bit feels criminal. The same goes for meat. When you buy a cow whole, you find a way to cook the entire cow, and you foster and maintain a relationship with the rancher. If you plant an apple orchard, you must eventually be ready to process two thousand pounds of apples at a time. You have to understand the land and be prepared for all the attendant work of maintaining the trees.

The pioneers knew all this. They relied on jamming, jarring, dehydrating, pickling, and curing their harvest in order to survive. What they didn't know was that they were paving the way for Utah's current food culture. Sure, you can still find Jell-O salad and fry sauce in various forms throughout Utah, but you'll also find wonderful restaurants—both casual and upscale, in tiny towns and big cities—that are embracing local traditions, tending their own gardens, buying from small farms, and focusing on seasonal and place-based fare.

This value system and knowledge embodies a true sustainability, a "waste not, want not" ethic that is rare in our present-day society, but lovingly ingrained in Utah's heritage. It's reverent in a deeply practical way. This is Utah food: born from the powerful need to survive and thrive in a harsh and wild landscape, and to make home and sustenance grow where you've planted yourself.

Blake Spalding and Jen Castle

GREEN CHILI TUMBLEWEED SCONES

PREPARATION TIME: 25 MINUTES
COOKING TIME: 40 MINUTES
MAKES: 8–12 SCONES

- 2 sticks (225 g) butter, in chunks
- 2¼ cups (295 g) all-purpose (plain) flour
- 1½ teaspoons baking powder
- ½ cup (100 g) sugar
- ½ cup (65 g) cornmeal
- 1 teaspoon salt
- ¼ teaspoon freshly ground black pepper
- 1 teaspoon granulated garlic
- 1 teaspoon Chimayó chili powder
- 1 egg
- 1 cup (240 ml) buttermilk
- ½ cup (120 g) roasted and chopped poblano peppers (see page 86 on how to roast chilies)
- ½ cup (75 g) blanched baby tumbleweeds, squeezed dry and chopped (you can substitute raw baby spinach cut in ribbons)
- ½ cup (55 g) grated Monterey Jack or cheddar cheese
- 1 tablespoon finely chopped fresh chives
- ¼ cup (60 ml) sour cream

[We hand-weed every acre in our fields. The tender little tumbleweed shoots are best when about 2 inches (5 cm) long. Remove the long pink roots by holding a bundle in your hand and cutting with scissors.]

Preheat the oven to 335°F (170°C/Gas Mark 3). Line a baking sheet with parchment paper.

In a stand mixer fitted with the paddle attachment, combine the butter, flour, baking powder, sugar, cornmeal, salt, pepper, garlic, and chili powder and paddle until the butter is cut in and the mixture is crumbly. Add the egg, buttermilk, and poblano peppers and mix gently and briefly, just until combined. Remove from the mixer and mix in the tumbleweeds, cheese, and chives gently by hand.

Transfer the dough to a lightly floured board. Form it into a square, pat it down, and roll it gently until it is 1½ inches (4 cm) thick. Using your hand, wipe the top of the dough with the sour cream, to all edges, evenly. Cut the dough into 8–12 triangles and place on the baking sheet.

Bake for 11 minutes. Rotate the pan front to back and bake until the tops are shiny and starting to brown, about 4 minutes longer.

GREEN CHILI–BRAISED LOCAL BEEF WITH ROASTED TOMATOES AND FARM GREENS

PREPARATION TIME: 15 MINUTES
COOKING TIME: 3 HOURS 30 MINUTES
SERVES 4–6

- 3 lb (1.4 kg) rump roast, chuck roast, bottom round, or brisket
- 2 tablespoons clarified butter
- 2 cups (425 g) canned fire-roasted diced tomatoes
- 2 cups (135 g) packed chopped kale or chard, with ribs, stems discarded
- ½–1 cup (120–240 g) diced roasted green chilies (depends on how hot you like it)
- 3 cloves garlic, sliced
- 2 teaspoons dried marjoram or 3 sprigs fresh
- 2 teaspoons salt
- ½ teaspoon freshly ground black pepper

[Our bookkeeper, Katie Awesome, raises cows for us. Wanting to use as much of the meat as we can, we love this dish as a way of using cuts from the chuck, brisket, and round. We serve the resulting delight with lots of the broth in a big bowl over a scoop of buttery polenta.]

Preheat the oven to 300°F (150°C/Gas Mark 2).

Cut the beef into 4-inch (10 cm) chunks.

In a 12-inch (30 cm) Dutch oven (casserole), heat the butter over medium to high heat until hot. Working in batches so as not to crowd the pan, sear the beef on all sides. Transfer the beef to a plate to collect juices. Add the tomatoes to the Dutch oven, still over heat, and use their juice to deglaze the pan. Remove from the heat.

Return the beef (and any juices) to the pan and add the kale, green chilies, garlic, marjoram, salt, and pepper. Add water to come up one-third of the way of the meat. Stir the liquids to mix in the spices and tuck the greens down between the meat chunks. Cover, transfer to the oven, and braise until a fork can twist easily in the meat, about 3 hours.

CORNMEAL-PINE NUT PEACH CRISP

PREPARATION TIME: 20 MINUTES
COOKING TIME: 45 MINUTES
SERVES: 8

For the filling:
- 7 cups (1.1 kg) peeled, sliced peaches
- 1 cup (200 g) sugar
- 4 tablespoons all-purpose (plain) flour
- 2 tablespoons fresh lemon juice

For the topping:
- 1 cup (130 g) all-purpose (plain) flour
- ⅔ cup (45 g) yellow cornmeal
- ⅔ cup (135 g) sugar
- 1 teaspoon salt
- ⅔ cup (150 g) very cold butter, cut into small pieces
- ½ cup (70 g) toasted pine nuts

[In Boulder we have many varieties of peaches and this crisp is one of our favorite ways to use them. Eat it with whipped cream, vanilla ice cream, or your bare hands.]

Preheat the oven to 375°F (190°C/Gas Mark 5). Butter a 9 x 13-inch (23 x 33 cm) baking dish.

For the filling: In a medium bowl, combine the peaches, sugar, flour, and lemon juice. Use your hands to really mix it well so no little flour lumps lurk anywhere. Spread the fruit mixture evenly in the baking dish and set aside.

For the topping: In a medium bowl, mix together the flour, cornmeal, sugar, and salt. Using your fingers or the paddle attachment of a stand mixer, work the butter pieces into the dry ingredients so the mixture looks like coarse crumbs. Mix in the pine nuts.

Cover the fruit evenly with the topping. Set it on a baking sheet to catch any juices that spill over. Bake until the fruit is bubbling and fork-tender and the topping is golden, about 45 minutes.

Seamus Mullen is chef-owner of Tertulia in New York City and author of *Hero Food* and *Real Food Heals*. He grew up in Vermont.

I have been cooking in New York City for years, but my first experiences in the kitchen were on the small farm I grew up on in my home state of Vermont. Nearly all my earliest memories involve food—from harvesting, cleaning, and freezing snap peas with my grandmother, to tapping sugar maples for sap and boiling it down to my state's most iconic ingredient: thick, dark, sweet, nutty maple syrup.

As a cook, I came of age with the best products within arm's reach. Vermonters, or at least the old-timers of my generation, are very industrious people who are jacks-of-all-trades. As a kid I didn't know a single Vermonter who *didn't* grow their own vegetables or raise their own hens for eggs (and stewing!). Most folks also foraged in the spring for fiddlehead ferns, morel mushrooms, and wild ramps. In hindsight, it's remarkable that a state with such a short growing season has such tremendous produce, but come summer, when I visit my parents, the rich flavor of tomatoes or eggplant from the garden reminds me just how nutrient-dense the soil is. Our rich cheesemaking tradition has gained modern traction with state-of-the-art dairies producing some of the country's most sophisticated cheeses. Going home, I am reminded of my favorite childhood moments, as those memories drift up from the pans on the stove, taking me back to my mother's tomato sauce, my dad's fresh baked bread, and my grandmother cooking the classic dishes of her childhood.

I grew up very close to my grandmother Mutti—exploring the woods with her, cooking out of her garden, and asking unending questions. Any free time I had as a kid I spent with a fishing pole in hand, in search of brook trout from the cold, steely waters in our local streams. My efforts weren't always successful, but when they were, I would take my catch back to my grandmother's house, always with tales of the bigger fish I *almost* caught, and we would cook them together.

Seamus Mullen

GENTLY ROASTED BROOK TROUT WITH SUMMER SQUASH

PREPARATION TIME: 30 MINUTES
COOKING TIME: 10 MINUTES
SERVES: 4

- 2 brook trout, filleted, skin on
- Salt and freshly ground black pepper
- ½ lb (225 g) mixed heirloom summer squash, cut into ½-inch (1.25 cm) pieces
- Small handful of cherry tomatoes (I love sweet Sun Gold cherry tomatoes)
- 1 shallot, quartered and separated into petals
- Finely grated zest and juice of 1 lemon, plus more juice for the shaved squash
- Leaves of 1 sprig fresh lemon thyme
- Leaves of 1 bunch fresh summer savory
- Leaves of 1 sprig fresh oregano
- 4 or 5 leaves fresh basil, torn
- 1 teaspoon Aleppo pepper or crushed chili flakes
- 4 tablespoons olive oil
- 1 tablespoon dry white wine
- A few pieces baby summer squash, sliced into ribbons on a mandoline

[My fondest memories of early childhood involve two things: fishing for trout and cooking with my grandmother. This dish is an ode to both.]

Preheat the oven to 350°F (180°C/Gas Mark 4).

Season the trout fillets with salt and pepper on all sides.

In a large bowl, combine the cut-up squash with the tomatoes, shallots, lemon zest, lemon juice, herbs, Aleppo pepper, and salt and black pepper to taste. Toss with 1 tablespoon of the olive oil and the wine. Evenly distribute on a rimmed baking sheet and slide the pan into the oven.

Meanwhile, in a large cast-iron skillet, heat 2 tablespoons of the olive oil over medium-high heat. Add the trout fillets, skin side down, and sear until golden and crispy, about 3 minutes.

Carefully transfer the fish from the skillet and place them skin side up on top of the vegetables in the oven. Finish cooking the trout in the oven until just cooked through, another 5 minutes. The squash should be bright in color and barely cooked, with a bit of toothiness.

In a small bowl, season the raw squash ribbons with salt, pepper, the remaining 1 tablespoon olive oil, and lemon juice to taste.

Divide the cooked vegetables evenly among 4 warm plates. Place a fillet atop each bed of vegetables and scatter each plate with a few raw squash ribbons. Serve immediately.

ASPARAGUS SALAD WITH MORELS, FIDDLEHEAD FERNS, AND BITTER GREENS

PREPARATION TIME: 15 MINUTES,
   PLUS SOAKING TIME
COOKING TIME: 25 MINUTES
SERVES: 4

- 1 bunch green asparagus, woody ends trimmed
- 1 bunch white asparagus, woody ends trimmed
- Salt and freshly ground black pepper
- 3 teaspoons olive oil, plus more for cooking
- 2 cups (50 g) loosely packed basil, parsley, sage, thyme, tarragon, and dill leaves
- 1 or 2 cloves garlic, peeled but whole, plus ½ clove, minced
- Finely grated zest of 1 lemon
- ¼ cup (75 g) dried morels
- ½ cup (120 ml) boiling water
- ½ lb (225 g) fresh morels
- 2 tablespoons (30 g) butter
- 1 tablespoon sherry vinegar
- ¼ cup (60 ml) white wine vinegar
- 2 tablespoons honey
- 1 teaspoon Dijon mustard
- 1 cup (240 ml) olive oil (I like Arbequina)
- 1 cup (160 g) fiddlehead ferns, quickly blanched in salted water and shocked in an ice bath
- 1 cup (20 g) dandelion greens, sorrel, or arugula
- ½ cup (50 g) Parmigiano-Reggiano cheese shavings (shaved with a vegetable peeler)

[This recipe brings me back to springtime, hunting morels and chanterelles with my mom in the thick stand of maples near our house, where they popped up among the spring green ferns after a heavy rain. My mom has a sixth sense for morels; she taught me to how to look for the trees that they like, how to check the soil, etc. And harvesting fiddlehead ferns is also a classic rite of spring in Vermont. You can use whatever wild salad greens you can find—I love using sorrel and dandelion greens—but this salad is just as delicious with spinach.]

Season the asparagus with salt and pepper and toss with a thin film of olive oil. Heat a large cast-iron skillet over high heat. Add the asparagus and cook until blackened and tender, about 5 minutes. Transfer to a bowl and add 2 cups (475 ml) of the oil, 1 cup (25 g) of the fresh herbs, the whole garlic, and the citrus zest. Let rest for 2 hours.

Soak the dried morels in the boiling water for 15 minutes. Reserving the soaking liquid, drain the morels and set aside. Meanwhile, soak the fresh morels in cold water for 5 minutes, changing the water three times to clean. Dry the morels very well.

In a large frying pan, heat 1 tablespoon of the olive oil over high heat. Add the butter and when it foams, add the fresh and dried morels, and cook for 5 minutes. Deglaze with the sherry vinegar. Season with salt and pepper and set aside in a warm place.

In a small bowl, mix together the reserved morel soaking liquid, the white wine vinegar, minced garlic, honey, mustard, and salt and pepper to taste. Transfer to a blender and blend thoroughly. With the blender running, drizzle in the olive oil.

Remove the asparagus from the marinade. In a large bowl, toss together the fiddleheads, greens, asparagus, and mushrooms. Season with salt and pepper. Dress, to taste, with the vinaigrette and divide among 4 chilled plates. Finish with a sprinkle of Parmigiano shavings on each plate and the remaining 1 cup (25 g) of torn fresh herbs.

GRILLED LAMB LOIN CHOPS WITH BRAISED MUSTARD GREENS AND SORREL SALSA VERDE

PREPARATION TIME: 25 MINUTES
COOKING TIME: 20 MINUTES
SERVES: 4

- 2 tablespoons olive oil
- 4 oz (110 g) fresh shiitake mushroom caps, cut into quarters
- 8 cups (1 lb/455 g) coarsely chopped mustard greens
- 4 cloves garlic, sliced
- 1 shallot, sliced
- 2 tablespoons white balsamic vinegar or champagne vinegar
- Kosher (coarse) salt and freshly ground black pepper
- 4 lamb loin chops
- Sorrel Salsa Verde, to taste (recipe follows)

[My parents were homesteaders in Vermont. My brother and I worked on the farm from a young age, helping to grow our own vegetables, bale our own hay, and raise and butcher livestock. My mom did a lot of the butchering at home. It wasn't until I got much older that I realized what an impact my upbringing had on my approach to food as a chef—I took for granted the beauty of raising our own animals and learning to cook with them. Just like any other kid, I wanted to be outside riding a bike or playing soccer. But in retrospect, I owe a great deal to my mother for teaching me and instilling in me the values of knowing where your food comes from—we were farm-to-table before that became a buzz phrase. I don't know too many moms who butcher their own meat, but I am proud to say that mine does.]

In a large saucepan, heat the olive oil over medium heat until it slips easily across the bottom of the pot. Add the shiitake mushrooms and cook for 2–3 minutes, then add the mustard greens and quickly wilt for 1 minute. Add the garlic and shallot and cook, stirring frequently (to ensure they don't burn as the greens start to sweat out their liquid), until translucent, about 3 minutes. Add the vinegar and let it reduce for 2–3 minutes. Season to taste with salt and pepper. Set aside.

Preheat a gas or charcoal grill (barbecue) to high heat.

Season the chops all over with salt and pepper. Place on the grill, turning the chops every few minutes, to sear and get nice grill marks, about 4 minutes per side. The internal temperature should read 125°F (52°C). Set aside to rest for 5–10 minutes before serving.

To serve, divide the braised mustard greens among 4 warm plates. Place a chop on top and finish with a drizzle of salsa verde. Serve immediately.

SORREL SALSA VERDE

PREPARATION TIME: 10 MINUTES
MAKES: 1½ CUPS (355 ML)

- 2 cups (55 g) sorrel leaves
- 1 cup (50 g) fresh parsley, leaves and small stems
- 1 cup (40 g) fresh mint, leaves and small stems
- 1 cup (240 ml) olive oil
- 1 tablespoon crushed chili flakes
- 1 clove garlic, peeled but whole
- Finely grated zest and juice of 4 lemons
- Salt and freshly ground black pepper

In a food processor, combine the sorrel, parsley, mint, olive oil, chili flakes, garlic, lemon zest, and salt and pepper to taste and process until smooth. Refrigerate until ready to serve. Just before serving, whisk in the lemon juice.

Michael W. Twitty is a culinary historian. He received the Taste Talks Pioneer Award and the *Saveur* Readers' and Editors' Choice awards for his blog Afroculinaria, devoted to African American historic foodways.

When I was seventeen, my dad shoved a piece of Virginia in my mouth—literally: a small chunk of blood-red clay from our family's ancestral farm in the south-central tobacco belt, dug out by a century-old shovel. He asked me if it tasted "like chocolate." It tasted like dirt. But leave it to my dad to teach me my first lesson in terroir. That Virginia farm, through the hard work of my great-great-grandparents, formerly enslaved on surrounding plantations, was the source of home-cured country ham, apple butter, okra, collards, and sorghum molasses and the best peaches in the county. Virginia, home to ancestors of each of my four grandparents, will always be where my roots lie as well as home to the best ham biscuits, peanut pie, and two of the greatest cooks in American history: James Hemings, chef to Thomas Jefferson, and Edna Lewis, the "Julia Child of the South."

In the years following the Civil War, a local humorist named George Bagby defined Virginia food as it once was. He reduced Virginia's cuisine to "bacon and greens," but not before he suggested that a Virginian needed "fried chicken, stewed chicken, broiled chicken and chicken pie; old hare, butter-beans, new potatoes, squirrel, cymlings, snaps, barbecued shoat, roas'n ears, buttermilk, hoe-cake, ash-cake, pancake, fritters, pot-pie, tomatoes, sweet-potatoes, June apples, waffles, sweet milk, parsnips, artichokes, carrots, cracklin bread, hominy, bonny-clabber, scrambled eggs, gooba-peas, fried apples, pop-corn, persimmon beer, apple-bread, milk and peaches, mutton stew, dewberries, batter-cakes, mushmelons, hickory nuts, partridges, honey in the honey-comb, snappin'-turtle eggs, damson tarts, catfish, cider, hot light-bread, and cornfield peas" as well. He forgot blue crab, oysters, clams, herring, black-eyed pea cakes, and peanut or okra soup, but we digress.

One of the biggest ingredients contemporary Virginians are heir to is a diverse cultural heritage starting with the nine state-recognized Native American nations. Tribes like the Mattaponi guard the old shad creeks, seeking to protect their ancestral fishing grounds. Virginia was home to the oldest surviving English settlement and the first Thanksgiving dinner in 1619, and its English, Welsh, Scots-Irish, and Scottish roots are evident across the Commonwealth. Virginia is the site of the oldest African presence in British North America; the transatlantic slave trade brought nearly 100,000 Africans here. Africa, Native America, and Europe mingle in the unique Virginia delicacy, Brunswick stew.

In the Old Dominion, you can experience German *fachsnacht* ("fox knots") doughnuts in the Shenandoah or *yok*, an early fusion of African American and Chinese American food, in the urban Tidewater, or pupusas and empanadas and yuca in northern Virginia. Virginia has a thriving wine industry, where grapes like Viognier and Norton flourish on old tobacco lands. One of the largest purvey-ors of Southern heirloom vegetable seeds is based in Mineral, and small producers trade in heritage apples and heritage-breed pork and poultry along with wild pawpaw and persimmon trees to recreate the edible land-scapes of our ancestors.

Even in progress and innovation, fashion and trend, Virginia looks back to move forward. All of this is a much easier way to taste Virginia than from my dad's shovel.

Sean Brock grew up in rural Virginia and is the James Beard Award-winning chef-partner of McCrady's, McCrady's Tavern, Husk, and Minero restaurants in Charleston, South Carolina; Nashville, Tennessee; and Atlanta, Georgia.

MUSCADINE-CUCUMBER GAZPACHO

PREPARATION TIME: 30 MINUTES,
   PLUS CHILLING TIME
COOKING TIME: 5 MINUTES
SERVES: 6

- 20 large muscadine grapes
- 6 lb (2.7 kg) cucumbers, peeled, halved lengthwise, and seeded
- ½ cup (120 ml) extra-virgin olive oil
- ½ cup (80 g) thinly sliced leek, white part only, washed and drained
- 6 slices white sandwich bread, crusts removed
- ½ cup (60 g) Marcona almonds
- 1 tablespoon sour cream
- Kosher (coarse) salt
- Sherry vinegar

[The inspiration for this dish was the classic Spanish white gazpacho, which often features grapes. I used the indigenous muscadine grape, a thick-skinned subgenus of some three hundred varieties that thrive in the heat and humidity of the South. Muscadine grapes have a unique flavor, musty and floral. They go well with the yeasty aromas of the bread and the fruitful zing of the sherry vinegar. Make sure to use good-quality vinegar and olive oil. You can taste the difference.]

Press the grapes through a fine-mesh sieve into a bowl to obtain the juice. Discard the skins, seeds, and pulp. Dice enough of the cucumbers to get 4 cups (535 g) dice. Run the remaining cucumbers through a juice extractor to get 2 cups (475 ml) juice.

In a medium frying pan, heat 1 tablespoon of the olive oil over medium-low heat. Add the leek and cook, stirring frequently, until translucent and tender, about 5 minutes. Let cool.

Working in batches if necessary, combine the muscadine juice, diced cucumbers, cucumber juice, the remaining 7 tablespoons olive oil, the leek, bread, almonds, and sour cream in a blender and blend until very smooth, about 5 minutes. Season to taste with salt.

Transfer to a container, cover, and refrigerate until well chilled. (Tightly covered, the soup will keep for up to 3 days in the refrigerator.)

When ready to serve, season the gazpacho with sherry vinegar.

RABBIT STEW WITH BLACK PEPPER DUMPLINGS

PREPARATION TIME: 25 MINUTES
COOKING TIME: 2 HOURS 10 MINUTES
SERVES: 6

For the dumplings:
- 3½ cups (455 g) very fine pastry flour, such as Anson Mills fine cloth-bolted pastry flour, sifted, and chilled in the freezer
- 1½ teaspoons baking powder
- ½ teaspoon kosher (coarse) salt
- 1 tablespoon freshly ground black pepper
- 1 stick (115 g) unsalted butter, frozen, grated on a cheese grater, and chilled in the freezer
- 1½ cups (355 ml) ice-cold whole-milk buttermilk

For the stew:
- 1 large rabbit (about 2 lb/910 g)
- 4 cups (640 g) finely diced white onions
- 2 cups (200 g) medium diced celery
- 2 cups (255 g) medium diced carrots
- 2 sprigs fresh thyme
- 1 fresh bay leaf
- 1 tablespoon (15 g) unsalted butter
- ¼ cup (30 g) all-purpose flour
- 1 tablespoon soy sauce
- 1 tablespoon hot sauce
- Kosher (coarse) salt and freshly ground black pepper

[By watching my mother, chicken and dumplings was one of the first dishes I learned how to make. Smelling that rich chicken aroma may have been a defining moment for me. I wanted to create a rendition for Husk. Since I will probably never best my mom's chicken version, I substituted rabbit.]

For the dumplings: Preheat the oven to 375°F (190°C/Gas Mark 5). Lightly butter a baking sheet.

In a large bowl, combine the chilled flour, baking powder, salt, and pepper and use the tips of your fingers to work in the frozen butter until the texture resembles coarse cornmeal. Stir in the buttermilk until combined. Turn the dough out onto a lightly floured work surface and knead until smooth and elastic, about 2 minutes. Use a rolling pin to roll the dough out into a round about ½ inch (1.25 cm) thick. Using a ½-inch (1.25 cm) round cutter, cut out the dumplings and put them, touching one another, on the prepared baking sheet. (Do not re-roll dough.)

Bake the dumplings until they just start to dry, about 10 minutes. It's important that they don't get any color—they will finish cooking in the stew. Let the dumplings cool. Pull them apart and set aside, uncovered, on a baking sheet; they can be kept at room temperature for up to 5 hours.

For the stew: Put the rabbit in a large pot and cover with water. (If you do not have a big enough pot, you can cut up the rabbit.) Bring to a simmer over high heat, skimming any scum off on the top. Add half the onions, half of the celery, half of the carrots, the thyme sprigs, and bay leaf. Reduce the heat to low, cover, and simmer until the leg meat easily pulls away from the bone, about 1 hour. Remove the rabbit from the pot and let cool. Strain the broth and reserve (discard the solids).

Wash the pot and heat it over medium-high heat until hot. Add the butter and when foaming, add the remaining onions and cook, stirring frequently, until translucent, about 4 minutes. Add the remaining celery and cook until just tender, about 2 minutes, then add the remaining carrots until just tender, about 7 minutes. Reduce the heat to medium, add the flour, and stir with a wooden spoon so it absorbs the fat. Continue to stir the roux constantly until it reaches a light golden color, about 10 minutes. Slowly stir in the reserved broth, and simmer until thickened, about 25 minutes.

While the broth is cooking, remove all the meat from the rabbit, discarding the skin, bones, cartilage, and tendons, and shred the meat.

Add the soy sauce and hot sauce to the thickened broth and season with salt and pepper. Add the shredded rabbit. (The stew can be made to this point up to 3 days ahead, cooled, and refrigerated; reheat it over medium heat when ready to add the dumplings.) Add the dumplings to the stew and simmer until cooked through, about 5 minutes. Divide the dumplings and stew among 6 warm bowls and serve.

Renee Erickson is a James Beard Award winner and co-partner of The Walrus and the Carpenter, The Whale Wins, Barnacle, Bar Melusine, Bateau, and General Porpoise. She is author of *A Boat, a Whale & a Walrus*.

When I think about the flavors of Washington, I think about Puget Sound.

I grew up just east of Seattle and we spent our summers up on the Tulalip Indian Reservation, north and then west out a bend in the water.

We had a really rustic cabin there, not fancy at all. My dad would commute back to the city for work, but my mother, brother, and I would stay all summer. It was idyllic.

Being on the water meant we had all the seafood we wanted. We ate plenty of salmon and shrimp, and sometimes we'd go across the water to another island to dig clams. But most of all, we ate Dungeness crab.

These days the crabbing season is limited, but back then you could crab every day. Catching crab isn't hard; you just need a boat and some traps and bait. We'd save fish scraps for bait, collecting salmon heads and bones in the freezer. Then we'd drop our traps and let them soak for a couple of hours, giving the crabs time to crawl in.

Now, as a chef, my favorite way to prepare crab is on the grill, finished with lots of butter. But back then, we'd eat crab every which way, just about every day. We'd make crab omelets, crab melts, and the fanciest noodle casseroles. But mostly, we'd just cook it plain and keep it in the fridge. Then we'd sit around the table and eat it cold, cracking it open and dipping it in butter.

For me, the best part about eating crab is that it's totally hands-on: You have to dig in and get messy. And it's rare that anybody cracks crab for an entire family—usually each person is on their own. So as we cracked our catch, night after night, there was nothing glamorous— except the fact that we were eating copious amounts of Dungeness crab.

We ate so much crab each summer that as kids we became not quite charmed by it—but in hindsight it was pretty epic. Today it's the ingredient that I hold closest in my memories of my upbringing, and it's still one of my favorite things to cook and eat. On my long list of "last meal" dishes, for sure, would be crab.

Renee Erickson

GRILLED DUNGENESS CRAB WITH HARISSA BUTTER

PREPARATION TIME: 15 MINUTES
COOKING TIME: 20 MINUTES
SERVES: 6

- Kosher (coarse) salt
- 3 (3½ lb/1.6 kg) fresh-caught Dungeness crabs
- 1 stick (115 g) unsalted butter
- ¾ cup (180 g) harissa

Set up a large bowl of ice and water. Bring a large pot of water to a boil. Season with salt until the water tastes like the sea.

Meanwhile, prepare a gas or charcoal grill (barbecue) for cooking to medium-high heat (about 425°F/220°C). Brush the grill rack clean.

Add the crabs to the water and cook for 5 minutes, or 1 or 2 minutes—longer if the crabs are substantially larger, or if they have been stored on ice. Plunge the cooked crabs into the ice bath and let sit until cool. Clean the crabs.

Meanwhile, in a small saucepan, combine the butter and harissa and melt over low heat, stirring occasionally.

Transfer the crabs to a platter and smear them liberally on both sides (and in all their cracks) with the harissa butter. (It's okay if the butter has firmed up a bit.)

Place the crabs on the grill, cover, and cook, turning once, until the butter has melted into the crevices of each shell, 2–3 minutes. Serve hot.

MANILA CLAMS WITH SPRING ONIONS, HERBS, AND CRÈME FRAÎCHE

PREPARATION TIME: 15 MINUTES
COOKING TIME: 35 MINUTES
SERVES: 4–6

- 2 tablespoons extra-virgin olive oil
- 2 spring onions (salad onions) the size of golf balls, halved and thinly sliced
- ¾ cup (180 ml) dry white wine
- ½ cup (120 ml) heavy (whipping) cream
- 1 tablespoon fresh lemon juice
- 1 teaspoon kosher (coarse) salt
- 5 lb (2.3 kg) Manila (carpetshell) clams, scrubbed
- ½ cup (115 g) crème fraîche
- 1 cup (50 g) loosely packed, roughly chopped sorrel
- 4 tablespoons roughly chopped fresh chervil
- 4 tablespoons fresh tarragon leaves
- Freshly ground black pepper
- Julienned zest of 1 small lemon
- Good bread, for serving

Heat a large heavy pan over medium heat. Add the oil, then the onions, and cook, stirring, until the onions begin to soften, about 3 minutes. Add the wine, cream, lemon juice, and salt. Increase the heat to high and bring to a boil. Add the clams, cover, and steam until all the clams have opened, about 5 minutes.

When the clams have opened (discard any that don't), add the crème fraîche and stir until it melts into the sauce, then add the sorrel, chervil, tarragon, and pepper to taste. Cook for another 1 or 2 minutes, then stir in about two-thirds of the lemon zest. Serve hot, garnished with the remaining lemon zest, with a hunk of bread for dipping.

Brent Cunningham is managing editor of The Food & Environment Reporting Network. He has been included in the *Best Food Writing* anthologies and is writing a book about West Virginia food culture.

When I tell people I'm from West Virginia, what they often imagine—narrow hollows, poverty, coal—is a mashup of reality and stereotype. But it wasn't my reality. I grew up in Charleston, the state capital, and in most ways my childhood was standard suburban America, circa 1970s. I rode my bike to the pool, caught fireflies at dusk, wore my hair long and my jeans wide, and played Asteroids at the video arcade.

That went for much of what I ate, too. It was the golden age of fast and processed food, and I popped open tubes of refrigerator biscuits, watched Steak-umm tiles shrivel in the frying pan, and savored the doughy centers of undercooked Pillsbury cinnamon rolls. When the first McDonald's opened in Charleston, it was an event. So was buying our first microwave.

In West Virginia, though, the past is never far away. And what I learned there about cooking and eating—what has endured and shapes my habits in the kitchen to this day—has nothing to do with Big Macs or microwaved food.

My mother's family was from Lincoln County, on the edge of the southern coalfields, a short drive from Charleston. Her parents were country people. I have a photo of my grandfather posing with a shotgun in one hand and two dead squirrels in the other. When they moved to the city at the tail end of the Great Depression, they brought their traditional foodways with them.

So I ate my share of "country food," as well, from leather britches and creasy greens to soupbeans and cornbread. My grandfather's entire backyard, sizable for the suburbs, was

a garden, and my grandmother canned and pickled and preserved what he grew. We even still ate the occasional squirrel or venison steak.

It isn't something I describe with the hushed reverence for "authenticity" that characterizes so much writing today about the foods we grew up with. These things were just part of our regular rotation of meals—but so was take-out pizza. Rather, the real culinary legacy of my Appalachian roots is a creativity born of thrift that persisted long after my family had left serious poverty behind.

Take beans and cornbread, that most iconic of Appalachian meals. For the uninitiated, beans and cornbread typically refers to pinto beans slow-cooked with some type of smoked, fatty pork—for us that meant a ham hock—and served with a skillet of cornbread. This provided the foundation for a series of meals over several days.

The life cycle of a pot of beans in our house began like this: On Friday night we sifted the dried beans to remove the tiny stones that occasionally made their way into the bag, then soaked the beans overnight. On Saturday morning, my father and I would get the hocks at Johnnies butcher shop, and the beans would simmer through the afternoon. When the sun got low, Mom spooned a heaping dollop of bacon grease from the jar in the refrigerator into a cast-iron skillet, and slid it into the oven to get smoking hot. The cornbread batter hissed and sputtered as she poured it into the hot skillet, the bacon grease pooling here and there on top. Soon we were sitting down to big bowls of rich, smoky beans, topped with chopped onion ▶

◄ and maybe some of my grandmother's canned tomatoes. I submerged my cornbread in the beans, creating a porridge of sorts; my sister studiously kept hers on the side, slathered in butter. Or margarine, actually; it was the 1970s, after all.

The next day, we'd eat a smaller bowl of beans alongside potatoes and onions (fried in bacon grease, of course), and some type of stewed green, either spinach or kale or creasy, a pungent cousin of watercress common in Appalachian gardens.

After that, the leftovers went in any number of directions. My mother would crumble stale cornbread in a tall glass of buttermilk for lunch (or dessert); the fried potatoes were paired with eggs and bacon for breakfast; and we would repeat that first meal another time or two. The point is that cheap, nutritious ingredients were turned into satisfying meals, and nothing was wasted. To let something spoil to the point where it had to be thrown out was considered a dereliction of one's duty as manager of the family larder.

It is a mantle I carry today, as chief cook and kitchen manager in my own home. I'm known, with a mix of exasperation and respect, as the "leftover king" for my ability to turn all manner of leftovers into meals that are, if not always guest-worthy, at least serviceable and satisfying. We waste very little food. And while the things I do with leftover beans today—top them with good tuna, radicchio, and shaved Parmesan, for instance—may be more refined than those Lincoln County options, it all still begins with a long simmer, a meaty hock, and a sizzling skillet.

Damian Heath is Chef of Lot 12 Public House in his hometown of Berkeley Springs, West Virginia. He has twice been a semifinalist for the James Beard Best Chef: Southeast award.

WILD RAMP VICHYSSOISE WITH GRILLED COUNTRY HAM AND CRÈME FRAÎCHE

PREPARATION TIME: 20 MINUTES
COOKING TIME: 1 HOUR
SERVES: 10–12

- 5 lb (2.3 kg) Yukon Gold and/or russet (baking) potatoes, peeled
- ⅓ cup (75 g) unsalted butter
- ½ lb (225 g) ramps (wild garlic), white part and some of the greens, chopped
- Salt and freshly ground black pepper
- Ground white pepper
- 1½ cups (355 ml) heavy (whipping) cream
- Grilled country ham, julienned, for garnish
- Crème fraîche or sour cream, for garnish

In a large pot of salted boiling water, cook the potatoes for about 40 minutes, until fork-tender.

Meanwhile, in a large saucepan, melt the butter over medium heat. Add the ramps and cook until softened, about 12 minutes. Add 3 cups (710 ml) water and simmer for 30 minutes. Season to taste with salt and both black and white pepper.

Drain the potatoes and return them to the pot. Add three-fourths of the ramp broth and 1 cup (240 ml) of the cream and purée with a hand blender. Season to taste. Add the remaining ½ cup (120 ml) cream and more ramp broth, if needed, for desired consistency.

Serve garnished with country ham and crème fraîche.

FETTUCCINE WITH WILD MORELS, WATERCRESS, AND ASPARAGUS

PREPARATION TIME: 1 HOUR
COOKING TIME: 30 MINUTES
SERVES: 6

- 1 lb (455 g) morels, halved
- 2 tablespoons (30 g) plus ⅓ cup (75 g) butter
- 1 lb (455 g) asparagus, woody ends trimmed, and cut on the diagonal into ¾-inch (2 cm) pieces
- 1 lb (455 g) fettuccine, cooked according to package directions, reserving ⅓ cup (80 ml) of the cooking water
- 1 lb (455 g) watercress, thick stems discarded
- Salt and freshly ground black pepper
- Grated Parmigiano-Reggiano or Pecorino Romano cheese, for serving

Soak the morels in warm water for 20 minutes to remove any debris; then rinse and pat dry.

In a large sauté pan, melt 2 tablespoons (30 g) of the butter over medium heat. Add the morels and cook until they begin to soften, 3–4 minutes. Add the asparagus and cook for 2 minutes. Add the pasta, reserved cooking water, and watercress. Toss for several minutes until tender and warm. Add the remaining ⅓ cup (75 g) butter in pieces and stir into the broth. Taste and season with salt and pepper. Garnish with grated cheese.

VENISON RAGU WITH PAPPARDELLE AND GRILLED VENISON LOIN

PREPARATION TIME: 20 MINUTES,
    PLUS OVERNIGHT MARINATING
COOKING TIME: 3 HOURS 40 MINUTES
SERVES: 6–8

For the loin and marinade:
- 4 tablespoons red wine
- 3 tablespoons olive oil
- ¼ cup (10 g) fresh herbs, such
  as oregano, savory, and marjoram
- Finely grated orange zest
- 1 teaspoon garlic powder
- Salt and freshly ground black pepper
- 2 lb (910 g) venison loin

For the ragu:
- 2 lb (910 g) venison leg, cubed
- Salt and freshly ground black pepper
- Sugar
- Olive oil
- ⅓ lb (150 g) pancetta, diced
- 18 cloves garlic, sliced
- ¾ cup (100 g) sliced shallots
- 1 lb (455 g) cremini (chestnut)
  mushrooms, quartered
- 1¾ cups (415 ml) red wine
- 1½ cups (360 ml) tomatoes, crushed
- 1¾ cups (415 ml) chicken stock
- 1 bay leaf
- ¼ teaspoon freshly grated nutmeg

For serving:
- 1 lb (455 g) pappardelle, cooked
  according to package directions
- Sprigs of fresh herbs for garnish
- Parmigiano-Reggiano or Pecorino
  Romano cheese
- Balsamic glaze

For the loin and marinade: In a bowl, stir together the wine, olive oil, herbs, orange zest, garlic powder, and salt and pepper. Rub the loin with the mixture. Wrap in plastic (clingfilm) and marinate overnight in the fridge.

For the ragu: Season the venison leg with salt and pepper and a little sugar. Heat a large Dutch oven (casserole) over high heat. When hot, add the olive oil and heat until just smoking. Working in batches if necessary, add the venison and sear all over. Remove the venison from the pan.

Reduce the heat to medium. Add the pancetta and render until crisp. Add the garlic, shallots, mushrooms, and enough olive oil to slicken everything. Cook until tender, about 10 minutes. Return the venison to the pot and add the wine, tomatoes, stock, bay leaf, and nutmeg. Simmer gently until tender, 2–3 hours. Add more stock if needed, but the ragu should be relatively thick. Season to taste with salt and pepper and a fresh grating of nutmeg.

Preheat a gas or charcoal grill (barbecue) to medium-high heat. Remove the loin from the marinade and grill for about 5 minutes per side, to medium-rare. Let it rest for 10 minutes, then slice on the diagonal.

To serve: In a large sauté pan, toss together the cooked pappardelle and ragu and warm gently. Divide the pasta among plates and top with the grilled loin. Garnish with the herbs, Parmigiano or Pecorino, and a drizzle of balsamic glaze.

Christine Muhlke is editor-at-large of *Bon Appétit* and a cookbook writer. She is from Wisconsin.

It took me a while to admit how much I love the food of Wisconsin. When I was growing up on Lake Michigan in Racine in the 1970s and 1980s, my state's cuisine was always a punch line. There was that smell when you drove past the sauerkraut factory. The lutefisk, gravlax, kringles, and other silly-to-pronounce Scandinavian foods that were part of every party. (My family had kringles shipped to us during a long vacation in Spain in 1980, and this was well before FedEx—and before Obama visited O&H Danish Bakery for jam-filled pastry rings.) The embarrassing chest freezer my parents bought to store the cow that they split with friends every year at the state fair, rounded out by bratwurst and kielbasa made by the local German butcher. (Also: We bought ice cream by the tub. And I'm an only child.) The fish fries up in Door County, often featuring tiny smelt fries. Frozen custard at Kopp's in Milwaukee—okay, that wasn't embarrassing. Cheese balls. Cheese curds! Port wine cheese spread. Cow-shaped cheddar bought at the Mars Cheese Castle. Brandy old-fashioneds, made with 7-Up. Oh, and beer. So much beer.

While I might have been mortified by the Wisconsin culinary stereotypes that were thrown at me when I would visit my father in California, I wouldn't disavow the true love of eating that growing up there had instilled in me.

For me, the bustle and abundance of the Dane County farmers' market in Madison provokes the same sense of hunger and awe that the Ferry Building market in San Francisco does, from the greens grown by Hmong farmers to the griddled bread cheese samples being toothpicked to the incredible wood-oven bread baked at Cress Spring

Bakery by Jeff Ford, who also hosts a pizza farm on summer weekends. (Pizza farms, in which guests visit a farm to eat pizza made on-site from just-harvested ingredients, are a Wisconsin phenomenon.) Then I'll buy a wheelie's worth of cheese at Fromagination—real name—and see which one of chef Tory Miller's restaurants is open. The South Korean–born Miller grew up cooking in his adopted German grandparents' diner in Racine. His love of food—his Wisconsin heritage—is infectious.

There is a pleasure in indulging in food that is connected to one's heritage. There is a pride in the beef, dairy, and vegetables grown and raised there.

Dave Swanson moved to Milwaukee, Wisconsin, in 1998. He is chef-owner of Braise, which has a culinary school, and he is a four-time James Beard Foundation nominee for Best Chef: Midwest.

CRISPY PIG WITH CREAMY POLENTA AND GOAT CHEESE

PREPARATION TIME: 20 MINUTES,
PLUS MARINATING TIME
COOKING TIME: 2 HOURS 45 MINUTES
SERVES: 6–8

- 3 lb (1.4 kg) slab of pork belly
- 4 tablespoons Simple Pork Belly Rub (page 704)
- ¼ cup (60 ml) sorghum syrup
- 1 tablespoon cider vinegar
- Salt and freshly ground black pepper
- ½ cup (80 g) fresh chèvre
- 2 tablespoons heavy (whipping) cream
- Creamy Polenta (page 704)

Note:
If the squares of pork belly are particularly fatty in some spots, they can be fairly easily trimmed of excess fat and reassembled. As the pieces of pork are reheated they will somewhat bind back together.

Place the pork belly fat side up in a nonreactive baking dish and season both sides with the rub, trying to coat as evenly as possible. Cover and refrigerate for at least 6 and up to 24 hours.

Meanwhile, in a small bowl, mix together the sorghum syrup, vinegar, and a pinch of salt and pepper. Set aside. In another small bowl, stir the chèvre and cream together to lighten the consistency. Refrigerate until serving time.

Position a rack in the center of the oven and preheat to 225°F (110°C/Gas Mark ¼).

Wrap the dish containing the pork belly with foil and bake for 2 hours. Remove from the oven and increase the oven temperature to 350°F (180°C/Gas Mark 4). Uncover the pork belly, return to the oven, and cook until the fatty layer is golden brown and crispy, about 30 minutes. Remove the meat from the oven and increase the oven temperature to 400°F (200°C/Gas Mark 6). Let the pork belly cool completely, then cut it into large squares about 3 ounces (85 g) each.

Meanwhile, make the polenta. As the polenta is cooking, place the pork belly pieces in the oven to reheat, about 10 minutes.

To serve, ladle some of the polenta on a plate, place the warmed pork belly on top, drizzle with the sorghum mixture, and top with a dollop of the chèvre mixture.

PORK BELLY RUB

PREPARATION TIME: 10 MINUTES
COOKING TIME: 10 MINUTES
MAKES: ABOUT 1 CUP (140 G)

- ¼ cup (35 g) kosher (coarse) salt
- ½ cup (100 g) sugar
- 1 tablespoon cumin seeds, toasted and ground
- 1 tablespoon garlic powder
- 1 tablespoon freshly ground black pepper
- ½ tablespoon yellow mustard seeds, toasted and ground
- 2 bay leaves, ground

Combine all the ingredients in a bowl. Mix well.

CREAMY POLENTA

PREPARATION TIME: 5 MINUTES
COOKING TIME: 35 MINUTES
MAKES: 10 CUPS (ABOUT 2.4 LITERS)

- 3 cups (710 ml) milk
- 2 cups (475 ml) heavy (whipping) cream
- 3½ cups (830 ml) chicken stock
- 4 tablespoons (60 g) butter
- 2 cups (265 g) cornmeal
- 1½ cups (135 g) freshly grated Parmesan cheese

Note:
If you made the polenta ahead and it stiffened up after sitting in your refrigerator, reheat it with a bit of milk or heavy cream.

In a wide pot (preferably double-bottomed to help prevent scorching), combine the milk, cream, stock, and butter and heat over medium heat. Once the butter melts into the liquids, begin to gradually add the cornmeal about ¼ cup (35 g) at a time, whisking after each addition. Bring to a simmer, then reduce the heat to a low simmer. Whisk frequently to cook evenly and eliminate any clumps. Scrape the bottom of the pot every few minutes to prevent scorching. Cook until the polenta has thickened slightly and does not have a gritty texture, about 30 minutes. Stir in the Parmesan cheese and serve immediately.

STEAMED PORK BUNS WITH SCALLION VINAIGRETTE AND SPICED PEANUTS

PREPARATION TIME: 1 HOUR 25 MINUTES,
 PLUS MARINATING AND RISING TIME
COOKING TIME: 2 HOURS 40 MINUTES
MAKES: ABOUT 15 BUNS

For the cured pork belly:
- 2 lb (910 g) pork belly
- 4 tablespoons Pork Belly Cure (page 706)

For the steamed buns:
- ½ teaspoon active dry yeast
- ½ cup (115 ml) warm water
- 2¼ cups plus 3 tablespoons (315 g)
 all-purpose (plain) flour
- 2 tablespoons sugar
- 1½ teaspoons kosher (coarse) salt
- 5 tablespoons hot water
- ¾ ounce (22 g) rendered pork fat

For serving:
- Scallion Vinaigrette, to taste (page 706)
- Crushed Spiced Peanuts, to taste
 (page 707)

For the cured pork belly: Place the pork belly fat side up in a non-reactive baking dish and sprinkle both sides with the pork belly cure, trying to coat as evenly as possible. Cover and refrigerate for at least 6 and up to 24 hours.

Position a rack in the center of the oven and preheat to 225°F (110°C/Gas Mark ¼).

Wrap the dish containing the pork belly with foil and bake for 2 hours. Remove from the oven and increase the oven temperature to 350°F (180°C/Gas Mark 4). Uncover the pork belly, return to the oven, and cook until the fatty layer is golden brown and crispy, about 30 minutes. Let cool completely, then cut the pork belly into small dice.

For the steamed buns: In a large bowl, mix together the yeast and warm water. Stir in 1¾ cups (245 g) plus 2 tablespoons of the flour and let sit for about 5 minutes to activate the yeast.

In the bowl of a stand mixer fitted with the paddle attachment, stir together the remaining ½ cup (65 g) plus 1 tablespoon flour, the sugar, and salt. Add the hot water and then gradually add the pork fat. Beat in the yeast mixture until it becomes a smooth, uniform ball. The dough should pull away from the sides of the bowl. Transfer the dough to a large bowl, cover, and let the dough rise in a warm draft-free area until doubled in volume, about 1½ hours.

Pull the dough into pieces the size of golf balls and roll into ovals with a rolling pin. Fold in half and let sit uncovered until doubled in size, about 30 minutes.

Steam the buns in a steamer basket for 15 minutes. Let the buns cool before slicing crosswise, through one of the long sides of the bun, to open up just one side.

When ready to serve, preheat the oven to 400°F (200°C/Gas Mark 6).

Reheat the pork belly in the oven for about 10 minutes. Some more of the fat will render off and the belly will further crisp up. At the same time, reheat the buns in a steamer basket. Lift the belly out of its rendered fat with a slotted spoon and fill the buns with it. Drizzle a generous amount of the scallion vinaigrette over the pork, then top with the crushed spiced peanuts.

PORK BELLY CURE

PREPARATION TIME: 10 MINUTES
COOKING TIME: 10 MINUTES
MAKES: 1 CUP (150 G)

- ¼ cup (35 g) kosher (coarse) salt
- ½ cup (100 g) sugar
- 5 whole star anise, toasted and ground
- 2¼ teaspoons Sichuan peppercorns, ground
- ½ tablespoon coriander seeds, toasted and ground
- ½ tablespoon black peppercorns, ground
- 1 teaspoon crushed chili flakes
- 1 tablespoon ground ginger
- 1 tablespoon garlic powder

Combine all the ingredients in a bowl. Mix well.

SCALLION VINAIGRETTE

PREPARATION TIME: 15 MINUTES
MAKES: 3¼ CUPS (770 ML)

- 1¼ cups (125 g) chopped scallions (spring onions)
- 2 tablespoons minced fresh ginger
- 2¼ teaspoons minced garlic
- 1 cup (240 ml) rice vinegar
- 1 tablespoon fish sauce
- 1 tablespoon Dijon mustard
- 2 teaspoons fresh lemon juice
- ½ tablespoon sesame oil
- 1 cup (240 ml) grapeseed oil

In a blender, combine the scallions (spring onions), ginger, garlic, vinegar, fish sauce, mustard, lemon juice, and sesame oil. Blend until homogenized, then, with the blender still running at medium-high speed, slowly drizzle the grapeseed oil until fully incorporated.

CRUSHED SPICED PEANUTS

PREPARATION TIME: 15 MINUTES,
   PLUS COOLING TIME
COOKING TIME: 15 MINUTES
MAKES: 2 CUPS (220 G)

- 2 egg whites
- 1 tablespoon heavy (whipping) cream
- ⅓ cup (65 g) sugar
- 1 teaspoon coriander seeds, toasted and ground
- 1 teaspoon ground Chinese cassia cinnamon
- ½ teaspoon ground white pepper
- ¼ teaspoon cayenne pepper
- 2 teaspoons salt
- ½ lb (225 g) roasted peanuts

Preheat the oven to 325°F (160°C/Gas Mark 3).

In a large bowl, with an electric mixer, beat the egg whites, cream, and sugar to firm peaks. Fold in the coriander, cinnamon, white pepper, cayenne, and salt.

Toss the peanuts with the egg white mixture until coated. Spread in a single layer on a baking sheet and bake until the egg white coating has set and the peanuts are slightly darker golden, about 15 minutes. Let the peanuts cool completely, then pulse in a food processor to the size of tiny pebbles.

SMOKED TROUT PARFAIT WITH CORNMEAL JOHNNY CAKES AND PEPPER JAM

PREPARATION TIME: 10 MINUTES
COOKING TIME: 5 MINUTES
SERVES: 5–6

- ½ cup (120 ml) fresh lemon juice
- ¾ cup (180 g) mascarpone cheese
- ½ cup (120 ml) sour cream
- 2 teaspoons (15 g) kosher (coarse) salt
- 4 ounces (115 g) smoked trout, skin removed and broken into 1-inch (2.5 cm) pieces
- Freshly ground black pepper
- 10 Cornmeal Johnny Cakes (page 708)
- ⅓ cup (80 ml) store-bought pepper jam

In a small saucepan, cook the lemon juice over medium heat until reduced to about 2 tablespoons, about 5 minutes. Let the lemon reduction cool.

In a bowl, gently fold about 2 teaspoons of the lemon reduction into the mascarpone. The mascarpone should begin to stiffen up a bit, but not separate. If it is not tightening up at all, add a little bit more lemon reduction. Fold in the sour cream and salt until just incorporated. Gently fold in the trout.

Serve a spoonful of trout parfait atop a warm johnny cake and garnish with a dollop of the pepper jam.

CORNMEAL JOHNNY CAKES

PREPARATION TIME: 10 MINUTES,
  PLUS COOLING AND RESTING TIME
COOKING TIME: 15 MINUTES
MAKES: 10 CAKES

- ½ cup (65 g) cornmeal
- ¾ cup (180 ml) boiling water
- ½ cup (120 ml) buttermilk
- ½ cup (120 ml) milk
- 1 egg
- 1 tablespoon olive oil
- ½ cup (65 g) all-purpose (plain) flour
- 1 teaspoon baking powder
- 2 teaspoons salt
- 3 tablespoons (45 g) butter

Place the cornmeal in a small heatproof bowl. Slowly pour in the boiling water, stirring to incorporate. Let cool to room temperature.

In a medium bowl, whisk together the buttermilk, milk, egg, and oil. Whisk the cornmeal into the buttermilk mixture in increments, beating out any lumps. In a separate bowl, combine the flour, baking powder, and salt. Lightly whisk the cornmeal/buttermilk mixture into the flour until incorporated. Let the batter rest for 20 minutes.

Working in 3 batches, in a large nonstick frying pan or cast-iron skillet, melt 1 tablespoon (15 g) butter over medium heat. Ladle or spoon batter by the ¼ cup (60 ml) into the pan, 3–4 pancakes in each batch, and cook until the center begins to bubble and the edges turn golden brown, about 3 minutes. Flip and cook through on the other side, about 2 more minutes.

CHOCOLATE POTS DE CRÈME

PREPARATION TIME: 15 MINUTES,
  PLUS RESTING AND CHILLING TIME
COOKING TIME: 45 MINUTES
SERVES: 8

- 14 oz (400 g) dark chocolate, chopped
- 2¾ cups (650 ml) plus 3 tablespoons heavy (whipping) cream
- 2¾ cups (650 ml) plus 2 tablespoons milk
- 12 egg yolks
- 5½ tablespoons sugar

Preheat the oven to 250°–300°F (95°–150°C).

Place the chocolate in a heatproof medium bowl. In a saucepan, bring the cream and milk to a boil. Pour the milk mixture over the chocolate to melt and mix until completely dissolved. In a separate bowl, beat together the egg yolks and sugar. While whisking constantly, slowly drizzle the chocolate mixture into the yolk mixture. Pour the custard into eight 8-ounce (240 ml) ramekins, ½ inch (1.25 cm) from the top of the ramekin.

Line a baking dish (large enough to fit all the ramekins) with a tea towel and arrange the ramekins in the dish. Bring a kettle of water to a boil, let rest 2 minutes, then fill the dish with water to come about halfway up the sides of the ramekins. Cover with foil and bake until just set (they should be slightly jiggly in the center, but will firm up as they rest), 30–40 minutes. Check to be sure the water never simmers more than a few bubbles here and there. If necessary, reduce the oven temperature.

Remove the ramekins from the baking dish. Let pots de crème rest at room temperature for 30 minutes before refrigerating until chilled.

Jeff Drew is chef and managing partner of the Snake River Grill in Jackson Hole, Wyoming. He was nominated three years in a row for Best Chef: Northwest by the James Beard Foundation.

Wyoming is a fisherman's paradise with more than 15,000 miles of fishing streams and 3,400 lakes, ponds, and reservoirs—which support seventy-six species of fish. The cutthroat trout is one of my favorites. Word has spread through the fly-fishing community about their spirited fighting ability and instinct.

Every year, September brings is the world cup of fly-fishing, the Jackson Hole One Fly. Anglers from around the world convene on our pristine rivers to compete in catching either the largest amount of, or the biggest, trout using just one fly.

If this conjures up images of the Robert Redford movie *A River Runs Through It*, with the lone individual, hip-deep in crystal-clear rushing water, silhouetted by the sunset—yes, it is that beautiful.

Out here in the West, most will say that fly-fishing is what "real" fishermen pursue. In fact, I have quite a few friends whose business cards list their title as "Fly-Fishing Guide." That profession carries more swagger and envy at the local bar than any lawyer or banker will find. Even we amateurs have memories of coming off the river and enjoying the freshest fish, all the while regaling our dinner companions with stories of the epic battle won on the water.

Becoming proficient at the sport of fly-fishing is no easy task, something I can tell you from personal experience. Like so many kids in Wyoming, my daughter learned to do it only a few years after learning how to ride a bike. I joined her for lessons, but after a few weeks she was still catching more trout.

Once caught and easily cleaned, this flaky light fish doesn't need much—it is excellent in myriad simple preparations. My favorite way is grilled whole with a little potato-bacon stuffing, or filleted and breaded with cornmeal or ground pecans and sautéed in butter. Both methods feature the skin left on and cooked until crispy—delicious!

Jeff Drew

WATERCRESS APPLE SALAD

PREPARATION TIME: 10 MINUTES
SERVES: 4

- 1 bunch watercress, thick stems trimmed
- 1 Fuji apple
- 1 tablespoon cider vinegar
- ½ tablespoon walnut vinegar
- 3 tablespoons corn oil
- ½ teaspoon minced shallot
- ¼ teaspoon kosher (coarse) salt
- Small pinch of freshly ground
  black pepper
- Small pinch of ground caraway seeds

Place the watercress in a medium bowl. Using a mandoline or sharp knife, shave the apple into thin half-moon slices and add to watercress. In a small bowl, whisk together both vinegars, the oil, shallot, salt, pepper, and caraway. Toss everything to combine.

PECAN-CRUSTED TROUT

PREPARATION TIME: 30 MINUTES
COOKING TIME: 10 MINUTES
SERVES: 4

- 1 cup (125 g) finely chopped pecans, toasted
- 1½ cups (160 g) dried breadcrumbs
- 4 tablespoons chopped fresh parsley
- 1 teaspoon chopped fresh rosemary
- ½ teaspoon kosher (coarse) salt
- ½ teaspoon freshly ground black pepper
- 4 rainbow trout fillets, skin on
- 1 stick (115 g) butter, melted
- ½ cup (120 ml) olive oil

[This is great served with Watercress-Apple Salad (page 710) and Horseradish Crème Fraîche (recipe follows).]

Preheat the oven to 425°F (220°C/Gas Mark 7).

In a bowl, mix together the pecans, breadcrumbs, parsley, rosemary, salt, and pepper. Pour the mixture onto a rimmed baking sheet.

On a second baking sheet, lay out the trout fillets skin side down. Brush the melted butter liberally over the trout. Press each fillet, buttered side down, into the breadcrumb mix so it sticks.

In a large ovenproof sauté pan, add the oil to the pan over medium heat and wait 1 minute for it to get hot. Gently place the trout, crumb side down, in the pan and cook for 3 minutes. Flip the fillets over onto the skin side and transfer the pan to the oven. Bake until the flesh is opaque and flakes easily with a fork, about 8 minutes.

Serve the trout on warm plates.

HORSERADISH CRÈME FRAÎCHE

PREPARATION TIME: 5 MINUTES,
PLUS 12 HOURS STANDING TIME
MAKES: ABOUT 1½ CUPS (360 ML)

- 1 cup (240 ml) heavy (whipping) cream
- 1 tablespoon fresh lemon juice
- 2 tablespoons prepared horseradish
- 4 tablespoons grated fresh horseradish
- Salt and freshly ground black pepper

In a bowl, combine the cream, lemon juice, and prepared horseradish and let sit in a cool, but not cold, place for about 12 hours.

Stir in the fresh horseradish and season to taste with salt and pepper.

IL IN IA

chili Colorado 212
cucumber salad with soy
and ginger 52
French fries 258
fried oysters 35
grilled marinated salmon with
sesame and ginger 180
huckleberry pie 286
onion rings 254, *255*
pan-seared bison fillets 204
pine pesto 543
prairie butter 138
raw oysters 34
Rocky Mountain oysters 40
sautéed wild mushrooms 250
slow-roasted salmon with
yogurt sauce 178, *179*
smoked trout morels 542
smoky chipotle bison pot roast 204
spudnuts 443
trout with fingerling potatoes 544
wheat berry pudding 369
white currant granité 544
wild nannyberry butter 472
wild strawberry freezer crisp 364
zwieback 428

ILLINOIS (IL) 545–7
American-style goulash 207
apple crumble 382
apple pie 281
apple slump 378
apple turnovers 302
boiled burbot 168
boiled cod with mustard sauce 167
chewy sugar cookies 344
Chicago steakhouse rub 456
Chicago–style deep-dish
pizza 112, *113*
Chicago–style hot dog 99
Chicago–style steak 130
chicken salad 70, *71*
chocolate cream pie 298
cinnamon rolls 426, *427*
classic American white bread 412
corn pierogi 547
cream of mushroom soup 77
dill pickles 473
dilly beans 476
hickory nut cake 326
hot German potato salad 60, *61*
Italian beef sandwich 97
lebkuchen 353
mayapple jelly 469
meat loaf 135
morning glory muffins 440

oatmeal raisin cookies 342
paczki 447
pan-fried Great Lakes fish with
lemon-parsley butter sauce 171
persimmon pudding 369
pierogi 116, *117*
pineapple upside-down cake 322
potato salad 60
prime rib roast beef 124
ranch dressing 480
rum raisin pie 287
sauerkraut and kielbasa 152
scrambled eggs with morel
mushrooms 399
shortbread 344
sloppy Joe 98
snickerdoodles 348, *349*
sweet corn elotes 546
swiss steak 132
venison stew with wild rice 206
wheat berry pudding 369
wild nannyberry butter 472
wild rice hotdish 166
wild strawberry freezer crisp 364
'inamona 457

INDIANA (IN) 548–53
American-style goulash 207
apple crumble 382
apple pie 281
apple slump 378
apple turnovers 302
beets with sour cream and
horseradish 233
boiled burbot 168
boiled cod with mustard sauce 167
chewy sugar cookies 344
chicken salad 70, *71*
chocolate cream pie 298
cinnamon rolls 426, *427*
classic American white bread 412
cream of mushroom soup 77
creamed corn 244
dill pickles 473
dilly beans 476
heirloom grits 553
hickory nut cake 326
hot German potato salad 60, *61*
Indiana wild mushrooms 549
lebkuchen 353
marinated slow-roasted
watermelon 550
mashed potatoes 256
meat loaf 135
morning glory muffins 440
nam prik green goddess dressing 551

oatmeal raisin cookies 342
persimmon pudding 369
pickled kumquats 553
pineapple upside-down cake 322
pork tenderloin sandwich 100
porter-braised pork cheeks over
heirloom grits with pickled
kumquats and crispy collards 552
potato salad 60
ranch dressing 480
rum raisin pie 287
scrambled eggs with morel
mushrooms 399
shortbread 344
sloppy Joe 98
snickerdoodles 348, *349*
sticky date pudding 370, *371*
swiss steak 132
tomatoes with roasted watermelon,
avocado, and cottage cheese 550
venison stew with wild rice 206
wheat berry pudding 369
wild nannyberry butter 472
wild rice hotdish 166
wild strawberry freezer crisp 364
Indiana wild mushrooms 549
injera 420

IOWA (IA) 554–7
American-style goulash 207
apple crumble 382
apple pie 281
apple slump 378
apple turnovers 302
boiled burbot 168
boiled cod with mustard sauce 167
boiled dressing 457
cabbage cooked in milk 234
chewy sugar cookies 344
chicken salad 70, *71*
chocolate cream pie 298
cinnamon rolls 426, *427*
classic American white bread 412
corn-Manchego tortellini 555
cream of mushroom soup 77
dill pickles 473
dilly beans 476
fresh egg noodles 235
hickory nut cake 326
Hilljack Cocktail 556
hot German potato salad 60, *61*
iceberg wedge salad with blue
cheese dressing 44, *45*
lebkuchen 353
lima bean bake 272
loosemeat sandwich 97

LESS THAN 5 INGREDIENTS RECIPES | 5 |

ABOUT THE AUTHOR

Gabrielle Langholtz writes about the intersection of food, culture, and ecology. She oversaw communications for New York City's farmers markets, was editor of *Edible Brooklyn* and *Edible Manhattan*, and wrote *The New Greenmarket Cookbook*. She has taught a master's degree course at New York University's Food Studies program, written for *House Beautiful*, been quoted in the *The New Yorker*, appeared in *Martha Stewart Living* and the *New York Times*, and worked for the national non-profit Wholesome Wave. A former vegetarian now married to a livestock farmer, she has visited scores of farms, milked cows and sheep, tapped sugar maples, and foraged ramps. Gabrielle has traveled to all fifty states.

AUTHOR ACKNOWLEDGEMENTS

Foremost, to Emily Takoudes, for inviting me to create this book, giving me the chance of a lifetime, and being open to my vision for it. Emily, I was in my kitchen when I read your first email about this project and my life has not been the same since. Thank you.

To Olga Massov, for sure-handedly stewarding this book's long journey to print, with eagle-eyed attention to every detail along the way.

To Ken Carlton, for urging me decades ago to leave *Fortune* for food and to leading by example.

To Rachel Wharton, whose knowledge of bookmaking and barbecue were fundamental to this book and other things in my life.

To Annie Hollister, my researcher, chief-of-staff, and priestess of spreadsheets who tracked contributors, created solutions with patience, and kept it all together.

To Marie Viljoen, one of the most beautiful humans I've met, and an immigrant who knows more about America's edible ecosystem than anyone I know. She opened my eyes, beginning with lambsquarter growing from a Brooklyn tree pit. She contributed greatly to the recipes with foraged ingredients.

To the many behind the scenes who helped develop recipes: Caroline Wright, who worked on cakes. Kelly Geary, who put her heart into the pies. Jessica Applestone, who provided enormous guidance on the meat recipes. And especially to Erin Merhar, who developed recipes for the South and Southwest, and worked on contributor recipes.

To Doug Adrianson for his tremendous help with the manuscript and to Kate Slate for copyediting the manuscript.

To the authors, chefs, and scholars who showed the world a different way to understand American food, especially: James Beard, Betty Fussell, Clementine Paddleford, Andy Fischer, Larry Forgione, Karen Hess, and Jane and Michael Stern.

To every chef and writer who contributed essays and recipes to this book and, moreover, for making American food a spectacularly beautiful living thing.

To my culinary coven: Jacqueline Langholtz, Irene Hamburger, Carol Diuguid, Mindy Fox, Jenny Dirksen, Kate Barney, Kristin Donnelly, Erin Gleeson, Nina Planck, Emery Van Hook, Raquel Pelzel, Chelsey Simpson, Fiona McBride, Susan Fields, and the Marla Nicolo sisterhood.

To Jennifer Unter for her guidance.

My husband and daughter, who for the past years while working on this book have occasionally eaten tested recipes, but mostly ate takeout while I typed.

And this book was made possible by Elizabeth Schula and her knowledge of American food — its history, culture, ingredients, traditions, and regions. Her skills at the stove, determination, and shared vow that this book include immigrant dishes are greatly appreciated.

- Butter should always be unsalted unless otherwise specified.

- All herbs are fresh and parsley is flat-leaf unless otherwise specified.

- Eggs, vegetables, and fruits are assumed to be medium size, unless otherwise specified.

- Milk is always whole, unless otherwise specified.

- Garlic cloves are assumed to be large; use two if yours are small.

- Ham means cooked ham, unless otherwise specified.

- Cooking and preparation times are for guidance only, as individual ovens vary. If using a convection (fan) oven, follow the manufacturer's instructions concerning oven temperatures.

- Some of the recipes require advanced techniques, specialist equipment, and professional experience to achieve good results.

- To test whether your deep-frying oil is hot enough, add a cube of stale bread. If it browns in thirty seconds, the temperature is 350–375°F/180–190°C, about right for most frying. Exercise a high level of caution when following recipes involving any potentially hazardous activity, including the use of high temperature and open flames. In particular, when deep-frying, add the food carefully to avoid splashing, wear long sleeves, and never leave the pan unattended.

- Some recipes include raw or very lightly cooked eggs. These should be avoided particularly by the elderly, infants, pregnant women, convalescents, and anyone with an impaired immune system.

- For tough cuts of meats such as variety meats (offal), a pressure cooker can be used to reduce cooking times. Follow the manufacturer's instructions for use.

- Exercise caution when making fermented products, ensuring all equipment is spotlessly clean, and seek expert advice if in any doubt.

- All herbs, shoots, flowers, and leaves should be picked fresh from a clean source. Exercise caution when foraging for ingredients; any foraged ingredients should only be eaten if an expert has deemed them safe to eat.

- Mushrooms should be wiped clean.

MEASUREMENT NOTES

- Both imperial and metric measures are used in this book. Follow one set of measurements throughout, not a mixture, as they are not interchangeable.

- All spoon measurements are level.

- 1 teaspoon = 5 ml; 1 tablespoon = 15 ml. Australian standard tablespoons are 20 ml, so Australian readers are advised to use 3 teaspoons in place of 1 tablespoon when measuring small quantities.

- When no quantity is specified, for example of oils, salts, and herbs used for finishing dishes, quantities are discretionary and flexible.

Phaidon Press Limited
Regent's Wharf
All Saints Street
London N1 9PA

Phaidon Press Inc.
65 Bleecker Street
New York, NY 10012

phaidon.com

First published 2017
© 2017 Phaidon Press Limited

ISBN 978 0 7148 7396 1

A CIP catalogue record for this book
is available from the British Library and the Library
of Congress.

Commissioning Editor: Emily Takoudes
Project Editor: Olga Massov
Production Controller: Nerissa Vales
Photography: Danielle Acken
Design & Illustration: Julia Hasting
Typesetting: Ana Rita Teodoro

Printed in China

The publisher would like to thank Emilia Terragni, Vanessa Bird,
Elizabeth Ellis, Sophie Hodgkin, Annie Hollister, Dorothy Irwin,
Isaac Klein, Anna Kovel, Carmen Ladipo, Lesley Malkin, João
Mota, Eve O'Sullivan, Elizabeth Schula, Kate Slate, and Tracey
Smith for their contributions to the book.

CONTRIBUTING FOOD WRITERS & CHEFS BY STATE

ALABAMA
SCOTT PEACOCK
FRANK STITT

ALASKA
CHRISTOPHER NICOLSON

ARIZONA
GARY PAUL NABHAN

ARKANSAS
P. ALLEN SMITH
MATTHEW MCCLURE

CALIFORNIA
JONATHAN GOLD
ALICE WATERS

COLORADO
EUGENIA BONE
HOLLY ARNOLD KINNEY

CONNECTICUT
MICHAEL STERN
GABE MCMACKIN

DELAWARE
SAM CALAGIONE
HARI CAMERON

FLORIDA
NORMAN VAN AKEN

GEORGIA
NICOLE A. TAYLOR
HUGH ACHESON

HAWAII
RACHEL LAUDAN
MARTHA CHENG

IDAHO
KEVIN HUELSMANN
KRIS KOMORI

ILLINOIS
PAUL KAHAN
STEPHANIE IZARD

INDIANA
JONATHAN BROOKS

IOWA
JEREMY JACKSON
ANDY & CARRIE SCHUMACHER

KANSAS
CARL THORNE-THOMSEN

KENTUCKY
ADAM SACHS
EDWARD LEE

LOUISIANA
BRETT ANDERSON
JOHN BESH

MAINE
ANDREW TAYLOR & MIKE WILEY

MARYLAND
JOHN SHIELDS
JEREMIAH STONE

MASSACHUSETTS
CORBY KUMMER
BARBARA LYNCH

MICHIGAN
ARI WEINZWEIG
ANITA LO

MINNESOTA
WINONA LADUKE
ANDREW ZIMMERN

MISSISSIPPI
MARTHA FOOSE
JOHN CURRENCE

MISSOURI
DANNY MEYER
COLBY & MEGAN GARRELTS

MONTANA
SEABRING DAVIS
ANDY BLANTON